Mass Media and Society

4th Edition

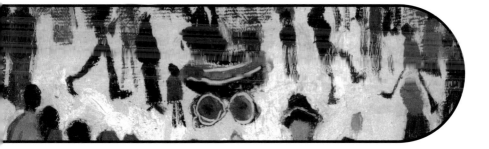

Mass Media and Society

4th Edition

Edited by James Curran and Michael Gurevitch

Hodder Arnold

A MEMBER OF THE HODDER HEADLINE GROUP

First published in Great Britain in 2005 by
Hodder Arnold, an imprint of Hodder Education
and a member of the Hodder Headline Group,
an Hachette Livre UK Company,
338 Euston Road, London NW1 3BH

www.hoddereducation.co.uk

The advice and information in this book are believed to be true and
accurate at the date of going to press, but neither the authors nor the publisher
can accept any legal responsibility or liability for any errors or omissions.

British Library Cataloguing in Publication Data
A catalogue record for this book is available from the British Library

Library of Congress Cataloging-in-Publication Data
A catalog record for this book is available from the Library of Congress

ISBN 978 0 340 88499 7

4 5 6 7 8 9 10

Typeset in 10/13 Adobe Garamond by Servis Filmsetting Ltd, Manchester
Printed and bound in India by Replika Press Pvt. Ltd

What do you think about this book? Or any other Hodder Education title?
Please visit our website: www.hoddereducation.co.uk

Contents

List of Contributors

Linda Aldoory, Assistant Professor of Communication at the University of Maryland

Jay G. Blumler, Professor Emeritus, University of Leeds

Karen Boyle, Lecturer in Film and Television Studies at the University of Glasgow

Kalyani Chadha, Director of the Media, Self and Society Program at the University of Maryland, College Park

Joseph Man Chan, Professor, School of Journalism and Communication, Chinese University of Hong Kong

James Curran, Professor of Communications at Goldsmiths College, University of London

Peter Dahlgren, Professor of Media and Communication Studies at Lund University, Sweden

Robert M. Entman, Professor of Communication and Political Science, North Carolina State University

Nicholas Garnham, Emeritus Professor of Media Studies, University of Westminster

Christine Geraghty, Professor of Film and Television Studies at University of Glasgow

Peter Golding, Professor of Sociology and Head of Department of Social Sciences, Loughborough University

Michael Gurevitch, Professor, Philip Merrill College of Journalism, University of Maryland

Dan Hallin, Professor of Communication at the University of California, San Diego

David Hesmondhalgh, Senior Lecturer in Media Studies in the Faculty of Social Sciences at the Open University

Anandam P. Kavoori, Associate Professor of Telecommunications and Broadcast News at the University of Georgia

Chin-Chuan Lee, Chair and Professor of Communications, City University of Hong Kong

Tamar Liebes, Professor and Chair in the Department of Communication at the Hebrew University of Jerusalem, and presently a Fellow at the Hebrew University's Institute of Advanced Studies

Sonia Livingstone, Professor of Social Psychology in the Department of Media and Communications, London School of Economics and Political Science

Paolo Mancini, Professor at the Dipartimento Istituzioni e Società, Università di Perugia

Daniel Miller, Professor of Material Culture, Department of Anthropology, University College London

Graham Murdock, Reader in the Sociology of Culture, Department of Social Sciences, Loughborough University

Zhongdang Pan, Professor, Department of Communication Arts, University of Wisconsin, Madison

Shawn J. Parry-Giles, Associate Professor of Communication and Director of the Centre for Political Communication and Civic Leadership at the University of Maryland

Naomi Sakr, Media Research Consultant and Research Associate at the University of Westminster

Michael Schudson, Professor of Communication and Sociology at the University of California, San Diego

Don Slater, Reader of Sociology at the London School of Economics and Political Science

Clement Y.K. So, Associate Professor, School of Journalism and Communication, Chinese University of Hong Kong

Daya Kishan Thussu, Professor of International Communication at the University of Westminster

Barbie Zelizer, Professor and Raymond Williams Chair of Communication in the Annenberg School for Communication, University of Pennsylvania

Introduction to the Fourth Edition

This book has grown almost into a mini-series. It really began life in 1977 under the title, *Mass Communication and Society*, as a course reader for a pioneering Open University media course. All three of the editors (then including Janet Woollacott, who subsequently left academic life) wanted to break free from the dominance of 'communications', the way in which the subject had been conceived in the USA and exported around the world. Instead, we wanted to promote an alternative tradition that drew upon a variety of different disciplines and tapped into the critical traditions of European social thought. The great-great-grandparent of this edition consequently foregrounded critical social theory and Marxism (largely absent from communications research) and set up a debate between this radical, 'European' tradition and the taken-for-granted, liberal-pluralist approach that underpinned much media work in the USA. The book did well: it was reprinted in Britain, and published in American and Spanish editions.

This prompted us to edit in 1991 a successor volume, called *Mass Media and Society*. Despite the slight change of title, this was in all but name a second edition. It had the same three-part, organizing framework as *Mass Communication and Society*, repeated the same 'radical versus liberal-pluralist' debate, and was again published by Arnold. However, in updating the book, we drew attention in passing to a new revisionist trend. The 'new revisionism' – in essence an attack on the fundamentalist positions of a pioneer generation of radical media researchers by people who mostly originated in the radical tradition – became the main thematic focus of the next edition, published in 1996. Four years later, after this debate had become exhausted, we changed tack completely. The next edition, published in 2000, made globalization its main theme, and gave more space to the study of popular culture since this was an area where important work was taking place. These revisions seemed to resonate with both students and teachers, and successive editions reprinted numerous times, as well as appearing in Chinese, Greek, Korean and Japanese.

Each new edition thus sought to identify key new developments in the field, and to contribute to their development. However, this thematic orientation was always set within a wider 'textbook' framework in which we attempted to cover the compass. Each edition included essays on a range of topics or approaches that we felt ought to be covered: such as media political economy, feminism, political communication and democracy, the sociology of media organizations, the production of meaning and media influence. However, what was

1

thought to be the staple diet of the field changed, to some degree, between editions. There was also a cumulative shift in two other respects. The reader became less British and, in relative terms, more international. Reprinted essays that loomed large initially gave way to newly commissioned work in later editions.

This time around, *Mass Media and Society* foregrounds new media studies. This is partly because new communications technology – and in particular the Internet and the Web (still designated conventionally with a capital I and W as a way of registering public awe and wonder, just as the press was given an honorific, capital P in the nineteenth century) – is changing the communications process in important ways. It is also because the new media literature has gone beyond its early technophiliac, cult-fan phase. It has built up a solid core of evidence, and hosts a range of important debates. 'New media' studies are now an essential part of the syllabus. Indeed, new media feature in the majority of essays in this book, and are the specific concern of three chapters.

This edition continues the trend of previous editions in that it is more international in orientation than before. This is registered in the range of countries that fall within its purview: from Ghana to Qatar, China to Sweden, India to Jamaica. However, this desire to resist the parochialism of much media research is offset by our conviction that we should pay more heed to the increasing global pre-eminence of the USA. Consequently, we have given more critical attention than in any previous edition to the workings of the American media and political system.

This new edition has also continued with the policy of having a major blood transfusion every five years or so. Fourteen out of its twenty chapters are new, while the remaining six chapters have all been revised.

Since most readers will dip into this book, rather than read it straight through, it may be helpful to provide a brief guide to what it contains. The chapters on the internet are distributed in different parts of the book. They start, in Section I, with Sonia Livingstone's overview of new media studies. Instead of offering a potted and dull résumé of the literature on this new phenomenon – so typical of a certain style of textbook – Livingstone focuses on two case study themes: on whether the internet has modified or exacerbated social inequality, and whether it has significantly changed political participation and the nature of democracy. Her cautious conclusions illustrate why she rejects the position that sees new communications technology as being outside society, and impacting upon it. Needed, she argues, is a synthesis that recognizes the influence of both technology and society in shaping new media, though one that tends towards what she calls 'soft [social] determinism'.

This debate about what shapes new media, and their wider influence, is taken up in an ambitious, comparative ethnographic account of the net, web and mobile phone. Daniel Miller and Don Slater argue that the different cultures of Ghana and south Asia give rise to divergent ways in which the net is being used and appropriated (though, in both contexts, the net is viewed as a gateway to modernity). The divergent cultures and local contexts of Jamaica and Trinidad also help to explain why the mobile phone took off in the former, and the internet in the latter. However, this is also attributed in part to different government and business policies. The authors thus invoke both a political economy and cultural explanation. This synthetic approach is pursued to its logical conclusion by Miller and Slater who argue that economic and cultural influences became entwined in the different historic evolutions of Jamaica and Trinidad, and that these in turn shaped their respective capitalism, politics and culture that influenced how new media were used.

The third essay in the new media triptych is Nicholas Garnham's guided tour of the information society debate. These comprise, as he points out, a number of different interpretations of the impact of new communications technology linked to different understandings of economic and social change. They are encapsulated by certain labels or concepts that have been frequently invoked at different points during the last three decades; 'leisure society', 'post-industrial society', 'new economy', 'e-business', 'post-fordism', 'third wave' economic development and so on. Garnham goes through each in turn, and concludes that they are all to varying degrees flawed. Indeed, all studies, he concludes, that claim that new communication technology is a central driver of the economy should be viewed with profound scepticism.

These three contributions are situated within a general framework that monitors the field. Thus, Section I is concerned with general perspectives of the role of the media in society. Karen Boyle looks at post-feminist media studies, arguing that its preoccupation with the discourse of representation has led it to lose sight of the ways in which men continue to exercise power in the real world. Christine Geraghty offers a critical account of the development of a literary studies approach to analysing meaning in popular fiction. Kalyani Chadha and Annandam Kavoori point to the growing global convergence of media policy and media formats, but argue unfashionably that the nation-state and nation are important filters that interpret, mediate and also limit through regulation this global convergence. Graham Murdock and Peter Golding outline a distinctive tradition of media political economy, concerned with justice, equity and the public good, that they have played a prominent role in developing. Jay Blumler and Michael Gurevitch survey the enormous changes that have taken place in the relationships between political actors, media and audiences during the recent period. James Curran focuses attention on the conflict between the needs of democracy and of the market, and outlines how these can be resolved.

Section II of the book is concerned with media systems, organizations and cultures. It begins with David Hesmondhalgh's survey of the production of entertainment, centring on the sociology of organization and political economy approaches but noting also important new entrants into the field. This is matched by Michael Schudson's account of the sociology of news organizations – significantly revised in its new version here to incorporate work undertaken in a wide range of countries, as well as modifying its original position in intriguing ways. It is complemented by Barbie Zellizer's argument for stepping outside studies of journalism as an industry, an organization or an occupation by, instead, conceiving of journalism as a culture.

While the first part of this section is concerned with the media in general, the second half travels to specific destinations. Daniel Hallin and Paolo Mancini outline three contrasting models of the media – liberal, democratic corporatist and polarized pluralist – that operate in North America and western Europe (with similarities elsewhere). Naomi Sakr contrasts the repressive media regime of Saudi Arabia and the coercive system in coalition-occupied Iraq with the rise of state-sponsored public service broadcasting in Qatar. Robert Entman offers an externalist view of the US media system, arguing that it is strongly influenced by its political context of a 1.5 party system. Daya Thussu contends that global news networks are mostly strongly influenced by the US foreign policy agenda, and advance the 'soft power' of the USA.

Section III is concerned with media representations, mediations and influence. The opening two essays by Miller and Slater and Garnham that have already been outlined, are concerned with the internet. These are followed by Lee, Chan, Pan and So's analysis of the way in which the same event was reported and interpreted in very different ways around the world, reflecting the divergent national interests, collective memories and ideological/cultural traditions of the countries where different media were based. Linda Aldoory and Shawn Parry-Giles examine the articulation of gender and race, pointing, among other things, to ways in which media sometimes both eroticize and 'otherize' women of colour. Tamar Liebes provides an overview of the development of audience research that takes account of changes in methodology, conceptions of society and the nature of the audience. The book concludes with an essay by Michael Gurevitch and Peter Dahlgren that examines the nature of civic culture in the context of transforming media systems, changing public orientations and evolving liberal democracy.

Acknowledgements

Our thanks go to contributors who put up with requests for revisions, and to Deborah Edwards, Eva Martinez and Abigail Woodman at Arnold who encouraged the conception and delivery of this new edition. We would like to express also our gratitude to Richard Smith for all his help on this edition.

Media and Society: General Perspectives

chapter one

Critical Debates in Internet Studies: Reflections on an Emerging Field

SONIA LIVINGSTONE

Telling the story of the internet

In recent years, the story of the internet, a decentralized, global communications network mediated by the conjunction of computers and telecommunications, has been retold often enough for a consensus to have emerged. Drawing on the longer history of telecommunications, along with accounts of a century's innovations in computing, the story of the internet is generally traced to its origins in the 1960s, making 'internet studies' a very recent field. Key moments include ARPANET's first decentralized communications network in 1969, the introduction of email in 1975, followed by usenet and bulletin board services, the many interim innovations born of interactions between scientists and hackers in the 1970s, Unix users' tradition of the 'open source movement' during the 1980s, the development of hypertext language by Tim Berners-Lee in 1989, the first client browser software in 1991 leading to the world wide web and, bringing the internet widespread recognition beyond the technological elite, US Senator Al Gore's championing of the 'national information infrastructure' (the NII) in the early 1990s. Following this, Microsoft introduced (or privatized) the internet for the mass market with the Windows browser Microsoft Explorer in 1995, and the internet became widely used among businesses and public elites in Western societies by the mid 1990s (Castells, 2002; Slevin, 2000; Winston, 1998).

In its core infrastructure, there has been little technological change over the past decade, notwithstanding vast increases in speed, scale, content and complexity. However, socially this has been a decade of rapid and significant changes, with the internet becoming an everyday technology, diffusing through homes, schools and workplaces by the late 1990s. In 2003, 76 per cent of Americans had used the internet, and 65 per cent had home access (USC, 2004); the rate of internet diffusion in the USA is such that it took just seven years to reach 30 per cent of households, a level of penetration that took 17 years for television and 38 years for the telephone (Rice, 2002). In the UK, 58 per cent of UK adults had used the internet by February 2004, with 49 per cent of UK households having internet access in December 2003 (ONS, 2004). The World Internet Project (2004) found that 66 per cent in Sweden (in 2002) had used the internet, 50 per cent in Japan (in 2002), 46 per cent in Germany (in 2002), 24 per cent in Taiwan (in 2000) and 18 per cent in Hungary (in 2001). Despite the rapidity of the diffusion process, there are considerable cross-national differences (Norris 2001) though, it seems, a levelling-off in access.

If the key 'facts' of the story are agreed, the meaning of those 'facts' is often contested. It is beyond the scope of this chapter to consider technological and infrastructural debates, but it is our purpose to consider the social, political, cultural and economic debates over the internet's shaping, significance and consequences for society. The internet today faces considerable challenges precisely because of its astonishing success. There are problems of scale and capacity, of network architecture and infrastructural robustness, of international legal and regulatory frameworks, and of public trust, security and e-crime, all these accompanying the opportunities widely associated with the internet – its potential for enhancing global communication, revitalizing the democratic process, facilitating economic development and trade, reconfiguring social relations and identities, and many others. The signs are growing that the once-anarchic, perhaps emancipatory internet is subject to increasing attempts to privatize, commercialize, control and profit from the activities of consumers online. Some of these are defended as a neo-liberal freeing of the market, online as well as offline. Others are hotly contested precisely as incursions into public freedoms, privacy and rights. In seeking to understand these phenomena, we must ask, what's new about the internet, what are its characteristics, what opportunities and dangers does it afford, why is it used as it is, in whose interests, and how could things be otherwise?

Complicating attempts to understand the social shaping and consequences of the internet is the way in which it continues to change – the scope of the world wide web is expanding exponentially, newsgroups are losing popularity while blogs are on the rise, instant messaging has displaced chat rooms for many users, e-commerce was slower to take off than expected while email proved the opposite, an unexpected 'killer application' not dissimilar to the surprise success of text messaging, and various, increasingly powerful mobile devices are reaching the market. Hence research must be specific about its focus. The singularity of 'the internet' is particularly problematic, for it refers to a diverse collection of technologies, forms and services bundled together (notably, the world wide web, email, multi-player gaming, e-commerce, newsgroups, peer-to-peer file-sharing, etc.). Yet 'it' (i.e. 'the internet') is often treated, misleadingly, as unitary in academic, public and policy discourses.

What is 'internet studies'?

What are the contours of this emerging field? A parallel story to that of the rise of the internet can be told about the emergence of 'internet studies', though the struggles for control are not quite so hotly fought nor the stakes so high. Still, like the internet itself, internet studies is by no means settled as an intellectual endeavour. Its disciplinary roots are diverse, its methods barely formed and its politics much contested. Moreover, its continually-evolving object of study, being a moving target for research, sets a challenging pace to the entire project. However, the highly time-sensitive claims about technological change are linked to much longer-term and more fundamental changes in society, thereby linking 'internet studies' to 'information studies' through concepts such as the information society, knowledge society, information age and network society (Castells, 2002; Dutton, 1999; Webster, 2002). This, more than the focus on technology, brings a rich vein of theoretical development and argument into the field, together with the necessity of a multidisciplinary or, perhaps better, interdisciplinary perspective.

So, again like the Internet itself, internet studies moved beyond the specialized fields of computer science and technology studies in the mid 1990's drawing in scholars across the academy from the arts to political science, from anthropology to photography and perhaps receiving the most enthusiastic reception in those relatively new and interdisciplinary fields of study – information studies, media studies, science and technology studies, and cultural studies. The *Journal of Communication* featured a symposium on the internet in 1996, with editors Newhagen and Rafaeli already arguing for a complex, empirically grounded analysis of the internet. The *Journal of Computer-Mediated Communication*, begun in 1996, proved quickly successful, *Information, Communication and Society* began in 1998, *New Media and Society* in 1999, and others followed. The first international conference of the *Association of Internet Researchers* (AoIR) brought these diverse fields together face-to-face (as well as online) in 2000, and no visitor to the library or bookshop could miss the overwhelming explosion of academic books with 'internet' (or 'digital', 'wired', 'cyber' or 'online') in their titles. Still one may wonder, does the institutionalization of internet studies mean that a distinct discipline is being born? Or that definite progress is being made?

At the time of writing, internet studies is less institutionalized than, say, media studies or cultural studies. Nonetheless, scholars have sought to identify distinct stages in the development of academic research on the internet. Wellman (2004: 124) describes the first 'age of internet studies' as 'punditry rides rampant', an optimistic celebration of the transformative potential of the internet during the mid 1990s, peppered with dystopian prognostications from the sceptics. Around the time of the dotcom bust at the turn of the twenty-first century, the second age turned to a more serious engagement with evidence, seeking to document users and uses of the internet (see also Lievrouw and Livingstone, 2002; Miller and Slater, 2000). As Wellman and Haythornthwaite (2002: 4) put it, current research studies the internet 'as it descends from the firmament and becomes embedded in everyday life'. The hope is that the third age – the present – will make the move 'from documentation to analysis' (Wellman, 2004: 27).

In this chapter I will consider whether progress is being made towards the theoretical explanation and critical analysis, following both the defusing of the hype and documentation of descriptions of the place of the internet in society. Certainly, any such progress, like technological developments in the underlying infrastructure, has followed a haphazard path of problems, solutions and yet more problems, rather than the well-planned roll-out of a coherent programme. Yet, even though 'there is clearly an internet research generation in the making' (Castells, 2002: x), I shall not argue for the birth of a new academic discipline but rather for a new and provisional field, inevitably since it is tied to a fast-changing technology, that – appropriately – takes its key theories and methods from long-established disciplines in the social sciences and beyond. For if the internet is changing society, it is to theories of society that we must turn for an analysis of these changes.

Disciplinary origins and orientations

Labelling a field has consequences for how it is recognized, valued and connected to neighbouring fields. The study of 'information and communication technology' (ICT) is perhaps the broadest term used to refer to the field. 'New media studies' anchors the research agenda in a long history of media and communications studies. 'Information studies' instead links it to research in library and information studies, information systems and technology studies. So, if the term 'internet' in 'internet studies' is not a simple one, the term 'studies' is no less tractable, and 'internet studies', should, if it were not too tiresome, retain quote marks throughout this chapter. 'Internet studies', then, is a field of inquiry which, while greatly stimulated by the global diffusion of the internet, has a longer intellectual history, bringing together diverse strands of research (e.g. on the economics of information, on cybernetics, on the social psychology of face-to-face communication, on the sociology of mass consumption and on media studies' accounts of previously-new media such as the video recorder or computer games). Consequently, internet studies draws on, if not necessarily draws together, academic disciplines spanning information systems, psychology, economics, media studies and sociology, anthropology and cultural studies, among others.

The case for asserting the existence of, and importance of, internet studies lies, however, less in the distinctiveness of its theory or methods than in the distinctiveness of its object. There have been many attempts to specify just what is interesting and significant about the internet, while seeking to avoid a definition likely to become quickly outdated. Key features of new media, typical of the internet, are outlined in Lievrouw and Livingstone (2002):

- First, new media shape and are shaped by society in a manner that is 'recombinant', meaning that 'new media systems are products of a continuous hybridization of both existing technologies and innovations in interconnected technical and institutional networks' (p. 8). This contributes to the difficulty of determining what is 'new' or not new about the internet (Jankowski *et al.*, 1999), and undermines simple causal claims about the role of technology in social change: as Castells (2002: 1) says, while networks are not inherently new to history, 'they have taken on a new life in our time by becoming information networks, powered by the internet'.

- Second, 'the point-to-point "network" has become accepted as the archetypal form of contemporary social and technical organization', with the term 'network' referring to 'a broad, multiplex connection in which many points or "nodes" (persons, groups, machines, collections of information, organizations) are embedded' (p. 8). This fits with a society increasingly structured according to a 'network of networks' (Castells, 2002), and challenges the dominant 'one-to-many' frame of mass communication by adding in also one-to-one and many-to-many communication into the mix.

- Third, 'ubiquity', this not simply in the sense that all members of society may use new media (for many still lack access) but in the sense that new media 'are ubiquitous because they affect everyone in the societies where they are employed . . . Banking systems, utilities, education, law enforcement, military defence, health care and politics . . . are all dependent on extensive ICT systems for record-keeping, monitoring and transmitting

information – activities that affect anyone who deals with these services or activities'
(pp. 8–9).

- Fourth, interactivity, the means by which the internet and other new media 'give users the means to generate, seek and share content selectively, and to interact with other individuals and groups, on a scale that was impractical with traditional mass media' (p. 9). Even though selectivity, interaction and content creation each have a longer history through other media and, of course, face-to-face communication, it is their specific recombination on a vast scale that mediates a new and challenging set of social consequences.

These key features of the internet provide a common focus for researchers in internet studies. But the social and communicative shifts that they refer to rest on more fundamental shifts. This means that claims for the distinctiveness of the internet are more productively focused on the processes of information, communication and power mediated by the internet – facilitating the technologically mediated extension of human abilities to communicate across time and space and so enabling a greatly increased degree of connectedness among social actors worldwide – than on the technology itself. Many social trends also contribute to shaping the changing conditions of communication – trends in the nature and production of economic goods and services, in the labour market, transport systems, language, etc. These often are analysed in terms of Bell's 'post-industrial society', defined as 'the emergence of a new economic order characterised by the central importance of information and theoretical knowledge, and by a shift from a goods-producing to a service society' (Golding, 2000: 169).

To get a better sense of the field as currently developing, I examine two domains in detail, below. I shall then discuss three critical debates in internet studies in order to draw out some tentative conclusions.

Case 1: From the Digital Divide to Digital Inclusion

Defining the problem

On the premise that 'exclusion from these [internet-mediated economic, social, political, cultural] networks is one of the most damaging forms of exclusion in our economy and in our culture' (Castells, 2002: 3), concerns over the gap between the digital (or internet) haves and have-nots have stimulated much debate and research on barriers to the supposed freedoms enabled by the internet. The 'digital divide' is conceived on all levels from the global, where it is primarily an economic phenomenon that distinguishes developed from developing countries, to the national level, where factors of geography, socio-economic status and ethnicity prove crucial, and the domestic level, where gender and generation stratify contexts of access and use.

These different levels invite very different kinds of empirical projects, from the cross-national comparison of economic flows, employment trends in the information and other sectors and emerging practices of national and international e-commerce, to detailed critiques of national information infrastructure policy and implementation, population surveys comparing internet access and use across diverse constituencies within a nation and, at the most micro level, ethnographic studies of the meanings and practices of internet access and use in the home, school, community or workplace.

Developing the research agenda

Several phases can be distinguished in the developing research agenda. First, in the early to mid 1990s, the focus was on who has access to a computer, then to the internet, and who does not. Digital divide research followed diffusion theory (Rogers, 1995) in seeking to predict the acquisition path for the new medium from its introduction and take up by privileged, early adopters to mass ownership across society. The assumption was generally made that the internet is an unquestioned public and economic good to which all citizens have the right of access (as advocated during the 1990s by the USA's Information Infrastructure Task Force and, in Europe, by the Bangemann Report; Liff *et al.*, 2002), a neo-liberal assumption challenged by critical scholars (Golding, 2000). Beyond charting statistics on access in relation to such stratifying factors as region, age and socio-economic status, this phase led to the setting of policy targets. In the UK, the government announced a target of getting 'everyone online' by 2005. In the USA and elsewhere, attention also focused on those who were 'falling through the net' (Compaine, 2001).

A growing body of research showed that the divide between digital haves and have-nots was reducing but by no means was the gap closing, this suggesting instead a continual shifting of the goal posts and, consequently, the failure of the dichotomy itself. Indeed, increasing ICT access seemed to maintain rather than eliminate distinctions between the relatively more and less advantaged. It became widely recognized that a more complex view, going beyond a simple dichotomy of haves and have-nots, was therefore required (Selwyn, 2004). Not all agreed, however. Compaine (2001: 325) adopts a strictly diffusion approach to argue that the digital divide is rapidly closing, and that the market can be left to itself: he suggests we should 'declare the war won', for 'the overwhelming weight of the data . . . all point in a direction that is historically consistent and socially positive'. This, he argues, is precisely a triumph for capitalism, for it is economic pressures towards innovation and competition that systematically drive down costs and extend accessibility to maximize the market.

For most researchers, however, the second phase switched focus to examine the quality of access, 'the new technological divide' (Castells, 2002). As the platforms for internet access (computer, mobile phone, digital television and a growing range of personal devices), quality of internet access (dial-up, broadband) and the range of locations to go online all diversified, the question increasingly became, 'access where, how and to what?' Following a business model of continual expansion, updating and specialization, technological innovation is a moving target, requiring of the user a recurrent rather than one-off investment (Golding, 2000) in which, once again, social stratification matters. On the basis of her substantial cross-national review, Norris (2001) concludes that increasing internet penetration serves to exacerbate rather than reduce inequalities, precisely because the internet is unlike simple media and consumer goods in which a more-or-less stable technology diffuses from the early adopters to the mass market. For the internet, the 'chameleon-like capacity of digital technologies to morph, converge, and reappear in different guises' (Norris, 2001: 17) maximizes the conditions for maintaining distinctions. Hence 'the' digital divide was reconceptualized as a continuum, with 'degrees of marginality' (Murdock, 2002. 387), and in the plural, as a number of different divides.

The emphasis on equality shifted to that of equity, for providing everyone with equal access is all but impossible in a fast-moving, commercial context in which access is largely privatized within homes and workplaces. On the other hand, seeking to ensure that everyone has a fair or equitable chance is more achievable. In practice, this means a policy of compensatory interventions to ensure that the disadvantaged have at least minimal provision of internet access. Indeed, this phase saw numerous community-based initiatives to provide internet access targeted towards marginalized, 'hard-to-reach' communities. Many pilot projects sprang up to bring internet access and support to deprived inner-city communities, to ethnic minorities, to the elderly or disabled, and so forth (e.g. Phipps, 2000). Frustratingly, however, the many and valiant attempts to collate and share best practice and lessons learned were undermined by the difficulties encountered. These initiatives proved highly resource intensive, uncertain as to their purpose, often underused, and difficult to sustain. Warschauer (2003) offers three telling accounts of well-meaning attempts to bring the internet to excluded communities: in each case the problems encountered, resulting in generally disappointing outcomes, amply demonstrate why 'access is not enough'. Rather, multiple factors – material, economic, social, cultural, technical – crucially mediate access and use of the internet (Livingstone, 2002; Murdock *et al.*, 1995).

In the third phase, 'digital inclusion' has become the new policy goal, linking ICT provision to wider debates over social inclusion and exclusion, and inviting research on the multiple paths to inclusion and the multiple barriers leading to exclusion (Liff *et al.*, 2002; Selwyn, 2004). While not leaving behind the ever-growing requirements of quality access for all, this also brings to the fore questions of meaningful use, of the social contexts of use, and of people's motivation and levels of skill. Moreover, as more aspects of daily life are mediated by the internet, digital skills must be reframed also, seen no longer as the simple extension of basic skills (typing, updating software, installing filters, etc.) but also more ambitiously in terms of literacy (or capacity or competencies) (Livingstone, 2002). The present research agenda, then, assumes that 'the ability to access, adapt, and create new knowledge using new information and communication technology is critical to social inclusion in today's era' (Warschauer, 2003: 9). Perhaps initiatives grounded less in technology and more in people's motivations and social contexts of daily life can be more successful. While still resource-intensive (in both online and, especially, offline resources), Warschauer offers evidence that marginalized groups more successfully gain internet-related skills and literacies when they come together for a community-based project meaningful to their circumstances; not, in other words, to learn to use a computer, but rather to use computing and other resources in order to address the neighbourhood crime problem, or create a student newspaper, or participate in the development of local citizens' rights, etc.

Lessons learned

The dominant metaphor in the digital divide debate is that of a race, with some getting ahead and others left behind. The necessity of running seems taken for granted, since everyone seems to be joining in, though the gains waiting at the winning post are less than clear, and nor is it established that running this race is preferable to other routes to inclusion (e.g. tackling poverty or improving education or strengthening the public sphere). Still, this metaphor is instructive in its emphasis on competition, a central feature of capitalist societies. The lesson of the second phase of the research agenda is surely that even if policies could be put in place to ensure that everyone finishes the race, still some will get on the tracks earlier, arrive at the winning post first, and so get a head start in subsequent races. Little is surprising here, for research in internet studies repeatedly shows 'the persistence of familiar patterns of social structure and experience' (Golding, 2000: 180). More pessimistically, Norris (2001: 17) concludes that 'even if the basic digital divide shrinks gradually over time, it is naïve to believe that the virtual world can overturn fundamental inequalities of social stratification that are endemic throughout postindustrial societies, any more than it is likely to overcome world poverty'.

Still, with more modest ambitions than that of countering inequality, the research community continues to devote its efforts to identifying the conditions under which access to information and communication technologies (computing, digital technologies, most often the internet) can exacerbate or alleviate pre-existing levels of inequality and exclusion. The third phase faces many research questions in pursuing the argument that 'social context, social purpose, and social organization are critical in efforts to provide meaningful information and communication technology access' (Warschauer, 2003: 201). And this in turn can stimulate a range of policy interventions to address the barriers and enablers, now focused more on the 'real' social factors contextualizing internet use than on the provision of technology, in order to use ICT to broaden and deepen social inclusion (e.g. Liff *et al.*, 2002; Phipps, 2000).

Case 2: Online Participation and E-Democracy
Defining the problem

Stimulated by new opportunities to communicate, connect and deliberate online, in a context in which the mass communication model, with its centralized organization, elite gatekeepers and established relations with institutions of power no longer has a monopoly, many have sought to explore whether the internet can facilitate political participation and so revitalize the far-from-perfect democratic process. In the debate over e-democracy, the public or user is positioned not as consumer or skilled worker (as in the digital divide debate) but rather as citizen. In policy circles also, it is increasingly asserted that 'internet access has become a basic entitlement of citizenship in the digital age' (Murdock, 2002: 386; see also Gandy, 2002) and that there threatens to be what Norris (2001: 12) terms a 'democratic divide', distinguishing 'those who do and do not use the multiple political resources available on the internet for civic engagement'.

In recent decades, political scientists have been charting, with mounting concern, the steady decline in political participation by the public, across many countries, as measured by such indicators as voter turn-out, party loyalty and representation in decision-making bodies (Bennett, 1998; Coleman, 1999; Dahlgren, 2003). Since this decline has coincided with the spread of mass media into daily life, media critics have scrutinized every dimension of the media's relations with political institutions and the public sphere. While some ask whether the media are responsible for the withdrawal from civil society (Putnam, 2000), others are intrigued that the public seems to be reconstituting community online, discovering common interests with a potentially huge network of like-minded peers, developing new skills, building alternative deliberative spaces, raising the possibility of a virtual public sphere. So, by contrast with the (somewhat stereotypical) characterization of traditional organizations in democratic societies, structured in accordance with elite hierarchy, representation and accountability, the internet is celebrated for its alternative features – the stress placed on trust, inclusiveness, transparency, action and, above all, deliberation. Can it be that, 'replacing traditional civil society is a less conformist social world . . . characterised by the rise of networks, issue associations, and lifestyle coalitions facilitated by the revolution in personalized, point-to-point communication' (Bennett, 1998: 745)?

Following Habermas (1969/89), Bentivegna (2002) argues that the internet is 'democratic' in the sense that, while each of its features is not intrinsically new, in combination, the internet introduces a qualitative shift in the potential for democratic communication. The features she identifies are: interactivity, enabling citizens to be senders as well as receivers of messages; co-presence of vertical and horizontal communication, facilitating not only communication between elites and citizens but also communication among citizens; disintermediation, by which the power of traditional gatekeepers is undermined in favour of more direct communication among interested parties; communication costs, greatly reducing the entry barriers to participation for small groups, social movements and individuals; the speed of communication, transforming the potential for information dissemination, flexible organization and mobilization across considerable geographic range; and the absence of boundaries, permitting the relatively free circulation of information, opinion and proposals among all interested parties. Here, then, is a rich agenda for empirical research on public participation.

Developing the research agenda

As in the digital divide debate, the early hyperbolic claims for the transformative potential of the internet to right the ills of democracy were quickly superceded. Research shifted to examining rather more modest claims for internet-mediated communication as complementing – rather than replacing – existing channels for political deliberation and action. In so doing, research draws on a long-standing theoretical debate over whether deliberative and participatory models of democracy – seemingly more fitted to the internet – offer an improvement over the well-established but apparently ailing representative model of democracy. So, while some research does explore how traditional political elites use the internet to promote their political goals more effectively (Graber et al., 2004), most research has pursued the possibilities for online deliberation and active participation by the public in the political process.

Worldwide there has been an explosion in projects and initiatives – at global, national and, most often, local levels – to exploit the potential of the internet to draw citizens into civic participation and so enhance democratic partic ipation (Tsagarousianou et al., 1998). However, most projects occur in the 'wired' West, since in non-democratic regimes, such as China, Cuba and Singapore, governments seek to restrict or censor any form of online political deliberation (Graber et al., 2004). One success was the UK Citizens Online Democracy in 1997, which conducted the first online scrutiny of proposed government legislation (the Freedom of Information White Paper); one-third of the many who participated were individual citizens, deliberating with each other and with the government minister responsible (Coleman, 1999; Tumber, 2001). Another was the USA's Move On campaign to persuade Congress to drop impeachment proceedings against Bill Clinton in 1999, mobilizing half a million online messages sent by citizens to Congress (Graber et al., 2004).

At the level of local communities, Rakow's (1999) account of a 'televillage' in North Dakota, USA, provides valuable lessons for the democratizing potential of the internet in community decision-making, though her story ends depressingly when, in a secret business deal, the local (commercial) paper takes over the (public) city website. In the Blacksburg Electronic Village (Kavanaugh and Patterson, 2002), things went awry for a different reason, for although in this community the internet was used effectively to mediate local, social capital-building activities, those involved were precisely those in the community who were already actively involved, already high in civic engagement and social status, the internet merely providing a new conduit for their established interests and activities. In that case, Jankowski (2002) observes that the wired community had been constructed top-down by local elites, positioning ordinary residents as consumers rather than citizens from the start. Even when online community is organized in a more inclusive, democratic fashion as a virtual public sphere, it seems that familiar social patterns are reasserted online. For example, in the Digital City Amsterdam, 'now one of the largest online communities in the world' (Slevin, 2000: 68), citizens transferred offline norms online in order to govern this space (limiting space for each 'resident', banning pornography, vandalism, harassment, etc.), rather than developing new and original forms of social organization.

So, perhaps we should ask not whether the internet can reinvigorate participation among the many but whether it provides an effective tool for those few already committed to participation? Here empirical support is easier to find, both in relation to established political elites and for alternative social movements. Examples of online participation within new social movements include the Zapatistas in Mexico, who used the internet imaginatively and effectively to organize, disseminate and stimulate grass roots activism for a previously marginalized cause, and the international protest in Seattle in 1999 over the globalization policies of the World Trade Organization (Kahn and Kellner, 2004).

In researching e-democracy, it is difficult to determine whether the evidence points to social transformation or merely to a modest increase in levels of participation. Assuming there is more evidence for the latter, it is also difficult to determine whether the absence of dramatic change is best explained by a lack of public interest in participation or by the relative lack of importance of the internet as an enabler of participation. Rather, in response to new forms of networked politics (Graber et al., 2004), the internet continues to develop and change, 'new web forms of design, such as web logs and wikis, have evolved the internet's hypertextual architecture. even as such online phenomena as hacker culture, terrorism, and hactivist militancy have emerged from the technical-fringe to become a central feature of everyday life on the world wide web' (Kahn and Kellner, 2004: 88), resulting in the 'permanent campaign' (for example, against Nike's exploitative labour practices, or against Microsoft's anticompetitive business strategies) characteristic of late modernity (Graber et al., 2004).

Lessons learned

Neither the data nor the theory are so contested in this domain as much as the conclusions to be drawn from them. The pessimists concede that much political activity – publicity, mobilizing, informing, lobbying, consulting, advocacy – is now conducted online, but consider that there is little evidence that political activity is thereby increased or improved as a consequence, for 'politics as usual will probably prevail' (Graber et al., 2004: 97). Moreover, if judged according to Habermasian ideals of the public sphere (1969/89), they argue that 'the virtual political sphere clearly fails the test' (Murdock, 2002: 389), being insufficiently inclusive, interactive or consequential. At the worst, 'individualisation, unequal access, and disenfranchisement may be the outcome of net politics' (Golding, 2000: 176).

The optimists, however, argue that it is too early to judge, but that the embryonic signs provide grounds for hope (Dahlgren, 2003; Hampton and Wellman, 2002; Papacharissi, 2004), for 'politics in cyberspace is attempting to redefine itself in the light of the profound changes affecting the social system in the past decades by exploiting the internet's intrinsic potential' (Bentivegna, 2002: 51). Norris (2001) too concludes on a note of cautious optimism, not because a ringing endorsement of e-democracy is possible, but because of the encouraging if tentative evidence that the internet permits a more open space for debate among a wider diversity of political actors, amplifying small voices that might otherwise not be heard, facilitating rapid, flexible responses to events, ready sharing of information both locally and globally, and some critical challenges to the establishment.

As is also evident in the digital divide debate, e-democracy initiatives require considerable efforts (energy, time, technology, funding) to start up and maintain, both offline as well as online. They also require commitment from political elites if they are not to become 'merely' a discussion among citizens; it is particularly difficult to link the outcome of deliberation (on or offline) to political action or community consequences (Hampton and Wellman, 2002). Problematically too, though familiar from research on knowledge gaps (Bonfadelli, 2002), it seems easier to attract the already interested or politically active than it is to draw in new initiates to democratic deliberation: consequently, initiatives directed at the marginalized risk instead further advantaging the privileged. And, most worryingly, it is not yet clear how robust such initiatives are against the potential to undermine, disrupt or transform democratic spaces into authoritarian, reactionary or extreme spaces.

How ambitious should research be in seeking to change politics? Is Coleman (1999: 69) right that 'the emergence of the internet presents . . . the possibility of a qualitative shift in the practice of political communication, as significant for the pre-millennial 1990s as TV was for the 1960s . . . [with] hitherto unprecedented possibilities for citizens' deliberation and public input to decision-making processes' (Coleman, 1999: 69). If so, this opens up an agenda examining the communicative conditions under which open deliberation can be effective online, the creativity of (h)activist strategists versus the dominance of the elite publicity machine, the commitment of political elites to participatory ideals (rather than merely to more publicity), the continued emergence of innovative online forums and tactics, the willingness of the public to trust and to commit (on and offline), and so forth. This agenda can keep internet studies busy for years to come. Yet even after this, we may still also find ourselves worrying, with McChesney (1996: 108), that 'the issue here is not whether a citizen-based, nonprofit sector of cyberspace can survive in the emerging regime . . . rather, the key issue is whether the nonprofit, non-commercial sector of cyberspace will be able to transform our societies radically for the better'.

Varieties of Critique in Internet Studies

In this chapter I have pointed to some key debates and developments in the new field of internet studies, including debates over the focus of the field itself. I have also examined two cases within the field: that of the digital divide, now digital inclusion, and that of online participation or e-democracy. As these demonstrate, developments in internet studies depend on a rigorously critical reception by the academy, contesting claims, introducing alternative evidence and pointing to biases or oversimplifications. In this final section I explore more carefully the nature of these critical debates, arguing that 'critique' within the academy means at least three distinct ways of approaching theory and evidence within (and beyond) internet studies. These are, first, 'analytic critique' – a cautious and sceptical analysis that stays within the terms of the argument to interrogate claims being made for internet-related societal changes; second, 'explanatory critique' – the contrasting of competing arguments or explanations for observed changes, which in internet studies is typically cast in terms of technological versus social determinisms; and third, 'ideological critique' – in which the underlying interests at stake in driving these changes are identified from conflicting critical/Marxist and neo-liberal world views. Let us examine these varieties of critique in turn.

What's new?

Internet studies have been stimulated by the dramatic sense that the internet could change everything, so the world will never be the same again; this idea has brought attention, resources and talent to the research agenda. At the same time, the academy has devoted considerable energy to critiquing these claims for change; as Golding (2000: 166) sceptically observes, 'we are, it seems, always on the cusp of a new sociality'. Indeed, the research literature is full of sensible warnings against getting caught up in hyperbole, swayed by moral panics or rushing down blind alleys endemic to popular and policy discussion. These public discussions typically assert a powerful narrative of progress or decline, with the internet cast as angel or villain in the moves towards global understanding, loss of tradition, rise in surveillance, loss of privacy, new forms of creativity or new levels of risk.

As the cases of the digital divide and e-democracy both show, the internet has not (yet) made a dramatic difference to either inequality or participation in society, though more modest changes are evident as we learn not only more about the internet but more about how the internet is, and can be, embedded in everyday circumstances. When Jankowski et al. (1999: 6) asked 'what's new about new media?' in *New Media and Society*, it was to prioritize these provisional, contingent claims that they invited 'work which seeks to analyse "newness" through comparison between the old and the new, in their social and cultural contexts'. Five years on, asking 'what's changed about new media', Lievrouw (2004) argues that the field has become characterized less by uncertainty and more by the banality of its topic as new media become part of the mainstream of everyday life.

This banality has its upsides – for example, it provokes us to become more theoretical, now that much of the basic descriptive work has been done; and its downsides – as some of the more radical possibilities become obscured by emerging norms surrounding the technology. We must continue to be sceptical of claims for change, weighing evidence, clarifying concepts, acknowledging the limits of research. For example, in arguing for continuities rather than a radical break with the past, Webster (2002: 22) rejects the term 'information society' (though not the importance of information) because, he argues, the case has not been established that 'quantitative increases in information lead to qualitative social changes' – and indeed, the case for the qualitative changes so often claimed is a difficult one to make. In relation to e-democracy, we have seen how difficult it is to determine whether the evidence points to social transformation or merely to a modest increase in levels of participation, and whether this is best explained by a lack of public interest in participation or by the relative lack of importance of the internet as an enabler of participation. Or is the problem more prosaically a methodological one, that the right questions have not yet been asked, or the best measures used, or sufficient resources put into the initiatives being evaluated?

Increasingly, academics are expected to predict, and so intervene in, events that shape the future, despite their considerable and warranted wariness about engaging in futurology (Silverstone, 1997). Widely varying assessments of the pace and urgency of social and technological change frame debates about the internet. Indeed, there are genuine difficulties in measuring social change. The social consequences of print, for example, became evident only after centuries of change, beginning with the invention of the printing press in the fifteenth century, playing a key role in the Protestant Reformation in Europe through the sixteenth and seventeenth centuries, and then with the achievement of mass literacy (via mass education) in the eighteenth and nineteenth centuries (Luke, 1989). The 'internet revolution', if such it is, is supposedly occurring on a scale of decades, years or even months, hyped by technologists, business and, it must be said, by governments. The difficulty for research lies in balancing attention to standards and precautions required for intellectual and empirical rigour with the demand of producing timely findings and recommendations to contribute to public and policy agendas.

Accounting for change

The claim that every aspect of society – from work to family life, from politics to entertainment, from religion to sexuality – is affected by innovations in information and communication technologies all too easily lends itself to the kind of technological determinism that still so often now widely critiques. As Raymond Williams noted, 'in *technological determinism, research and development* have been assumed as self-generating. The new technologies are invented as it were in an independent sphere, and then create new societies or new human conditions' (1974: 13). Rather than casting technological innovation as the cause and society as the effect, social science instead seeks to understand how 'the technological, instead of being a sphere separate from social life, is part of what makes society possible – in other words, it is constitutive of society' (MacKenzie and Wajcman, 1999: 23). The internet, far from being 'a single medium which sprung fully formed into our lives less than a decade ago' (Lievrouw and Livingstone, 2002), is like other innovations in undergoing a lengthy and highly social process of research, development and design, hand in hand with the co-construction of a 'market' and its 'needs' (Mansell and Silverstone, 1996; Winston, 1998).

To counter the claims of technological impact or determination, Woolgar (2002: 14–19) proposes five 'rules' for understanding developments within what he calls, with a deliberate question mark, the 'virtual society?'. These are, first, the importance of contextualization, namely that 'the uptake and use of the new technologies depend crucially on local social context'; second, the assumption of inequality, that 'the fears and risks associated with new technologies are unevenly socially distributed'; third, the consistent empirical evidence against displacement of the real, for 'virtual technologies supplement rather than substitute for real activities'; fourth, the counter-intuitive observation, 'the more virtual the more real', based on findings that the growth of online activities/spaces has in unexpected ways intensified, remediated or stimulated innovation also in offline activities and spaces; and fifth, contra claims about the death of distance, since efforts to transcend the local and promote the global turn out to depend on specific local practices and identities, 'the more global the more local'.

These rules are clearly consonant with our two case studies and they offer a useful heuristic for anticipating the social processes that shape and contextualize the development and diffusion of new media. But they make little or no reference to the specifics of the technology itself and so risk replacing technological determinism with an equally simple sociological determinism. Though advocates of both these positions can be found in the literature, others are seeking a more subtle 'soft determinism', for 'everything that is important is what happens in the mediations, which dissolves these dualisms' (Miller *et al.*, 2004: 79). One approach is to treat technologies as texts, as designed and interpreted within particular social contexts that facilitate certain social options and close off others.

Agre (2004: 27) endorses this, arguing that 'every system affords a certain range of interpretations, and that range is determined by the discourses that have been inscribed into it'. Relatedly, Lessig (1999) argues that cyberspace is regulated at the level of the internet codes: these inscribe cultural norms, encode institutional imperatives, configure possible uses, prioritize certain activities and interests over others and establish the line between what is public and what is private online in subtle but crucial ways. Internet users, like mass audiences, are faced not with the onslaught of technological impacts but with the challenge of interpreting texts flexibly and meaningfully, guided and also constrained by textual and contextual factors (Livingstone, 2004). Note the verbs used here, for they mark discursively the shift in the argument – from strong determinism's language of impact, effect and transformation, positioning the technology as outside society and impacting upon it, to soft determinism's language of reconfiguring, establishing, affording, positioning the technology as precisely part of society and, by encoding its meanings and practices, in turn contributing to it. The question of whether the internet is to be judged 'democratic' as a medium, for example, will be answered differently depending whether one means that it is inherently democratic, or democratic to the extent that we have made it so.

Eschewing simple determinisms then, internet studies should now critically develop both the soft-determinist claim that 'core economic, social, political, and cultural activities throughout the planet are being structured by and around the Internet' (Castells, 2002: 3), and the social shaping claim that 'people, institutions, companies, and society at large, transform technology, any technology, by appropriating it, by modifying it, by experimenting with it' (Castells, 2002: 4). Neither can be studied satisfactorily in isolation from the other. Some would then take a further step towards social critique which 'situates technology within the underlying unequal power relationships that exist in society' (Warschauer, 2003: 209). This raises questions not only about the explanations in contention within internet studies but also about their politics and values.

Change for the better?

Many introductions to internet (or new media or ICT) studies describe a polarization between optimists and pessimists, as illustrated by our two case studies. Since this optimistic/pessimistic framing is not typical of the social sciences, we might ask why? Often, the optimist/pessimist discourse is introduced for rhetorical purposes, in order to disavow both positions (set up as 'straw men') and so legitimate a more cautious and grounded perspective in their place. More significantly, the pivotal role of social change in framing technology–society relations is responsible, rendering the field heavily future-oriented and policy-directed, despite social scientists' preference for analysing the past and present. With this future-orientation comes a focus, implicitly or explicitly, on values, even on political ideologies. However, when the optimist/pessimist positions are more seriously debated one of several underlying oppositions appears to be at stake.

One opposition is that between administrative and critical schools of communication research, defined by Lazarsfeld (1941) in the early days of mass communication research. He sought to distinguish research that takes its agenda from, and produces recommendations useful for, public policy, from research which maintains a critical distance from established institutions. We can gloss over this by contrasting those who consider it the responsibility of research actively to shape social and technological change with those who consider it their role to produce independent knowledge that critiques the strategic activities of the establishment (Levy and Gurevitch, 1994). In internet studies it seems as if the optimists work within the normative social framework in order to contribute towards 'making things better' while the pessimists stand outside in order to remind them when the public interest is not after all being served.

A second debate discernible within the optimism/pessimism polarity is that between the political economy versus cultural studies schools of communication research (Ferguson and Golding, 1997; Mosco, 1996). The political economists tend towards pessimism for similar reasons to the critical communication scholars, for macro-level analyses of the exploitation of the public interest to further the interests of the elite, characteristic of capitalism, unsurprisingly generate a pessimistic critique. Unlike critical communications scholars, however, who maintain their independence, the political economists also argue for policy interventions that might alleviate inequalities, improve participation, reduce invasions of privacy, increase public accountability of governance structures, and so forth. For example, McChesney (1996: 100) argues not only that 'capitalism encourages a culture that places a premium on commercial values and downplays communitarian ideals' but he also argues for structural media reform, for increasing regulation in the public interest and for limiting the antidemocratic consequences of the major media conglomerates (see also Mansell, 2004; McChesney, 2000).

On the other hand, the optimism evident within cultural studies is unlike that of administrative scholars. Instead, it seeks to identify forms of evasion or resistance among the public, whether ordinary people, particular subcultures or new social movements, so that some subversion of or alternatives to the dominant order is achieved (see Curran *et al.*, 1996; Seiter, 1999). Here the work on cultural analysis of mass media audiences is extended to new media so as to reveal the ways in which, through the interstices and indeterminacies of (mediated) social structures, people in their daily lives manage to evade, resist or reconstruct normative meanings or practice (Livingstone, 2004).

A third debate also motivates the rehearsal of the optimist/pessimist rhetoric, this being between modernist versus postmodernist views. Where late modern accounts stress the continuities from life offline to life online (e.g. Livingstone, 2002; Miller and Slater, 2000; Webster, 2000), postmodern accounts radically rethink the key terms to open up new and exciting possibilities. For example, Poster (2001: 175) explores the role of the internet within a postmodern democracy 'that opens new positions of speech, empowering previously excluded groups and enabling new aspects of social life to become part of the political process'. The radical nature of this claim becomes clear not just from his argument that 'the age of the public sphere as face-to-face talk is clearly over' (p. 181) but more importantly from his suggestion that 'the public sphere as a homogeneous space of embodied subjects in symmetrical relations, pursuing consensus through the critique of arguments and the presentation of validity claims' (pp. 181–2) is also over. In electronically mediated discourse, operating within what Poster terms 'the mode of information' (or 'virtualisation'), we find instead 'new forms of decentralized dialogue', 'new combinations of human–machine assemblages, new individual and collective "voices"' (p. 182). Others are developing postmodern arguments in other domains. Kress (2003) asks how the visual, hypertextual, always-open representational forms of the world wide web permit new ways of thinking and understanding, by contrast with the linear, hierarchical, closed formats and thinking of the modernist era of print. Kellner (2002) extends this argument to suggest that, if forms of representation are radically changing, so then are the possibilities for literacy and hence for education, enabling more democratic and creative styles of learning.

There is little resolution to be had here. Those seeking to counter the postmodern position (Golding, 2000; Webster, 2002; Wellman and Haythornthwaite, 2002) do not convince those excited by the potential of the internet to prompt radically challenging ways of thinking. In empirical terms, our two case studies suggest that researchers have been more successful in tracking the (re-)emergence of familiar cultural norms, social conventions and everyday anxieties than they have in documenting radical or alternative forms of consumption, communication and community-building, except perhaps among a highly motivated and generally elite minority of internet enthusiasts (e.g. Snyder, 1998; Turkle, 1995). But other cases may have led to different, less conservative conclusions. After all, research on the internet is still in its early stages, the internet itself only having been widely available for ten years, and even then only in wealthy parts of the world.

Internet studies have moved on from the early days of speculative hyperbole towards a solid grounding in empirical research, even if this remains tentative in its preliminary conclusions. They have also moved on from the assumption of a separate domain, 'cyberspace', clearly distinct from the 'real world'. Thirdly, they have moved away from simple assertions of technological determinism in favour of either social determinism or 'soft' technological determinism. The research agenda continues to be contested by scholars taking more optimistic or more pessimistic approaches, working within more market liberal or more critical frameworks, from a late modern or postmodern stance. And the research agenda continues to expand as ever more aspects of everyday life, once (and still) the subject of other social sciences (from anthropology to criminology, from economics to psychology), 'go online' and so also fall under the (one hopes capacious) umbrella of 'internet studies'.

References

Agre, P. (2004) 'Internet Research: For and Against', in M. Consalvo *et al.* (eds), *Internet Research Annual*, vol. 1. New York: Peter Lang.

Bennett, L. (1998) '1998 Ithiel De Sola Pool Lecture: The Uncivic Culture: Communication, Identity, and the Rise of Lifestyle Politics', *Political Science and Politics*, 31 (4), 740–61.

Bentivegna, S. (2002) 'Politics and New Media', in L. Lievrouw and S. Livingstone (eds), *The Handbook of New Media*. London: Sage, pp. 50–61.

Bonfadelli, H. (2002) 'The Internet and Knowledge Gaps: A Theoretical and Empirical Investigation', *European Journal of Communication*, 17 (1), 65–84.

Castells, M. (2002) *The Internet Galaxy: Reflections on the Internet, Business, and Society*. Oxford: Oxford University Press.

Coleman, S. (1999) 'The New Media and Democratic Politics', *New Media and Society*, 1 (1), 67–73.

Compaine, B. M. (ed.) (2001) *The Digital Divide: Facing a Crisis or Creating a Myth?* Cambridge MA and London: MIT Press.

Curran, J., Morley, D. and Walkerdine, V. (eds) (1996) *Cultural Studies and Communications*. London: Edward Arnold.

Dahlgren, P. (2003) 'Reconfiguring Civic Culture in the New Media Milieu', in J. Corner and D. Pels (eds), *Media and the Restyling of Politics*. London: Sage, pp. 151–70.

Dutton, W. (1999) *Society on the Line: Information Politics in the Digital Age*. Oxford: Oxford University Press.

Ferguson, M. and Golding, P. (eds) (1997) *Cultural Studies in Question*. London: Sage.

Gandy, O. H. (2002) 'The Real Digital Divide: Citizens versus Consumers', in L. Lievrouw and S. Livingstone (eds), *The Handbook of New Media*. London: Sage, pp. 448–60.

Golding, P. (2000) 'Forthcoming Features: Information and Communications Technologies and the Sociology of the Future', *Sociology*, 34 (1), 165–84.

Graber, D. A., Bimber, B., Bennett, W. L., Davis, R. and Norris, P. (2004) 'The Internet and Politics: Emerging Perspectives', in H. Nissenbaum and M. E. Price (eds), *Academy and the Internet*. New York: Peter Lang, pp. 90–119.

Habermas, J. (1969/89) *The Structural Transformation of the Public Sphere: An Inquiry into a Category of Bourgeois Society*. Cambridge, MA: MIT Press.

Hampton, K. N. and Wellman, B. (2002) 'The Not So Global Village of Netville', in B. Wellman and C. Haythornwaite (eds), *The Internet in Everyday Life*. London: Blackwells, pp. 345–71.

Jankowski, N. W. (2002) 'Creating Community with Media: History, Theories and Scientific Investigations', in L. Lievrouw and S. Livingstone (eds), *Handbook of New Media: Social Shaping and Consequences of ICTs*. London: Sage, pp. 34–49.

Jankowski, N., Jones, S., Samarajiva, R. and Silverstone, R. (1999) 'Editorial', *New Media and Society*, 1 (1), 5–9.

Journal of Communication (1996) Symposium on 'The Net', J. Newhagen and S. Rafaeli (eds).

Kahn, R. and Kellner, D. (2004) 'New Media and Internet Activism: from the "Battle of Seattle" to Blogging', *New Media and Society*, 6 (1), 87–95.

Kavanaugh, A. L. and Patterson, S. J. (2002) 'The Impact of Community Computer Networks on Social Capital and Community Involvement in Blacksburg', in B. Wellman and C. Haythornwaite (eds), *The Internet in Everyday Life*. London: Blackwells, pp. 325–44.

Kellner, D. (2002) 'New Media and New Literacies: Reconstructing Education for the New Millenium', in L. Lievrouw and S. Livingstone (eds), *The Handbook of New Media: Social Shaping and Consequences of ICTs*. London: Sage, pp. 90–104.

Kress, G. (2003) *Literacy in the New Media Age*. London: Routledge.

Lazarsfeld, P. F. (1941) 'Remarks on Administrative and Critical Communications Research', *Studies in Philosophy and Science*, 9, 3–16.

Lessig, L. (1999) *Code, and Other Laws of Cyberspace*. New York: Basic Books.

Levy, M. R. and Gurevitch, M. (eds) (1994) *Defining Media Studies: Reflections on the Future of the Field*. New York: Oxford University Press.

Lievrouw, L. (2004) 'What's Changed About New Media? Introduction to the Fifth Anniversary Issue of New Media and Society', *New Media and Society*, 6 (1), 9–15.

Lievrouw, L. and Livingstone, S. (eds) (2002) *Handbook of New Media: Social Shaping and Social Consequences*. London: Sage.

Liff, S., Steward, F. and Watts, P. (2002) 'New Public Places for Internet Access: Networks for Practice-based Learning and Social Inclusion', in S. Woolgar (ed.), *Virtual Society? Technology, Cyberbole, Reality*. Oxford: Oxford University Press, pp. 78–98.

Livingstone, S. (2002) *Young People and New Media*. London: Sage.

————(2004) 'The Challenge of Changing Audiences: or, What is the Audience Researcher to do in the Internet Age?', *European Journal of Communication*, 19 (1), 75–86.

Luke, C. (1989) *Pedagogy, Printing and Protestantism: The Discourse of Childhood*. Albany, NY: State University of New York Press.

MacKenzie, D., and Wajcman, J (eds), (1999) *The Social Shaping of Technology*, 2nd edn. Buckingham: Open University Press

Mansell, R. (2004) 'Political Economy, Power and New Media', *New Media and Society*, 6 (1), 96–105.

Mansell, R. and Silverstone, R. (1996) (eds), *Communication by Design. The Politics of Information and Communication Technologies*. Oxford: Oxford University Press.

McChesney, R. W. (1996) 'The Internet and U.S. Communication Policy-Making in Historical and Critical Perspective', *Journal of Communication*, 46 (1), 98–124.

——(2000) *Rich Media, Poor Democracy: Communication Politics in Dubious Times*. New York: The New Press.

Miller, D. and Slater, D. (2000) *The Internet: An Ethnographic Approach*. London: Berg.

Miller, D., Slater, D. and Suchman, L. (2004) 'Anthropology', in H. Nissenbaum and M. E. Price (eds), *Academy and the Internet*. New York: Peter Lang, pp. 71–89.

Mosco, V. (1996) *The Political Economy of Communication: Rethinking and Renewal*. London: Sage.

Murdock, G. (2002) 'Review Article: Debating Digital Divides', *European Journal of Communication*, 17 (3), 385–90.

Murdock, G., Hartmann, P. and Gray, P. (1995) 'Contextualizing Home Computers: Resources and Practices', in N. Heap *et al.* (eds), *Information Technology and Society: A Reader*. London: Sage, pp. 269–83.

Norris, P. (2001) *Digital Divide: Civic Engagement, Information Poverty, and the Internet Worldwide*. Cambridge: Cambridge University Press.

Office-for-National-Statistics. (2004, April) *Internet Access: 12.1 Million Households Now Online*, www.statistics.gov.uk.

Papacharissi, Z. (2004) 'Democracy Online: Civility, Politeness, and the Democratic Potential of Online Political Discussion Groups', *New Media and Society*, 6 (2), 259–83.

Phipps, L. (2000) 'New Communications Technologies: A Conduit for Social Inclusion', *Information, Communication and Society*, 3 (1), 39–68.

Poster, M. (2001) *What's the Matter with the Internet?* Minneapolis: University of Minnesota.

Putnam, R. D. (2000) *Bowling Alone: The Collapse and Revival of American Community*. New York: Simon and Schuster.

Rakow, L. F. (1999) 'The Public at the Table: from Public Access to Public Participation', *New Media and Society*, 1 (1), 74–82.

Rice, R. (2002) 'Primary Issues in Internet use: Access, Civic and Community Involvement, and Social Interaction and Expression', in L. Lievrouw and S. Livingstone (eds), *Handbook of New Media: Social Shaping and Consequences of ICTs*. London: Sage, pp. 109–29.

Rogers, E. M. (1995) *Diffusion of Innovations*, vol. 4. New York: Free Press.

Seiter, E. (1999) *Television and New Media Audiences*. New York: Oxford University Press.

Selwyn, N. (2004) 'Reconsidering Political and Popular Understandings of the Digital Divide', *New Media and Society*, 6 (3), 341–62.

Silverstone, R. (1997) 'New Media in European households', in U. T. Lange and K. Goldhammer (eds), *Exploring the Limits: Europe's Changing Communication Environment*. Berlin: Springer-Verlag, pp. 113–34.

Slevin, J. (2000) *The Internet and Society*. Cambridge: Polity.

Snyder, I. (ed.) (1998) *Page to Screen: Taking Literacy into the Electronic Era*. London and New York: Routledge.

Tsagarousianou, R., Tambini, D. and Bryan, C. (1998) (eds), *Cyberdemocracy: Technology, Cities and Civic Networks*. London: Routledge.

Tumber, H. (2001) 'Democracy in the Information Age: The Role of the Fourth Estate in Cyberspace', *Information, Communication and Society* 4 (1). 95–112.

Turkle, S. (1995) *Life on the Screen: Identity in the Age of the Internet*. New York: Simon and Schuster.

USC (2004, September) *The Digital Future Report: Surveying the Digital Future Year Four – Ten Years, Ten Trends*. USC Annenberg School, Center for the Digital Future (www.digitalcenter.org).

Warschauer, M. (2003) *Technology and Social Inclusion: Rethinking the Digital Divide*. Cambridge, MA: MIT Press.

Webster, F. (2002) 'The Information Society Revisited', in L. Lievrouw and S. Livingstone (eds), *Handbook of New Media: Social Shaping and Consequences of ICTs*. London: Sage, pp. 22–33.

Wellman, B. (2004) 'The Three Ages of Internet Studies: Ten, Five and Zero Years Ago', *New Media and Society*, 6 (1), 123–29.

Wellman, B. and Haythornthwaite, C. (2002) *The Internet in Everyday Life*. London: Blackwells.

Williams, R. (1974) *Television: Technology and Cultural Form*. London: Fontana.

Winston, B. (1998) *Media Technology and Society: A History: From the Telegraph to the Internet*. London: Routledge.

Woolgar, S. (2002) 'Five Rules of Virtuality', in S. Woolgar (ed.), *Virtual Society? Technology, Cyberbole, Reality*. Oxford: Oxford University Press, pp. 1–22.

World Internet Project (2004) (www.worldinternetproject.net/, consulted 26/10/04).

chapter two

Feminism Without Men: Feminist Media Studies in a Post-Feminist Age

KAREN BOYLE

Post-ing feminism

The terms 'feminism' and 'post-feminism' are widely used both in the media and in media studies, yet their meaning is difficult to pin down. As Amanda Lotz writes:

> Confusion and contradiction mark understandings of feminism in US popular culture at the turn of the 21st century. Surveying the terrain of both feminist theory and popular discussions of feminism, we seem to have entered an alternate language universe where words can simultaneously connote a meaning and its opposite (Lotz, 2001: 105).

This article considers how this confusion and contradiction impacts upon feminist media studies, focusing on the ways in which 'post-feminism' features in these debates. The final section works through these issues in relation to *Buffy the Vampire Slayer* and feminist criticism of the show.

At the outset, a definition of terms must be provided, although this is no easy task. Indeed, a quick perusal of any book dealing with feminist theory provides an array of feminisms: liberal feminism, socialist feminism, radical or revolutionary feminism, lesbian feminism, black feminism, postmodern feminism, first-, second- or third-wave feminisms to name just a few. Clearly, these feminisms are defined less by commonality than by difference – of membership, generation, allegiance with other political movements, modes of organization and relationship to the academy – but they do share a common recognition of gendered inequality and a determination to change that reality. Or, as bell hooks (2000: 1) puts it: 'feminism is a movement to end sexism, sexist exploitation, and oppression'. So, until sexism, sexist exploitation and oppression have been consigned to the dustbin of history, there will be a need for feminism.

In this context, what can 'post-feminism' offer?

If defining feminism is complicated, then defining post-feminism is even more so, requiring a definition both of the feminism to be 'post-ed' and of the 'post-ing' itself. The feminism most often at stake here is second-wave feminism, which, in both the UK and the USA, can be dated to the development of the women's liberation movement (WLM) in the late 1960s. Many contemporary writers – whether they define themselves as post-feminist or not – characterize the WLM as a consensus-based political movement, noting the movement's rejection of conventional modes of femininity and its assumption of a universalized feminist sisterhood (e.g. Brooks, 1997; Hollows, 2000). There is a certain amount of truth in this characterization. There was (and still is) a tension between feminism and femininity that alienated many women, and the 1960s–70s movement was rightly criticized – particularly by women-of-colour, lesbians and working-class women – for ignoring structural differences between women in the often naïve conception of 'sisterhood' (e.g. Carby, 1982; hooks, 1982). However, it is not true that the second wave completely failed to recognize difference (Richardson, 1996). In the British context, for example, debates at the National Women's Liberation Movement conferences held between 1971 and 1978 repeatedly foregrounded women's different positions of privilege in relation to regional, class and sexual identities. Difference, here, was not simply an issue for theory (though it *was* an issue for theory), but related to the organization and priorities of the movement itself. At the regional and local levels, groups organized around single issues (including reproductive rights, wages for housework and violence against women) or sought to bring women together on the basis of commonality *and* difference, in relation, for example, to racial, ethnic or national identities, class, sexuality or experience of motherhood.[1]

However, what is perhaps most worrying about the (re-)construction of the second wave as a period of consensus is the way this functions to take the movement out of feminism or to equate movement with the 'post' era (see Brooks, 1997). Feminism's practices have never remained static but have developed and responded to change, both in the contemporary period and in feminism's first wave (see Littlewood, 2004: 149–50). Acknowledging difference, then, is not to 'post' feminism, but to *do* feminism. As hooks (2000: 58) argues:

> There has been no contemporary movement for social justice where individual participants engaged in the dialectical exchange that occurred among feminist thinkers about race which led to the re-thinking of much feminist theory and practice. The fact that participants in the feminist movement could face critique and challenge while still remaining wholeheartedly committed to a vision of justice, of liberation, is a testament to the movement's strength and power. It shows us that no matter how misguided feminist thinkers have been in the past, the will to change, the will to create the context for struggle and liberation, remains stronger than the need to hold on to wrong beliefs and assumptions.

The understanding of feminism upon which post-feminism relies is, therefore, flawed. To be clear, this is not to argue that there is one authentic feminism that post-feminism has simply misunderstood. Rather, it is to point to the very multiplicity of feminisms – within as well as outside of the second wave – and the inherent difficulty of attempting to fix feminism in order to 'post' it.

The meaning of the 'post' in post-feminism also requires consideration. Broadly speaking, there are three overlapping ways in which the term is used – to imply a periodization, a rejection or a development of second-wave feminism – and I will briefly consider each of these, reflecting on the way their meanings are constructed in popular representations and by feminist media critics. It should also be noted, however, that I am – of necessity – glossing over important national and disciplinary differences in the usage of the term (Lotz, 2001: 112). Partly, this is a practical decision – mapping the terrain is already complicated enough and my aim is to give a broad overview of debates rather than a strictly comprehensive account – but it is also an acknowledgement that the ways in which discourses about (post-) feminism circulate, within media studies and within the media, are not bound by national or disciplinary boundaries even as they may exhibit national or disciplinary peculiarities.

Periodizing feminism

In implying a periodization, post-feminism speaks of a time *after* feminism.

As Sarah Projansky (2001: 70) notes, the death of (second-wave) feminism has been regularly proclaimed in the media since the early 1980s. The reasons given for its passing are two-fold: either feminism's successes have rendered the movement obsolete because women now have equality; or, feminism's failures have rendered the movement obsolete in demonstrating the absurdity of feminist demands and the intractability of material differences based on gender. However, to go back a step, the very existence of feminism's second wave depends upon a first wave (usually associated with the struggle for suffrage). To the extent that it ignores this legacy and reduces all feminisms to one feminist moment (in the late 1960–1970s), post-feminism is profoundly ahistorical (Brunsdon, 1997a: 102).

Moreover, proclaiming the 'death' of feminism in this way depends upon an assumption that feminism's movement is a linear one. This is difficult to sustain, not least because so much feminist work has to be continually rediscovered by new generations (Spender, 1982). As a result, constructing a feminist lineage is fraught with difficulty. For example, Ann Brooks' (1997) attempt to fix writers and ideas within a chronology culminating in post-feminism leads her to describe Ann Kaplan's work of the early 1980s as 'pre-postfeminist' and Teresa de Lauretis' work of the same period as 'early postfeminist'. Both of these designations imply that there is a moment, in time as well as in theory, before which it is not possible to talk of post-feminism and after which it is not possible to talk about feminism without qualification (hence, 'pre-postfeminism' rather than simply 'feminism'). Leslie Heywood and Jennifer Drake (1997: 4) attempt to fix their moment even more precisely, defining feminists born between 1963 and 1974 as third wavers. Clearly, the history of feminist theory and practice is important. However, it is difficult to see how this kind of fixing of pre-feminist, feminist, post-feminist *moments* is useful on a theoretical, political or even on a personal, level. After all, how many of us experience feminism in this way?

To give a personal example: my birthdate places me within Heywood and Drake's third wave and my teenage years were clearly shaped by the gains of the second wave, but I only encountered feminist activism and theory as a young adult in the academy. This academic encounter – which privileged the texts and theories of the second wave – led to my involvement with feminist organizations working to challenge male violence and support women survivors, an ongoing involvement that feeds into my academic writing and thinking about feminism and the media. How I 'do' feminism (and how I do feminist media criticism) therefore continues to shift as I encounter new ideas, practices and challenges and as – through my academic work – I encounter old ideas, practices and challenges that are, nevertheless, new to me. I am continually learning about feminism's present and its history, and that conjunction shapes the kind of feminism I 'do'. But it also makes the need to fix and precisely define that feminism impossible and rather redundant. On a broader scale, the intellectual effort to fix and define feminism(s) is often counter-productive in that it makes feminism and feminists (not sexism, sexist exploitation and oppression) the subject of our criticism.

One result of this within feminist media studies is that we have numerous studies that explore the 'feminism' of women-centred media texts, but very little work that examines the daily playing out of gender relations in non-feminist or male-centred shows. 'Post-feminism' has been a key concept in much of this scholarship since the early 1990s (Lotz, 2001). Brunsdon (1997a: 81–102), for example, uses the term in an essay on *Working Girl* (Nichols, 1987) and *Pretty Woman* (Marshall, 1990) to signal how these films are formed by, yet disavow, feminism. She argues that the female protagonists have a specific relation to femininity, being neither trapped in femininity (pre-feminist), nor rejecting of it (feminist), but, rather, using it to their own advantage in the workplace and the bedroom. Whilst the heroines' uses of femininity often look decidedly pre-feminist, their desires and aspirations – for career advancement, equality in interpersonal relationships, financial independence and sexual satisfaction – are expressed in a vocabulary that is historically specific in its debt to feminism. It is precisely this combination of traditional femininity with the gains of second-wave feminism that many cultural critics – both within and outside of the academy – have labelled post-feminist.

For these critics, post-feminism is not a movement or theory, but a way of acknowledging the complex relationship to feminism exhibited in mainstream cultural texts and, indeed, the term is sometimes used as though it is synonymous with popular feminism. It is the apparent tension between feminism and femininity that is central here and, as a result, a majority of this work is concerned with women and girls. So, for example, we have numerous studies addressing the (post-)feminist attributes of Madonna (Schwichtenberg, 1993), *Sex and the City* (Arthurs, 2003; Henry, 2004; Kim, 2001), *Ally McBeal* (Kim, 2001; Moseley and Read, 2002) and *Buffy the Vampire Slayer* (Daugherty, 2002; Owen, 1999; Vint, 2002), to name just a few of the most popular topics. Of course, it is not incidental that these texts/ performers have also become central to popular debates about feminism, from the much-discussed *Time* cover (29 June 1998) that used Ally McBeal to symbolize the death of feminism, to debates in the quality press about whether Madonna/Carrie/Ally/Buffy and others can be defined as 'feminist'. As Moseley and Read (2002) convincingly argue, it is important for feminist cultural critics to engage with and interrogate these popular (post-)feminisms. However, my concern is that we allow the popular debate to set the parameters of our own study. Thus, the emphasis of much of this work is on women (critics) judging women (performers, characters) on behalf of a third group of women (viewers, fans, consumers) who look to the media for suitable role models.

In discussing the suitability of these characters as role models for (other) women, it is important to note that physical appearance and dress are recurring concerns. Whilst there are important questions to be asked about the media's construction of feminine beauty, there is a danger that this obsessive focus on women's appearance as the marker of their worth – albeit, this time as feminist role models – replicates the construction of women as objects of the (male) gaze in the mainstream media. The emphasis on appearance and clothing also contributes to the construction of feminism as an out-dated fashion or performance, associated with repression and replaced by this season's post-feminism with its lipgloss, designer shoes and push-up bras. In other words, much of this criticism emphasizes the (re-)construction of the self rather than providing a framework for action.

In a paper reflecting on the field of feminist television scholarship, Brunsdon (2004) makes a broadly similar argument, noting that much recent work in the field has taken the form of what she dubs the 'ur-feminist article'. This ubiquitous article begins by noting how a text (or character) aimed at women or focusing on women characters has been denounced or claimed by feminists and goes on to explore whether the text/character fits the author's definition of feminism. Thus, the very project of much feminist television criticism involves an articulation of dis-identity, as though it is only possible for the critic to identify herself (or her object of study) as feminist by saying what kind of a feminist she/ it is not. Moreover, to the extent that feminist television criticism has developed around this ur-article, it has focused primarily on character, appearance and story with the result that other aspects of the television text – seriality, flow, aesthetics, sound and so on – have been rather marginalized. Feminism, not television, has become the critical focus.

Rejecting feminism

While the term post-feminism has a certain validity in describing the simultaneous debt to and disavowal of feminism in contemporary media discourse, it is less useful as a description of feminist theory and activism as it consigns that theory and activism to the past and erases its future. For, if post-feminism represents the evolution of the second wave then it is also implies the end of the sequence: how can there be a third, fourth or fifth wave post (i.e. after) feminism? It is in this sense that post-feminism has been associated with a rejection of, or backlash against, feminism.

Post-feminism and the backlash are not new phenomena. Indeed, Susan Faludi (1992: 70) notes that the term post-feminism first surfaced in the US press in the 1920s and was used to construct an opposition between younger women and their feminist elders at the very point that feminist gains began to re-shape the public sphere. In the contemporary context, Faludi links the re-invention of post-feminism to the political conservatism of the 1980s and the attempt to solicit women's consent for anti-women policies by presenting feminism, rather than sexism and oppression, as the source of women's discontent. For Faludi, then, post-feminism is virtually synonymous with the backlash, both in the moments of their emergence and in their ideological projects of pitting generations of women against one another.

The construction of post feminism as generational requires comment. Admittedly, the language, organization, style and even some of the key demands of the 1970s' women's movement seem alien to many daughters of the second wave. However, this does not mean that a decisive and antagonistic split is necessary. Indeed, those identifying themselves as third-wave feminists often have a clear sense of how their own politics and activism continue and develop the struggles of an earlier, but still active, generation.[2]

In contrast, the label 'post-feminist' – certainly as it is applied in the media – is more often used to indicate a decisive break with and rejection of the more radical politics of second-wave feminism. Nowhere was this more apparent than in the early 1990s when books by Camile Paglia (1993), Naomi Wolf (1994), Katie Roiphe (1994) and Christina Hoff Sommers (1994) very publicly asserted that it was feminism (and not the backlash) that was failing women, and young women in particular. These writers – variously labelled as post-feminists, anti-feminists, power feminists and new feminists – have little in common, except, perhaps, a general concern with rejecting what they argue is the 'victimizing' tendency of radical feminism and with exploring women's autonomy and sexual desire. Their arguments are, in many ways, attractive. It is, after all, much less depressing to think about what gives us pleasure than to focus on situations where women are relatively powerless, and easier to change the self than to change society. Indeed, the individual is the main focus of these books and while these authors typically criticize feminism's second wave for ignoring differences between women, the fierce individualism of these texts allows for little constructive consideration of difference. The extensive media coverage these authors received on both sides of the Atlantic replicated this individualism, turning the authors' physical appearances and personal lives into the subject of analysis. This Projansky (2001: 71) describes as an antifeminist feminist post-feminism: a feminism that insists upon the death of other feminisms in proclaiming its own birth.

The post-feminism born out of this conjuncture is a feminism that is focused on the aspirations and possibilities for individual women (typically, white, affluent, American women) but rejecting of second-wave feminism's demands for structural change. In particular, this post-feminism seems designed to let men (and patriarchy) off the hook, either by celebrating men's feminism or by turning individual men into objects of fun and derision whilst affirming the ideal of masculinity. This phenomenon is not, of course, consigned to theoretical texts and, indeed, a number of feminist media critics and commentators have explored its manifestation in popular culture. For example, in their analyses of rape representations in US film and television, both Projansky (2001) and Moorti (2002) demonstrate that it is on-screen men who most frequently give voice to feminist arguments and teach women about feminism, often in the face of other women's opposition. It might seem counter-intuitive to argue that this is an antifeminist move, however, when men are cast as 'better' feminists than women, women (and feminists) are once more positioned as redundant.

The redundancy of women was, of course, taken a stage further in many texts emerging during the 1980s where women were, quite literally, absent. It was this absence that led Tania Modleski (1991) to describe the post-feminist age as 'feminism without women', a description that has two meanings, pointing both to a feminist anti-essentialism (of which, more later), and to the triumph of a male feminist perspective that excludes women. It is important to emphasize that Modleski's 'feminism without women' is a popular feminism, that is, it is (post-)feminism *as represented* in media texts (factual and fictional), rather than a development within theory – and, indeed, it is in this guise that post-feminism has most often featured in media criticism.

However, while Modleski saw women being obliterated in the cultural landscape of the 1980s, any review of feminist media studies must conclude that it is men who are missing in action. Feminist media studies' focus on women is not, however, a post-feminist innovation. For example, Brunsdon (1997b) identifies four main categories of *feminist* television scholarship: the real world of women working in television; content analyses of the presence of women on the screen; textual studies of programmes for and about women; and studies focusing on female audiences. More specifically, in the introduction to *Feminist Television Criticism*, Brunsdon *et al.* (1997: 1) suggest that feminist television criticism is defined by an engagement, 'with the problems of feminism and femininity – what these terms mean, how they relate to each other, what they constitute and exclude'. Yet, despite its women-centredness, much of this work sets about deconstructing the very category 'woman', with the result that it becomes very self-reflexive, individualistic and difficult to relate to a feminist politic. Indeed, in the early twenty-first century, we seem to have reached a point where the legacy of feminism in relation to both television content and television scholarship is being repeatedly, indeed almost exclusively, measured by the performances of individual women and girls (Madonna, Carrie, Ally, Buffy etc.). The critical focus on individual women allows the challenge of feminism to disappear as it is positioned as a lifestyle choice (being feminist) rather than a movement (doing feminism). If feminism is equated with women's agency, choice and subjectivity, then questions about gender, about structural inequalities, discrimination, oppression and violence are allowed to slip from view.

Finally, it is instructive to consider the gleeful men-bashing indulged in by female-centred 1990s texts such as *Bridget Jones' Diary* (Fielding, 1997) or *Sex and the City* (1998–2004) which are also routinely dubbed 'post-feminist' by critics. In a *Guardian* column reflecting on *Sex and the City's* first series, Charlotte Raven (1999) describes the show's male characters as:

> commitment-phobes, smug marrieds, posers, nerds, swingers, clingers, workaholics, slackers, culture bores, philistines, predators, romantics, porn freaks, computer geeks, emotional illiterates, needy jerks, fastidious queens, slobs, liars, confessors, fashion victims, dorks, virgins, perverts, twentysomething bimbos, thirtysomething creeps, fortysomething saddos and – most contemptible of all – losers with tiny dicks.

– hardly a prestigious role-call. It is not surprising, therefore, that many of the column inches devoted to *Sex and the City* were reports on the battle of the sexes. Yet, whilst this battle might look considerably different to that conducted by the feminist men of Projansky and Moorti's rape narratives, there are important parallels: both pre-empt feminist critiques of male power and privilege by showing men to be either willing to give up that power (feminist) or incapable of wielding power (pathetic). In both instances power is dispersed to the point where it becomes impossible to analyse the structural inequalities that have concerned feminists. To return to Raven:

[Feminists'] man-hating wasn't a bar room grudge but a response to a political situation. It wasn't about individuals – most feminists got on fine with individual men, even as we also denounced masculinity as an idea. These days, the situation is reversed. The modern man-hater hates specific men but worships the idea of masculinity.

Nevertheless, it would be too simplistic to state that authors such as Roiphe or programmes such as *Sex and the City* are simply anti-feminist, for both the texts themselves and the extensive public debate they generate also provide feminism's most public face. As Projansky (2001: 70) argues in her discussion of yet-another magazine editorial proclaiming the 'death' of feminism, such texts ensure that feminism lives on in the public imaginary even if only to instigate the question about its demise. Or, as Faludi (1992) argues, the intensity of the backlash is very real evidence of the clear and present danger to the status quo that feminism represents.

Developing feminism

In this section I want to consider how the term 'post-feminism' is used to describe a regeneration and development of feminist theory within the context of broader developments in postmodernism and post-structuralism. 'Feminism without women' in this context refers to an antiessentialist challenge to the very category 'woman' (and 'man', though this is rarely made explicit) and the abandonment of grand narratives and universalizing theories. For antiessentialists, it should not matter whether we do our feminism without women or without men: the point is that gender-categories *per se* are mutable. But it is important to ask: Whose interests are best served by such a deconstruction?

For Brooks (1997: 4), whose *Postfeminisms: Cultural Theory and Cultural Forms* provides a valuable summary of these debates, the term 'post-feminism' denotes a 'conceptual shift within feminism from debates about equality to debates about difference'. A fundamental problem with this formulation is, of course, the way in which it reduces the history and diversity of feminisms to one strand of the 1960s–70s movement (liberal, or equity feminism), suggesting that feminism depended upon a consensus (however fragile) among women and an ignorance of the differences that shape our experiences under patriarchy. For Brooks, the recognition of difference so fundamentally challenged feminism as to warrant the invention of this new label, though many of the critics she cites (including bell hooks) resist the post-feminist label and, instead, see their work as contributing to the development of *feminist* theory and practice.

It is also worth noting that this version of post-feminism is largely an academic one – that is, it is based in theory rather than practice – and has had particular currency in writing about the media and culture. This is, in part, due to the emphasis on discourses rather than on overarching structures. Yet it is also a reflection of the fact that it is far easier to destabilize gender in the representational field than in our daily lives where our gender-presentation continues to have very concrete material effects. It is telling, in this respect, that Brooks devotes much of her chapter on post feminism and popular culture to a consideration of Madonna, a performer whose continual re-invention of herself works to destabilize categories of gender and sexual identity. However, at this juncture, it is important to ask how Madonna's performances relate to the lived experiences of other women (see Schwichtenberg, 1993). Lisa Henderson, for example, notes that whilst cultural critics might celebrate the destabilization of fixed gender and sexual identities in Madonna's performances, the political struggles of feminists and queer activists depends upon fixing these identities, both for our own protection and because these identities remain the basis of material inequalities in the social world:

> It is difficult, finally, to acknowledge the divided self and engage the pleasure of masquerade while at the same time fighting a strikingly antagonistic legal and social system for your health, your safety, your job, your place to live, or the right to raise your children. Indeed, this is the other contradiction of lesbian and gay resistance: to be constructionists in theory, though essentialists as we mobilize politically, demanding that the state comply because this, after all, is *who we are*, not who we are today or who we have become in recent history (Henderson, 1993: 123).

Part of the difficulty with much contemporary (post-)feminist writing on the media is that the link between the representational and material spheres has been severed as studies of representational practices have become divorced from a broader feminist political project and history. Moreover, the destabilizing of the category 'woman' has – in practice – led to a very narrow focus on individual women as the objects of study. As a result, much of this writing ends up replicating the focus on the white, middle-class self that was the basis of the critique of the second wave, the difference being that post-feminists do not claim any universal status for this self. In focusing on the individual it becomes, by definition, almost impossible to say anything meaningful about difference: what can an analysis of Madonna, Carrie, Ally or Buffy tell us about differences between women? More damagingly, the failure to connect these analyses to a broader feminist praxis makes the analyses – no matter how interesting and well argued – seem rather pointless. As Modleski (1991: 15) puts it:

> The once exhilarating proposition that there is no 'essential' female nature has been elaborated to the point where it is now often used to scare 'women' away from making any generalizatons about or political claims on behalf of a group called 'women'.

Making the personal political should not mean that the personal is the *only* site of political contestation and change. In short, if analysing Madonna can only tell us about Madonna then, frankly, why should we bother?

My intent in providing this brief survey of these complex debates is not to try to fix the meaning of post-feminism once and for all – indeed, this seems to be a rather pointless, if not impossible, task – but to highlight the way in which these 'post-ings' repeatedly focus on women, feminism and femininity as the problem, as the objects of investigation and critique.

As a result, much recent feminist media studies presents a feminism at war with itself and the political relevance of feminism is in danger of being lost. Moreover, whilst all this deconstructing of the female gender has been going on, men and masculinity have, once again, been allowed to slip under the radar: hence my reformulation of Modleski's title. As a political theory and practice, feminism without men is surely as limited as feminism without women.

Buffy binaries and *Buffy*'s boys

So far, my argument has been fairly abstract. The remainder of this article seeks to rectify this by providing a case study centred on *Buffy the Vampire Slayer*. My intention is not to argue that *Buffy* (or Buffy) is or is not feminist; rather, I want to consider the ways in which the show's 'feminism' has been framed in existing criticism and how this framing has allowed other issues of importance to feminism (and to *Buffy*) to escape critical scrutiny.

In an oft-quoted account, *Buffy* creator Joss Whedon describes the show as,

> my response to all the horror movies I had ever seen where some girl walks into a dark room and gets killed. So I decided to make a movie where a blonde girl walks into a dark room and kicks butt instead (Whedon quoted by Early, 2001).[3]

Whedon's creation tale is the starting point for numerous articles (both popular and academic) dealing with the show's feminism and, indeed, Whedon's willingness to use the f-word in discussing the show's ideology and appeal has meant that *Buffy*'s relationship to feminism has been consistently foregrounded both on-screen and in responses to the show.

The blonde girl in question is, of course, Buffy Summers (Sarah Michelle Gellar), a former cheerleader who is also the vampire slayer. The first two seasons repeatedly return to the apparent incongruity of conjoining 'Buffy' with 'vampire slayer' and play on and with characters' and viewers' expectations of the blonde girl, expectations that clearly change as show and character develop. Nevertheless, in the early seasons, a large part of the show's humour and drama comes from the apparent conflict between the demands and gains of feminism and femininity, and it is this conflict – and the various ways in which it is played out within the show and in secondary texts – that has been the major concern of those interested in its relationship to feminism. Patricia Pender (2002: 35), for example, notes that much of the debate revolves around opposing value judgements about the feminist credentials of the central character and the show: 'Put simply, is *Buffy* good or bad?' As a physically strong, assertive and sexually desiring heroine Buffy is claimed as a (good) feminist. As a young woman concerned with her appearance, clothing and desirability to the opposite sex, she is a bad feminist, but – depending on the position of the author – she might still be a good post-feminist. For many critics, the combination of feminism and femininity places *Buffy* firmly in the 'post' era.

Asking the question 'is *Buffy* good or bad' for feminism seriously limits the scope of feminist enquiry to how we define feminism and construct a feminist identity. Moreover, to return to Lotz, with confusion and contradiction marking popular definitions of feminism, it should hardly be surprising that the same characteristics are variously read as feminist, antifeminist or post-feminist, and celebrated or condemned on these grounds by different critics. To give an example, Buffy's appearance is a central concern in many early responses to the show. Buffy – as played by Gellar – is blonde, petite, nubile, perfectly made-up and, above all, fashionable. Her favoured daywear in the early seasons is a short skirt, spaghetti-strap top and high heels: clothing designed to expose and shape her body according to conventional standards of feminine beauty. For some critics, this conjunction of feminism and femininity is to be celebrated in extending feminism's appeal to a new generation of women and girls; for others, it compromises the show's feminist premise by constructing Buffy/Gellar as a sexualized object.[4]

I am less interested here in which group of critics is 'right' than in the fact that Buffy and/or Gellar are so often the focus of critical consideration. The reason often given to justify this is their importance as role models for young girls who use media figures to help them construct their own sense of identity and agency (e.g. Vint, 2002). Yet, this depends upon a very limited notion of identification and fails to account for the possibilities and pleasures of cross-sex identification and same- and cross-sex desire. Indeed, while Whedon talks about selling feminism to boys as a major concern,[5] boy fans have been the subject of little (if any) feminist scholarship. As Anthony Easthope (1986: 1) pointedly argued nearly 20 years ago, the effect of this critical interest in women is to allow masculinity to pass itself off as natural and universal, placing it beyond critique.

Moreover, much of the good Buffy/ bad Buffy debate fails to consider the show *as television*. In other words, this criticism (particularly in its more populist versions) is a harking back to the 'images of women' approach that characterized feminist critiques of the media in the late 1960s and early 1970s and paid little attention to medium specificity (Walters, 1995). For example, whilst the concern regarding sex-object-Buffy may well be justified at a meta-textual level (Vint, 2002), the television show rarely constructs Buffy as the object of a sexualized male gaze. It is undoubtedly true that her daywear – in the early seasons in particular – is flesh-shaping and exposing; however, the camera rarely lingers on or fetishises her body. Further, when it comes to night-time slayage, Buffy rarely wears such obviously sexualized attire: indeed, when she does – as in Season 2's opening episode 'When She Was Bad' – it is a sign that all is not well. More typically, in fight scenes Buffy is shown in long shot, her face and form obscured by shadow and dark lighting as well as by her loose clothing and long hair.[6] Combined with the specular and narrative privileging of the woman's point of view in the show, this makes it difficult to argue that *Buffy* privileges a male gaze in any straightforward way (Daugherty, 2002).

As Pender also notes (2004), the need to resolve Buffy/ *Buffy*'s feminist credentials seems to serve for some critics as a justification of their own engagement, preventing an acknowledgement of the show's complexities and contradictions. I am reminded here of Modleski's warning that feminist media criticism risks becoming increasingly narcissistic, 'based on an unspoken syllogism that goes something like this: "I like *Dallas*; I am a feminist; *Dallas* must have progressive potential" ' (1991: 45). One of the implications of this in *Buffy* studies has been a marked reluctance among feminists to consider the show's less liberatory aspects – such as its treatment of race and class – as though this would somehow tarnish the object of study (Pender, 2004). Alternatively, a post-feminist approach might seek to embrace these contradictions as part of the post-feminist fabric of the show. In either case, the effect is the same: the marginalization of difference and an emphasis on the individual.

To the extent that we allow the popular television text – and the growing body of critical work on such texts – to define our 'feminism', we marginalize many of the most important challenges feminism *as a movement* posed and continues to pose. From my own perspective, as a feminist working mainly on gendered violence, it is pertinent to note that whilst (post-) feminist action heroines have been the subject of recurring critique within feminist media studies (e.g. Early and Kennedy, 2003; Helford, 2000; Inness, 1998; Tasker, 2004), there has been relatively little academic work that considers media representations of male violence from a perspective informed by feminism. In this respect, the critical silence on male violence in *Buffy* – particularly from those critics interested in the show's relationship to feminism – can be read as evidence of the way that the post-feminist frame works to banish the spectre of the radical ('victim') feminist and her analysis of patriarchy. Yet, radical feminism is more than a spectral form in the show itself, which – although inconsistent on this point – often seems to offer a surprisingly radical analysis of the systematic nature of male violence. My intent here is not to demonstrate that *Buffy* conforms to my version of feminism (as in Brunsdon's ur-article), but rather to point to some of the themes that are too often neglected within feminist media studies in this 'post-feminist' age.

Buffy's primary focus may be to 'take back the night' for the living, but it is notable that the undead and demonic are – with few exceptions – male.[7] This, in itself, is hardly exceptional – content analyses of prime-time television consistently find that the majority of both perpetrators and victims of on-screen violence are white males (Center for Communication and Social Policy, 1997, 1998a, 1998b; Gunter and Harrison, 1998) – but the very routine nature of male violence should surely make it more, not less, worthy of feminist comment and analysis (Boyle, 2004). Yet, the first book-length feminist studies of television violence were not published until the early 2000s (Cuklanz, 2000; Moorti, 2002; Projansky, 2001) and it is notable that all these studies focus on a very specific form of violence, namely rape. Certainly, *Buffy*'s treatment of sexual violence is worthy of feminist attention. However, so too are unexceptional, routinized examples of male violence which may, indeed, be invisible as violence given the cultural value attached to aggression as an expression of normative masculinity. Where *Buffy* is relatively unusual (and potentially radical), is in the way in which this link between heterosexual-masculinity and violence is critically and provocatively kept in view. This is perhaps most explicit in the figure of Caleb (Nathan Fillion), the final season's misogynist villain, but comments about the aggressive and morally questionable behaviour of men, as a group, are made throughout. Interestingly, it is often left to recurring male figures to comment on the limits of masculinity. When the hapless Xander (Nicholas Brendon), is possessed by a hyena in 'The Pack' (1.06), for example, Buffy's Watcher, Giles (Anthony Stewart Head), resists labelling his sexually aggressive, condescending behaviour as demonic:

> Giles: Xander's taken to teasing the less fortunate? [. . .] And there's been a notable change in both clothing and demeanour? [. . .] And otherwise all his spare time is spent lounging about with imbeciles?
> Buffy: It's bad isn't it?

Giles: It's devastating, he's turned into a 16 year-old boy. Course, you'll have to kill him

Buffy: Giles I'm serious

Giles: So am I, except for the part about killing him. Testosterone is a great equalizer, it turns all men into morons. He will, however, get over it. [. . .] Buffy, boys can be cruel. They tease. They prey on the weak. It's a natural teen behaviour pattern.

Although Giles' essentialist account is quickly proved wrong, he is not wrong in pointing out that a level of aggression, competition and misogyny is an accepted part of normative constructions of masculinity within the Buffyverse (and beyond). This recognition of what men as a group stand to gain from violence (both in terms of their status with other men, and in terms of material and sexual power), whilst central to feminist critiques, is in direct contrast to accounts of male violence in other mainstream media contexts where the focus is typically on drawing a clear distinction between violent men (monsters, beasts, perverts, fiends) and 'normal' men (Benedict, 1992; Boyle, 2004). In contrast, *Buffy* continually draws parallels between its monsters and its men, making masculinity both visible and problematic.

Admittedly, this might not seem immediately obvious from the above example where 'evil' Xander, possessed by a hyena, is, quite obviously, *not* Xander. More generally, in the early episodes there does appear to be a relatively clear-cut distinction between man (the conscious, socially situated agent) and monster (the inhuman, asocial beast) that is underlined by the *mise-en-scène*: the monsters look monstrous, inhabit dark spaces on the margins of Sunnydale and are often in full or partial shadow. Yet, such an *absolute* distinction is difficult to sustain. The vampire, the werewolf and the possessed teen are liminal figures: humans who become monsters and retain the human's visage (at least some of the time) and memories. One of the more interesting complexities of the Angel/Angelus character,[8] for example, is that it is the demonic Angelus who has the most in common with Liam, the drunken, sexually aggressive and immoral man the vampire once was. As Angel comments in 'Doppelgangland' (3.16), the traces of the vampire are in the human. Equally, those who are introduced as demons frequently express human emotions and complexities. As major characters move from one position to another any ideas of 'absolute' evil become increasingly complicated and this, too, is visually rendered through changes in costume, make-up, lighting and so on. Whilst it could be argued that this destabilization of identity is quintessentially post-feminist, to follow this argument is once more to re-direct the focus of our enquiry from a quintessentially feminist issue (gendered violence), to feminism itself.

Finally, *Buffy*'s centuries-old demons are also associated with the past and, specifically, with a pre-feminist past that they bring with them into the show's present. In this sense, while Buffy (the character and the show) might be beneficiaries of feminism, it is clear from the outset that Sunnydale is not a post-patriarchy. In other words, an analysis of the Buffyverse (like an analysis of our own world), demonstrates the difficulty of fixing pre-feminist, feminist, and post-feminist *moments* and the necessity of considering movement, organization and behaviour at both the individual and societal level.

In conclusion, as feminist media critics we need to continually keep in focus the ways in which our analyses of cultural texts contribute to broader struggles both within and outside of the academy. We need to think about our methods, about our objects of study and, perhaps most importantly, about the *purpose* of our study. For example, examining representations of men's violence against women has long been seen as part of the broader feminist struggle to challenge and de-naturalize that violence – as the preceding discussion of *Buffy* begins to suggest. As Benedict (1993) argues, changes in representation not only follow on from changes in reality, they can also lead the way. This is why struggles over language and meaning matter and why analysing, challenging and changing how we – and others – speak about or otherwise represent men's violence (or other forms of gendered realities and inequalities) is an important part of feminism's transformative project. This does not mean that feminists cannot also study music videos, or shoe shopping, or romance novels, but it helps to remind us that in all our work we need to retain a sense of the broader picture. In this respect, we cannot afford to lose sight of how debates about feminism (and feminists) are used within the media. It is hardly surprising that disputes over the feminist identities of figures such as Madonna, Carrie, Ally or Buffy have received such widespread media attention for, as I have argued in this article, such a focus allows the more difficult challenges posed by feminism – challenges to male privilege and power, to the lived tensions of all of our daily lives – to slip from view. To let these debates define our 'feminism' in the early twenty-first century would be a truly regressive move.

Notes

1 To get to grips with the diversity of debate it helps to get beyond academic sources and examine documents produced within the movement – newsletters, conference materials, oral histories and so on. These documents can be accessed in a variety of feminist archives, including (in the UK) the Glasgow Women's Library (see http://www.womens-library.org.uk/), the Women's Library (see http://www.thewomenslibrary.ac.uk/) and the Feminist Library (see http://www.feministlibrary.org.uk/).

2 See, for example, essays collected in Heywood and Drake (1997), Mirza (1997) and in Gillis *et al.* (2004).

3 Buffy made her first appearance in a 1992 film, written by Whedon and directed by Fran Rubel Kuzui.

4 For more on this, see Fudge (1999), Owen (1999), Pender (2002), and Vint (2002).

5 Whedon comments: 'If I can make teenage boys comfortable with a girl who takes charge of the situation, without their knowing that's what's happening, it's better than sitting down and selling them on feminism' (cited in Esmonde, 2003).

6 The need to disguise the stunt doubles used in the fight sequences provides a practical reason for this.

7 Whedon himself describes *Buffy* as a chance for horror's prototypical blonde girl to 'take back the night' (in Esmonde, 2003), an allusion to on-going feminist campaigns. *Not once* in 144 episodes does Buffy battle a lone female or an all-female gang in her patrols. This is not to suggest that *Buffy*'s female characters never act violently with evil or morally questionable intent, but morally reprehensible violence does *not* bring female characters together in the way that it routinely unites male gangs.

8 Angel (played by David Boreanaz) is Buffy's first love. A vampire cursed with a soul, Angel loses that soul (reverting to Angelus) after he and Buffy have sex.

References

Arthurs, J. (2003) '*Sex and the City* and Consumer Culture: Remediating Postfeminist Drama', *Feminist Media Studies*, 3 (1).

Benedict, H. (1992) *Virgin or Vamp: How the Press Covers Sex Crimes*. New York and Oxford: Oxford University Press.

———(1993) 'The Language of Rape', in E. Buchwald *et al.* (eds), *Transforming a Rape Culture*. Minneapolis: Milkweed.

Boyle, K. (2004) *Media and Violence: Gendering the Debates*. London: Sage.

Brooks, A. (1997) *Postfeminisms: Feminism, Cultural Theory and Cultural Forms*. London: Routledge.

Brunsdon, C. (1997a) 'Post-Feminism and Shopping Films', in C. Brunsdon (ed.), *Screen Tastes: Soap Opera to Satellite Dishes*. London: Routledge.

———(1997b) 'The Role of Soap Opera in the Development of Feminist Television Criticism', in C. Brunsdon (ed.), *Screen Tastes: Soap Opera to Satellite Dishes*. London: Routledge.

———(2004) 'Feminism, Post-Feminism, Martha and Nigella', Paper presented at: Interrogating Post-Feminism: Gender and the Politics of Popular Culture, University of East Anglia, 2–3 April 2004.

Brunsdon, C., D'Acci, J. and Spigel, L. (1997) 'Introduction', in C. Brunsdon *et al.* (eds), *Feminist Television Criticism: A Reader*. Oxford: Oxford University Press.

Carby, H. V. (1982) 'White Woman Listen! Black Feminism and the Boundaries of Sisterhood', in Centre for Contemporary Cultural Studies (ed.), *The Empire Strikes Back: Race and Racism in 70s Britain*. London: Hutchinson.

Center for communication and social policy (ed.)(1997) *National Television Violence Study*, vol. 1. Thousand Oaks: Sage.

———(1998a) *National Television Violence Study*, vol. 2. Thousand Oaks: Sage.

———(1998b) *National Television Violence Study*, vol. 3. Thousand Oaks: Sage.

Cuklanz, L. M. (2000) *Rape on Prime Time: Television, Masculinity and Sexual Violence*. Philadelphia: University of Pennsylvania Press.

Daugherty, A. M. (2002) 'Just a Girl: Buffy as Icon', in R. Kaveney (ed.), *Reading the Vampire Slayer: An Unofficial Critical Companion to* Buffy *and* Angel. London: Tauris Parke.

Early, F. (2001) 'Staking Her Claim: *Buffy the Vampire Slayer* as Transgressive Woman Warrior', *Journal of Popular Culture*, 35 (3).

Early, F. and Kennedy, K. (eds) (2003) *Athena's Daughters: Television's New Women Warriors*. Syracuse, NY: Syracuse University Press.

Easthope, A. (1986) *What A Man's Gotta Do: The Masculine Myth in Popular Culture*. London: Paladin.

Esmonde, J. (2003) 'Ghoul Power: Buffy Sticks it to the System', *New Socialist*, No. 40. Available at: www.newsocialist.org/magazine/40.html (Accessed August 2004.)

Faludi, S. (1992) *Backlash: The Undeclared War Against Women*. London: Chatto & Windus.

Fielding, H. (1997) *Bridget Jones' Diary: A Novel*. London: Picador.

Fudge, R. (1999) 'The Buffy Effect: Or, a Tale of Cleavage and Marketing', *Bitch*, No. 10. Available at: www.bitchmagazine.com/ (Accessed September 2004.)

Gillis, S., Howie, G. and Munford, R. (eds) (2004) *Third Wave Feminism: A Critical Exploration*. London: Palgrave Macmillan.

Gunter, B. and Harrison, J. (1998) *Violence on Television: An Analysis of Amount, Nature, Location, and Origin of Violence in British Programmes*. London: Routledge.

Helford, E. R. (ed.) (2000) *Fantasy Girls: Gender in the New Universe of Science Fiction and Fantasy Television*. Lanham: Rowman & Littlefield.

Henderson, L. (1993) 'Justify Our Love: Madonna and the Politics of Queer Sex', in C. Schwichtenberg (ed.), *The Madonna Connection: Representational Politics, Subcultural Identities and Cultural Theory*. Boulder: Westview Press.

Henry, A. (2004) 'Orgasms and Empowerment: *Sex and the City* and the Third Wave Feminism', in K. Arkass and J. McCabe (eds), *Reading Sex and the City*. London: I. B. Tauris.

Heywood, L. and Drake, J. (1997) 'Introduction', in L. Heywood and J. Drake (eds), *Third Wave Agenda: Being Feminist, Doing Feminism*. Minneapolis: University of Minnesota Press.

Hollows, J. (2000) *Feminism, Femininity and Popular Culture*. Manchester: Manchester University Press.

hooks, b. (1982) *Ain't I a Woman: Black Women and Feminism*. London: Pluto.

———(2000) *Feminism is for Everybody: Passionate Politics*. London: Pluto.

Inness, S. A. (1998) *Tough Girls: Women Warriors and Wonder Women in Popular Culture*. Philadelphia: University of Pennsylvania Press.

Kim, L. S. (2001) ' "Sex and the Single Girl" in Postfeminism', *Television and New Media*, 2 (4).

Littlewood, B. (2004) *Feminist Perspectives on Sociology*. Harlow: Pearson.

Lotz, A. D. (2001) 'Postfeminist Television Criticism: Rehabilitating Critical Terms and Identifying Postfeminist Attributes', *Feminist Media Studies*, 1 (1).

Mirza, H. S. (1997) *Black British Feminism: A Reader*. London: Routledge.

Modleski, T. (1991) *Feminism Without Women: Culture and Criticism in a 'Postfeminist' Age*. London: Routledge.

Moorti, S. (2002) *Color of Rape: Gender and Race in Television's Public Spheres*. Albany: State University of New York Press.

Moseley, R. and Read, J. (2002) ' "Having it *Ally*": Popular Television Post-Feminism', *Feminist Media Studies*, 2 (2).

Owen, S. A. (1999) '*Buffy the Vampire Slayer*: Vampires, Postmodernity and Postfeminism', *Journal of Popular Film and Television*, 27 (2).

Paglia, C. (1993) *Sex, Art and American Culture*. London: Penguin.

Pender, P. (2002) ' "I'm Buffy and You're . . . History": The Postmodern Politics of Buffy', in R. V. Wilcox and D. Lavery (eds), *Fighting the Forces: What's at Stake in* Buffy the Vampire Slayer. London: Rowman & Littlefield.

———(2004) 'Whose Revolution Has Been Televised?: *Buffy*'s Transnational Sisterhood of Slayers'. Paper presented at: Slayage Conference on *Buffy the Vampire Slayer*, Nashville, June 2004. Available at: www.slayage.tv/SCBtVS_Archive/index.htm (Accessed August 2004.)

Projansky, S. (2001) *Watching Rape: Film and Television in Postfeminist Culture*. New York and London: New York University Press.

Raven, C. (1999) 'All Men Are Bastards: Discuss . . .' *The Guardian*, 9 February.

Richardson, D. (1996) ' "Misguided, Dangerous and Wrong": On the Maligning of Radical Feminism', in D. Bell and R. Klein (eds), *Radically Speaking: Feminism Reclaimed*. London: Zed.

Roiphe, K. (1994) *The Morning After*. London: Hamish Hamilton.

Schwichtenberg, C. (ed.) (1993) *The Madonna Connection: Representational Politics, Subcultural Identities and Cultural Theory*. Boulder: Westview Press.

Sommers, C. H. (1994) *Who Stole Feminism? How Women Have Betrayed Women.* New York: Simon & Schuster.

Spender, D. (1982) *Women of Ideas and What Men Have Done to Them: From Aphra Behn to Adrienne Rich.* London: Routledge & Kegan Paul

Tasker, Y. (2004) 'Family/ Romance: Reading the Post-Feminist Action Heroine'. Paper presented at: Media Research Conference, University of Tampere, January 2004. Available at: www.uta.fi/laitoksct/tiedotus/Mediatutkimuspaivat/PAPERIT/MTP04YvonneTasker.pdf (Accessed September 2004.)

Vint, S. (2002) 'Killing us Softly? A Feminist Search for the "Real" Buffy', *Slayage: The On-line International Journal of Buffy Studies* 5 www.slayage.tv (Accessed August 2004.)

Walters, S. D. (1995) 'From Images of Women to Woman as Image', in S. D. Walters, *Material Girls: Making Sense of Feminist Cultural Theory.* Berkeley and London: University of California Press.

Wolf, N. (1994) *Fire With Fire: The New Female Power and How to Use It.* New York: Fawcett Columbine.

▶ chapter three

Representation, Reality and Popular Culture: Semiotics and the Construction of Meaning

CHRISTINE GERAGHTY

Introduction

This essay is concerned with representation and textual analysis. Its starting point is semiotics, the language of signs which had a key role in the development of media studies. Semiotics seemed to offer a scientific approach to the construction of meaning, an alternative to the traditional emphasis on quality in literary criticism which was largely unhelpful when applied to mass media products. To some extent, the language of semiotics has entered into broader cultural discussions; 'iconic' has become a term of praise for a photograph rather than a semiotic term for a signifier which makes meaning through a resemblance to what it signifies. In general, though, media studies has moved away from some of the grander claims of semiotics and has recognized that an understanding of how the media create meaning must involve questions of, for instance, media ownership, the diversity of audiences and economic and technological developments. Nevertheless, I would suggest that the particular forms of cultural texts are important both to the pleasure we take in them and the use we make of them. The concept of representation has underpinned much work in media studies and in this essay I am going to look at particular examples of textual analysis in order to examine how questions of representation have been used in media analysis and suggest some of the strengths and limitations of this approach.

To re-present, to mediate, to image – if we make into active verbs the nouns we use so commonly in communications and media studies – representation, media, image – we can see how powerfully the language we have at our disposal frames our understanding. What it suggests is a process whereby a pre-existing given, whether it be a physical object or philosophical abstraction, is translated so that it can be comprehended and experienced by a recipient, an observer, an audience. In the process, the mediation may be presented as reflection with the implication that the original is relatively unchanged by the process; or there may be questions of bias, distortion, re-framing so that somehow the purity of the original is lost. A particular relationship is established by this vocabulary in which the reader or viewer is involved in recognizing, checking, reconstructing the original from the media production – the photograph, the television series, the newspaper article – or else is taken in or absorbed by it. What is at stake in the process of transmission which we so readily associate with the media?

Work on representation in the media is crucially marked by the development of semiotics in linguistics and the application of its techniques to communications systems which also involve images. Accounts of the work on language systems developed through semiotics can be found in more detail elsewhere [1] but it is important to note certain principles. Semiotics was significant in work on the media because it attempted to break the notion of mediation and to show that the key relationship within a language system was not between a word and its referent, a pre-existing object to which the word referred; instead it was argued that a word's meaning was established through its relationship with other words and that it was recognized because it was different from other words – 'cat' was 'cat' because it was not 'mat' or 'cot'; further, what it signified or referred to was not a particular cat but the concept of a cat. This had important consequences for how language systems, and by extension other communications systems, might be conceived. It created a structure in which the key relationships were inside the language system rather than between language and something conceived of as being outside language, in the 'real world'; indeed, the 'real world' did not pre-exist language but was constructed through it. Semiotics also emphasized the abstraction of language systems in which a word referred to a concept rather than a particular object; it proposed that language did not spring naturally from a relationship between word and object but was based on conventions which the users of a language had to learn.

Abstraction, convention, construction – these were all concepts that were to have important consequences in the development of studies of the media, particularly in studies of photography, film, television and the press, all of which involved representation based on visual images as well as spoken or written language. By bringing these concepts to bear, it was possible to see, for instance, that a photograph was composed not just in the usual sense by the photographer but by conventions of colour, lighting and subject which helped to fix meaning; that films were understood through the way in which they referred to each other in generic systems; that newspaper layout and the composition of headlines were not determined by what happened 'out there' but by the conventions internal to the press. Most importantly, semiotics challenged the notion of transparency in mediation – the media as a window through which we see the world or a mirror in which reality is reflected. The notion that the language of the image was 'rhetoric' (Barthes, 1977) and was based on construction not reflection, undermined some key value judgements in the area. If language was not a process of reflection, why were the mimetic claims of realism so highly valued as compared with the non-realist forms of, for example, melodrama? If media texts were a construction, what was the significance for audiences of their claims to represent reality?

I will come back to some of these questions in looking at particular examples but it is important at this stage to note that the prevalence of visual images in the media posed particular problems for the use of semiotics. For in visual representation relying on photography it could be argued that the relationship between the image and the object imaged was not abstract or arbitrary, was indeed iconic. A photograph of a cat might signify the concept of a cat but it also relied on the concept of resemblance by referring to this cat, at this moment, in this place. Barthes in 'Rhetoric of the image' reflects on the way in which the photograph's capacity to record 'reinforces the myth of photographic "naturalness"' and generates 'an awareness of its having-been-there' (Barthes, 1977: 44). For Bill Nichols, writing about documentary film, the link between the visual sign and the particular object it refers to 'anchors the image in the specificity of the given moment' (Nichols, 1990: 108) and 'refers us back to the historical' (p. 111). Even in fiction, the visual image can generate a sense of something beyond the initial construction. John Wayne, constructed as a star through his films and publicity material, plays a dying man in *The Shootist* (Siegal/US/1976) but part of the meaning of his fictional character is generated by the visible signs of his own final illness. Thus the double reference of the visually recorded image, to the particular as well as the general, to the local as well as the abstract, remained a problem to those who wanted to adapt the insights of semiotics to the study of media texts.

Semiology has been criticized for promoting too narrow a focus on texts and for being too hermetically sealed in its own systems to allow for analysis of the processes of historical change. In addition, concern has been expressed within communications studies at the adoption of semiotic approaches for visual languages that lack 'anything equivalent' to the stable vocabulary, syntax and grammar of 'natural language' (Corner, 1986: 53). As Ellen Seiter put it, in a statement on television which could be applied to other media forms, 'because television is based on weaker codes than those that govern verbal languages, it is, as a system of communication, unstable; it is constantly undergoing modification and operates by conventions rather than by hard-and-fast rules' (Seiter, 1992: 49). Accepting these limitations, I nevertheless want to look at three forms of media representations in the context provided by semiotics' emphasis on language as a construction in order to tease out the possibilities and limitations of this approach.

Understanding a photograph

The first example that I want to recall and use is that of a photograph, or rather a series of photographs taken and used in the press when Charles and Diana, then the British Prince and Princess of Wales, were on an official visit to South Korea in November 1992. The photographs showed us two people, one male one female, formally dressed, unsmiling, as they turned away from each other to gaze abstractly out of the frame. The images are a professional construction, taken by the many photographers accompanying the royal tour, cropped to focus attention on the two figures, isolated from each other, the two heads, looking away. Thus framed and laid out on the front pages of the British press, they entered into the international circulation of images.

In understanding such images, we bring a number of frameworks to bear, a number of discourses that help to organize meaning. We draw on different kinds of knowledge and a study of that process suggests that the meaning of a photograph is not hidden or immanent in the picture but is constructed through a range of different signifying practices. During the process of recognition and understanding, we relate what we see in a photograph, the visual signs, to a wider set of understandings. Some of these may be signified directly from what is in the photograph; others depend on cultural knowledge which can be activated by the photograph.

Take Diana's hat, for instance. The photographs tell us which particular hat Diana was wearing that day and avid royal watchers may be able to recognize it. But the hat also, if we understand what certain kinds of dress signify, tells us that this is a formal occasion with all that that implies in terms of being on best behaviour. It is also a sign of how royalty are marked as different from 'ordinary' women who do not, in modern Europe, wear hats very often. And if we have experience of the way in which Diana was perceived to operate as a fashion leader we may also be drawn to judge her physical appearance; does the hat suit her? Thus, in understanding the photograph, we are called on to use our knowledge of codes of dress that operate both inside and outside photography in order to understand some of its meaning.

The photographs depict two people, a man and a woman. These need to be identified through cultural knowledge as members of the British royal family. The capacity to identify and name these people may be accompanied by a set of associations with hierarchy, history and tradition which surround royalty in Britain. In this context the pair may be understood to be participating in a particular kind of formal occasion at which they have themselves a representative function. But set against that understanding of the formal roles and traditions of British royalty may be a more scurrilous discourse of gossip and speculation about the behaviour of some members of the royal family, including these two. Thus, the photograph can be understood through the associations that invoke the privileged position and private stresses of the modern royal family.

The photographs therefore may be placed in these kinds of general contexts and for some press photographs this may be enough. The British press and magazines such as *Hello* frequently featured photographs of Diana that could be understood almost entirely in the context of royalty, fashion and glamour – this is what she was wearing, isn't she dazzling? But press photographs often need to be understood in the context of news – this photograph is important at this point because it tells us something new. The meaning of the photograph then has to be established more clearly so that the viewer is guided to the appropriate response.

One way of doing this is, to use Barthes' term, to 'anchor' the meaning through the written text that accompanies it. The written text then rules out as inappropriate certain meanings and underlines others as being correct; we do not necessarily have to follow this guidance but other readings run the risk of being deemed irrelevant or deviant. In this example the written text warned us that it was not enough to understand the photograph through discourses of fashion or the royal family. To do so would be to miss the point of the unsmiling faces turned away from each other. This is underlined by headlines such as 'Charles and Diana Face New Crisis' and articles which began 'This is the picture which reveals the rift between the Prince and Princess of Wales. The physical and emotional distance between them is clear' (*Daily Mail*, 3.11.92). The written text thus focuses attention on one specific aspect of the photograph, the demeanour of the couple, and suggests, quite forcibly, that this is where the photograph's meaning must be found.

A number of professional practices allow this anchoring to take place: it is conventional in newspapers to accompany photographs with headlines and captions in order to make their meaning more stable; it also conventional that photographs are used to support written text and to provide evidence that backs up journalists' stories. But the practice is also supported by other discourses which encourage us to understand the photograph in this way. By reading the photograph as 'the breakup of the marriage' we place it in the context of a narrative, the story of the marriage which has been told through the media – in the press, on television, in books. Narrative organization encourages us to make sense of a story by looking for the way in which one event causes or has an effect on the next and by associating individual participants with particular character traits. At this point in the Charles and Diana story the overarching narrative has moved from the bachelor prince choosing a suitable bride through the fairytale wedding and the birth of two sons to the estranged couple trapped in an unhappy marriage. This narrative is not the invention of any one journalist or indeed the media as a whole. It is a structure that draws on different kinds of stories – fairy tales, family sagas, the movement from adolescence to adulthood – and provides the means to make sense of a mass of information, selecting what is significant and giving it meaning. Thus, a photograph of Charles and Diana can be understood through where it is placed in that story. The narrative encourages a reading that emphasizes the turned away heads, the gazes out of the frame, the sense that being trapped in the official car is the physical equivalent of the trap of their marriage. But could the South Korean photographs have been used earlier in the marriage to signify the way in which the happy couple took their formal duties seriously and performed them well, not daring to look at each other in case personal happiness distracted them from serious affairs of state?

Charles and Diana are, of course, public figures and most of us cannot call on direct knowledge to understand their photographs in the way we might with our own photos. But, in some senses, our direct experience is called on to create meaning – not our experience of Charles and Diana but of our own personal lives. The story of the royal couple straddles the public and the personal spheres, spheres which we are used to thinking of as separate. On the public side are placed issues of economics, employment, the law, the constitution; on the personal side, are falling in love, getting married, having children. The two spheres are actually inseparable but in general the public sphere is conceived of as the place for experts – politicians, economists, judges – while we all deemed to have varying degrees of experience of the private sphere. It is that expertise that we bring to bear on the photograph of Charles and Diana. We are not asked to scrutinize the faces of politicians at a summit meeting for signs of likes and dislikes; the formal photographs used suppress that kind of inquiry. But to understand how the South Korean photographs speak of the breakup of this marriage we can call on our own experience. We use our particular experiences of relationships to create a generality (this is how such couples look) to apply to a particular couple (yes, Charles and Diana are in trouble).

And so we are back with the photograph and the way in which it seems to offer a particular access to reality, the sense that it offers evidence of the truth if we can bring to it the right keys. The more general discourses I have been describing are locked back into a discourse specific to photography – that of impassively recording private emotions, of catching and exposing moments whose significance might otherwise be lost and of searching out that which the participants might wish to conceal. The discourses I have described above – of dress, of royalty, of the personal sphere – can be used to make meaning because they are channelled through the photograph's apparent promise to make this particular moment available to our gaze.

In analysing a photograph in this way I want to stress two points in particular. Firstly, our understanding of the photograph is based on a play between the particular and the general, between the specifics of the image and the general discourses of photography, social structures and personal behaviour. These more general associations are what Barthes called connotations or 'a body of "attitudes" ' (1977: 47) which are used to fix the meaning of a particular image. This process is not a game of 'free association' but almost its opposite, of ruling out a range of possibilities in favour of those that make sense in terms of our more general social experience. The associations, though they will vary from reader to reader, also provide the common basis for discussing the photograph; the less the common ground is shared – Who is Princess Di? Why aren't they speaking? – the less there is a basis for communication. Secondly, Barthes suggests that it is through connotations that an individual image is connected with the ideological formations of the society that produces it. Barthes speaks of 'a body of "attitudes" ' because the knowledges we bring to bear on the photograph are also positions – on romance, on royalty, on the ability of a photograph to tell us the truth. These positions are not monolithic, but again, unless we can place ourselves within a range of attitudes to, for instance, the British royal family, the photograph will lack significance in that discourse. And, indeed, in discussing the photographs of the royal visit, it is important to note that meanings based on an understanding of South Korean mores are likely to be lost on British audiences. Thus, an active role is given to the audience in this process of understanding since meaning depends not on the photograph itself but on the resources of the viewer. This does not mean we can be content with the lazy cliché that 'everyone sees things differently'; instead what is offered is ways of thinking about how those differences are structured and can in their turn be understood. The viewer may be active but is not free.

The story of Diana of course had a tragic ending which was itself subject to many interpretations and which is now something that we bring to bear in reading the photographs of her married life. But it is worth pointing to the way in which, before her death, she had tried to provide 'the anchor' to her own image, to wrest the meaning of her photographs away from the commentators. Significantly, she used television to do this through the 1995 *Panorama* interview. Television has the added dimension of sound, and frequently on the news, for instance, there is a disjuncture between sound and image as the commentators tell the viewers how to interpret what they are seeing, doing the task performed by written copy in the newspapers. In her television interview, Diana was trying to get over that disjuncture by speaking for herself about what her image meant. The attempt was the more audacious since it meant re-defining what the language of royalty might signify. Thus, she claimed the title of queen but used the language of romance to do so, suggesting that she wanted to be thought of as 'the Queen of Hearts'. The reception of this language in the interview, which women were much more supportive of than men, underlined the importance of considering gender in seeking to understand representation.[2]

Representation and gender

We make sense of a news photograph in the context of its claim to represent reality, its evidential or documentary status. But questions about representation and the mediation of reality also arise with fictional material. In this section I want to consider how the question of women's representation in soaps led on to more general issues of the relationship between soap opera and women viewers.

Much of the impetus for early work on the representation of women came from the feeling that the available 'images of women' were not adequate, generating the common complaint, 'We're not really like that'. It is a complaint which can be made by any group that feels itself to have an identity which is misrepresented by the media and is most consistently made by those who feel themselves to have little power within media institutions and little control over what they do. The complaint 'women are not really like that' rests on a number of assumptions that need to be unpicked. Firstly, it suggests that an important function of the media is to make realistic representations, an assumption which, as we saw earlier, depends on the concept of mediation between the audience and what is being represented. Secondly, it asserts the importance of the representation at least getting closer to what 'we are really like'. This is not necessarily a naïve position but one which rests on an understanding of the way in which the typical is used in media representations to highlight certain common characteristics that are deemed important. Representation then takes on the representative function of showing what a particular group is like to others and therefore has a public function. Thirdly, there is in the complaint a sense that a more accurate representation is important to those being represented because it affects how they see themselves. The question of realistic representations is thus a complex one in which their power in public and private constructions of identity is at stake.

In this context we need to consider what is meant by 'real'. Julie D'Acci in her account of the US programme *Cagney and Lacey* quotes some comments from fans of the programme which provide a useful starting point. One writes, 'When I watch these two women working together being friends, fighting, loving and surviving it's so believable . . . I can think of no other show I've ever seen that's had real women, ordinary, living, breathing women as its stars' (D'Acci, 1994: 179); and another, 'I know I speak for all women when I say it's about time there has been a television show which portrays two real and human women who are successful as police detectives. . . . We prefer to watch a show which has as its stars people like ourselves living probable and possible lives' (p. 178). In both these examples we get a sense of the importance of the representative quality of the two characters who seem real because they are ordinary, recognizable because they are 'like us'. But these responses indicate the demand for a particular kind of reality in which the women characters also embody positive characteristics – they work, they survive, they are friends. So what is being welcomed by these viewers is a representation that will be positively helpful to women trying to live such a life, and educational to those who are dismissive about what women can do. D'Acci quotes another letter which is quite specific about this. 'Most importantly, though, it is the only show on television today which is an honest and thorough example of the roles which women . . . play in our society today' (p. 180).

This demand by women viewers for a more positive representation of women characters can be seen in some feminist television theory of the late 1970s/early 1980s, particularly in feminist writing on soap opera. Terry Lovell commented on the presence of 'strong independent women' in *Coronation Street*, welcoming an important extension of the range of imagery which is offered to women within popular forms' (Lovell 1981: 52). In *Women and Soap Opera* (1991), I pointed to the way in which female friendship and a solidarity between women is an important factor in British and US prime-time soaps.

Feminist theorists have however been cautious about the progressive model of which *Cagney and Lacey* is an example. For such writers, the intervention of semiotics and its subsequent developments had made the double call for realism and role models problematic. An emphasis on realism seemed to depend on a failure to recognize the constructed nature of representation and to be rooted in a belief that a perfect transparency could be achieved. Griselda Pollock, for instance, in 1977, argued that it was 'a common misconception to see images as merely a reflection, good or bad, and compare "bad" images of women (glossy magazine photographs, fashion advertisements etc) to "good" images of women ("realist" photographs, of women working, housewives, older women, etc)'. Instead Pollock argued that 'one needs to study the meanings *signified* by woman in images' (my emphasis, p. 26) but in doing so she recognized a gap growing between the call for more realistic representation of women within feminism generally and the work on signification being undertaken by feminists working on representation.[3] In a rather separate but related development, there was concern that the desire for a positive role model seemed to privilege one type of woman over others and involved rejecting 'more "feminine" traditional roles' in a way that seemed to collude with male denigration of them. Instead, feminist critics in media and cultural studies turned to the programmes such as soap operas and prime-time melodramas which were, for many women, a source of pleasure with a view to examining the way in which they constructed femininity and represented women's lives.

One important recognition was that realism should not necessarily be equated with the surface detail of everyday life. Ien Ang's *Watching Dallas* suggested that, despite the programme's surface glamour and its apparent distance from the day-to-day lives of its international audiences, viewers found a psychological believability, particularly in the character of Sue Ellen, which enabled them to recognize and identify with her emotional difficulties. Indeed, Ang argued that the melodramatic format of *Dallas* allowed for the expression of these emotions in a more direct and forceful way than the restrictions of realism allowed. Experiences were represented in such a way that they could be felt rather than merely observed. This notion of the personal sphere of emotion, elaborated by critics such as Charlotte Brunsdon (1981, 1991), was of crucial importance in developing work on how women were represented and what they signified. The separation of the public and private sphere, which we saw in play in potential readings of the royal photographs, was identified as a key device in both defining femininity and denigrating it. The domestic space of the home and the problems of personal relationships, particularly in the family, are constructed as being female concerns; the work needed to keep the home and family going is not given the same recognition or status (let alone pay) as that performed in the public sphere. Soap opera, it was argued, was one of the few formats on television which both acknowledged the nature of women's work in the private sphere and endorsed it. Soap operas may represent women in the traditional roles (the mother, the bitch) which so outraged the fans of *Cagney and Lacey* but did not identify them as 'lesser'. The women in soaps were portrayed as wives, mothers, daughters, girlfriends and many of the stories revolved around the emotional problems generated by these relationships. What was important however, and what gave women viewers pleasure, was the care and intensity with which the problems in these relationships were played out and the value given to women's role in maintaining them.

In endorsing soap operas and the relationship they establish with women viewers, feminist media theorists, including myself, found themselves in a somewhat paradoxical position. Awareness of the processes of signification meant that such writers distanced themselves from complaints about the misrepresentation of women on television while at the same time the re-evaluation of soap opera meant that, in media theory, feminism was strongly associated with programmes that privileged the traditionally feminine associations between women and emotions. Carrying this further, some writers have seen, in the relationship created between soaps operas and their female audiences, the possibility of a separate 'gendered, oppositional space' in which women may 'produce their own meanings and strategies' (Seiter *et al.*, 1991: 244). In such accounts, women viewers' recognition of and identification with the representative world of soaps works with the discussion and gossip associated with soap opera viewing to create a space in which women might express the inexpressible. In this space, it is argued, what Mary Ellen Brown calls 'a feminine discourse' (Brown, 1990: 190) can be established in which emotional relationships can be discussed in terms of power and the subordinated position of women in their social roles can be acknowledged by women viewers. In this analysis, the viewer is not merely active in the process of understanding media products, as we saw in the previous section, but also resistant. In the gendered space of soap-watching, women viewers may recognize the constraints under which women operate and acknowledge the pain they cause or mockingly defy them. Soaps allow them to recognize not so much real women but the reality of their own oppressed position.

Work on soap opera has been extremely fruitful in opening up work on representation and it has gone well beyond the textual analysis associated with semiotic work on representation. It has drawn attention to the constructions of femininity and masculinity which frame our understanding and has demanded that attention be paid to the intimate detail of the audience's relationship with particular modes of representation. Two more general processes should be noted in this work. Firstly, it is rooted in the notion that soap operas can be understood not so much as a mass media product imposing a particular kind of representation on women from above but as a product of popular culture, claimed from below, because it can support women's resistance to male domination. Thus, while production issues may be interesting, the meaning and importance of the representations lie with the audience. And secondly, the emphasis in this work has been on how meaning is established within the context of domestic viewing and in private talk between women viewers. The call for greater realism in the images of women seemed to indicate a need for a public acknowledgement of the importance of representation and a change in how such representations are produced. Work on soaps, on the other hand, placed a greater value on the pleasures made available to women viewers in the private sphere and the possibilities of resistance in consumption. The argument thus moved on to what was deemed to be more private and hidden terrain, the space of the feminine. In opening up this private space, work on soap opera which sprang out of second-wave feminism made a contribution to the development of post-feminist work which is discussed by Karen Boyle elsewhere in this volume (Chapter 2).

Representation and factual entertainment

Programmes such as soaps, with the exception of some British programmes, make little claim to the realist project of reflecting the world; for other programmes, however, engagement with events and issues of debate in the public world is crucial to their success. In this final section I want to turn to a range of programmes which come under the heading factual entertainment and to consider the issues raised in terms of representation by what are often controversial formats. This type of television programming takes real people and either records or reconstructs events in their lives or puts them into invented situations to test them out. In looking at such programmes I want raise further questions about representation, to focus in particular on the increasingly blurred lines between factual and fictional presentation of material in this area and ask how far the tools provided by semiotics are adequate for their analysis.

This kind of television format can be traced back to programmes in which dramatic events are represented through video footage recorded at the time and/or reconstructions. Sarah Kozloff saw the blurring of fact and fiction as crucial to such programmes, describing the US programme *Rescue 911* as blending 'reenactments and documentary footage, actors and "real people", to recreate the "true stories" of victims of life-threatening situations, victims who were saved by the assistance of emergency personnel' (Kozloff, 1992: 73). In some cases these programmes use the notion of public service as a guarantee of their good intent. Typical in this is the BBC's *Crimewatch UK*, produced with the active cooperation of the police, which seeks to involve the public by using reconstructions of crimes to prompt viewers to ring in with information which might solve them; or *Rescue 911*, which frames each story with suggestions on how accidents might be avoided or ameliorated by the actions of ordinary people as well as those of the emergency personnel; or *Police Stop*, which provides a stern commentary on the perils of bad driving to accompany the bumps and crashes featured in the official video footage.

Alongside these moral purposes, however, the programmes also employ and place a value on devices that are more usually the property of fiction. The stories of *Rescue 911* are, as Kozloff indicates, 'excruciatingly suspenseful' (p. 73), relying on fast cutting, action hidden from the protagonists but not the viewer, and a piling up of incident. The compressed nature of the story means that characters are flat rather than rounded and are used to stand for positions and emotions (victim, fearful mother). This together with the exemplary nature of the stories gives them a melodramatic tone not normally associated with the narrative devices of documentary practice. Programmes such as *Crimewatch UK*, which reconstruct murder or violent attacks, inevitably show women or the elderly in the vulnerable positions made familiar by crime fiction, in the dark streets or hearing suspicious noises within the fragile home. The attraction of *Police Stop* is to allow a viewing of the crashes and spills made familiar in feature film car chases, with music or humorous comment to accompany the less serious episodes. These programmes do not try to present themselves merely as reports or to disguise their construction, their use of narrative and other devices more commonly associated with fiction. Instead they make construction overt, presenting re-construction as part of their attraction, inviting the audience to be engaged in the emotional pull of the drama as well as to play the part of concerned public citizens.

Despite this, these programmes gain urgency and immediacy from the fact of their basis in real people's lives. Kozloff suggests that the suspense of *Rescue 911* is based in part on our sense that the stories have 'the unpredictability, the unforeseeable "messiness," of "real life"' and that 'the show capitalizes on a certain "reality effect" – knowing that the action really transpired along these lines makes the peril and the stakes much higher than they would be in an overtly fictional text' (1992: 74). *Crimewatch UK* reiterates the reality of the events it deals with by its use of surveillance video recordings, the interviews with relatives or survivors and the emphasis on dates and times which, quite apart from their value to the detecting process, give a particular sense of being there. The blurred video images of *Police Stop*, far from detracting from the programme, reinforce its sense of being fleetingly captured from another source which had different purposes, reality caught literally as it moves.

The unease engendered in this combination of fictional display and documentary appeal seems to be present in the punctuation which Kozloff uses in her description of *Rescue 911*; the inverted commas around 'real people', 'real life' and 'reality effect' indicates an understandable uncertainty about the status of the concepts that are being referred to by these television images. For if these images are signifiers like any other why should they be marked as different except that our entertainment relies precisely on them being different? This distinctive emphasis on a reality base has extended in the 1990s to a wide range of programmes including the docu-soaps such as *Hotel* (1997) on British television and the US daytime talk shows such as *Rikki Lake* and *Springer*. The talk shows, in particular, draw attention to their construction and theatricality (Shattuc, 1998) but the allegation that the shows actually make up, rather than provoke, the emotional displays on which they rely calls into question their status. It is not just their integrity but their value as entertainment that is diminished if they are revealed as only construction. Certainly, scandal was provoked in Britain when it was alleged in 1999 that the BBC One talk show, *Vanessa*, had been using fake guests, recruited by an entertainment agency, and the show was pulled off the air.

Other reality programmes, though, seem to have dispensed almost entirely with their referent in a pre-existing world.[4] Instead, television actually creates a separate world which is continually surveilled for our entertainment. These reality television programmes have provided formats that have proved successful worldwide. In *Big Brother*, a house is built which is physically cut off from the outside world and constructed around spaces that will generate appropriate activity – hot tubs, the diary room, the sofas. In *Survivor* and *I'm a Celebrity: Get Me Out Of Here!*, contestants are isolated in carefully organized versions of nature which provide a graded series of tests and dilemmas. In *Wife Swap*, we have real husbands and wives but the programmes focus not on the day-to-day reality of their marriages but on what happens when the wives are placed in a strange home and expected to run a new family. In all these cases the environment, even when it existed before the show, has what Corner calls 'a fully managed artificiality' (2002: 256), created by both the transformation of the physical surroundings and the very fact that the participants are knowingly on display all the time. The relationship between reality and its representation seems to have been severed leaving such programmes in the realm of semi-improvised performances of sometimes scandalous activities choreographed, to varying degrees, by the production team and the participants who have been specifically cast for their group dynamics. Jane Roscoe, in her discussion of the Australian version of *Big Brother*, emphasizes that 'producers are very clear about this being a constructed event, rather than "real life"' (2001: 481) and cites one producer who compares the programme to 'a soapie where the actors get to write the script' (p. 480).

Nevertheless, as with emergency and chat shows, the referencing of reality is an important element of these created-for-TV programmes. Annette Hill's study of the British audiences for factual entertainment found that they preferred programmes such as docu-soaps, which observed real situations, or the emergency shows, which provided public service information. But even with programmes such as *Big Brother*, Hill found that audiences, though very conscious of the performative aspects of the programme, were looking for some kind of authenticity, some kind of relationship, we might say, between the signifier and a signified in the real world. The relationship found was that between emotional expressions – of anger, joy, surprise, despair – and the real self of the contestant; the moments of extreme emotional expression were taken to be revealing so that, as one respondent put it, commenting on a particularly fraught exchange, '"I don't think that was put on, I think that was very real"' (Hill, 2002: 335). Thus Hill suggests that those viewers who enjoy *Big Brother* do so because of a belief that

> when contestants in BB are faced with emotionally difficult situations, they often reveal their 'true' selves. Audience attraction to judging levels of authenticity in BB is primarily based on whether contestants stay true to themselves, rather than when the program is truthful in its depiction of contestants (p. 336).

This hunt for moments of revelation takes us quite a long way from the notion that the iconic nature of visual images, the resemblance between signifier and signified, grounded them in the specificity of a particular moment. Indeed, what Hill describes is much more like Ang's suggestion that viewers of *Dallas* were seeking emotional realism made possible by melodramatic formats. Reality television appears to mark the point at which this form of television actually loses contact with the documentary roots which provided some signs of a relationship with reality. But perhaps such programmes are popular because they are a way of both recognizing the mediations, performances and contortions of the mass media and still retaining faith in a notion of reality which has to be reached through constructions that are overtly fictional rather than documentary. Waiting for revelation is no longer enough; moments of extreme pressure are instead constructed as a way of punching through to the signified.

Problems still remain though. The different kinds of programmes I have discussed in this section are all based on the use of people who have an existence outside the programmes' images. Nichols has suggested limitations to the semiotic approach when it comes to documentary generally. He comments on the way in which such an approach takes images of people as signifiers with meaning dependent on their relation to other elements in the signifying chain. 'Useful as this approach may be to the refutation of the notion of transparency between image and reality', he goes on, 'it does not quell the disturbances semiosis sets up in the bodies of those who have their image "taken". Legal principles of privacy, libel, and slander attest to some of the dimensions of conflict' (Nichols, 1991: 271). This warning applies even more to reality television. While semiotics has been helpful in thinking through the implications of the visual image for the viewer's understanding, it does not provide a framework for addressing the political, moral and ethical questions that arise over the position of the viewed.

Conclusion

In looking at issues of representation through these three case studies, I have tried to show the ways in which semiotic methods with their emphasis on construction and convention have been helpful in analysing how images are understood in the mass media. Through such analysis, media theory has begun to describe the complex process of understanding which we bring to a newspaper photograph, a television fiction or a piece of video footage and challenged the notion, so deeply embedded in our commonsense responses, that visual images rely on revelation rather than construction and process. In addition, semiotics drew attention to the possibilities of an active role for the audience in understanding such constructions and paved the way for work on the relationship between text and viewer which has been explored for instance in feminist writing on soaps. But I have marked also points where it seems to me that semiotics led to something of an impasse. Such a moment occurred when, as Pollock described, feminists tried to make a bridge between 'images of women' and 'real women'. In writing on soap opera and women's fiction, it was possible to move out of that dilemma by working with the grain of feminine/female representations and find the possibilities of resistance within them. Factual shows that use reality as entertainment also raise questions about representation which are difficult to think through in a framework bound by semiotics. As with soaps it would be possible to focus on the possibilities of audience resistance, as Shattuc (1998) does, by stressing the way in which audience members are translated into performers and given a partial access to the telling of their own story. Nevertheless, questions still remain about who has power to control and organize meaning and how those meanings are understood and used. To answer these questions, we need political and ethical frameworks and audience research methods that go beyond the vocabulary of representation.

Notes

1 Helpful general accounts can be found in Culler (1976), Turner (1990) and Seiter (1992) among others while Branston and Stafford (2003) offer numerous practical examples.

2 Useful studies of the Diana phenomenon, written immediately after her death, can be found in *Screen*, Spring 1998, and in *Planet Diana*, 1997.

3 The article was mainly concerned with photography but similar arguments were made about images on film and television.

4 Raphael (2004) discusses the legal challenges to the use of found footage in US emergency shows. Programmes that generate their own reality run fewer risks in this respect.

References

Ang, I. (1985) *Watching Dallas*. London: Methuen.

Barthes, R. (1977) *Image – Music – Text*, S. Heath (translator). London: Fontana.

———(1993) *Camera Lucida*. London: Vintage

Branston, G. and Stafford, R, (2003) *The Media Students Book*, 3rd edn. London: Routledge.

Brown, M. E. (1990) 'Motley Moments: Soap Opera, Carnival, Gossip and the Power of Utterance', in M. E. Brown (ed.), *Television and Women's Culture*. London: Sage.

Brunsdon, C. (1981) 'Crossroads Notes on Soap Opera', *Screen*, 22 (4).

———(1991) 'Pedagogies of the Feminine: Feminist Teaching and Women's Genres', *Screen*, 32 (4).

Corner, J. (1986) 'Codes and Cultural Analysis', in R. Collin *et al.* (eds), *Media, Culture and Society*. London: Sage.

———(2002) 'Performing the Real Documentary Diversions', *Television and New Media*, 3 (3).

Culler, J. (1976) *Saussure*. London: Fontana.

D'Acci, J. (1994) *Defining Women: Television and the Case of Cagney and Lacey*. Chapel Hill: University of North Carolina Press.

Geraghty, C. (1991) *Women and Soap Opera*. Oxford: Polity Press.

Hill, A. (2002) '*Big Brother*: The Real Audience', *Television and New Media*, 3 (3).

Kozloff, S. (1992) 'Narrative Theory and Television', in R. Allen (ed.), *Channels of Discourse*. London: Routledge.

Lovell, T. (1981) 'Ideology and Coronation Street', in R. Dyer (ed.), *Coronation Street*. London: British Film Institute.

Nichols, B. (1990) 'Questions of Magnitude', in J. Corner (ed.), *Documentary and the Mass Media*. London: Edward Arnold.

———(1991) *Representing Reality*. Bloomington and Indianappolis: Indiana University Press.

Pollock, G. (1977) 'What's Wrong With Images of Women?', *Screen Education*, Autumn, no. 24.

Raphael, C. (2004) 'The Political Economic Origins of Reali-TV', in S. Murray and L. Ouellette (eds), *Reality TV Remaking Television Culture*. New York: New York University Press.

Re:Public (1997) *Planet Diana Cultural Studies and Global Mourning*. Kingswood: Research Centre in Intercommunal Studies, University of Western Sydney Nepean.

Roscoe, J. (2001) '*Big Brother* Australia Performing the Real Twenty-Four-Seven', *International Journal of Cultural Studies*, 4 (4).

Screen (1998) 'Flowers and Tears: The Death of Diana, Princess of Wales', 39 (1).

Seiter, E. (1992) 'Semiotics, Structuralism and Television', in R. Allen (ed.), *Channels of Discourse*. London: Routledge.

Seiter, E., Borchers, H., Kreutzner, G. and Warth, E. (1991) 'Don't Treat us Like we're so Stupid and Naive': Towards an Ethnography of Soap Opera Viewers', in E. Seiter, *et al.* (eds), *Remote Control*. London: Routledge.

Shattuc, J. (1998) '"Go, Rikki": Politics, Perversion and Pleasure in the 1990s', in C. Geraghty and D. Lusted (eds), *The Television Studies Book*. London: Arnold.

Turner, G. (1990) *British Cultural Studies*. London: Routledge.

chapter four

Culture, Communications and Political Economy

GRAHAM MURDOCK AND PETER GOLDING

Introduction

Everyone, from politicians to academics, now agrees that public communications systems are part of the 'cultural industries'. The popularity of this tag points to a growing awareness that media organizations are both similar to and different from other industries. On the one hand, they clearly have a range of features in common with other areas of production and are increasingly integrated into the general industrial structure in three key ways. Firstly, telecommunications and computer networks provide the essential infrastructure that allows businesses to coordinate their activities across widely dispersed sites of activity. Secondly, as the major arena for advertising, the commercial media play a pivotal role in matching consumer demands to production. Thirdly, media corporations are significant economic actors in their own right, employing substantial numbers of people and making major contributions to export flows. On the other hand, it is equally clear that the goods they manufacture – newspapers, advertisements, television programmes and feature films – play a pivotal role in organizing the images and discourses through which people make sense of the world. Many acknowledge this duality rhetorically, but go on to examine only one side, focusing either on the textual construction and consumption of media meanings or the economic organization of media industries. What distinguishes the critical political economy perspective outlined here, is precisely its focus on the interplay between the symbolic and economic dimensions of public communications. It sets out to show how different ways of financing and organizing cultural production have traceable consequences for the range of discourses, representations and communicative resources in the public domain and for the organization of audience access and use.

Critical political economy of communications – straw men and stereotypes

Some terms become notoriously loose in practice, acquiring the status of cliché or slogan rather than analytical precision. One such term in our field is 'critical' analysis. The dichotomy between empirical (often implying simply quantitative) work and more theoretical concerns became equated rather loosely with the distinction between administrative (meaning commissioned by the media companies by and large) and critical work (meaning broadly marxisant). This division was always false.

The approach we outline here is clearly critical, but in a sense which necessarily engages with empirical research, and which has no qualms about addressing issues of pragmatic and policy concern. It is critical in the crucial sense that it draws for its analysis on a critique, a theoretically informed understanding, of the social order in which communications and cultural phenomena are being studied.

This is a characteristic which it shares with another major tradition of research – cultural studies. Both are centrally concerned with the constitution and exercise of power, and both keep their distance from the liberal pluralist tradition of analysis with its broad acceptance of the central workings of advanced capitalist societies (Curran, 1990: 139). But this shared general stance conceals long-standing differences of approach, generated by the divergent intellectual histories of these traditions, and sustained by their very different locations on the contemporary academic map. Whereas critical political economy has been institutionalized within faculties of social science, and draws its major practitioners from the ranks of people trained in economics, political science and sociology, departments and programmes of cultural studies are still mostly situated in humanities faculties and mainly pursued by scholars drawn from literary and art historical studies, and from anthropology and other disciplines concerned with the micro politics of everyday meaning making. As a result, the two groups tend to approach communications with rather different interests and reference points, even when there is a strong desire to cut across disciplinary boundaries, as there often is.

Much work in cultural studies focuses on the moment of exchange, when the meanings carried by media texts – television programmes, popular romances or computer games – meet the interpretations that readers bring to them, or when the possibilities for self-expression and communication offered by internet message boards or camera phones are mobilized. These micro studies are absolutely essential to a proper understanding of how people sustain their social relations, construct their identities and invest their lives with meaning, but they offer only one half of a full analysis. The other half requires detailed investigation of the wider structures that envelop and shape everyday action, looking at how the economic organization of media industries impinges on the production and circulation of meaning and the ways in which people's options for consumption and use are structured by their position within the general economic formation. Exploring these dynamics is the primary task for a critical political economy of communications.

What is critical political economy?

Critical political economy differs from mainstream economics in four main respects. Firstly, it is holistic. Secondly, it is historical. Thirdly, it is centrally concerned with the balance between capitalist enterprise and public intervention. And, finally, and perhaps most importantly, it goes beyond technical issues of efficiency to engage with basic moral questions of justice, equity and the public good.

From 'the economy' to economic dynamics

Mainstream economics sees the 'economy' as a separate domain in which media economics has the specialized task of investigating how 'changing economic forces direct and constrain the choices of managers, practitioners and other decision makers across the media' (Doyle, 2002: 2). In contrast, critical political economy is interested in the general interplay between economic organization and political, social and cultural life. In the case of the cultural industries we are particularly concerned to trace the impact of economic dynamics on the range and diversity of public cultural expression, and on its availability to different social groups. These concerns are not of course exclusive to critical commentators. They are equally central to political economists on the right. The difference lies in the starting points of the analyses.

Liberal political economists focus on exchange in the market, as consumers choose between competing commodities on the basis of the utility and satisfaction they offer. The greater the play of market forces, the greater the 'freedom' of consumer choice. Over the last two decades, this vision has gained renewed credence with governments of a variety of ideological hues. Born again in their faith in Adam Smith's hidden hand of 'free' competition, they have pushed through programmes of 'marketization' designed to extend the scale and scope of market mechanisms and to install market criteria of evaluation as the primary yardsticks against which the performance of all media organizations, including those still in the public sector, will be judged (see Murdock and Golding, 2001). Against this, critical political economists follow Marx in shifting attention from the realm of exchange to the organization of property and production, both within the cultural industries and more generally. They do not deny that cultural producers and consumers are continually making choices, but point out that they do so within the limits set by wider structures.

Where mainstream economics focuses on sovereign individuals, critical political economy starts with sets of social relations and the play of power. It is interested in seeing how the making and taking of meaning is shaped at every level by the structured asymmetries in social relations. These range from the ways the relations between press proprietors and editors or journalists and their sources impact on news reporting, to the way that television viewing or home computer use is affected by the organization of domestic life and power relations within households. These concerns are of course widely shared by researchers who are not political economists. What marks critical political economy out as distinctive is that it always goes beyond situated action to show how particular micro contexts are shaped by general economic dynamics and the wider formations they sustain. It is especially interested in the ways that communicative activity is structured by the unequal distribution of material and symbolic resources.

Developing an analysis along these lines means avoiding the twin temptations of instrumentalism and structuralism. Instrumentalists focus on the ways that capitalists use their economic power within a commercial market system to ensure that the flow of public information is consonant with their interests. They see the privately owned media as instruments of class domination. This case is vigorously argued in Herman and Chomsky's book, *Manufacturing Consent: The Political Economy of the Mass Media* (1988). They develop what they call a 'propaganda model' of the American news media, arguing that 'the powerful are able to fix the premises of discourse, to decide what the general populace is allowed to

see, hear and think about, and to "manage" public opinion by regular propaganda campaigns'
(1988: xi, see also, Herman, 2000, and Klaehn, 2002). They are partly right. Government
and business elites do have privileged access to the news, large advertisers can operate as a
latter-day licensing authority, selectively supporting some newspapers and television
programmes and not others, and media proprietors can determine the editorial line and
cultural stance of the papers and broadcast stations they own. But by focusing solely on these
kinds of strategic interventions they overlook the contradictions in the system. Owners,
advertisers and key political personnel cannot always do as they would wish. They operate
within structures that constrain as well as facilitate, imposing limits as well as offering
opportunities. Analysing the nature and sources of these limits is a key task for a critical
political economy of culture.

At the same time, it is essential to avoid structuralism which conceives of structures as
building-like edifices, solid, permanent and immovable. Instead, we need to see them as
dynamic formations which are constantly reproduced and altered through practical action. In
his review of news studies, Michael Schudson argues that political economy relates the
outcome of the news process directly to the economic structure of news organizations, and
that 'everything in between is a black box that need not be examined' (Schudson, 1989: 266).
This is a misreading. Although some studies confine themselves to the structural level of
analysis, it is only part of the story we need to tell. Analysing the way that meaning is made
and re-made through the concrete activities of producers and consumers is equally essential to
the perspective we are proposing here (see Deacon and Golding, 1994; Murdock, 2003). The
aim is 'to explain how it comes about that structures are constituted through action, and
reciprocally how action is constituted structurally' (Giddens, 1976: 161).

This in turn requires us to think of economic determination in a more flexible way. Instead
of holding on to Marx's notion of determination in the *last* instance, with its implication that
everything can eventually be related directly to economic forces, we can follow Stuart Hall in
seeing determination as operating in the *first* instance (Hall, 1983: 84). That is to say, we can
think of economic dynamics as playing a central role in defining the key features of the general
environment within which communicative activity takes place, but not as a complete
explanation of the nature of that activity. At the same time, critical political economy continues
to insist on the need to begin any analysis with the organization of production. Against this
some analysts of the cultural industries have argued that since production, distribution and
consumption constitute an integrated circuit and that 'you have to go the whole way round
before your study is complete' (Du Gay *et al.*, 1997: 4) it does not matter where you enter this
circle. This argument is attractive but flawed. Whilst it is clearly the case that production and
consumption are mutually constitutive, as Vincent Mosco points out, 'mutuality does not
mean equal influence' (Mosco, 1996: 5–6), and since 'production is processually and
temporally prior to consumption' (Born, 2000: 406) it remains the logical place to start.

From events to processes

Critical political economy is also necessarily historical, but historical in a particular sense. In
the terms coined by the great French historian, Fernand Braudel, it is interested in how 'the

fast-moving time of events, the subject of traditional narrative history' relates to the 'slow but perceptible rhythms' that characterize the gradually unfolding history of economic formations and systems of rule (Burke, 1980: 94). Five historical processes are particularly central to a critical political economy of culture: the growth of the media, the extension of corporate reach; commodification; the universalization of citizenship; and the changing role of state and government intervention.

The extension of mediatization, which Thompson describes as 'the general process by which the transmission of symbolic forms becomes increasingly mediated by the technical and institutional apparatuses of the media industries' (1990: 3–4) makes the media industries the logical place to begin an analysis of contemporary culture.

Media production has been increasingly commandeered by large corporations and moulded to their interests and strategies. This has long been the case, but the reach of corporate rationales has been considerably extended in recent years by the sale of public assets to private investors (privatization), the introduction of competition into markets that were previously commanded by public monopolies (liberalization) and the continuing squeeze on publicly funded cultural institutions. Corporations dominate the cultural landscape in two ways. Firstly, an increasing proportion of cultural production is directly accounted for by major conglomerates with interests in a range of sectors, from newspapers and magazines to television, film, music and leisure goods and services. Secondly, corporations that are not directly involved in the cultural industries as producers can exercise considerable control over the direction of cultural activity through their role as advertisers and sponsors. The financial viability of commercial broadcasting, together with a large section of the press, depends directly on advertising revenue, whilst more and more of the other 'sites where creative work is displayed', such as museums, galleries and theatres, 'have been captured by corporate sponsors' and enlisted in their public relations campaigns (Schiller, 1989: 4).

The extension of corporate reach reinforces a third major process – the commodification of cultural life. A commodity is a good that is produced in order to be exchanged at a price. Commercial communications corporations have always been in the business of commodity production. At first, their activities were confined to producing symbolic commodities that could be consumed directly, such as novels, newspapers or theatrical performances. Later, with the rise of new domestic technologies such as the gramophone, telephone and radio set, cultural consumption required consumers to purchase the appropriate machine (or 'hardware') as a condition of access. Before they could make a telephone call they had to buy a hand set and rent a line. Before they could listen to the latest hit record at home they had to have a gramophone or, later, a radio set. This compounded the already considerable effect of inequalities in disposable income, and made communicative activity more dependent on ability to pay. As we shall see, the higher a household's income, the more likely it is to own key pieces of equipment – a telephone, a video cassette recorder, a home computer – and hence the greater its communicative choices.

At first sight, advertising-supported broadcasting seems to be an exception to this trend, since anyone who has a receiving set has access to the full range of programming. They do not have to pay again. However, this analysis ignores two important points. Firstly, audiences do contribute to the costs of programming in the form of additions to the retail price of heavily advertised goods. Secondly, within this system, audiences themselves are the primary commodity. The economics of commercial broadcasting revolves around the exchange of audiences for advertising revenue. The price that corporations pay for advertising spots on particular programmes is determined by the size and social composition of the audience it attracts. And in prime time, the premium prices are commanded by shows that can attract and hold the greatest number of viewers and provide a symbolic environment in tune with consumption. These needs inevitably tilt programming towards familiar and well-tested formulas and formats and away from risk and innovation, and anchor it in common-sense rather than alternative viewpoints. Hence the audiences' position as a commodity serves to reduce the overall diversity of programming and ensure that it confirms established mores and assumptions far more often than it challenges them.

Policies and ethics

From its inception, political economy has been particularly interested in determining the appropriate scope of public intervention. It is therefore inevitably involved in evaluating competing policies. It is concerned with changing the world as well as with analysing it. Classical political economists and their present-day followers start from the assumption that public intervention ought to be minimized and market forces given the widest possible freedom of operation. Critical political economists, on the other hand, point to the distortions and inequalities of market systems and argue that these deficiencies can only be rectified by public intervention, though they disagree on the forms that this should take.

Arguments within political economy on the proper balance between public and private enterprise are never simply technical however. They are always underpinned by distinctive visions of what constitutes the 'public good'. Adam Smith ended his career as a professor of moral philosophy. He saw markets, not simply as more efficient, but as morally superior. Because they gave consumers a free choice between competing commodities, only those goods that provided satisfaction would survive. At the same time, he saw very clearly that the public good was not simply the sum of individual choices, and that private enterprise would not provide everything that a good society required. He identified particular problems in the sphere of culture, and recommended various public interventions to increase the level of public knowledge and provide wholesome entertainment. Critical political economy takes this line of reasoning a good deal further, linking the constitution of the good society to the extension of citizenship rights.

The history of the modern communications media is not only an economic history of their growing incorporation into a capitalist economic system, but also a political history of their increasing centrality to the exercise of citizenship, which we can define in its broadest sense as 'the right to participate fully in social life and to help shape the forms it might take in future' (Murdock, 1999: 8). Translating this right from a high-sounding rhetoric into an everyday reality, however, requires that people have access to a range of cultural and communicative resources that support participation. These include: access to the information, advice and analysis that enables them to know their rights and to pursue them effectively; access to the broadest possible range of interpretation and debate on areas that involve political choices; the right to have one's experiences, beliefs and aspirations represented without distortion or stereotyping; and the right to participate in public culture by speaking in one's own voice, registering dissent and proposing alternatives. Like Adam Smith, even the staunchest present-day advocates of maximizing market freedoms in communications admit that commercial provision is unlikely to provide all these resources or make them equally available to everyone. As an influential British committee on broadcast finances, chaired by the convinced free marketeer, Sir Alan Peacock, noted; 'there will always be a need to supplement the direct consumer market by public finance for programmes . . . supported by people in their capacity as citizens and voters but unlikely to be commercially self-supporting in the view of broadcast entrepreneurs' (Home Office, 1986: 133).

In an effort to address these 'market failures' and counter the commodification of communicative activity, complex democracies have developed a range of cultural institutions funded out of taxation. These include: museums with free entry, public libraries, subsidized concerts and performances, and arguably, most import of all, because of its centrality in everyday experience, public service broadcasting. These initiatives break with the logic of commercial provision in two fundamental ways. Firstly, where commodities are sold as personal possessions, public cultural services are offered as public goods which are equally available to all. As John Reith, the first Director General of Britain's public service broadcaster, the BBC, proudly noted: the Corporation's programming 'may be shared by all alike, for the same outlay, and to the same extent . . . there need be no first and third class'. (Reith, 1924: 217–18). Secondly, rather than targeting their audiences as individual consumers of particular media products and services (as with cable subscription services) or of the goods promoted in the advertising that surrounds commercial broadcast programming or printed editorial matter, public media address their audiences first and foremost as members of moral and political communities.

Critical political economy in practice: three core tasks

To illustrate the concerns and distinctive priorities of a critical political economy of communications we briefly outline three key areas of analysis. The first is concerned with the manufacture of cultural goods, to which, as we noted earlier, political economy attaches particular importance in its presumption of the limiting (but not completely determining) impact of cultural production on the range of cultural consumption. Secondly, we examine the political economy of texts, to illustrate ways in which the representations present in media products are related to the material realities of their production and consumption. Finally, we assess the political economy of cultural consumption, to illustrate the relation between material and cultural inequality which political economy is distinctively concerned to address.

The production of meaning as the exercise of power

Philip Elliott, in a bleak reading of developments in Britain in the early 1980s, suggested that the public space available for collective debate and deliberation was being seriously eroded by technological and economic developments that were promoting 'a continuation of the shift away from involving people in societies as political citizens of nation states towards involving them as consumption units in a corporate world'. Intellectuals, in particular, were being robbed of those public forums in which they could engage in their culture of political discourse (Elliott, 1982: 243–4). Investigating how changes in the array of forces which exercise control over cultural production and distribution and limit or liberate public cultural space is a focal question for the political economy of communications.

In practice this directs attention to two key issues. The first is the pattern of ownership of media companies and its consequences for the exercise of control over their activities. The second is the nature of the relationship between state regulation and communications institutions. We can briefly review each of these in turn.

Media concentration and owner control

The steadily increasing amount of cultural production controlled by large corporations has long been a source of concern to theorists of democracy. They saw a fundamental contradiction between the ideal that public media should operate as a 'public sphere' and the reality of concentrated private ownership. They feared that proprietors would use their property rights to restrict the flow of information and open debate on which the vitality of democracy depended. These concerns were fuelled by the rise of the great press barons at the turn of the century. Not only did proprietors such as Pulitzer and Hearst in the USA and Northcliffe in England own chains of newspapers with large circulations, but they clearly had no qualms about using them to promote their pet political causes or to denigrate positions and people they disagreed with.

These long-standing worries have been reinforced in recent years by the emergence of multi-media conglomerates with significant stakes across a range of central communications sectors and a significant presence in all the world's major markets. The present ownership of the major Hollywood film studios illustrates this process well.

The Warner Brothers studio is a subsidiary of Time Warner, a conglomerate that includes the Time magazine publishing empire, the Little Brown book publishing group, the major cable channels CNN and HBO, and AOL's internet interests.

Twentieth Century Fox is part of Rupert Murdoch's News Corporation which has major newspaper publishing holdings in the USA, Australia and the UK, substantial book publishing interests grouped around the HarperCollins brands and significant stakes in television in key markets including the USA (through the Fox Network), the UK (through the BSkyB satellite channels) and Asia (through the Star satellite service).

Paramount Pictures is now owned by Viacom which also controls the CBS television network in the USA, the Simon and Schuster publishing group, and a number of key cable channels, including MTV, the children's service Nickelodeon and The Movie Channel.

The rise of these comprehensive communications conglomerates adds a new element to the long-standing debate about potential abuses of owner power. It is no longer a simple case of proprietors intervening in editorial decisions or firing key personnel who fall foul of proprietors' political philosophies. Cultural production is also strongly influenced by the commercial strategies built around 'synergies' which exploit the overlaps between the company's different media interests. The group's newspapers may give free publicity to their television stations or the record and book divisions may launch products related to a new movie released by the film division. The effect is to reduce the diversity of cultural goods. Although in simple quantitative terms there may be more commodities in circulation, they are more likely to be variants of the same basic themes and images.

In addition to the power they exercise directly over the companies they own, the major media moguls also have considerable indirect power over smaller concerns operating in their markets or seeking to break into them. They establish the rules by which the competitive game will be played. They can use their financial power to drive new entrants out of the marketplace by launching expensive promotional campaigns, offering discounts to advertisers or buying up key creative personnel. Firms that do survive compete for market share by offering similar products to the leading concerns and employing tried and tested editorial formulae.

The powers of the major communications corporations and their cultural and geographical reach are currently being extended by the worldwide romance with 'free' markets coupled with the move towards digital technologies. For the first time, all forms of communications – written text, statistical data, still and moving images, music and the human voice – can be coded, stored and relayed using the same basic digital array of zeros and ones, the language of computing. As a result, the boundaries that have separated different communications sectors up until now are being rubbed away. We are entering the era of convergence. The potentials are impressive. Cultural products flow between and across media in an increasingly fluid way. New combinations become possible. Consumers can use, in principle, the upgraded telecommunications and cable networks to call up materials of their choice from vast electronic archives and libraries whenever they wish and in whatever combinations and sequences they desire. Enthusiasts present these possibilities as ushering in the transfer of power from owners to audiences. One of the most vocal celebrants is Rupert Murdoch. As he told a conference in September 1993, 'I must add (with maybe a tiny touch of regret) that this technology has liberated people from the once powerful media barons' (quoted in Greenslade, 1993: 17). Because, in the age of digital technology, 'anybody will be able to start media, or get anything they want for the price of a phone call' he sees his power and the influence of other major media owners diminishing drastically (quoted in Bell, 1993: 25).

The spectacle of one of the most powerful of the present-day media moguls cheerfully writing his own business obituary is attractive but deeply flawed. The fact that consumers will have access to a wider range of cultural goods, provided they can pay (a point we shall come back to presently), does nothing to abolish the control exercised by media moguls. In the emerging environment, power will lie with those who own the key building blocks of new communication systems, the rights to the key pieces of technology and, even more importantly, the right to the cultural materials – the films, books, images, sounds, writings – that will be used to put together the new services. And in the battle for command over intellectual properties, media moguls have a sizeable advantage since they already own a formidable range of the expressive assets that are central to public culture, and this range is steadily increasing through acquisitions, mergers and new partnerships. Moreover, the geographical reach of these conglomerates is being rapidly extended as governments around the world embrace 'free' market disciplines and allow the major communications companies access to previously closed or restricted markets. The opening up of markets in the former territories of the Soviet empire and in China (which in 2004 significantly relaxed restrictions on foreign ownership in its domestic media market) and India are simply the most substantial instances in a widespread trend.

The forward march of marketization

The last two decades have seen a variety of marketizing policies introduced in a wide range of countries, sometimes in response to disillusion with interventionism and state management, sometimes as a way of accelerating modernization, and sometimes as a condition of loans from international agencies or membership of the World Trade Organization. At an institutional level there has been a concerted effort to reduce the scope of the public sector and enlarge the corporate sector. Major public cultural enterprises, such as the state-owned telecommunications utilities and the French TF1 television network, have been sold to private investors, and liberalization policies have introduced private operators into markets that were previously closed to competition. In 1980 only two out of 18 Western European countries, Italy and the UK, had dual television systems with commercial and public service operators in competition. By 1997 this had become the norm with dual systems installed in 12 further countries (see Siune and Hulten, 1998: 27). At the same time, the primary purpose of regulatory regimes has been redefined. As Philip Lowe, the Director General for Competition in the European Commission, recently explained: 'the emphasis has shifted from protection of some broadly defined "public interest" towards opening up markets, ensuring free and fair competition between producers and promoting the interests of consumers' (Lowe, 2004: 1). This reliance on competition law to regulate corporate activity coupled with the installation of the 'consumer' rather than the citizen as the central figure in the communications landscape marks a comprehensive capture of public policy by market thinking. The net effect of these changes has been greatly to increase the potential reach and power of the major communications companies, and to reinforce the danger that public culture will be commandeered by private interests. Charting these shifts in the balance between commercial and public enterprise and tracing their impact on cultural diversity is a key task for a critical political economy.

Free markets and strong states

Observing the progressive enlargement of the market sector and the retreat from public interest regulation, it is tempting to conclude that the state now plays a less and less important role in organizing communications in contemporary capitalist societies. This is a mistake since it ignores two key areas where state intervention has been markedly extended in recent years: the reorganization of surveillance, and the expansion of government information management.

Modern nation states have always employed surveillance systems to identify potential threats from outside their borders and monitor dissenters and subversives at 'home'. At the same time commercial companies have developed their own extensive monitoring systems to identify consumer preferences and track audience behaviour. Up until recently these systems remained parallel but separate. The 9/11 attacks on the Twin Towers and the Pentagon however have prompted a fundamental re-think. The failure of conventional intelligence to identify a number of the hijackers in advance has been met with plans to widen the surveillance net and mobilize every available data source. The result has been the increasing 'convergence and integration of very different kinds of surveillance – police, intelligence, and consumer' (Lyon, 2003: 89). Because they may declare positions and preferences, reveal motivations and point to social connections and networks, people's use of communications and cultural facilities are a major focus for this new, inclusive, monitoring system. In the USA, for example, the Patriot Act gives the FBI the power to demand customer records for Internet service providers and other communication providers such as libraries and bookstores (American Civil Liberties Union, 2004: 12).

In the UK recent years have witnessed the growing use of surveillance techniques. As Taylor notes, 'Over the past thirty years in particular, considerable advances in technology have dramatically increased the powers of the state to carry out surveillance upon its citizens' (2003: 66). The growing use of CCTV in public places, or of phone-tapping and similar techniques, has increasingly seemed to many critics to have outgrown any rational justification for their use in detecting or deterring crime. By 2003 one estimate suggested that 'there may be as many as 4.2 million cameras in the UK or 1 for every 14 of the population' (McCahill and Norris, 2003). A rhetorical focus on the 'fight against terrorism' was used, in both the UK and the USA, to warrant a range of measures enhancing the state's capacity to record, monitor and inhibit the activities of residents and citizens. In the UK the government-appointed Information Commissioner was reported (*The Times*, 16 August 2004) expressing his 'anxiety that we don't sleepwalk into a surveillance society where much more information is collected about people, accessible to far more people shared across many more boundaries than British society would feel comfortable with'. His fears, focused on proposed new databases, were reflected in a swathe of measures announced in 2004 as the final legislative programme of the second Blair administration, including the introduction of digital identification using ID cards.

But the state is not only a regulator of communications institutions. It is itself a communicator of enormous power. How this power is exercised is of major interest to a political economy of culture. Governments are inevitably anxious to promote their own views of the development of policy, and to ensure that legislative initiatives are properly understood and supported. In recent years this desire has fostered a rapid growth in communications activity, so that by 1990 the government had become the second biggest advertiser in the country (see Golding, 1990: 95). Between 1986 and 1992 UK government advertising increased in real terms by 16 per cent, having more or less doubled in the previous decade (Deacon and Golding, 1994: 6). Allocations to the Government Information and Communication Service (GICS) and its predecessors rose from £607,000 in 1996–97 to over £4 million in 2002–03 (*Hansard*, 14 January 2004: Col. 767W). Growing public unease about this growth, and not least the reputation of the 'New Labour' government for using spin, especially as formulated by Mr Blair's close associate and director of communications,

Alastair Campbell, prompted an inquiry under an experienced broadcasting executive (Phillis, 2004). The report began with a stark assertion of 'The three-way breakdown in trust between government and politicians, the media and the general public' (p. 2) and recommended the abolition of the GICS.

Communications researchers have commonly analysed this process as one in which the state effectively gives subsidies to media organizations by reducing the effort required to discover and produce information for their audiences. As Gandy defines the term, an information subsidy 'is an attempt to produce influence over the actions of others by controlling their access to and use of information relevant to those actions' (Gandy, 1982: 61). In an increasingly public relations state the provisions of such subsidies can range from the entirely healthy distribution of essential information with which to explain and facilitate public policy, to the nefarious management of news in which 'being economical with the truth' becomes an accessory of political life (see Golding, 1986, 1994).

The British government's anxiety to control communications reached an apogee in 2004 following a ferocious row with the BBC over the Corporation's coverage of the Iraq war. Tension between the ideal of public service broadcasting as a public watchdog on abuses of power and the instincts of government to restrain critical comment has coloured the history of UK broadcasting from its inception in the 1920s. However, the broadcast on BBC radio, in May 2003, of an unscripted news report that suggested the government had deliberately 'sexed up' its dossier of information about Saddam Hussein's development of and capacity to deploy weapons of mass destruction, brought this tension to an unprecedented level of intensity. In the ensuing row a report on the events by a distinguished judge, Lord Hutton, led directly to the resignation of both the Director-General and the Chair of Governors of the BBC. While the report was widely received by the press as unfairly biased against the BBC (not usually favoured by commercial press acclaim, but on this occasion subject to the unexpected camaraderie of attack by a common enemy), the damage was done. The increasing benefits of hindsight cast widening shadows of doubt over the fairness of the Hutton report, but nonetheless it remained clear that the BBC would be 'put under heavy pressure from inside and out over its coverage of news and its editorial procedures. With a charter renewal looming, it is vital that the Corporation treads carefully . . .' (Anon., 2004: 3).

The corporatization of public culture

As the fierce row between the BBC and the Labour Government over the drafting of the public dossier laying out the case for invading Iraq makes clear, public communications organizations may find themselves caught in an escalating crossfire between strong states and free markets. Marketizing policies do not simply redraw the boundaries between institutional sectors, they also alter the way public institutions operate and see themselves. Indeed, corporatization polices, which require or cajole public bodies into behaving like private enterprises, are a central strand in the marketization process. In 1989, for example, the New Zealand government, then dominated by fundamentalist free market thinking, passed a Broadcasting Act which transformed the country's public broadcaster, Television New Zealand (TVNZ), into a State Owned Enterprise whose first obligation was to return a profit to the Treasury. To fulfil this remit, though still nominally a public enterprise (with no shareholders), TVNZ launched an aggressive drive to maximize ratings for prime-time programming in competition with the newly arrived commercial competitor, TV3. The result, as in advertising-driven broadcasting systems generally, was a marked bias 'toward what does not strain at the leashes of familiarity and acceptability' (Blumler, 1991: 90). Similar tendencies, though not as marked, were also evident in a number of European television systems as more and more public broadcasters topped up their revenues by selling advertising and entered into competition firstly with commercial cable and satellite services and secondly with newly introduced commercial terrestrial channels. Although the BBC successfully fended off attempts to persuade the government to privatize it or require it to carry ads on its major channels, it too was caught up in the drive for corporatization.

In the mid 1990s in an effort to alter the balance of trade in cultural goods the government nominated the BBC as a 'national champion' and encouraged it to capitalize on its reputation as vigorously as possible in the expanding global marketplace for television programming created by the growth of home video, satellite and cable systems. As an official report noted, to enable the Corporation to 'create and sustain a United Kingdom presence in an international multi-media world' the government has encouraged it 'to develop its commercial activities, seeking private sector partners and finance' (HMSO, 1994: 24). The BBC responded. Its commercial arm, originally known as BBC Enterprises, was relaunched as BBC World, a number of co-production agreements were struck with American companies, and a major effort was made to sell the formats to successful entertainment shows in major international markets. Commercial gains can carry cultural costs however. As programme makers find themselves under greater pressure to take account of the requirements of the international marketplace there is likely to be less diversity, less creative risk-taking and more reliance on tried and tested formats and established reputations. Success in the marketplace places a major question mark against the future of public service broadcasting.

The more commercial revenue it generates, the weaker the case for continuing to fund its activities out of the public purse. As a Government Committee noted when the expansion of the Corporation's commercial activities was just getting underway, 'should the BBC find a new, profitable commercial role . . . it might be very difficult, if not impossible, to justify the existence of the licence fee at all' (National Heritage Committee, 1993: para. 105).

Although many free marketeers would be only too happy to see the BBC privatized, as we noted earlier, a number concede that market provision is unlikely to produce the full range of cultural resources required for participatory citizenship. One solution is to retain 'public service programming' as a particular, specialized category of output that merits public subsidy but to argue that it is not necessary to have dedicated public broadcasting institutions in order to produce it. In line with the principles of market competition, access to programme funding then becomes 'contestable' and open to anyone on a project by project basis. Once again, this proposal found its most enthusiastic supporters in New Zealand where the government set up a grant-giving body, New Zealand on Air, to dispense public funds to programme makers. There were two major problems. Firstly, projects were only funded if they could demonstrate that one of the channels was committed to broadcasting the finished programme or series. But channel controllers were often reluctant to assign slots, particularly if the programme dealt with controversial subjects, since lower ratings meant lost advertising revenues. It was safer to schedule a familiar programme with a known audience. Secondly, because public service programmes were often one-offs and scattered across the available channels there was little possibility of building audiences over time.

The reinvention of public goods

The marketization of public cultural provision has not gone unopposed, however. In common with governments in a number of countries, the British government is eager to encourage viewers to migrate to digital television and radio services so that the spare spectrum capacity released by switching off the old, bulky analogue systems can be auctioned off or reassigned to non broadcast users. In pursuit of this objective it has supported the BBC's launch of a cluster of additional digital channels, which can be viewed for no extra payment other than a single outlay on a digital converter box. The success of this initiative has prompted its commercial competitors to complain that the Corporation is simply duplicating services that are readily available on subscription on cable and satellite platforms. The BBC's new children's channel has been a particular bone of contention. In reply supporters argue that children have a right to watch programming tailored to their needs without being bombarded with advertising designed to incorporate their imagination and play into the consumer system and that households have a right to access this provision for the minimal possible outlay.

These arguments reassert the fundamental principle that public broadcast programming is a public good, equally available to everyone with a suitable receiving set, and designed to offer a diversity of experiences, representations and stimulations, not to promote consumerism. This rejection of commodification has been taken a stage further in the BBC's plans for a Creative Archive. This aims to make as much of the Corporation's past programming as possible available at no charge over the internet, allowing viewers to download whatever they wish and to re-use it in whatever way they choose, provided it is not for commercial gain. By making this huge cultural resource freely available the Corporation hopes to stimulate a wide range of creative activity among audience groups. Even so, the bulk of public culture will continue to be produced by the professional personnel employed in the media industries.

Contextualizing cultural work

The production of communications is never merely a simple reflection of the interests of the public agencies and private corporations who own or control the broad range of capital plant and equipment which make up the means by which cultural goods are made and distributed. The media industries are made up of men and women working within a range of codes and professional ideologies, and an array of aspirations, both personal and social. These ambitions can be idealized; much cultural production is routine, mundane and highly predictable. But the autonomy of those who work within the media is a matter of substantial interest to political economists since it has a direct bearing on the diversity of cultural production. Their aim is to discover how far this autonomy can be exercised given the constraints of the broad economic structure we have described above, and to what extent the economic structure of the media prevents some forms of expression from finding a popular outlet and audience.

An example can illustrate the point. Successive Royal Commissions have remarked on the significant absence within the British media of a popular newspaper with political sympathies to the radical left. The last Royal Commission on the Press, for example, concluded that 'There is no doubt that over most of this century the labour movement has had less newspaper support than its right-wing opponents and that its beliefs and activities have been unfavourably reported by the majority of the press' (House of Commons, 1977: 98–9). 'There is no doubt', it went on, 'that there is a gap in political terms which could be filled with advantage' (p. 110). Many journalists would sympathize with this view. As senior Fleet Street commentator Tom Baistow has lamented, 'For millions of Left, Centre and agnostic Don't Know readers there is no longer any real choice of newspapers' (Baistow, 1985: 57). To explain this political economists will examine the impact of shifts in advertising support and ownership to discover why this gap exists, and why, therefore, opportunities for the expression of radical views of the political left do not routinely find space in the organs of the British national press. In 1997 the general election in the UK returned a Labour government under Tony Blair with a landslide majority, a quite extraordinary shift in the political landscape accompanied by dramatic changes in the apparent political affiliations and enthusiasms of some national newspapers. Plainly this did not happen because a large number of journalists had a common and sudden reverse in political vision. But some proprietors, in keen recognition of the collapse in popular support for the Conservative government of John Major, were swift to recognize the need to back a winning horse, and to safeguard their own future needs in relation to the next government's likely inclinations in the field of media regulation.

The complex interplay between proprietorial interests, economic imperatives and the cultural production is of central concern to critical political economy (Deacon *et al.*, 2001). To trace the consequences of these relations, however, it needs to go beyond the broad delineation of structural dynamics and assess their concrete impacts on daily practice, recruitment and professional ideology. This requires detailed study of how cultural workers go about their jobs, the way sources of varying power and authority engage in 'agenda-building', and the link between what industrial sociologists have traditionally characterized as market situation and work situation.

The political economy of cultural production, then, is very much concerned with tracing the concrete consequences of broad patterns of power and ownership for the work of making media goods. To see where this takes us in the analysis of what gets produced we need to move on to the political economy of media output.

Political economy and textual analysis

Research in cultural studies has been particularly concerned with analysing the organization of media texts and tracing their role in sustaining systems of domination. As it has developed, this work decisively rejected the notion that the mass media act as a transmission belt for a dominant ideology and developed a model of the communications system as a field or space, in which contending discourses, offering different ways of looking and speaking, struggle for visibility and legitimacy. But outside of televised political speeches, discourses are seldom available for public consumption in their raw state. They are reorganized and recontextualized to fit the particular expression form being used. Discourses about child abuse, for example, might well feature in a variety of television programmes, ranging from public health advertisements, to news items, investigative reports, studio discussion programmes, or episodes of soap operas or police series. Each of these forms has a major impact on what can be said and shown, by whom, and from what point of view. In short, cultural forms are mechanisms for regulating public discourse.

We can distinguish two dimensions to this process. The first has to do with the range of discourses that particular forms allow into play; whether they are organized exclusively around official discourses, or whether they provide space for the articulation of counter-discourses. The second concerns the way that the available discourses are handled within the text, whether they are arranged in a clearly marked hierarchy of credibility which urges the audience to prefer one over the others, or whether they are treated in a more even-handed and indeterminate way which leaves the audience with a more open choice.

If cultural studies is primarily interested in the way these mechanisms work within a particular media text or across a range of texts, critical political economy is concerned to explain how the economic dynamics of production structure public discourse by promoting certain cultural forms over others. Take for example the increasing reliance on international co-production agreements in television drama production. These arrangements impose a variety of constraints on form as the partners search for subject-matter and narrative styles that they can sell in their home markets. The resulting bargain may produce an Americanized product which is fast moving, based on simple characterizations, works with a tried and tested action format and offers an unambiguous ending. Or it may result in a variant of 'televisual tourism' which trades on the familiar forms and sights of the national cultural heritage (Murdock, 1989a). Both strategies represent a narrowing of the field of discourse and inhibit a full engagement with the complexities and ambiguities of the national condition. The first effects a closure around dominant transatlantic forms of story-telling, with their clearly marked boundaries and hierarchies of discourse. The second reproduces an ideology of 'Englishness' which excludes or marginalizes a whole range of subordinate discourses.

This general perspective, with its emphasis on the crucial mediating role of cultural forms, has two major advantages. Firstly, it allows us to trace detailed connections between the financing and organization of cultural production and changes in fields of public discourse and representation in a non-reductive way, that respects the need for a detailed investigation of textual organization. Indeed, far from being secondary, such an analysis is central to the full development of the argument. Secondly, by stressing the fact that media texts vary considerably in their degree of discursive openness, it offers an approach to audience activity that focuses on structured variations in response. However, in contrast to some recent work on audience activity which concentrates on the negotiation of textual interpretations and media use in immediate social settings, critical political economy seeks to relate variations in people's responses to their overall location in the economic system

(Murdock, 1989b). Of course, this cannot explain everything we need to know about the dynamics of response, but it is a necessary starting point.

Consumption, use and everyday creativity: sovereignty or struggle

Curiously, an influential version of free market philosophy has had considerable currency in much work within cultural studies. In an attempt to contest the apparent simplistic determinism of a view which sees audiences as the passive dupes of all powerful media, some writers have asserted the sovereignty of viewers and readers to impose their own meanings and interpretations on commercially produced material. The customer, though perhaps a little bruised, is still ultimately sovereign. For writers with more critical or radical instincts it is a view that has unleashed a populist romance in which the downtrodden victims caricatured by crude economic determinists are revealed as heroic resistance fighters in the war against cultural deception. As we noted earlier, this argument is based on studies of people's close encounters with media texts and communications technologies which takes little or no account of the ways everyday activities are constrained as well as enabled by people's location in wider economic and social formations. The task of critical political economy is to examine the organization of these barriers and to trace their impact on the choices open to audiences and users. These barriers are both material and symbolic (see Murdock and Golding, 2004).

Where communications goods and facilities are available only at a price, access to them will inevitably be limited by the disposable spending power of individuals and households. Taking Britain as an example, spending on services generally has grown significantly in the last generation. From 1976 to 2003 spending on leisure goods and services has increased from 10 per cent to 18 per cent of household expenditure. Between 1971 and 2002 household expenditure in general grew to an index of 235, taking 1971 as 100. But on recreation and cultural goods and services this figure was 570, and on communication 828 (Office for National Statistics, 2004a). Within this global figure spending within the home has risen as a proportion, linked most significantly to the television set as an increasingly dominant hub of leisure time and expenditure. On average by the turn of the century British men were spending about 2 hours each week day and nearly 3 hours daily at the weekend using TV, radio or video (figures for women being slightly lower) (Office for National Statistics, 2004b: Table 13.4). As the range of hardware required for such activities grows, however, so too does the demand on private expenditure necessary to participate in them.

These shifts in expenditure patterns reflect a gradual change in lifestyles across the population, but these are experienced very differentially among different groups. In 2002–03 weekly expenditure on recreation and culture was £86.30 among professional and managerial groups, but only £57.20 among manual workers and £44.00 for the unemployed (Office for National Statistics, 2004b: Table 6.3). Lower income households inevitably spend a higher proportion of their disposable resources on essentials such as clothing, food and housing, while spending on communication goods and services is inescapably restricted. The disposable spending required for these goods and services is thus tilted increasingly towards

Consumer Durable	Higher Professional (%)	Intermediate (%)	Routine Occupations (%)	Economically Inactive (%)	All (%)
Colour TV	100	99	99	98	99
DVD player	66	66	60	25	50
Home computer	93	74	50	30	57
Fixed telephone	98	94	84	91	92

Table 4.1. UK household ownership of selected consumer durables among different socioeconomic groups (2003).

Source: www.nationalstatistics.gov.uk/STATBASE/Expodata/Spreadsheets/D8745.xls

more affluent groups. This has radical implications for their availability if they remain commodities in the marketplace rather than services in the public sector.

As Table 4.1 shows, ownership of and access to communications is clearly differentiated by income within the UK population. This becomes more sharply true for recent innovations in information and communication technology. This gap has become a matter of intense policy debate also in the USA, where a series of reports by the National Telecommunications and Information Administration have charted what has widely become known as the 'digital divide'. The most recent such report addresses the growing importance of broadband access for membership of the new information society. It notes that, 'The number of households willing to pay a premium over the cost of a basic dial-up connection for broadband access more than doubled between September 2001 and October 2003, growing from 9.9 million to 22.4 million. Underlying this growth is an evolution in the way people are connecting to the Internet. One in five (19.9 percent) U.S. households and over one-third (36.5 percent) of Internet households [in 2003] have a high-speed connection' (US Dept of Commerce, 2004: 3). Detailed data in the reported survey shows that while 85 per cent of households in 2003 with incomes above $100,000 are internet users, this figure fell to 38 per cent among households with incomes between $15,000 and $25,000. The figure for Hispanic households was little over half that for white households (37 per cent to 65 per cent) (US Dept of Commerce, 2004: Appendix Table 1). Broadband access and use similarly differentiates the population. Table 4.2 shows the digital divide in the UK. Broadband connections are relatively expensive compared with a basic home computer with dial-up internet access. As Manuel Castells has noted, unequal internet access is a moving target so that just as 'the huddled masses finally have access to a phone-line Internet, the global elites will already have escaped into a bigger circle of cyberspace' (Castells, 2001: 256). Many advanced uses of desktop computers, such as video streaming, require the extra speed and capacity of broadband connections. Without it these possibilities are denied. Consequently, limited spending power is a deterrent not only to initial purchase but to full and flexible use.

	1998–99	2002–03
Poorest 10 per cent	1	12
Third decile group	2	23
Fifth decile group	4	42
Seventh decile group	10	57
Richest decile group	32	85
All households	10	46

Table 4.2. Households with home access to the internet by gross income decile group (UK).

Source: adapted from www.nationalstatistics.gov.uk/STATBASE/Expodata/Spreadsheets/D6937.xls

This apparent widening divide is not a blip in the statistics, nor is it likely to be transitional as we stampede towards digital ubiquity. Unlike domestic household goods diffused in previous decades, this gap is unlikely to diminish substantially, owing to two factors. Firstly, income and wealth differentials themselves have sharply widened in recent decades. Between 1979 and 1998 in the UK the number of employees with earnings below the Council of Europe 'decency threshold' rose from 7.8 million (38 per cent) to 10.6 million (49 per cent) (Stewart, 1999). From the mid 1990s while poverty levels in the UK (still among the worst in Europe) were eased, inequality widened, due especially to accelerating advantage at the top end. The authors of an authoritative study on these data concluded that 'the level of inequality inherited after the big inequality rise of the 1980s has not been much reversed, and income inequality remains near a 40-year high' (Goodman and Oldfield, 2004: vii). In 2002, while the wealthiest 5 per cent in the UK owned 43 per cent of marketable wealth, the bottom 50 per cent of the distribution held just 5 per cent of the total wealth between them. This gap had widened from 35 per cent and 8 per cent in 1991 (Office for National Statistics, 2004b: Table 5.26).

The second reason to anticipate the digital gap being widened is to do with the goods themselves. They require regular updating and replacement, disadvantaging groups with limited spending power and cumulatively advantaging the better off. Owning video or computer hardware requires expenditure on software, owning a phone means spending money on using it. Owning a PC generates demand for add-ons – a printer, a scanner and in time (probably no more than four years) the need to replace the basic machine. The migration from dial-up connection to broadband involves further recurrent expenditure. Thus limited spending power is a deterrent not only to initial purchase but to regular use. Once again the general figures disguise sharp divisions among social groups. For example, telephone ownership among single parents with more than one child is lower than for the general population. Research by the industry regulator in 2003 showed that while on average 7 per cent of UK consumers had no telephone, this figure rose to 15 per cent among the unemployed, and 12 per cent in areas of high deprivation (Ofcom, 2003: Fig. 3b). In other words many such households are excluded from a communication resource for which they might be argued to have particular need.

However, not all expenditure on communications goods involves expensive acquisition of equipment. Television programmes can be viewed once you have a set to watch them on, as most people do, while many cultural materials are available as public goods; they are paid for from taxation as a common resource — public library books, for example. This is not a static situation, however. For political economists a shift in the provision and distribution of cultural goods from being public services to private commodities signals a substantial change in the opportunity for different groups in the population to have access to them. If television channels, or individual programmes, are only accessible by price, as in subscription systems, then the consumption of television services will be significantly governed by the distribution of household incomes. The growth of multiple channel television and pay-per-view services will impose increasing demands on limited disposable incomes, and will increasingly differentiate the range of material accessible to various groups across the income gradient. Similar considerations would come into play if, for example, public libraries were to make greater use of powers to charge, as was proposed in a government Green paper in 1988, even though, at the time, such proposals were shelved (Office of Arts and Libraries, 1988). By imposing the discipline of price on cultural goods they acquire an artificial scarcity. It is for this reason that the political economy of cultural consumption has to be especially concerned with material inequalities.

Critical political economy is not only concerned with monetary barriers to cultural consumption, however. It is also interested in the ways in which social location regulates access to other relevant resources. Central to this analysis is the attempt to trace the consequences of differing positions in the system of 'production', understood not simply as paid labour but as the complex intersection of waged work and domestic labour, including the work of caring. Four kinds of non-monetary resources are relevant to a full understanding of consumption and audience activity – time, space, access to social networks and command of the cultural competencies required to interpret and deploy media materials in particular ways.

Time, particularly true leisure time, is a highly unevenly distributed resource, and as much research in domestic settings has shown, access to unaccounted for time, time for oneself, is strongly stratified by gender. Women's prime responsibility for the 'shadow work' (Illich, 1981) of shopping, cleaning, cooking and nurturing has fundamental consequences for their relation to the mass media. Not only are their choices often constrained by the prior demands of husbands and children, but the fact that no one else in the family is regenerating their affective resources leads them to look for other ways of maintaining psychological support. For example, where men mostly use the telephone instrumentally, to 'get things done', women often use it expressively, to sustain social networks. What appears from the outside as trivial gossip, is experienced from the inside as an emotional life-saver. The 2000 UK Time Use Survey found that, 'overall, men spent more time in paid employment than women – an average of 3 hours 48 minutes a day for all men, compared with just over 2 hours a day for all women. Conversely men spent less time than women doing household tasks (cooking and washing up, housework, and washing and ironing) – an average of 2 hours a day compared with 3 hours and 35 minutes for women' (Office for National Statistics, 2004b: 196).

Access to space is also a key resource which structures communicative choices, though it has so far been relatively little studied. The experience of watching television will differ depending on whether it is viewed in 'a room of one's own', in a living room, kitchen or other communal family space, or in a public site such as a bar. What is at issue here is the shifting spatial organization of privatized and sociable consumption and its implications for media experience. In order to map these varying mixes of spatial zones we need to trace their links to the dynamics of production and the patterns of geographic mobility and immobility, social separation and solidarity, and psychological identification and antipathy, that these generate.

An analysis of 'production' is also central to understanding the differential distribution of social networks and cultural competencies. One of the strongest empirical traditions within cultural studies – running from studies of youth subcultures to research on differential 'readings' of television texts – has concerned itself with how social locations provide access to cultural repertoires and symbolic resources that sustain differences of interpretation and expression (Morley, 1983).

But critical political economy needs to go a stage further to explore how access to systems of meaning, particularly those offering frameworks of interpretation that cut across the grain of the cultural mainstream, is linked to involvement in the social sites that generate and sustain them, and how these sites in turn are being transformed by political economic changes more generally, as contemporary 'production' moves, shifts and recomposes. What happens to the micro cultures of neighbourhoods in the face of urban redevelopment? How does de-industrialization and the shift from manufacturing to services alter occupational cultures and the critical cultures produced by the labour movement? How are the cultural relations between local and global formations reshaped by the migratory and diasporic movements of labour? These questions can only be tackled by reconnecting the analysis of communications with the political economy and cultural sociology of the contemporary world.

Conclusion

People depend in large measure on the cultural industries for the images, symbols and vocabulary with which they interpret and respond to their social environment. It is vital, therefore, that we understand these industries in a comprehensive and theoretically adequate way which enables the analysis of communications to take its place at the heart of social and cultural research. We have argued that a critical political economy provides an approach that sustains such an analysis, and in so doing have illustrated, in a preliminary way, the origins, character and application of such an approach. Much remains to be done, both theoretically and empirically, however, before we can claim to have fully established a critical political economy of communications.

Bibliography

American Civil Liberties Union (2004) *The Surveillance-Industrial Complex: How the American Government is Conscripting Businesses and Individuals in the Construction of a Surveillance Society.* New York: American Civil Liberties Union.

Anon. (2004) 'Editorial', *British Journalism Review*, 15 (1), 3–5.

Baistow, T. (1985) *Fourth Rate Estate: An Anatomy of Fleet Street*. London: Comedia.

Bell, E. (1993) 'Days of the Media Baron are Over', *The Observer Business News*, 5 September, p. 25.

Blumler, J. G. (1991) 'Television in the United States: Funding Sources and Programme Consequences', in J. G. Blumler and T. Nossiter (eds), *Broadcasting Finance in Transition: A Comparative Handbook*. Oxford: Oxford University Press.

Born, G. (2000) 'Inside Television: Television Studies and the Sociology of Culture', *Screen*, 41 (4), 404–24.

British Market Research Bureau (BMRB) (1999) *Is IT For All?* London: BMRB.

Burke, P. (1980) *Sociology and History*. London: George Allen & Unwin.

Castells, M. (2001) *The Internet Galaxy: Reflections on the Internet, Business and Society*. Oxford: Oxford University Press.

Curran, J. (1990) 'The New Revisionism in Mass Communication Research: A Reappraisal', *European Journal of Communication*, 5 (2–3), 135–64.

Deacon, D. and Golding, P. (1994) *Taxation and Representation: The Media, Political Communication, and the Poll Tax*. London: John Libbey.

Deacon, D., Golding, P. and Billig, M. (2001) 'Press and Broadcasting: "Real Issues" and Real Coverage', *Parliamentary Affairs*, 54 (4), 666–78.

Doyle, G. (2002) *Understanding Media Economics*. London: Sage.

Du Gay, P., Hall, S., Jones, L., MacKay, H. and Negus, K. (1997) *Doing Cultural Studies: The Story of the Sony Walkman*. London: Sage.

Elliott, P. (1982) 'Intellectuals, the "Information Society", and the Disappearance of the Public Sphere', *Media, Culture and Society*, 4, 243–53.

Fiske, J. (1989) *Understanding Popular Culture*. London: Unwin Hyman.

Gandy, O. (1982) *Beyond Agenda-Setting: Information Subsidies and public policy*. Cresskill, NJ: Ablex.

Giddens, A. (1976) *New Rules of Sociological Method*. London: Hutchinson.

Golding, P. (1986) 'Power in the Information Society', in G. Muskens and C. Hamelink (eds), *Dealing with Global Networks: Global Networks and European Communities*. Tilburg: IVA.

———(1990) 'Political Communication and Citizenship: The Media and Democracy in an Inegalitarian Social Order', in M. Ferguson (ed.), *Public Communication: The New Imperatives*. London: Sage, pp. 84–100.

———(1994) 'Telling Stories: Sociology, Journalism and the Informed Citizen', *European Journal of Communication*, 9 (4), 461–84.

———(2000) 'Forthcoming Features: Information and Communications Technologies and the Sociology of the Future', *Sociology*, 34 (1), 165–84.

Goodman, A. and Oldfield, Z. (2004) *Permanent Differences? Income and Expenditure Inequality in the 1990s and 2000s*. London: Institute for Fiscal Studies.

Greenslade, R. (1993) 'Sky is Not the Limit', *New Statesman and Society*, 10 September, pp. 16–17.

Hall, S. (1983) 'The Problem of Ideology – Marxism Without Guarantees', in B. Matthews (ed.), *Marx: A Hundred Years On*. London: Lawrence & Wishart, pp. 57–85.

———(1986) 'Media Power and Class Power', in J. Curran *et al.* (eds), *Bending Reality: The State of the Media*. London: Pluto, pp. 5–14.

Herman, E. S. (2000) 'The Propaganda Model: A Retrospective', *Journalism Studies*, 1 (1), 101–12.

Herman, E. S. and Chomsky, N. (1988) *Manufacturing Consent: The Political Economy of the Mass Media*. New York: Pantheon.

Home Office (1986) *Report of the Committee on Financing the BBC*, Cmnd 9824, London: HMSO.

HMSO (1994) *The Future of the BBC: Serving the Nation Competing World Wide*, Cmnd 2621. London: HMSO.

House of Commons (1977) *Royal Commission on the Press: Final Report*, Cmnd 6810. London: HMSO.

Illich, I. (1981) *Shadow Work*. London: Marion Boyars.

Klaehn, J. (2002) 'A Critical Review and Assessment of Herman and Chomsky's Propaganda Model', *European Journal of Communication*, 17 (2), 147–82.

Lowe, P. (2004) 'Media Concentration and Convergence: Competition in Communications', *Speech to the Oxford Media Convention*, 13 January.

Lyon, D. (2003) *Surveillance after September 11*. Cambridge: Polity Press.

McCahill, M. and Norris, C. (2003) 'Estimating the Extent, Sophistication and Legality of CCTV in London', in M. Gill (ed.), *CCTV*. Leicester: Perpetuity Press.

Morley, D. (1983) 'Cultural Transformations: The Politics of Resistance', in H. Davis and P. Walton (eds), *Language, Image, Media*. Oxford: Blackwell, pp. 104–17.

Mosco, V. (1996) *The Political Economy of Communications: Rethinking and Renewal*. London: Sage.

Murdock, G. (1989a) 'Televisual Tourism', in C. W. Thomsen (ed.), *Cultural Transfer or Electronic Colonialism?* Heidelberg: Carl Winter-Universitatsverlag, pp. 171–83.

———(1989b) 'Audience Activity and Critical Inquiry', in B. Dervin *et al.* (eds), *Rethinking Communication. vol. 2: Paradigm Exemplars*. London: Sage, pp. 226–49.

———(1999) 'Rights and Representations: Public Discourse and Cultural Citizenship', in J. Gripsrud (ed.), *Television and Common Knowledge*. London: Routledge, pp. 7–17.

———(2003) 'Back to Work: Cultural Labour in Altered Times', in A. Beck (ed.), *Cultural Work: Understanding the Cultural Industries*. London: Routledge, pp. 15–36.

Murdock, G. and Golding, P. (1974) 'For a Political Economy of Mass Communications', in R. Miliband and J. Saville (eds), *The Socialist Register 1973*. London: Merlin Press.

———(1978) 'Theories of Communication and Theories of Society', *Communication Research*, 5 (3), 390–456.

———(2001) 'Digital Possibilities, Market Realities: The Contradictions of Communications Convergence', in L. Panitch and C. Leys (eds), *A World of Contradictions: Socialist Register 2002*. London: Merlin Press, pp. 111–29.

———(2004) 'Dismantling the Digital Divide: Rethinking the Dynamics of Participation and Exclusion', in A. Calabrese and C. Sparks (eds), *Toward a Political Economy of Culture: Capitalism and Communication in the Twenty-First Century*. Lanham: Rowman & Littlefield, pp. 244–60.

National Heritage Committee (1993) *The Future of the BBC Volume 1: Report and Minutes of Proceedings*. London: HMSO.

Ofcom (2003) *Consumers' Use of Fixed Telephony*. London: Ofcom.

Office for National Statistics (2004a) www.statistics.gov.uk/STATBASE/Expodata/Spreadsheets/D8562.xls

———(2004b) *Social Trends 34*. London: HMSO.

Office of Arts and Libraries (1988) *Financing Our Public Library Service: Four Subjects for Debate*. Cmnd 324. London: HMSO.

Phillis, B. (2004) *An Independent Review of Government Communications*. London: Cabinet Office.

Reith, J. (1924) *Broadcast Over Britain*. London: Hodder & Stoughton

Schiller, H. I. (1989) *Culture Inc: The Corporate Takeover of Public Expression*. New York: Oxford University Press.

Schudson, M. (1989) 'The Sociology of News Production', *Media, Culture and Society*, 11 (3), July, 263–82.

Siune, K. and Hulten, O. (1998) 'Does Public Broadcasting Have a Future?', in D. McQuail and K. Siune (eds), *Media Policy: Convergence, Concentration and Convergence*. London: Sage, pp. 23–37.

Stewart, M. (1999) 'Low Pay, No Pay Dynamics', in *Persistent Poverty and Lifetime Inequality*. HM Treasury Occasional Paper No. 10.

Taylor, N. (2003) 'State Surveillance and the Right to Privacy', *Surveillance and Society*, 1 (1), 66–85.

Thompson, J. B (1990) *Ideology and Modern Culture: Critical Social Theory in the Era of Mass Communication*. Oxford: Polity Press.

US Dept. of Commerce (2004) *A Nation Online: Entering the Broadband Age*. Washington: Economics And Statistics Administration, National Telecommunications And Information Administration.

Welch, C. (1994) 'Whose Economic Upturn?', *The New Review*, Nov/Dec Low Pay Unit.

chapter five

Globalization and National Media Systems: Mapping Interactions in Policies, Markets and Formats

KALYANI CHADHA AND ANANDAM KAVOORI

Introduction

As an explanatory concept, globalization is a relatively new one. Indeed, while the word 'global' is over 400 years old and many argue that the phenomenon itself can in some form be traced back to the sixteenth century, the use of the term globalization in a processual sense only occurred in the 1960s, and it was not until over 20 years later that the use of the term became widespread. Yet despite its recent conceptual lineage as well as a lack of consensus about its definition and significance, the notion of globalization, perceived both within empirical trends such as the trans-nationalization of capital flows and production, the growth of supranational political and economic organizations, the migration of people and the emergence of seemingly universalized patterns of culture and consumption (Albrow, 1990; King, 1991), as well as the intensified subjective consciousness of these trends, has gathered considerable currency within both academic and popular discourse. As Malcolm Waters puts it:

> We can define globalization as a social process in which the constraints of geography on economic, political, social and cultural arrangements recede, in which people become increasingly aware that they are receding and in which people act accordingly (Waters, 2001: 5).

Thus defined, globalization implies a world reconfigured in spatial and temporal terms, marked by the heightened interconnectedness of commodities, capital, people, places, ideas and images over time (Appadurai, 1990; Featherstone, 1990, 1995). While this development is perceived as having implications at a multiplicity of levels, with some viewing it as the worldwide triumph of capitalist democracy (Fukuyama, 1992), others seeing it as the internationalization of civilization without the constraints of nation-states (Ohmae, 1995) and yet others characterizing it as the final epoch of finance capitalism, the notion of globalization has been widely used in relation to contemporary changes in culture and communication. In fact, a significant thrust of the globalization debate within social science theory has focused on the cultural implications of the phenomenon, specifically changes in socio-cultural processes and forms of life. On the one side of the globalization debate are those who (usually drawing on neo-Marxist and functionalist positions) argue that the phenomenon is primarily driven by the desire of developed capitalist nations to perpetuate their economic and cultural hegemony by penetrating markets across the globe, resulting in the emergence of what one commentator has called pan-capitalism (Teheranian, 1999).

Indeed, to many scholars of this persuasion, globalization appears as little more than yet another variant of Western domination. This perception is especially acute in the realm of culture, where the concentration of communication resources among a few dominant actors in the developed world and the consequent flow of cultural production from these actors to locales around the world, is seen as resulting in the growth of uniformity and homogeneity brought about by the consumption of similar material and cultural products (Amin, 1997; Latouche, 1996). In this perspective, globalization is conceptualized as a phenomenon that results not in the emergence of an open international order, as often asserted by its supporters, but rather in the pervasive transfer of meaning and values to diverse cultural milieus and their eventual transformation on cultural and ideological lines, similar to major media players such as the USA, who dominate the global media marketplace.

On the other side of this debate are theorists who, while recognizing the presence of Western media and cultural products associated with globalization, contest the notion that global media flows represent either a form of domination or even a type of one-way traffic. Instead, they argue that there is a contra flow of culture from the periphery to the centre as well as between geo-cultural markets, especially in the area of television and films (Sinclair *et al.*, 1996). As Barker (1997: 5) puts it, 'Globalization is not to be seen as a one-way flow of influence from the west to the "rest", rather, globalization is a multi-directional and multi-dimensional set of processes.'

These scholars who tend to view globalization as 'a form, a space or field made possible through improved means of communication in which different cultures meet and clash' (Featherstone, 1995), also question assumptions regarding homogenization as a result of the diffusion of Western culture. In their account then, the forces of fragmentation and hybridity are equally strong and in fact affect all societies that are enmeshed within the processes of globalization. In the words of Tomlinson (1991: 175), 'the effects of cultural globalization are to weaken the cultural coherence in all individual nation-states, including economically powerful ones'. Consequently, as they see it, globalization is characterized by de-centred and heterogeneous cultural developments (Featherstone, 1995; Waters, 2001) and represents a 'complex, overlapping, disjunctive order which cannot be understood in terms of existing center–periphery models' (Appadurai, 1990: 296).

Considerable discussion about globalization has thus essentially been framed around the poles of cultural homogenization and cultural heterogenization, the global and the local. In fact, Appadurai (1990) has argued that the central problem of today's global interactions is the tension between cultural homogenization and heterogenization. And while the role of media is certainly acknowledged in this discussion, it tends to be conceptualized as either the purveyor of homogenizing fare (Mattelart, 1983; Schiller, 1976) or as a force that offers mass-mediated experiences to those who would otherwise live in largely local contexts (Giddens, 1990; Tomlinson, 1994). As a result, what is often overlooked in such analyses of globalization that are framed in terms of the opposing polarities of the global and the local, is the structural and institutional transformation of media systems that has occurred in the context of the phenomenon at the *national* level. This is not surprising, given that the relevance and strength of the nation-state as an institution has been frequently questioned by both those who take a positive view of globalization, seeing it as promoting global markets and liberal democracy (Archibugi and Held, 1995; Fukuyama, 1992) as well as those who view the phenomenon in a more dystopian light (McChesney, 1999).

Nonetheless, this position is deeply problematic. For while the idea that 'globalization as a process that supersedes geographical borders erodes the power of the state has become conventional wisdom', it is evident that despite the 'challenging and changing conditions', faced by nation-states such as 'the remarkable global expansion of media corporations, facilitated by the liberalization and privatization of media systems worldwide', that have reduced 'states' ability to exercise power and maintain information sovereignty' (Waisbord and Morris, 2001: ix), the rumours of the death of the nation-state have been vastly exaggerated.

Indeed, as Straubhaar (2002) points out, although the global market pushes for certain kinds of commercial and financial structures, the political economy of the nation-state still plays a crucial role in determining the structure, nature and organization of media industries. This is especially true of the electronic media, where not only are patterns of consumption still overwhelmingly national, but state authorities continue to play a central role in broadcasting, and even transnational flows of programming are ultimately mediated by national considerations and policies. Hence even though globalization theorists sometimes underestimate the power of the state, the evidence would seem to indicate that the nation state continues to provide the basic frame of reference for media systems throughout the world.

Consequently, in this chapter we propose an analysis that focuses on the interplay between the processes of globalization and media systems, to understand how media systems have evolved and developed in recent decades, by inserting the national into the discussion. We undertake this through an empirical exploration of global developments in electronic media markets, policies and institutions, audiences and formats, through the prism provided by case studies of diverse national settings. These case studies have been chosen not only from the perspective of ensuring geographic range but also because they constitute significant examples of the policy, market and media content trends that have emerged within national media environments in the context of globalization.

On the basis of our exploration of these case studies, we argue that the intersection of the forces of globalization with the media systems of nation-states has engendered profound and widespread changes in global media landscapes that are typically manifest in the adoption of increasingly market-oriented media policies by nation-states, the rapid emergence of national media conglomerates as well as the domestication of global formats to conform to national tastes and preferences. Consequently, drawing on these empirical trends we propose that the analysis of globalization and its impact on media systems should not only include the frequently overlooked level represented by the national but also that the framing of the issue should be enlarged to move beyond the global/local dichotomy towards a model that focuses on the real transformation of media systems that has occurred in recent years, engendering a pattern of convergent trends in terms of media policies, market and format related developments, in nation-states across the world.

Media policies and institutions

In the course of the last two decades, the media sector has been decisively and irrevocably transformed by the globalization of electronic media and what were once highly controlled and regulated industries, often dominated by public service or governmental broadcasters. Manifest variously in the proliferation of powerful technologies of distribution such as cable and satellite systems, the emergence of increasingly integrated markets as well as the growth of international conglomerates that purvey a variety of entertainment services worldwide, this transformation of the media has been seen as the consequence of a series of technological, political, economic and ideological changes whose roots can be traced back to the 1980s (Dyson and Humphreys, 1988, 1990).

In technological terms, these changes have included the emergence of new technologies of distribution such as satellite and cable services that challenged existing assumptions of spectrum scarcity, created new demand for programming and most importantly made possible rapid and economical transmission of programming worldwide. In economic terms they have comprised a shift towards information and service-based economies, resulting in increased pressures to liberalize the sector in the interests of consumer choice, efficiency and competitiveness; changes in global trade regimes that enabled the emergence of markets for media products across the globe. And finally, in ideological terms, they have meant a profound international move in the direction of neo-liberalism that called for the replacement of state intervention in sectors such as the media by market-friendly policies. Together, these developments have had significant implications for nation-states, creating a new range of both pressures and opportunities with which they have had to contend, as well as necessitating the re-evaluation and reformulation of media policy frameworks within diverse national contexts (Braman and Sreberny-Mohammadi, 1996).

National media policies: the move towards the market and the challenge to public broadcasting

A country where changes in media policy became apparent relatively early was the USA, where the Reagan administration made a concerted effort to deregulate the media industry, spurred not only by ideological imperatives but also by the growing awareness of the importance of the media sector in the context of national economic growth. As Hollifield (2003) points out, while manufacturing jobs were being lost to competitors overseas, American policy-makers recognized that as the dominant player in the global media and communications sector, the USA could effectively deploy its media industries as an engine of economic advancement. Consequently, they sought to capitalize on this advantage by removing restrictions on media industries in order to support their growth and expansion overseas, and pushed aggressively for their inclusion within international trade agreements such as the Uruguay Round of the General Agreement on Trade and Tariffs (GATT), the North American Free Trade Agreement (NAFTA) and the World Trade Organization (WTO) treaties that were designed to compel nations to open their markets to 'free trade' in media products.

This trend towards media deregulation was further accelerated with the passage of the Telecommunications Act of 1996, as well as recent attempts by the Republican-dominated Federal Communications Commission to further relax rules determining ownership and operation of television stations. But while the USA has come to be characterized by an increasingly deregulated and hyper-commercial media system where the market rules, a development that has had wide-ranging implications for the media sector both at home and abroad (Herman and McChesney, 1997), the perception of policy transformation has somehow been less profound than one might expect. This is perhaps because the USA (under pressure from the National Association of Broadcasters), has long chosen to organize its broadcasting sector on almost exclusively commercial lines, and has historically had comparatively little governmental oversight of its media organizations (McChesney, 1999).

Similarly, in Latin America, where many countries adopted a model of commercial broadcasting similar to their northern neighbour, although there has been a definitive trend towards the further consolidation of market-friendly policies, through the privatization of state-owned television stations as in Mexico, Argentina, Colombia and Chile, as well as the easing of restrictions on cross ownership and foreign direct investment as in Brazil, the long-standing presence of the commercial style of broadcasting historically favoured by the region's political elite has meant that policy changes, while certainly consequential, have appeared to represent a continuum rather than a completely new turn (Fox and Waisbord, 2002).

Instead, it is in the areas elsewhere in the world where broadcasting has historically operated within a more regulated environment, whether under public service organizations or government-controlled broadcasters, that the most transformative policy shifts have occurred. In Western Europe, for example, where (despite national variations) broadcasting was predicated on the notion of public service, provided by 'specially mandated, non-commercially driven, publicly owned and funded and publicly accountable', organizations (Brants and De Bens, 2000: 9), there has been a profound change in the media policy landscape in recent decades, driven by many of the types of changes that were significant in the North American case (Dyson and Humphreys, 1990; Humphreys, 1996).

Demonstrated in the growing ascension of policies of 'marketization', this change has been part of a larger paradigmatic shift whereby nation-states moved away from the Keynesian consensus that prevailed in the post-war years and sought to replace the expanded welfare and regulatory functions that had come to characterize them with market-oriented strategies and policies (Dahlgren, 2000). In the case of the media this has signified an erosion of the policy frameworks that had defined and held in place the model of public service broadcasting that, in one form or another, had characterized most of Western Europe, with the notable exception of Luxembourg, where commercial broadcasting was always in place.

According to Murdock and Golding (1999), the shift towards market-oriented policies has typically involved steps such as:

- Privatization or the sale of communication assets to private investors, such as the sale of the major French television network TF1 to private investors as well as the proposed sale of the Danish public service television station TV2 and the Spanish regional broadcaster Canal 9.

- Liberalization or the introduction of competition into monopoly broadcast markets as, for example, in the case of Norway, Germany, Belgium, Spain, France, Sweden and Greece.

- Corporatization or the emphasis on a corporate model of functioning by public service organizations such as the BBC's launch of profit-oriented entities such as BBC Research, BBC Resources and BBC Monitoring, that provide commercial, creative, technical and production services to businesses and consumers as well as its push into the international marketplace through services such as BBC World.

Concurrent with this move towards market mechanisms there has been a parallel effort to relax or modify the programme obligations associated with public service broadcasting for new entrants as well a push towards greater commercialization whereby public broadcasters are encouraged or even required to organize their activities according to market principles, including relying on advertising revenues as a source of finance. This has resulted in a series of changes, the most notable of which have been the breakdown of the long-standing monopoly of public service broadcasters, an explosion of commercial channels and the emergence of a dual system of broadcasting, characterized by both public service and private entities. Indeed, this shift is clearly discernible in the hard numbers that show that while in the early 1980s, in the 17 nations that comprise Western Europe, there were 40 public service channels and only four commercial channels, and these were limited to three countries (Britain, Luxembourg and Finland), the current situation is very different. At present we find that while the number of public channels is almost 60, the number of terrestrial commercial channels has jumped to over 70. In addition, there are also hundreds of private cable and satellite channels that are aimed at local or regional audiences.

Furthermore, according to the European Audiovisual Observatory, public funding for public broadcasting organizations has fallen, resulting in increased dependence on commercial income, especially advertising revenues, for which they have to compete with the growing number of commercial broadcasters (European Audiovisual Observatory, 2002). This has in many cases resulted in significant declines in public broadcasters' share of advertising revenue, particularly as their audiences have also fallen. In fact, in 1998 the market share of national public channels in Germany, Greece, France, Finland, Belgium, Italy and the Netherlands was less than that of national private channels, while in Sweden, Norway, Portugal and the UK, public broadcasters were hanging onto a marginal lead (Brants and De Bens, 2000).

While in Western Europe changes in media policies and institutions can be linked to a complex combination of factors associated with globalization, in Eastern and Central Europe, where substantial changes have characterized the media sector, the principal impetus for change was provided by the fall of communism, an event whose onset can be linked to the forces of expanding capitalism and the emergence of new transmission technologies. Indeed, here the shift has perhaps been even more dramatic, involving the overthrow of monopolistic state-owned, party-controlled electronic media. But although the original aim of post-communist reformers was to establish pluralistic and democratic broadcasting media that were independent of the government and allowed for active participation by diverse voices, this has not quite come to pass (Jackubowicz, 1995). For while formal censorship has largely disappeared in the region, it has proved quite difficult for former state broadcasters to turn themselves into real public broadcasters. In part, at least, this has been due to the region's political climate where governments have been reluctant to cede control, and examples abound of governmental attempts to interfere in the workings of broadcasting organizations as in the case of the efforts of the ruling parties in Serbia, Romania and Bulgaria to assert their authority over former state broadcasters (Sparks, 2000). Additionally, the move towards public broadcasting has also been negatively impacted by the serious financial crises caused by the withdrawal or reduction of state subsidies and the inadequate availability of public funding in the region (Brunner, 2002).

Consequently, most of Central and Eastern Europe has come to be characterized by a dramatic growth in private commercial broadcasting, both in radio and television, typically in conjunction with foreign capital. This trend was inaugurated in the Czech Republic, which was the first country to issue a licence for commercial television broadcasting to TV Nova which draws about 65 per cent of the national audience, and has emerged in countries across the region in a veritable bandwagon effect. For example, in Poland commercial broadcasters have emerged in both cable and satellite as well as terrestrial networks, while in Hungary where in addition to commercial channels accessible via satellite and cable, there are two private terrestrial broadcasters in the form of the Scandinavian Broadcasting Service (SBS)-owned TV2 and Bertelsmann's RTL-Klub. And even in Bulgaria and Romania, where political interference in the media sector has been very marked, there has been a shift towards privatization and liberalization of broadcasting (European Audiovisual Laboratory, 2000).

As in the case of Western Europe, the emergence of private commercially-based broadcasters has also posed a significant challenge to the former state broadcasters in terms of finance and audiences. According to a report published in 2003 by the European Federation of Journalists, public broadcasters in Hungary, Romania, the Czech Republic and Bulgaria have almost uniformly lost audiences, and as a result of changes in media legislation have also found themselves receiving decreasing support from the state while having to compete for advertising revenues with private operators. In the Czech Republic, where broadcasting no longer receives state subventions, the public broadcaster Czeska Televize has been faced with budget shortfalls, especially since it only receives about 15 per cent of the national advertising revenue. Similar problems also beset Hungary's MTV, Bulgaria's BNT as well as Slovakia's public broadcaster (European Audiovisual Laboratory, 2000).

Thus while the dual broadcasting model, containing a mix of public and private broadcasting, has emerged in the countries of Central and Eastern Europe, it is apparent that public broadcasting, which was only recently established in this region, is confronted with even greater challenges than in Western Europe and that the overall policy shift orientation is clearly in the direction of greater liberalization and commercialization. A similar policy shift is also discernible in Asia where over the course of the last decade or so public or state-owned broadcasting monopolies have been increasingly dismantled and the sector opened to private operators. Indeed, while the degree and extent of the changes has certainly varied across nation-states, there has been a marked and pervasive shift in the character of media broadcasting organizations that were originally established in order to achieve a variety of national objectives ranging from the dissemination of educational messages and development strategies to the promotion of national unity and integration. As Kitley (2003: 4) points out:

> In the former Western colonies of South East Asia, television was developed as a central element in the political and cultural processes of nation-building. In Malaysia, Singapore and Indonesia, nation-building was the prime motivation for the creation of state-owned public television services, just as it was in the centrally-planned People's Republic of China.

And while he does not refer to India, there too television was introduced to achieve specific national goals. But although state-controlled broadcasting monopolies endured for several decades after their establishment, in the last 15 years or so they have been impacted by a range of developments, many of which are associated with globalization. These include the international diffusion of pro-liberalization policy prescriptions (often from financial institutions such as the IMF), the desire of nations to benefit economically from the emergence of the so-called information economy and, perhaps most significantly, the emergence of new technologies of transmission that have brought a wave of foreign programming into the historically regulated and closed broadcasting systems of Asia.

In the shifts that have consequently resulted within media policy regimes in this region, not only have private, commercial providers been increasingly allowed to enter the broadcasting sector, but former monopolists have been pushed to adopt a more corporate mode of operations that relies less on public finance and more on commercial revenue generation. For instance, in India the introduction of a general policy of economic liberalization in 1990, combined with the growth of unregulated cable television and the introduction of satellite television services that immediately registered significant urban audiences such as STAR TV and Zee TV, resulted in significant changes in the broadcasting sector. Specifically, these changes involved the government's recognition of private commercial broadcasting, the reduction of budgetary support to the state broadcaster Doordarshan as well as the issuing of a mandate that the latter raise its own revenues through commercial activities such as advertising and sponsored programming. In addition, the state-launched DD Metro, an entertainment-oriented commercially funded channel, aimed at urban areas where it was losing viewers to cable and satellite channels, used its legal and institutional power aggressively to obtain the rights for programming materials that were likely to attract large audiences and advertising and finally, building on an existing pattern of limited state–private cooperation, allowed the sale of time slots on Doordarshan channels to private producers (McDowell, 1999).

Moreover, the government also eased restrictions on the operations of private broadcasters, such as allowing them to own and operate commercial satellite systems, enabling them to uplink directly from India using Indian or foreign satellites (provided they meet certain criteria), allowing foreign direct investment in the media sector, and introducing a Convergence Bill that seeks to open up the country's proposed DTH platform to private use. The result has been an explosion in the growth of private channels that currently number over 40, and reach approximately 42 million cable and satellite homes in the country. And although the state broadcaster Doordarshan continues to draw a large audience, reaching about 105 million television homes, this is primarily due to its reach in the rural areas ('Media Penetration in India', 2003). In urban areas, Doordarshan has witnessed both a migration of audiences and advertisers (particularly during prime time) to satellite channels such as STAR Plus, Zee TV and Sony Entertainment Television's flagship channel who now account for the majority of India's television advertising pie ('Balanced Budgets', 2003).

This tectonic shift in India's media policy, manifest both in the transformation of the state broadcaster, Doordarshan, and the growth of private commercial broadcasting, is also mirrored to some degree in China. In the Chinese context the motivation for change was provided by the government's move to transform state-owned organizations such as the national government broadcaster CCTV into self-supporting entities (as part of a set of larger economic reforms), as well as its desire to accommodate demands for advertising venues by business groups who have emerged as a result of China's growing integration with the international economy (Yan, 2000).

Some of these changes have included substantial reductions in state support to media enterprises such as the national broadcaster CCTV (which now receives only a quarter of its revenue from the government), as well as a growing emphasis on revenue generation by national and provincial television stations, whether through advertising and other commercial activities such as programme sales, commercial sponsorships or related businesses such as audiovisual production and cable stations. Furthermore, the Chinese government has authorized the establishment of commercially oriented 'economic' radio and television stations, such as the Shanghai Oriental Television Station, that enjoy considerably greater autonomy in their operations than the so-called 'people's stations'. In fact, China recently took an unprecedented step in this direction when it issued television production licences to eight privately owned domestic companies to provide television programming (Collier, 2003). Thus even though Chinese broadcasting remains state owned, its increasing market orientation is apparent (Zhao, 1998).

Similarly, in Indonesia, where TVRI (Televisi Republik Indonesia) had served as the ideological voice of the state, by the late 1980s the state's control of broadcasting was being challenged by external satellite programmes and smuggled video cassettes. Simultaneously there was growing pressure from private domestic enterprises anxious to take advantage of the new technologies of transmission, and the combination of these factors eventually played a critical role in the breakup of TVRI's monopoly and the introduction of commercial broadcasting in the country (Kitley, 2003). Between 1990 and 1991 five new privately owned commercial channels were introduced onto the Indonesian broadcasting landscape. These new entrants (RCTI, SCTV, TPI, ANTEVE and IVM) have drawn audiences away from TVRI, as have the recently introduced satellite broadcasting and pay television channels, posing a serious threat to public broadcaster according to Idris and Gunaratne (2000).

As in the case of neighbouring Indonesia, television had been a state monopoly in Malaysia and had been established in order to weld the diverse ethnic groups that inhabited the country, into a nation. By the late 1970s, however, audiences were increasingly dissatisfied by Radio Television Malaysia (RTM)'s didactic programming, and seeking alternatives to it. Reacting to this growing 'threat', which was resulting in declining viewers and advertising revenues for RTM, the government sought to introduce a national commercial channel, TV3, whose licence was held by a private group in 1985. Two years later the government also reduced subsidies to RTM under the Broadcasting Act of 1988, and in 1995 it authorized a second private commercial channel, MetroTV, as well as Mega TV, a private terrestrial cable broadcaster. Finally, in 1998 it passed the Multi Media and Communications Act in which it called for the restructuring of RTM into an organization that was free to generate its own revenues.

This trend towards commercialization can also be discerned in countries such as Thailand and Singapore, where in recent years private operators have been allowed to enter the broadcasting market and government channels have begun to contract production to private producers, as in the case of Thailand's television channels 5, 9 and 11 (Ekachai, 2000).

From this discussion of media policies and institutions it is evident that there has developed an observable shift within the framework of media policies and institutional structures in the direction of the market, within national contexts across the world. This shift, which has usually occurred in response to the technological and economic imperatives associated with globalization, is manifest specifically in the introduction of competition into state or public broadcasting systems, resulting in the emergence of dual broadcasting systems, as well as the transformation of state/public broadcasters on commercial lines. And while national trajectories vary in terms of the degree of changes that they manifest, it is undeniable that the rules of the broadcasting game have been in an unprecedented state of flux for some time and that many of the old institutional certainties and normative prescriptions that characterized it no longer hold.

This said, it is however necessary to keep in mind that while the marketization of the broadcasting sector has advanced significantly, almost nowhere has the model of state or public broadcasting been completely abandoned in favour of a purely market-based model of the American type. In fact, in many cases public broadcasting organizations have been encouraged to undertake a process of adaptation (albeit through the adoption of more market-oriented policies), enabling their continued survival. Concurrently, it is also essential to underline that contemporary developments that signal a market orientation do not by any means imply the demise of the nation-state, as has also often been predicted (Ohmae, 1995). Indeed, one can make the case that not only do nation-states continue to establish and enforce gate-keeping policies related to broadcasting technology and content (Chadha and Kavoori, 2000), but even media policy shifts resulting in enhanced liberalization of electronic media have typically been introduced at the initiative of nation-states seeking to respond not only to the 'threats' posed by globalization (although these clearly play a role), but also in the pursuit of national economic growth or to benefit domestic corporations and enable participation by domestic elites in the global marketplace. Thus despite how one might perceive eventual outcomes, ultimately it would seem that national policies continue to play a critical role in the making of media policies and working of institutions in that they 'filter and mediate globalization, outlining its limits and possibilities' (Waisbord and Morris, 2001: 6) as they negotiate its dynamics.

Media markets and conglomerates

A significant aspect of contemporary media developments has been the emergence of huge media conglomerates whose reach extends across the globe. Although the globalization of media and markets is not an entirely novel development, there having existed a long tradition of international trade in media products, its current scope and scale are certainly unprecedented and have resulted in far-reaching changes in the economics and management of media enterprises (Thussu, 2000). Underlying this global expansion are specific economic factors, as Priest (1994) points out. First, media products have relatively low reproduction costs. Second, they can be resold without requiring any additional outlay by producers, and hence once production costs are covered, they generate pure profits for their owners. And in the risky environment of media production where the profitability of a product can only be assessed after its production, these factors, combined with technological changes, have played a key role in pushing companies to distribute their products on the largest scale possible. In fact, by 2002, 100 per cent of the top 10 media companies and at least 25 per cent of the top 25 media groups found themselves engaged in some type of overseas activities (Higgins *et al.*, 2001).

Much of the attention regarding the growth of media conglomerates has been focused on the activities of the big few, i.e. AOL–Time Warner, ABC–Disney, NBC–Vivendi, Bertelsmann, News Corporation, Sony and CBS–Viacom, who have moved aggressively to become global players, based on the considerable advantages that they enjoy in terms of access to large domestic markets (such as the USA) as well as the ability to benefit from the synergies that exist between the companies that they own. However, often overlooked in the expressions of shock and awe (depending on one's perspective), regarding the growth of these global oligopolies, is a parallel development.

The rise of national multi-media conglomerates

This is the emergence of multi-media conglomerates within nation-states that are engaged both in the consolidation of their position in broadcasting at home, as well as, in many cases, expansion into cultural–linguistic, geo-linguistic and diasporic markets abroad (Straubhaar, 2002; Wilkinson, 1995). The growing presence of such conglomerates is significant because they possess many of the elements on which the growth of the existing global giants has been based. For instance, they usually have access to sizeable domestic and oftentimes geographic and cultural–linguistic markets as well. Furthermore, while the scale on which they operate is smaller, they have considerable success in generating advertising revenues. And finally, they often also enjoy other advantages that give them considerable operating leverage. These include their frequent closeness to governments and political elites, their exemption as 'national enterprises' from certain types of regulatory restrictions and gate-keeping policies that typically target 'foreign' media entities, and above all their ability to provide audiences with culturally and linguistically 'proximate programming' (Chadha and Kavoori, 2000).

Some of the most major examples of such conglomerates come from Latin America in the form of Brazil's O Globo, Mexico's Grupo Televisa, Venezuela's Grupo Cisneros and Argentina's Grupo Clarins. Globo, Brazil's most powerful commercial broadcaster with 113 stations, claims almost 80 per cent of the prime-time audience and garners over 60 per cent of the country's total advertising expenditure (de Melo, 1995). In addition, it also owns the dominant cable network, Cabo Globo, a satellite service Globosat, 15 radio stations and is currently one of the largest players in the Latin American television market, selling its telenovelas to 20 countries on a regular basis, among them Portugal, Italy and the USA, where racy Brazilian soap operas are widely watched on Spanish-language channels.

Like O Globo, the Mexican conglomerate Grupo Televisa also has an extremely dominant position at home and has similarly expanded into markets outside its base country. Benefiting from the close relationship between the Azcarraga family, which controls Televisa and the PRI party which ran Mexico from 1929 to 2000, the company's holdings include 250 television stations and four networks, partial ownership in 17 radio stations, majority stakes in the leading cable television company Cablevision and the Latin American satellite broadcaster Innova (Hoover Online, 2004). The leading commercial broadcaster in Mexico, where it claims 75 per cent of the prime-time audience, Televisa also has a stake in Univision, the leading Spanish broadcaster in the USA, and produces 47,000 hours of programming, such as telenovelas, which it supplies to countries all over South America (Malkin, 2001). Like Televisa and Globo, both the Cisneros and Clarins groups dominate the media scene in their home countries of Venezuela and Argentina, respectively.

In Asia, India with its 80 million television households has also witnessed the growth of several domestic conglomerates, the most significant of which is the Zee network. Launched in 1992, as a single, entertainment-oriented satellite channel aimed at the Indian mass market, Zee TV soon emerged as a market leader, drawing large numbers of viewers with its mix of Hindi films and film-related programmes, serials, game and talk shows. By the mid 1990s it was widely acknowledged that Zee had changed the face of broadcasting in India and had expanded into other media businesses as well. These included the establishment of other satellite channels such as Zee Cinema and Zee News and the acquisition of Siticable, one of the country's largest cable multi-system operators (Thussu, 1998). Zee was also one of the first Indian companies to recognize the potential of broadcasting overseas to geo-cultural and diasporic populations and currently claims to reach 250 million viewers in 120 countries.

While the political connections that supported the rise of national media companies in Latin America are less obvious in the Indian case, Zee has nevertheless benefited from its relationship with successive Indian governments and its projection of itself as an 'Indian' company ('Zee Merges', 2003). Recently, a Zee-backed company became the first private entity to receive the Indian government's permission to launch direct-to-home satellite services, while the News Corp-owned Star TV still has an application pending ('Zee First to Start', 2003). Zee has also managed to continue to uplink its services directly from India despite the presence of a higher than permissible level of foreign equity in its structure (while other foreign companies have been barred from doing so), and even received an extension on a deadline to comply with government regulations (Subramanian, 2004).

In Hong Kong, an example of a national multi-media corporation is Television Broadcasts Ltd, or TVB as it is better known. TVB not only dominates the broadcasting scene with its Cantonese Jade Channel (commanding more than three quarters of the island's viewers), but recently also entered into an agreement to launch a pay-TV network as well. Originally a terrestrial broadcaster, TVB has investments in affiliation and production companies, satellite services and subscription companies and is also the world's largest producer of Chinese programming, exporting over 6,000 hours of programmes globally to over 40 countries, including mainland China and Taiwan, using both direct sales and its Jade Channel (Groves, 1994).

Even in Europe, where mono rather than multi-media concentration has been the norm, multi-media conglomerates have begun to emerge at the national level. These include Roularta, Belgium's largest media group, which in addition to owning domestic television and radio channels, also has a stake in Dutch and Portugese television channels; the largest privately owned media group in Spain, Grupo Prisa, which besides interests in newspapers, radio, cable (Sogecable) and television (Localia TV) nationally, also owns television stations and other media properties in Bolivia (where it purchased a 70 per cent stake in the country's main media group) and other parts of Latin America; Scandinavian companies such as Denmark's Egmont, Finland's Sanoma WSOY and Norway's A-Pressen group, who not only have myriad media properties at home but are also expanding overseas, particularly into Central and Eastern Europe and the Baltic Republics (Williams, 2003).

The rise of such multi-media conglomerates in varied contexts in many ways parallels the emergence of the vertically integrated global companies (albeit on a much smaller scale), and as in their case, has implications at multiple levels. Indeed, the trend toward media consolidation represented by such companies poses a significant challenge to the pluralism of ideas and diversity of culture, both within nation-states as well as in external markets, where the presence of companies whose programming and financial decisions are made outside, often has a profound impact on communities. Similarly, their relationships with political elites while giving them the latitude to operate freely, also results in their unwillingness to challenge the status quo.

In the case of Latin America, for example, the Brazilian company Globo, which had strong ties to successive military regimes, actively worked to suppress information about a popular movement for electoral democracy in the 1980s. In Mexico, Televisa's conservative soap operas have tended to reinforce the country's iniquitous and hierarchical socio-economic system, while broadcasters selling media products to China have avoided any political critiques of the regime. Moreover, their emphasis as expanding commercial enterprises on revenue generation has meant a focus on profitable, almost exclusively entertainment-oriented programming, whether in the form of Hindi film-related shows such as those first produced by Zee TV in India, the Latin American telenovelas or TVB's Chinese dramas. Emerging national multi-media corporations it would thus seem are reinforcing the trends associated with the workings of global media companies, sometimes by emulation of their operational templates and, increasingly, by entering into alliances with them.

Media formats

In addition to shifts within media policies and markets, a major development associated with globalization within the last decade has been the expansion of media formats, first developed in the West (usually in the USA), ranging from television news to soaps, talk-shows, quiz shows and, most recently, reality television into varied national contexts. For many critics of globalization this development has once more resurrected concerns regarding Western cultural imposition (via replication), of American media formats that structure local audience and subject them to the commercially driven, consumer-oriented discourse that such programming usually entails.

On the other side of this equation are the postmodernists who, according to Kellner, argue that global culture makes possible unique appropriations and reworkings of global products and signifiers all over the world, resulting in the emergence of new forms of hybrid syntheses of the global and the local, thus proliferating difference and heterogeneity (Kellner, web document). Lost in the homogenization/heterogenization debate between these two sides are two important issues: the processes of such domestication (Gurevitch *et al.*, 1991) and the contextual frame in which they take place. Gurevitch *et al.* define domestication as the process by which 'media maintain (simultaneously) both global and culturally specific orientation' (p. 206).

National domestication of global media formats

Following this line of argument, we suggest here that not only do media formats undergo a process of domestication and adaptation, but also that the contextual frame within which this occurs is fundamentally national. As defined by Moran (2004b), 'a format is an economic and cultural technology of exchange that has meaning not because of a principle but because of a function or effect' (p. 6), and the function or effect that they refer to lies in the specificities of cultural transfer and reproduction of these media formats. Thus, in the words of Thomas (2003: 39),

> the practice of television programs cloning among developing countries must be contextualized within particular cultural and economic contexts. This is critical to understanding both the apparent divergence and convergence of practices of the television industry as well as of reception by audiences as compared to those of the developed world.

The first task is to assess the range of such programming and its implications for national audiences. The range in India alone is impressive. It includes police dramas (*C.A.T.S.* from *Charlie's Angels*), sitcoms (*Hello Friends* from *Friends*), soap operas (*Tara* from *The Bold and the Beautiful*), game shows (*Family Fortunes* from *Family Feud*) and news (*Aaj Tak* from *CNN/Headline News* and *Star Report* from the *Fox Report*).

The rise of such media formats has to be problematized in the context of the rapid growth of television in India, from two channels to over 80 in one decade. While the transference of these media formats is partly an institutional response to the imperatives of filling long hours of programming, it also signals a *linguistic and demographic* shift. In its original form, for example, *CNN/Headline News* often catered only to those well educated in English. The shift to a local product in the local language, such as *Aaj Tak* news in India, signals a specific kind of domestication, a *national* orientation that speaks to the audience as a linguistic, majoritarian entity.

Aaj Tak is also important as a model for us to think through issues of market formats as they relate to issues of globalization. The second author of this chapter was one of the chief consultants in the design and training of journalists for *Aaj Tak*, and can speak to the organizational and pedagogical news philosophies that result in the reproduction of these market formats. Echoing the work of Lisbeth Clausen (2004) on the domestication of global news formats in the case of Japan, we would like to suggest that in the case of *Aaj Tak*, news producers at the national broadcast stations work in the space between the global and the national, based on a specific model of audience orientation: national, populist and working/middle class. It tried using the rubric of the *CNN/Headline News* model to undertake the domestication of news (via the dominant frame of national identity).

This has been reflected in its eschewing the formal Hindi espoused by the state broadcaster and replacing it with informal Hindi; in editorial philosophy (with a focus on national stories over international ones); of storytelling over talking heads (anchor-read story); and in the dynamics of news gathering itself where the key issues were those of the kinds of cameras to be used and the number of people on a crew. They successfully negotiated management philosophies aimed at lowering costs and argued essentially for a culturally relevant model for news gathering based on what they identified as quintessentially 'Indian' conditions.

Indeed, *Aaj Tak* has emerged as more than just successful media format. It has come to define and set the standard for an entirely new cultural vocabulary around information and the role of news in India. It is in a very real sense a *national* media phenomenon that despite the use of a global media format, reflects a *national* articulation of concerns very specific to the Indian case: the struggles over Hindutva and secularism, Hindu–Muslim riots, caste wars and cricket. Besides *Aaj Tak*, perhaps the most successful adaptation of media formats in India is that of *Kaun Banega Crorepati* (KBC), a licensed adaptation of *Who Wants to be a Millionaire?* by Star TV. This programme achieved the highest ever ratings in India and spawned numerous quiz-show clones among its rival channels such as Zee TV and Sony ET (Thomas, 2003). The success of KBC can easily be read as an example of cultural synchronization, the inevitable result of globalization. But as in the case of *Aaj Tak*, what we see with KBC is a process of national localization. Framed with the master text of Amitabh Bachchan (a national icon of Bollywood) and its India-specific questions, the show has become a success story for Star TV, emphasizing the success of national programming for a global conglomerate.

In the same vein, while clones of the MTV music channel have proliferated globally, they reflect both linguistic adaptation as well as a presentation style that reflect national cultural tastes and preferences. For example, in East Asian countries not only do most music channels (including MTV-Asia) avoid violent and sexually explicit music videos but the choice of music is carefully tailored to accommodate preferences for what veejay David Wu calls 'syrupy ballads about love lost and found', usually by Cantonese pop stars (Mufson, 1994). Similarly, in South Asia, music channels devote a considerable amount of airtime to programming related to Hindi films and film music, hosted by Indian veejays whose patter is that peculiar mix of Hindi and English, or Hinglish, that typifies urban India. And finally, in even in Europe, music channels such as the German language VIVA or the Dutch TMF have adapted the MTV model to reflect national tastes and artists (Roe and De Meyer, 2000).

In addition to these national domestications of media formats, as Richards and French (2000) point out, there are numerous other examples of the complex adaptation of Western television formats to fit indigenous viewing appeal, such as China's culturally-specific version of *Sesame Street*, or Taiwan's popular epic drama *Pao the Judge*, which while drawing on the stylistic conventions of Westerns serials, are nevertheless based in terms of content on national folklore and historical myths (Richard and French, 2000: 11).

Even in countries such as the Philippines, with its historical mix of foreign influences and its tradition of importing American programming, not only was *Who Wants to be a Millionaire?* translated into the country's lingua franca, Tagalog (despite the fact that English was well-understood by the upper and middle classes), but more importantly, as Keane (2004) points out, the show was most successful after it was 're-versioned', by leading local content provider ABS–CBN, into a show called *Game Ka Na Baa* or *Are You Ready for the Game?* Indeed, even in Japan, the most Westernized of the Asian countries, shows such as *Survivor* have been significantly adapted. As the producer of the Japanese version explains it, 'while the main feature of the US version is the exposure of naked human nature, as witnessed in betrayals and plots forged among contestants to expel a particular rival, the Japanese version places more focus on the inner mental conflicts of each challenger' (Iwabuichi, 2004: 25).

Similarly, while Australian networks have embraced a global media phenomenon, i.e. reality television, as an increasingly cost effective way to produce media content, and have imported many such series including *The Mole, Temptation Island* and *Survivor*, they have also begun to move away from the traditional policy of import substitution towards greater adaptation of formats in the form of shows such as *Big Brother* which was recently remade and broadcast in Australia in 2001 with specifically Australian 'touches' such as the transformation of the eviction of house residents into an outdoor event (Moran, 2004a).

In the words of Venzo, such production and 'consumption of such popular media phenomenon within local visual scenes requires us to think more contextually than the general framework of globalization allows' (Venzo, 2003: 1). This quality manifests itself most prevalently when so-called global television products such as *Big Brother* and *Temptation Island* are produced outside a dominant culture such as America. Despite their global qualities, such as aesthetics, narrative similarities and the capacity for multiplatforming, these programmes when produced and consumed in Australia often produce culturally specific images, characters and references that deny, rather than invoke, the dominant popular discourses and institutions that spawned them (Venzo, 2003: 4).

In fact we find that although there exists a widespread diffusion of successful 'Western' formats, largely due to the inherent uncertainty of the media business that leads producers to prefer tried and tested formats rather than potentially risky original concepts, the overwhelming preference of national audiences for culturally and linguistically resonant programming (Ferguson, 1993; De la Garde, 1994; Silj, 1992; Silj and Alvarado, 1988) results in the adaptation of these formats based on the cultural sensibilities of the national context into which they are imported. Globalization, then, does not seem to result in the wholesale cultural homogenization of national audio-visual systems as has been assumed, but rather in a complex and selective process of appropriation, as indicated by the adaptation and deployment of formats in various countries.

Globalization and national media systems: moving beyond the global/local dichotomy

Based on the trends examined here it is evident that not only are media and globalization closely intertwined but also that their relationship is not merely an instrumental one. While it is true that the media play a self-evident technological role as one of the drivers of globalization (and indeed one might argue that there could be no globalization without them), they simultaneously engage with and are transformed by its dynamics. In other words, there exists a dialectical interplay between these two elements that is negotiated and articulated at the level of the nation-state, resulting in far-reaching structural and institutional changes within national media landscapes. These changes include a pattern of commercialization of broadcasting frequently at the initiative of the state, the emergence of nationally based multi-media conglomerates as well as the national domestication of formats. Despite some variations, these developments are manifest in a range of national contexts, and underscore the necessity of developing a model of media globalization that recognizes the continuing role of the national and conceptualizes the phenomenon in terms of a convergence of policy orientations, market developments and programming trends within countries, rather than the somewhat Manichaean homogenization versus heterogenization debate that does little to illuminate the complexities of contemporary media developments as they are manifest across national contexts around the globe.

References

Albrow, M. (1990) 'Globalization, Knowledge and Society', in M. Albrow and E. King (eds), *Globalization, Knowledge and Society*. London: Sage.

Amin, S. (1997) *Capitalism in the Age of Globalization*. London: Zed Books.

Appadurai, A. (1990) 'Disjuncture and Difference in the Global Cultural Economy', in M. Featherstone (ed.), *Global Culture. Nationalism, Globalization and Modernity*. Newbury Park, CA: Sage.

Archibugi, D. and Held, D. (eds) (1995) *Cosmopolitan Democracy*. Cambridge: Polity Press.

'Balanced Budgets' (2003, December) Television Asia. LexisNexis.

Barker, C. (1997) *Global Television*. Malden, MA: Blackwell.

Braman, S. and Sreberny-Mohammadi, A. (1996) *Globalization, Communication and the Transnational Civil Society*. Cresskill, NJ: Hampton Press.

Brants, K. and De Bens, E. (2000) 'The Status of TV Broadcasting in Europe', in J. Wieten *et al.* (eds), *Television Across Europe*. London: Sage.

Brunner, R. (2002) 'How to Build Public Broadcasting in Post-Socialist Countries'. Retrieved from www.medienhilfe.ch

Chadha, K. and Kavoori, A. (2000) 'Media Imperialism Revisited: Some Findings from the Asian Case, *Media, Culture and Society*, 22.

Clausen, L. (2004) 'Localizing the Global, Domestication" Processes in International News Production', *Media, Culture and Society*, 26.

Collier, A. K. (2003, 3 September) 'China Opens Production Sector'. South China Morning Post, p. 2.

Dahlgren, P. (2000) 'Key Trends in European Television', in J. Wieten *et al.* (eds), *Television Across Europe*. London: Sage.

De la Garde, R. (1994) 'Cultural Development: State of the Questions and Prospects for Quebec', Canadian Journal of Communication, 19.

de Melo, J. M. (1995) 'Development of the Audiovisual Industry in Brazil from Importer to Exporter of Television Programming', *Canadian Journal of Communication*, 20 (3).

Dyson, K. and Humphreys, P. (1988) *Broadcasting and New Media Policies in Western Europe*. London: Routledge.

———(1990) *The Political Economy of Communications*. London: Routledge.

Ekachai, D. (2000) 'Thailand', in S. A. Gunaratne (ed.), *Handbook of the Media in Asia*. New Delhi: Sage.

European Audiovisual Laboratory (2000) 'The Financing of Public Service Broadcasting in Selected Central and East European Countries', *IRIS Legal Observations*. Strasbourg: Council of Europe.

European Audiovisual Observatory (2002) *Statistical Yearbook 2002. Film, Television, Video and New Media in Europe*. Strasbourg: Council of Europe.

Featherstone, M. (1990) 'Global Culture: An Introduction', in M. Featherstone (ed.), *Global Culture. Nationalism, Globalization and Modernity*. Newbury Park, CA: Sage.

———(1995) *Undoing Culture: Globalization, Postmodernism and Identity*. London: Sage.

Ferguson, M. (1993) 'The Mythology About Globalization', *European Journal of Communication*, 7 (1).

Fox, E. and Waisbord, S. (2002) 'Introduction', in E. Fox and S. Waisbord (eds), *Latin Politics, Global Media*. Austin, TX: University of Texas Press.

Fukuyama, F. (1992) *The End of History and the Last Man*. London: Hamish Hamilton.

Giddens, A. (1990) *The Consequences of Modernity*. Cambridge: Polity Press.

Groves, D. (1994, 6 April) 'Oz Report Eyes Asia, Says Relationships Key to Market', *Daily Variety*, p. 198.

Gurevitch. M., Levy, M. and Roeh, I. (1991) 'The Global Newsroom: Convergences and Diversities in the Globalization of Television News', in P. Dahlgren and C. Sparks (eds), *Communication and Citizenship: Journalism and the Public Sphere in the New Media Age*. London: Routledge.

Herman, E. and McChesney, R. (1997) *The Global Media: The New Missionaries of Corporate Capitalism*. London: Cassell.

Higgins, J. M., McClellan, S. and Kerschbaumer, K. (2001, 27 August) 'Top 25 Media Companies', *Broadcasting and Cable*, 17.

Hollifield, C. A. (2003) 'The Economics of the International Media', in A. Alexander *et al.* (eds), *Media Economics: Theory and Practice*. Mahwah, NJ: Lawrence Earlbaum Associates.

Hoover Online. Grupo Televisa S. A. Retrieved from premium.hoovers.com/subsribe/co/factsheet. xhtml?ID=51043

Humphreys, P. (1996) *Mass Media and Media Policy in Western Europe*. Manchester: Manchester University Press.

Idris, N. and Gunaratne, S. A. (2000) 'Indonesia', in S. A. Gunaratne (ed.), *Handbook of the Media in Asia*. New Delhi: Sage.

Iwabuchi, K. (2004) 'Feeling Glocal: Japan in the Global Television Format Business', in A. Moran and M. Keane (eds), *Television Across Asia. Television Industries, Program Formats and Globalization*. London: RoutledgeCurzon.

Jakubowicz, K. (1995) 'Media Within and Without the State: Press Freedom in Eastern Europe', *Journal of Communication*, 45 (4).

Keane, M. (2004) 'Asia: New Growth Areas', in A. Moran and M. Keane (eds), *Television Across Asia. Television Industries, Program Formats and Globalization*. London: RoutledgeCurzon.

Kellner, D. 'Globalization and the Post Modern Turn'. Retrieved from gseis.ucla.edu/courses/ed235a/dk/GLOBPM

King, A. D. (1991) 'Introduction', in A. D. King (ed.), *Culture, Globalization and the World System: Contemporary Conditions for the Representation of Identity*. Binghampton, NY: Department of Art and Art History, State University of New York at Binghampton.

Kitley, P. (2003) 'Introduction: First Principles – Television, Regulation and Transversal Civil Society in Asia', in P. Kitley (ed.), *Television, Regulation and Civil Society in Asia*. London: RoutledgeCurzon.

Latouche, S. (1996) *The Westernization of the World: The Significance, Scope and Limits of the Drive Towards Global Uniformity*, R. Morris (translator). Cambridge: Polity Press.

Malkin, E. (2001, 25 October) 'Emilio Azcarraga, 31, is Remaking Mexico's Televisa in His Own Image', *Business Week*. LexisNexis.

Mattelart, A. (1983) *Transnationals and Third World: The Struggle for Culture*. South Hadley, MA: Bergin & Garvey.

McChesney, R. (1999, 29 November) 'The New Global Media', *The Nation*.

McDowell, S. D. (1999) *Globalization, Liberalization and Policy Change. A Political Economy of India's Communications Sector*. New York: St Martin's Press.

'Media Penetration in India' (2003, 16 July) 'Times of India'. LexisNexis.

Moran, A. (2004a) 'Distantly European: Australia in the Global Television Format Business', in A. Moran and M. Keane (eds), *Television Across Asia. Television Industries, Program Formats and Globalization*. London: RoutledgeCurzon.

——— (2004b) 'Television Formats in the World. The World of Television Formats', in A. Moran and M. Keane (eds), *Television Across Asia. Television Industries, Program Formats and Globalization*. London: RoutledgeCurzon.

Mufson, S. (1994, 4 December) 'Far Eastern Exposure for Veejays', *The Washington Post*. LexisNexis.

Murdock, G. and Golding, P. (1999) 'Common Markets: Corporate Ambitions and Communications Trends in the UK and Europe', *Journal of Media Economics*, 12 (2), pp. 117–32.

Ohmae, K. (1995) *The End of the Nation State: The Rise and Fall of Regional Economies*. London: HarperCollins.

Priest, W. C. (1994) 'An Information Framework for the Planning and Design of "Information Highways"', Retrieved from www.eff.org/Groups/CITS/Reports/cits_nii_framework_ots.report.

Richards, M. and French, D. (2000) 'Globalization and Television: Comparative Perspectives', *The Cyprus Review*, 12.

Roe, K. and De Meyer, G. (2000) 'Music Television: MTV-Europe', in J. Wieten, G. Murdock and P. Dahlgren (eds), *Television Across Europe*. London: Sage.

Schiller, H. (1976) *Communication and Cultural Domination*. New York: International Arts and Sciences Press.

Silj, A. (1992) 'Italy: An Introduction', in A. Silj (ed.), *The New Television in Europe*. London: Libbey,

Silj, A. and Alvarado, M. (eds), *Fast of Dallas: The European Challenge to American Television*. London, British Film Institute

Sinclair, J., Jacka, E. and Cunningham, S. (eds) (1996) *New Patterns in Global Television: Peripheral Vision*. New York: Oxford University Press.

Sparks, C. (2000) 'Media Theory After the Fall of Communism', in J. Curran and M-J. Park (eds), *De-Westernizing Media Studies*. London: Routledge, pp. 35–49.

Straubhaar, J. (2002) '(Re)asserting National Television and National Identity Against the Global, Regional and Local Levels of World Television', in J. M. Chan and B. McIntyre (eds), *In Search of Boundaries*. Westport, CT: Ablex Publishing.

Subramanian, N. (2004, 9 August) 'Government Approval Hangs Cloud Over Zee Business Channel Plans', *Business Line*. Lexis Nexis.

Teheranian, M. (1999) *Global Communication and World Politics: Domination, Development and Discourse*. London: Lynne Reiner.

Thomas, O. (2003) 'Flattery or Plagiarism? Television Cloning in India', *Media Development*, 4.

Thussu, D. K. (1998) 'Localizing the Global: Zee TV in India', in D. K. Thussu (ed.), *Electronic Empires: Global Media and Local Resistance*. London: Arnold.

——(2000) *International Communication. Continuity and Change*. London: Arnold.

Tomlinson, J. (1991) *Cultural Imperialism: A Critical Introduction*. London: Pinter.

——(1994) 'A Phenomenology of Globalization? Giddens on Global Modernity', *European Journal of Communication*, 9 (2).

Venzo, P. (2003) 'Think Global-Watch Local TV', *Metro Magazine*, Winter. Retrieved from findarticles.cpm/p/articles/107422835

Waisbord, S. and Morris, N. (2001) 'Rethinking Media and State Power', in N. Morris and S. Waisbord (eds), *Media and Globalization*. Lanham, MD: Rowman and Littlefield.

Waters, M. (2001) *Globalization*. Routledge: London

Wilkinson, K. (1995) *Where Culture, Language and Communication Converge: The Latin-American Cultural Linguistic Market*. Austin, TX: University of Texas-Austin.

Williams, G. (2003) 'European Media Ownership: Threats on the Landscape'. Brussels: European Federation of Journalists.

Yan, L. (2000) 'China', in S. A. Gunaratne (ed.), *Handbook of the Media in Asia*. New Delhi: Sage.

'Zee First to Start Direct-to-Home Services' (2003, 30 July) 'BBC Monitoring International Reports', LexisNexis.

'Zee Merges Overseas Entities to Broadcast Zee TV from India' (2003, 16 December), *Asia Pulse*. LexisNexis.

Zhao, Y. (1998) *Media, Markets and Democracy in China: Between the Party Line and the Bottom Line*. Urbana, IL: University of Illinois Press.

chapter six

Rethinking the Study of Political Communication

JAY G. BLUMLER AND MICHAEL GUREVITCH

Introduction

Different fields of study call for different degrees of re-thinking and revision. Consequently, scholars working in diverse disciplines may be differentially obliged to take retrospective looks at the conceptual underpinnings of their fields. In part, this has to do with the 'hardness' or 'softness' of the fields concerned; in part it hinges on the pace of change in the societal, technological and intellectual environments in which their enquiries are situated. Whether a field of study is 'hard' or 'soft' is, of course, a matter of judgement, but it could be argued that the less the basic paradigm of a field of enquiry needs to adapt to the impact of external changes, the more it could claim 'hardness'; the more vulnerable the conceptual structure of a given field to the vagaries of external change, the 'softer' it is and the greater the need to reconsider and re-frame it in the light of changing conditions.

Gauged by this criterion, the physical sciences are clearly less exposed to sources of paradigm shift than the social sciences. The seeming immutability of the laws of nature offers greater protection to the paradigms on which those sciences are based and to their theoretical underpinnings. Of course, as Thomas Kuhn has taught us, the physical sciences are also subject to paradigmatic changes, but these arise more from accumulating weaknesses in the explanatory power of a given paradigm than from changes in their objects of study. The social sciences, by comparison, clearly require greater theoretical and conceptual alertness. Processes of social, political and cultural change are bound to impact on the conceptual frameworks developed and deployed by sociologists, economists and political scientists, since the phenomena which they examine and the issues they study are continually being transformed. It is more difficult to discern enduring structures, rules and generalizations when the societal kaleidoscope keeps revolving, confronting us with ever-changing, new and different patterns.

A good case in point is the field of political communication, the scholars and practitioners of which must continually adapt to changes both in the communication technologies by which political messages are produced and disseminated and in the structure and culture of the surrounding social and political system.[1] Thus, Blumler and Kavanagh (1999) maintain that over the relatively short period since the end of World War II, the organization of political communication has passed through three successive – if overlapping – phases in many Western democracies. First was a time (in the late 1940s and 1950s) when much political communication, reflecting partisan positions and beliefs associated with relatively strong and stable political institutions, enjoyed fairly ready access to the mass media. Next came the age of limited-channel nationwide television, expanding the mass political audience and elevating the news media to ever more powerful institutional standing *vis-à-vis* parties and governments. The third, current and still emerging, period is marked by a proliferation of the main means of communication both within and beyond the mainstream mass media and is therefore an age of communication abundance.

This latest transition is a confusing time for the study of political communication. Swanson (1999: 205) finds it particularly 'complex, volatile and . . . chaotic'. Four impulses appear most responsible for such unsettlement.

First, the communication problems of political parties, the prime seekers of electoral support in representative democracies, have been acutely aggravated by profound social changes. The huge reservoirs of social support on which they relied in the past – relatively coherent and party-minded social class, workplace and neighbourhood groupings – have dried up or dwindled. Instead politicians have had to court backing from a more consumerist, individualistic, volatile and sceptical electorate on the basis of issues and appeals of the moment. Trying to implement and sustain an effective strategy for communicating to such a public must often seem like an unceasing scramble.

Second, advances in audio-visual technology have instituted a more elaborate, fragmented, competitive and commercially geared media system. This not only hosts many more channels but also an exploding variety of journalistic formats and services, ranging from news flashes to conventional bulletins to 24-hour news, as well as an equally diverse set of 'infotainment' formats, talk shows and the like. This has increased uncertainty for all wishing to get their political messages into circulation – over where best to place them and how they might fare in the maelstrom of follow-up questioning, comment and criticism. Moreover, the responses to all this of individual citizens, who are better placed than ever before to relate to both politics and to communication as they personally choose, are more difficult to predict and master.

Third, new, though still embryonic, modes of political communication are being injected into the system via the surging dissemination of the internet and other interactive sources of information and opinion. Many questions with no clear answers as yet arise from this. How will the hitherto dominant political and media institutions adapt their offerings to it? Will they be seriously rivalled by other forces keen to exploit it? Will the internet mainly supplement the mainstream news media or increasingly supplant them? Will the availability of large stores of information, easy access to a wide range of sources, and mechanisms for the exchange of views and information transform people's expectations of how they should be addressed and served as citizens? Will present inequalities between the information-rich and information-poor be increased or levelled? Will representative democracy itself be challenged by more participatory, plebiscitary or populist models? Although the answers to these questions are still hidden in the future, the forecasters are divided at present into two camps – the optimists and the sceptics. Optimists maintain that the internet will usher in an era of liberated and empowered citizens, turning consumers of political messages into originators and producers of political communication. The sceptics (such as Davis, 1999) claim that thus far the internet has not proven to be a revolutionary innovation and that as yet there is little evidence of the expected rosy future. Obviously, only time will tell.

Fourth, the geography of communication is also in flux. National boundaries no longer define communication systems so distinctly, as the organization and flow of mass communications are being internationalized. Satellite technology has extended and speeded coverage of events throughout the world. Media economics – escalating production costs allied to limits on domestic revenues – has increased the importance of foreign markets. New genres packaged for global sale (e.g. MTV, CNN) have emerged (Ferguson, 1990). A few giant media conglomerates are vying for transnational supremacy. Many people have increasing access to non-national sources of entertainment, information, play, sociability – and politics. Politicians and pressure groups increasingly strive to reach and influence international audiences. Every now and then the contours of a global public sphere seem to be emerging.

If we are to make sense of such a turbulent scene, we need to select some key points of anchorage from which to view and analyse it. What might these be? Much of our own past work (cf. Blumler and Gurevitch, 1981, 1995; Gurevitch and Blumler, 1977) was predicated on the view that an understanding of the processes of political communication required a systemic perspective, i.e. one in which the different components of the system – media institutions and professionals; political institutions, parties and political advocates; audience members placed at the receiving end of the output produced by these institutions; and the surrounding socio-political environment – interact and impact upon each other, such that change in one triggers adaptive changes in the rest of the system. We believe that the application of such a framework to present conditions – considering how each of the elements in this model is being affected by the various changes outlined above – could still be clarifying.

The shifting political communication terrain
Political advocates

Our point of departure here is the 'competitive struggle to influence and control popular perceptions of key political events and issues', which takes place in all democracies nowadays among politicians and spokespersons of other interests and causes wishing to shape public policy (Blumler, 1990: 103). Much of this involves a 'competition for access' to the major communications media of the time, in which the 'material and symbolic advantages' of the various advocates 'are unequally distributed' (Schlesinger, 1990: 77).

Several developments in such publicity competition have stemmed from the waning of party loyalties and deference to authority among members of the public. First, effective communication to the electorate through the mass media has become even more important for government leaders and vote-seeking politicians, needing to gain each day (as it were) the approval they formerly could count on over longer stretches of time. This has impelled a thorough-going professionalization of the parties' communication activities, in which specialist consultants assume responsibility for proactive news management, campaign and message design, and research-based political marketing (Mancini, 1999a; Mayhew, 1997). Second, pressure groups and other sources of advocacy have put relatively less emphasis than in the past on lobbying inside governments, legislatures and parties and more on communication of their concerns and stands through the mass media. This helps them to build and sustain membership support and to create agendas to which governments must respond. And third, the terms of politicians' involvement in competition for media access have shifted to their disadvantage.

Until the 1980s the prevailing system tended to give 'a rather privileged position in political communication output to the views of already established power holders' (Blumler and Gurevitch, 1981: 489). Although political leaders had to heed the demands of other groups as well, they often managed this by incorporating their representatives into networks of formal and informal consultation, in which broadly shared assumptions about policy goals, and how conflict over them should be negotiated, prevailed. More radical groups, moved by different normative stances and policy priorities, tended to be excluded, not only from policy discourse but also from media access – unless they engaged in newsworthy protests and demonstrations, in which case they risked provoking pejorative coverage depicting them as disruptive and violent extremists (see McLeod, 1995).

But latterly the pecking order of political voices in the news has altered. For one thing, the political newshole is shrinking. In the USA, Britain and other advanced democracies the main news media are devoting relatively less space and time to the activities of governments and statements of politicians (Lee, 1999; Negrine, 1999; OECD, 1996). For another, politicians face increased competition for media publicity from a much wider range of advocates who operate outside the political parties, including advertisers, pollsters, interest groups and diverse social causes and movements. It is true that certain material and symbolic advantages still accrue to leaders of political institutions owing to their authority as elected representatives of the people and their power to make laws and execute policies affecting society as a whole. Nevertheless, 'official' politicians must fight harder to get their messages noticed and passed on in their preferred terms, while media tolerance has apparently increased for stances that would previously have seemed beyond the pale. At times the central publicity tussle pits a government or a political party against a well-organized, well-resourced and media-savvy pressure group or social movement rather than the opposing party. In 1999 Britain, for example, some of the Blair government's most difficult communication struggles arose from conflict with consumer groups and the environmental lobby (over genetically engineered foods), a countryside alliance (over fox-hunting, farmers' reduced incomes and rural decline generally) and the campaign for freedom of information (over the initially modest terms of its proposals for abolishing the Official Secrets Act). Another example is the big publicity battle that raged, during the Seattle conference later in the same year of the World Trade Organization, between governments of the richer countries and a disparate alliance of ecologists, human rights groups and trade unionists.

Many factors underlie this shift in the structure of media access for political advocates. One is increased journalistic scepticism about politicians' claims and assertions, which is reinforced by their belief that many members of the public are also unwilling to take politicians' utterances at face value. Related to this is the affronted sensitivity of journalists to leading politicians' attempts to manage the news in their favour, an effort they can sometimes neutralize by bringing in other critical voices. In the prevailing atmosphere of political disenchantment, coverage of party conflict, organized as government vs. opposition, may have also lost some of its appeal – as if too often stale and predictable.

Flows of communication to and through the media have also been affected by trends in the overall relationship of modern society to the political arena. On the one hand, a heightened awareness has developed in recent years of every citizen's entitlement to a decent life in a wide range of spheres – at work, in health, education, social security, public transport, the environment, etc. But on the other hand, a host of problems have arisen in most of these areas, which are not amenable to immediate solution and which, at best, politicians can only hope to ameliorate gradually over the longer term. As Bennett *et al.* (1999: 18) summarise:

> First, rising standards of living and security may encourage people to be less
> likely to defer to authorities, be they government or media. Second, the bar
> of public expectations for institutions and their leaders may have been raised
> over time.

And this tension between personal expectations and social conditions affords alert non-party pressure groups many opportunities to publicize their values and demands in the media – e.g. through coverage of research they may have sponsored on worsening social trends in their fields or of opinion surveys they have conducted on people's experiences and problems in such fields.

Finally, today's much expanded media system has helped to prise open the previously rather narrow funnel of access to electoral audiences. There are now many more outlets in which groups can try to place their messages in the hope of eventually achieving their wider circulation throughout the rest of the system as well.

Professional mediators

Like politicians, professional political journalists have also been slipping down a salient pecking order – that of access to news time and space for their reports inside their media organs. Of course demand for their contributions fluctuates in response to the flow of events – increasing during election campaigns, at times of high political crisis, or when controversy rages over weighty decisions of state. But the intensified competitive pressures on media organizations arising from communication abundance and increased commercialism have tended to diminish political journalists in two ways.

First, they have lost status. Partly this is because they no longer address the entire attentive nation through a small number of authoritative channels. There are now many more outlets through which people can follow politics, none of which can rule the roost as before. Partly it is because politics must compete with the increased availability in most of those outlets of entertainment, sport and other more beguiling fare. This has been accompanied by an upsurge of other forms of specialist journalism, which compete with political journalism for resources, space and appeal – e.g. financial journalism, sports journalism, celebrity journalism, fashion journalism, etc.[2] Partly the loss of status stems from the increased exposure of many journalists' media employers to a market logic, which subjects politics like everything else to the levelling impact of a profit-and-loss calculus. This calls into question the previously sheltered position that political journalism used to enjoy inside many media organizations.

Several consequences flow from this loss of standing. 'Sacerdotal' approaches to political coverage, wherein certain political events are regarded as inherently deserving of ample and serious coverage, have become less common. Politics must fight for its place in reporting and scheduling more often on the basis of its news value or likely audience appeal. Examples include drastic reductions of party convention coverage by the US networks, similar reductions in verbatim reporting of parliamentary debates by Britain's broadsheet press, and the near-demise of long-form analytical documentaries in many national broadcasting systems. Another consequence is the blurring of past distinctions between the 'quality' and 'tabloid' press and an upsurge of 'infotainment' approaches to politics. To get noticed, political journalists must learn to accommodate civic with hedonistic values. In addition, as market competition intensifies and politics is knocked off its pedestal, the ethics of political journalism becomes less careful and less closely policed. Davis and Owen (1998) ascribe the decline in traditional standards in part to the fact that many of the new media outlets are not bound by any notion of public service or by the norms of objective journalism. More generally, political coverage in the new conditions comes more often under review and pressure to demonstrate its compatibility with media organizations' goals, entailing a retailoring of such output if necessary.

Second, as with political advocacy, so too has the range of significant actors involved in the professional mediation of politics been broadened. The more or less bounded and coherent circle of political journalists who in the past boarded the same 'bus' to follow the same political personalities (Crouse, 1972) has been diluted and bypassed. The big players of political journalism no longer command the field they once dominated so prominently. They are now jostled by many new and less inhibited makers and breakers of news, sources of commentary and investigative pursuers and purveyors of scandal in talk shows, tabloids and internet web sites. One of the more significant developments here is the role played by entertainers and popular culture professionals in the political arena (e.g. stand-up comics and talk show hosts) as well as the tabloidization of news and current affairs magazines. The professional political journalist now shares the stage with media professionals who come from the entertainment side of the industry, whose celebrityhood provides them with considerable clout, and with whose perspectives and offerings they must somehow engage.

The audience for political communication

This component of the political communication process is changing in three important respects: in structure; modes of reception; and in role.

First, new media conditions tend to fragment the political audience, though to what extent and along what lines is not entirely clear and needs to be empirically monitored over time. With the multiplication of channels and outlets, the size of the mass audience for political news is undoubtedly reduced, and a diversification of political communication forms, catering for more distinct audience sectors, is facilitated. 'Balkanization' is probably an overly extreme metaphor for present-day audience structures. The saturation of our media environment with round-the-clock coverage of the top stories of the day ensures that almost everyone, even some who 'don't want to know', will be reached by news about major political events and conflicts. What may differ most across outlets and their audiences is how those stories are framed, analysed and followed up in diverse arenas and styles of commentary and discussion.

Nevertheless, two fault lines of audience differentiation may deepen with the advance of communication abundance. Political communication may increasingly address the particular identities and concerns of culturally distinct sub-groups – though such a process may vary cross-nationally according to how far the societies concerned are already culturally segmented and polarized. And the audience may be structured even more than at present by variables of political stratification (interest, knowledge and a propensity actively to seek out more information), as some in the population absorb little more than the daily political headlines and occasional tabloid stories, while others use the internet to explore the panorama of political issues and ideas more widely and deeply.

Second, media abundance is likely to change how political messages are received by audience members, though again research is needed to clarify along what lines. Much audience reception in the new conditions may turn on a tension between a greater freedom to choose, and an increased inability to avoid, political materials. Thus, with so many communication channels and forms available, it is obviously easier for people to look for and stay with that which interests them and to turn off whatever does not. Yet because political communication often blends with a flow of other materials nowadays, people can be exposed to it inadvertently as it crops up in genres and formats not usually designated as 'political'. All that said, however, media abundance does appear to introduce a greater element of flexibility into people's approaches to political communication. By multiplying and diversifying the possibilities of audience patronage across a wide range of media and information sources, it allows some individuals to be 'specialists', spending extensive amounts of time consuming favourite materials, and other individuals to be 'eclectics', sampling a broader miscellany of media fare. Again a potential for restructuring the audience arises here, differentiating political cognoscenti from 'hit-and-run' followers of public affairs and from 'anti-politicals', who may try so far as possible to close their eyes and ears to politics in the media.

But a third audience-related shift may be even more important than the others. Until recently much political communication was a straightforwardly top-down affair. The issues of the day were mainly defined and discussed by politicians, journalists, experts and interest group leaders for reception and consideration by voters. The former were predominantly actors, the latter recipients of political communication. But today it sometimes seems as if the 'audience' has broken out of that pigeonhole into a different role – like that of a 'producer' or an 'actor' (though lacking the focused intentionality of other actors in the system).[3]

In part this change stems from the increased choice inherent in an expansion of media abundance that can cater more closely for individual preferences. Thus, a combination of the decline of network news, the coming of 24-hour news, and the emergence of the world wide web as a news medium have arguably shifted 'some of the editorial process to the viewers' (Pope, 1999: 57). But it is an outcome as well of those strong currents of populism that have lately been suffusing the worlds of both politics and the media. These also emanate from the expansion of media outlets, which 'has created new opportunities and pitfalls for the public to enter the political world' (Delli Carpini and Williams, 2001). But they derive additionally from the decline of ideology, leaving a sort of legitimacy gap that populism helps to fill; from the growth of political marketing as an adjunct to campaign strategy; and from the diminished standing of political, media and other elites in popular eyes.

Consequently, communicators who wish to inform, persuade or simply hold the attention of their auditors must adapt more closely than in the past to what ordinary people find interesting, relevant and accessible. More efforts are made to engage voters in news stories by featuring the comments of ordinary citizens. The voiced opinions of men and women in the street are being tapped more often in a veritable explosion of populist formats and approaches: talk shows; phone-ins; solicitation of calls, faxes and e-mails for response by interviewed politicians; studio panels confronting party representatives; larger studio audiences putting questions to politicians through a moderator; and town meetings of the air, deliberative polling and televised People's Parliaments. Moreover, leading political and media organizations regularly conduct research into ordinary people's preferences, tastes and images of their own efforts and personalities – to help them keep in touch with the public mood and to stand a better chance of winning electoral support or audience share, respectively.

All this may be transforming the agenda-setting process, giving the audience-public (or its 'public opinion' as presented in polls, market research and media reports) a more active role in it than was previously the case. Although the news media are frequently depicted as front-line 'agenda setters', one can always ask: Who sets the agenda for them? When a partial answer refers to the initiatives and statements of politicians, the same question can be raised: Who puts the words in the politicians' mouths? And when the answer to that question is cast in terms of politicians' advisers, communication experts and pollsters, again the question can be put: From where do these people get their ideas? Presumably a main source is poll results, focus groups, etc., i.e. members of the public. We thus have a sort of circle of agenda-setting, to which the audience element now appears at least as contributory as that of the others.

The surrounding environment

As much of the above has intimated, the socio-political field in which political communicators operate has become far more complex and fluid than before. Curtin (1999) even terms the present situation an 'era of indeterminacy' for all involved in cultural and political expression. This heightens their difficulties of comprehension, adaptation and control.

In part this arises from the increased intractability of the central problems of politics, such as those of economic management, safeguarding the environment, escalating demands and costs of social provision, and rising rates of crime, drug abuse and other indicators of social breakdown. In part, it stems from the intensified competition by which all communicators are affected. But it is also the product of a host of increased uncertainties. When voters' loyalties are more volatile, what policies and messages stand the best chance of bringing them into your camp — and for how long? When people have more identities to assume, through which ones are they most likely to respond to particular events, initiatives and appeals? When the issues on the publicity agenda are more numerous and diverse, to which should communicators give highest priority? When the voices accorded access to the media are more numerous and diverse, which are most likely to ring sympathetic bells with the general public? When more outlets for political communication are available in our elaborated media system of television, press, radio, news magazines and the internet, how can messages be most effectively designed to suit their diverse 'demand characteristics' and to appeal to their diverse audiences? And when the very boundaries that previously structured the political communication field seem to be dissolving – e.g. between 'political' and 'non-political' popular-culture genres, between 'quality' and 'tabloid' approaches to politics, between journalists serving audiences as 'informers' and as 'entertainers', and between 'mass' and 'specialist' audiences – how can one know what to say most persuasively to whom through what channel?

A new form of political communication system?

Out of the convergence of many recent trends – especially the continuing advance of media innovation and abundance, the acceleration of social change with its numerous unpredictable consequences, the fragmentation of social orders, the de-throning of political institutions, people's increased expectations of personal autonomy, and the resulting proliferation and diversification of communicators, issue agendas and media outlets – a new form of political communication system does seem to be emerging. How might it be most appropriately characterized? Although it is too early to discern its ultimate shape, three broad, and possibly enduring, features stand out at this stage in contrast to past arrangements.

Porous politics

First, what counts as 'political' has become less clear-cut than previously. Highly significant in this respect has been the entry of popular culture into politics. During George W. Bush's campaign for the presidency in 2000, for example, the question of Bush's intellectual suitability for presidential office was being pursued in the USA by jokes from talk show hosts Jay Leno and David Letterman.[4] Earlier in the same year President Clinton was the butt of their (and others') jokes about his involvement with Monica Lewinsky. Was he being treated thereby as a politician, or an ordinary man with the usual sex drives, or both? At any rate, entertainment has become a more significant source of people's perceptions of politics. This development can be expressed in various ways – as a matter of politics being 'cut down to size', or of the 'de-ghettoization of politics'. But politics has undoubtedly broken out of the shells of respect, deference and distance from people's daily lives in which it had formerly been enclosed. There is now a less identifiable core of what counts in some delimited sense as 'the political'.

It follows that people's experiences of 'the political' may become more divergent as well. When there was a more identifiable core, most people would have tuned in to more or less the same personalities, ideas and problems that constituted politics in the media. But now they are more likely to follow those facets of a more sprawling and amorphous political field which they individually notice or that happen to have reached them when using the media for other purposes.

As part and parcel of the same tendency there has been an increased politicization of other domains of life – as with sex, gender and family relations. Politics is increasingly a prime definer of many other areas of social life and is consequently being viewed through a multiplicity of other lenses. Thus, virtually everything becomes in principle raw material for treatment as a public issue. Politics is more all-embracing.

Might such an expanded notion of 'the political', less tightly focused and more entertainment-laced, affect people's ability to make choices as citizens and their ability to find material in the media designed to clarify those choices? Such a question may be less pressing at election time. For when politicians campaign for support, when the media cover their campaigns, and when voters respond to them, all tend to revert to the more 'official' sense of what politics and citizenship are about, a core set of top-of-the-agenda choices and issues for determination through the established political institutions. But whether such a compartmentalization can be sustained – and how completely if at all – remains to be seen.

Thus, 'third-age' political communication could be said to pivot on a master tension between 'infinite' politics (politics is everything and is open to all modes of communication – entertaining as well as informing) and a more conventionally 'bounded' politics (that which is characteristically processed through the official institutions and departments of state).

System integration

Second, for many reasons democratic political communication systems are less closely integrated than formerly. In part, this is due to the sheer abundance of the present media system, in which there are many 'more channels, chances and incentives to tailor political communication to particular identities, conditions and tastes' (Blumler and Kavanagh, 1999: 221). Partly it is because the aggregating power of the major parties – their ability to draw into themselves and to coordinate a broad range of political demands under a few alternative umbrellas – has weakened. They are more often buffeted by a multiplicity of conflicting demands, posed from the outside – in the media and on the streets, as it were. And in great part, it is because the mutual understandings, ground rules and informal networks that once prevailed between political and journalistic elites, shaping much of their behaviour and output, are no longer so influential. In increasingly fragmented and competitive political and media markets, such understandings tend to lose their binding force (Sanders et al., 1999). There is also the fact that each side of the old 'political-media complex' (Swanson, 1992) has become less dependent on the other: journalists can turn to many other sources than politicians to keep their stories moving; and politicians have a wider choice of media outlets in which to place their messages.

In addition, a marked divergence seems to be surfacing in the new political communication system between the processes and assumptions that underlie the institutions

of territorial representative democracy and the goals and assumptions that animate the
increasingly assertive and media-aware organizations of so-called 'civil society'. Britain, for
example, is said by Alderman (1999: 140) to 'have become two nations politically' on the one
hand, that of [the] two parties which continue to monopolise power at the parliamentary and
governmental level and, on the other, that of the single issue groups and protest movements,
whose membership has long since outstripped the active grassroots support the parties can
call upon'. Beck (1992/1997) terms the latter 'arrangements from below' or 'subpolitics',
when referring to the politicizing activities of social movements, advocacy and pressure
groups which coalesce and vie with each other in attempts to influence the exercise of
political power by mobilizing communication pressures on its holders through media-
reported events, protests, statements, surveys and agitation (Eide and Knight, 1999). Their
increased visibility and clout are potentially disintegrative, because the raison d'être of such
bodies is to promote particular values, interests and demands with little regard for their
relations to other values and claims or to the availability of resources in the public purse.

This divergence has attracted polarized evaluations among commentators. Some tend to
celebrate the upsurge of subpolitics, regarding its welter of clubs, professional associations,
causes and pressure groups as a more vigorous and authentic alternative to the machinations
of politicians and the alleged failure of the state as a moral and participatory project
(McLellan, 1999). But others tend to deplore the new state of affairs, because, in contrast to
party-controlled politics, which can make 'the whole greater than the parts', interest group
politics is intrinsically single-minded and divisive, involving the 'accumulation of mere
enthusiasms with no certainty of overall coherence' (Seymour-Ure, 1999: 49).

Perhaps the divergence between these two arenas should not be exaggerated. After all,
governments and parties are still in the business of trying to build supportive coalitions of
multiple interests. But this has undoubtedly become more difficult. Governments have more
often to take decisions on contested issues in the face, simultaneously, of party-political
opposition, interest group pressures and media-framed coverage. This is a complex and
multifaceted terrain, which communication research has tended to neglect. Although the
literature is full of studies of government–media relations on the one side, and includes many
studies of how the media have portrayed various social movements and interest groups on the
other, there is a dearth of work that focuses on the interplay of all these elements. Case studies
of the interrelations among government, media and active interest groups in high-profile issue
areas are much needed.

But the question of system integration may also be considered from two other angles.
One concerns the staying power of the so-called 'political – media complex'. As Swanson
(1999: 205) points out:

> From the 1960s forward . . . political communication has been . . . explained by
> scholars essentially as the product of a well-understood dynamic between
> political actors and parties on the one hand, and mainstream news media on the
> other hand, with both soliciting the attention and consideration of the public.

Despite the recent destabilization of both these communicators, it would be premature to
close the scholarly books on them. Leading politicians still enjoy unique authority as elected

law-makers, just as top professional journalists still enjoy unique prestige arising from their regular access to such figures. And neither group will submit passively to all the new found challenges to their positions. Indeed, recent research has documented how assiduously the best-funded candidates and largest media organizations in the USA have been adapting their strategies and offerings to the new medium of the internet in order to maintain their dominance as primary players in the flow of political communication and information. Its author consequently predicts that the news organizations and government entities with the 'most influence on the mass news dissemination business' will hitch the web so successfully to their wagons that their materials 'will become the primary information sources for internet users of the future'.

Otherwise, we should not lose sight of certain interconnecting influences by which key institutions and actors are affected and constrained in even our more loosely organized political communication systems. Three important sources of such system-wide 'integration' may be identified.

One arises from the imperative for most attempts to influence political opinion to be funnelled nowadays through a 'media-constructed public sphere' (Schulz, 1997). As Castells (1997) puts it:

> It is not that the media 'controls' politics as such, rather that they have come to create and constitute the space in which politics now chiefly happens for most people in so called 'advanced' societies . . . Whether we like it or not, in order to engage in the political debate we must now do so through the media.

As noted in the section on political advocacy, however, it has become an increasingly demanding task to operate effectively in this space, one for which expert assistance is now regarded as indispensable. Neither publicity amateurs nor subject specialists can manage this on their own. Consequently, almost all would-be political advocates – not only political parties and candidates but also the leading cause and interest groups that compose 'civil society' – must *professionalize* their approaches to media publicity and hire the services of personnel skilled in such activities as planning campaigns, conducting and interpreting opinion research, adapting to the schedules and formats of diverse media outlets, and addressing the news values and working practices of journalism. Despite its increased social and political fragmentation, then, the new political communication system is as if integrated by the impact of an increasingly commanding and self-confident elite of professional communicators, whose members work for all political publicity seekers and share perspectives, strategies and insights across those diverse sponsors, not only domestically but also internationally (Plasser, 1999).

Second, it follows that in a media-constructed public sphere, certain formative characteristics of *media organization* will exert cross-system influences on a society's flow of political communications. How far the media are commercially organized or oriented to public service and their social responsibilities, for example, will tend to shape that flow, as will the intensity of the competition that prevails among the main media for audiences and revenues.

Finally, how political advocates and professional mediators fashion their communications for optimal reception by their audiences will be affected by certain system-spanning tenets of *political culture*, which may vary across different societies. For example, political cultures may differ 'in the degree to which they value the political sphere itself as a dignified and important realm of activity, communal involvement in which deserves to be promoted' (Gurevitch and Blumler, 1977: 283); 'in the degree to which they embrace or resist populism – or the principle of *vox populi, vox dei*' (Blumler and Gurevitch, 2000); and in the basic stock of historically derived 'ideas in good currency' (Schon, 1971), on which rivals in the battle for public opinion may periodically draw when striving to frame contested issues in terms which they hope will appeal to journalists and their target publics.

Democracy and the media

Third, the new political communication system is hosting many explorations of new meanings, expectations and potentials of 'democracy' and 'citizenship'. In Hannerz's (1999: 403) words:

> These days the notion of 'citizenship' is coming into prominence again; not only in a legal sense, but as a key word in debates over desirable combinations of rights, responsibilities and competences in the late 20th century, soon 21st century, world.

Three root sources have combined to fuel this process: a widespread belief that democracy as conventionally interpreted is in trouble and that shortcomings of mainstream media coverage of politics are largely to blame for its 'crisis' (Blumler and Gurevitch, 1995); the rising tide of populism in cultural, political and media quarters, which upgrades the value of heeding the views and preferences of ordinary people; and an impression that certain qualities of the new media could be enlisted behind more active forms of political participation. Often mentioned as potentially redemptive features of the new media are: the availability of large stores of information for citizens to tap without the prior intervention of media gatekeepers or other mediators; more emphasis on the substance of political conflict in contrast to conventional journalists' heavy treatment of it as a 'game'; interactivity, enabling citizens to find things out for themselves rather than passively receiving or ignoring what is given; and the creation of virtual forums, enabling exchanges between citizens and officials and discussions of current issues among citizens themselves.

The new democratic strivings have been expressed in many ways, both normatively and practically. Most influential among the normative manifestations has been Habermas's (1989) concept of the 'public sphere', depicted as a space in which people can discuss civic issues on their merits without distortion by pressures of state or market institutions. This is put forward as an ideal, in light of which existing political communication arrangements can be criticized, their reform conceived, and certain practices approximating the desired standards be welcomed. Thus, Livingstone and Lunt (1994) have discussed the conformity of talk shows and audience discussion programmes to Habermas's standards, while Larson (1999: 143) contends that the increased coverage of 'people in the street' by US network news during the 1996 Presidential campaign 'was consistent with the notion of a public sphere'. Another normative expression is the civic journalism movement in the USA, which urges news organizations to assume some responsibility for revitalizing public communication, notably by identifying voters' most pressing concerns, creating forums in which those concerns can be aired and obliging politicians to address them.

In practical terms, not only have the schedules of broadcasting organizations been peppered with discursive formats centring on ordinary people's political views and experiences (as itemized in the section on the audience above), but in many countries, the governmental process itself has been opened to new participatory efforts through public consultations over national and local issues. Pratchett (1999), for example, notes the recent development in Britain of a wide-ranging 'public participation agenda', including the creation by public bodies of citizens' panels, citizens' juries, focus groups and community planning forums. Similarly, Tambini (1999) has surveyed the emergence in Europe and the USA of 'civic networks', i.e. attempts to use new media technology, particularly the internet, to improve participation in local democratic processes. Describing this as 'a global trend', he states that 'New information systems and civic networks' are being 'opened by local authorities every week' (p. 308).

Much of this is in its infancy, and the jury is still out on the exercises concerned, some of which have in any case been conceived as trials and experiments. This is not the place to consider their detailed implementation, achievements and problems. In conclusion we would only make two points that have been somewhat neglected in recent discussions of democracy and the media.

One is to warn against unthinking adherence to tacitly anarchic notions of civic communication. Democratic deliberation and participation can be significantly advanced only through institutions and procedures that are specifically designed to realize such goals. For example, the mere creation of more space in the news for coverage of the forces of 'civil society' should not be taken as a sign that the mass media are becoming exemplars of Habermas's public sphere, especially if what is mainly reported are demonstrations, confrontations with the police, emotional outpourings and slogans, lacking placement in some broader framework of considered debate. This point is underscored by a recent study of discussion forums on the internet, in which there is apparently little real exchange of views. Instead, discrete assertions by scattered individuals tend to predominate in an atmosphere that favours 'the loudest and most aggressive' contributors. For their part, the possibility that some promoters of populist and participatory schemes in broadcasting or national and local government are going through such motions chiefly for their own instrumental ends (to attract large audiences, to appease critics or just to seem accessible) rather than to enrich democracy, cannot be excluded. Much empirical research and sifting of evidence about motives, structures, practices and outcomes are therefore needed before the prospects for deploying new communication technologies to enhance the constructive involvement of citizens in public affairs can be properly assessed.

Second, amidst all the revisionist ferment, time should also be spared to consider a new sort of normative issue posed by key features of the new political communication system. With social change proliferating advocates and issues for consideration, and with media change creating more channels for them to appear and be aired in, in such a system there may be more chances for more numerous voices to be heard, more problems to be brought to people's attention, and more chances for people to find what they want to hear, see or know about. But it may also be more difficult to put all this together 'at the centre'. The contrast could be between a public sphere of cacophony and one of coherent communication: How can the system as a whole and the individuals holding diverse roles within it sort out the cacophony when making their respective choices? And how many will be deterred by the apparent 'embarrassment of riches' and give up the effort altogether?

Buddy, can you paradigm?

The introductory theme of this essay was the relative vulnerability of paradigms prevalent in the social sciences to the vagaries of change. There, however, the full implications of such 'softness' for our particular field were left open. How should they be faced? Does turbulence in the technological and social environment in which processes of political communication are conducted today require its scholars to go back to the conceptual drawing board? Clearly there have been many changes in the phenomena of political communication and in the issues raised for research and evaluation. But has its generative ground altered so fundamentally as to demand a new paradigm of political communication analysis?

Our answer to this question is both a 'yes' and a 'no'!

On the one hand, new concepts and research approaches are needed to take account of the increased diversification that is affecting political communication at all levels.[5] Such diversification applies, for example, to: the instruments by which political communications are carried and therefore shaped (ranging from television to the internet); the main sources of political advocacy; the numerous issues such advocates place on the societal agenda and the differing perspectives on political reality they project; expansion of the range of media practitioners beyond the ranks of traditional political correspondents to include not only notionally 'non-political' genres in mainstream media but also originators of messages from outside the familiar media organizations; models of democracy (including representative and direct, 'top-down' and 'bottom-up' variants); and ways in which citizens may tap into, process and use the multiplicity of available streams of information and ideas. Consequently, all theories of political communication impact which have presumed mass exposure to relatively uniform bodies of political content – such as those of agenda-setting, the spiral of silence and the cultivation hypothesis – must be re-thought.

On the other hand, it appears from our detailed review that a 'systems' perspective on political communication processes is still valid and useful. In taking stock of what has been happening, it was clarifying to focus on a triad of actor types (advocates, mediators and audiences) situated in an environmental field; to specify possible influences on their mutual relations; and to identify overall patterns that may be resulting from their interactions. It is true that political communication systems have become more fluid and hence more difficult to comprehend at any given moment, before the kaleidoscope turns and they change again. Yet so long as we acknowledge that fluidity and are prepared to incorporate it into our analytical efforts, the approach presented here should continue to serve us well into the foreseeable future.

Notes

1 For a full discussion of the main sources of change in political communication systems, see Blumler and Gurevitch (1995: 204–6).

2 Citing a content survey of regional dailies over several recent decades, Simons (1999) notes that in the USA in recent years 'business news has been, far and away, the fastest-growing editorial segment in the nation's newspapers, if not in all media'.

3 See Rhodes (1996) for a rigorous discussion of the problems involved in representing collectivities (such as 'the public' or 'the audience') as actors.

4 According to Bruni (1999), Bush 'is the one whose failure on a televised pop quiz about lesser-known world leaders launched a thousand quips, helping to turn him into Leno's favorite target. "George Bush released his new slogan today: He'll get tough with What's-His-Name", Leno joked last month. This month, Letterman cracked, "The guy may have bonehead stamped all over him".'

5 For a full discussion of diversification, see Blumler and Kavanagh (1999: 221–3) and Mancini (1999b).

Bibliography

Alderman, K. (1999) 'Parties and Movements', *Parliamentary Affairs*, 52 (1), 128–30.

Beck, U. (1992) *Risk Society: Towards a New Modernity*. London, Newbury Park and New Delhi: Sage.

———(1997) *The Reinvention of Politics: Rethinking Modernity in the Global Social Order*. Cambridge: Polity Press.

Bennett, W. L. and Manheim J. B. (2001) 'The Big Spin: Strategic Communication and the Transformation of Pluralist Democracy', in W. L. Bennett and R. M. Entman (eds), *Mediated Politics: Communication in the Future of Democracy*. Cambridge and New York: Cambridge University Press.

Bennett, S. E., Rhine, S. L., Flickinger, R. S. and Bennett, L. M. (1999) ' "Video Malaise" Revisited: Public Trust in the Media and Government', *Harvard International Journal of Press/Politics*, 4 (4), 8–23.

Blumler, J. G. (1990) 'Elections, the Media and the Modern Publicity Process', in M. Ferguson (ed.), *Public Communication: The New Imperatives*. London, Newbury Park and New Delhi: Sage.

Blumler, J. G. and Gurevitch, M. (1981) 'Politicians and the Press: An Essay on Role Relationships', in D. D. Nimmo and K. R. Sanders (eds), *Handbook of Political Communication*. Beverly Hills and London: Sage.

———(1995) *The Crisis of Public Communication*. London and New York: Routledge.

———(2001) 'Americanization Reconsidered: UK-US Communication Comparisons Across Time', in W. L. Bennett and R. M. Entman (eds), *Mediated Politics: Communication in the Future of Democracy*. Cambridge and New York: Cambridge University Press.

Blumler, J. G. and Kavanagh, D. (1999) 'The Third Age of Political Communication: Influences and Features', *Political Communication*, 16 (3), 209–30.

Bruni, F. (1999) 'Jabs at Bush Put Focus on Question of Intellect', *New York Times on the Web*, 8 December 1999.

Castells, M. (1997) *The Power of Identity*. Oxford: Blackwell.

Crouse, T. (1972) *The Boys on the Bus*. New York: Ballantine Books.

Curtin, M. (1999) 'Feminine Desire in the Age of Satellite Television', *Journal of Communication*, 49 (2), 55–70.

Davis, R. (1999) *The Web of Politics: The Internet's Impact on the American Political System*. Oxford and New York: Oxford University Press.

Davis, R. and Owen, D. (1998) *New Media and American Politics*. Oxford and New York: Oxford University Press.

Delli Carpini, M. X. and Williams, B. A. (2001) 'Let us Infotain you: Politics in the New Media Environment', in W. L. Bennett and R. Entman (eds), *Mediated Politics: Communication in the Future of Democracy*. Cambridge and New York: Cambridge University Press.

Eide, M. and Knight, G. (1999) 'Public/Private Service: Service Journalism and the Problems of Everyday Life', *European Journal of Communication*, 14 (4), 525–47.

Ferguson, M. (1990) 'Electronic Media and the Redefining of Time and Space', in M. Ferguson (ed.), *Public Communication: The New Imperatives*. London, Newbury Park and New Delhi: Sage.

Gurevitch, M. and Blumler, J. G. (1977) 'Linkages Between the Mass Media and Politics: A Model for the Analysis of Political Communication Systems', in J. Curran, M. Gurevitch and J. Woollacott (eds), *Mass Communication and Society*. London: Edward Arnold.

Habermas, J. (1989) *The Structural Transformation of the Public Sphere: An Enquiry into a Category of Bourgeois Society*. Cambridge, MA: MIT Press.

Hall, S., Critcher, C., Jefferson, T., Clarke, J. and Roberts, B. (1978) *Policing the Crisis: Mugging, the State and Law and Order*. London, Macmillan.

Hallin, D. and Mancini, P. (2004) *Comparing Media Systems: Three Models of Media and Politics*. Cambridge and New York: Cambridge University Press.

Hannerz, U. (1999) 'Reflections on Varieties of Culturespeak', *European Journal of Cultural Studies*, 2 (3), 393–407.

Larson, S. G. (1999) 'Public Opinion in Television Election News Beyond Polls', *Political Communication*, 16 (2), 133–45.

Lee, M. (1999) 'Reporters and Bureaucrats: Public Relations Counter-Strategies by Public Administrators in an Era of Media Disinterest in Government', *Public Relations Review*, 25 (4).

Livingstone, S. and Lunt, P. (1994) *Talk on Television: Audience Participation and Public Debate*. London and New York: Routledge.

Mancini, P. (1999a) 'New Frontiers in Political Professionalism', *Political Communication*, 16 (3), 231–45.

———(1999b) 'A "Technology Theory" of Political Communication', Paper presented to a Conference on Technological Innovation and Political Communication, Perugia, December 1999.

Mayhew, L. H. (1997) *The New Public: Professional Communication and the Means of Social Influence*. Cambridge and New York: Cambridge University Press.

McLellan, D. (1999) 'Then and Now: Marx and Marxism', *Political Studies*, 47 (5), 955–66.

McLeod, D. M. (1995) 'Communicating Deviance: The Effects of Television News Coverage of Social Protest', *Journal of Broadcasting and Electronic Media*, 39 (1), 4–19.

Negrine, R. (1999) 'Parliaments and the Media: A Changing Relationship?', *European Journal of Communication*, 14 (3), 325–52.

Organization for Economic Cooperation and Development, (1996) *Ministerial Symposium on the Future of Public Services*. Paris: OECD.

Plasser, F. (1999) *Tracing the Worldwide Proliferation of American Campaign Techniques*. Vienna: Center for Applied Political Research.

Pope, K. (1999) 'Network and Cable TV', *Media Studies Journal*, 13 (2), 52–7.

Pratchett, L. (1999) 'New Fashions in Public Participation: Towards Greater Democracy?', *Parliamentary Affairs*, 52 (4), 616–33.

Rhodes, R. A. W. (1996) 'The New Governance: Governing without Government', *Political Studies*, 44 (4), 652–67.

Sanders, K., Bale, T. and Canel, M. J. (1999) 'Managing Sleaze: Prime Ministers and News Management in Conservative Great Britain and Socialist Spain', *European Journal of Communication*, 14 (4), 461–86.

Schlesinger, P. (1990) 'Rethinking the Sociology of Journalism: Source Strategies and the Limits of Media-Centrism', in M. Ferguson (ed.), *Public Communication: The New Imperatives*. London, Newbury Park and New Delhi: Sage.

Schon, D. (1971) *Beyond the Stable State*. London: Temple Smith.

Schulz, W. (1997) 'Changes of the Mass Media and the Public Sphere', *Javnost – the Public*, 4 (2), 57–71.

Seymour-Ure, C. (1999) 'Are the Broadsheets Becoming Unhinged?', in J. Seaton (ed.), *Politics and the Media: Harlots and Prerogatives at the Turn of the Millennium*. Oxford: Blackwell.

Simons, L. M. (1999) 'Follow the Money', *American Journalism Review*, 21 (10), 55–68.

Swanson, D. L. (1992) 'The Political-Media Complex', *Communication Monographs*, 59, 397–400.

——(1999) 'About This Issue' (Introduction to a Symposium on A Third Age of Political Communication), *Political Communication*, 16 (3), 203–7.

Tambini, D. (1999) 'New Media and Democracy: The Civic Networking Movement', *New Media and Society*, 1 (3), 305–29.

Tedesco, J. C. (2004), 'Changing the Channel: Use of the Internet for Communication about Politics', in L. L. Kaid (ed.), *Handbook of Political Communication Research*, Mahwah, NJ: Lawrence Erlbaum Associates.

Underwood, D. (2001) 'Reporting and the Push for Market-Oriented Journalism', in W. L. Bennett and R. M. Entman (eds), *Mediated Politics: Communication and the Future of Democracy*. Cambridge and New York, Cambridge University Press.

chapter seven

Mediations of Democracy

JAMES CURRAN

Introduction

Many of the received ideas about the democratic role of the media derive from a frockcoated world where the 'media' consisted principally of small-circulation, political publications and the state was still dominated by a landed elite. The result is a legacy of old saws, which bear very little relationship to contemporary reality. They need to be reassessed.[1]

Discussion of the media's democratic role is intimately bound up with a debate about the media's organization and regulation. Indeed, the classic liberal theory of a free press on which we still rely was refined and elaborated in the nineteenth century as part of a political campaign for press deregulation (Curran, 1978). Rethinking classic liberal theory necessarily implies a reappraisal of media policy.[2]

In short, the literature on media and democracy is in need of a removal van to carry away lumber accumulated over two centuries. What should be discarded, what should be kept and how the intellectual furniture should be rearranged is something that needs to be thought about in a new way.

Free market watchdog

The principal democratic role of the media, according to traditional liberal theory, is to act as a check on the state. The media should monitor the full range of state activity, and fearlessly expose abuses of official authority.

This watchdog role is said in traditional liberal theory to override in importance all other functions of the media. It dictates the form in which the media system should be organized. Only by anchoring the media to the free market, in this view, is it possible to ensure the media's complete independence from government. Once the media become subject to state regulation, they may lose their bite as watchdogs. Worse still, they may become transformed into snarling Rottweilers in the service of the state.

This orthodox view is especially well entrenched in the USA. For instance, Kelley and Donway, two American political scientists of conservative sympathies, argue that any reform of the media, however desirable, is unacceptable if it is 'at the cost of the watchdog function. And this is the inevitable cost. A press that is licensed, franchised or regulated is subject to political pressures when it deals with issues affecting the interests of those in power' (Kelley and Donway, 1990: 97). This reservation is restated by the communitarian political theorist, Stephen Holmes as a rhetorical question: 'Doesn't every regulation converting the media into a "neutral forum" lessen its capacity to act as a partisan gadfly, investigating and criticising government in an aggressive way?' (Holmes, 1990: 31). Even many American analysts with strong reformist views share the same fear. 'I cannot envision any kind of content regulation, however indirect,' writes the media critic Carl Stepp, 'that wouldn't project government into the position of favouring or disfavouring some views and information over others. Even so-called structural steps aimed at opening channels for freer expression would post government in the intolerable role of super-gatekeeper' (Stepp, 1990: 194).

This free market argument was deployed with great effect in the USA to justify broadcast deregulation. Television channels were 'freed' from the fairness doctrine which required them to present alternative views on controversial issues of importance (Baker, 1998). Rules restricting media concentration were also relaxed (McChesney, 2004).

A parallel campaign was mounted in Britain. As the media magnate, Rupert Murdoch, succinctly put it, 'public service broadcasters in this country [Britain] have paid a price for their state-sponsored privileges. That price has been their freedom' (Murdoch, 1989: 9). Although this rhetoric encountered more opposition in Britain than in the USA, it influenced the government of the day. Regulation of commercial broadcasting content was reduced, and anti-monopoly restraints were eased during the 1990s and early 2000s (Curran and Seaton, 2003; Goodwin, 1998).

The liberal watchdog argument proved effective in the campaign to 'liberalize' broadcasting because it was based on a premise that was widely accepted. Regulation of the press, other than through the 'ordinary' law of the land, had been successfully opposed in both the USA and Britain on the grounds that it would stifle free expression, and curtail critical scrutiny of power. Thus, the American Supreme Court struck down in 1974 a press right of reply law in Florida on the grounds that it would 'chill' critical debate (Barron, 1975). Similarly, the last Royal Commission on the Press in Britain opposed in 1977 any form of selective newspaper subsidy because 'it would involve in an obvious way the dangers of government interference in the press' (Royal Commission on the Press, 1977: 126).

Market liberals had only accepted extensive regulation of broadcasting on the grounds that the limited number of airwave frequencies made it a 'natural monopoly' (Royal Commission on the Press, 1977: 9; cf. Horwitz, 1991). When the number of television channels multiplied with the introduction of advanced cable and satellite, this 'special case' argument was undermined. What was right in principle for the press was now applicable, it was argued, to broadcasting. Television should be set free.

Attention has focused for the sake of brevity on Britain and the USA. However, a very similar sequence of argument and pressure occurred in many other countries. The same freedom rhetoric was invoked; the same opportunities beckoned with the development of new television channels; and a shift towards broadcasting deregulation followed (Aldridge and Hewitt, 1994; Avery, 1993; Catalbas, 2000; Curran and Park, 2000; Herman and McChesney, 1997; Humphreys, 1996; Page and Crawley, 2001; Papathanassopoulos, 2002; Raboy, 1996; Tracey, 1998, among others).

Limits of the 'watchdog' perspective

The traditional public watchdog role of the media is thus invoked to legitimize the case for broadcasting reform, and strengthen the defence of a free market press. At first glance, this approach would seem to have much to commend it. After all, critical surveillance of the state is an important aspect of the democratic functioning of the media, as is demonstrated for example by Caco Barcello's revelations of the cold-blooded murder of black and mestizo suspects in the 1990s by Sao Paulo's military police (Waisbord, 2000a: 34–5) or, in 2003, by the American television network CBS's disclosure of the abuse of prisoners in the Abu Ghraib detention centre in Iraq.

However, this argument is not as clear-cut as it seems. While the watchdog role of the media is enormously important, it is perhaps quixotic to argue that it is so paramount that it should dictate media policy. After all, even many so-called 'news media' allocate only a small part of their content to public affairs[3] – and a tiny amount to disclosure of official wrongdoing. In effect, the liberal orthodoxy defines the main democratic purpose and organizational principle of the media in terms of what they do *not* do most of the time.

The watchdog argument also appears timeworn in another way. Traditionally, liberal theory holds that government is the sole object of press scrutiny. This stems from the traditional idea that government is the 'seat' of power. However, this fails to take account of shareholder and other forms of authority. A revised conception is needed in which the media are conceived as being a check on the abuse of all sources of power in both the public and private realms.

This modification diminishes the case for 'market freedom' since it can no longer be equated with independence from corporate power. A significant section of the world's media has been taken over by major industrial and commercial concerns such as the General Electric, Toshiba, Fiat, Bouyges and Santo Domingo groups, in a development that extends from the USA and Japan to Hungary and Colombia (Curran and Park, 2000; Herman and McChesney, 1997; Kelly *et al.*, 2004; McChesney, 2004; Tunstall and Machin, 1990). A number of media organizations have also grown into huge leisure conglomerates with major investments straddling a number of interests such as television, film, music, newspapers, books and net enterprises. Concern should no longer be confined to the media's links to big business: the media *are* big business.

The conglomeration of news media mostly took place during the last three decades. It gave rise sometimes to no-go areas where journalists were reluctant to tread for fear of stepping on the corporate toes of a parent or sister company (Bagdikian, 1997; Curran and Seaton, 2003; Hollingsworth, 1986). It is also claimed plausibly that the media are in general less vigilant in relation to corporate than public bureaucracy abuse because they are part of the corporate business sector (McChesney, 1997).

Market corruption

The classic liberal response to these criticisms is that the state should be the main target of media scrutiny because the state has a monopoly of legitimated violence, and is therefore the institution to be feared most. For this reason, it is especially important to establish a critical distance between the media and the governmental system through private, media ownership.

This seemingly persuasive argument ignores the way in which the world has changed since the early eighteenth century when 'Cato' (1983 [1720]) set out with such powerful eloquence the press watchdog thesis. A magnetic field of mutual advantage has developed within the media–political realm. Governments need the media because they have to woo a mass electorate. At the same time, governments' sphere of activity has expanded enormously, so that a wide range of official policies potentially affect the profitability of media organizations. For their part, the media have become more market-driven and expansionist, and are therefore more concerned that governments adopt market-friendly policies.

These cumulative changes have given rise to a relationship that, while sometimes adversarial, is also prone to corruption. This is highlighted by Chadwick's (1989) pioneering research which shows that a number of media entrepreneurs formed a tactical alliance with the Labour government in Australia in the late 1980s as a way of securing official permission to consolidate control over Australia's commercial television and press. This resulted in an unprecedented number of editorial endorsements for the Labour Party in the 1987 election as well as opportunistic fence-sitting by some traditionally anti-Labour papers. Similarly, Rupert Murdoch removed the critically independent BBC World News service from his Asian Star satellite system in 1994, and vetoed HarperCollin's publication of ex-Hong Kong governor Chris Patten's memoirs in 1998, because he wanted to curry favour with the Chinese government in order to obtain permission to expand his operations in China. In much the same way the Argentine media tycoon, Eduardo Eurnekian, axed a critical television report on the building of an expensive airstrip on President Menem's private property. At the time Eurnekian was bidding for (and duly obtained) a major stake in Argentina's privatized airports (Waisbord, 2000b).

Indeed, the potential for media corruption was enormously increased by the deregulatory policies that were pursued during the last two decades. How broadcasting franchises were allocated, under what conditions, and whether limits on media consolidation were relaxed, affected the financial prospects of leading media corporations. This created an environment that encouraged the development of non-aggression pacts, typified by the tacit alliance that was cemented in 1996 between New Labour leader, Tony Blair, and Rupert Murdoch, the head of the largest private media corporation in Britain. Tabloid hounds pursuing Labour were called to heel in response to very strong signals that a New Labour government would enable Murdoch's monopolist empire to expand (Curran and Seaton, 2003).

In other words, the market can give rise not to independent watchdogs serving the public interest but to corporate mercenaries which adjust their critical scrutiny to suit their private purpose.

Market suppression

Still more serious is the way in which the market can silence media watchdogs altogether. Many privately owned media organizations supported right-wing military coups in Latin American countries (Fox, 1988; Waisbord, 2000b). This collusion was typified by

El Mercurio, which backed the military coup in Chile, loyally supported the Pinochet dictatorship and largely overlooked its violation of human rights. Similarly, the Globo television network gave unconditional support to the military regime in Brazil, while most of Argentina's privately owned media failed to investigate state-sponsored 'disappearances' during the period of military rule. Less dramatically, private media in Taiwan 'not only accepted authoritarian rule', according to Lee (2000: 125), 'but also helped to rationalize it' during the period before 1987. In each case, these collaborations with authoritarian states arose because media controllers were allies of those in government: indeed, private media were an integral part of the system of power.

Even in societies where market-based media have a more independent and critical relationship to government, appearances can be deceptive. Media attacks on official wrongdoing can follow private agendas. 'Fearless' feats of investigative journalism, in these circumstances, are not necessarily the disinterested acts undertaken on behalf of the public that they appear to be. For example, a seven-person team from Northwestern University examined six investigative stories exposing official fraud, failure or injustice that appeared in the American media in the period 1981–1988 (Protess *et al.,* 1991). All these stories, it turned out, were initiated and sourced by well-positioned power holders. In most cases, media tip-offs were part of a conscious agenda-building strategy by 'policy elites' who were preparing the ground for a policy change or were engaged in boosting their personal reputations. Media disclosure can be best understood, according to this debunking account, as an aspect of elite management in which the public were regularly sidelined.[4]

Even press disclosure of the Watergate scandal (exposing high-level Republican involvement in the 1972 break-in into the Democrat headquarters and President Nixon's subsequent cover-up, leading to his forced resignation) is not immune from this demythologizing approach. It has gone down in legend as an example of intrepid journalists doggedly tracking down the truth, and changing the course of history. In fact, most of the press's independent investigation took the form of receiving pre-culled information from state officials. Furthermore 'the moving force', according to Gladys and Kurt Lang (1983: 301), 'behind the effort to get to the bottom of Watergate came neither from the media nor public opinion but from political insiders' who maintained pressure for the story to be pursued, and to be recognized as important. This elite guidance, the Langs suggest, was a mixed blessing. It resulted in Watergate being defined narrowly by the news media as a legal-juridical issue, which limited unduly the reform of the political system that followed after Nixon's resignation.

What all these examples point to is the inadequacy of the neo-liberal model that explains the media solely in terms of market theory. The media are assumed to be independent, and to owe allegiance only to the public, if they are funded by the consumer and organized through a competitive market. This theory ignores the many other influences which can shape the media, including the political commitments and private interests of media shareholders, the influence exerted through news management and the cultural power of leading groups in society. In short, this extremely simplistic theory fails to take into account the wider relations of power in which the media are situated. This is a key point to which we shall return when we consider other aspects of the media's democratic role.

State control

If private media are subject to compromising constraint, so too of course are public media. There is no lack of examples where public broadcasters have acted as little more than mouthpieces of government (Curran and Park, 2000; Downing, 1996; Sparks, 1998; Waisbord, 2000a). These cautionary experiences reveal the variety of levers that governments can pull to get the broadcasting they want. Public broadcasters have been subject to direct censorship through restrictive laws and regulations; licences to broadcast have been allocated to government supporters; broadcasters have been encouraged to censor themselves in response to a variety of pressures (public criticism, private intimacy, information management, financial pressure, the threat of privatization or the loss of a television franchise); and journalists who cannot be intimidated have been summarily sacked, jailed or even killed.

However, a qualifying note needs to be introduced at this point. The media literature is bedevilled by a system logic that assumes state-linked media serve the state, and business-controlled media slavishly support corporate interests. This ignores or downplays countervailing influences. Privately owned media need to maintain audience interest in order to be profitable; they have to sustain public legitimacy in order to avoid societal retribution; and they can be influenced by the professional concerns of their staff. All these factors potentially work against the total subordination of private media to the political commitments and economic interests of their shareholders. Likewise, the long-term interest of public broadcasters is best served by developing a reputation for independence that wins public trust, and sustains political support beyond the duration of the current administration. In many liberal democracies the ideal of broadcasting independence is not only pursued by broadcasting staff for professional reasons, but is supported also by the political elite partly out of self-interest. Senior politicians of all major parties know they will need access to broadcasting when they are voted out of office.

The autonomy of publicly regulated broadcasting is also supported by a system of checks and balances. While this varies from country to country, it usually includes in western Europe a number of the following features: a constitutional guarantee of freedom of expression; formal rules requiring broadcasting impartiality, enshrined in law; civic society or all-party representation on broadcasting authorities; funding by licence fee rather than direct government grant; competition between broadcasters for audiences; diversity of broadcasting organizational structures; and the devolution of authority within them (Humphreys, 1996; Kelly *et al.*, 2004; Raboy, 1996). The ultimate safeguard of broadcasting independence is that generally it has the support of the public.

This can result in a pattern of reporting that confounds dogma. For example, the privately owned, deregulated American television system provided more uncritical reporting of the 2003 Iraq War, was more uncritical of official coalition government positions, and gave less space to dissent, than did the state-linked or owned television system in Britain (Seib, 2004; Tumber and Palmer, 2004). What happened was thus the very opposite to what we are encouraged to expect.

Two further examples illustrate this qualification, firstly in relation to shareholder control. In April 1984 the chief executive of Lonrho, Tiny Rowland, intervened to protect the corporation's profitable investments in Zimbabwe. One of Lonrho's many newspapers, the

London-based *Observer*, was about to report that the Zimbabwe army had massacred civilians in the country's dissident Matabele province. Lonrho's relations with the Zimbabwe government were already strained since Lonrho had backed the losing party in the recent election. The corporation had also been widely attacked in Zimbabwe as a relic of colonial power. Anxious to avoid further trouble, Rowland told his editor, Donald Trelford, not to run the story. Trelford refused and was backed by the paper's staff and independent directors. The dispute at the paper was leaked, and Rowland was widely criticized. He hastily backed down to avoid further public censure (Curran and Seaton, 2003).

The second example illustrates journalistic resistance to state control. In 1988, Thames Television, part of the British publicly regulated ITV network, made a programme, *Death on the Rock*, which reported in effect that a British army Special Air Service (SAS) unit had unlawfully killed unarmed members of an Irish Republican Army (IRA) active-service unit in Gibraltar. The programme also claimed that the official version of this event was misleading. The Foreign Secretary, Sir Geoffrey Howe, asked the commercial television regulatory authority, the Independent Broadcasting Authority (IBA), to veto the programme on the technical grounds that it would prejudice the official inquest that was due to take place. The IBA refused and the programme was transmitted on 28 April 1988.

This was not the end of the saga. The government made known its anger at the decision. Its displeasure was echoed by much of the press, which lambasted the programme as bad and irresponsible journalism. 'TV slur on SAS' was the *Daily Star*'s headline (29 April 1988). 'Fury over SAS "trial by TV" ', reported the *Daily Mail* (29 April), which also published a television review calling the programme 'a woefully one-sided look at the killings'. The *Sunday Times* ran several articles that impugned the reliability of the programme's main witness, and cast doubt on the programme's claims.

This public flak failed to intimidate. Thames Television ordered an internal enquiry which hailed the programme as 'trenchant' and its makers as 'painstaking and persistent' (Windlesham and Rampton, 1989: 143). The programme was given subsequently the top annual (BAFTA) award of the television industry in a symbolic act which deliberately snubbed both the government and the Conservative press. Thames Television then rubbed salt in political wounds by repeating the programme in May 1991, as an example of outstanding journalism.

But if these two examples illustrate professional aspirations for independence in both the public and private sectors, it should be remembered that these aspirations are not equally supported. The political culture of liberal democracies is very alert to the threat posed by governments to the freedom of public media, but is much less concerned about the threat posed by shareholders to the freedom of private media. Government ministers are attacked if they seek to dictate the content of public television broadcasts, yet proprietors are not exposed to equivalent criticism if they seek to determine the editorial line of their media properties. Elaborate checks and balances have been established in old liberal democracies to shield public media from the state. Yet, equivalent checks have not yet been developed to shield private media from corporate abuse.[5]

In sum, an unthinking, catechistic subscription to the free market is not the best way to secure fearless media watchdogs that serve democracy. Instead, practical steps should be taken to shield the media from the corruptions generated by *both* the political and economic systems.

Settling of accounts

Since the discussion so far has followed a number of twists and turns, it may be helpful to reiterate here our central claim. The conception of the media as a democratic watchdog is important but it does not legitimize, as neo-liberals claim, a free market system. This is for a number of reasons. Market pressures can lead to the downgrading of investigative journalism in favour of entertainment, while corporate ties can subdue critical surveillance of corporate power. More importantly, controllers of market-based media are not necessarily independent. They can muzzle media surveillance of government because they are government supporters or because they want to secure a regulatory favour. The market, in short, does not guarantee critical scrutiny of either public or private power.

Pressures can also be brought to bear to silence media watchdogs with links to the state. However, elaborate defences have been developed in some countries to prevent ministers from intimidating public broadcasters in contrast to the much weaker protections that have been constructed against shareholder abuse.

Information and debate

The watchdog perspective of the media is defensive. It is about protecting the public by preventing those with power from overstepping the mark. However, the media can also be viewed in a more expansive way, in liberal theory, as an agency of information and debate that facilitates the functioning of democracy.

In this view, free media brief the electorate, and assist voters to make an informed choice at election time; they provide a channel of communication between government and governed; and they provide a forum of debate in which people can identify problems, propose solutions and reach a consensus.

All this can be best achieved, it is maintained, through the free market. The freedom of the market supposedly allows anyone to publish an opinion, thus ensuring that all significant points of view are aired. It also means that people are exposed through market competition to contrary views and sources of information, and this makes for good judgement and wise government. As American jurist, Oliver Holmes, declared in a much-quoted statement, 'the best test of truth is the power of the thought to get itself accepted in the competition of the market . . .' (cited in Barron, 1975: 320).

As with the watchdog perspective, there is much to commend this approach. It assumes that democracies need informed and participant citizens to manage their common affairs. It also believes that public debate is more likely to produce rational and just outcomes if it takes account of different views and interests. At the heart of this approach – what is called in the USA the republican tradition – is an admirable stress on the need for civic information, public participation, robust debate and active self-determination.

There is, however, one flaw at its centre: its wide-eyed belief in the free market. Its espousal of neo-liberalism undermines what it sets out to achieve in four different ways.

First, the high costs of market entry curtail the freedom to publish. When liberal press theory was first framed, it really was the case that groups of ordinary people could set up their trestle-table, so to speak, in the main market place of ideas because it was relatively cheap to publish. Great national newspapers were launched in 1830s Britain with minimal outlays (Curran, 1002), More or less £20 million is needed to establish a new national broadsheet, and more than this to establish a new popular cable television channel in Britain.[6] While there are still some media sectors where costs are low, these tend to be marginalized or have low audiences. A lone website is virtually free but it does not have the same communicative power as a mass television channel or newspaper.

Second, the free market undermines the provision of information (Hamilton, 2004). The dynamics of this process are explored by Curran *et al.* (1980) in relation to the British press. Pioneer market research undertaken for publishers over a 40-year period showed that human-interest stories consistently obtained the highest readership scores because they appealed to all categories of reader, whereas public affairs had a minority following concentrated among certain social groups. Competitive market pressure to maximize sales resulted in public affairs coverage giving way to more universally popular human-interest content. Indeed, by the late 1970s, public affairs accounted for less than 20 per cent of the editorial content of the national popular press. A comparable process is now developing in mass television. In Britain, for example, the 10 o'clock *News* on the main commercial channel, ITV1, was shifted in 1999 to 11 p.m. to make way for entertainment. Pressure from the regulator (Independent Television Commission) led to the return of the *News* at 10 p.m. on some days in 2000, and then a compromise 10.30 p.m. slot. The weakening of the regulator resulted, however, in the halving of international coverage in ITV's current affairs programmes between 1988 and 1998 (Barnett and Seymour, 1999: 16).

Third, the free market generates information-rich media for elites, sustained by advertising, and information-poor media for the general public. The result, in many countries, is a polarization between prestige and mass newspapers. Something rather similar is now developing in the public space being constructed around the emergent Euro-polity. High-information newspapers, magazines and television channels serve a Euro-elite but not the general public (Schlesinger, 1999).

Fourth, the market undermines intelligent and rational debate. Market-oriented media tend to generate information that is simplified, personalized, decontextualized, with an emphasis on action rather than process, visualization rather than abstraction, stereotypicality rather than human complexity (Gitlin, 1990; Hallin, 1994; Inglis, 1990; Iyengar, 1991; Liebes, 1998). Thus, there was a spectacular increase in the reporting of crime in local American television news during the 1990s, partly because it was cheap, dramatic and popular. This resulted in a rising proportion of people thinking that crime was the most important problem facing the USA, even when crime rates were actually falling (Patterson, 2003). Local TV news also tended to focus on decontextualized acts of crime by black perpetrators on white victims in ways that strengthened racial stereotypes and animosity towards African Americans (Iyengar, 2000).

Ironically, successful public service broadcasting systems come closest to embodying the liberal ideal of informed, rational and inclusive public debate. They give priority to public affairs programmes, reasoned discussion and (in some systems) pluralistic representation. This is because they put the needs of democracy before those of profit, and are supported in this objective by a legal and regulatory framework. However, this approach implies an intellectual adjustment. It means abandoning seventeenth-century fears of the leviathan state (when absolutist military authority was viewed with good reason as an ever-present threat) and recognising that the democratic state, elected by the people, can extend the sphere of information and public debate in the interests of sustaining a healthy democracy.

Voice of the people

Representing people to authority is, in liberal theory, the third key democratic function of the media. In one version this is the culmination of the media's mission. After having briefed the people and staged a debate, the media relay the public consensus that results from this debate to government. In this way the government is exposed to the popular will between elections, and is subject to public supervision when it makes new laws. As Thomas Carlyle (1907: 164) famously proclaimed, the press is 'a power, a branch of government with an inalienable weight in law-making'.

The introduction of opinion polls took some of the wind out of this 'fourth estate' argument. More often now the claim is made simply that the media speak for the people, and represent their views and interests, in the public domain. The assumption is that 'the broad shape and nature of the press is ultimately determined by no one but its readers' (Whale, 1977: 85) because the press must respond in a competitive marketplace to what people want, and express their views and interests. As a consequence the privately owned press – and, by extension, the privately owned broadcasting system – speak up for the people.

This argument is advanced so frequently that it is necessary to explain in some detail why it is fundamentally flawed.

Market failures

The influence of the consumer is reactive rather than proactive. It is exerted through choosing between what is available in the marketplace. The extent of real market choice is consequently central to how much influence the consumer has. If choice is curtailed, then consumer power is correspondingly diminished.

Up until the early 1980s, consumer choice was strongly constrained by media oligopoly in the press, television and most other sectors. This cosy world was shattered by the rise of satellite, cable, video, the internet and digitization. These innovations expanded the range of media products, established new niche markets and extended competition. For a time it seemed as if oligopolistic market control would be ended, and the public would be greatly empowered.

The response of leading media producers to this threat was a well-judged combination of political lobbying and market adaptation. They secured in many countries a relaxation of restrictions on media concentration by arguing initially that the increase in the number of media outlets diminished the need for regulation, and subsequently that concentration was necessary in order to compete effectively in the global market and invest in generating greater consumer choice. Liberalization opened the door for even larger multimedia giants to emerge, seeking to achieve economies of scope facilitated by the flexibility of digital technology. The form that this consolidation took varied in different countries. For instance, in the USA, a number of film and television companies merged to establish an axis around which other media interests were grouped, whereas in Germany the main axis of consolidation was press and television. However, it is by no means clear that the enlargement of media businesses led to a substantial increase of market concentration in the media industries as whole, whether in the USA or in Europe, because total media output rose rapidly after 1980 (Compaine and Gomery, 2000; Hesmondhalgh, 2002). In some sectors (most notably the newspaper press and book publishing) the trend was towards increased concentration, while in others (most notably television) the trend was in the opposite direction. Overall, the major conglomerates mostly rode out the storm and maintained their leading position despite the threat posed by new competition. Thus, the established press and television news media in both Britain and the USA succeeded in dominating the most visited news websites (Curran and Seaton, 2003; McChesney, 1999).

If one defensive response to market fragmentation was corporate concentration, another was attempted global conquest. The introduction of new ways of delivering television programmes provided an opportunity to break into formerly protected national markets, while privatization policies led to the sale of state media assets. However, this global expansionist strategy ran into mounting resistance. New centres of media production, from Taiwan to Brazil, developed to challenge the might of the transnational 'majors', mostly with headquarters in the USA (Sinclair *et al.*, 1996). In many countries, television audiences showed a strong preference for their national product. The adaptive response of transnational media corporations to these setbacks was, increasingly, to 'think global but act local'. They formed alliances with leading national media corporations, in this way strengthening the forces of national oligopoly. They brought to these alliances formidable weapons: additional financial resources, cross-media promotion, popular production formulae, accumulations of stock and often a global distribution network.

The first key factor limiting consumer power is, thus, the maintenance of corporate oligopoly. The second factor, already referred to, is high market entry costs. This is interpreted in traditional liberal analysis in a restricted way as tending to exclude insights that might enhance public enlightenment. This overlooks its key significance as an invisible form of censorship which excludes social groups with limited financial resources from competing. The result is a market system which is not genuinely open to all, but which is controlled by corporate wealth. While some media controllers have proved to be consumer-led pragmatists, others have exerted significant influence to advance right-wing or strongly pro-market views.

These latter are subject to a number of constraints, a point illustrated by the remarkable career of Rupert Murdoch. He has always been willing to rein in his ideological commitments in order to gain regulatory favours from politicians, to conform to state-imposed impartiality rules, or even to woo audiences with subversive material (such as the television series, *The Simpsons*), if the situation required it. But informing his last 30 years, and indeed giving to it a certain principled continuity, has been a steadfast determination to promote, *wherever possible*, right-wing values (Chenoweth, 2001; Leapman, 1983; Munster, 1985; Shawcross, 1993). As one of his former editors, Andrew Neil, records: 'Rupert expects his papers to stand broadly for what he believes: a combination of right-wing republicanism from America mixed with undiluted Thatcherism from Britain . . .' (Neil, 1996: 164), a view echoed by other senior Murdoch employees (Evans, 1983; Giles, 1986). This resulted in his entire global newspaper empire, and some of his television interests such as Fox News, supporting the 2003 Iraq War. What has assisted Murdoch, and fellow ideologues, is that the link between media and public opinion that used to exist has been weakened because the media have become more entertainment-centred. This has increased the relative freedom of media controllers to pursue their private agendas provided that they do not bore or upset their audiences.

The third limitation on consumer influence derives from the operation of the market. High sales or ratings produce not only large receipts but also major economies of scale (and consequently lower unit costs). This generates strong pressure, in mass markets, for media producers to converge towards the conventional and mainstream. This has been offset by the expansion of niche provision for specialized markets during the last two decades. However, this has tended to be geared more towards the affluent than low-income groups because the former have more money to spend. This distortion is further accentuated by advertising funding, which tends to exert a gravitational pull towards upscale, profitable audiences (Baker, 1994; Curran, 1986; D'Acci, 1994). Market democracy is a universe where individuals do not have equal votes.

The claim that market expansion has led to more consumer choice thus needs to be viewed critically. More media outlets do not necessarily mean 'more of the same', as some left-wing critics maintain. But what it does mean is that the expansion of choice is always *pre-structured* by the conditions of competition. In a contemporary context, this means provision for unequal consumers in oligopolistic markets where entry is generally restricted by high costs.

Comparative perspective

If privately owned media are not automatically the voice of the people, whom then do they represent? The answer to this question depends partly upon the configuration of power to which the media are linked.

In authoritarian corporatist societies, political power tends to be monopolized by the ruling party, and maintained through a clientelist system of patronage that binds together different social groups within the structure of the party and the state. The 'will of the people' represented by the media tends to be defined by the ruling party. This broadly corresponds to the situation in contemporary Malaysia (Nain, 2000) and the one that prevailed until recently in Korea (Park *et al.*, 2000), Taiwan (Lee, 2000) and Mexico (Hallin, 2000). In these societies the news media can be influenced politically more by the interaction of factions within the dominant party than by consumers. According to Hallin, the liberalizing changes that occurred in late 1980s Mexican television, for example, were due to pressure not so much from the general public as from a determined reformist faction within the ruling party which pushed the old guard controlling commercial television 'kicking and screaming' into a more pluralistic mould (Hallin, 2000: 103).

In liberal corporatist societies, a consensus is formed through consultation between government and organized interests. The system is 'liberal' in the sense that political parties tend to affiliate; the armed forces are firmly under the control of civic authority and freedoms are not undermined by coercive measures. But within this system the consensus of society tends to be defined by the major players; to prevail whichever party is in power; and to be echoed by the media. Essentially, this defines the system of power that operates in most northern European countries, although as Dahlgren (2000) notes in an acute analysis of Sweden, the balance of advantage within the corporatist system is shifting in favour of economic power.

In still other societies, power is organized in a more fluid and less stable way. To take a maverick example, in immediate post-Communist Russia an oligarchy established a leading position in the economy, a stranglehold over national media and a strong presence within the state (McNair, 2000). This power group directed the main commercial television channels, under its control, to join public broadcasting in providing partisan support for its chosen candidate, Boris Yeltsin, and helped to secure his re-election despite his obvious shortcomings. However, the oligarchy was challenged by Yeltsin's successor, President Putin, and despite being reconstituted no longer holds the sway that it once did.

Thus, one key variable influencing media representations is the way in which power is organized within the political system. Another significant influence is the degree to which the prevailing power network coheres. If disagreements develop within it, these are generally reproduced in the media. In such situations the media can operate in a way that seems to exemplify liberal theory. Tip-offs from rival, elite groups can trigger investigative journalism; their conflicts can generate media debate; and the consensus arising from this debate can be relayed to government. But in these situations the initiative for change usually comes from within the structure of power rather than from the people.

However, another important contextual influence is the extent to which control is maintained over public debate. An energized civil society, well-developed alternative networks of ideas and news sources, idealistic media staff and radical consumer pressure can combine to detach part of the media from the prevailing system of power.

This is a necessarily condensed alternative view to that of private media as tribunes of the public. What it stresses is the need to take account of the full range of influences shaping journalism, in social contexts that are different and cannot be reduced to a single, liberal market interpretation of the media as the voice of the consumer.

Media, politics and entertainment

The growth of media entertainment raises issues that are less straightforward than they are often presented to be.[7] On the one hand, democracies need extensive and intelligent media coverage of public affairs. This is for a number of reasons, two of which need to be emphasized in particular. Citizens in democracies have responsibilities that go with the rights of popular sovereignty: for example, a citizenry ought to consider in an informed way whether the killing of foreign citizens in its name is necessary or should be opposed. Secondly, a certain level of political awareness, public debate and participation has to be sustained if elite domination and manipulation is to be avoided. As Alexander Meikeljohn (1983: 276) succinctly puts it, 'self-government is a nonsense unless the "self" which governs is able and determined to make its will effective'.

On the other hand, self-government does not only take the form of law-making and public administration. Self rule, in any meaningful sense of the word, is also based on collective regulation through public norms. These are the tacit rules, conventions and expectations that guide our behaviour in everyday life. These norms influence how we fulfil a social role (such as that of parent), understand a sense of obligation (for example as a child of ageing parents), and relate to others in myriad social situations (for example, by behaving differently in someone else's house than in our own). These norms are, in a broad sense, collectively arrived at, maintained and enforced. They are acquired through early socialization, internalized and sustained through social interaction. But they can also be weakened, strengthened or change over time in response to collective processes. Public norms – like laws – are one of the ways in which society governs itself.

Media entertainment plays an important role in the maintenance and revision of public norms. Thus, one genre of human interest stories affirm public norms through the ritual degradation of transgressors. This is typified by a two-page spread in the *Daily Mail* (Britain's second biggest selling daily) reporting a woman who went on holiday with her lover, and left her children uncared for, under the headline 'Is This Britain's Most Selfish Mother?' (*Daily Mail*, 8 March, 2003). This style of tabloid journalism has a counterpart in film and television melodrama in which the transgressor is symbolically punished by coming to an unhappy end.

However, another genre of entertainment opens up social norms for public debate. Television talk shows often enable those under attack to answer back, and for studio audiences to participate, thus enabling the validity and application of public norms to be openly discussed. Some television fiction takes the form of open texts in which contrasting norms are juxtaposed, and the tension between them is left unresolved. For example, an episode of the successful TV series *Sex and the City* features a woman who elects to surrender her successful career as the manager of an art gallery to become a full-time mother.[8] Views for and against this decision are presented in dramatic dialogue between friends, and in a comment from a job interviewee. But what was the right thing to do was left open-ended, implicitly inviting the viewer to decide between the competing claims of parenthood and career. This is typical of a certain style of entertainment that connects to changing social mores, and invites a collective re-evaluation of a particular set of social norms.[9]

Different perspectives, values and experiences need to gain adequate expression in entertainment if the media are to facilitate an inclusive form of normative debate. Differences ought, ideally, to be expressed over a spectrum of programmes in a form that extends human understanding and insight. In the context of growing tensions between the Christian west and Islamic world, it is worth citing the wisdom of the Hutchins Report published more than half a century ago:

> The truth about any social group, though it should not exclude its weaknesses
> and vices, includes also recognition of its values, its aspirations, and its common

humanity . . . If people are exposed to the inner truth of the life of a particular group, they will gradually build up respect for and understanding of it (Hutchins Report, 1947, 57).

Media entertainment does not only contribute to self-government through normative regulation. It also influences the political process in numerous indirect ways. Media entertainment influences understandings of the world, and moral and social values, which affect political life. It facilitates the exploration of self, and the formation of social identity, that influences political allegiances. Normative debates conducted partly through entertainments result in periodic 'settlements' that can result in new legislation. Media entertainment can also contribute to new understandings of what is 'political', and influence the public agenda. There are so many ways, in short, that entertainment penetrates the world of politics (and vice versa) that it is difficult to understand why these two things should have been viewed for so long as being analytically distinct.

And yet, it is worth insisting on some form of separation. Politics is practised primarily in order to regulate in a collective way, on the basis of agreed procedures, the institutions of the state responsible for law making, law enforcement, foreign relations, tax collection and public provision. It is also a civilizing response to the enormous inequalities generated by all market systems. These inequalities are mitigated through the transfer of resources and payments from the rich to the poor, and from the fortunate to the unfortunate, through the authorization of the democratic state. The nature and extent of these social transfers are determined by democratic politics.

Major decisions by society, made through the state, need to be influenced by informed public debate. Television entertainment is not the best way of understanding the nature of the real world, nor of discussing the merits of alternative policies. There needs also to be intelligent and informative journalism that sustains the workings of democracy. If entertainment crowds out prime-time coverage of public affairs on mass television, still the principal medium of public information, democracy becomes starved and anorexic.

Unfortunately, the world's only superpower has a market-driven, entertainment-centred media system that leaves large numbers of its citizens politically ignorant. A comparative survey found that, in 1994, Americans were very much less informed about international affairs than Europeans (Dimock and Popkin, 1997). A 2001 survey found Americans were less informed about the causes of global warming than the populations of most other advanced countries (Brechin, 2003).[10] Various survey organizations reported that a substantial number of Americans, after the 2003 Iraq War, still believed that the Hussein regime was directly involved in the 9/11 attacks, and that the USA did in fact discover weapons of mass destruction.[11]

Additional media objectives

The traditional liberal approach to media diversity is to conceive of it in terms of the market. The number of competing media outlets or distribution of market shares becomes the yardstick of media pluralism. The assumption is that, if there is a significant level of competition, there is no lack of diversity – a view regularly endorsed in American legal judgements (Baker, 1977; Horwitz 1991).

This ignores where opinions come from. Indeed, usually absent from this market competition approach is any recognition that ideas and systems of representation are part of the discursive arsenal which competing groups use to advance their interests. This argument can be pitched in a simple and rudimentary way in terms of party agendas. Political parties on the right tend to emphasize low tax, law and order, and national security, while those on the left tend to stress welfare provision and employment, because these are areas in which they are traditionally thought to be strong by voters. Rival political parties consequently vie with each other to get television to make their 'issues' the dominant ones of the election campaign.

A comparable but more complex process of contestation takes place between rival social groups at the level of ideology. Different ways of making sense of society, different codes and explanatory contexts, different premises and chains of association privilege some social interests as against others. The media's role is never solely confined to imparting information: it always involves arbitrating between the discursive frameworks of rival groups. Which frameworks are included or excluded can affect collective opinion and, through the political process, the distribution of resources and life chances in society.

For this reason, media pluralism cannot be equated just with competition. It should be conceived as a contest that is *open* to different social groups to enter. One implication of this is that media pluralism has sometimes to be defended through structural reforms that widen social access to public debate or extend social representation. Anti-monopoly controls that prevent market domination by one company is not enough if the market as a whole is rigged by high entry costs in favour of those with large financial resources.

In addition, diversity should not be conceived only in terms of securing a mass media system that represents a plurality of views and perspectives. It has a further dimension in terms of grassroots media organization. One part of the media system should assist social groups to constitute themselves and clarify their objectives. In what ways they are best served as a social group is not something that springs pre-formed into people's consciousness as a consequence of their social circumstances. It needs to be explored through internal group processes of debate (Baker, 2000).

A democratic media system needs therefore a well-developed, specialist sector, enabling different social groups to debate within their terms of reference issues of social identity, group interest, political strategy and social–moral values. Part of this sector should also aid sectional groups to become and remain organized. Activist minority media should assist collective organizations to recruit support; provide an internal channel of communication for their members; and transmit their concerns and policy proposals to a wider public. In other words, the representative role of the media includes helping civil society to be effective.

If one revised objective is for the media system to give adequate expression to differences and conflicts within society, another should be for the media system to promote conciliation. This is not something that features in market libertarian understandings of the democratic role of the media, which emphasizes individual freedom of expression within an idealized understanding of the market. But the experience of societies such as Northern Ireland, former Yugoslavia and Sri Lanka where communal hatreds have become entrenched is a reminder of the need for members of society to coexist with each other in some degree of mutuality. The media system should, at some level, promote a sense of common identity by enabling different groups to communicate with each other, share collective memories and relate to symbols of collective unity. It should sustain the culture of civil democracy, characterized by a sense of being connected to society, a shared commitment to the ideal of objectivity (i.e. the shared pursuit of truth rather than cynical advocacy of whatever serves a prior conclusion), an orientation towards the public interest rather than exclusive concern for what's-in-it-for-me, and a belief in the efficacy of the democratic state based on the recognition that there are some worthwhile goals that cannot be secured through individual action alone.

The media should also assist the functioning of the democratic system – the principal way in which conflicts are 'settled' through arbitration in self-governing societies. This includes informing the electorate about the political choices involved in elections in a way that helps to constitute these as defining moments for collective decision. The media need also to be responsive to the demands of civil society, and maintain pressure for adequate responses to them from the governmental system. It is also important that opposition representatives are adequately reported between elections, not only to sustain public dialogue and a democratic check on government, but also to ensure that 'losers' among the electorate do not feel disenfranchised.

Most discussion of media and democracy is centred on the nation-state because this is where democracy is primarily practised. However, a global regulatory order – constituted by the World Trade Organization, the International Monetary Fund, the United Nations and other agencies – has come into being that is imperfectly accountable to national governments and national publics, and is not subject to adequate media scrutiny. Powerful global forces, most notably the deregulated global financial markets and transnational business corporations, are even less scrutinized and publicly accountable. While an international debate takes place mediated through the media, this tends to be dominated by powerful states and institutions (Hallin, 1994; Thussu, 2000). A global civil society is emerging, but it is too fragmented by linguistic differences, distorted by global inequality, subdivided into self-referencing constituencies and insufficiently wired to the structures of decision-making to be as yet fully effective. Further thought needs to be given to how the media can assist its growth and strengthening – an issue to which we shall return.

These revised goals seem, at first sight, contradictory or intangible. Is not the objective of securing forceful expression of conflict and uncompromising difference in the media completely at odds with the desire for a media system that promotes social conciliation? How does one relate the regulation of media through national governments (still the principal way in which it is done) with the needs of a changing world order?

Towards a working model

The starting point of what is advocated can be outlined first in general terms. The needs of the market conflict with those of democracy. However, for over 80 years, there has been a sustained attempt in western Europe, and elsewhere, to reconcile these two things through state reform of the media. What is proposed here may be viewed, especially in America, as either undesirable or unrealistic. But in fact all that this model does is to assemble and composite different features of media policy pursued in different European countries. It is in this sense a manifesto of 'actually existing' Social Democracy and its first cousin, European Christian Democracy: a European alternative to the American neo-liberal model (as distinct from its admirable social responsibility model) being extolled around the world.

Its architectural principle is that the media are not a single institution with a common democratic purpose. Rather, different media should be viewed as having different functions within the democratic system, calling for different kinds of structure and styles of journalism.

The model can be viewed at a glance in Figure 7.1. It has a core sector, constituted by general interest television channels which reach a mass audience. This is where different individuals and groups come together to engage in a reciprocal debate about the management of society. This core sector is fed by peripheral media sectors, three of which are intended to facilitate the expression of dissenting and minority views. The *civic* media sector consists of channels of communication linked to organized groups and social networks. The *professional* media sector occupies a space in which professional communicators relate to the public on their own terms, with the minimum of constraint. The *social market* sector subsidizes minority media as a way of promoting market diversity and consumer choice. To this is added a conventional *private* sector which relates to the public as consumers, and whose central rationale within the media system is to act as a restraint on the over-entrenchment of minority concerns to the exclusion of majority pleasures.

This media system is organized in different ways, and connects to different segments of society in order to enhance its diversity. Publicly accountable in multiple ways, it is intended to be broadly representative of society. Above all, its design is intended to create spaces for the incubation and communication of opposed viewpoints, and a common space for their mediation.[12] Both the detail and the thinking behind this outline are explored further below.

Fig 7.1 Working model of a democratic media system.

Civic media sector

The civic media sector supports the activist organizations of civil society. These are defined to include political parties as well as new social movements, minority groups and sub-cultural networks. Political parties have a particularly strategic role in liberal democracies as organizations that aggregate interests, distribute costs, define electoral choices and offer avenues for influencing society as a whole as distinct from promoting single issues. They are badly in need of rejuvenation and, often, democratization. Their decline makes it still more imperative that the other organizations of civil society are effective in voicing the concerns of the public.

The civic media sector can be viewed analytically as having three main tiers (although these sometimes overlap in practice). The first consists of media, such as party-controlled newspapers or social movement websites, which provide a link between civil society organizations and the wider public. They are generally propagandist, and seek to build support for a partisan perspective and set of objectives. The second tier consists of sub-cultural media, such as gay or lesbian magazines, which relate to a social constituency rather than an organized group. These can have an important 'constitutive' function that facilitates organizational effectiveness: in particular, they can promote a sense of social cohesion and common identity, and clarify values and goals through internal processes of discussion (Gross, 2002). The third tier consists of intra-organizational media, such as trade union journals, whose main purpose is in principle to reinforce collective identity, hold leaderships to account to rank-and-file members, assist in the sharing of relevant information and experience, and provide a context for developing new ideas and initiatives.

The civic media sector is in trouble. Party-controlled newspapers have been in decline throughout the Western world for a very long time. Many politically aligned magazines have an uncertain future. The intra-organizational media of the civic sector are dwarfed by the products of corporate public relations such as company videos and magazines. Only sub-cultural media, in some areas, are flourishing.

There are two ways in which the civic media sector can be reinvigorated. One strategy is to award grants to the media of civil society organizations, from websites to membership journals, to enhance their communication effectiveness. For example, in Norway the weekly journals of the political parties, immigrant groups and other organizations receive financial support, amounting in 1995 to £2.6 million (Murschetz, 1998: 297). The case for doing this is the same as for public funding of political parties. It is a way of facilitating the working of democracy, and supporting collective organizations as a public interest counterweight to private corporate interests.

The alternative, more ambitious strategy is to assign spectrum, technical facilities and some public funding to civil society organizations linked to the size of their memberships. This would enable civil society to control, through lease and time-share arrangements, television and radio channels. This approach is derived from the Dutch public service broadcasting system which assigns national public television channels to seven main organizations, and a considerable number of smaller bodies, that are judged to be representative of Dutch society. These are largely ideological, religious or social organizations. Their share of airtime, technical facilities and public funding is determined by membership levels (registered through payment of a fixed membership due or subscription to an organization's television programme guide) (Brants, 2004; Brants and McQuail, 1997; Nieuwenhuis, 1993). While this approach has not proved entirely successful as a way of organizing general public service television channels, it has perhaps more merit as a way of allocating *minority* public communication facilities.

Social market sector

The social market sector consists of minority media, operating within the market, which are supported by the state. Its purpose is to promote media pluralism and diversity of ownership.

One aim of social market policy is to enhance producer access to the market. Thus, all European countries have some form of anti-monopoly media legislation, one aim of which is to prevent market domination from excluding new market entrants (Commission of the European Communities [CEC], 1992). Broadcasting organizations within countries of the European Union are required to commission a set quota of programmes from independent production companies. In addition, newspapers in France have the legal right to be distributed, subject to an administration charge for returns. Norwegian film-makers, an endangered species, are able to get their films exhibited in Norway as a consequence of the country's municipal ownership of cinemas.

A second aim of the social market approach is to facilitate the establishment of new media by providing seed finance. In Austria, preferential loans are available to consortia seeking to acquire premises and plant to launch a newspaper. The level of production support for new films in France makes it the leading film-making country in Europe. In Britain, valuable frequency was allotted to a national public television channel (Channel 4) which commissions rather than makes programmes specifically for minorities. This gave minority programme-makers (and subsequently art-house film-makers) two vital things: money to make programmes, and a means of reaching a significant audience. The channel is funded by advertising, and proved so successful in reaching a young, lucrative audience that it was able to dispense with an initial cross-subsidy arrangement.

A third aim is to sustain minority media through a drip feed of selective subsidy. This is typified by the press subsidy schemes developed in Nordic countries, with variants in Austria and the Netherlands (Murschetz, 1998; Skogerbo, 1997). Thus in Sweden, grants encourage cost-cutting co-operation between rivals, particularly in the area of distribution, as a way of helping vulnerable papers. A graduated production subsidy also goes to non-market leaders, calculated neutrally in relation to circulation and volume of newsprint without reference to editorial politics. It is administered by a public body, with all-party representation. Its effect has been to keep alive a local political press, and sustain a greater degree of editorial diversity than would otherwise exist (Hulten, 2004). Its further unplanned consequence has been to promote internal debate within the party-aligned press since public subsidies loosened dependence on party. However, the support system sustains relatively mainstream newspapers. An equivalent scheme in Norway preserves more diverse publications, including a remarkable cultural Marxist daily, *Klassekampen*.

There are cautionary lessons to be learnt from the social market approach. The traditional neo-Keynesian justification for selective subsidy is that 'secondary' producers (such as minority papers or European film-makers) have lower scale economies than their larger rivals, and need compensatory support if they are to survive. However, this has resulted in public money being spent on worthy films that have never gained a commercial release, and have as a consequence been virtually unseen (CEC, 1994). Even the Swedish press subsidies scheme is now running into difficulties because rising levels of public funding are needed for it to continue to be effective (Weibull, 2003). Rather than seek to remodel markets according to neo-Keynesian precepts, it is probably better to set up a public trust, with all-party representation, with a brief to promote media pluralism as effectively as possible within a defined budget. This will almost certainly result in money being diverted from the high-cost sectors of film and newspapers where the social market sector is most developed, in favour of low-cost sectors where limited money will go further in terms of fostering media diversity.

There is also a case for funnelling support towards certain project categories: minority media that the market will not support (for example, political weeklies, a class of publication that fails to deliver a coherent consumer market that advertisers want, and consequently relies unhealthily on handouts from millionaires); distribution agencies, the weak link of the minority media sector most notably in the music industry; innovatory forms of media organization; and ventures that exploit the potential of new technology (most notably the internet).

Professional media sector

The professional media sector should be composed of media which are under the control of professional communicators, or which are organized in a form that gives staff maximum creative freedom. This is the only part of the proposed media plan that does not already exist in prototype, and for this reason may seem especially fanciful. Precedents could be cited in the form of individual media organizations that operate as public trusts, co-operatives or public interest ventures (Dowmunt, 1993; Downing, 2001). However, the 'professional sector' concept really derives from the de-politicized, British model of public service broadcasting during its heyday.

The professional media sector could consist of one minority television and radio channel. It should be publicly funded in order to be insulated from market pressure. Yet, it should be free from public regulation. Its staff would be in the enormously privileged position of being more independent than any of their peers.

This autonomy should assist the professional media sector to scrutinize the state and other centres of power. It should also help to forge a distinctive form of journalism. Journalists working for market media are increasingly entertainers; those working for civic media are advocates; while those in public service broadcasting are constrained by an obligation to mediate a 'balanced' perspective. By contrast, journalists in the professional sector should be guided by truth-seeking.

Hopefully, the professional sector will also promote a renaissance of socially relevant television drama. Just as novelists in the second half of the nineteenth century expanded the boundaries of conscience and understanding, and offered arresting interpretations of social change that galvanized public debate in Russia, France, Britain and elsewhere, so television dramatists should occupy a similar place in the imaginative landscape of contemporary society, and generate comparable public reflection about the direction in which society is moving.

Private sector

A private enterprise media sector should also be part of this blueprint. It will make the media system as a whole more responsive to popular pleasures. It will also tend to privilege right-wing perspectives. This is a positive feature of the plan, enhancing its pluralism.

In principle, the private sector should be subject to minimal regulation other than public law. However, the private television sector will need to be subject to a public service regime to prevent it from subverting the core public service system. Monopoly controls ought to be retained. There is also a strong case for supporting the independence of staff in large multimedia corporations as a way of resisting pressures for uniformity arising from media concentration, and as a way of restraining corrupt forms of cross-media promotion. This could be achieved by legally underwriting the freedom of editors and their equivalents, and introducing new procedures for staff participation in senior appointments (Curran, 1995). Another approach, adopted in the Austrian press, is for the editorial independence of journalists to be protected in legally binding contracts.

Public service core

The core media sector is where people come together to engage in a reciprocal debate about the management of society. This core sector is best organized as competing public service organizations in order to be inclusive and avoid excluding people by price. It gives prominence to public affairs, reports the news with due impartiality and gives space to different views. The version of the public service approach adopted here – the democratic corporatist model – has the additional advantage of seeking to reflect the diversity of society.

This model is exemplified by German television (with democratic corporatist variants in Sweden, Norway, Denmark and elsewhere). German public service television is a devolved, federal system subject to regional administration. It is controlled by representative broadcasting councils which lay down a broad strategy and appoint the chief executive. These councils have democratic representatives appointed on the basis of one of three methods, depending upon the region. In some states, representatives are nominated by organizations representing business, labour, politics, consumers, pensioners, women, tenants, education and other leading institutions or groups. In other states, council members are appointed by the local state assembly and government, usually in proportion to the current party balance. In still other states, the method of securing council members is a mix of these civil society and parliamentary models (Hickethier, 1996; Kleinsteuber, 2004; Kleinwachter, 1998; Sandford, 1997).

This emphasis on representative pluralism is reinforced by the German constitution ('basic law') which lays down that 'everybody has the right to free expression and publication of his opinion in word, writing and picture and the right to obtain information without hindrance from sources generally accessible' (cited in Kleinsteuber and Wilke, 1992: 79). This is interpreted by the Constitutional Court to mean that significant groups in society must be given the opportunity to air their viewpoints within the overall programme schedule of television, including entertainment as well as information programmes. What makes this different from the more limited American First Amendment is that it underwrites not only freedom of expression but also the audience's right of access to diverse viewpoints.

The representative pluralism of German television is further strengthened by its independence from the central state. This independence is secured as a consequence, paradoxically, of television's politicization. This is perhaps best exemplified by the Arbeitsgemeinschaft der Rundfunkanstalen Deutschlands (ARD), which is made up of local organizations formed into a national network. ARD organizations in left-wing regions tend to have radical broadcasting councils and a radical tradition of programme-making, while the opposite is the case in right-wing regions. Their combined output is fed into a nationally networked schedule, producing a mix of radical and conservative elements. Opposed political tendencies are also embedded in the decentralized management structure of ARD in a way that prevents federal government control.

This pluralistic approach to organizing a general television system can have shortcomings in practice. The German version, for example, over-represents political parties, and under-represents other important groups, such as immigrants, in the management of television. But the democratic corporatist model of television, when implemented successfully, is a good way of enabling society to commune with itself.

Global web journalism

The internet has proved to be an effective organizing tool of the emergent global civil society because it is cheap, international and interactive (Donk et al., 2004). However, although the net has lowered entry costs, the actual establishment cost of an online website such as OpenDemocracy – covering the generation of content, overheads, web design and maintenance, sub-editing, translation, administration and promotion costs – amounted to well over a million pounds even though it relied on free contributions (Curran, 2003). However, the success of this venture, funded principally by American charities such as the Ford Foundation, demonstrates what can be achieved. It provides an open, pluralistic, interactive and intelligent channel of debate and discussion between people in different parts of the globe. Its inspirational lead should now be followed by an international consortium of public service broadcasters which should establish a global public service website commissioning quality articles, hosting discussions and facilitating access to its informational resources. Its remit should be to contribute, in whatever way possible, to the building of a global civil society that seeks to hold to account the new international order.

Conclusion

Implicit in this outline is a complex set of requirements for a democratic media system. It should empower people by enabling them to explore where their interest lies; it should support sectional group identities and assist the functioning of organizations necessary for the effective representation of group interests; it should sustain vigilant scrutiny of the government and centres of power; it should provide a source of protection and redress for weak and unorganized interests; and it should create the conditions for real societal agreement or compromise based on an open discussion of differences rather than a contrived consensus based on elite dominance. This can be best realized through the establishment of a core public service broadcasting system, encircled by a private, social market, professional and civic media sectors. These latter will strengthen the functioning of public service broadcasting as an open system of dialogue, and give added impetus to the collective, self-organized tradition of civil society.

Notes

1 My thanks go to staff and students at the Department of Communications, University of California San Diego, for helpful suggestions incorporated into the original essay on which this chapter is based; and to fellow members of the Annenberg Press Commission whose discussions influenced my reformulation of its argument here.

2 'Liberal' is a confusing word, meaning different things in Britain and the USA. It is used here in its British historical sense of thought, emphasizing individualism, freedom, tolerance and free trade.

3 Estimates for the proportion of public affairs content in mass media are provided by Curran and Seaton (2003), Strid and Weibull (1988), Neuman (1986) and Abramson (1990).

4 In its key final chapter this admirable, thought-provoking book fails to distinguish between progressive and conservative elites. This distinction offers a way of reinterpreting the authors' conclusions.

5 In this context it is worth noting that the *Observer*, when it was owned by Lonrho, was different from most privately owned media in having 'independent directors', largely selected by the staff, who played a key role in seeking to defend the paper's editorial integrity.

6 These estimates are based on the start-up and run-in costs, respectively, of *The Independent* and *Live TV*, as estimated by senior executives working for these ventures.

7 For a full discussion of these issues, see Curran (2005).

8 *Sex and the City*, Season 4, episode 55 (*Time and Punishment*).

9 Normative attitudes towards mothers with small children going out to work has in fact changed significantly during the last two decades in Britain. See Crompton *et al.*, (2003).

10 This was a consequence not only of under-reporting, but also of how global warming was reported, to judge from Dispensa and Brulle (2003).

11 Even in September 2003, 24 per cent of Americans thought that weapons of mass destruction had been found in Iraq (P.I.P.A. Survey, September 2003). My thanks go to Shanto Iyengar for pointing this out to me.

12 This outline corresponds broadly with Habermas's reconception of the public sphere (Habermas, 1996), although it conceives the role of public service broadcasting differently. For further discussion of the issues raised by Habermas's work, see Curran (2002).

References

Abramson, J. (1990) 'Four Criticisms of Press Ethics', in J. Lichtenberg (ed.), *Mass Media and Democracy*. New York: Cambridge University Press.

Aldridge, A. and Hewitt, R. (eds) (1994) *Controlling Broadcasting*. Manchester: Manchester University Press.

Avery, R. (ed.) (1993) *Public Service Broadcasting in a Multichannel Environment*. White Plains, NY. Longman.

Bagdikian, B. (1997) *The Media Monopoly*, 5th edn. Boston: Beacon Press.

Baker, C. (1994) *Advertising and a Democratic Press*. Princeton, NJ: Princeton University Press.

———(1997) 'Giving the Audience What it Wants', *Ohio State Law Journal*, 58 (2).

———(1998) 'The Media that Citizens Need', *University of Pennsylvania Law Review*, 147 (2).

———(2000) *Media, Markets and Democracy*. New York: Cambridge University Press.

Barnett, S. and Seymour, E. (1999) *A Shrinking Iceberg Travelling South*. London: Campaign for Quality Television.

Barron, J. (1975) *Freedom of the Press for Whom?* Ontario: Midland Book.

Brants, K. (2004) 'Netherlands', in M. Kelly *et al.* (eds), *The Media In Europe*. London: Sage.

Brants, K. and McQuail, D. (1997) 'The Netherlands', in B. Ostergaard (ed.), *The Media in Western Europe*, 2nd edn. London: Sage.

Brechin, S. (2003) 'Comparative Public Opinion and Knowledge of Global Climate Change and the Kyoto Protocol: The US versus the World?', *International Journal of Sociology and Social Policy*, 23 (10).

Carlyle, T. (1907) *On Heroes, Hero-Worship and the Heroic in History*. London: Chapman and Hall.

Catalbas, D. (2000) 'Broadcasting Deregulation in Turkey: Uniformity Within Diversity', in J. Curran (ed.), *Media Organisations in Society*. London: Arnold.

Cato, (1720) 'Of Freedom of Speech: That the Same is Inseparable from Publick Liberty', *Cato's Letters*, No. 15, 4 February. Reprinted in H. Bosmajian (ed.) (1983) *The Principles and Practice of Freedom of Speech*, 2nd edn. Lanham: University Press of America.

Chadwick, P. (1989) *Media Mates*. Melbourne: Macmillan.

Chenoweth, N. (2001) *Virtual Murdoch*. London: Secker & Warburg.

Commission of the European Community, (1992) *Pluralism and Media Concentration in the Internal Market*. Brussels: CEC.

———(1994) *Report by the Think Tank on the Audiovisual Policy in the European Union*. Luxembourg: CEC.

Compaine, B. and Gomery, D. (2000) *Who Owns the Media*, 3rd edn. Mahwah, NJ: Lawrence Erlbaum.

Crompton, R. Brockmann, M. and Wiggins, R. (2003) 'A Woman's Place . . . Employment and Family Life for Men and Women', in A. Park *et al.* (eds), *British Social Attitudes: The 20th Report*. London: Sage.

Curran, J. (1978) 'The Press as an Agency of Social Control: An Historical Perspective', in G. Boyce *et al.* (eds), *Newspaper History*. London: Constable.

———(1986) 'The Impact of Advertising on the British Mass Media', in R. Collins *et al.* (eds), *Media, Culture and Society: A Critical Reader*. London: Sage.

———(1995) *Policy for the Press*. London: Institute for Public Policy Research.

———(2002) *Media and Power*. London: Routledge.

———(2003) 'Global Journalism: A Case Study of the Internet', in N. Couldry and J. Curran (eds), *Contesting Media Power*. Lanham, MA: Rowman & Littlefield.

————(2005) 'What Democracy Requires of the Media', in G. Overholser and K. Jamieson (eds), *The Press*. New York: Oxford University Press.

Curran, J. and Park, M. Y. (eds), (2000) *De-Westernizing Media Studies*. London: Routledge.

Curran, J. and Seaton, J. (2003) *Power Without Responsibility: The Press, Broadcasting and New Media in Britain*, 6th edn. London: Routledge.

Curran, J., Douglas, A. and Whannel, G. (1980) 'The Political Economy of the Human-Interest Story', in A. Smith (ed.) *Newspapers and Democracy*. Cambridge, MA: MIT Press.

D'Acci, J. (1994) *Defining Women*. Chapel Hill, NC: University of Carolina Press.

Dahlgren, P. (2000) 'Media and Power Transitions in a Small Country: Sweden', in J. Curran and M-Y Park (eds), *De-Westernizing Media Studies*. London: Routledge.

Dimock, M. and Popkin, S. (1997) 'Political Knowledge in Comparative Perspective', in S. Iyengar and Reeves, D. (eds), *Do The Media Govern?*, Thousand Oaks, CA: Sage.

Dispensa, J. M. and Brulle, R. (2003) 'Media's Social Construction of Environmental Issues: Focus on Global Warming – a Comparative Study', *International Journal of Sociology and Social Policy*, 23 (10).

Donk, W., Loader, B., Nihon. P. and Rucht, D. (2004) *Cyberprotest*. London: Routledge.

Dowmunt, T. (1993) *Channels of Resistance*. London: British Film Institute.

Downing, J. (1996) *International Media Theory*. London: Sage.

————(2001) *Radical Media*, 2nd edn. Boston: South End Press.

Evans, H. (1983) *Good Times, Bad Times*. London: Weidenfeld and Nicholson.

Fox, E. (ed.) (1998) *Media and Politics in Latin America*. London: Sage.

Giles, F. (1986) *Sundry Times*. London: John Murray.

Gitlin, T. (1990) 'Blips, Bites and Savvy Talk: Television and the Bifurcation of American Politics', in P. Dahlgren and C. Sparks (eds), *Communication and Citizenship*. London: Routledge.

Goodwin, P. (1998) *Television Under the Tories*. London: British Film Institute.

Gross, L. (2002) *Up from Invisibility: Lesbians, Gay Men and the Media in America*. New York: Columbia University Press.

Habermas, J. (1996 [1992]) *Between Facts and Norms*. Cambridge: Polity.

Hallin, D. (1994) *We Keep America on Top of the World*. London: Routledge.

————(2000) 'Media, Political Power, and Democratization in Mexico', in J. Curran and M-Y. Park (eds), *De-Westernizing Media Studies*. London: Routledge.

Hamilton, J. (2004) *All the News That's Fit to Sell*. Princeton, NJ: Princeton University Press.

Herman, E. and McChesney, R. (1997) *The Global Media*. London: Cassell.

Hesmondhalgh, D. (2002) *The Cultural Industries*. London: Sage.

Hickethier, K. (1996) 'The Media in Germany', in T. Weymouth and B. Lanizet (eds), *Markets and Myths*. London: Longman.

Hollingsworth, M. (1986) *The Press and Political Dissent*. London: Pluto Press.

Holmes, S. (1990) 'Liberal Constraints on Private Power?: Reflections on the Origins and Rationale of Access Regulation', in J. Lichtenberg (ed.), *Mass Media and Democracy*. New York: Cambridge University Press.

Horwitz, R. (1991) 'The First Amendment Meets Some New Technologies: Broadcasting, Common Carriers, and Free Speech in the 1990s', *Theory and Society* 20(1), 21–72.

Hulten, O. (2004) 'Sweden', in M. Kelly *et al.* (eds), *The Media In Europe*. London: Sage.

Humphreys, P. (1996) *Mass Media and Media Policy in Western Europe*. Manchester: Manchester University Press.

Hutchins Report, (1947) *A Free and Responsible Press*, Chicago: University of Chicago Press.

Inglis, F. (1990) *Media Theory*. Oxford: Blackwell.

Iyengar, I. (2000) 'Media Effects: Paradigms for the Analysis of Local Television News', in S. Chambers and A. Costain (eds), *Deliberation, Democracy and the Media*. Lanham, MA: Rowman and Littlefield.

Iyengar, S. (1991) *Is Anyone Responsible? How Television Frames Political Issues*. Chicago: University of Chicago Press.

Kelley, D. and Donway, R. (1990) 'Liberalism and Free Speech', in J. Lichtenberg (ed.), *Mass Media and Democracy*. New York: Cambridge University Press.

Kelly, M., Mazoleni, G. and McQuail, D. (eds) (2004) *The Media in Europe*. London: Sage.

Kleinsteuber, H. (2004) 'Germany', in M. Kelly *et al.* (eds), *The Media In Europe*. London: Sage.

Kleinsteuber, H. and Wilke, P. (1992) 'Germany', in B. Ostergaard (ed.), *The Media in Western Europe*. London: Sage.

Kleinwachter, W. (1998) 'Germany', in D. Goldberg *et al.* (eds), *Regulating the Changing Media*. Oxford: Oxford University Press.

Lang, G. and Lang, K. (1983) *The Battle for Public Opinion*. New York: Columbia University Press

Leapman, M. (1983) *Barefaced Cheek*. London: Hodder & Stoughton.

Lee, C. (2000) 'State, Capital and Media: The Case of Taiwan', in J. Curran and M-Y Park (eds), *De-Westernizing Media Studies*. London: Routledge.

Liebes, T. (1998) 'Television's Disaster Marathons: A Danger for Democratic Processes?', in T. Liebes and J. Curran (eds), *Media, Ritual and Identity*. London: Routledge.

McChesney, R. (1997) *Corporate Media and the Threat to Democracy*. New York: Seven Stories Press.

———(1999) *Rich Media, Poor Democracy*. Urbana: University of Illinois Press.

———(2004) *The Problem of the Media*. New York: Monthly Review Press.

McNair, B. (2000) 'Power, Profit, Corruption, and Lies: The Russian Media in the 1990s', in J. Curran and M-Y Park (eds), *De-Westernizing Media Studies*. London: Routledge.

Meikeljohn, A. (1983) 'The Rulers and the Ruled', in H. Bosmajian (ed.), *The Principles and Practice of Freedom of Speech*. Lanham: University Press of America.

Munster, G. (1985) *Rupert Murdoch*, Ringwood. Australia: Viking.

Murdoch, R. (1989) *Freedom in Broadcasting* (MacTaggart Lecture). London: News International.

Murschetz, P. (1998) 'State Support for the Daily Press in Europe: A Critical Appraisal', *European Journal of Communication*, 13 (3).

Nain, Z. (2000) 'Globalized Theories and National Controls: The State, the Market, and the Malaysian Media', in J. Curran and M-Y Park (eds), *De-Westernizing Media Studies*. London: Routledge.

Neil, A. (1996) *Full Disclosure*. London: Macmillan.

Neuman, W. (1986) *The Paradox of Politics*. Cambridge, MA: Harvard University Press.

Nieuwenhuis, A. J. (1993) 'Media Policy in the Netherlands: Beyond the Market?', *European Journal of Communications* 7(2).

Page, D. and Crawley, W. (2001) *Satellites over Asia*. New Delhi: Sage.

Papathanassopoulos, S. (2002) *European Television in the Digital Age*. Cambridge: Polity.

Park, M-Y., Kim, C-N. and Sohn, B W. (2000) 'Modernization, Globalization, and the Powerful State: The Korean Media' in J Curran and M Y. Park (eds), *De-Westernizing Media Studies*. London: Routledge

Patterson, T. (2003) *The Vanishing Voter*. New York: Vintage.

Protess, D., Cook, F., Doppelt, J., Ettema, J., Leff, D. and Miller, P. (1991) *The Journalism of Outrage*. New York: Guilford Press.

Raboy, M. (ed.) (1996) *Public Broadcasting for the 21st Century*. Luton: University of Luton Press

Royal Commission on the Press 1974–77 Final Report, (1977). London: HMSO.

Sandford, J. (1997) 'Television in Germany', in J. Coleman and B. Rollet (eds), *Television in Europe*. Exeter: Intellect.

Schlesinger, P. (1999) 'Changing Spaces of Political Communication: The Case of the European Union', *Political Communication* 16.

Seib, P. (2004) *Beyond the Front Lines*. Basingstoke: Palgrave.

Shawcross, W. (1993) *Murdoch*. London: Pan.

Sinclair, J., Jacka, E. and Cunningham, S. (1996) *New Patterns in Global Vision*. Oxford: Oxford University Press.

Skogerbo, E. (1997) 'The Press Subsidy System in Norway', *European Journal of Communication*, 12 (1).

Sparks, C. (1998) *Communism, Capitalism and the Mass Media*. London: Sage.

Stepp, C. (1990) 'Access in a Post-Responsibility Age', in J. Lichtenberg (ed.), *Mass Media and Democracy*. New York: Cambridge University Press.

Strid, I. and Weibull, L. (1988) *Mediesveridge*. Goteborgs: Goteborgs University Press.

Thussu, D. (2000) *International Communication*. London: Arnold.

Tracey, M. (1998) *The Decline and Fall of Public Service Broadcasting*. Oxford: Oxford University Press.

Tumber, H. and Palmer, J. (2004) *The Media and the War*. London: Sage.

Tunstall, J. and Machin, D. (1990) *The Anglo-American Connection*. Oxford: Oxford University Press.

Waisbord, S. (2000a) *Watchdog Journalism in South America*. New York: Columbia University Press.

———(2000b) 'Media in South America: Between the Rock of the State and the Hard Place of the Market', in J. Curran and M-Y Park (eds), *De-Westernizing Media Studies*. London: Routledge.

Weibull, L. (2003) 'The Press Subsidy System in Sweden: A Critical Approach', in N. Couldry and J. Curran (eds), *Contesting Media Power*. Lanham, MA: Rowman & Littlefield.

Whale, J. (1977) *The Politics of the Media*. London: Fontana.

Windlesham, L. and Rampton, R. (1989) *The Windlesham/Rampton Report on Death on the Rock*. London: Faber & Faber.

Media Systems, Organizations and Cultures

chapter eight

The Production of Media Entertainment

DAVID HESMONDHALGH

Introduction

Entertainment has often been treated as second best to news and current affairs in media sociology. The sense of mere diversion clings to the term and it is hard to escape the feeling in a lot of media teaching and research that entertainment represents the leftovers, once the more politically urgent issues surrounding news have been thoroughly digested. And entertainment is not only secondary to news, it loses out to art too. Entertainment ought to be pleasurable (even if much of it can be downright miserable) but the term art implies something much deeper: works of creative imagination which, at their best, elevate audiences and societies, rather than just providing amusement. In practice, the line between art and entertainment is often hard to draw – both involve communication via symbols, and give rise primarily to aesthetic experiences that have little or no further function. Because of these problems of definition and status, many prefer alternative terms such as culture or popular culture to entertainment, and cultural industries or creative industries rather than entertainment industries. In spite of its relatively humble status in media studies, the way in which entertainment comes to us, its production, has generated a substantial academic literature. There has been a boom in this literature in recent years, and this makes now an apposite time to survey the field. So this chapter examines this area of study and assesses what it can tell us about the media and society.

An initial distinction can be made between the different *levels* at which the production of entertainment has been studied.

- Studies of the production of individual texts, or series of texts (e.g. Tulloch and Alvarado, 1983, on *Doctor Who*; Levine, 2001, on *General Hospital*). Sometimes, analysis of production will take place in the context of larger studies of particular texts, including other aspects such as reception, or textual analysis (e.g. Gripsrud, 1995, on *Dynasty*). Television very much dominates studies at this level.

- Studies of the production of a particular genre, or group of genres, usually within a particular industry or medium over a particular period (e.g. Grindstaff, 2002, on TV talk shows; Raphael, 2004, on reality TV crime programmes). Again, this will often be part of a wider study of a genre (e.g. Laing, 1985, on punk).

- Studies of a particular occupational group within a particular industry or medium (Cantor, 1971, on Hollywood TV producers; Kealy, 1979, on sound mixers/record producers).

- Studies of a production organization or corporation (Elliot *et al.*, 1983, on MTM; D..., 2004, on the BBC).

- Studies of an entire industry, often within a particular national context, over a particular prescribed period (Falicov, 2000, on Argentinian film; Ma, 1999, on Hong Kong TV), often within the context of a study of an entire medium (Frith, 1981, on Anglo-American rock; Coser *et al.*, 1982, on books in the USA; Bordwell *et al.*, 1985, on Hollywood; Barker, 1999, on 'global television').

- Studies of entire sets of entertainment-related industries (Ryan, 1992, on the corporate form of cultural production; Miège, 1989, on the cultural industries; Scott, 2000, on cities and cultural production; Caves, 2000, on the creative industries).

This gives a sense of the huge scope of the academic field, and there are many relevant non-academic studies too. Much of the work (not necessarily that cited above) tends towards informative description, with little attempt to build or develop theory. But such theoretical foundations are necessary to make systematic sense of the relationship between entertainment production and society. What major *theories* of the production of media entertainment structure the field? Since the 1970s, there have been two major groups of theoretical approach.

The first group of approaches emerged in the USA in the late 1960s and early 1970s. It grew out of the functionalist sociology of the post-war years, but reacted against it and also against Marxism by, to use their terms, rejecting the idea that culture could be read off from the structure of society (Peterson and Anand, 2004). Instead, the emphasis was on looking at the production of entertainment and art, but also at other 'cultural' forms, such as science and religion, in order to reveal the social construction of practices which might otherwise be taken for granted. Many of these studies analysed a wide variety of factors in the production of culture, including technology, law and regulation, industry structure, organizations, occupations and market structure (Peterson, 1985). But within mainstream sociology of culture's approach to entertainment, there is a striking focus on the close analysis of media production *organizations*, reflecting a longstanding preoccupation of US sociology with this important concept. For this reason, I'll call this group *mainstream organizational sociology of culture* – mainstream because it has dominated cultural sociology in the English-speaking world.

The second group consists of *political economy approaches to the media*. Political economists are in essence sociologists of culture but they have tended to operate in media and communication studies, and on the margins of sociology. These approaches share a commitment to understanding the production and consumption of symbols in modern societies in terms of questions of justice, power and equality (one highly influential approach within this category is outlined by Peter Golding and Graham Murdock in Chapter 4 in this volume); but in practice the focus has tended to be on production.

The big division between these groups of approaches is a political one. Political economists are either explicitly Marxian or are on the radical left of social democracy, whereas the organizational sociologists tend to adopt a more descriptive, neutral tone, whatever their own political positions might be. As Hirsch (1972: 644) put it in a highly influential study, the organizational approach 'seldom enquires into the functions performed by the organization for the social system but asks rather, as a temporary partisan, how the goals of the organization may be constrained by society'. Acting as temporary partisans of media organizations would be a form of false objectivity for political economists. It is important to note their different methodological orientations too: the organizational sociologists lean towards micro-empirical studies of organizations, whereas political economists incline more towards theory and the use of secondary data on industry trends (though there is a radical sociology of media organizations – the major work is Gitlin, 1983 – which shares many of the assumptions of political economy).

Some important studies of media entertainment production do not fall comfortably into either of these categories, but many do. As will be clear by now, this is a division that fits in strongly with the neo-Marxian/liberal-pluralist split which structured the predecessor to the present collection (Curran and Gurevitch, 1977) and its first edition. While in other areas, radicals and liberal-pluralists have converged, in studies of media entertainment production, the Marxian/liberal-pluralist split has been remarkably resilient. If there has been convergence, it has been that more and more individual studies of particular texts or genres draw on perspectives associated with both organizational and political economic theories; but the two theoretical positions remain distinct. Recently, though, there have been significant new entries into the field and these can be grouped into three.

Firstly, there has been a new interest in entertainment production on the part of *economics* and of the three intertwined areas of *management, business* and *organizational studies* (which, for simplicity's sake, I will refer to as management studies from now on). This interest derives not only from the increasing size and economic significance of the entertainment industries, though that is certainly a factor. It also stems from a view, widely held in social science in the 1990s (e.g. Lash and Urry, 1994) that the cultural industries have certain characteristics which are becoming more and more a part of economic and organizational life generally. In particular, there has been a surge of interest in the idea of 'creativity' in management studies (Davis and Scase, 2000; Jeffcut and Pratt, 2002) and it seems that academics in this area have turned to the study of the 'creative industries' in the hope that this will reveal secrets about how to unlock the creativity of employees in organizations of all kinds (Tschmuck, 2003).

Secondly, there has been an increasing interest amongst *geographers* in entertainment production, as part of studies of the spatial distribution of the cultural industries (Scott, 2000). But related to this there has also been considerable work on the location of entertainment institutions from *cultural policy* and *arts management studies*, as governments attempt to boost the prosperity and attractiveness of cities, towns and regions through cultural industries quarters, 'creative clusters' and the like (Landry and Bianchini, 1995).

A third grouping of research has been influenced by *cultural studies* and by those parts of sociology influenced by post-structuralism. For years, there has been considerable animosity between scholars associated with political economy approaches and those associated with cultural studies (I try to summarize these spats in Hesmondhalgh, 2002). Much of the most-cited empirical work in cultural studies has primarily concerned questions of identity and consumption. But in recent years have been an increasing interest in the production of media entertainment within that field, as we shall see.

So we have five groups of approaches, two established, and three emergent. The two established areas represent distinctive theories, whereas some of the new entrants are, as we shall see, more theoretically ambitious than others. In what ways, if any, should we redraw the map of studies in this sub-field of media entertainment production in the light of these new developments? How can we assess the relative strengths of the different approaches? To address these questions, I want to look at how these different groups of approaches have addressed three fundamental issues. These are as follows:

- Organization: What is the process by which media entertainment comes to us? How is its production organized?

- Ownership, size and strategy: How important are the size and ownership of the entertainment corporations, and what is the role of smaller companies? Related to this are debates about the size of the entertainment business as a whole.

- Work: What is the nature of work in the entertainment industries?

Organization

Political economists and organizational sociologists agree that the entertainment industries make products that are primarily aesthetic, symbolic or expressive, rather than serving 'a clearly utilitarian function' (Hirsch, 1972: 642). Meaning and aesthetic value are not just incidental to these cultural products, but integral. So, for many writers in these traditions, the relationship between production and output is a central concern. In other approaches to culture, particularly in the arts and humanities, these relationships have been understood through the lens of ideas of talented individual creators (authors – and the term refers to creators in all fields, not just books).

Mainstream sociology of culture has questioned this view. Howard Becker's classic *Art Worlds* (1982), for example, argues that even works that seem to involve primarily one creator, such as painting, are dependent on a great array of other people. In Becker's words, 'art worlds, rather than artists, make works of art' (p. 198). Linked to this idea is the notion that creativity is incremental, that artists do not create out of a vacuum, but innovate by tiny steps, modifying conventions.

The sociological emphasis on complexity and collaboration in production derives from a strong democratic and levelling impulse. It implies that art and entertainment are not just something to be delegated to the special few, they are the products of social interaction. This critique of authorship and of individual creativity was echoed in a cognate but different form in literary and art theory, which began to question the way that the meaning and cultural significance of works of art were 'read off' the lives and intentions of authors (most famously, Barthes, 1976).

Yet the problem of authorship has refused to go away. Outside of sociological and literary theory, romantic, individualist notions of creativity still reign supreme in discourses about art and entertainment. Watch any TV documentary or read any newspaper or magazine article tracing the work of a film-maker, musician or writer: the emphasis is nearly always on the achievements of great individuals, rather than on the many and various people involved in making entertainment. In a world where authorship is ascribed more than ever, as commentary on media production proliferates, the critique of authorship begs the question of who does what in complex culture-making organizations, and what it means to say that a film, TV programme or album is 'by' someone. In a 1980 article, political economist Graham Murdock made an important suggestion which has not been heeded enough in the years since. Analysis of media entertainment organizations, he said, ought not to liquidate authorship (as Born, 1993, points out, that would run the danger of denying agency to cultural producers); instead, it ought to examine how notions of authorship operate in different types of production, legitimating certain aesthetic and economic practices over others. So, in order to stake a claim to artistic status, projects are conceived and marketed as the product of a particular author; the US television subscription channel HBO's TV series *Six Feet Under*, for example, was marketed as having been 'created by' Oscar-winning film writer Alan Ball. In areas of entertainment less concerned with artistic status, and more with commercial success, star names – singers, actors, presenters – are attached to products (recordings, films, TV shows) but their authorship is less forefronted in marketing and publicity; creative control is not necessarily ceded to these figures.

This helps us to see the issue of authorship as integrally related to an even bigger issue in studies of media entertainment production: the tensions between art or creativity[1] and commerce. A great number of empirical studies, many of them from mainstream organizational sociology of culture, show, implicitly or explicitly, the tensions between creativity and commerce in the everyday workings of media organizations. In a classic account, Coser *et al.* (1982) showed how the book industry had been consistently anxious about 'commercialization' for nearly a century, but they also showed that the rise of the blockbuster novel had in fact led to increased commercial pressures in trade publishing in the 1970s. Baker and Faulkner (1991) examined the effects of the rise of the blockbuster movie in the late 1970s on the division of roles in major Hollywood film productions. Business and artistic domains separated out: producers acted as directors much less often in order to concentrate on business issues; track records of commercial success became more important, and led more and more directors and scriptwriters to take on combined director/writer roles. However, cultural studies approaches to the production of music have had important things to say about the relationship of creativity and commerce too. Frith (1981) showed how rock's claims to artistic status derived from its commercial success, in the context of a cultural moment which heard that music as the expression of the authentic experience of youth. Mass culture was, temporarily and tenuously, reconciled with art.

Such detailed studies are important and valuable. But some studies, from both political economy and organizational sociology, have gone even further, by attempting to *theorize* how the creativity/commerce split is manifested in modern media organizations. Central to such efforts is the fundamental distinction, made by both political economy and organizational sociology, between the 'creative' stage of production and other stages involving getting cultural products to audiences. Some clearing-up of terminology is necessary here. These stages are often labelled production and distribution (Garnham 1990, Hirsch 1978), but distribution makes it sound as though the main issue concerns delivery (vans and transmitters) when actually it concerns information and persuasion. A better breakdown of the stages of cultural production is as follows, adapted from Ryan (1992):

- Creation – where the 'original' of a product is conceived and executed, usually by teams. Creation is a better term than Hirsch's production, which I think is best reserved for the whole process of making and circulating cultural goods prior to their purchase and experience by audiences.

- Reproduction – where the product is duplicated.

- Circulation – this includes delivery (transmission, wholesaling and retailing) but more importantly, it involves marketing and publicity.

Early work in organizational sociology of culture argued that distribution (reproduction and circulation in our terms) in the cultural industries was organized along *bureaucratic* lines, but that production (creation in our terms) by contrast was organized according to *craft* principles (see Hirsch, 1972, for a seminal account), and that this combination of contrasting forms was highly distinctive. Bureaucracies, characteristic of much modern factory production and of modern state government, provided continuity of employment and status to employees, but monitored employees closely, and provided hierarchies of command (Weber, 1978). Craft administration, however, was characterized by short-term contracts, with certain key features of the work determined by the rules and conventions of the craft to which workers belonged, rather than by hierarchical command. It is this hybrid characteristic of the cultural industries, combining characteristics of craft and bureaucratic production, which has made it of special interest to management studies in recent years, as bureaucratic styles of governance have come under increasing attack (see Davis and Scase, 2000: 1–12).

Political economy approaches broadly concur with this view, namely that the separate and distinctive organization of creation and circulation is extremely important for understanding the cultural industries. But they emphasize control, conflict and contradiction (the three cons) much more strongly. Importantly, in the most developed accounts, they also lay considerable stress on a *historical* understanding of production. The French sociologist Pierre Bourdieu (1996), whose ideas are closer to political economy than to the US organizational sociologists, showed how, in the nineteenth century, the idea that painters and writers should be autonomous of political power and commercial imperatives gradually created a particular structure of cultural production, divided between large-scale production for primarily short-term commercial products, and 'restricted' or small-scale production, where artistic success was the main goal (and where, for businesses, the hope was that artistic success would lead to long-term financial rewards). Bourdieu hardly dealt with popular culture at all, and failed to show how the rise of the cultural industries affected the structure of the field of cultural production in the twentieth century; but his work has provided the fullest analysis available of the importance of the creativity/commerce pairing in cultural production

The principle of autonomy for creators leads to a distinctive problem for owners of capitalist media businesses: how to make original and marketable cultural products but also at the same time discipline the creative process (Ryan, 1992). Recognition of such conflict is not altogether missing from the liberal-pluralist sociology of culture tradition (see DiMaggio, 1977: 443) or indeed from the more recent management studies literature (Jeffcut *et al.*, 2000; Lampel *et al.*, 2000). But whereas political economists portray creativity/commerce tensions as *struggles* over cultural work and creative output, organizationalists tend to portray them as technical *problems*, to be resolved by managerial strategy.

How are these tensions resolved organizationally? Ryan points to the crucial importance of a strand of managers who act as mediators between, on the one hand, the interests of often shirty, independent creators and, on the other, those of the owners and executives of companies, who seek to make profit out of creative labour.

Ryan calls these mediators 'creative managers'. Mainstream organizational sociology of culture has also recognized the centrality of these mediators. An important contribution here was by Paul DiMaggio (1977), who refined the craft/bureaucratic distinction discussed above by arguing that cultural (i.e. symbol) production was actually characterized not by craft administration but by a previously unrecognized system called 'brokerage administration', where 'brokers' mediate between competing interests – most importantly, between creative autonomy and managerial control. DiMaggio then distinguished in turn between 'pure' brokerage systems, where, for example, publishing editors have considerable discretion to deal with creative personnel (authors, designers), and 'centralized' brokerage systems, where brokers intervene much more strongly in the creative process on behalf of managers, such as in prime-time television, where TV scripts must be constantly submitted to TV networks for approval (see Bielby and Bielby, 1994).

There are other strategies too for controlling tricky creators besides the intervention of creative managers or brokers. Ryan argues that over the latter part of the twentieth century, cultural industry businesses, including the entertainment businesses which are our concern here, attempted increasingly to rationalize the creative stage of production by introducing 'formatting', whereby creative managers create plans for products, based on genre rules and conventions, and present them to creative personnel. Nevertheless, the pursuit of artistic freedom remains part of this rationalized system: if creators are commercially successful, they can win some of the autonomy which modern societies believe that 'artists' should have. This is why some star creators – performers, directors, producers – gain not only huge financial rewards from their work, but also considerable slack to do what they please. This is always a provisional autonomy, however, and one very much dependent on continued success. Perhaps the most notable example of such autonomy was the deal that film director Stanley Kubrick had with Warner Brothers studios from the 1960s until his death in 1999 (and some would argue that it led to some very poor films). Returning to the question of authorship, such cases suggest that, when discussing the creative contribution of particular individuals, it is important to bear in mind considerations regarding contracts and working practices. Kubrick in his later years really can be thought of as the primary author of the films marketed under his name; the authorship of most films is more tangled.

Entertainment businesses face other distinctive problems, besides the awkward notion of creative autonomy. In particular, as both political economy and organizational approaches stress, the cultural industries are marked by high levels of risk and uncertainty, not only because of their limited control over creators, but also because they cannot quite predict which products are going to resonate with other media (which are essential for publicizing media products) and with audiences. Entertainment organizations have long been required to devote considerable resources to marketing and publicity. Even in 1972, Paul Hirsch wrote of the need to 'co-opt' media publicity by the extensive use of 'contact men' (a term which could hardly be used of the much more feminized armies of PR staff employed by entertainment businesses today). But as media products have proliferated, and as much of the product is generic and 'formatted' in nature, those products that are not marked by the names of star performers can be difficult to distinguish. How can audiences and publicity media, such as television and radio stations, decide which of the dozens of historical sagas, or pop singles, or softcore porn videos available in shops or over the internet are worthy of special attention above all the others? This leads to a situation in which media businesses are forced to spend ever higher amounts of money on marketing and publicity, so that, for example, Hollywood marketing budgets now threaten to exceed production budgets (see Dale, 1997: 31). There is also evidence of a huge increase in the use of market research across all entertainment businesses over the last few decades (see Toynbee, 2006). The growth of marketing and publicity means that, within media entertainment organizations, those personnel who deal with such issues are now more powerful and influential, and increasingly 'advise' during the creation stage. For some, especially those influenced by political economy, this may involve a threat to the notion of artistic autonomy which, while based on a fictitious notion of creative endeavour, in that creativity can never really be autonomous of social or economic forces, creates space for innovation and – sometimes – politically challenging products.

So, to summarize, organizational sociology and political economy accounts such as Ryan's are in agreement that control over circulation (marketing and publicity) is an absolutely fundamental feature of the cultural and entertainment industries; and that art and artistic autonomy have crucial implications for the organization of production in the entertainment industries. Extrapolating from such accounts, we can say that, at the broadest level of analysis, the distinctive organizational form of contemporary media entertainment production involves relatively loose control of the creative stage, and relatively tight control of the circulation stage (see Hesmondhalgh, 2002). However, within this consensus, there is an important difference of emphasis. For those oriented towards political economy, and some versions of cultural studies (e.g. Negus, 1992) the key point is that creativity/commerce tensions are manifested in 'conflict over control and autonomy in the work situation' (Elliott, 1982: 147) and in continuing struggles in media production, whereas organizational sociologists and their management studies heirs tend to see entertainment businesses as involved in a more-or-less successful and rational effort to deal with the social and cultural constraints they face.

Ownership, size and strategy

I began this survey with a discussion of differing approaches to the organisation of entertainment production, because this is the most direct way into an understanding of the way cultural products reach their audiences. It has to be said that while there are some fine political economy studies that pay close attention to the organizational issues under discussion (Elliott, 1982; Murdock, 1980; Ryan, 1992), this has not always been a strong point with political economy. Rather, the emphasis in many political economy accounts has been on the ownership and market structure of the media, and the business strategies used by large corporations as they seek to dominate markets. Organizational sociologists have shown much less interest in these issues.

Many of the major entertainment markets have a similar structure: an oligopoly of large firms have a very large share of the market, as high as 80 or 90 per cent in some countries; a fairly high number of smaller firms co-exist alongside these firms. In any market, large businesses pursue a number of strategies to reinforce and build their position. The crucial ones in the entertainment industries are as follows (and these are overlapping categories):

- mergers and acquisitions
- conglomeration
- vertical integration
- internationalization.

To these we might add other emerging strategies noted by a literature from accounting and finance studies, involving financing measures such as the spreading of financial risk (Phillips, 2004). Political economy accounts have consistently traced the operation of these strategies over the last few decades (Schiller, 1976, and McChesney, 2004, are prominent analysts). The strategies have been applied in a more uneven way than some accounts suggest, and they by no means guarantee success. For example, many of the big mergers and acquisitions carried out in the entertainment industries, such as the widely hyped linking of AOL and Time Warner in 2000, have left the companies concerned saddled with huge debt, and have brought about considerable organizational problems. But the key fact remains: large corporations dominate the entertainment industries. Big companies have got bigger, more intertwined with other companies and sectors, more integrated and more international.

These developments are closely related to the growth in markets for cultural products. The cultural industries have grown as a result of increasing leisure time and disposable income over the last century, and because cultural businesses have worked hard to attract consumers to spend time and money on their products. The steady growth of cultural markets – much of it entertainment-based – has led some commentators to argue that culture is now no longer peripheral to the economy, but is becoming increasingly central (Lash and Urry, 1994). Some have even made this claim for the entertainment industries. Noting that 'entertainment is in many parts of the world the fastest-growing sector of the economy', media management consultant Michael Wolf has extrapolated from this that 'entertainment has found itself at the forefront of economic growth and cultural evolution' (Wolf, 1999: 5) – a very different and much more problematic claim. For even the biggest entertainment-led corporations continue to be dwarfed by the finance, banking, energy and automobile companies. While entertainment – broadly defined to include live entertainment and sport as well as media entertainment – may be overtaking some other key sectors, such as clothing, as a percentage of household expenditure in some countries, in most countries in the world, even defined in these very broad terms, entertainment is still a small component of a country's economy – though not, of course, of its culture.

While organizational sociology and management studies, with some exceptions, tend to treat the growth of the big corporations as an inevitable feature of media business, political economy approaches worry about the potentially damaging implications for modern societies. However, it is important to distinguish some different concerns about the size and power of large entertainment corporations, which are sometimes blurred in analysis. These are standardization/homogenization, ownership and control and the power of entertainment corporations in society.

Standardization/homogenization

The very earliest critiques of the growth of the cultural industries were concerned about the standardization of the goods created and circulated by these companies. In the words of Adorno and Horkheimer, forerunners of political economy approaches to the media, 'Under monopoly all mass culture is identical' (1977: 349). Although few political economists would put the issue anything like so polemically, and the best approaches emphasize the complex and contradictory nature of cultural products (see Miège, 1989, for a critique of Adorno and Horkheimer), these concerns have persisted. The political economist Vincent Mosco (1995: 258) has made an important distinction between multiplicity (the sheer number of products) and diversity (whether these products are really substantially different from each other on crucial issues of public concern). These concerns have also been intermittently present in mainstream organizational sociology of culture; a classic study by Peterson and Berger (1975) aimed to show, not altogether successfully, that diversity in popular music was inversely related to the degree of concentration in the industry. In general, though, sociology of culture has tended to reject the mass culture approach of a previous generation (not just Adorno and Horkheimer, but also liberal critics of the industrialization of culture). DiMaggio (1977), for example, argued that while some industries produced standardized products, others did not, and that there was diversity across modern societies as a whole. And even within political economy, the radical critique of standardization under oligopoly conditions has proved difficult to sustain. In fact, by the 1980s, political economists and others were turning to models that criticized cultural production on the basis of the social fragmentation it brought about, rather than on the grounds of standardization, by using the theory of the public sphere developed by the German philosopher Jurgen Habermas (1989/1962). (This is the basis, for example, of much of Croteau and Hoynes, 2001.) Nevertheless, it still remains possible and important to talk about situations in which the range of available expression in a particular medium or genre might become narrowed under the aegis of entertainment businesses with similar perspectives, especially when combined with a particular political conjuncture. Gitlin, for example, from a broadly political economy perspective, showed this taking place in his study of US prime time TV in the late 1970s and early 1980s, with issues of poverty, unemployment and ethnic difference almost disappearing from prime-time screens.

Ownership and control

A key concern of political economy approaches is whether, via their ownership of the means of communication, including of course entertainment, the wealthy and powerful are able to impose their values on audiences. The problem here is essentially that of ideology, of meaning in relation to power, though that term has a bewilderingly complex history. Other approaches have, at the very most, been only tangentially interested in this issue. It is all the more surprising then that there have been so few organizational studies from political economy that have attempted to theorize the exertion of ideological control in the actual making of entertainment (there have been more in the case of news). Part of the reason perhaps is that it is difficult to observe such control, because it is indirect – and here, again, we return to the way that creative autonomy remains present even in the contemporary, commercialized production of media entertainment. Recent political economy accounts, influenced by cultural studies, have stressed that entertainment corporations still manage to produce texts that can be argued to be subversive. Perhaps the most striking example is *The Simpsons*, produced by Rupert Murdoch's Fox Television (see Hesmondhalgh, 2001, and Downey, 2006). CBS, at the time part of the RCA empire, funded, distributed and marketed (heavily) the records of the great leftist punk group The Clash. These might be exceptions, sops to rebellious or cynical sections of society, but they are a reminder that the values of wealthy owners are not simply reflected in entertainment products. However, corporations still exert control over the allocation of budgets and schedules; the right to hire and fire is still heavily influenced by corporate policy, which comes down from senior executives.

The power of entertainment corporations in society

If debates about ownership and ideological control are difficult to prove empirically, more certain is that the huge resources of the large entertainment corporations give them considerable power to influence the way in which cultural production is carried out in society, and how the rewards for making entertainment are distributed (see the next section). Whenever governments go about reforming media law and regulation, it is absolutely guaranteed that the major corporations and the trade associations they dominate will work extremely hard to persuade governments to undertake measures that will favour them. An important recent example of this was a reform to US copyright law in 1998, which extended the length of copyright ownership protection after an author's death from 50 years to 70 years, under pressure from the powerful corporations that owned many of the most important copyrights. Congress has extended the term of copyright retrospectively eleven times in the last 45 years, in response to corporate lobbying (see Lessig, 2002: 107).

These are all concerns that political economy approaches have addressed far more than any of the other main theoretical approaches discussed in this chapter, and they have surely been right to do so, even if the debates surrounding these issues remain unresolved. But it is important to remember that small and medium-sized enterprises, including micro-companies continue to play an important role in entertainment too. Alongside the music majors, hundreds of small record companies operate in nearly all the advanced industrial countries. Most film companies are organized around particular projects. The important role of small companies is partly explained by the relatively low entry costs surrounding creation and reproduction (it does not cost that much to make a record, or produce a magazine). But there are cultural factors too, as discussed in the previous section. In many areas of media entertainment, among audiences and intermediaries such as journalists, small companies are considered to be where the most creative and innovative production is likely to take place; in some cases, actual cultural forms have been named after these small, 'independent' companies (indie rock, independent cinema).

Small companies have played an important part in debates about changes in the entertainment industries. In the 1980s, various commentators began to analyse shifts in advanced industrial economies, noting a decline in mass production, an increased emphasis on the targeting of niche markets, and in some cases a subsequent return to craft forms of production (Piore and Sabel, 1984; various contributors to Hall and Jacques, 1989), along with various associated organizational changes, such as the increased use of subcontracting and freelancing, and new relations between large and small companies. Some used the term 'post-Fordism' to describe this new era beyond the Fordism of mass production; some preferred the terms 'flexible specialization' or 'restructuring'. These debates were an important factor in drawing management studies academics to the study of media entertainment production, where these features had arguably been present for many years (Robins, 1993). Others were drawn by an interest in the concept of entrepreneurship to the study of industries where small businesses are abundant, and where the products are perhaps a little sexier than some other areas of study (Leadbeater and Oakley, 1999). Such debates about post-Fordism and flexible specialization attracted the attention of geographers from the 1980s onwards, because they involved important issues concerning regional and urban development (Christopherson and Storper, 1989). Geographers noted that cultural businesses tended to 'agglomerate' in particular locations, and the spatial distribution of the entertainment industries became a major topic of interest (Scott, 1988). It then linked up with an increasing interest amongst policy-makers, on a national and local level, with the cultural and creative industries as sectors that might replace dying industries with new sources of employment, and which might also make cities more attractive places to invest (Bianchini and Parkinson, 1993). This in turn has occasioned a further surge in work in management studies and cultural policy studies on the creative industries, including further studies of entrepreneurship and small companies (Bilton, 1999).

Some of this work makes valuable contributions to understanding the extent and distribution of employment in the growing cultural industries (Pratt, 1997; Scott, 2000). Some of it makes important interventions in local and regional cultural policy, pointing to the unforeseen consequences of top-down initiatives and seeking to direct money towards grass-roots production (O'Connor and Wynne, 1996). The focus on city locales helps to ground the study of media entertainment production in the actual places where so many producers live and work, and looks at an aspect of the effects of such production on urban spaces which had been relatively neglected (Zukin, 1982, was a groundbreaking work in this respect). At times, there is significant overlap with the concerns of political economy (Christopherson, 1996; Scott, 2000: 204–16). Elsewhere in these new waves of literature, however, there is little sign of effort to engage with the systematic analysis of the dynamics of production explored in the political economy and sociology of culture literature. There is much loose talk of a transition to an informational economy, or of a new economy based around culture. At times, there is evidence of complacency about the social repercussions of entertainment production. The relations between media entertainment production and questions of social power, central to the political economy tradition, are often – though not always – missing. This suggests an urgent need for these new strands of literature to engage with the best contributions to political economy and sociology of culture approaches; and in turn for political economy and sociology of culture to engage with questions of space and local policy.

Entertainment work

Perhaps the most promising area for interdisciplinary dialogue in the study of media entertainment production is the analysis of work. No examination of media production could be complete without thinking about the working lives and rewards of its key workers – and yet this has been a surprisingly neglected topic in media and cultural studies (see Beck, 2003, for an exception). However, more recently the subject of entertainment work has been taken up in a number of areas. There are, though, real tensions between the different approaches.

A significant strand of management studies has addressed the changing nature of work and careers in modern societies. The notion of the 'boundaryless career' (Arthur and Rousseau, 1996) refers to a range of supposedly newer forms of employment, which involve moving between different employers to work on different projects, and drawing validation from networks outside the organization in which people work. Careers in the entertainment industries have always taken this form, and so there has been considerable interest in management studies and elsewhere in working patterns associated with these industries. Candace Jones (1996), for example, reports on how, following the break-up of the Hollywood studio system in the 1950s, film production increasingly came to be organized as a series of one-off projects, each one separately financed. It is hard not to get a sense in some of the management studies literature that the new mobile career represents a better, brighter future than the supposedly dour world of traditional organizations (see Anand et al., 2002, and the concept of the 'creative career'). But studies of labour markets and income patterns for artists by economists and sociologists suggest that the world of entertainment can be a difficult one for those who choose to work there. Towse (1992) summarized the findings of studies of the characteristics of artistic labour forces in the following way:

1. artists tend to hold multiple jobs

2. there is a predominance of self-employed or freelance workers

3. work is irregular, contracts are short-term, there is little job protection

4. career prospects are uncertain

5. the distribution of earnings is highly skewed (i.e. unequal)

6. artists are younger than other workers

7. the workforce appears to be growing.[2]

Given factors 3, 4 and 5 here, it is striking that there is no shortage of workers aiming to fulfil the growing demand for artistic labour. Why do more and more people, many of them very young, appear to want to work in the entertainment business? Menger (1999: 554) usefully distinguishes three different explanations for this phenomenon. The first is the labour of love explanation (Freidson, 1990) – artists, or symbol creators, have a strong sense of a 'calling', of potential fulfilment, and they are prepared to take the risk of failure. A second set of explanations claims that artists might be risk-lovers or, like lottery players, simply have not considered properly how likely it is that they will fail (though success and failure is not quite as arbitrary as in a lottery). A third explanation is that artistic work brings non-monetary, psychological rewards. Artistic work is attractive because of some of the features noted earlier, such as high levels of personal autonomy. And there are others too: a sense of community, the possibility of self-actualization, and potentially high degrees of recognition, even celebrity. Some argue that contemporary labour markets function by balancing differences, so that work that has these non-monetary rewards is compensated less. But, as Menger points out, these non-monetary benefits apply very unevenly in artistic (and entertainment) work. And there are non-monetary downsides too, associated with job insecurity and maintaining networks.

While organizational sociologists and management academics will usually point out job insecurity and income disparities amongst entertainment and cultural workers, they tend to take a cool, neutral stance towards these factors. Others, particularly those influenced by Marxism, are more inclined to interpret such phenomena as exploitation. Marx of course wrote prolifically about work under capitalism, and his work was taken up by Marxian analysts of 'labour process theory' in the 1960s and 1970s who wanted to look at developments since the nineteenth century (most notably Braverman, 1974). The labour process theorists argued that the twentieth century had seen a series of transformations that brought about the real subordination of workers. According to such theorists, capitalists sought to cheapen labour – especially craft work – in two main ways: first, deskilling; second, separating out key forms of knowledge from the rest of production, and placing that knowledge in the hands of management. Rationalization via new technology and new forms of management was seen by labour process theory as the main means of controlling and cheapening labour. Labour process theory was mainly concerned with the modern manufacturing factory and other sites of manual labour, and there was very little study of cultural and entertainment work. Surprisingly, political economy of culture writers have done little to fill this gap, with the notable exception of Ryan (1992), who, as we have already seen, argued that entertainment businesses attempted to rationalize cultural production via formatting from the 1950s onwards, but were only partly successful, because long-standing discourses about creative and artistic work helped to protect the craft-like creative stage of production. To reiterate, the emphasis in Ryan's account is on conflict, control and contradiction.

Labour process theory has been widely criticized by Weberian sociologists, management academics and by other Marxians for a variety of sins, including overestimating capitalist control and the degradation of work, and understating the countervailing role of the state and labour organizations. One notable strand of critique came from writers influenced by the French historian and social theorist Michel Foucault. These writers argued that Marxian and mainstream sociological debates about labour and power downplayed and misunderstood the subjectivity of workers. Subjectivity, they argued, could not be explained by an analysis of the political–economic structures of capitalism, but should be looked at as the product of particular 'technologies' – or discourses – of self, of what it meant to be a person (Wilmott, 1990). This post-structuralist critique of labour process theory has been taken up by Gillian Ursell in an important article which attempts to apply both Marxian and post-structuralist accounts to work in the television industry. For Ursell, Foucauldian insights might be used 'not to refute labour process theory but to move it on' (Ursell, 2000:810). Ursell's research attempts to do this by showing, in Marxian fashion, that television production prays upon its workers like a vampire, 'ingesting youngsters at low prices from a large pool provided by the education system, working newcomers and established hands remorselessly, and discarding the older and less accommodating at will' (p. 816). But she also shows, through interviews, in a manner consistent with Foucault, that the 'vampire is seductive. . . . Television production can be a type of work which allows for the exploration, expression and actualization of the sensual dimensions of creativity' (p. 821). For Ursell, television workers, seeking reputation, acclaim and self-fulfilment through work are implicated in (though not necessarily to blame for) their own working conditions.

This type of analysis has resonances with new developments in cultural studies, an academic area which, after some years of paying relatively little attention to production, has begun to pay attention to the issue of work in the entertainment industries. McRobbie (2002), for example, analyses how notions of creativity, talent and work are being redefined in those burgeoning micro-businesses of the cultural sector associated with young people, including fashion and design, but also entertainment industries such as clubbing, recording and magazine journalism. She echoes Ursell in pointing to the 'utopian thread' involved in the 'attempt to make-over the world of work into something closer to a life of enthusiasm and enjoyment' (McRobbie, 2002: 523) but also how this leads to a situation where, when things go wrong, young people entering these creative worlds of work can feel that they only have themselves to blame. McRobbie also notes an increasing conformism in the sector, where difficult ethical and political questions are frowned upon, as 'speed and risk negate ethics, community and politics' (p. 523). The distinctively cultural-studies contribution here is an ability to read the political implications of changing cultural values. This suggests a promising avenue for making connections between such studies of the world of entertainment work, and the nature of the entertainment texts produced (although McRobbie does not explore this direction in her article). Such connections can be seen in another work influenced by cultural studies and by feminism, Laura Grindstaff's *The Money Shot* (2002). Building on the important sociological work of Arlie Hochschild on 'emotional labour', Grindstaff reveals the intense and demanding work that goes on behind the scenes of talk shows, mainly on the part of young, middle-class women, to produce those displays of feeling on the part of 'ordinary' people, which are, in Grindstaff's words, the equivalent of the orgasm in pornography. 'the hallmark of the genre, central to its claim to authenticity' (p. 20).

Looking ahead

Such studies further suggest the potential fruitfulness of new approaches to the study of media entertainment production. But in general, the 'new entrants' to the field have not yet formed into significant new theories of entertainment production in a way that would challenge the longstanding pre-eminence of political economy and organizational sociology – and it will be interesting to see whether such theoretical challenges are offered in the years ahead. In the meantime we can expect the study of media entertainment production to proliferate, just as its object of study undoubtedly will. The best work is likely to be produced by those researchers who work across such disciplinary divides, combining the methods and ethical concerns associated with the different fields, but emerging with their own distinctive visions of this important area of inquiry.

Notes

1 The term creativity is used widely and loosely. The reference here is clearly to creativity in the sense of making entertainment/artistic products – i.e. symbolic creativity – rather than, say, scientific problem-solving. For an important treatment of creativity, see Negus and Pickering (2004).

2 Many studies take 'artists' to mean actors, musicians, dancers, writers, etc. working in the subsidized arts sector, but in fact many such performers work primarily in the commercial entertainment sector. The above characteristics very much apply to that larger sector.

References

Adorno, T. and Horkheimer, M. (1977) 'The Culture Industry: Enlightenment as Mass Deception', in J. Curran and M. Gurevitch (eds), *Mass Communication and Society*. London: Edward Arnold, pp. 349–83.

Anand, N. Peiperl, M. A. and Arthur, M. B. (2002) 'Introducing Career Creativity', in M. Peiperl *et al.* (eds), *Career Creativity*. Oxford: Oxford University Press, pp. 1–11.

Arthur, M. B. and Rousseau, D. M. (eds) (1996) *The Boundaryless Career*. New York and Oxford: Oxford University Press.

Baker, W. E. and Faulkner, R. R. (1991) 'Role as Resource in the Hollywood Film Industry', *American Journal of Sociology*, 97 (2), 279–309.

Barker, C. (1999) *Global Television*. Oxford: Blackwell.

Barthes, R. (1976) 'The Death of the Author', in R. Barthes, *Image/Music/Text*. London: Fontana.

Beck, A. (ed.) (2003) *Cultural Work*. London: Routledge.

Becker, H. S. (1982) *Art Worlds*. Berkeley: University of California Press.

Bianchini, F. and Parkinson, M. (1993) *Cultural Policy and Urban Regeneration*. Manchester: Manchester University Press.

Bielby, W. T. and Bielby, D. D. (1994) '"All Hits are Flukes": Institutionalised Decision Making and the Rhetoric of Network Prime-Time Program Development', *American Journal of Sociology*, 99 (5), 1287–1313.

Bilton, C. (1999) 'Risky Business: the Independent Production Sector in Britain's Creative Industries', *Cultural Policy*, 6 (1), 17–39.

Bordwell, D., Staiger, J. and Thompson, K. (1985) *The Classical Hollywood Cinema*. London, Melbourne and Henley: Routledge and Kegan Paul.

Born, G. (1993) 'Against Negation, for a Politics of Cultural Production: Adorno, Aesthetics, the Social', *Screen*, 34 (3), 223–42.

————(2004) *Uncertain Vision*. London: Secker & Warburg.

Bourdieu, P. (1996) *The Rules of Art*. Cambridge: Polity.

Braverman, H. (1974) *Labor and Monopoly Capital*. New York: Monthly Review Press.

Cantor, M. G. (1971) *The Hollywood TV Producer*. New York: Basic Books.

Caves, R. E. (2000) *Creative Industries*. Cambridge: Harvard University Press.

Christopherson, S. (1996) 'Flexibility and Adaptation in Industrial Relations: The Exceptional Case of the US Media Entertainment Industries', in L. S. Gray and R. L. Seeber (eds), *Under the Stars: Essays on Labor Relations in Arts and Entertainment*. Ithaca and London: ILR Press.

Christopherson, S. and Storper, M. J. (1989) 'The Effects of Flexible Specialisation on Industrial Politics and the Labor Market: The Motion Picture Industry', *Industrial and Labor Relations Review*, 42, 331–47.

Coser, L. A., Kadushin, C. and Powell, W. W. (1982) *Books: The Culture and Commerce of Publishing*. New York: Basic Books.

Croteau, D. and Hoynes, W. (2001) *The Business of Media*. Thousand Oaks: Pine Forge Press.

Curran, J. and Gurevitch, M. (eds) (1977) *Mass Communication and Society*. London: Edward Arnold.

Dale, M. (1997) *The Movie Game*. London: Cassell.

Davis, H. and Scase, R. (2000) *Managing Creativity*. Buckingham and Philadelphia: Open University Press.

DiMaggio, P. (1977) 'Market Structure, the Creative Process and Popular Culture: Towards an Organizational Reinterpretation of Mass-culture Theory', *Journal of Popular Culture*, 11 (2), 436–52.

Downey, J. (2006) 'Large Media Corporations: Do Size, Ownership and Internationalisation Matter?', in D. Hesmondhalgh, (ed.) *Media Production*. Maidenhead and Milton Keynes: The Open University/The Open University Press.

Elliott, P. (1982) 'Media Organizations and Occupations: An Overview', in M. Gurevitch *et al.* (eds), *Culture, Society and the Media*. London: Methuen, pp. 142–73.

Falicov, T. (2000) 'Argentina's Blockbuster Movies and the Politics of Culture under Neoliberalism, 1989–98', *Media, Culture and Society*, 22, 327–42.

Feuer, J., Kerr, P. and Vahimagi, T. (1984) *MTM 'Quality Television'*. London: British Film Institute.

Freidson, E. (1990) 'Labors of Love: A Prospectus', in K. Erikson and S. P. Vallas (eds), *The Nature of Work: Sociological Perspectives*. New Haven: Yale University Press, pp. 149–61.

Frith, S. (1981) *Sound Effects*. New York: Pantheon.

Garnham, N. (1990) *Capitalism and Communication*. London: Sage.

Gitlin, T. (1983) *Inside Prime Time*. New York: Pantheon.

Grindstaff, L. (2002) *The Money Shot: Trash, Class, and the Making of TV Talk Shows*. Chicago: University of Chicago Press.

Gripsrud, J. (1995) *The Dynasty Years*. London and New York, Routledge.

Habermas, J. (1989/1962) *The Structural Transformation of the Public Sphere*. Cambridge: MIT Press.

Hall, S. and Jacques, M. (eds) (1989) *New Times*. London: Lawrence and Wishart.

Hesmondhalgh, D. (2001) 'Ownership is Only Part of the Media Picture', *openDemocracy*, www.opendemocracy.net.

———(2002) *The Cultural Industries*. London and Thousand Oaks: Sage.

Hirsch, P. M. (1972) 'Processing Fads and Fashions: An Organization-set Analysis of Cultural Industry Systems', *American Journal of Sociology*, 77, 639–59.

———(1978) 'Production and Distribution Roles Among Cultural Organizations: On the Division of Labor Across Intellectual Disciplines', *Social Research*, 45 (2), 315–330.

Jeffcut, P. and Pratt, A. C. (2002) 'Editorial: Managing Creativity in the Cultural Industries', *Creativity and Innovation Management*, 11 (4), 225–33.

Jeffcut, P., Pick, J. and Protherough, R. (2000) 'Culture and Industry: Exploring the Debate', *Studies in Culture, Organizations and Societies*, 6, 129–43.

Jones, C. (1996) 'Careers in Project Networks: The Case of the Film Industry', in M. B. Arthur, and D. M. Rousseau, (eds), *The Boundaryless Career*. New York and Oxford: Oxford University Press, 58–75.

Kealy, E. (1979) 'From Craft to Art: The Case of Sound Mixers and Popular Music', *Sociology of Work and Occupations*, 6, 3–29.

Laing, D. (1985) *One Chord Wonders*. Buckingham: Open University Press.

Lampel, J., Lant, T. and Shamsie, J. (2000) 'Balancing Act: Learning from Organizing Practices in Cultural Industries', *Organization Science*, 11 (3), 263–9.

Landry, C. and Bianchini, F. (1995) *The Creative City*. London: Demos.

Lash, S. and Urry, J. (1994) *Economies of Signs and Spaces*. London: Sage.

Leadbeater, C. and Oakley, K. (1999) *The Independents: Britain's New Cultural Entrepreneurs*. London: Demos.

Lessig, L. (2002) *The Future of Ideas: The Fate of the Commons in a Connected World*. New York: Vintage.

Levine, E. (2001) 'Toward a Paradigm for Media Production Research: Behind the Scenes at General Hospital', *Critical Studies in Mass Communication*, 18 (1), 66–82.

Ma, E. K-W. (1999) *Culture, Politics and Television in Hong Kong*. London: Routledge.

McChesney, R. W. (2004) *The Problem of the Media*. New York: Monthly Review Press.

McRobbie, A. (2002) 'Clubs to Companies: Notes on the Decline of Political Culture in Speeded up Creative Worlds', *Cultural Studies*, 16, 516–31.

Menger, P.-M. (1999) 'Artistic Labor Markets and Careers', *Annual Review of Sociology*, 25, 541–74.

Miége, B. (1989) *The Capitalization of Cultural Production*. New York: International General.

Mosco, V. (1995) *The Political Economy of Communication*. London: Sage.

Murdock, G. (1980) 'Authorship and Organization', *Screen Education*, 35, 19–34.

Negus, K. (1992) *Producing Pop*. London: Edward Arnold.

Negus, K. and Pickering, M. (2004) *Creativity and Culture*. London and Thousand Oaks: Sage.

O'Connor, J. and Wynne, D. (eds) (1996) *From the Margins to the Centre*. Aldershot: Arena.

Peterson, R. A. (1985) 'Six Constraints on the Production of Literary Works', *Poetics*, 14, 45–67.

Peterson, R. A. and Anand, N. (2004) 'The Production of Culture Perspective', *Annual Review of Sociology*, 30, 311–34.

Peterson, R. A. and Berger, D. G. (1975) 'Cycles in Symbol Production: The Case of Popular Music', *American Sociological Review*, 40, 158–73.

Phillips, R. (2004) 'The Global Export of Risk: Finance and the Film Business', *Competition and Change*, 8, 2.

Piore, M. and Sabel, C. (1984) *The Second Industrial Divide*. New York: Basic Books.

Pratt, A. C. (1997) 'The Cultural Industries Production System: A Case Study of Employment Change in Britain, 1984–91', *Environment and Planning A*, 29, 1953–74.

Raphael, C. (2004) 'The Political Economic Origins of Reali-TV', in S. Murray and L. Ouellette (eds), *Reality TV: The Re-making of Television Culture*. New York: New York University Press.

Robins, J. A. (1993) 'Organization as Strategy: Restructuring Production in the Film Industry', *Strategic Management Journal*, 14, 103–18.

Ryan, B. (1992) *Making Capital from Culture*. Berlin and New York: Walter De Gruyter.

Schiller, H. (1976) *Communication and Cultural Domination*. White Plains, New York: International Arts and Sciences Press.

Scott, A. J. (1988) *New Industrial Spaces*. London: Pion.

———(2000) *The Cultural Economy of Cities*. London and Thousand Oaks: Sage.

Towse, R. (1992) 'The Labour Market for Artists', *Richerce Economiche*, 46, 55–74.

Toynbee, J. (2006) 'The Media's View of the Audience', in D. Hesmondhalgh (ed.) *Media Production*. Maidenhead and Milton Keynes: The Open University/The Open University Press.

Tshmuck, P. (2003) 'How Creative are the Creative Industries: A Case of the Music Industry', *The Journal of Arts Management, Law, and Society*, 33 (2), 127–41.

Tulloch, J. and Alvarado, M. (1983) *Doctor Who, The Unfolding Text*. London: Macmillan.

Ursell, G. (2000) 'Television Production: Issues of Exploitation, Commodification and Subjectivity in UK Television Labour Markets', *Media, Culture and Society*, 22, 805–25.

Weber, M. (1978) 'Bureaucracy', in M. Weber, *Economy and Society*. Berkeley: University of California Press, pp. 956–1005.

Wilmott, H. (1990) 'Subjectivity and the Dialectics of Praxis: Opening up the Core of Labour Process Analysis', in D. Knights and H. Wilmott (eds), *Labour Process Theory*. London: Macmillan, 336–78.

Wolf, M. J. (1999) *The Entertainment Economy*. London: Penguin.

Zukin, S. (1982) *Loft Living*. Baltimore: Johns Hopkins University Press.

▶ chapter nine

Four Approaches to the Sociology of News

MICHAEL SCHUDSON

Introduction

This essay, in its original 1989 appearance and in several published revisions, has proposed that there are three distinct approaches to explaining how news is produced: political–economic, sociological and cultural perspectives. These categories remain visible in this latest revision, but they do not seem to me as satisfactory as they once did.

There are two problems with them. The first problem is that the category of 'political economy' obscures more than it reveals, and I have at last abandoned it, setting up separate discussions of 'economic' and 'political' approaches to the study of news-making. 'Political economy', meant to conjure up a nineteenth-century intellectual breadth in which the study of economics was not divorced from moral philosophy, in practice has been a term adopted by left-leaning scholars critical of neo-classical economics. They objected to the way conventional economics 'naturalizes' the market, as if market mechanisms exist in a pristine condition undirected or unstructured by political and legal decisions. This was an important step forward. However, the term 'political economy' in communication studies did not simply recognize that economic and political spheres are interrelated but smuggled in the Marxist theorem that economics is fundamental and political structures secondary. Analysis of media institutions – almost always analysis of capitalist media institutions – condemned media organizations for their profit orientation. The ways different political institutions structure media institutions and media markets differently rarely became a topic of interest. This is a profound weakness. Happily, it has been remedied in a fundamental way by the publication of Daniel Hallin and Paolo Mancini's *Comparing Media Systems* (2004) and, though there are other important and relevant works that also take political institutions seriously and examine how formative political choices structure the media (Starr, 2004), I shall borrow especially from Hallin and Mancini.

The second problem is more difficult. Earlier editions of this essay took it for granted that the analytical approaches it discusses together exhaust the factors that contribute to the production of news. This is an assumption I now reject. It is simply not true that social, cultural, political and economic factors separately or together can explain why news is the way it is. Social, cultural, economic and political forces do in fact structure news production. But they do not produce news out of nothing. They act on 'something' in the world. The 'something' they work on are events, happenings, occurrences in the world that impress journalists and their audiences with their importance or interest, their remarkable-ness, their noteworthiness. The forces of journalism act on these things but do not (necessarily) produce them. Journalism can and does produce noteworthy events – in press conferences, interviews and so forth. These are directly created by journalists or by other people acting with journalists in mind. Corporations, non-profit organizations, governments and social movements often act with the intention of making news, and so one might say that journalism indirectly manufactures events originating in these groups. But journalists do not create hurricanes or tornados, elections or murders. They do not create Christmas or rock concerts or the Olympics. They shape them, but they do not shape them just as they choose. Michelangelo created 'David', and there are political, economic, social and cultural factors that would help explain how he did so. But Michelangelo did not create the statue out of nothing. He made it out of marble. And even though he carefully selected which marble to use, he was in some measure the servant of that marble and its distinctive features. The marble's own properties placed limiting conditions on what the artist could do and so influenced in essential ways what the artist arrived at.

In the past, I joined nearly all other social scientists who study the news in speaking of how journalists 'construct the news', 'make news' or 'socially construct reality'. 'News is what newspapermen make it', according to one study (Gieber, 1964: 173). 'News is the result of the methods newsworkers employ', according to another (Fishman, 1980: 14). News is 'manufactured by journalists' (Cohen and Young, 1973: 97) in the words of a third.

In the most elementary way, this is obvious. Journalists write the words that turn up in the papers or on the screen as stories. Not government officials, not cultural forces, not 'reality' magically transforming itself into alphabetic signs, but flesh-and-blood journalists literally compose the stories we call news. Journalists make the news just as carpenters make houses and scientists make science.

This point of view does not make much headway with professional journalists. 'News and news programmes could almost be called random reactions to random events', a British reporter told sociologist Graham Murdock. 'Again and again, the main reason why they turn out as they do is accident – accident of a kind which recurs so haphazardly as to defeat statistical examination' (Murdock, 1973: 163). I now see that this journalist had a good point. Journalists confront the unexpected, the dramatic, the unprecedented, even the bizarre. In fact, they very likely confront more of this 'event-driven' news than they did a generation ago (Lawrence, 2000). This calls for social scientists to alter their almost exclusive preoccupation with 'institution-driven' news. Understanding how the institutions and practices of news-making interact with 'events' should be a leading challenge for the sociology of news.

The sociology of the production of news goes back at least to Max Weber (1921, 1946), who wrote of the social standing of the journalist as a political person; Robert Park (1922, 1923), an ex-journalist himself, who wrote about the US immigrant press and news itself as a form of knowledge; and Helen MacGill Hughes (1940), who wrote an early study of human interest stories. 'Gatekeeper' studies in the 1950s took the next step. Social psychologist Kurt Lewin coined the term 'gatekeeper' and several scholars (White, 1950;

Gieber, 1964) applied it to journalism. David Manning White studied a middle-aged wire editor at a small American newspaper. For one week, 'Mr Gates' (as White called him) made available to the researcher every piece of wire copy, both those he rejected and those he selected to print in the paper. He then wrote down a reason for rejecting the wire story he turned down. Some of these reasons were not very illuminating – 'not enough space'. Others were technical or professional – 'dull writing' or 'drags too much'. Still others were explicitly political – 'propaganda' or 'He's too Red'. These last greatly influenced White's conclusion that the personal prejudices and preferences of gatekeepers make the news, although Mr Gates' political views explained just 18 out of 423 of the news items he rejected.

If Mr Gates' judgements can be attributed to personal subjectivity, we should expect some variation among wire editors in a larger sample. Walter Gieber found otherwise in a study of 16 wire editors in Wisconsin. All the editors selected news items in the same way. They were not doing politics in selecting the news. They were doing a rote task. The typical editor was 'concerned with goals of production, bureaucratic routine and interpersonal relations within the newsroom' (Gieber, 1964: 175). Gieber's analysis is a refutation, not an extension, of White's.

The term 'gatekeeper' is still in use. It provides a handy metaphor for the relation of news organizations to news products. But, surprisingly, it leaves 'information' or 'news' sociologically untouched. Who gets to be a gatekeeper and why? Who writes the news items that reach the gatekeepers? Under what constraints and with what expectations? The gatekeeper metaphor tries to fix news-making at one point along a circuit of interactions and does not examine the circuit as a whole.

Then what approaches might work better? Four perspectives on news-making are commonly employed. The first two traditions relate the outcome of the news process to the structure of the economy and the state, respectively. The third approach comes primarily out of sociology, especially the study of social organization, occupations and professions, and the social construction of ideology. This perspective tries to understand how journalists' efforts on the job are constrained by organizational and occupational demands. Fourth, a 'cultural' approach emphasizes the constraining force of broad cultural traditions and symbolic systems, regardless of the structure of economic organization or the character of occupational routines.

The value of each of the four perspectives varies depending on what aspect of 'news' one wants to explain. Is it the conservative, system-maintaining character of news? Or is it the very opposite – the extent to which the press in liberal societies is adversarial or even nihilistic, system-attacking or system-denigrating, cynical about government or derisive of a society's core values? Analysts may want to understand the finer features of the news: Why does it focus on individuals rather than systems and structures? Why is news so heavily dependent on official sources? Why has there been a 'tabloidization' of news around the world in the past decades? Each of the perspectives that I will now review may be more useful with some of these questions than with others.

The economic organization of news

The link between the larger structures of state, market and society and day-to-day practices in journalism is, as Graham Murdock has observed, 'oblique' (Murdock, 1973: 158). Even the link between ownership of news organizations and news coverage, a topic of perennial interest, is not easy to determine – and it grows more difficult by the day as public and commercial systems of ownership mix and blend and interact (Nerone 1991). In some cases, patterns of ownership can be tied to specific habits of reporting. Curran *et al.* (1980) ask why elite and mass-oriented newspapers in Britain provide such different fare even though reader surveys find that different classes prefer to read similar materials. They explain that advertisers find value in papers that attract a small, concentrated elite audience; the expense of reaching an 'upscale' audience is lower if a large share of this audience can be addressed through a single publication without having to pay the expense of reaching thousands of extraneous readers.

In other cases, a link between ownership and market structure on the one hand and news content on the other is not apparent. In Europe, it is not clear that public and private broadcasters differ systematically in the ways they present political news and current affairs (Brants, 1998: 328). Despite the commercialization of news organizations in Europe in the past several decades, and a consequent shift toward more dramatic forms of news discourse, the total political content of news remains high and has in some instances even increased (Hallin and Mancini, 2004: 281). Research on the impact of chain ownership compared with independent ownership of American newspapers on news content has been inconclusive (Demers, 1996) or 'tepid' (Baker, 1994: 19). A recent assessment finds no consistent support for the belief that independent news outlets offer more diverse content than those run by corporate conglomerates or that locally owned media are better for diversity than national chains. 'Sometimes corporate media giants homogenize, and sometimes they do not. Sometimes they shut people up and stifle dissent, and sometimes they open up extra space for new people to be visible and vocal . . . because diversity sometimes serves their interests . . .' (Gamson and Latteier, 2004).

Some scholars write as if corporate ownership and commercial organizations necessarily compromise the democratic promise of public communication (McChesney, 1997), but the evidence is more nearly that the absence of commercial organizations, or their total domination by the state, is the worst case scenario. In Latin America, government officials benefited more from state-controlled media than did the public; for Latin American policy-makers in the recent wave of democratization, 'strong control, censorship, and manipulation of the mass media during authoritarian and democratic regimes have deeply discredited statist models' (Waisbord, 1995: 219). South Korean journalism is more free since political democratization began in 1987 than it was under the military regime of the early 1980s when 700 anti-regime journalists were dismissed, the Minister of Culture could cancel any publication's registration at will, security agencies kept the media under constant surveillance, and the Ministry of Culture routinely issued specific guidelines on how reporters should cover events (Lee, 1997). Still, in the new Korean media system, market considerations create new forms of internal censorship, old expectations of politicians – that they should receive favourable media treatment – persist, and cultural presuppositions of deference to a king-like president weaken the capacity of the media to exercise its putative liberties.

Not that market-dominated systems and state-dominated systems are always easy to distinguish. Yuzhei Zhao offers a detailed and persuasive account of the blending of commercial and state-controlled media in post-Tiananmen Square China (Zhao, 1998). After Tiananmen Square, the government tightened controls on the media, closed down three leading publications whose coverage it judged too sympathetic to the protesters, replaced editors at other newspapers and required all news organizations to engage in self criticism. The state continues to monitor political news, but pays less attention to coverage of economics, social and environmental issues. In all cases, self-censorship rather than heavy handed party control is the operating system (Polumbaum, 1997).

Despite the tightening of party control, a proliferation of sensational, entertainment-oriented tabloids has offered the established press serious competition for advertising revenues. Media outlets in the 'commercial' sector remain political organs, catering to the Party's propaganda needs but trying to 'establish a common ground between the Party and the people' through its choice of what topics to cover (Zhao, 1998: 161). The commercial media have grown rapidly while the circulation of the traditional Party organs has dropped. While Party control of the media remains powerful everywhere, even at Central China Television, the most influential station in the country, new news shows have tested the limits and sought to please the public as well as the Party leadership. The journalists are 'dancing with chains on' (Zhao, 1998: 121).

The new blends of state, independent and commercial news media, the mixed patterns of ownership and control, do not even have names, let alone theories to explain them. Zhao, for lack of any better term, describes the Chinese system as a 'propagandist/commercial model' of the media (p. 151). Nor is there any accounting in media theory for the degree and extent of corruption in Chinese journalism. News sources routinely pay for journalists' travel, hotel and meals when they report out-of-town events ('three-warranty reporting'), some journalists moonlight as public relations agents for businesses, and journalists and news organizations receive cash, negotiable securities, personal favours and gifts not only from business clients but even from government clients seeking favourable coverage (pp. 72–93). Journalists' salaries are low and 'few . . . can resist the temptation offered by one paid news report that can bring in a red envelope with as much as a whole month's salary, not to mention an advertising deal worth years of salary' (p. 87). There are not only a variety of political and economic structures of news production, but each gives rise to its own characteristic evasions, collusions and corruptions.

Fewer and fewer corporations control more and more of the American news media (Bagdikian, 1997). Major media conglomerates control more and more of the world's media. Where media are not controlled by corporations, they are generally voices of the state. Under these circumstances it would be a shock to find the press a hotbed of radical thought. But, then, critical or radical thought in any society at any time is exceptional. In all political and economic systems, news 'coincides with' and 'reinforces' the 'definition of the political situation evolved by the political elite' (Murdock, 1973: 172). This basic intuition has long seemed incontestable. However, in the perennial debates about whether the news media in liberal democratic societies are 'lap-dogs' of power or 'watch-dogs' for the public, there is growing reason to seek out a new model or metaphor since the media so obviously serve both roles. The best proposal may be that of Susan Pharr in a paper on the Japanese media. Pharr argues that the news media have taken on the role of 'trickster' once played by jesters, diviners and minstrels, the insider–outsider whose independence makes its relationship to state and society so complex and ambivalent. The trickster is by no means simply a megaphone for ruling elites, but neither is it an unbridled critic of power. The trickster is 'as likely to tweak as to condemn' and often does both at once. While the media tricksters do not simply reproduce existing power, their overall effect as critics is 'to disperse, dissipate, or fragment any effort on the part of the audience to agree on a systematic critique of the established order or to forge an alternative construction of reality that calls for profound political and social change' (Pharr, 1996: 35). They reveal tensions, they evaluate critically, they horrify by attending to the grotesque and obscene, and they help build social bonds by placing common fare for reflection before society as a whole. This is a complex image but it may offer opportunities for improving studies of the media that simpler models have not provided.

A rigid view that sees the media working hand-in-glove with other large corporations to stifle dissent or promote a lethargic public acceptance of the existing distribution of power (Herman and Chomsky, 1988) is entirely inconsistent with what most journalists in democratic societies commonly believe they are doing. It also fails to explain a great deal of news content, especially news critical of corporate power (Dreier, 1982) or news of corporate scandals, conflicts, illegalities and failures.

One might prefer a more flexible theoretical stance – that the media reinforce the 'cultural hegemony' of dominant groups; that is, that they make the existing distribution of power and rewards seem to follow from nature or common sense and so succeed in making oppositional views appear unreasonable, quixotic or utopian – perhaps even to the dissenters themselves. But 'hegemony' also explains too much. It offers no account of how progressive social change happens when it does, despite 'hegemonic' media. The concept of 'hegemony' requires more subtle deployment if it is to be used at all. The ability of a capitalist class to manipulate opinion and create a closed system of discourse is limited; ideology in contemporary capitalism is contested terrain. The ability of a socialist bureaucracy to create closure has faced few legal or political impediments. The question to ask is: What role does the media play in the midst of or in relationship to social change? The behaviour of the American press in questioning the Vietnam war may have emerged precisely because the political elite did not know its own mind. It was deeply divided. Even then, the press seems largely to have gone about its normal business of citing official leaders – but at a time when officials were at odds with one another (Hallin, 1986). The result was that the media did not reinforce existing power but amplified elite disagreements in unsettling and unpredictable ways.

A strictly economic explanation of news is very appealing to journalists themselves. In fact, it is in many respects as obvious to working journalists as to critical scholars that 'MBAs rule the newsroom', to borrow the title of a popular work (Underwood, 1995), that pleasing Wall Street investors rather than serving conscience is increasingly the task of publishers, that editors more than ever are seeking news that will sell, and that nothing is so corrupting of journalism as the hegemony of the dollar (Downie and Kaiser, 2002; Sumpter, 2000). Recent work on American television and print news by James Hamilton uses quantitative data imaginatively to argue that trends toward 'soft news' content are a direct result of news organizations' efforts to reach certain elusive demographic groups (particularly women aged 18 to 34). TV news counts men and women over 50 as regular viewers, but younger women, whose purchasing decisions are of special interest to advertisers, are only occasional viewers. News producers thus make extra efforts to attract their attention, and that means either reducing the emphasis on politics altogether or focusing on political issues (gun control and education, for example) likely to draw them in (Hamilton 2004: 189).

Financial considerations are normally decisive in news organizations' adoption of new technologies. But there has been little academic attention to the concrete consequences of the technological transformation of news production, both in print and in television. Beginning in the 1970s, newspapers saw the introduction of personal computers, pagination (the electronic assembly of pages), online and database research, remote transmission and delivery, digital photo transmission and storage. The technologies are generally introduced to reduce labour costs and to provide the technical capability to make the newspaper more 'user-friendly', with more interesting and attractive page design. What influence does this technological change have on the news product? Anthony Smith (1980) was probably the first to draw comprehensive attention to the issue, but his work has not been followed up with the same analytic skill. We know that new technologies have moved elements of newspaper production from the 'backshop' to the newsroom, increased the amount of time editors spend on page make-up, and improved spelling. Some observers suggest that the ability of foreign correspondents to send copy home by satellite has led to more and shorter stories on timely events rather than fewer, longer, more analytic, and less time-bound work (Weaver and Wilhoit, 1991: 158–9). In a study of CNN international news from 1994 to 2001, Livingston and Bennett (2003) find that new technologies such as the videophone and other mobile, convenient, hand-held equipment for live reporting from remote locations, have increased the amount of event-driven rather than institution-initiated news. They conclude that this has produced less change in the news than one might imagine since official voices are still generally inserted into these stories and still dominate CNN reporting. Still, this is a lively arena for new research.

Scholars, critics and journalists have often viewed recent technological and market changes with alarm. The anecdotal evidence here is sobering, but the baseline of comparison is feebly depicted. The worst incidences of contemporary journalism get compared with the remembered best of another era; there is a need for more careful comparison and more broadly conceived research frameworks.

The political context of news-making

Both states and corporations that own news organizations limit free expression, but this does not make the comprehensiveness and severity of their means, the coherence of their motives, or the consequences of their controls the same. Public criticism of state policy is invariably easier in liberal societies with privately owned news outlets than in authoritarian societies with state or private ownership. In China, published criticism of the state has been tightly constrained; newspapers, it is said in China, 'swat flies but don't beat tigers'. (Polumbaum, 1994: 258).

Economic perspectives in Anglo-American media studies have generally taken liberal democracy for granted and so have been insensitive to political and legal determinants of news production. Increasingly, economic determinism has been recognized as a serious deficiency. In the 1980s in Europe, in the face of a threat to public broadcasting from conservative governments sympathetic to commercialization, scholars came increasingly to see in public broadcasting a pillar of a free public life (Garnham, 1990: 104–14). Increasingly, there have been efforts to articulate a view of 'civil society' where the media hold a vital place and attain a degree of autonomy from both state and market – as in the best public service broadcasting (Keane, 1991).

This correctly suggests that, within market societies, there are various institutional forms and constitutional regimes for the press. Rosario de Mateo's (1989) sketch of the newspaper industry in Spain during the Franco regime, the transition to democracy, and the full restoration of democracy makes it clear that private, profit-making newspapers put ideological purity as their first priority under Franco. After Franco, however, the same private, profit-making press has emphasized profits first while providing more opportunity for freedom of expression. Where state-operated media in authoritarian political systems serve directly as agents of state social control, both public and privately owned media in liberal societies carry out a wider variety of roles, cheer-leading the established order, alarming the citizenry about flaws in that order, providing a civic forum for political debate and acting as a battleground among contesting elites. Pnina Lahav and her colleagues have usefully surveyed press law in seven democratic societies. Lahav concludes that Sweden and the USA protect free expression better than the UK, France and the Federal Republic of Germany with 'a more elitist attitude toward the press' (Lahav, 1985: 4).

The distinction between 'market' and 'state' organization of media, or between commercial and public forms of broadcasting, masks important differences within each category. Public broadcasting may be a quasi-independent corporation or be directly run by the government, its income may come from fees only (Japan, Britain and Sweden), or also from advertising (Germany, France, Italy), or from the government treasury (Canada). In Britain, Cabinet ministries determine fee levels while in Japan, France and Germany, parliament makes the decision (Krauss, 2000). Each of these variations creates (and results from) a distinct politics of the media. In Norway, since 1969, and in Sweden, France and Austria since the 1970s, the state has subsidized newspapers directly, especially to strengthen newspapers offering substantial political information but receiving low advertising revenues. These policies have sought to stop the decline in the number of newspapers and so to increase public access to a diversity of political viewpoints. The size of the subsidies has fallen off in recent years as governments have come to place more faith in market principles and the virtues of economic efficiency (Murschetz, 1998; Skogerbo, 1997).

From time to time there is serious ideological contestation in liberal democracies. Just how it takes place differs depending on the political institutions that govern the press. Hallin and Mancini (2004) distinguish broadly among three media systems in the 18 European and North American democracies they examined. The Mediterranean or southern European media system has relatively low newspaper penetration; that is, the print media have been largely oriented to elites, they tend to emphasize advocacy or highly politicized rather than neutral and professional styles of journalism, they have strong formal and informal links to political parties, and their commercial organization and drive is generally weak. Hallin and Mancini trace this pattern to political systems of high ideological diversity, strong and often authoritarian states, and a weak or delayed development of liberal institutions and rational–legal authority.

In contrast, northern and central European democracies typically have a 'democratic corporatist' system, characterized by high newspaper penetration, a quasi autonomous profession of journalism more differentiated from political careers and political parties than in southern Europe, a moderately developed commercialism, and, especially in northern Europe, relatively high levels of state regulation of private media. However, where state regulation in southern Europe has periodically meant state censorship, regulation in northern Europe has typically been state subsidies on behalf of press freedom or in pursuit of increasing ideological diversity in the press.

Finally, there is the North Atlantic or liberal model, to be found in its extreme form in the USA and in more moderate form in Britain and Canada. Newspaper penetration is intermediate here between the highs of northern Europe and the lows of southern Europe, professional autonomy is high and jealously guarded, the favoured journalistic model centred on providing information rather than providing commentary or advocacy, although the British model welcomes commentary more than the American. Commercialism is highly developed and powerful, and there is a greater divorce between the media and political parties than in the other systems. The role of the state is more limited in the liberal model than in the other models; even where public broadcasting is powerful, as in Britain, it is relatively well insulated from political control by the state.

Hallin and Mancini (2004) do not presume that any one of these models is the one to which the others are tending or, in the best of all possible worlds, should be tending. They deny that the liberal model is an end-point that the other systems will eventually approximate. Their underlying claim is that political democracy in the West over a century or more has developed a variety of relatively stable, relatively enduring systems for integrating the media and politics. Theirs is a plea to recognize that democracy is not one system but a set of differentiated forms. There are, to be sure, signs of the spread of the liberal model in the recent past. In northern Europe, for example, the close ties of newspapers and parties has declined sharply. In Denmark in 1960, only 14 of 88 newspapers were independent of political parties; by 2000, it was 24 of 33 (Hallin and Mancini, 2004: 179). Finnish newspapers with political affiliation controlled 70 per cent of the market in 1950, but only 15 per cent by 1995 (p. 252). Systems dominated by public broadcasting have become mixed systems with commercial broadcasting making major inroads. The impact of the American model elsewhere in the world has been large, both in the intensity of its commercialism and in the influence of its institutions for journalism education, promoting an information-centred, autonomous professionalism. Even so, Hallin and Mancini argue that a number of factors, including notably the persistence of important differences in the political and legal systems of the European democracies, will keep the diversity of media/political models from collapsing into variations of the liberal model.

All of this concerns journalism in societies with strong and relatively stable states; the problems of journalism in societies with weak states are of a different order. In Colombia, 133 journalists were murdered between 1978 and 1997. Where states are weak or disintegrating, and where journalists nonetheless dare to report on paramilitary organizations, drug cartels or government corruption, reporters and their news organizations become the targets of harassment, threat and assassination (Waisbord, 2002).

The social organization of newswork

In an influential essay, Harvey Molotch and Marilyn Lester (1974) created a typology of news stories according to whether the news 'occurrence' is planned or unplanned and, if planned, whether its planners are or are not also promoting it as news. If an event is planned and then promoted as news by its planners, this is a 'routine' news item. If the event is planned by one person or organization but promoted as news by someone else, it is a 'scandal'. If the event is unplanned, it becomes news as an 'accident'.

For Molotch and Lester, it is a mistake to try to compare news accounts with 'reality' in the way journalism critics ordinarily do, labelling the discrepancy as 'bias'. Instead, they reject the assumption that there is a real world to be objective about. For them, the news media reflect not a world 'out there' but 'the practices of those who have the power to determine the experience of others' (p. 54).

In 1974 this strong conviction of the subordination of knowledge to power announced a liberating insight. Thirty years later, it looks overstated, failing to recognize that one of the constraints within which journalists operate is the need to write 'accurately' about actual – objectively real – occurrences in the world, whoever planned them and however they came to the media's notice. The reality-constructing practices of the powerful will fail (in the long run) if they run roughshod over the world 'out there'. If the hypotheses of Livingston and Bennett (2003) and Lawrence (2000) are correct, then it is increasingly true that event-driven news is important and that it can displace even the most carefully orchestrated institution-driven grabs for media attention (Schudson, 2003).

Still, an emphasis on the social organization of journalism and on the interaction of journalists and their sources has reinforced economic and political perspectives that take news-making to be a reality-constructing activity governed by elites. Emphasizing the power of government officials to direct the attention of journalists, Mark Fishman's study at a middle-sized California newspaper found that journalists are highly attuned to bureaucratic organizations of government and that '*the world is bureaucratically organized for journalists*' (Fishman, 1980: 51). One of the great advantages of dealing with bureaucracies for the journalist is that the bureaucracies 'provide for the continuous detection of events' (p. 52). The government bureaucrat provides a reliable and steady supply of the raw materials for news production.

One study after another agrees that the centre of news generation is the link between reporter and official, the interaction of the representatives of news bureaucracies and government bureaucracies (Bennett, 1994: 23–29; Cohen, 1963: 267; Gans, 1979: 116; Schlesinger and Tumber, 1994). 'The only important tool of the reporter is his news sources and how he uses them', a reporter covering state government in the USA told Delmer Dunne (1969: 41). Stephen Hess confirms this in his study of Washington correspondents. He found reporters 'use no documents in the preparation of nearly three-quarters of their stories' (Hess, 1981: 17–18). Hess does not count press releases as documents – these are, of course, another means of communication directly from official to reporter. It is clear that the reporter–official connection makes news an important tool of government and other established authorities. Some studies, accordingly, examine news production from the viewpoint of the news source rather than the news organization (Cook 1989) or focus on the links between reporters and their sources in 'source–media analysis' (Schlesinger and Tumber, 1994: 28).

A corollary to the power of the government source or other well legitimated sources is that 'resource-poor organizations' have great difficulty in getting the media's attention (Goldenberg, 1975). If they are to be covered, as Todd Gitlin's study of American anti-war activities in the 1960s indicated, they must adjust to modes of organizational interaction more like those of established organizations (Gitlin, 1980).

Reporter–source studies have implications for evaluating the power of media institutions as such. Media power looms especially large if the portrait of the world the media present to audiences stems from the preferences and perceptions of publishers, editors and reporters unconstrained by democratic controls. However, if the media typically mirror the views and voices of established (and democratically selected) government officials, then the media are more nearly the neutral servants of a democratic order. To note a recent instance, policy experts blamed graphic scenes of starving people shown on American television news for what they judged a hasty and unwise military intervention in Somalia in 1992. But the networks picked up the Somalia story only after seven senators, a House committee, the full House, the full Senate, a presidential candidate and the White House all publicly raised the issue. When the media finally got to it, they framed it very much as Washington's political elites had framed it for them (Livingston and Eachus, 1996; Mermin, 1997). This does not mean the TV stories made no difference; clearly they rallied public interest and public support for intervention. But where did the TV story come from? From established, official sources.

The consistent finding that official sources dominate the news is invariably presented as a criticism of the media. If the media were to fulfil their democratic role, they would offer a wide variety of opinions and perspectives to encourage citizens to choose among them in evaluating public policies. But there is an alternative view also consistent with democratic theory. What if the best to hope for in a mass democracy is that people evaluate leaders, not policies? What if asking the press to offer enough information, history and context for attentive citizens to make wise decisions on policies before politicians act is asking the impossible? It may be a more plausible task for the media, consistent with representative democracy, that citizens assess leaders after they have acted (Zaller, 1994: 201–2).

Despite the academic consensus that official opinion dominates in the news, several studies suggest that this conclusion has been overdrawn. An instructive study of the *New York Times'* coverage of the US–Libya crisis of 1985–86 finds that the news diverged from mirroring official US government opinion in two respects. News overemphasized Congressional views that challenged the administration's position – a journalistic attraction to finding conflict and representing alternative views gave critics of the administration more weight in the pages of the newspaper than independent measures suggested they actually held in the Congress. Moreover, there was much more citing of foreign sources, many of them critical of the US position, than the researchers expected, and they concluded that in a 'decentered, destabilized international political system' this is likely to endure (Althaus *et al.*, 1996: 418).

Second, Regina Lawrence's account of how the news media cover police brutality finds that more voices – and more critical voices – enter into the construction of news stories when the stories originate in events rather than institutions. As she writes, 'Event-driven discourse about public issues is often more variable and dynamic than institutionally driven news, ranging beyond established news beats and drawing on a wider variety of voices and perspectives' (Lawrence, 2000: 9). Although she acknowledges that institutionally driven problem construction remains predominant, she sees a trend toward event-driven news. The latter has problems of its own – it is often 'sensationalized, hyperbolic, and overheated'. Even so, it can often be the mechanism (as in a number of prominent cases of police brutality) whereby public officials and public institutions are scrutinized and held accountable (p. 187). The continued and ever-growing competition in news coverage, concentration of ownership notwithstanding, the growing accessibility of sensational news through video and photography, from the Rodney King beating in Los Angeles in 1991 to the photos of American prison guard brutality at Abu Ghraib prison in Iraq in 2004, contribute to the plausibility of Lawrence's hypothesis that event-driven discourse is growing; as it does, the 'officials dominate the news' mantra must be qualified.

There has been more attention to reporter–official relations than to reporter–editor relations, a second critical aspect of the social organization of newswork. Despite some suggestive early work on the ways in which reporters engage in self-censorship when they have an eye fixed on pleasing an editor (Breed, 1955: 80), systematic sociological research has not been especially successful in this domain. Certainly case studies of newswork regularly note the effects – usually baleful – of editorial intervention (Crouse, 1973: 186; Gitlin, 1980: 64–5; Hallin, 1986: 22). Mortensen and Svendsen (1980) pay explicit attention to various forms of self-censorship in Danish newspapers. Generally, however, studies do not look at the social relations of newswork from the editor's desk. Sumpter (2000) offers a useful review of literature on the editors' role in constructing news, suggesting, as newspaper audiences shrink, editorial decisions are increasingly guided by anxiety to please the audience.

Most research, then, has focused on the gathering of news rather than on its writing, rewriting and 'play' in the press. This is unfortunate when research suggests that it is in the *play* of a story that real influence comes. Hallin (1986), Herman and Chomsky (1988) and Lipstadt (1986) all argue that in the press of a liberal society such as the USA lots of news, including dissenting or adversarial information and opinion, gets into the newspaper. The question is *where* that information appears and how it is inflected. Hallin suggests there was a 'reverse inverted pyramid' of news in much reporting of the Vietnam war. The nearer the information was to the truth, the farther down in the story it appeared (p. 78).

If more work develops on the relations of reporters and editors inside the newsroom, it can learn much from the comparative studies initiated by Wolfgang Donsbach and Thomas Patterson and reported by Donsbach (1995) and further developed in a careful British–German comparison by Esser (1998). Where there are many job designations in a British newsroom, all personnel in a German newsroom are *Redakteurs*, editors or desk workers, who combine the tasks of reporting, copy-editing, editorial or leader writing and commentary. Where editors read and edit the work of reporters in a British or American newspaper, what a *Redakteur* writes goes into print without anyone's exercising supervision.

Different historical traditions have led to different divisions of labour and different understandings of the possibility and desirability of separating facts from commentary.

Who are the journalists in news organizations who cover beats, interview sources, rewrite press releases from governments, business and occasionally take the initiative in ferreting out hidden or complex stories? If organizational theorists are correct, it does not matter. Whoever they are, they will be socialized quickly into the values and routines of daily journalism and will modify their own personal values 'in accordance with the requisites of the organization' (Epstein, 1973: xiv). A cross-national survey implicitly supports this view: despite different national cultures, despite different patterns of professional education, and despite different labour patterns of journalists (some in strong professional associations or unions, some not), the stated professional values of the journalists do not differ greatly (Sparks and Splichal, 1989). Surveys in Germany likewise find relatively modest differences in journalists' occupational norms between those trained in the West and those who entered the field through the state and party-run schools and media organizations of the former German Democratic Republic (East Germany) (Hagen, 1997: 14).

It is best to be cautious about this survey data. Twice as many East Germans as West Germans (25 per cent to 11 per cent) say a journalist should be a 'politician using alternative means' (Hagen, 1997: 14). Even when journalists uphold the same nominal values, they may do so for different reasons. In communist Poland, journalists were strongly attached to professionalism, not out of occupational autonomy but as a refuge from 'the unpleasant push and pull of political forces' (Curry, 1990: 207). Professionalism protected the Polish journalist from manipulation by the Communist Party, government bureaucrats and the sponsoring organization of each newspaper. Even so, it has proved difficult for journalists in Eastern Europe to shed a sense of journalism as a form of political advocacy (Jakubowicz, 1995: 136–7). We may simply not comprehend the discrepancy between 'professional values' revealed in surveys and actual journalistic practice (De Smaele, 1999: 180).

Whether there is a convergence of journalistic practices and precepts is an important question. There are signs of a shared professional culture, promoted by what has been called 'the global newsroom' (Gurevitch *et al.*, 1991). Political journalists from different countries (Italy, the Soviet Union, the USA) covering the same international event all adopted common themes and a common orientation to addressing 'humanity' rather than particular national audiences (Hallin and Mancini, 1991). Convergence may increase as Western public agencies, private corporations, and non-profit organizations promote a liberal model of market-based journalism in Eastern Europe and the former Soviet Union (Mickiewicz, 1998). Convergence of a different sort exists among foreign correspondents from countries who congregate in the same capital cities and, in the past two decades, in a set of African cities from which they can get quickly to the latest African crisis point where their stories regularly affirm an 'Afro-pessimism' (Hannerz, 2004: 129).

Journalists at mainstream publications everywhere accommodate to the political culture of the regime in which they operate. Still, the ideals of journalistic professionalism may incline journalists toward acting to support freedom of expression. In China, some journalists have developed a professional devotion to freedom of expression and have been a pressure group for the liberalization of press laws (Polumbaum, 1993; Zhao, 1998). In Brazil under military rule in the 1960s and 1970s, reporters grew adept at sabotaging the government's efforts at censorship (Dassin, 1982: 173–6).

Some American scholars have insisted that professional values are no bulwark against a bias in news that emerges from the social backgrounds and personal values of media personnel. Lichter *et al.* (1986) made the case that news in the USA has a liberal 'bias' because journalists at elite news organizations are themselves liberal. Their survey of these journalists finds that many describe themselves as liberals and tend to vote Democrat, although their liberalism was much more pronounced on social than on economic issues.

The Lichter *et al.* approach has been criticized for failing to show that the news product reflects the personal views of journalists rather than the views of the officials whose positions they are reporting (Gans, 1985). American journalists, more than their counterparts in Germany, are committed to their ideology of dispassion, their sense of professionalism, their allegiance to fairness or objectivity (Donsbach, 1995). They have a professional commitment to shielding their work from their personal political leanings. Moreover, their political leanings tend to be weak. Several close observers find leading American journalists not so much liberal or conservative as apolitical (Gans, 1979: 184; Hess, 1981: 115). Still, the liberalism of the US elite media on social issues such as abortion and gay and lesbian rights seems clear, at least; the *New York Times'* ombudsman agrees on this point with his newspaper's conservative critics (Okrent, 2004). The source of that liberalism, however, if Hamilton (2004) is right, may be less the views of the journalists than the efforts of the news organization managers to appeal to certain demographic groups (younger women) whose views on these topics tend to be liberal.

Critics and activists who advocate the hiring of more women and minorities in the newsroom share the intuition of Rothman and the Lichters (1986) that the personal values journalists bring to their jobs will colour the news they produce. While this has been an especially hot issue in the USA, there are comparable concerns about the unrepresentativeness of newsrooms elsewhere, as in Robin Jeffrey's documentation of the absence of Dalits (untouchables) in Indian news organizations (Jeffrey, 2001). New hiring practice to develop a newsroom more representative of the population by gender and ethnicity should thus transform the news product itself. News should become more oriented to groups often subordinated or victimized in society. Some anecdotal evidence (Mills, 1990) suggests that a changing gender composition of the newsroom does influence news content, but other reports from both the USA and Israel suggest that definitions of news have not dramatically changed (Beasley, 1993: 129–30; Lavie and Lehman-Wilzig, 2003). In the USA there has probably been more concern that the growing affluence of national journalists, who report by fax and phone and access data bases from their computers, will separate journalists from direct contact with the poor or others who live in places unpleasant to visit than there has been hope that more minorities and women in the newsroom will make the press more responsive to a broader constituency.

Social constraints on newswork come not only from the news organizations that reporters work for directly, but from patterns of news-gathering that bring reporters from different publications under the influence of one another. In the USA there is criticism of 'pack journalism', where reporters covering the same beat or same story tend to emphasize the same angle and to adopt the same viewpoint. In Japan, a kind of bureaucratized 'pack journalism' has become entrenched. 'Reporters' clubs' are organizations of reporters assigned to a particular ministry, and most basic news comes from reporters in these clubs. Since most clubs are connected to government agencies, news takes on an official cast. The daily association of reporters at the clubs contributes to a uniformity in the news pages, reporters are driven by what is described as a 'phobia' about not writing what all the other reporters write (Feldman, 1993: 98, 120–3; Freeman, 2000; Krauss, 2000).

A social organizational perspective insists that news is not a report on a factual world but 'a depletable consumer product that must be made fresh daily' (Tuchman, 1978: 179). It is not a gathering of facts that already exist; indeed, as Tuchman has argued, facts are defined organizationally – facts are 'pertinent information gathered by professionally validated methods specifying the relationship between what is known and how it is known . . . In news, verification of facts is both a political and a professional accomplishment' (pp. 82–3). Yes, but. Yes, events in the world do not magically transform themselves into news; but the process of news production takes place not in a vacuum-packed world containing only journalists and government officials but in a permeable world where journalists respond to occurrences that neither they nor their sources control or anticipate.

Little has been said here about the differences between print and television news. There is much to say, of course, but in terms of the basic news-gathering tasks, less than meets the eye. Most television news stories come from print sources, especially the wire services (Krauss, 2000). Despite the global prominence of CNN, it has far fewer correspondents and bureaus outside the USA than the leading global wire services – Agence France-Presse, Associated Press and Reuters (Moisy, 1996). News outlets, television as much as print, rely overwhelmingly on these services.

American evidence suggests that, at least for national news, print and television journalists share a great deal in their professional values. Separate studies of how print and TV journalists use experts, for instance, reveal that in foreign policy coverage, both prefer former government officials to other kinds of experts (Hallin et al., 1993; Steele, 1995). What Janet Steele calls the 'operational bias' in TV news – selecting for experts who personally know the key players, who have strong views on a limited range of policy alternatives, and who will make short-term predictions – are also characteristics print journalists seek. Even the television preference for experts who can turn a good phrase is one that print journalists share.

Cultural approaches

In social-organizational approaches, the fact that news is 'constructed' suggests that it is *socially* constructed, elaborated in the interaction of the news-making players with one another. But the emphasis on the human construction of news can be taken in another direction. Anthropologist Marshall Sahlins has written in a different context that 'an event is not just a happening in the world; it is a *relation* between a certain happening and a given symbolic system' (Sahlins, 1985: 153). Social-organizational approaches do not focus on the cultural givens within which everyday interaction happens in the first place. These cultural givens, while they may be uncovered by detailed historical analysis, cannot be extrapolated from features of social organization at the moment of study. They are a part of culture – a given symbolic system, within which and in relation to which reporters and officials go about their duties.

Most understandings of the generation of news merge a 'cultural' view with the social-organizational view. It is, however, analytically distinct. Where the social organizational view finds interactional determinants of news in the relations between people, the cultural view finds symbolic determinants of news in the relations between 'facts' and symbols. A cultural account of news helps explain generalized images and stereotypes in the news media – of predatory stockbrokers just as much as hard-drinking factory workers – that transcend structures of ownership or patterns of work relations. Foreign correspondents, whether American, Swedish, British or Japanese, tend to pick up and reproduce conventional story lines in their reporting: '. . . in Jerusalem reporting, conflicts between Arabs and Israelis and between the secular and the Orthodox; from Tokyo, stories of difference, even weirdness; from Johannesburg, apartheid and its undoing and, on a larger African stage, perhaps tribalism, chaos, despots, and victims' (Hannerz, 2004: 143). British mass media coverage of racial conflict has drawn on elements of the British cultural tradition 'derogatory to foreigners, particularly blacks. The media operate within the culture and are obliged to use cultural symbols' (Hartmann and Husband, 1973: 274). Frank Pearce, in examining media coverage of homosexuals in Britain (1973), takes as a theoretical starting point anthropologist Mary Douglas's view that all societies like to keep their cultural concepts clean and neat and are troubled by 'anomalies' that do not fit the pre-conceived categories of the culture. Homosexuality is an anomaly in societies that take as fundamental the opposition and relationship of male and female; thus homosexuals provide a culturally charged topic for story-telling that reaffirms the conventional moral order of society and its symbolic foundation. News stories about homosexuals may be 'an occasion to reinforce conventional moral values by telling a moral tale' (Douglas, 1973: 293).

A cultural account of this sort can explain too much; after all, news coverage of homosexuality has changed enormously, a universal cultural anxiety about anomalous categories notwithstanding. A 1996 study of US news coverage concludes that gays and lesbians appear much more in the news than 50 years ago, are covered much more 'routinely' as ordinary news subjects rather than moral tales (Alwood, 1996: 315).

Similarly, broad cultural explanations of the prevalence and character of crime news (Katz, 1987) must also be evaluated with some caution. While it makes sense that broad and long-lasting phenomena – such as heavy news coverage of crime over two centuries across many societies – will have deep cultural roots, it is also important to recognize fashions, trends and changes in crime coverage. Joel Best (1999) explains that some newly-defined crimes receive only occasional or episodic press coverage and others, with better institutionalized support in a 'victim industry', receive more systematic and ongoing treatment. General cultural and specific social-organizational dimensions of news interact.

Journalists may resonate to the same cultural moods their audiences share even if they typically know little about their audiences. Herbert Gans found that the reporters and editors he studied at US news weeklies and network television programmes 'had little knowledge about the actual audience and rejected feedback from it'. They typically assumed that 'what interested them would interest the audience' (Gans, 1979: 230). But journalists, like other writers, address an 'implied audience' and it would be instructive to know more about how this image of the reader is constructed in the journalists' minds.

A cultural account of news is also relevant to understanding journalists' vague renderings of how they know 'news' when they see it. The central categories of newsworkers themselves are 'cultural' more than structural. Stuart Hall has observed that the 'news values' or 'news sense' that journalists regularly talk about 'are one of the most opaque structures of meaning in modern society. All "true journalists" are supposed to possess it: few can or are willing to identify and define it . . . We appear to be dealing, then, with a "deep structure" whose function as a selective device is un-transparent even to those who professionally most know how to operate it' (Hall, 1973: 181). Gaye Tuchman's observation on American journalists parallels Hall's on the British when she writes that 'news judgment is the sacred knowledge, the secret ability of the newsman which differentiates him from other people' (Tuchman, 1972: 672).

Getting an analytical grip on this sacred knowledge is difficult. The cultural knowledge that constitutes 'news judgement' is too complex and too implicit to label simply 'ideology' or the 'common sense' of a hegemonic system. News judgement is not so unified, intentional and functional a system as these terms suggest. Its presuppositions are in some respects rooted much more deeply in human consciousness and can be found much more widely distributed in human societies than capitalism or socialism or industrialism or any other particular system of social organization and domination can comprehend. Patriarchal and sexist outlooks, for instance, may well be turned to the service of capitalism, but this does not make them capitalist in origin nor does it mean that they fit capitalist structures especially well.

A specific example may illustrate the many dimensions of this problem. Why, Galtung and Ruge (1970) ask, are news stories so often 'personified'? Why do reporters write of persons and not structures, of individuals and not social forces? They cite a number of possible explanations, some of which are 'cultural'. There is cultural idealism – the Western view that individuals are masters of their own destiny responsible for their acts through the free will they exercise. There is the nature of story-telling itself, with the need in narrative to establish 'identification'. There is also what they call the 'frequency-factor' – that people act during a time-span that fits the frequency of the news media (daily) better than do the actions of 'structures' that are much harder to connect with specific events in a 24-hour cycle.

Is this last point a 'social structural' or a 'cultural' phenomenon? In some respects it is structural; if the media operated monthly or annually rather than daily, perhaps they would speak more often of social forces than of individuals. Indeed, examining journalism's 'year-end reviews' would very likely turn up more attention to social trends and structural changes than can be found in the daily news. But, then, is the fact that the press normally operates on a daily basis structural or cultural? Is there some basic primacy to the daily cycle of the press, of business, of government, of sleeping and waking, that makes the institutions of journalism inescapably human and person-centred in scale?

Or might there be some more or less universal processes of human perception that lead to an emphasis on the individual? Does this have less to do with something peculiarly American or Western or capitalistic than it does with what psychologists refer to as the 'fundamental attribution error' in human causal thinking – attributing to individuals in the foreground responsibility or agency for causation that might better be attributed to background situations or large-scale trends or structures? That news definitions and news values differ across cultures can be demonstrated by comparative research. For instance, the Soviet media, like Western media, operated on a daily cycle, but very little of the news treated happenings in the prior 24 hours (Mickiewicz, 1988: 30). Soviet news organizations operated according to long-range political plans and stockpiled stories and editorial to meet political needs (Remington, 1988: 116). The sense of immediacy taken by Western media to be a requirement of news (and often taken by critics to be an ideologically loaded weakness of journalism) is not, the Soviet case would suggest, an invariant feature of bureaucratic organization, occupational routines or a universal diurnal human rhythm. It is rooted instead in a nation-specific political culture.

So one need not adopt assumptions about universal properties of human nature and human interest (although it would be foolish to dismiss them out of hand) to acknowledge that there are aspects of news-generation that go beyond what sociological analysis of news organizations is normally prepared to handle. Richard Hoggart has written that the most important filter through which news is constructed is 'the cultural air we breathe, the whole ideological atmosphere of our society, which tells us that some things can be said and that others had best not be said' (Bennett, 1982: 303). That 'cultural air' is one that in part ruling groups and institutions create but it is in part one in whose social context their own establishment takes place.

The cultural air has both a form and content. The content, the substance of taken-for-granted values, has often been discussed. Many studies, in a number of countries, have noted that violent crimes are greatly over-reported in relation to their actual incidence (Katz, 1987: 57–8). Over-reporting takes place not only in the popular press but (to a lesser degree) in the mid-market and quality press, too (Schlesinger and Tumber, 1994: 185). Gans (1979) describes the core values of American journalism as ethnocentrism (surely a core value in journalism around the world although more pronounced in the USA than in many places), altruistic democracy, responsible capitalism, small-town pastoralism, individualism and moderatism. These are the unquestioned and generally unnoticed background assumptions through which news in the USA is gathered and within which it is framed.

If elements of content fit conventional notions of ideology (Gans calls them 'para-ideology'), aspects of form operate at a more subtle level. Assumptions about narrative, story-telling, human interest and the conventions of photographic and linguistic presentation influence news production. Weaver (1975) has shown some systematic differences between the inverted-pyramid structure of print news and the 'thematic' structure of television news; Schudson (1982) has argued that the inverted-pyramid form is a peculiar development of late nineteenth-century American journalism and one that implicitly authorized the journalist as political expert and helped redefine politics itself as a subject appropriately discussed by experts rather than partisans; Hallin and Mancini (1984) demonstrate in a comparison of television news in Italy and the USA that formal conventions of news reporting often attributed to the technology of television by analysts or to 'the nature of things' by journalists in fact stem from features of a country's political culture. All of this work recognizes that news is a form of literature and that among the resources journalists work with are the traditions of story-telling, picture-making, and sentence construction they inherit from their own cultures, with a number of vital assumptions about the world built in.

Reporters breathe a specifically journalistic, occupational cultural air as well as the air they share with fellow citizens. The 'newsroom' of journalism are not only social, emerging out of interactions among officials, reporters and editors, but literary, emerging out of interactions of writers with literary traditions. More than that, journalists at work operate not only to maintain and repair their social relations with sources and colleagues but their cultural image as journalists in the eyes of a wider world. Robert Manoff shows how television news reporters deploy experts in stories not so much to provide viewers with information but to certify the journalist's 'effort, access, and superior knowledge' (Manoff, 1989: 69). Zelizer (1990) has demonstrated the ways that reporters in American broadcast news visually and verbally establish their own authority by suggesting their personal proximity to the events they cover. Regardless of how the news was in fact 'gathered', it is presented in a style that promotes an illusion of the journalists' adherence to the journalistic norm of proximity. The reality journalists manufacture provides not only a version and vision of 'the world' but of 'journalism' itself.

Cultural form may also refer to language itself. Prognostications of a 'global village' unified by new globe-spanning satellite communications founder on the persistent strength of local and regional language loyalties and national identities. While CNN (Cable News Network) was by 1993 available in 140 countries, relatively small proportions of viewers regularly tune in. Euronews, similarly, if on a smaller scale, is a five-language satellite-transmitted news channel begun in 1994 and available to millions is already experiencing the difficulties of one-world broadcasting in a multinational, multicultural human scene (Parker, 1994).

Most research on the culture of news production takes it for granted that, at least within a given national tradition, there is one common news standard among journalists. This is one of the convenient simplifications of the sociology of journalism that merits critical attention, and might indeed be a point at which a lot of current assumptions about how journalism works begin to unravel. Reporters who may adhere to norms of 'objectivity' in reporting on a political campaign (what Daniel Hallin calls the 'sphere of legitimate controversy') will not blink to report gushingly about a topic on which there is broad national consensus (the 'sphere of consensus') or to write derisively on a subject that lies beyond the bounds of popular consensus (the 'sphere of deviance') (Hallin, 1986: 117). It is as if journalists were unconsciously multilingual, code-switching from neutral interpreters to guardians of social consensus and back again without missing a beat. Elihu Katz and Daniel Dayan have noted how television journalists in Britain, the USA, Israel and elsewhere who narrate live 'media events' rather than ordinary daily news stories abandon a matter-of-fact style for 'cosmic lyricism' (Katz and Dayan, 1992: 108). Yoram Peri shows that the same code-switching took place in Israeli print journalism in covering the martyred Prime Minister Yitzhak Rabin. In life, Rabin walked in the sphere of legitimate controversy, but in death he was absorbed into the sphere of consensus (Peri, 1997).

Although cultural explanations of news often overlap with social explanations, sometimes they conflict. The most striking example of this is research by Scott Althaus that challenges the view that news reproduces the array of elite opinion among the sources journalists rely on.

Althaus finds, to the contrary, that US news reports on American foreign policy over-represent views critical of administration action. Why should this be? Not, Althaus concludes, because the media oppose a particular administration but because they are following journalistic norms that emphasize balance and journalism's eagerness for drama and conflict (Althaus, 2003).

Conclusions

The approaches to the study of news I have reviewed all have advanced an understanding of the media by focusing on the specific institutions and the specific processes in those institutions responsible for creating news. Most studies, regardless of the approach they take, begin with a normative assumption that the news media *should* serve society by informing the general population in ways that arm them for vigilant citizenship. I agree that this is one goal the news media in a democracy should try to serve, but it is not a good approximation of what role the news media have historically played – anywhere. The news media have always been a more important forum for communication among elites (and some elites more than others) than with the general population. In the best of circumstances, the fact of a general audience for the news media provides a regular opportunity for elites to be effectively embarrassed, even disgraced, as Brent Fisse and John Braithwaite show in their cross-national study of the impact of publicity on corporate offenders (Fisse and Braithwaite, 1983). The combination of electoral democracy with a free press, economist Amartya Sen has argued, has prevented famines even when crops have failed (Sen and Dreze, 1989). But even in these cases the 'audience' or the 'public' has a kind of phantom existence that the sociological study of news production has yet to consider in its theoretical formulations.

Of course, the four perspectives I have discussed do not account for all that we might want to know. They may help to explain historical changes in news, but to the extent that these changes emerge from broad historical forces, any research focused on the news institutions themselves is likely to fall short. Take just one important example. There is a shift, reported in a number of studies from around the world, toward reporting styles that are more informal, more intimate, more critical, and more cynically detached or distanced than earlier reporting. One can look at British television interviewing, which changed from a style formal and deferential toward politicians to a more aggressive and critical style (Scannell, 1989: 146), or Japanese broadcasting, which has become 'more cynical and populist' in the past several decades (Krauss, 1998: 686), or a journalism less deferential to power and more part of a culture of 'critical scrutiny' as in Sweden (Djerf-Pierre, 2000) or more aggressive, scandal-seeking reporting in Brazil, Argentina and Peru (Waisbord, 1997: 201). Or one can point to more melodramatic reporting in Norway (Eide, 1997: 179) or a style both more critical and more intimate in the Netherlands (van Zoonen, 1991) or, in many countries, more mocking and satirical. There is some evidence that the German press has resisted these trends (Wilke and Reinemann, 2001) but the developments are remarkably widespread. This transformation of public culture around the globe marks a profound shift in the character of cultural authority whose dynamics and whose consequences have yet to be understood.

References

Althaus, S. L. (2003) 'When News Norms Collide, Follow the Lead: New Evidence for Press Independence', *Political Communication*, 20, 381–414.

Althaus, S. L., Edy, J. A., Entman, R. M. and Phalen, P. (1996) 'Revising the Indexing Hypothesis: Officials, Media, and the Libya Crisis', *Political Communication*, 13, 407–21.

Alwood, E. (1996) *Straight News: Gays, Lesbians, and the News Media*. New York: Columbia University Press.

Bagdikian, B. (1997) *The Media Monopoly*, 5th edn. Boston: Beacon Press.

Baker, C. E. (1994) *Ownership of Newspapers: The View from Positivist Social Science*. Cambridge, MA: Joan Shorenstein Center on Press, Politics, and Public Policy, Research Paper R-12, Harvard University.

Beasley, M. (1993) 'Newspapers: Is There a New Majority Defining the News?', in P. J. Creedon (ed.), *Women in Mass Communication*. Newbury Park, CA: Sage.

Bennett, T. (1982) 'Media, "Reality", Signification', in M. Gurevitch *et al.* (eds), *Culture, Society and the Media*. London: Methuen, pp. 287–308.

Bennett, W. L. (1994) 'The News About Foreign Policy', in W. L. Bennett and D. L. Paletz (eds), *Taken by Storm: The Media, Public Opinion, and US Foreign Policy in the Gulf War*. Chicago: University of Chicago Press, pp. 12–40.

Best, J. (1999) *Random Violence: How We Talk About New Crimes and New Victims*. Berkeley: University of California Press.

Blumler, J. G. (1997) 'Origins of the Crisis of Communication for Citizenship', *Political Communication*, 14, 395–404.

———(1999) 'Political Communication Systems All Change: A Response to Kees Brants', *European Journal of Communication*, 14, 241–49.

Blumler, J. G. and Gurevitch, M. (1995) *The Crisis of Public Communication*. London: Routledge.

Brants, K. (1998) 'Who's Afraid of Infotainment?', *European Journal of Communication*, 13, 305–35.

Breed, W. (1952, 1980) *The Newspaperman, News and Society*. New York: Arno Press.

———(1955) 'Social Control in the Newsroom: A Functional Analysis', *Social Forces*, 33, 326–55.

Cohen, B. C. (1963) *The Press and Foreign Policy*. Princeton: Princeton University Press.

Cohen, S. and Young, J. (eds) (1973) *The Manufacture of News: A Reader*. Beverly Hills: Sage.

Cook, T. E. (1989) *Making Laws and Making News: Media Strategies in the U.S. House of Representatives*. Washington, DC: Brookings Institution.

Crouse, T. (1973) *The Boys on the Bus*. New York: Ballantine.

Curran, J., Douglas A. and Whannel G. (1980) 'The Political Economy of the Human-Interest Story', in A. Smith (ed.), *Newspapers and Democracy*. Cambridge, MA: MIT Press, pp. 288–342.

Curry, J. L. (1990) *Poland's Journalists: Professionalism and Politics*. Cambridge: Cambridge University Press.

Dassin, J. (1982) 'Press Censorship and the Military State in Brazil', in J. L. Curry and J. R. Dassin, *Press Control Around the World*. New York: Praeger, pp. 149–86.

De Mateo, R. (1989) 'The Evolution of the Newspaper Industry in Spain, 1939–87', *European Journal of Communication*, 4, 211–26.

Demers, D.(1996) 'Corporate Newspaper Structure, Editorial Page Vigor, and Social Change', *Journalism and Mass Communication Quarterly*, 73, 857–77.

De Smaele, H. (1999) 'The Applicability of Western Media Models on the Russian Media System', *European Journal of Communication*, 14, 173–89.

Djerf-Pierre, M.(2000) 'Squaring the Circle. Public Service and Commercial News on Swedish Television, 1956–99', *Journalism Studies*, 1, 239–60.

Donsbach, W. (1995) 'Lapdogs, Watchdogs and Junkyard Dogs', *Media Studies Journal*, Fall, 17–30.

Downie, L. and Kaiser, R. G. (2002) *The News About the News*. New York: Alfred A. Knopf.

Dreier, P. (1982) 'Capitalists vs. the Media: An Analysis of an Ideological Mobilization Among Business Leaders', *Media, Culture and Society*, 4, 111–32.

Dunne, D. D. (1969) *Public Officials and the Press*. Reading, MA: Addison-Wesley.

Eide, M. (1997) 'A New Kind of Newspaper? Understanding a Popularization Process', *Media, Culture and Society*, 19, 173–82.

Elias, N. (1996) 'Changes in European Standards of Behaviour in the Twentieth Century', in N. Elias, *The Germans*. New York: Columbia University Press, pp. 23–43.

Epstein, E. J. (1973) *News From Nowhere*. New York: Random House.

Esser, F. (1998) 'Editorial Structures and Work Principles in British and German Newsrooms', *European Journal of Communication*, 13, 375–405.

Feldman, O. (1993) *Politics and the News Media in Japan*. Ann Arbor: University of Michigan Press.

Fishman, M. (1980) *Manufacturing the News*. Austin: University of Texas Press.

Fiss, B. and Braithwaite J. (1983) *The Impact of Publicity on Corporate Offenders*. Albany: State University of New York Press.

Freeman, L. A. (2000) *Closing the Shop: Information Cartels and Japan's Mass Media*. Princeton: Princeton University Press.

Galtung, J. and Ruge, M. (1970) 'The Structure of Foreign News: The Presentation of the Congo, Cuba and Cyprus Crises in Four Foreign Newspapers', in J. Tunstall (ed.), *Media Sociology: A Reader*. Urbana: University of Illinois Press, pp. 259–98.

Gamson, J. and Latteier, P. (2004) 'Do Media Monsters Devour Diversity?', *Contexts*, 3, 26–32.

Gans, H. J. (1979) *Deciding What's News: A Study of CBS Evening News, NBC Nightly News, Newsweek and Time*. New York: Pantheon.

———(1985) 'Are U.S. Journalists Dangerously Liberal?', *Columbia Journalism Review*, November/December, 29–33.

Garnhan, N. (1990) *Capitalism and Communication*. London: Sage.

Gieber, W. (1964) 'News Is What Newspapermen Make It', in L. A. Dexter and D. Manning, *White, People, Society and Mass Communications*. New York: Free Press.

Gitlin, T. (1980) *The Whole World Is Watching*. Berkeley: University of California Press.

Goldenberg, E. (1975) *Making the Papers*. Lexington, MA: D.C. Heath.

Gurevitch, M., Bennett, T., Curran, J. and Woollacott, J. (eds) (1982) *Culture, Society and the Media*. London: Methuen.

Gurevitch, M., Levy, M. R. and Roeh, I. (1994) 'The Global Newsroom: Convergences and Diversities in the Globalization of Television News', in P. Dahlgren and C. Sparks (eds), *Communication and Citizenship*. London: Routledge.

Hagen, L. (1997) 'The Transformation of the Media System of the Former German Democratic Republic After the Reunification and Its Effects on the Political Content of Newspapers', *European Journal of Communication*, 12, 5–26.

Hall, S. (1973) 'The Determination of News Photographs', in S. Cohen and J. Young, (eds), *The Manufacture of News: A Reader*. Beverly Hills: Sage, pp. 176–90.

Hallin, D. C. (1986) '*The Uncensored War': The Media and Vietnam*. New York: Oxford University Press.

———(1994) *We Keep America on Top of the World*, London: Routledge.

Hallin, D. C. and Mancini, P. (1984) 'Speaking of the President: Political Structure and Representational Form in U.S. and Italian Television News', *Theory and Society*, 13, 829–50.

———(1991) 'Summits and the Constitution of an International Public Sphere: The Reagan-Gorbachev Meetings as Televised Media Events', *Communication*, 12, 249–65.

———(2004) *Comparing Media Systems: Three Models of Media and Politics*. Cambridge: Cambridge University Press.

Hallin, D. C., Manoff, R. K., and Weddle, J. K. (1993) 'Sourcing Patterns of National Security Reporters', *Journalism Quarterly*, 70, 753–66.

Hamilton, J. T. (2004) *All the News That's Fit to Sell*. Princeton: Princeton University Press.

Hannerz, U. (2004) *Foreign News: Exploring the World of Foreign Correspondents*. Chicago: University of Chicago Press.

Hartmann, P. and Husband, C. (1973) 'The Mass Media and Racial Conflict', in S. Cohen and J. Young (eds), *The Manufacture of News: A Reader*. Beverly Hills: Sage, pp. 270–83.

Herman, E. S. and Chomsky N. (1988) *Manufacturing Consent*. New York: Pantheon.

Hess, S. (1981) *The Washington Reporters*. Washington, DC: The Brookings Institution.

———(1984) *The Government/Press Connection*. Washington, DC: The Brookings Institution.

Hughes, H. M. (1940) *News and the Human Interest Story*. Chicago: University of Chicago Press.

Jakubowicz, K. (1995) 'Media Within and Without the State: Press Freedom in Eastern Europe', *Journal of Communication*, 45 (4), 125–39.

Jeffrey, R. (2001) '(Not) Being There: Dalits and Indian Newspapers', *South Asia*, 24, 225–38.

Kalb, M. (1998) 'The Rise of the "New News": A Case Study of Two Root Causes of the Modern Scandal Coverage'. Cambridge, MA: Joan Shorenstein Center on Press, Politics, and Public Policy, Discussion Paper D-34.

Katz, E. (1998) 'And Deliver Us From Segmentation', in R. G. Noll and M. E. Price, (eds), *A Communications Cornucopia*. Washington, DC: The Brookings Institution, pp. 99–112.

Katz, E. and Dayan. D. (1992) *Media Events: The Live Broadcasting of History*. Cambridge, MA: Harvard University Press.

Katz, J. (1987) 'What Makes Crime "News"?', *Media, Culture and Society*, 9, 47–76.

Keane, J. (1991) *Liberty of the Press*. Cambridge: Polity Press.

Krauss, E. (1998) 'Changing Television News in Japan', *Journal of Asian Studies*, 57, 663–92.

———(2000) *Broadcasting Politics in Japan: NHK TV News*. Ithaca, N.Y.: Cornell University Press.

Lahav, P. (ed.) (1985) *Press Law in Modern Democracies: A Comparative Study*. New York: Longman.

Lavie, A. and Lehman-Wilzig, S. (2003) 'Whose News? Does Gender Determine the Editorial Product?', *European Journal of Communication*, 18, 5–29.

Lawrence, R. G. (2000) *The Politics of Force: Media and the Construction of Police Brutality*. Berkeley: University of California Press.

Lee, J. (1997) 'Press Freedom and Democratization: South Korea's Experience and Some Lessons', *Gazette*, 59 (2), 135–49.

Lichter, S. R., Rothman, S., and Lichter, L. S. (1986) *The Media Elite: America's New Powerbrokers.* Bethesda, MD: Adler and Adler.

Lipstadt, D. (1986) *Beyond Belief: The American Press and the Coming of the Holocaust 1933–1945* New York: Free Press.

Livingston, S. and Bennett, W. L. (2003) 'Gatekeeping, Indexing, and Live-Event News: Is Technology Altering the Construction of News?', *Political Communication,* 20, 363–80.

Livingston, S. and Eachus, T. (1996) 'Humanitarian Crises and U.S. Foreign Policy: Somalia and the CNN Effect Reconsidered', *Political Communication,* 12, pp. 413–29.

Mancini, P. (1991) 'The Public Sphere and the Use of News in a "Coalition" System of Government', in P. Dahlgren and C. Sparks (eds), *Communication and Citizenship.* London: Routledge, pp. 137–54.

Manoff, R. K. (1989) 'Modes of War and Modes of Social Address: The Text of SDI', *Journal of Communication,* 39, 59–84.

Matthews, M. N. (1996) 'How Public Ownership Affects Publisher Autonomy', *Journalism and Mass Communication Quarterly,* 73, 342–53.

Mazzoleni, G. (1995) 'Towards a "Videocracy"? Italian Political Communication at a Turning Point', *European Journal of Communication,* 10, 291–319.

McChesney, R. W. (1997) *Corporate Media and the Threat to Democracy.* New York: Seven Stories Press.

Mermin, J. (1997) 'Television News and American Intervention in Somalia: The Myth of a Media-Driven Foreign Policy', *Political Science Quarterly,* 112, 385–403.

Mickiewicz, E. (1988) *Split Signals: Television and Politics in the Soviet Union.* New York: Oxford University Press.

———(1998) 'Media, Transition, and Democracy: Television and the Transformation of Russia', in R. G. Noll and M. E. Price (eds), *A Communications Cornucopia.* Washington, DC: The Brookings Institution, pp. 113–37.

Mills, K. (1990) *A Place in the News.* New York: Dodd, Mead.

Moisy, C. (1996) 'The Foreign News Flow in the Information Age'. Cambridge, MA: Joan Shorenstein Center on Press, Politics, and Public Policy, Discussion Paper D-23.

Molotch, H. and Lester, M. (1974) 'News as Purposive Behavior: On the Strategic Use of Routine Events, Accidents, and Scandals', *American Sociological Review,* 39, 101–12.

Mortensen, F. and Svendsen, E. N. (1980) 'Creativity and Control: The Journalist Betwixt His Readers and Editors', *Media, Culture and Society,* 2, 169–77.

Murdock, G. (1973) 'Political Deviance: The Press Association of a Militant Mass Demonstration', in S. Cohen and J. Young (eds), *The Manufacture of News: A Reader.* Beverly Hills: Sage, pp. 156–75.

———(1982) 'Large Corporations and the Control of the Communications Industries', in M. Gurevitch, T. Bennett, J. Curran and J. Woollacott (eds), *Culture, Society and the Media.* London: Methuen, pp. 118–50.

Murdock, G. and Golding, P. (1977) 'Capitalism, Communication and Class Relations', in J. Curran, M. Gurevitch and J. Woollacott (eds), *Mass Communication and Society.* London: Edward Arnold, pp. 12–43.

Murschetz, P. (1998) 'State Support for the Daily Press in Europe: A Critical Appraisal', *European Journal of Communication,* 13, 291–313.

Noam, E. (1991) *Television in Europe.* New York: Oxford University Press.

Okrent, D. (2004) 'Is the New York Times a Liberal Newpaper?', *New York Times,* 25 July, Section IV, p. 2.

Park, R. E. (1922) *The Immigrant Press and Its Control.* New York: Harper.

————(1923) 'The Natural History of the Newspaper', *American Journal of Sociology*, 29, 273–89.

Parker, R. (1994) 'The Myth of Global News', *New Perspectives Quarterly*, 11, 39–45.

Pearce, F. (1973) 'How To Be Immoral and Ill, Pathetic and Dangerous, All At the Same Time: Mass Media and the Homosexual', in S. Cohen and J. Young (eds) *The Manufacture of News: A Reader*, Beverly Hills: Sage, pp. 284–301.

Peri, Y. (1997) 'The Rabin Myth and the Press: Reconstruction of the Israeli Collective Identity', *European Journal of Communication*, 12, 435–58.

Pharr, S. J. (1996) 'Media as Trickster in Japan: A Comparative Perspective', in S. J. Pharr and E. S. Krauss (eds), *Media and Politics in Japan*. Honolulu: University of Hawaii Press.

Polumbaum, J. (1993) 'Professionalism in China's Press Corps', in R. V. Des Forges, L. Ning and W. Yen-bo (eds), *China's Crisis of 1989*. Albany: SUNY Press, pp. 295–311.

————(1994) 'To Protect or Restrict: Points of Contention in China's Draft Press Law', in P. B. Potter (ed.), *Domestic Law Reforms in Post-Mao China*. Armonk, N.Y.: M. E. Sharpe, pp. 247–69.

————(1997) 'Political Fetters, Commercial Freedoms: Restraint and Excess in Chinese Mass Communications', in C. Hudson (ed.), *Regional Handbook of Economic and Political Development*, vol. l. Chicago: Fitzroy Dearborn.

Remington, T. F. (1988) *The Truth of Authority: Ideology and Communication in the Soviet Union*. Pittsburgh: University of Pittsburgh Press.

Rivers, W. (1962) 'The Correspondents After 25 Years', *Columbia Journalism Review*, 1, 4–10.

Robinson, M. J. and Sheehan, M. A. (1983) *Over the Wire and On TV*. New York: Russell Sage Foundation.

Rosten, L. C. (1937) *The Washington Correspondents*. New York: Harcourt, Brace.

Sahlins, M. (1985) *Islands of History*. Chicago: University of Chicago Press.

Scannell, P. (1989) 'Public Service Broadcasting and Modern Public Life', *Media, Culture and Society*, 11, 135–66.

Schlesinger, P. and Tumber, H. (1994) *Reporting Crime: The Media Politics of Criminal Justice*. Oxford: Clarendon Press.

Schudson, M. (1982) 'The Politics of Narrative Form: The Emergence of News Conventions in Print and Television', *Daedalus*, 111, 97–113.

————(1994) 'Question Authority: A History of the News Interview in American Journalism, 1860s–1930s', *Media, Culture & Society*, 16, 565–87.

————(1995) *The Power of News*. Cambridge, MA: Harvard University Press.

————(2003) *The Sociology of News*. New York: W. W. Norton.

Sen, A. and Dreze, J. (1989) *Hunger and Public Action*. Oxford: Clarendon Press.

Sigal, L. V. (1973) *Reporters and Officials*. Lexington, MA: Lexington Books.

Skogerbo, E. (1997) 'The Press Subsidy System in Norway', *European Journal of Communication*, 12, 99–118.

Smith, A. (1980) *Goodbye Gutenberg*. New York: Oxford University Press.

Sparks, C. (1991) 'Goodbye, Hildy Johnson: The Vanishing "Serious Press"', in P. Dahlgren and C. Sparks (eds), *Communication and Citizenship*. London: Routledge, pp. 58–74.

Sparks, C. and Splichal, S. (1989) 'Journalistic Education and Professional Socialisation', *Gazette*, 43, 31–52.

Starr, P. (2004) *The Creation of the Media: Political Origins of Modern Communications*. New York: Basic

Books.

Steele, J. E. (1995) 'Experts and the Operational Bias of Television News: The Case of the Persian Gulf War', *Journalism and Mass Communication Quarterly*, 72, 799–012.

Sumpter, R. S. (2000) 'Daily Newspaper Editors' Audience Construction Routines. A Case Study', *Critical Studies in Mass Communication*, 17, 334–46.

Tuchman, G. (1972) 'Objectivity as Strategic Ritual: An Examination of Newsmen's Notions of Objectivity', *American Journal of Sociology*, 77, 660–79.

——(1976) 'Telling Stories', *Journal of Communication*, 26, 93–7.

——(1978) *Making News: A Study in the Construction of Reality*. New York: Free Press.

Underwood, D. (1995) *When MBA's Rule the Newsroom*. New York: Columbia University Press.

Van Zoonen, L. (1991) 'A Tyranny of Intimacy? Women, Femininity and Television News', in P. Dahlgren and C. Sparks (eds), *Communication and Citizenship*. London: Routledge, pp. 217–35.

Waisbord, S. (1994) 'Knocking on Newsroom Doors: The Press and Political Scandals in Argentina', *Political Communication*, 11, 19–33.

——(1995) 'Leviathan Dreams: State and Broadcasting in South America', *Communication Review*, 1, 201–26.

——(1997) 'The Narrative of Exposes in South American Journalism', *Gazette*, 59, 189–203.

——(2000) *Watchdog Journalism in South America*. New York: Columbia University Press.

——(2002) 'Anti-press Violence and the Crisis of the State', *Harvard International Journal of Press/Politics*, 7, 90–109.

Weaver, D. and Wilhoit, G. C. (1991) *The American Journalist*. 2nd edn. Bloomington: Indiana University Press.

Weaver, P. (1975) 'Newspaper News and Television News', in D. Cater and R. Adler (eds), *Television as a Social Force*. New York: Praeger.

Weber, M. (1921, 1946) 'Politics as a Vocation', in H. Gerth and C. W. Mills (eds), *From Max Weber: Essays in Sociology*. New York: Oxford University Press, pp. 77–128.

White D. M. (1950) 'The Gatekeeper: A Case Study in the Selection of News', *Journalism Quarterly*, 27, 383–90. Also reprinted in L. A. Dexter, and D. M. White, (eds), *People, Society, and Mass Communications*. New York: Free Press, 1964.

Wilke, J. and Reinemann, C. (2001) 'Do the Candidates Matter? Long-Term Trends of Campaign Coverage – A Study of the German Press Since 1949' *European Journal of Communication*, 16, 291–314.

Zaller, J. (1994) 'Elite Leadership of Mass Opinion: New Evidence from the Gulf War', in W. L. Bennett and D. L. Paletz (eds), *Taken by Storm: The Media, Public Opinion, and US Foreign Policy in the Gulf War*. Chicago: University of Chicago Press, pp. 186–209.

Zelizer, B. (1990) 'Where is the Author in American TV News? On the Construction and Presentation of Proximity, Authorship, and Journalistic Authority', *Semiotica*, 80, 37–48.

Zhao, Y. (1998) *Media, Market, and Democracy in China: Between the Party Line and the Bottom Line*. Urbana: University of Illinois Press.

chapter ten

The Culture of Journalism

BARBIE ZELIZER

Introduction

Journalism is a world of contradiction and flux, held in place by those with central access and stature while challenged by those on its margins. Since journalism's beginnings, it has been shaped by outliers to the journalistic world. A long list of luminaries, including Charles Dickens, Samuel Johnson, George Orwell, Ernest Hemingway, Andre Malraux, Martha Gellhorn and Joan Didion, all made clear that who is a journalist and what constitutes journalism remain categories to be challenged on craft, professional, moral, political, economic and technological grounds. Today, the challenge has been taken up by individuals with seemingly less notable credentials, less notable primarily because the challenge they pose is too close to be considered with perspective: From bloggers and reality television to Matt Drudge, Jim Romanesko and Jon Stewart, a list of 'as ifs' in the world of journalism shows yet again that we still have not found a way to account for journalism's internal messiness and flexible contours. Embarrassingly, hundreds of years into its consideration, we still reference journalism in ways that are limited, narrow and by definition incomplete, preferring instead what Peter Dahlgren (1992) critiqued as a metonymic grasp of the phenomenon. As news scholars, we can do better.

Seeing journalism through the lens of culture offers one way to do that. The construct of culture offers a way to repair the long-standing neglect of journalism's contradictions while attending to the flux of its territory. Had there been a clear way to account for the culture of journalism, the journalistic work of Dickens and his long list of cronies, arguably among the more interesting journalistic personalities, might have expanded the boundaries of what counts, or not, as journalism. Outliers such as political cartoonists, tabloid hacks, political satiricists, photojournalists and bloggers might all have been given at least qualified membership in the club. For recognizing journalism as a culture – a complex web of meanings, rituals, conventions and symbol systems – and seeing journalists, who provide different kinds of discourse about public events, as its facilitators offers a way to think about the phenomenon by accounting for its changing, often contradictory dimensions. By definition, then, the culture of journalism provides a way to both think about journalism more broadly and in conjunction with its internal variance.

Using culture as a construct

Thinking about journalism though the construct of culture is a notion derived from various academic concentrations, including research on the sociology of culture, an interest in constructivism in philosophy, a turn in anthropology and folklore toward the analysis of symbols and symbolic forms, a move toward ethnography in linguistics, and scholarship in cultural history, cultural criticism and cultural studies.[1] In different ways, each arena has drawn scholars toward thinking about culture as an analytical locus and by extension about journalism as one of its venues.

An emphasis on culture forces consideration of different sides of the journalistic world than are common to mainstream news scholarship. Attention to the collective codes of knowledge and the belief systems by which journalists are presumed to make sense of the world has its roots in an array of academic arenas, including early work in humanistic sociology (Berger, 1963; Park, 1925, 1940), symbolic interactionism (Blumer, 1969) and cultural anthropology (Geertz, 1973; Lukes, 1975). Each points in different ways to the utility of using culture as a way to understand journalism, both as a frame of mind and as patterned conduct. Work on Marxism and cultural criticism (Eagleton, 1995; Williams, 1978, 1982), combined with the two separate strains of cultural studies in the UK and the USA (Carey, 1986; Hall, 1973; Hartley, 1982), lend a pragmatic focal point to journalism's study, where its subjectivity of expression, the constructed nature of its meanings for events, the politics of its identity building, and the grounding of each of these premises in practice come to the forefront of attention.

Alternately called the collective knowledge that journalists need to function as journalists (Park, 1940), the 'culturological' dimensions of the news (Schudson, 1991), and the examination of 'journalism as popular culture' (Dahlgren, 1992), this scholarship links the untidy and textured *matériel* of journalism – its symbols, rituals, conventions and stories – with the larger world in which journalism takes shape. Perhaps nowhere does this *matériel* have as much credence as when journalism operates less effectively than might be hoped. When journalism must navigate simultaneously both internal and external tensions, it becomes most vulnerable to criticism from the outside world. It is then, more so than in times of calm, that thinking about journalism through the construct of culture becomes most valuable.

There are three givens about the culture of journalism that offer an effective address to journalism. Each revolves around a fundamental question of definition, none of which is mutually exclusive:

1. What is the culture of journalism?
2. Who inhabits the culture of journalism?
3. What is the culture of journalism for?

Such questions come to the fore particularly when journalism is situated in crisis, as was seen during the recent, and still ongoing, war in Iraq. This chapter addresses public discourse on the US media and the war and shows how the regularly invoked notions for thinking about journalism's performance fall short as a way of evaluating the news. At the same time, thinking about US journalism through the prism of culture provides a more targeted appraisal of how news has unfolded during the Iraq war.

What is the culture of journalism?

More than just reporters' professional codes of action or the social arrangement of reporters and editors, the culture of journalism references a complex and multidimensional lattice of meanings for all those involved, 'a tool kit of symbols, stories, rituals and world views, which people use in varying configurations to solve different kinds of problems' (Swidler, 1906. 274). Allowing for a wide expanse of journalistic practices, the culture of journalism includes impulses that are counter-productive, contradictory and contrary to the supposed aims of what journalism is for. Culture recognizes journalism's various moments of creation and revision, with all of their problems, limitations, contradictions and anomalies, giving equal credence to the informal and formal, the high and low, the unarticulated and articulated, the implicit and explicit, and the contradictory and coherent. In effect, this means that seeing journalism through a cultural lens strategically and pronouncedly interrogates the articulated foundations for journalism and journalistic practice that may be taken for granted elsewhere in the academy.

The culture of journalism travels the uneven road of reading journalism against its own grain while giving that grain extended attention. It both sees journalism through journalists' own eyes, tracking how being part of the community comes to have meaning for them, and queries the self-presentations that journalists provide. Emphasizing 'the constraining force of broad cultural symbol systems regardless of the details of organizational and occupational routines' (Schudson, 1991: 143), the culture of journalism moves decidedly in tandem with but oppositionally to the pronounced and conventional understandings of how journalism works. Undercutting the pronounced sense of self that journalism professionals have long set forth regarding their practices and their position in the world, culture assumes that journalists employ collective, often tacit knowledge to become members of the group and maintain their membership over time (see, for example, Goodenough, 1981). Drawing from what Robert Park (1940) called 'synthetic knowledge' – the kind of tacit knowledge that is 'embodied in habit and custom' rather than that which forms the core of formalized knowledge systems – this forces attention to the cues by which journalists think about journalism and the world. It also presumes that what is explicit and articulated as that knowledge may not reflect the whole picture of what journalism is and tries to be. [2]

Seeing journalism as culture thus allows for a wide range of attributes not included in other constructs for thinking about the phenomenon – notably, as a profession, an industry, an institution and a craft. Unlike the profession, which emphasizes the values, beliefs and practices by which journalists are constituted as professional beings, the culture of journalism presupposes a wide range of internal and external conventions that identify certain activities as journalistic but without the honorific aura attached to 'being professional'; by definition, this opens journalism's definition to activities that go under the radar of professionalism – in alternative venues such as the alternative press and the internet, in opinion-driven formats such as political satire, blogs and cartoons, and in forums situated explicitly on the margins of journalism if not beyond, such as the satirical comedy show and reality television. Unlike the industry, which targets the large-scale mechanistic, bureaucratic and technical processes by which journalism is set in place to address problems such as an eroding and ageing audience, media concentration and convergence, or economic profit, the culture of journalism allows for the craft-oriented dimensions of practice, aspects of work that have little to do with the efficiency, profit or workability of the news industry. It encourages attention to the viability and integrity of journalistic practices, where skills, ethics, individual maps and principles come to the forefront of attention regardless of whether or not they have impact on the survival of either a specific news organization or the industry as a whole. Unlike the institution, which focuses on journalism's role in the large-scale rendering of power in society, the culture of journalism targets how journalistic practices, routines and conventions take on meaning internally for and among journalists. And unlike the craft of journalism, which tracks the skills and qualities inherent in doing journalism as most relevant to journalists themselves, the culture of journalism situates its craft aspects in a larger picture that accounts for external exigencies as well. In each case, connections are made that link internal mind-sets about how the world works with the external arrangements by which social life is set in place.

The culture of journalism thus takes shape by bridging centres and margins. Variables that traditionally keep certain aspects or kinds of journalism distinct – hard news versus soft, mainstream news versus tabloid, journalists' verbal reports versus the visual images they use – are here repositioned as links across differences, consequently positioning journalism as a whole of disparate, changing, often self-contradictory impulses. The different tools of journalism, different kinds of journalism, and similarities between journalism and the world outside are brought together to illuminate the nuanced and textured character of journalism in all of its possibilities.

Perhaps nowhere was this as obvious as in the war in Iraq. Much of the US journalistic coverage of Iraq was evaluated in line with a professional lens – whether journalists were able to do their job impartially, accurately and with balance. Editorials and news articles hailed the way in which news organizations met the logistic and organizational challenges of covering war (e.g. Getler, 2003; Strupp, 2003b). Discussions focused largely on embedding, with professional organizations such as the Project for Excellence in Journalism organizing responses to what was largely seen as a relatively novel reporting arrangement ('Embedded Reporters', 2003). Other problems – a lack of reflection or scepticism, empathy with the troops, and unrepresentative or narrowly focused stories and visuals – arose over time: CNN reporter Christiane Amanpour noted that embedding failed to give 'a concise and broader context. [The network thinks] "live" brings more spontaneity, "keep it moving" is what they tell us' (cited in Lowry and Jensen, 2003: E1). Not surprisingly, public expectations of journalism remained 'at what may be a historic high' (Fisher, 2004: 2).

What these discussions obscured was that the default setting they invoked for considering war coverage was too narrowly defined. Not only did a very small percentage of journalists become embeds, but a focus on professionalism failed to predict the messiness that forced other changes and adaptations in journalism's practice as the war ensued. Such changes and adaptations were key to considering journalism as a culture. In fact, it was as a culture – through a shared reliance on meanings, rituals, conventions, symbol systems and consensual understandings – that much of the coverage took shape. Journalists struggled to make sense of the war in ways far broader than the guidelines offered by professionalism, for journalism's practice changed in a decidedly 'non-professional' direction: magnifying the voice of the political right, Fox News surpassed CNN as the top-rated cable news channel, raising questions about what kind of journalism much of the US public wanted. Although many journalists distanced themselves from 'its' kind of news, labelling it derisively 'the Fox effect' or the 'Fox formula' and ridiculing its 'opinionated news with an America-first flair' (Rutenberg, 2003a: B9), its popularity lingered nonetheless. Already during the war's early days, it provided twice as much coverage as did any of the US broadcast networks (Media Monitor, 2003) and was watched avidly by a marked percentage of the US public; by mid-2004, its still high popularity left an uneasy taste among many journalists who were left to navigate its increasingly mainstreamed voice.

Other changes took place on the left of political consensus. The ascent of al-Jazeera, a satellite network based in Qatar, not only created a presence that forced journalistic attention to aspects of the story not usually covered by Western journalism but it broadened the repertoire of practices by which war coverage could be implemented. While only as late as July of 2004 did the powers-that-be at al-Jazeera consider the establishment of a code of ethics, a long-sworn given at many Western news establishments (Johnson, 2004), a range of practices started at al-Jazeera began to be adopted by the US media as the war pushed on. Al-Jazeera's initially-contested displays of video footage of wounded US POWs and dead bodies of the coalition forces were critiqued widely in March of 2003, but by late 2004 similar images were being shown regularly across Western news media. The display of pre-taped videos by 'interested' individuals, a practice largely begun by al-Jazeera during the war in Afghanistan when it showed video tapes of Osama bin Laden to wide-ranging critique, also became a far more widespread practice by the time of the Iraq war. By mid-2004, pre-execution tapes filmed by Iraqi militias who were intent on beheading their video-taped captives if their demands were not met appeared as regularly in the Western news media as they did on al-Jazeera. In each case, practice migrated from the so-called margins to the centre, affording a different answer to the question of what is the culture of journalism. When considered through the lens of professionalism, such practices were addressed primarily insofar as they violated professional behaviour – an unsatisfactory address to what was transpiring, as the practices' widespread adoption soon attested.

Covering the war also involved an encounter with unpredictable and non-routine circumstances, many of which forced an adaptation of long-held journalistic beliefs, conventions and routines. Missed stories, erroneous interpretations and a loyalty to misleading sources all revealed craft limitations in situations in which reporters had 'their hands full trying to cover a bewildering, determined urgency' (CJR Comment, 2004: 6; also Mooney, 2004). The uncritical reportage regarding the claims of weapons of mass destruction forced the *New York Times* to publish an unprecedented *mea culpa* on its pages ('The *Times* and Iraq', 2004; 'Pause for Hindsight', 2004), while additional wrong judgements revealed other failings: tracking Ahmed Chalaby's strategically erroneous leads (McCollom, 2004), embodied most directly but by no means limited to *New York Times* reporter Judith Miller, highlighted the limitations of source–reporter behaviour. Elaborated stories about bio-weapons laboratories, the Jessica Lynch rescue story, the defection of Tariq Aziz, and uprisings in the south of Iraq, many of which were contested by al-Jazeera at the time of their reporting, were later found to be false, while 'figuring out Iraqi sentiment [became] one of the most complex journalistic endeavors in years' (Beckerman, 2004: 40). Even the erroneous initial reports of widespread looting of the Iraqi National Museum were later blamed on 'the difficult and imperfect nature of [war] reporting' (Lawler, 2003: 68). The media's reticence about pursuing the Abu Ghraib story turned the focus on an unsatisfactory journalistic performance when troubling reports emerged of reporters missing the story and of Dan Rather's lame attempt to justify CBS's two-week delay of its airing (Mitchell, 2004). As late as July of 2004, observers wondered whether journalists even knew how to cover battlefields that were overrun with terrorist activity (Eisendorf, 2004).

Each instance pointed to the basic fact that much of the war coverage, operating without the usual relays of grassroots information, international aid workers, and representatives of other non-governmental organizations, was off-base, and it took shape as much through improvisation, trial and error, and informal discussion as through predictable journalistic cues. Thinking about journalism as a culture offers a way to account for its unfolding contrary to long-held professional expectations and helps explain how an altering of long-standing assumptions – about what 'allies' mean, about which punitive behaviours prisoners 'deserve' – can force a change, albeit delayed or incremental, in journalistic practice. What this means is that in their first draft of the Iraq war, journalists did not always get the story fully right. It is no wonder that by mid-summer of 2004, documentary films such as *Fahrenheit 911*, *Control Room*, and *Outfoxed*, or theatrical productions such as *Embedded* rang a popular chord with the US public. They dared to address some of the issues left unaddressed by much of US journalism.

Technologically-driven questions also came to a curious forefront of the culture of journalism in Iraq, in that they were unrealistically glorified by the news industry. Predictions soared that the war would become online journalism's breakthrough event (Outing, 2003; Walker, 2003); in one view, web-based news coverage 'could define how future wars are covered' (Swartz, 2003). At the same time the US TV networks had been engaged in 'an "armaments race" of their own', with each of the networks and Fox News fully prepared to 'challenge CNN's superiority in battlefield reporting capability' (Biernatzki, 2003: 13). The availability of video satellite phones with compression technology made it possible for nearly every reporter to transmit stories first-hand; Baghdad alone sported close to 300 phone links and a dozen video links (Blumenthal and Rutenberg, 2003). This technological race for the most immediate and ongoing on-site relay drove the ratings for 24-hour news skyward. CNN's audience went up by some 393 per cent compared with the same week the previous year, and Fox News went up 379 per cent (Deans, 2003; also Allan and Zelizer, 2004: 7). News executives praised a technology that was 'lighter, cheaper, easier to transport, and sturdier' (Grossman, 2003: 6). Disputing reports that the new technologies incurred long-term losses for the news industry, Lawrence K. Grossman noted that war reporting might be 'the most efficient way a news division can spend its money, because so much of what the money is spent on gets on the air' (Grossman, 2003: 6).

What seemed to matter less was that in many instances technology overshadowed content. News magazines lamented that the immediacy of the web and video phones had made time into 'the enemy' (Sandler, 2003). Newspapers lamented an audience compelled by the quickest relay and consequently downwardly spiralling advertisements (Moses, 2003).

Many images and stories that technology provided 'in the end didn't amount to anything' (Doward, 2003). Long-standing problems of 'uneven translators, brutal deadlines, the difficulty of finding sources in an unfamiliar environment' (Beckerman, 2004: 41) remained, and the technological master, ever immediate, only made them more evident. Moreover, 'making frequent live transmissions . . . forced [reporters] to spend a great deal of time on the logistics and technology – time that could not be spent on gathering pictures and information for more complete stories. It turned out the technology was not quite ready for this war' (Friedman, 2003: 30).

In fact, the technological limitations on covering the wider story had a critical effect. The now-famous One-Man Mobile Uplink, caricatured during the late 1980s by Al Franken teetering under a massive satellite dish on *Saturday Night Live*, was reflected in Iraq when the reliance on extended technology rendered many front-line reporters unable to move freely. Embedded reporters offered hushed, somewhat frenzied accounts of the war that showed little more than the reporter's torso and offered on-site detail severely curtailed by military restriction, sandstorm and other circumstances. Though NBC correspondent David Bloom's much heralded 'Bloommobile' was equipped with high-quality, high-tech cameras that made 'other broadcasters drool with envy' (Friedman, 2003: 29), it was there that he met his death; moreover, his reports often provided little more than what the troops were eating or offered soldiers a chance to send regards home ('Embedded Reporters', 2003). While such accomplishments were hailed for offering some of the newest mobile technology to the industry, seen as a mark of improved efficiency, from the onset it was clear that certain kinds of reporting were being compromised. Telling news rather than collecting it became the motto of the day, a shortcoming of the US media more generally, as pointed out in the *State of the News Media 2004 Annual Report* (2004). Yet in Iraq it underscored the degree to which the 'toys' of journalism displaced those who operated them. Split screens, continual if static cameras, and an insistence to use them irrespective of what was being shown demonstrated, as the Project for Excellence in Journalism put it, that 'there is a tendency to use [technology] regardless of the news' it brings ('Embedded Reporters', 2003).

Appraising journalism in the Iraq war as the performance of an industry, a craft or a profession thereby offers less targeted evaluations of how journalism in Iraq has fared than does seeing it as a series of cultural arrangements and understandings. In that the culture of journalism references concerted action that activates conventional understandings to guide journalists in doing things in consensual ways, culture becomes one of the resources journalists draw upon to coordinate their activities as reporters, photographers and editors. Coverage of Iraq itself emerges as cultural too, relative to the givens of the groups and individuals engaged in its shaping and production.

Who inhabits the culture of journalism?

Who journalists are – or to frame the question more explicitly, who is included within the community of journalists? – is key to thinking about the culture of journalism. Derived from a sociological perspective that sees culture as a phenomenon produced by people instead of the anthropological view that sees culture as antecedent to people (Becker, 1986), the culture of journalism is given shape by the people who inhabit its terrain. Journalists to a large extent help shape the news.

Who is a journalist? Traditionally this question has been addressed by attending to the activities that journalists are expected to fulfil: a journalist expresses 'a judgment on the importance of an item, engages in reporting, adapts words and metaphors, solves a narrative puzzle, assesses and interprets' (Adam, 1993: 79). And yet the people who inhabit journalism are not equally regarded; nor are they given equal credence. While tensions over the boundaries of who is a journalist stretch from the United Nation's inclusion of field producers to the impact of the Iraqis taking freelance photographers into custody, differences persist more broadly. The distinctions between central and peripheral roles associated with professional groups engaged in creative activity (Becker, 1984) reflect a fundamental and long-standing ambivalence over who 'gets' to be called a journalist. Tabloid journalists have long been denied legitimacy by mainstream reporters, and those who report from alternative political streams, such as Victor Navasky or John Pilger, are often left out of journalism's 'who's who'. Photojournalists only became ranking members of journalistic professional associations in the 1940s, a full 80 years after images made their way into news, and only 50 years later did they take on leadership positions (Zelizer, 1998).

Much of the tension over who is a journalist comes from some of the prevailing notions for thinking about journalism. When seen as a profession, those who do not ascribe to norms of professional behaviour are kept outside of the community. In this regard, all of the populations mentioned above – tabloid journalists, political columnists, photojournalists – remain excluded. Seeing journalism as a craft is no more inclusive, for those who do not perform pre-defined requisite skills remain among those positioned beyond the boundary; all we need consider are the various discussions in the trade press about whether online reporters are journalists (Singer, 2003). When seen as an industry, journalists tend to get categorized through lists of 'relevant personnel' that are demarcated by division, hiding the fact that many journalists today work at more than one task simultaneously (Cottle, 2000). Operating increasingly from a financial point of view, US news organizations make decisions even about news personnel that at times undermine journalism's newsgathering function.

By contrast, seeing journalism as a culture offsets the boundary-marking that tends to exclude certain reporters or kinds of reporters from the community. Cultural conventions offer a way to unite journalists in patterned ways with people who are regularly excluded, even while they might consider themselves bona fide journalists. Cultural understandings also include people who are situated beyond the boundaries of the journalistic community, people who are not journalists and do not claim to be – film-makers, essayists, playwrights, poets and politicians. Each is similarly involved in diverse modes of cultural argumentation, expression, representation and production, such as when film-maker Oliver Stone claimed to ask questions in the film *JFK* about the Kennedy assassination that reporters missed (Zelizer, 1992). Thinking about the people who inhabit this culture, then, by definition broadens the population, precisely in ways that challenge the narrowed attempts to maintain territorial boundaries set in place by traditional scholarship.

This way of thinking has particular resonance when addressing the war in Iraq. Early discussions about embedded reporters, heralding a 'gee whiz quality' through which journalism's impending war coverage was initially appraised (Friedman, 2003: 29), set those who were embedded apart from those who were not. Those few hundred who accepted the arrangement received assistance with rations, medical attention, fuel and communications and were subject to some 50 contractual conditions (Boyd-Barrett, 2004: 81). The embedded reporters' work was subsidized by the Pentagon and overseen by public relations experts; none was assigned to Iraqi families, humanitarian agencies or anti-war groups (Schechter, 2003). Embedding provided TV reporters with unmatched access, though limited to a three-week ground war, and overlooked the fact that a large group of less institutionally supported reporters worked from a different vantage point. Called unilaterals, scores of US reporters went to cover the war from non-embedded positions, excluded from military transports and often paying their own way. Some chose not to be embedded so as to preserve freedom of movement, many were young and inexperienced, and several died in the first days of the war. And yet, as Michael Massing commented, 'the US military believed that only reporters who were officially embedded had the right to protection' (Massing, 2003: 33–5). Caught in the middle, the unilaterals were resented by the US military and had to sneak into Iraq across an officially closed border; they did, however, secure stories of civilian casualties, a broader context, and other complications of the war in a way that the embeds, who offered mostly on-site detail, did not (Donvan, 2003). How these reporters fared was as much a part of the journalistic community as the experiences of their more protected colleagues. In many views, 'embedding did not live up to advance billing' (Friedman, 2003: 29). And if nothing else, the contrast between the embedded and non-embedded reporters underscores the degree to which journalists make the news.

Within the recognized press corps too, observers critiqued some of its more marginal members. The early snafus surrounding Peter Arnett, whose interview with Iraqi TV cost him his job on MSNBC and landed him an alternative position with the British *Daily Mirror*, and Geraldo Rivera, whose drawing of a map in the sand pulled him away from the troops and repositioned him in Kuwait, cost both journalists one week's worth of air time. Jokes circulated freely about MSNBC reporter Ashleigh Banfield, whose changing hair colour and designer sunglasses were topics of discussion in the Afghanistan war but whose criticism of US war reporting in Iraq generated extensive name-calling (Rutenberg, 2003b). Some pondered the inclusion of 'reporters' for *People* magazine or MTV; called 'inexperienced', their coverage was said to be 'checkered', 'chancy' and 'super slick' (cited in Sims, 2003). Mainstream journalists continued to be rattled by online websites (Singer, 2003).

Perhaps the single most outstanding critique about the membership of the journalistic community in Iraq had to do with the weakening of journalism's borders in two directions – blogs and online journalism, and satirical comedy – and the related introduction of new community members in both regards. From the beginning, bloggers actively and systematically told the story of the war in their own words. Calling themselves 'personal journalists' – as contrasted with either 'professional' or 'amateur' reporters (Allan, 2004: 357) – these online diarists linked together information, opinion and intimate detail in ways thought to supplement the stories provided by recognized news outlets. They tended not to provide breaking news as much as focus attention on news reported but buried by the mainstream news organizations. Many saw the war in Iraq as their 'breakthrough'. In *Newsweek* reporter

Steven Levy's words, the blogs 'finally found their moment' as bombs struck Baghdad, when they were able to provide 'an easy-to-parse overview for news junkies who wanted information from all sides, and a personal insight that bypassed the sanitizing Quisinart of big media news editing' (cited in Allan, 2004: 358).

Prominent here was Salaam Pax, an invented *nom de guerre* for a 29-year-old architect living in Baghdad, who posted English language warblogs from September 2002 onward. Ranging in scope, the postings included humorous accounts of everyday life and angry responses to the events taking shape around him. Critically, this was 'embedded reporting of a different order' (Allan, 2004: 361), and the bloggers saw themselves doing what journalists did not. In Salaam Pax's words, 'I was telling everybody who was reading the web log . . . what the streets looked like . . . It is just somebody should be telling this because journalists weren't' (cited in Allan, 2004: 361).

In like fashion, online journalism sites run by marginal members of the journalistic community repeatedly provided access to information deemed inappropriate by the mainstream news organizations. When a furore erupted over the display of pictures of flag-draped coffins of US soldiers in April of 2004 and mainstream news organizations were prohibited from showing the photos, images instead appeared on a website run by Russ Kick – www.memoryhole.org; Kick had secured nearly 300 photos through a Freedom of Information Act request. When grisly photographs of the charred corpses of American contractors in Fallujah, Iraq, appeared that same April, non-US news organizations and their websites published footage of the bodies being beaten, dragged and hanging from the bridge. Following that display, the *Wall Street Journal* published a front-page rejoinder, separated from surrounding text in bold type, admitting that while US television showed 'unusual restraint' in airing the images, 'graphic photos and video were widely available on the Web, even on sites owned by traditional media. The ready availability of raw material has altered news decision-making' ('A Complex Picture', 2004). The paper followed that admission with an article where it pondered the fact that 'viewers now can seek out controversial images on the Internet even if mainstream news outlets avoid them' (Angwin and Rose, 2004: B1). Professional organizations also accommodated online journalism following the Fallujah coverage by publishing explicit guidelines on 'how to introduce truly disturbing images online' (Outing, 2004).

The war also drew significant attention from satiricists, comedians and late-night talk-show hosts, and through much of 2003 it remained the leading topic of jokes by late-night TV comedians Jay Leno, David Letterman and Conan O'Brien (Media Monitor, 2003). Satirical comedian Jon Stewart lampooned the prosecution of the war on Comedy Central's nightly comedy show, *The Daily Show*. Called by Bill Moyers a 'compendium of news interviews, and features, held up to a fractured mirror to reveal a greater truth' (Moyers, 2003), Stewart's show nonetheless raised the ire of various mainstream journalists, particularly so when his following reached significant proportions among US youth; as many people aged 18–29 received their news from TV comedy programmes *The Daily Show* and *Saturday Night Live* as from the nightly news (Pew Research Center for the People and the Press, 2004).

A similar case could be made, though on predictably debatable grounds, about the amateur photographers who took scores of digital photographs of the atrocities committed in

Abu Ghraib prison while serving in the US military. Though these photographs' display in the media was more serendipitous than intentional, it nonetheless raised the question of how what Susan Sontag labelled 'trophies' (Sontag, 2004: 27) extended the boundaries of who ~~provides the news beyond journalists themselves. As Sontag put it, where once~~ photographing war was the province of photojournalists, now the soldiers themselves are all ~~photographers – recording their war, their fun, their observations of what they find~~ picturesque, their atrocities – and swapping images among themselves and emailing them around the globe' (p. 27).

In each case, journalism changed by virtue of who inhabited its culture. It became, at least for a time, less authoritative, less reverent, in places more critical, more partisan and even ironic. And it became so in a way that spoke reams about the coverage of other kinds of public events. The 2004 annual report of the Project for Excellence in Journalism noted that only three of eight media sectors saw audience growth that year – ethnic media, alternative media and online media (*State of the Media*, 2004). It is no surprise, then, that during the 2004 US Presidential campaign, three dozen bloggers were given full press credentials at the Democratic national convention in August, prompting reporters to call 2004 'the year of the blog' (Lee, 2004: 7). If nothing else, this is evidence that when marginal members inhabit the community of journalists, they have impact, albeit delayed.

What is the culture of journalism for?

The most prevalent view of journalism focuses on its capacity to convey information. This view, which is primarily institutional in nature, sees journalism through its political effect, its role in maintaining an active and healthy body politic, and its impact on the public good. Journalism is considered a power-rendering institution, and scholars look at its influence on the surrounding community, its prestige, and its strength in asking what journalism is for. Much of this view has to do with notions of journalism being 'for' a culture, with an emphasis on what journalism does 'for' – and, in some views, 'to' – the public.

By contrast, the culture of journalism sees journalists as being 'in' a culture, viewing journalists not only as conveyors of information but also as producers of culture. Seeing journalism as a culture suggests that journalists themselves are part of the culture to which they report. How and to what degree journalism works for the people who create it is as important as the role it plays for its public. In this regard, journalists impart preference statements about what is good and bad, moral and amoral, and appropriate and inappropriate in the world, and their preference statements implicitly or explicitly shape the news. Journalists' positioning as the creators and conveyors of views about how the world works is linked with the positioning of their audiences, who make sense of the news in ways that reflect their own identity politics (Zelizer, 1993, 2004). Seeing journalism as culture thus goes beyond an emphasis on information relay and helps keep journalism's study in step with some of the more contemporary news developments, which, as already mentioned, have expanded to the unlikely places of satirical comedy shows, blogs, talk shows, cybersalons and reality television.

Coverage of the Iraq war rendered discussions of the public good somewhat unsatisfying, if for no other reason than 'good' journalism encountered obstacles. The shortcomings of the

US news media in Iraq have already been discussed. But the most visible discussion of the war coverage was stuck on the question of journalism's presumed optimum impact on the public. Much of this institutionally driven discourse focused on the issue of patriotism, with journalism's performance evaluated as to whether or not it worked for the public good. Despite the fact that initially readers' letters ran against the war ('War and the Letters Page', 2003), the climate for reportorial judgement was nonetheless set: CNN's lead morning anchor, Paula Zahn, said on-air after hearing a familiar song, 'If that rendition of the Star Spangled Banner doesn't stir you, I don't know what will', while an anxious observer saw 'US newsrooms bewitched by the war' (Moscou, 2003). US flags temporarily appeared on reporters' lapels and permanently adorned the studios of Fox News and MSNBC. The words 'we' and 'us' cluttered the US coverage, and professional organizations such as the Poynter Institute and the Project for Excellence in Journalism lobbied continual overviews of what to do about patriotism in the news.

While the question of how patriotic and impartial one could be was never fully resolved, it reduced the internal flux of covering Iraq into an overly coherent prism of patriotic behaviour without accounting for what was fast becoming the forefront of its operation. Particularly egregious was the degree to which the media bought into the US administration's line on the war. In the *Columbia Journalism Review*'s view, 'did the media fall for the Pentagon's spin? In a word, yes' (Smith, 2003: 28). But beyond the effect on information was the impact on journalistic performance itself: activities among journalists that were not explicitly supportive of the troops were labelled unpatriotic. The emergence of the so-called 'Fox Effect' (Rutenberg, 2003a), by which commentators regularly skewered anyone who did not strut out his or her patriotism, established a different playing ground for journalists used to protected borders on the issue of national sentiment. It was the 'cheerleading, can-do tone that infected too much of the reporting' (Smith, 2003: 8). And though charged with jingoism, Fox News lingered as the ratings leader in cable news.

The emphasis on patriotism obscured attention to what was a key aspect of journalistic coverage of Iraq – physical safety. What journalists were supposed to do reflected how well their capacity to report melded with their capacity to stay alive, shaped by concerns over physical danger and well-being, but such concerns rarely made it into the enthusiastic game plans for coverage laid out initially by US news organizations. Those accounts – given energized headlines like 'TV's Battle Plan' (Storm, 2003), 'Wire Services Deploy Their Own Troops' (Astor, 2003) and 'Papers Say They're Ready' (Strupp, 2003a) – bore the parameters of upbeat industrial overviews, telling readers excitedly how many reporters were going to Iraq or how they were to be transported; very little initial attention was paid to the question of physical danger. In one *Boston Globe* reporter's view, her preparation for entering a war zone was brief and non-comprehensive (personal comment, March 2003). Executives at news organizations admitted that they were also slow to provide counselling for reporters returning from combat (cited in Strupp, 2003c). Although war correspondents remained at risk for developing severe mental problems from covering war, particularly post-traumatic stress disorder (PTSD), with one in four certain to develop some problem after returning to the homefront, many lacked health insurance (Feinstein, 2003). One 16 year-old veteran with the *Christian Science Monitor* and no previous combat experience before Iraq said she remained jittery once back from the front and weeks later had yet to begin reading the news again (cited in Strupp, 2003c).

Danger's effect on journalistic practice quickly and consistently took its toll on the coverage. In the war's initial stages, the proximity to danger enhanced journalists' dependence on the embedding arrangements provided by the US and coalition forces, even when doing so meant the provision of less satisfying news stories. But even embedding could not shield reporters from their environment, as the deaths of certain journalists attested. Later in the war, when the hotels housing the press corps were strafed by coalition forces, non-Western reporters and some Western journalists claimed that they were being targeted (Massing, 2003). Such concerns reached a high point by mid 2004, following an increase in instances of threat, abduction and murder, when reporters began to keep to their hotel rooms, locked down in the middle of Baghdad and reporting on places such as Sadr City and Fallujah from afar. Online reporter Dahr Jamail, writing for the website Electronic Iraq, pointed to a 'horrendous disparity between what is really occurring on the ground and what the Western corporate media chooses to report . . . Even stories that were on the front pages stateside are regularly being covered from the press room and not the field' (cited in Schechter, 2004). Ridiculed by US deputy defence secretary Paul D. Wolfowitz in late June 2004 that they were too scared to get out and tell the story of the war, US journalists vied with the impression, created largely by obsequious video cameras manned by Iraqi nationals, that 'anyone can go anywhere in Iraq, even if it isn't true' (Fisher, 2004: 2). Calling the war coverage an 'experiment in war journalism', seen through the eyes of 'an Iraqi housewife, a college student, and a veteran of the Iran–Iraq war' and others who could go anywhere more freely than reporters, the *New York Times* admitted that it remained still too early to evaluate the strengths – and weaknesses – of what it called 'this novel reporting arrangement' (Fisher, 2004: 2). The fact that the paper offered such an evaluation 16 months into the war belied how ill-prepared much of Western media was for the physical dangers that awaited reporters. As Hassan Fattah, the founding editor of the English-language newspaper *Iraq Today*, commented, 'perhaps the most important – and difficult – decision any journalist in a war zone has to make is when to get out' (Fattah, 2004: 62). There is little room in traditional thinking about journalism that makes such a decision a natural option to providing coverage. And when the question of 'what journalism is for' is decided in conjunction with its impact on the public, the question of opting out of coverage is not viable.

The question of what journalism is for remains a largely unarticulated set of assumptions for evaluating journalistic practice, but in wartime, such evaluations move decidedly in the direction of the public good. Central to their realization, however, is the good of the reporters themselves, whose often compromised positions in wartime make necessary a more targeted focus on their circumstances. Such a view is offered when thinking about journalism as culture, in that seeing journalism through a cultural lens puts journalists back where they belong – part of the culture on which, to which and for which they report.

The culture of journalism

Seeing journalism through the lens of culture thus facilitates the examination of facets of journalism that have not been examined in much traditional news scholarship. These have always included features that regularly play out in newsmaking – how to connect form and content, how to navigate the often strategic but always changing relation between 'facts' and symbols, how to improvise in making news, how to accommodate the uneven and often unpredictable function of images, collective memories and journalism straitjackets.

But seeing journalism through culture helps focus attention on aspects of journalism that go under the radar of other ways of thinking about journalism. In Iraq, this involved journalists who wrestled with their patriotism, worked for online or alternative news media, learned new practices from marginal members of the community, cringed under the limitations created by technology, and worried over their physical safety. With no clear or universal answer to any of the dilemmas these issues created, seeing journalism as culture allows for their presence. It admits and works around the contradictions between what journalists would like to do and what they actually can do. It keeps tabs on the fluctuating definitions, boundaries, conventions and practices by which journalism is implemented, particularly in crisis situations such as wartime. And it does so by seeing journalism from the bottom up, without the prejudice of insisting that journalism conform to predetermined notions of a profession, an industry, an institution or a craft.

All of this suggests that seeing journalism through a cultural lens creates and proceeds from its own strategic dissonance: despite the prevalence of arguments for journalism's universal nature, the culture of journalism presupposes that journalistic conventions, routines and practices are dynamic and contingent on situational and historical circumstance. It offers a view of journalism that is porous, relative, non-judgemental and flexible. Given the troubling, uncontrollable and unclear horizons that contemporary journalists face, it may be that this is the best that we, as news scholars, can offer them in navigating their future.

Notes

1 For a more extended discussion of these issues, see Zelizer (2004).

2 For more on this, see Zelizer (2004).

References

Adam, G. S. (1993) *Notes Toward a Definition of Journalism*. St Petersburg, FL: Poynter Institute.

Allan, S. (2004) 'The Culture of Distance: Online Reporting of the Iraq War', in S. Allan and B. Zelizer (eds), *Reporting War: Journalism in Wartime*. London: Routledge, pp. 347–65.

Allan, S. and Zelizer, B. (eds) (2004) *Reporting War: Journalism in Wartime*. London: Routledge.

Angwin, J. and Rose, M. (2004) 'When the News is Gruesome, What's Too Graphic?', *Wall Street Journal*, 1 April, p. B1.

Astor, D. (2003) 'Wire Services Deploy Their Own Troops', *Editor and Publisher*, 27 February.

Becker, H. (1984) *Art Worlds*. Berkeley: University of California Press.

———(1986) 'Culture: A Sociological View', in *Doing Things Together*. Evanston, IL: Northwestern University Press, pp. 11–24.

Beckerman, G. (2004) 'In Their Skin', *Columbia Journalism Review*, March/April, 40–3.

Berger, P. (1963) *Invitation to Sociology: A Humanistic Perspective*. Garden City, NY: Doubleday.

Biernatzki, W. (2003) 'War and Media', *Communication Research Trends*, 22 (3), 2–31.

Blumenthal, R. and Rutenberg, J. (2003) 'Journalists are Assigned to Accompany Troops', *New York Times*, 14 February, p. A11.

Blumer, H. (1969) *Symbolic Interactionism: Perspective and Method*. Englewood Cliffs, NJ: Prentice Hall.

Boyd-Barrett, O. (2004) 'Understanding: The Second Casualty', in S. Allan and B. Zelizer (eds), *Reporting War: Journalism in Wartime*. London: Routledge, pp. 25–42.

Carey, J. W. (1986) 'The Dark Continent of American Journalism', in R. K. Manoff and M. Schudson (eds), *Reading the News*. New York: Pantheon, pp. 146–96.

CJR Comment (2004) 'Out of Sight, Out of Mind', *Columbia Journalism Review*, July/August, 6.

'Complex Picture, A' (2004) *Wall Street Journal*, 1 April, p. A1.

Cottle, S. (2000) 'New(s) Times: Towards a "Second Wave" of News Ethnography', *Communications*, 25 (1), 19–41.

Dahlgren, P. (1992) 'Introduction', in P. Dahlgren and C. Sparks (eds), *Journalism and Popular Culture*. London: Sage, pp. 1–23.

Deans, J. (2003) 'Fox Challenges CNN's US Ratings Dominance', *The Guardian*, 27 March.

Donvan, J. (2003) 'For the Unilaterals, No Neutral Ground', *Columbia Journalism Review*, May–June, 35–6.

Doward, J. (2003) 'Sky Wins Battle for Rolling News Audience', *The Observer*, 6 April.

Eagleton, T. (1995) *The Crisis of Contemporary Culture*. London: Oxford University Press.

Eisendorf, R. J. (2004) 'Are Terrorists Hijacking the News?' *San Francisco Chronicle*, 19 July, p. B7.

'Embedded Reporters: What Are Americans Getting?' (2003). Washington, DC: Project for Excellence in Journalism.

Fattah, H. (2004) 'Goodbye, Baghdad', *Columbia Journalism Review*, July/August, 62.

Feinstein, A. (2003) *Dangerous Lives*. Toronto: Thomas Allen.

Fisher, I. (2004) 'Reporting, and Surviving, Iraq's Dangers', *New York Times*, 18 July, section 4, 1–2.

Friedman, P. (2003) 'TV: A Missed Opportunity', *Columbia Journalism Review*, May/June, 29–31.

Geertz, C. (1973) *The Interpretation of Cultures*. New York: Basic Books.

Getler, M. (2003) 'Close Up and Vivid Reporting', *Washington Post*, 30 March.

Goodenough, W. (1981) *Culture, Language, and Society*. Reading, MA: Addison-Wesley.

Grossman, L. J. (2003) 'War and the Balance Sheet', *Columbia Journalism Review*, May–June, 6.

Hall, S. (1973) 'The Determinations of News Photographs', in S. Cohen and J. Young (eds), *The Manufacture of News*. London: Sage.

Hartley, J. (1982) *Understanding News*. London: Methuen.

Johnson, P. (2004) 'From Al-Jazeera, A Code of Conduct', *USA Today*, 18 July.

Lawler, A. (2003) 'Lifting the Fog of the Bias War', *Columbia Journalism Review*, November/December, 68–9.

Lee, J. (2004) 'Year of the Blog? Web Diarists Are Now Official Members of Convention Press Corps', *New York Times*, 26 July, p. P7.

Lowry, B. and Jensen, E. (2003) 'The "Gee Whiz" War', *Los Angeles Times*, 28 March, p. E1.

Lukes, S. (1975) 'Political Ritual and Social Integration', *Sociology*, 9 (2), May, 289–308.

Massing, M. (2003) 'The High Price of an Unforgiving War', *Columbia Journalism Review*, May/June, 33–5.

McCollam, D. (2004) 'The List: How Chalabi Played the Press', *Columbia Journalism Review*, July/August, 31–7.

Media Monitor, (2003) *The Media Go to War*. Washington, DC: Center for Media and Public Affairs, 17 (2) July/August.

Mitchell, G. (2004) 'Where Was Press When 1st Iraq Prison Allegations Arose?' *Editor and Publisher*, 13 May.

Mooney, C. (2004) 'The Editorial Pages and the Case for War', *Columbia Journalism Review*, March/April, 28–34.

Moscou, J. (2003) 'Newsrooms Bewitched by Iraq War', *Editor and Publisher*, 30 January.

Moses, L. (2003) 'How Would Iraq War Affect Advertising?' *Editor and Publisher*, 5 March.

Moyers, B. (2003) 'In Depth: Bill Moyers Interviews Jon Stewart', *Now With Bill Moyers*, PBS Transcript, 11 July.

Outing, S. (2003) 'War: A Defining Moment for Net News', *Editor and Publisher*, 26 March.

———(2004) 'How to Introduce Truly Disturbing Images Online', posted on www.poynteronline.org, 1 April.

Park, R. E. (1925) 'The Natural History of the Newspaper', in R. E. Park *et al.* (eds), *The City*. Chicago: University of Chicago Press, pp. 80–98.

———(1940) 'News as a Form of Knowledge', *American Journal of Sociology*, 45, March, 669–86.

'Pause for Hindsight, A' (editorial) (2004) *New York Times*, 16 July.

Rutenberg, J. (2003a) 'Cable's War Coverage Suggests a New "Fox Effect" on Television', *New York Times*, 16 April, p. B9.

———(2003b) 'From Cable Star to Face in the Crowd', *New York Times*, 5 May, p. C1.

Sandler, L. (2003) 'Magazine War Coverage: Time is the Enemy', *Los Angeles Times*, 24 March.

Schechter, D. (2003) *Embedded: Weapons of Mass Deception: How the Media Failed to Cover the War in Iraq*. New York: News Dissector.

———(2004) 'Misreporting the Iraqi Uprising', posted on www.mediachannel.org, 8 April.

Schudson, M. (1991) 'The Sociology of News Production, Revisited', in J. Curran and M. Gurevitch (eds), *Mass Media and Society*. London: Edward Arnold, pp. 141–59.

Sims, A. C. (2003) 'Music Channels are "N-Synch" with War Coverage', Fox News, 25 February.

Singer, J. B. (2003) 'Who Are These Guys? The Online Challenge to the Notion of Journalistic Professionalism', *Journalism: Theory, Practice and Criticism*, 4 (2), 139–63.

Smith, T. (2003) 'The Real-Time War: Hard Lessons', *Columbia Journalism Review*, May/June, 26–31.

Sontag, S. (2004) 'Regarding the Torture of Others', *New York Times Magazine*, 23 May, 24–9, 42.

State of the News Media (2004) Annual Report. Washington, DC: Project for Excellence in Journalism, 2004.

Storm, J. (2003) 'TV's Battle Plan', *Philadelphia Inquirer*, 11 March.

Strupp, J. (2003a) 'Papers Say They're Ready to Cover Iraq War', *Editor and Publisher*, 27 February.

———(2003b) 'Papers Roll Out "Special" Forces', *Editor and Publisher*, 23 March.

Strupp, J. (2003c) 'Out of Embed, But Facing Trauma?', *Editor and Publisher*, 24 April.

Swartz, J. (2003) 'Iraq War Could Herald a New Age of Web Based News Coverage', *USA Today*, 19 March.

Swidler, A. (1986) 'Culture in Action: Symbols and Strategies' in *American Sociological Review* 51, April, 273–86.

'The *Times* and Iraq' (editorial) (2004) *New York Times*, 26 May.

Walker, L. (2003) 'A Medium Meets Its War', *Washington Post*, 20 March.

'War and the Letters Page: Who's Counting?' (2003) *Columbia Journalism Review*, May/June, 10.

Williams, R. (1978) 'The Press and Popular Culture: An Historical Perspective', in G. Boyce *et al.* (eds), *Newspaper History from the Seventeenth Century to the Present Day*. Beverly Hills, CA: Sage, pp. 41–50.

———(1982) *The Sociology of Culture*. New York: Schocken.

Zelizer, B. (1992) *Covering the Body: The Kennedy Assassination, the Media, and the Shaping of Collective Memory*. Chicago: University of Chicago Press.

———(1993) 'Journalists as Interpretive Communities', *Critical Studies in Mass Communication*, 10, September, 219–37.

———(1998) *Remembering to Forget: Holocaust Memory Through the Camera's Eye*. Chicago: University of Chicago Press.

———(2004) *Taking Journalism Seriously: News and the Academy*. Thousand Oaks, CA: Sage.

Zelizer, B. and Stuart A. (2002) (eds), *Journalism After September 11*. London: Routledge.

chapter eleven

Comparing Media Systems

DANIEL C. HALLIN AND PAOLO MANCINI

Introduction

The comparative method has been fundamental to the the development of social theory since the late nineteenth century. Curiously, however, it has played little role in the field of communication. The old classic *Four Theories of the Press* (Siebert *et al.*, 1956: 1) set out to answer the question: 'Why does [the press] apparently serve different purposes and appear in widely different forms in different countries?' The limited progress communication scholars have made in addressing the question is eloquently symbolized by the very fact that *Four Theories of the Press* is still widely used as a framework for comparison worldwide, even though it contained little analysis of the way media systems actually operated, and only really addressed the media in the USA, Britain and the Soviet Union.

Why did a tradition of comparative research fail to develop for so long? The field of communication shifted to a focus on media effects rather than media systems: most of the research in the generation following *Four Theories of the Press* was about how particular media messages affected attitudes and beliefs of individual audience members, not about the media as institutions within a wider social and political system. Communication research also developed in a context where professional education was often dominant. Journalism schools were intended to pass on a model of how journalism 'ought' to be done, and comparative research seemed much too 'relativistic' and impractical from this point of view. American and British educators, especially, believed they knew the right way to do journalism, and were more interested in passing this on to the rest of the world than in exploring other media models. *Four Theories of the Press* reflected this normative approach, focusing on 'the authoritarian libertarian, social responsibility and Soviet communist concepts of what the press *should* be and do' (this was its subtitle, emphasis added), rather than on how the media actually interacted with other institutions, groups and interests in society. Only in recent years has a real tradition of comparative research begun to emerge in communication, and only recently, for other reasons we will not try to explore here, have scholars in comparative politics and political sociology begun to take an interest in the media.

Why comparative analysis?

Comparative analysis in social theory can be understood in terms of two basic functions: its role in concept formation and clarification and its role in causal inference.

It is valuable, in the first place, because it sensitizes us to variation and to similarity, and this can contribute powerfully to the refinement of our conceptual apparatus. Most of the literature on the media is highly ethnocentric, in the sense that it refers only to the experience of a single country, yet is written in general terms, as though the model that prevailed in that country were universal. This style of research has often held media researchers back from asking why media systems have the particular characteristics they do. Important aspects of media systems are assumed to be 'natural', or in some cases are so familiar that they are not perceived at all. Because it 'denaturalizes' a media system that is familiar to us, comparison forces us to conceptualize more clearly what aspects of that system actually require explanation. Our own comparative work began with the experience of exactly this type of insight. Comparing US and Italian TV news in the early 1980s, familiar patterns of news construction, which we had to some extent assumed were the natural form of TV news, were revealed to us as products of a particular system. We were thus forced to notice and to try to account for many things we had passed over, for example the highly interpretive character of American compared with Italian TV news, a characteristic which contradicted common assumptions about 'objective' journalism in the American system (Hallin and Mancini, 1984).

If comparison can sensitize us to variation, it can also sensitize us to similarity. In the USA, for example, media coverage of politicians has become increasingly negative over the past few decades. We typically explain that change by reference to historical events such as Vietnam and Watergate, as well as changes in the conduct of election campaigns. This trend, however, is virtually universal across Western democracies – which suggests that particular historical events internal to the USA are not an adequate explanation. Comparative analysis, in other words, can protect us from false generalizations, but can also encourage us to move from overly particular explanations to more general ones where this is appropriate.

The second reason comparison is important in social investigation is that it allows us in many cases to test hypotheses about the interrelationships among social phenomena. 'We have only one means of demonstrating that one phenomenon is the cause of another: it is to compare the cases where they are simultaneously present or absent', wrote Émile Durkheim in *The Rules of Sociological Method* (1965). This has become the standard methodology in much of the social sciences, particularly among those interested in analysing social phenomena at the system level, where variation will often not exist in a single-country study. This is a more advanced use of comparative analysis, since it assumes that the basic work of clarifying concepts and dimensions or 'variables' for comparison has already been done. For the most part, comparative study in communication is still too primitive to be able to do this very systematically. We do believe, however, that comparative analysis has great potential to help us sort our relationships between media systems and their social and political settings, and will try to suggest some key relationships between characteristics of political history and political systems, on the one hand, and media systems, on the other. This does not mean that we have to see these relations in terms of one-way causality between discrete 'independent' and 'dependent' variables; in some cases such a model may be appropriate, but in most cases, we believe, the relation between political and media systems must be seen in terms of the co-evolution of the media system with other social structures.

Media system models

In this chapter we present the results of a comparative analysis of media systems in 18 countries of western Europe and North America (Hallin and Mancini, 2004). We organize the discussion in terms of three models which we call the Polarized Pluralist Model, characteristic of southern Europe (France, Greece, Italy, Portugal and Spain), the Democratic Corporatist Model, characteristic of northern and central Europe (Austria, Belgium, Denmark, Finland, Germany, Netherlands, Norway, Sweden and Switzerland) and the Liberal Model, characteristic of what could be called the north Atlantic region (Canada, Ireland, the UK and the USA).

Several qualifications are important to stress here. The groups of countries we discuss under the three ideal types are not homogeneous, and it is important to recognize their differences as well as their similarities. Many media systems can be considered as mixed cases, combining elements of more than one model. Figure 11.1 gives a graphic summary of the way we see the relation of individual cases to the ideal types represented by the three models. As the figure suggests, we see the media systems of France, Britain, Belgium and certain other countries very much as mixed cases, and few cases really coincide exactly with the ideal types, though we will not be able to deal extensively with these variations here.

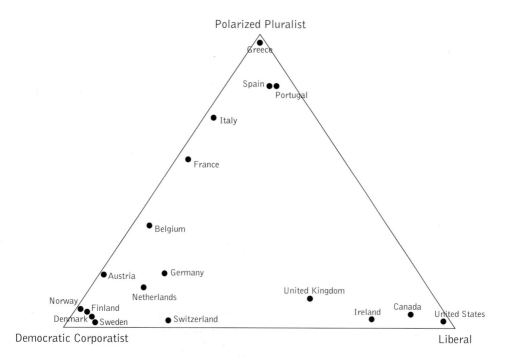

Figure 11.1 Relation of individual cases to the three models.

It is also important to keep in mind that individual media systems are also not *internally* homogeneous. This was another limitation of *Four Theories of the Press*: it gave the impression that each media system had a certain philosophical core which was reflected in each element of the system. In fact, real media systems often involve elements that evolved in different historical or structural contexts and operate according to different logics, or divisions of labour between different parts of the system. It is common, for example, that print media, at least at the national level, reflect a logic of 'external pluralism', with different newspapers or magazines representing different political tendencies. Broadcast media, on the other hand, were typically characterized by very limited channel capacity in their early days, and were required by law to be internally pluralistic.

Finally, media systems are not static. Change over time, in fact, is a central focus of our study. One thing we try to show is that media system development is 'path dependent', and that we cannot understand why media systems are as they are without looking back at the historical roots of their development. Our model emphasizes a particular phase in the development of the North American and European media systems; the models we describe were most distinct from the 1940s to the 1980s. We take the nation-state as the unit of analysis for comparison, because media systems have been organized primarily on a national basis for several centuries. It is not self-evident that this will always be true. Globalization, commercialization and other forces have made national media systems less distinct than they were a generation ago. It is conceivable that the differences we describe here will eventually disappear altogether; at present, however, they remain significant, even if they are less dramatic than in the past.

Dimensions of comparison

In comparing the three media system models we will focus on four dimensions or clusters of variables:

1. Development of the mass press. One of the most obvious differences between media systems is that rates of newspaper circulation vary dramatically. In Norway, about 720 newspapers are sold per 1,000 population, in the USA, about 260, in Greece, about 80. These patterns were set in the late nineteenth century, and have persisted despite dramatic changes in economic development and political structure. They reflect different patterns of social development, histories of the press, and roles the press has played in political and social life. Most basically, a distinction can be drawn between systems in which the press is directed at the mass public, and systems where it is directed at an educated, politically-active elite, and serves the process of bargaining and debate within that elite. Differences in the use and role of electronic media are much less marked, particularly since the introduction of commercial broadcasting in Europe.

2. Political parallelism. In some systems, the organization of the media system closely reflects the main lines of division within the political system; in other systems the relation is much looser. This is often referred to as party–press parallelism, though today, when few newspapers have clear identifications with a single political party, it is more useful to use the

more general term political parallelism. In the past, many newspapers had *organizational ties* with political parties or trade unions. Party papers were not necessarily directly controlled by their respective parties, but often were owned by associations connected with them – groups of readers, for example, made up of supporters of a particular party. Party press parallelism is also manifested in the character of *news content*, including the degree to which media discourses and discourses of partisan politics coincide, in *career patterns of journalists* and in the *patterns of readership or viewership*. In Spain, for example, in 1993, 74 per cent of the readers of the newspaper *ABC* voted for the conservative Partido Popular, compared with only 14 per cent of the readers of *El País* (Gunther *et al.*, 2000: 46).

3. Journalistic professionalism. This is a tricky concept, and we will only be able in this chapter to touch on some of the issues that arise in trying to use it in comparative analysis. We define it here in terms of three interrelated criteria: the degree to which journalists enjoy autonomy in exercising their functions; the degree to which journalism has developed distinct shared norms and standards of practice, separate from those of other social 'fields', to use Bourdieu's term (particularly the field of party politics); and finally the degree to which journalists see themselves and are seen by society as serving the public as a whole rather than particular sectors or actors. Journalistic professionalism is sometimes, though not always, manifested in formal institutions such as journalists' unions, professional associations and press councils.

4. The role of the state. Media systems vary significantly in the degree and kind of state involvement. Most European countries developed primarily public broadcasting systems, for example, while the USA had no such system at the national level until 1967, and it remains a small part of the media system. Some systems have extensive press subsidies, others do not. In some, the broadcast regulators are relatively party-politicized, in others they are more autonomous and professionalized, similar to a central bank.

Table 11.1 summarizes our three models in terms of these four dimensions. In the following sections of this chapter we summarize the principal characteristics of the three models, and explain why distinct systems arose in different groups of countries, connecting the development of media systems with historical patterns of political and social development.

The Polarized Pluralist Model

Balzac once described the press as:

The word adapted to express everything which is published periodically in politics and literature, and where one judges the works both of those who govern and of those who write, two ways of leading men (quoted in Ferenczi, 1993: 28).

In southern Europe the press developed as part of the worlds of literature and, above all, of politics, much more than of the market. This path of development produced a media system characterized by a lower-circulation, elite-oriented press, a lower level of professionalization of journalism, a high degree of political parallelism and strong involvement of the state in the media sector.

	Mediterranean or Polarized Pluralist Model (France, Greece, Italy, Portugal, Spain)	Northern European or Democratic Corporatist Model (Austria, Belgium, Denmark, Finland, Germany, Netherlands, Norway, Sweden, Switzerland)	North Atlantic or Liberal Model (Britain, USA, Canada, Ireland)
Newspaper industry	Low newspaper circulation, elite politically-oriented press	High newspaper circulation; early development of mass circulation commercial press	Medium newspaper circulation; early development of mass circulation commercial press
Political parallelism	High political parallelism; external pluralism, commentary-oriented journalism; parliamentary or government model of broadcast governance – politics-over-broadcasting systems	External pluralism especially in national press; historically strong party press; shift toward neutral commercial press; politics-in-broadcasting system with substantial autonomy	Neutral commercial press, information-oriented journalism; internal pluralism (but external pluralism in Britain); professional model of broadcast governance – formally autonomous system
Professionalization	Weaker professionalization; instrumentalization	Strong professionalization; institutionalized self-regulation	Strong professionalization; non-institutionalized self-regulation
Role of the state in the media system	Strong state intervention; press subsidies in France and Italy; periods of censorship; 'savage deregulation' (except France)	Strong state intervention but with protection for press freedom; press subsidies, particularly strong in Scandinavia; strong public-service broadcasting	Market dominated (except strong public broadcasting in Britain and Ireland)

Table 11.1. The three models: media system characteristics

The readers of nineteenth-century Italian newspapers, as Ricuperati (1981: 1087) puts it, were 'a public made up of erudites, theologians, university professors, members of scientific academies: a strong presence of clergymen'. As battles between conservative and liberal forces increased, the press increasingly became a means of fighting them, and a principal vehicle by which a man of ambition might enter the world of politics. Circulation rates were relatively low, reflecting lower literacy rates, a strong separation between urban and rural culture, and an elite-centred pattern of political participation. France was a partial exception to this pattern; newspaper circulation rates were quite high there during the late nineteenth and early twentieth centuries. But even in France the press was never as profitable as in countries such as Britain, Germany or the USA, and circulation rates eventually fell. Enzo Forcella, an Italian journalist, once wrote,

> a political journalist, in our country, can count on fifteen thousand readers: the ministers and subsecretaries (all of them), members of Parliament (some), party and trade unions leaders, the top clergy and those industrialists who want to show themselves well informed. The rest don't count, even if a newspaper sells three hundred thousand copies . . . the whole system is organized around the relation of the journalist to that group of privileged readers' (Forcella, 1959: 451).

In the 1970s, more market-oriented newspapers began to emerge in southern Europe, in the form of papers such as *La Repubblica, El País, Diario 16* and *El Periodico de Catalunya*; Spain is one of the few countries in the world with rising newspaper circulations over the past couple of decades. But southern European newspapers still tend to be sophisticated products with relatively small, educated readerships. Their circulation is especially limited among women, reflecting a history of gender differences in literacy rates as well as the political character of the press and the historical exclusion of women from the world of politics. In Portugal 58 per cent of men and 24 per cent of women read a newspaper in a typical week (World Association of Newspapers, 2001). Electronic media are the true mass media of southern Europe.

Political parallelism

Political parallelism is high in southern Europe. As the quotation by Balzac suggests, the journalism of the region is historically more a journalism of ideas than of information or entertainment. The purpose of a newspaper has, historically, been to shape opinion among the politically active population and to advance the process of bargaining among political factions. The party press played an important role in France and Italy – the two countries in the region with the longest history of democracy and the ones with the most developed mass political parties, especially in the period just after World War II. The style of journalism has emphasized commentary, and although informational styles have gained ground in recent years, newspapers in the Polarized Pluralist countries still mix commentary and reporting more than those of the other two systems. The press is characterized by external pluralism and political diversity, with a wide range of newspapers – and to some extent also electronic media – reflecting different political viewpoints. (The principal exception is the local press in

France, the only strong local press in southern Europe.) *La Repubblica*, the pioneeer in more market-oriented journalism in Italy, always had a strong identity as a paper of the Left, while almost all media in Spain, print or broadcast, are divided between two political camps, one close to the Partido Popular and one close to the Socialist PSOE. Public broadcasting in Italy, meanwhile, has been organized according to the *lottizazione* which divides political power among the parties, while public broadcasting in the other countries of the region has been under the effective control of the political majority, with France moving in the 1980s toward a more independent public broadcasting system.

Professionalization

Professionalization of journalism, meanwhile, has developed recently, and is not as strong as in the Liberal or Democratic Corporatist systems. Nineteenth-century newspapers, as Ortega and Humanes (2000:125) put it for the Spanish case, 'valued more highly writers, politicians and intellectuals' than reporters, and journalism was 'a secondary occupation, poorly paid, and to which one aspired as a springboard to a career in politics'. The status of reporters has improved. Still, journalistic autonomy is lower than in other systems. One comparative survey of journalists (Donsbach and Patterson, 1992) found 7 per cent of German journalists reporting that 'pressures from editors and senior management' were an 'important factor' in their jobs, compared with 13 per cent in the USA, 15 per cent in Britain and 27 per cent in Italy. Journalists at Spain's public broadcaster launched a major protest in 2004 against political manipulation of the news, which is indeed characteristic of the Spanish system. The limited autonomy of journalists in southern Europe reflects a pattern of 'instrumentalization', in which industrialists or politicians buy newspapers or other media outlets less for the purpose of making money than intervening in the political world. In Greece, as Papathanassopoulos (2001) notes, 'give me a ministry or I'll start a newspaper' is a traditional political threat. There are some exceptions to this pattern, especially in France, where there was a strong reaction against instrumentalization of the press after World War II, and journalists gained substantial control of many newspapers. At *Le Monde*, journalists retain substantial ownership rights and the right to elect the Director of the paper.

Distinct standards of professional practice are also less developed in southern Europe. In Italy, even though it is the only country in Europe in which access to an official Order of Journalists is controlled by an entrance exam, a code of ethics was only established in the 1990s, and surveys show it still enjoys only limited agreement among Italian journalists. The only press council in southern Europe is in Catalonia. And as the pattern of instrumentalization suggests, there is not a strong norm that media institutions should serve society as a whole; they are traditionally seen as representing particular parties, factions or interests.

Role of the state

The state plays an important, and often interventionist role in the Polarized Pluralist system. In part, this is because media have been weak economically, and therefore have been dependent on the state, as well as on support from private interests desirous of a political voice. Through much of their history, the countries of southern Europe have been under dictatorship, and the media have been censored or controlled by the state or ruling party (as with the Fascist press in Spain). In democratic periods, too, however, the role of the state has been strong. France and Italy have the highest levels of press subsidy in Europe. The state has often owned media enterprises, either in whole or in part, sometimes through parastatal companies (which have also been important advertisers). The French government, for example, invested in the *périfériques*, commercial radio stations based outside France, which, during the period when public service broadcasting had a legal monopoly, provided significant competition. Political actors often become involved in organizing the financing of the sale of a media outlet or the creation of a new one.

There is also, however, another side to the role of the state in southern Europe. In many cases, its grasp exceeds its reach, and because of political factionalism and clientelism, it does not always regulate media as effectively as the state in other systems. The most obvious example here would be Italy, where the political system failed to establish a regulatory system for broadcasting after the Italian Supreme Court invalidated the monopoly of public broadcasting in the 1970s. Berlusconi's empire was built in that regulatory vacuum. Traquina (1995) talks about a pattern of 'savage deregulation' in Portugal in the 1980s and 1990s, and this term applies in many ways to most of the region. The exception is France, which has always had an effective central state: the Conseil Supérieur de l'Audiovisuel is a strong regulatory agency by world standards.

Political history, structure and culture

The historical roots of this media system lie in the fact that the institutions of the *ancien régime* in Europe – feudalism and patrimonialism, the monarchy and the Catholic or Orthodox Church – were particularly strong in southern Europe, and as a result, the transition towards modernity and liberal institutions was relatively long and conflicted. When democracy was established in the region, it tended toward the form Sartori (1976) called polarized pluralism, a kind of political system characterized by relatively large numbers of political parties with distinct ideologies spanning a wide spectrum, including parties opposed to the basic institutions of capitalism and of democracy. Not all the countries of southern Europe fit Sartori's classic model; Spain and Portugal, for example, have a smaller number of parties today than a classic polarized pluralist system. But all share the history in which Sartori's pattern was rooted, and much of its political syle.

The development of the media system was profoundly shaped by this history. The strength of the *ancien régime*, first of all, slowed the growth of the mass circulation press in a variety of ways: mass literacy was never a priority in the counter-reformation tradition, for example, and patrimonialist patterns of social organization were associated with private control rather than public circulation of information. Political polarization was closely connected with political parallelism in the media: the wide spectrum of ideological perspectives that contended in southern Europe meant that claims of political neutrality or the idea that 'fact' could be separated from 'opinion' seemed naïve or opportunistic. Professionalization was limited by the strong politicization of the press, as actors outside journalism tended to remain in control, and differences within the profession made it difficult to achieve consensus on professional norms. The strong role of the state in southern Europe – both in society and in the media system – reflected both the relative weakness of the market and the bourgeoisie, and the politicization of society.

The Democratic Corporatist Model

The first 'corantos', forerunners of the modern newspaper, originated in trading cities such as Amsterdam, Antwerp, Frankfurt and Cologne. The press developed early and strongly in northern and north-central Europe for several reasons: the early development of merchant capitalism, which required a flow of public information; high literacy rates, encouraged by the Protestant Reformation; and a relatively early introduction of liberal institutions, including press freedom. The first official recognition of press freedom was in Sweden in 1766. The 'Democratic Corporatist' countries are characterized by high rates of newspaper circulation and many-layered print media markets, combining national, regional and in most countries strong local newspapers, and often both a tabloid and broadsheet press.

Political parallelism

In the Polarized Pluralist system, newspapers developed as part of the world of politics. In the Liberal system, as we shall see, commercial newspapers displaced newspapers established to represent parties and other organized social groups. In the Democratic Corporatist system, a strong commercial press developed alongside a strong party press and other media connected to organized social groups, and though the party press has declined in the last generation, a significant degree of political parallelism remains in the countries of northern Europe. The development of the press in this region was motivated partly by the needs of growing merchant communities. But it was also motivated by political conflict. The Reformation was followed by the Thirty Years War (1618–48) which involved most of the countries in this part of Europe. Modern political propaganda originated in this conflict, which created a tradition of using the print media as a means to influence opinion in the public sphere.

The religious and political divisions that began with the Reformation combined with divisions of language, class and ideology to create plural societies composed of highly self-conscious and organized social groups. One of the means by which these groups organized themselves and contended for influence in the public sphere was by creating their own newspapers and eventually, in some countries, other media. Party papers and others connected to organized social groups combined with the commercial press to develop the strong habits of newspaper-reading that characterize the region. The social networks of these groups were important means of distributing newspapers, and the habit of newspaper-reading in part reflected the culture of group solidarity. Through the first half of the twentieth century, virtually all newspapers, commercial or what we might call 'representative', had clearly-identified partisan affiliations. Denmark, for example, had what was know as the 'four-party press system' in which any city of significant size had one paper associated with each of the four major political parties.

The concentration of newspaper markets began weakening party and other representative papers by the middle of the century. But party papers were still important through the 1970s, particularly in Austria and in Scandinavia. Høyer and Lorentzen (1977) estimated that in the early 1970s party-affiliated papers represented 92 per cent of the press in Denmark, 87 per cent in Norway and 97 per cent in Sweden, and large percentages of journalists, particularly in the socialist press, were active in politics, holding party or public office. By the end of the century, true party papers had almost disappeared. Denmark had 14 Social Democratic papers in 1960, and 7 through the 1970s and 1980s, but the last of these closed in 2001. These changes in newspaper markets went along with shifts in journalistic style toward more information-oriented reporting with considerably less mixing of commentary and reporting than in earlier years.

Nevertheless, a significant degree of political parallelism still exists in the countries where the Democratic Corporatist Model developed. The national (or what the Germans call super-regional) press is still characterized by external pluralism, with a newpaper representing a variety of ideological tendencies, and political coverage reflecting partisan slants consistent with these tendencies. In the Dutch case, for example, newspapers, once tied to the separate ideological and religious 'pillars' into which Dutch society was organized (Protestant, Catholic, Liberal and Socialist), 'gradually redefined their substantive profiles, a process that in some instances resulted in substantive distinctiveness and in others in indistinct "catchallism". Most national papers opted for distinctiveness in order to appeal to audiences differentiated along left–right and lifestyle lines' (van der Eijk, 2000: 312). Research by Donsbach and Patterson (2004) shows that in Germany the political views of journalists are fairly strongly correlated with the political orientation of the medium they work for, while in the USA there is no such correlation.

Another manifestation of the importance of parties and organized social groups in the Democratic Corporatist system lies in the fact that public broadcasting systems and councils that regulate commercial broadcasting are in some cases based on representation of such groups. In the Dutch case, social groups actually ran public broadcasting directly, with time allocated to broadcasting associations rooted in the four pillars. These associations still exist in public broadcasting, though their significance is much diminished in a world where commercial broadcasting is dominant. In Germany and Austria parties and other 'socially relevant groups' are represented on broadcasting councils, and in Belgium – a bit more similar to the Polarized Pluralist system – the parties dominate public broadcasting. This contrasts with the Liberal notion – reflected in the tradition of the BBC – that broadcasting should be 'above politics'. The British tradition holds that if public broadcasting is to serve the society as a whole, parties and organized social groups must be kept *out* of its governance; the continental European tradition often tends toward the view that all such interests must be allowed *in* to the process.

Professionalization

The Democratic Corporatist Model combines many media system characteristics that are often assumed to be incompatible, mainly because media studies has generally taken the Liberal Model as the norm. The combination of strong commercial with a strong political press is one manifestation of this. Another is the fact that in the Democratic Corporatist system a high level of political parallelism has coexisted with a high level of journalistic professionalization. Journalistic autonomy is relatively high in the Democratic Corporatist system. As we have seen, Patterson and Patterson's comparative survey found Common journalists least likely to report pressures from senior editors and management. Even at papers directly connected to political parties, journalists eventually shifted toward an attitude that they should 'not take orders from either politicians or organizations' (Hadenius, 1983: 300). Many of the Democratic Corporatist countries have laws intended to protect the autonomy of journalists against intervention by media owners, and protections for journalists in public broadcasting are also strong. Consensus on journalistic ethics is also strong compared with other systems, cutting across political divisions and creating a culture in which the media are seen as institutions serving society as a whole, even where they also have political tendencies. Strong journalists' unions and professional associations developed early in Democratic Corporatist countries, and these introduced codes of ethics that enjoy high degrees of consensus. The Democratic Corporatist Model has much more formal organization of the profession of journalism than other systems. This is manifested in the fact that most of the Democratic Corporatist countries have Press Councils, and these are among the strongest such institutions in the world (though in countries such as Austria and Germany, where an important sensationalist press exists, they are of limited use in regulating this sector).

The role of the state

Here again there are two sides to the Democratic Corporatist Model. A Swedish newspaper wrote in the 1970s:

> In our view the state has a responsibility for the mass media. Firstly, it has the responsibility to ensure that freedom of expression and freedom of the press are formally and in reality guaranteed by legislation. Journalists must be guaranteed the right to seek information and to disseminate their knowledge. However, the state's responsibility is wider than this. In the service of democracy and its citizens the state has a responsibility to create and maintain an information and press system that will accommodate many and diverse voices (Gustafsson, 1980: 104).

This conception combines the Liberal principle of limited government and press freedom in the 'negative' sense that state control of media and information is restricted, with a positive conception of state responsibility for developing the media as a social institution. As we have seen, northern European countries were early adopters of press freedom as well as rights of access to public information. They also have strong welfare states, however, and this is manifested in media policy as in other areas. They have particularly well-funded and 'pure' public broadcasting systems, that is, systems with little or no advertising revenue. Many have systems of press subsidy, which were introduced in the 1970s to slow concentration of newspaper markets and to prevent commercial papers from entirely displacing the papers representing social groups and parties. They also have relatively strong regulation of media industries, with rules for example on advertising to children or on journalistic autonomy in news organizations.

Political history, structure and culture

Northern and north-central Europe differ from southern Europe in two ways that matter to us here. First, the cultural tradition of the Reformation prevailed in much of the region, and this was more favourable than the counter-Reformation tradition to the development of the press and the public sphere. Second, while the social structure of southern Europe was dominated by large landowners (including the monarchy and Church), small independent producers had a much larger role in northern and north-central Europe, including merchants and artisans in many of the cities of Germany, Switzerland and the Low Countries, and 'yeoman' farmers in Scandinavia. These differences meant that conservative forces were weaker in the north relative to the forces of liberalism, and the consolidation of liberal institutions happened earlier, without the protracted conflict that occurred in the south. The strength of small independent producers also encouraged the self-organization of subcommunities which we have seen is characteristic of this region.

In the 1920s, when economic crisis and political polarization produced a breakdown of democracy in much of Europe, the smaller countries of northern Europe developed Democratic Corporatism as a means of preserving social solidarity. This involved institutionalizing a process of bargaining among diverse social groups, which were already by this time extremely well organized. Austria and Germany, whose social and political histories were somewhat more similar to those of southern Europe, suffered extreme polarization during this period (the German Weimar Republic is among the classic cases of Polarized Pluralism), but adopted much of the Democratic Corporatist model after World War II.

Democratic Corporatism, and the historical pattern in which it developed, are closely connected with the media system we have examined. Protestantism and early liberalism contributed to the development of the mass circulation press. The strength of organized social groups also contributed to the development of the mass circulation press, and to the strength of political parallelism. At the same time, the Democratic Corporatist system offered fertile ground for the consolidation of journalistic professionalism. Journalists organized, as did other subgroups in society. As Katzenstein (1985) points out, moreover, Democratic Corporatism combined diversity of parties and organized social interests with a high degree of consensus on the rules of the political game and a sense of a common interest transcending ideological differences. In this context, it is not surprising that journalists too, despite their relatively politicized role, were able to move toward consensus on their own rules of the game. The Democratic Corporatist bargain, finally, involved a major expansion of the welfare state, and this was manifested in state support for a diverse media system as it was in state support for many other social objectives.

The Liberal Model

The most distinctive characteristic of the Liberal Model is the early development of commercial media, and their eventual displacement of party papers and other media that served organized social groups rather than the market. A commercial newspaper industry began to develop earliest in the USA, which was also the only major industrialized country to develop a broadcasting system that was almost purely commercial, until the formation of a relatively small public broadcasting system in 1967. Britain also introduced commercial broadcasting in the 1950s, a generation before most of the rest of Europe. The dominance of commercial media combined with elements of political culture to produce lower levels of political parallelism in many cases, though the British press is an important exception. Journalistic professionalism is relatively high, though not as formally institutionalized as in the Democratic Corporatist Model. A smaller role for the state is another of the defining characteristics of the Liberal Model, though there are again important exceptions.

Development of the mass circulation press

In the USA and Britain, literacy rates were high (though less so in the slaveholding South in America), press freedom, the market, and representative political institutions were all developed early, creating favourable conditions for the early development of newspapers. In the US case, newspapers were primarily business enterprises from a very early date, and with the introduction of the penny press in the 1830s, a strong commercial mass circulation press began to develop. In Britain, taxation of the press delayed its commercial development until the 1850s, but it took off rapidly in the late nineteenth century. In Britain, newspaper circulation rates today are comparable with those in many of the Democratic Corporatist countries, at more than 400 sold per thousand population. In the other countries covered here they are a bit lower, about 260 per thousand in the USA, 205 in Canada and 190 in Ireland.

Political parallelism

As in the other models examined here, the early development of the press in the Liberal Model was strongly connected with the world of politics. In Britain, newspapers began to develop as the pattern of government and opposition in parliament emerged, and political factions subsidized newspapers to advance their causes. In the USA, Tocqueville connected the prominent role of the newspaper in American life to the development of voluntary associations, and the expansion of the penny press was intimately connected to the expansion of the franchise in the 1820s and the subsequent development of mass parties. Early mass-circulation newspapers in all four countries (Britain, the USA, Canada and Ireland) usually had strong partisan affiliations. The commercial press, however, mostly displaced the kinds of media directly tied to parties and trade unions which remained so important in the Polarized Pluralist and Democratic Corporatist models. There is an important debate in media studies in the Liberal countries about whether the triumph of commercial media should be seen as liberating the media from political control, or as enhancing the power of commercial interests within the public sphere.

In the USA and Canada political parallelism declined substantially during the first half of the twentieth century. Journalistic culture came to be dominated by the principles of political neutrality and separation between the media and the institutions of political life, and 'catch-all' media which avoided identification with political parties or tendencies for the most part prevail. Patterson and Donsbach (1993) asked journalists in the USA, Britain, Sweden, Germany and Italy to place parties and major news organizations on the political spectrum from left to right. European journalists located the media across a wide spectrum, while American journalists put them all in the centre, between the Republican and Democratic parties. The decline of political parallelism in North America results from a combination of changes in political culture and media markets. The dominance of liberal ideology means that ideological differences between parties are smaller in the Liberal system (especially in the USA and Ireland) than in the other systems examined here, and in the US case there was a shift at the end of the nineteenth century towards a negative view of the role of parties. At the same time, the concentration of newspaper markets produced economic incentives for newspapers to avoid distinct partisan identities.

There is an important exception to this pattern, however. In Britain, broadcasting is marked by strong norms of internal pluralism and political neutrality. But the press remains partisan, probably as strongly so today as anywhere in Europe except Greece and Italy. This is especially true of the tabloid press, which dominates the British newspaper market as nowhere else in the world, and which in most elections campaign openly and stridently as partisan champions. In this sense, the common notion of an 'Anglo-American model' of journalism is a bit misleading. US and British newspapers do share an emphasis on information and narrative rather than commentary of the sort that once dominated in continental Europe, but they are in other ways very different. The higher degree of political parallelism in the British press is probably due both to differences in political culture – British parties have been more unified and ideologically coherent – and differences in media markets. American newspaper markets are primarily local monopoly markets; Britain has a competitive national market in which newspapers have an incentive to differentiate their product through their political stances. In the USA, with the deregulation of broadcasting and the multiplication of television channels, political parallelism is actually beginning to re-emerge in electronic media, with Fox News, especially developing a distinct political appeal. As has historically been the case with the British press, the new partisan media in the USA slant toward the Right.

Professionalization

Professionalism of journalism developed relatively strongly in the Liberal Model. Commercialization of the media meant hiring large corps of reporters and editors; journalism developed into a distinct occupational group and also a distinct form of discourse, with its own rules different from those of partisan debate. In the US case, formal education in journalism became well-institutionalized. At one time, instrumentalization of the press was common in the Liberal system. Its form was a bit different from that of the Polarized Pluralist Model, since media owners had their base of power within media industries, rather than outside them. But press 'barons', such as Lord Beaverbrook or William Randolf Hearst, clearly used their media properties to exercise influence in the political world. This pattern declined in the mid-twentieth century, as political parallelism in general declined, especially in North America. Media owners distanced themselves from the politcal world, and journalists, who in theory were committed to politically-neutral practices of reporting, obtained more autonomy within news organizations. This pattern was what *Four Theories of the Press* referred to as the 'social responsibility' model. In the case of broadcasting, organizations such as the BBC and CBS developed strong cultures of professional autonomy and public service, and the 'trusteeship model' of broadcast regulation, which required licence holders to 'serve the public convenience and necessity', encouraged this in US commercial broadcasting as well. Journalistic autonomy probably peaked in the Liberal countries in about the 1960s and 1970s. Since that time growing commercial pressures have eroded it and interventionist owners have become somewhat more common, with Rupert Murdoch and Canadian publisher Conrad Black symbolizing the trend.

Journalistic professionalism is not as formally instutionalized in the Liberal Model as in the Democratic Corporatist Model. The USA and Ireland, for example, have no Press Councils. Britain does, though the domination of the British newspaper market by highly competitive tabloids weakens its effectiveness. Quebec has a strong Press Council, while some other Canadian provinces have weaker ones.

Role of the state

The Liberal Model is, by definition, a system in which the role of the state is relatively limited. None of the liberal countries has significant press subsidies, for example. In the US case, the First Amendment to the Constitution occupies a privileged place in contemporary legal doctrine that makes many kinds of state regulation which are common in Europe untenable politically and legally, including right of reply laws and most regulation of communication in electoral campaigns.

At the same time, the role of the state is not insignificant even in the Liberal Model: the state has always played a significant role in the development of capitalism, and this is no less true in the media sphere. In Britain, the Liberal political tradition is mixed with a more statist conservative tradition and with important elements of Democratic Corporatism, and this is reflected in a strong public broadcasting system, relatively strong regulation of commercial broadcasting, certainly compared with the USA, and, in a different way, by the Official Secrets Act. In Canada and Ireland, Liberalism is modified by concerns about national identity, which have motivated state support for public broadcasting, and in the Canadian case controls on imported media products.

Even in the US case, the state has played an important role in the media system in many ways. The state created the basic infrastructure for the expansion of commercial media through the postal system and an extensive early system of public education, and in the early nineteenth century subsidized newspapers substantially through patronage. It also created a legal framework that was for the most part favourable to the expansion of media and the public sphere, although at times restricting them, particularly in matters of 'morality' – which is the principal exception today to the trend towards deregulation of media. Research on journalism in the Liberal countries has also shown substantial state influence on the content of the news, partly because of the strength of the culture of 'national security' in post World War II America and Britain.

Political history, structure and culture

The bourgeois revolution occurred early in Britain, and liberal institutions were transferred to British colonies. The USA never had a feudal past; its political culture was characterized by a dominant liberal consensus from very early (Hartz, 1955), and as Starr (2004) points out, it had no tradition of state or aristocratic patronage of arts and culture, so its public sphere was rooted in the market from a very early date. The republican culture that developed in the northern colonies of the USA placed a high value on an open flow of information.

Besides the obvious fact that a liberal political system meant a relatively strong development of market institutions in relation to the state, several other aspects of the political system that resulted from the early bourgeois revolutions in the Liberal system are worth noting here. Because liberalism became dominant early, the political spectrum is narrower in the Liberal system, and this made journalistic professionalization and the notion of a 'neutral' media serving society as a whole more plausible and more practical. Even partisan tabloids in Britain claim to speak not for a particular class or ideological group but for 'the people'. The liberal countries also saw a strong development of what Max Weber called rational–legal authority, which was pushed by business and by middle class reform movements in the late nineteenth century to rationalize public administration and make it more predictable and efficient for commerce. Rational–legal authority, which also developed strongly in the Democratic Corporatist system, was favourable to the development of a similarly 'neutral' profession of journalism. Finally, the Liberal system involves a relatively fragmented, individualistic model of political representation, and tends to be hostile to the kinds of organized social interests that play such a central role in the Democratic Corporatist system.

Conclusion

We conclude with a few words about the relevance of our three models to other media systems beyond the 18 countries covered here. Our analysis is based on what is known as a most similar systems design. We deliberately stayed away from the kind of universalistic theory proposed in *Four Theories of the Press*. We wanted to focus on a group of cases small enough that we could take reasonable care in the research we did on each case and that the conceptual framework needed to understand them would not be overly complex. We do not intend our framework to be applied to the rest of the world without modification. We do think that it will be of some relevance as a point of comparison, nevertheless. What we call the Liberal Model has become the dominant model throughout the world: it serves as a normative model for practitioners everywhere, and the forces of globalization have diffused its institutions and practices almost everywhere – though they are certainly not reproduced exactly in different political and cultural contexts. At the same time, we suspect that the Polarized Pluralist Model is the most relevant of our three models to understanding the actual functioning of media systems in most of the world where, as in southern Europe, capitalism and liberal democracy have developed late, and political polarization often continues to be strong. Elements of the Democratic Corporatist system are probably less commonly found, though there may be parallels in many systems, particularly in East Asia, where collectivist cultural and political traditions are strong. Certain East Asian countries do share with the countries of northern Europe the distinction of having the highest newspaper circulation rates in the world. We hope that our research will serve as an example of how to do comparative analysis, how to think about media systems and their relation to political history, structure and culture, rather than as a set of categories for classifying media systems.

References

Donsbach, W. and Patterson, T. (1992) 'Journalists' Roles and Newsroom Practices: A Cross-National Comparison', Paper presented at 42nd Conference of the International Communication Association, Miami.

————(2004) 'Political News Journalists: Partisanship, Professionalism and Political Roles in Five Countries', in F. Esser and B. Pfetsch (eds), *Comparing Political Communication: Theories, Cases and Challenges*. Cambridge: Cambridge University Press.

Durkheim, É. (1965) *The Rules of Sociological Method*. New York, Free Press.

Ferenczi, T. (1993) *L'invention du journalisme en France*. Paris: Librairie Plon.

Forcella, E. (1959) 'Milleciquecento lettori', *Tempo Presente*, no. 6.

Gunther, R., Montero, J. R. and Wert, J. I. (2000) 'The Media and Politics in Spain: From Dictatorship to Democracy', in R. Gunther and A. Mugham (eds), *Democracy and the Media: A Comparative Perspective*. Cambridge: Cambridge University Press.

Gustafsson, K-E. (1980) 'The Press Subsidies of Sweden: A Decade of Experiment', in A. Smith (ed.), *Newspapers and Democracy. International Essays on a Changing Medium*. Cambridge, MA: MIT Press, pp. 104–26.

Hadenius, S. (1983) 'The Rise and Possible Fall of the Swedish Party Press', *Communication Research*, 10 (3), 287–311.

Hallin, D. C. and Mancini, P. (1984) 'Speaking of the President: Political Structure and Representational Form in U.S. and Italian TV News', *Theory and Society*, 13, 829–50.

————(2004) *Comparing Media Systems: Three Models of Media and Politics*. Cambridge: Cambridge University Press.

Hartz, L. (1955) *The Liberal Tradition in America*. New York: Harcourt, Brace & World.

Høyer, S. and Lorentzen, P. E. (1977) 'The Politics of Professionalization in Scandinavian Journalism', in M. Berg *et al.* (eds), *Current Theories in Scandinavian Mass Communication Research*. Grenada: GMT.

Katzenstein, P. J. (1985) *Small States in World Markets: Industrial Policy in Europe*. Ithaca: Cornell University Press.

Ortega, F. and Luisa Humanes M. (2000) *Algo Mas Que Periodistas: Sociología de una Profesión*. Barcelona: Editorial Ariel.

Papathanassopoulos, S. (2001) 'Media Commercialization and Journalism in Greece', *European Journal of Communication*, 16 (4), 505–21.

Patterson, T. E. and Donsbach, W. (1993) 'Press–Party Parallelism: A Cross-National Comparison', Paper presented at the Annual Meeting of the International Communication Association. Washington, DC.

Ricuperati, G. (1981) 'I giornalisti italiani fra poteri e cultura dalle origini all'Unità', in *AA. VV.* (various authors), *Storia d'Italia*, pp. 1085–1132. Torino: Einaudi.

Sartori, G. (1976) *Parties and Party Systems: A Framework for Analysis*. Cambridge: Cambridge University Press.

Siebert, F. S., Peterson, T. and Schramm, W. (1956) *Four Theories of the Press.* Urbana: University of Illinois Press.

Starr, P. (2004), *The Creation of the Media: Political Origins of Modern Communications.* New York. Basic Books

Traquina, N. (1995) 'Portuguese Television: The Politics of Savage Deregulation', *Media, Culture & Society,* 17 (7), 223–38.

van der Eijk, C. (2000) 'The Netherlands: Media and Politics between Segmented Pluralism and Market Forces', in R. Gunther and A. Mugham (eds), *Democracy and the Media,* Cambridge: Cambridge University Press, pp. 303–42.

World Association of Newspapers (2001) *World Press Trends.* Paris.

▶ chapter twelve

Media Policy in the Middle East: A Reappraisal

NAOMI SAKR

Introduction: questions asked after 9/11

In the aftermath of the suicide attacks that killed some 3,000 people in the USA on 11 September 2001, the state of the Middle East's media began to attract unprecedented international attention. Broadly speaking, there were two reasons for this unwonted interest. One arose from the fact that 15 of the 19 hijackers on that day were Saudi nationals. Suddenly, for people outside Saudi Arabia, the socialization of a generation of young Saudis became a focus of concern. The kingdom's school textbooks were scoured for anti-Western messages and its media assessed for complicity in promoting intolerance (Doumato, 2003; Prokop, 2003). Criticism was levelled at the Arab media in general. Testifying before a US Congressional committee, the head of a private media-monitoring organization based in Washington claimed that the government-controlled media in Arab states 'frequently' carried articles openly supportive of, or even calling for, terrorist attacks against the USA (Whitaker, 2002). A second reason for ever-closer media scrutiny developed with the rise and rise of al-Jazeera, the pan-Arab satellite channel that had started up in the tiny Gulf state of Qatar in 1996. When the US government reacted to 9/11 by dropping bombs on Afghanistan, al-Jazeera's unique position inside the country and its access to exclusive videotape of the Saudi-born dissident, Osama bin Laden, earned instant recognition for the al-Jazeera brand around the world. It also provoked fierce arguments about whether the channel was inciting its viewers to violence, or doing the exact opposite by opening a space for verbal fire as an alternative to killing (Sakr, 2004a).

For many media critics close to Arab society, the central issue was not incitement through television images (as distinct from incitement through actual events) but the widespread non-use of public channels of communication in the Arab world for the exchange of conflicting political and social views. By some accounts, the spilling over of 'dangerous radicalism' could be blamed on an absence of 'normal outlets for expression', resulting from censorship imposed by dictatorial regimes (The Economist, 2003). According to others, censorship was not the ultimate explanation. It could be circumvented, but only by imaginative people with a better understanding of political struggle and more knowledge about the way other societies operate (Rabbani and Hendriks, 2001: 26). The first *Arab Human Development Report*, compiled by Arab intellectuals under UN sponsorship, picked up on the multidimensional nature of what it called the 'freedom deficit' in Arab countries, including a lack of 'voice' (UNDP, 2002: 27). It took a broad view of the institutional context (formal and informal) in which freedoms were denied and stressed the 'deep complementarity' that exists in the Arab world between individual agency and social arrangements (UNDP, 2002: 20). The second report in the series homed in on obstacles to knowledge diffusion imposed by controls on the media (UNDP, 2003). But the two reports' mixed reception among their target audience indicated that conflicting diagnoses of the region's problems would retard change in the making of Arab media policy. Indeed, while policy analysts outside the Arab world looked for evidence of media liberalization inside the region, Arab governments targeted their energies at non-Arab media, through campaigns aimed at highlighting foreign misreporting of Middle East affairs.

Divergences such as these make it important to discover whether policy towards free expression through the media did change in Arab countries after 9/11. But they also illustrate the difficulties involved in discerning and assessing policy changes. That is why this chapter, before discussing media policies in three states, grapples with the more generally applicable issue of interpretation. Actions, practices and institutions are usually presented by means of narrative. Yet narratives differ depending on perspective, and there may be times when the contest between or among policy narratives reveals as much about power relations as the narratives themselves (Bevir and Rhodes, 2002; Brown, 2001: 8–17). Governments in North America and Europe as well as the Middle East took measures to restrict information flows in the wake of 9/11 and legitimized their actions by reference to security needs (Peters, 2003). Yet in no case could the respective definitions of security be taken at face value. Nor would any of the policy-makers in question characterize their own actions and those of others in the same terms. This chapter therefore draws on different viewpoints to analyse a number of media initiatives. It tries to determine where they came from, whose interests they served, and whether they represented in any sense a departure from policy hitherto.

Media policy analysis: some pathways

If analysing policy in any context holds unseen pitfalls, it is partly because policy simultaneously derives from, and impinges on, the political process. Regulation cannot be seen simply as the implementation of policy, because existing regulation is a contributory factor in the way policy gets made. It determines, among other things, the distribution of resources among competing interests (Hills, 2002: 12). In turn, access to resources influences the ordering of agendas. Institutions not only differ in their resources, but also in their built-in norms and rules; these, whether obviously or not, embody power relationships. Resources, rules and relationships all affect the way problems are identified, the way information about possible solutions is collated and the way objectives are prioritized. Recognizing this requires some modification to rational choice theory, which maintains that people make choices about courses of action based on what they believe is likely to bring them the most benefit. If this theory's capacity to explain the actions of collective policy-makers is to be maximized, it has to acknowledge that actors are not perfectly informed, that outside factors can affect the perception of preferences, and that equal, if different, benefits might accrue from alternative actions (Dunleavy, 1991). Thus, for example, exploring constraints on the availability of information, and identifying forces implicated in framing and predicting policy outcomes, are necessary tasks in analysing policy.

Both tasks turn the spotlight on the media. So does the business of discovering how – or even whether – various policy options are articulated. The making of policy implies a choice from among alternatives, but this does not mean that rejected options are always made explicit. Lukes (1974) consequently advocated a three-dimensional view of power that would allow for consideration not only of issues and potential issues but of the many ways in which potential issues and latent conflicts are kept off the agenda altogether. Where agendas for media policy are concerned, media organizations enjoy a privileged position. They can intervene by seeking to shape perceptions in accordance with their vested interests. The question posed at this point by theories of globalization is where such organizations are based. Influencing policy decisions may appear to be a relatively self-contained process in the context of a nation-state with stable representative government and a developed and diverse media system, as suggested by Hutchison's narrow state-based list of actors in the policy process (Hutchison, 1999: 125). Political scientists have long recognized, however, that the so-called realist approach to politics, which sees states as the most significant actors, does not adequately account for cross-border intervention by non-state players. Examples of transnational influence on media policy are legion and predate the upsurge in transnational connectivity of the 1980s, as illustrated by the role of US advertising interests in the spread of commercial television outside the USA (Curran and Seaton, 1997: 162; Tunstall, 1983: 38). Transnational corporations use their media outlets or media allies in pursuit of their own objectives, even when their primary base of operations is outside the country where the resulting policy outcomes are felt. They have helped to steer debates over privatization and deregulation (Hills, 1986), as Rupert Murdoch's News International did in the UK (Freedman, 2003; Goodwin, 1998).

Meanwhile international organizations such as the International Telecommunication Union and World Trade Organization have been harnessed to serve commercial policy objectives (Herman and McChesney, 1997: 109–14) and other multistate groupings, notably the European Union, have devised audio-visual policies in response (Collins and Murroni, 1996: 119–25). All of which demonstrates that only a schema of media policy-making as comprehensive as Raboy's global policy 'map' (Raboy, 2002: 7–9) will fit the bill. Raboy identifies seven categories of actor, from multistate organizations, groupings and clubs (such as the G8 group of leading economies) to the transnational private sector, civil society bodies and what he sees as institutionally 'homeless' ad hoc clusters that form around specific issues. The nation-state occupies one of the seven categories but, importantly, states in this model are seen as sites of communications and cultural policy-making, not unitary actors. Clearly, exposure to external influence varies among political systems. Even so, Hallin and Mancini (2004) report that national media systems in advanced capitalist societies have tended to become homogenized. They attribute the process to a mixture of exogenous as well as endogenous forces, including powerful media outlets such as CNN among the former. Noting the contribution of international bodies involved in lobbying and journalism training, they specifically mention the World Association of Newspapers (WAN), which they see as a conduit for the spread of an American model of the press (Hallin and Mancini, 2004: 256–8). The WAN example draws attention to interpenetration between categories of policy actor. Government agencies negotiate on behalf of business, private companies fund non governmental organizations, and so on (Wilkin, 2001: 132–3).

If exogenous forces have had this much impact on the media systems of countries with robust national institutions, how much do they affect those of countries once fashionably described as 'in transition'? As mentioned earlier, all sorts of groups outside the Middle East want to change Middle Eastern media policies. But governments in the region have sought to retain tight control over media structures and media content, to ensure that official perspectives on media policy are generally the only ones expressed. A non-state-centric analysis of pan-Arab satellite television in the 1990s revealed that Arab governments were firmly in the driving seat of regional broadcasting policy, despite appearances to the contrary (Sakr, 2001). Have backseat drivers taken over since September 2001? Investigating this calls for an exhaustive checklist of potential players. It also necessitates a framework for dissecting the policy-making process. Sorbets, drawing on insights from the vast literature on policy analysis, offers such a framework with his four 'levels' for analysing media policy in Europe. Loosely summarized, these involve analysis related to: deciding and prioritizing targets; correcting or replacing existing policies; formulating 'legitimate' needs; and adopting an overall policy posture (Sorbets, 1998: 184–6). In other words, contests over policy involve rhetorical as well as practical dimensions. Past actions have to be rationalized or de-legitimized. And any list of formally recognized needs is likely to be incomplete.

Features of the regional policy map

It is hard to consider the media policies of any Middle Eastern country *without* taking account of regional or international players. Reasons for this are linked to language and history. The fact that Arabic is understood across a large group of contiguous countries means that cross-border communication is not subject to the same obstacles it often encounters elsewhere. From the early days of Arab broadcasting there was often no clear distinction between domestic and international radio broadcasting, as countries competed to transmit political propaganda over as wide an area as possible (Boyd, 1999: 4–5). Pan-Arab satellite broadcasting followed this precedent. Given the difficulty of jamming incoming satellite signals or enforcing a ban on receiving equipment, the most usual response was for each state to create one or more satellite channels of its own. In Saudi Arabia and Lebanon, this task was assigned to private companies allied to the ruling elite. Transmitting their own government-controlled material by satellite enabled political leaders to claim they were keeping up with new media technology while also observing the need for 'responsible' content compatible with regional values and traditions (Sakr, 2001: 37–40). Information ministers collaborated across borders to impose a broadcasters' code of honour and prevent uncooperative stations from breaking ranks (pp. 158–64).

Media policies have also to be seen in the context of the region's shared history of colonization. One amply documented assessment maintains that neither Islam nor Arab culture define the Arab Middle East as much as its background of external intervention

(Henry and Springborg, 2001: 8). The corollary of this, according to Halliday, is that contemporary public discourse has been shaped by 'one ideology above all', namely nationalism. 'The post-1990 Middle Eastern debate on globalisation reproduces much of what was said in earlier times about Western imperialism' (Halliday, 2002: 41). Like all ideology, it serves to obscure the real choices that Middle Eastern states and their opponents confront (p. 50). Even so, it received a major boost in 2003 with the US-led invasion of Iraq. By using force, and rationalizing it with a discourse of human rights and democratization, policy-makers behind the invasion provided the perfect rationale for Middle Eastern leaders to define their own policy needs ever more starkly in terms of national sovereignty and independence, while portraying notions of rights and democracy as Western myths. Such portrayals carried weight with local populations, who were fully aware that the very same countries behind the invasion had traditionally supplied authoritarian regimes in the region with military and financial support. Nevertheless a G8 summit meeting in the USA in June 2004 agreed to forge ahead with a programme to strengthen 'freedom, democracy and prosperity' in the Middle East through contacts with governments, business and civil society (White House, 2004). The programme was intended to build on existing European–Mediterranean, US–Middle East and Japanese–Arab 'partnerships'.

Just by reflecting on the pan-Arab media landscape and the G8 discourse about promoting freedom, it becomes apparent that, in this policy environment, categories such as the nation-state, civil society and the transnational private sector, are simultaneously connected and fractured in perhaps unforeseen ways. For example, Arab non-governmental groups involved in activities such as journalism training, film-making and media monitoring have long been eligible for financial and moral support from Western governments, under the Euro-Med Programme and schemes run by the US Agency for International Development. Those who take up such opportunities, however, have exposed themselves to charges from both their peers and their own national governments of weakening national unity and contributing to intellectual and cultural dependency on the West (Sakr, 2004b). Meanwhile the tropes of freedom used to gloss G8 actions in the Middle East in 2003–2004 have been debunked by non-governmental media advocacy organizations based in the West.

At the same time, Arab governments are closely tied to private Arab media corporations, which may consequently collaborate more closely behind the scenes than outward appearances suggest. A path-breaking study of media policy-making in Lebanon has shown how far the conventions of confessionalism, whereby power is supposedly shared on the basis of religious affiliation, were instrumentalized in the allocation of broadcasting licences to conceal how much control over resources was exercised by the country's inter-confessional power elite (Dabbous-Sensenig, 2002). Meanwhile, the corporate–government relationship distorts elements of Arab media markets, such as advertising expenditure and audience measurement, making them unattractive to transnational media companies based elsewhere. If private US companies saw profits to be made from Arabic-language news media, the business of promoting US voices in Arab countries would not be left to US state-financed ventures such as Radio Sawa and al-Hurra TV.

What also emerges from this criss-crossing of interaction and rejection is the centrality of historical perspective. The events of 9/11 may have marked a rupture from one viewpoint, but not from others. Western commentary on the Middle East has been prone to treat events such as the oil price explosions of the 1970s or the Gulf war of 1991 as though they marked the start of Middle Eastern time. Yet social change is a process. Ruptures in one aspect should not be allowed to distract attention from continuity in others (Davis, 1991: 14–24). Therefore the analysis conducted here, although primarily focused on the three years after September 2001, attempts to take a view that is both wide with regard to potential players and reasonably long. The countries chosen are ones whose media were particularly close to cross-continental military and verbal hostilities, namely Saudi Arabia, Qatar and Iraq.

Struggles over the Saudi media's narrowly defined role

Members of the Saudi ruling elite have long been leading players in the pan-Arab media, funding newspapers and satellite channels based abroad, in London, Rome, Beirut and Dubai. The ruling family, which holds all key posts in central and provincial government and national security, is very large. It consists of many branches, whose heads do not necessarily share the same outlook on their own or their country's future. By investing in media operations beyond the kingdom's borders, senior princes have gained a say in national and regional affairs in ways that would not be possible within the confines of Saudi Arabia's own authoritarian media laws, even though these are issued by royal decree. The laws proscribe anything deemed to contradict the austere Wahhabi interpretation of Islam espoused by religious scholars descended from Mohammed bin Abdel-Wahhab, the ally of an eighteenth-century ancestor of the ruling Al Saud. The Al Saud gain legitimacy as rulers by ceding control over many aspects of daily life to the religious authorities. But, as demonstrated by the Saudi-funded media abroad, the partnership entails a constant, costly negotiation. Media censorship is legalized through many separate pieces of legislation, a flavour of which is contained in the preamble to the 2000 Law on Press and Publications. This guarantees 'freedom of expression within the framework of the Sharia and other existing rules'.

Given this context, it is perhaps not surprising that a simple list of official media-related decisions taken between September 2001 and September 2004 presents a confusing picture. It includes several measures that, by diversifying the kingdom's institutional base, seemed to promise more scope for expressing a greater diversity of views.[1] For example, plans were announced in December 2001 to create the first association to represent the interests of Saudi journalists; the association's constituent assembly took place in March 2003 and its board was elected (with two women members) in June 2004. Restrictions on entry visas for foreign journalists were relaxed during 2002, and in 2003 foreign news organizations were permitted for the first time to open offices in the kingdom. In April 2003 the interior minister repeated earlier promises about creating a National Human Rights Association, which came into being a year later. Saudi Radio and Television and the Saudi Press Agency, from being adjuncts of the Ministry of Information, were turned into public corporations, and a 24-hour state-run satellite news channel was created. This was launched in January 2004 with the name al-Ikhbariya, a pool of female news presenters, and a mission to present a 'new image' of the state. November 2003 marked the start of a weekly programme on domestic television showing debates in the country's 120-member Consultative Council, a body appointed by the king to advise on public affairs.

The list is confusing because it also includes, over the same three-year period, many examples of obvious and persistent censorship. Banning of certain foreign Arab newspapers continued and newspaper owners were ordered to sack or sideline several prominent pro-reform figures. Internet access, introduced as recently as 1999, was kept under tight centralized control. Crews from al-Jazeera were denied entry to Saudi Arabia in 2002, after the pan-Arab satellite channel aired critical commentary on a Middle East peace plan proposed by the kingdom's de facto ruler, Crown Prince Abdullah. In June 2003 the government initiated a process called the National Dialogue, involving six-monthly meetings among a few dozen male and female representatives of different social groups. But whereas participants in the meetings called unambiguously for free speech, their deliberations were conducted behind closed doors. The Riyadh Declaration on Human Rights, issued in October that year, made no reference to freedom of expression in any of its 23 points. Meanwhile the non-violent London-based Movement for Islamic Reform in Arabia reported efforts by the Saudi government in mid-2003 to close down its satellite operation, Islah (Reform) TV, through pressure on the French authorities and the Paris-based satellite company, Eutelsat, to block transmission from Hotbird.

Contradictory signals in the wake of 9/11 left Saudi journalists bemused. Abdel-Rahman al-Rashed, chief editor of the Saudi-owned pan-Arab daily *Asharq al-Awsat*, put his puzzlement to Crown Prince Abdullah in an interview in May 2002. 'We are really perplexed', he said. 'We see an unprecedented freedom in the Saudi media and we sometimes see strict censorship decisions. What is the state's policy at a time when technology does not leave scope for censoring opinions and information?' (al-Rashed, 2002). The prince's reply, in essence, repeated the formula of the Press and Publications Law, that freedom to talk about 'shortcomings' had to be balanced with 'patriotism'. Describing an uncontrolled press as a 'curse' to its society, Abdullah declared that everyone in Saudi Arabia, 'old and young', observed tradition. Newspapers, he said, should not become a 'pick for destruction and sabotage'.

Abhorrence of division became a recurring theme of official statements after two major suicide bombings against civilian targets in Riyadh in May and November 2003. Whereas the authorities had insisted that previous attacks had been conducted as part of expatriate feuds over alcohol sales, the scale of Saudi Arabia's 'own 9/11' meant that the role of Osama bin Laden's al-Qaida network inside the kingdom could no longer be denied. In the face of compelling evidence of internal insecurity, spokesmen for the government and religious authorities stressed national unity. A religious sheikh, taking part in a programme called *War on Terrorism* on Saudi TV's Channel 1 on 17 September 2003, exemplified the approach when he said that Saudi society was built on solidarity between the ruler and the people. 'Those in charge,' he said, 'from the highest authority to the most junior official, seek the well-being and reform of the people.'

The target of government policy implicit in such statements appeared to be preservation of the political status quo. Legitimate needs to be met by government media policy were said by ministers to include educating Saudi youth about the dangers of terrorism and extremist ideas. Yet they did not extend to allowing media outlets to criticize the clergy for teaching intolerance, otherwise outspoken Saudi journalists who engaged in such criticism would not have been sacked. The official posture was thus one of reaction to an agenda set, via transnational media, by a range of players inside and outside the country: al-Qaida; Saudi residents and exiles seeking peaceful constitutional reform; and Saudi Arabia's chief ally, the USA. By the end of October 2003 the Saudi government had spent $16 million on advertisements across the USA to counter hostile voices that were urging a reappraisal of US–Saudi ties. A spokesman for the Saudi embassy in Washington said the campaign, managed by the Virginia-based public relations firm Qorvis, was intended to counter criticism of the 'Saudi government, religion and culture' (Carey 2003).

However, it is illuminating to note that some of the mildly positive media-related initiatives announced or adopted after 9/11 stemmed from developments set in motion before that date. Facilitating entry to selected foreign media is one example. The head of the Saudi Arabian General Investment Authority told a London audience in June 2003 that his agency, set up in April 2000 to attract urgently needed foreign investment into Saudi Arabia, had a definite interest in seeing foreign media based in the kingdom. He suggested that more openness in this regard would promote better informed and more specialized coverage, which would in turn enhance international understanding of Saudi affairs (Abdullah bin Faisal bin Turki, 2003). Similarly, the human rights conference held in October 2003 could be seen as a product not of post-9/11 pressures but a sequence of events dating back to Crown Prince Abdullah's take-over from the ailing King Fahd in the late 1990s. Faced at that moment with plunging oil revenues and the soaring demands placed on state spending by a rapidly growing population in need of infrastructure, services and jobs, the government suddenly turned its attention to creating a regulatory environment attractive to foreign investors and suited to future membership of the WTO. Amnesty International seized the opportunity to remind international business of Saudi Arabia's poor record on human rights. In response, the government promised some reforms (Amnesty International UK, 2000: 6–7).

Another dimension to the policy dynamic lies in the multifaceted relationship between Saudi Arabia and the USA. Here fissures opened up between attitudes to the relationship on both sides. Saudi rulers turned to the USA for military protection after the 1990 Iraqi invasion of Kuwait, despite having spent huge sums on defence in previous years. Justifying the decision to invite US troops into the country called for considerable rhetorical contortions (al-Rasheed, 1996). The princes' interest in projecting a humane image of their regime to the US public after 9/11 reflected their continuing need for US military support. Conversely, Saudi citizens of all shades of opinion became increasingly hostile to the USA as US policy grew ever more demoralizing to the Palestinians. Reform prescriptions emanating from US sources were consequently perceived as counter-productive by Saudi reformists, because US intervention made them look like the 'agents of a foreign power' (Gresh, 2003: 5). Saudi rulers, keen not to look like imperialist lackeys themselves, chose to be selective in the US advice they took. When US government figures expressed disquiet at the imprisonment of Saudi human rights campaigners in March 2004, the Saudi foreign minister, Prince Saud al-Faisal, standing next to US Secretary of State Colin Powell at a press conference, criticized the detainees for seeking 'dissension when the whole country was looking for unity and a clear vision' (Ambah, 2004). Saudi newspapers carried only official statements about the arrests. Campaigners held in prison and put on trial in August 2004 were those who refused to promise not to talk to the press

In other words, despite internal and external pressures after 9/11, senior Saudi princes kept a tight grip on the power to decide what was, or was not, presented via the kingdom's domestic media as a legitimate need.

Qatar: costs and benefits of al-Jazeera

Debates about the content and impact of programmes shown on al-Jazeera can be fraught and somewhat inconclusive (Rugh, 2004: 232–6). Denunciations of an alleged 'anti-Western' or 'anti-American' bias became increasingly frequent as the channel covered US-led attacks on Afghanistan and Iraq in 2001–2003. Given the controversy, an attempt to shift the analytical spotlight away from al-Jazeera's output to its place in Qatari government policy may be a useful corrective to perceptions based solely on broadcast material. For example, one key point is that the government of Qatar, which funds al-Jazeera, is closely allied to that of the USA. Washington was first to accord diplomatic recognition to Sheikh Hamad bin Khalifa Al Thani when he came to power in 1995, in a coup that the ousted emir, Sheikh Hamad's own father, struggled – with help from some other Gulf states – to overturn. Under a bilateral security pact that gives the USA access to air and naval bases in Qatar, US forces used al-Udeid airbase for military operations against both Afghanistan and Iraq. Preparations to boost US facilities at al-Udeid, as an alternative to the Prince Sultan airbase in Saudi Arabia, began during the final months of 2001. The ceremony at which Qatar formally agreed to al-Udeid's use in the invasion of Iraq was shown live on al-Jazeera, eliciting outrage in sections of the Arab press.

Arguably, by providing (via al-Jazeera) a forum in which Arab resentment against US foreign policy was allowed to be expressed, the Qatari leadership could be seen to achieve a self-interested objective. It burnished its credentials as a defender of Arab interests, thereby pacifying qualms at home and in other Arab states about the ruling Al Thani clan's alliance with the USA. However, since conjecture on this point is unlikely to be corroborated by official statements, Qatari media policy in the wake of 9/11 has to be examined through actual decisions and the way they were explained. For a start, the ruler's personal commitment to the station's survival became clear. November 2001 was the point at which, under the terms of its original five-year start-up loan, al-Jazeera was supposed to become self-financing. But this goal had receded, as other Arab governments' fury at the channel's uncensored output had translated into an advertising boycott by firms anxious not to displease their political masters. When al-Jazeera not only kept going, but absorbed all the expense of covering the bombardment of Afghanistan and its repercussions around the world, as well as losing advertisements from US companies unhappy at this coverage, subventions from the royal court took on new significance. 'Al-Jazeera brings the government non-financial benefits', explained the channel's managing director at the time (Al-Ali, 2002).

The channel's financial security seemed to be confirmed by its expansion from then on. Although plans for a documentary channel and an English-language channel were repeatedly postponed, an English-language website was added to the Arabic one in 2003, and sports and children's channels were prepared during 2004. The same period saw the al-Jazeera Media Training and Development Centre set up in Doha with technical help from the BBC. Intended as a business venture that might eventually bring revenue back to al-Jazeera, the centre still required an initial subsidy. Reasons given by Qatari ruling family members as to why al-Jazeera was a worthwhile project usually revolved around freedom of expression being a norm in democratic societies. The emir, on a visit to Washington in October 2001, revealed to the press that he had received complaints about al-Jazeera from US officials. But, he said, Qatar was turning itself into a parliamentary democracy, which required that the media should have freedom and credibility (*Gulf Times*, 2001). The channel's chairman, Sheikh Hamad bin Thamer Al Thani, a cousin of the emir, took the same line. He recalled that Qatar had held municipal elections and was moving towards parliamentary elections. He also noted that women were taking part in the political process in Qatar, implying a further contrast with other Gulf states. 'I think this direction corresponds with the direction of the media, be it Al-Jazeera or lifting censorship on local Qatari newspapers', he said (TBS, 2001). As to state subsidies for al-Jazeera, these were routinely compared to public funding of the BBC.

It is noteworthy that US complaints about al-Jazeera, besides being aired in public, were directed to the Qatari government through diplomatic channels. In April 2004, the US secretary of state, Colin Powell, reportedly said that US–Qatari relations had been 'clouded' by al-Jazeera's coverage of events in Iraq. Mr Powell used the word 'intense' to describe discussions on the subject with the Qatari foreign minister, Sheikh Hamad bin Jassem bin Jabr, another cousin of the emir (O'Carroll, 2004). A few days later Sheikh Hamad bin Jassem resumed the discussions in Washington with US vice president Dick Cheney and defence secretary Donald Rumsfeld. He then said he would tell al-Jazeera to review its coverage, to be more professional and not to disseminate 'wrong information' (BBC, 2004). There followed two further media initiatives on Qatar's part, consisting of a media conference in Doha in July 2004 and the publication by al-Jazeera of a Code of Ethics. The latter stressed the validity and accuracy of reporting as a higher priority than getting a scoop. It promised to give 'full consideration to the feelings of victims of crime, war, persecution and disaster, their relatives, our viewers, and to individual privacies and public decorum'.

According to one of al-Jazeera's presenters, the Code of Ethics was a direct response to US pressure. Members of Qatar's ruling family had apparently urged the channel's managers to ensure that any future complaint about bias or inaccuracy would be proved groundless (Abdullah, 2004). The Code of Ethics was issued under relatively new management at al-Jazeera, at a time when both the managing director and editor-in-chief had held their positions for less than a year. Mohammed Jassem al-Ali, managing director since the channel's launch in 1996, was removed in May 2003, after being accused by Ahmad Chalabi, of the US-backed Iraqi National Congress, of allowing spies working for Saddam Hussein to infiltrate al-Jazeera. Al-Ali denied the charge. His permanent replacement, not appointed until October 2003, was Wadah Khanfar, a reporter in his mid-thirties who had re-established al-Jazeera's Baghdad bureau after the city fell to US troops. The editor-in-chief, Ahmad al-Shaikh, took up his post in March 2004, after his predecessor, Ibrahim Helal, left to join the BBC World Service Trust, working on media training for Arab journalists.

There can be little doubt that al-Jazeera, in addition to being a media institution, was conceived by its Qatari financiers as a component of foreign policy. Foreign relations are a central preoccupation for the ruler of a small country and one account of Qatar's foreign policy over several decades describes it as consistently aggressive (Aljalil, 2004, 11). In particular, Qatar's leaders had to work hard from the 1860s onwards to maintain a separate existence from their Saudi and Bahraini counterparts (Said Zahlan, 1998: 99–105). It is widely suggested that, by sponsoring al-Jazeera, Qatar acquired influence disproportionate to its size. Nevertheless, Qatar's ruler had to maintain a balancing act in relations with the USA. As world attention became more intensely focused on events in Afghanistan and the Middle East after 9/11, forces undermining al-Jazeera's viability also increased, through advertising boycotts, closure of its offices in Arab capitals, and denial of access to important Arab meetings.

The events recounted here suggest that, in the immediate aftermath of 9/11, the emir decided that the non-financial returns on his investment in al-Jazeera were sufficient. A year after 9/11 one staff member even intimated that the channel meant as much to Qatar as nuclear weapons did to Israel (Sakr, 2004c: 67). But three years after 9/11 the non-financial benefits had seemingly been eroded by the US administration's antipathy, as expressed by the State Department and the Pentagon. With the release of al-Jazeera's Code of Ethics, it emerged that a feasibility study had been commissioned on turning the network into a private company, offering shares via the Qatar stock exchange.

Media regulation in Iraq: contradictory foreign interventions

Regulatory regimes for the media changed several times in Iraq in the three years after September 2001. During 2002, as the threat of a US-led attack grew closer, the government of Saddam Hussein manoeuvred to allow wider internet and satellite access to the privileged few who could afford them after 12 years of impoverishment under UN sanctions. Youth TV and the newspaper *Babil*, both run by Saddam Hussein's son Udai, touched on controversial topics ignored by other government-controlled outlets (Razzouk, 2002). When the March 2003 invasion put the USA and UK in charge, in the name of the Coalition Provisional Authority (CPA), a period ensued when decisions about media treatment were sometimes attributed to the CPA itself and sometimes to the US-appointed Iraqi Governing Council. As scores of newspapers sprang up, many carrying more opinion than verified information, Paul Bremmer, the CPA's civilian head, declared a need for 'some orderly process' whereby publications would be licensed. He seemed to believe that licensing the printed press was standard procedure in democratic states (Whitaker, 2003). In June 2003, CPA Order No. 14 on Prohibited Media Activity outlawed any material, original or reported, deemed to incite violence or civil disorder or advocate returning the Iraqi Ba'ath Party to power. Mike Furlong, a US official in Baghdad, said there could be 'no room for hateful messages that will destabilize the emerging Iraqi democracy' (Daragahi, 2003: 48). Support for Order 14 within the CPA was not unanimous, however, not least because it lacked transparency, due process, or provision for appeal against the summary closure of media outlets. It was consequently modified at the end of June 2004, under the CPA's all-embracing Order 100, which organized the handover of sovereign powers to the freshly installed Interim Government of Iraq (IGI).

Along with the amended Order 14, the CPA's legacy included two more media laws that were intended to outlive the IGI and endure into the era of elected government in Iraq. Like Order 14, Orders 65 and 66 were promulgated as 'binding instructions or directives', designed to prevent the unelected interim government from commandeering institutions to serve its own ends. Order 65 established what was later renamed the National Communications and Media Commission (NCMC), to license and regulate broadcasting and telecommunications along similar lines to the Federal Communications Commission in the USA and Ofcom in the UK. Unusually, it was also charged (under Section 5, clause 'h') with 'encouraging' professionalism among journalists and self-regulation of the press. Order 66 transformed the Iraq Media Network (IMN), which had been established and funded by the USA, into a public service broadcaster. The Order's preamble said 'open and rigorous debate' was essential to develop the democratic process. It noted that public service broadcasting was uniquely capable of serving the 'viewing needs of a diverse public, including underrepresented national minorities and other niche segments of society'. Ironically, the IMN had actually reduced the number of TV voices in 2003, when it snatched existing transmission equipment that newly emerging local stations had tried to use. As for 'rigorous debate', Reuters protested to the Pentagon in January 2004 about brutal intimidation of three of its reporters by US troops. News from Iraq showed that this was by no means the only incident of its kind.

Orders 65 and 66 came about through the efforts of the CPA's Media Development Team, headed from August 2003 by Simon Haselock, holder of similar previous postings in Bosnia-Herzegovina and Kosovo. This small team's big mission referred not only to Iraq but to the whole Arab world. It was to create a media landscape that embodied the 'best democratic principles and to which the rest of the Arab world can aspire' (FCO, 2004). In approving a media system with a strong public service broadcaster, the CPA acknowledged advice received from international journalists' rights groups at a conference in Athens in June 2003. A document compiled jointly by the Baltic Media Centre, Index on Censorship and the Institute for War and Peace Reporting described US planning for media policy and development in Iraq as 'poor' and 'beset by problems', including internal rivalries, chaotic decision-making and *ad hoc* hiring of inexperienced staff (IMS, 2003). The document called on the USA to 'firmly separate its public diplomacy agenda from any media development strategies' and insisted that 'competent Iraqis' should be given greater control. Thus the Media Development Team envisaged that Iraqis would start managing the IMN when the management contract awarded to Harris expired at the end of 2004. In winning the contract, Harris, a US communications equipment manufacturer, had succeeded a defence contractor, Science Applications International Corporation (SAIC), under whose supervision IMN's television arm, al-Iraqiya, had failed to report Saddam Hussein's arrest in December 2003 for nearly 24 hours after it happened (Pincus, 2004). As subcontractors, Harris had selected two non-Iraqi firms: the Lebanese Broadcasting Corporation and a Kuwaiti publisher, al-Fawares.

Carefully crafted though they were, Orders 65 and 66 were not to the liking of the IGI. Neither UN Security Council Resolution 1546, setting out the timetable for Iraq's political transition, nor the Transitional Administrative Law (the interim constitution signed off by the Iraqi Governing Council in March 2004) gave the IGI explicit power to legislate. But, barely a week after taking office, the IGI gave itself surveillance powers over mail and telecommunications under a National Safety Law, and government officials let it be known that regulations put in place by the occupiers would no longer apply. In July 2004 the prime minister made the IGI-MC subordinate to a new body, the Higher Media Commission, which he put under the authority of a former intelligence officer, Ibrahim Janabi. The IMN's al-Iraqiya broadcast an IGI account of the new arrangements. On 27 July it denied a *Financial Times* report the same day, which had quoted Mr Janabi as saying that the media must not cross 'red lines'. Instead of red lines, Mr Janabi told al-Iraqiya there would be 'directives, or as they say in English, guidelines'. In August the IGI ordered a four-week closure of al-Jazeera's office in Baghdad, saying this had been recommended by the new commission. The closure, which was extended indefinitely the following month, followed a precedent set a year earlier by the Iraqi Governing Council when it suspended the Baghdad operations of both al-Jazeera and al-Arabiya, a Saudi-owned 24-hour news channel based in Dubai.

The US government refused to condemn the IGI's decision to ban al-Jazeera. An IGI statement on the ban accused al-Jazeera of being a mouthpiece for terrorist groups and contributing to instability in Iraq. According to an AFP report of 9 August, Adam Ereli, a US State Department spokesman, described the ban as a purely Iraqi decision, based on what the IGI felt to be in the interests of the people of Iraq. He said Washington believed the IGI was working to ensure a 'balance' between free and independent media and security needs. International press freedom groups disagreed.

The Committee to Protect Journalists and Reporters sans Frontières condemned the ban. The *New York Times* weighed in with an editorial on 10 August that described al-Jazeera as the 'Arab world's principal source of uncensored information'. The IGI had closed its Baghdad office, the paper said, to save Iyad Allawi, the prime minister, the embarrassment of having violence in Iraq made visible to a worldwide audience and to give his government a freer hand to 'abuse human rights and pursue personal political vendettas in the name of restoring law and order'. Later in August, in incidents reported first-hand by *The Times*, *The Guardian* and others, Iraqi police threatened violence against journalists who stayed in Najaf to cover a stand-off between US forces and supporters of the rebel Shia cleric, Moqtada al-Sadr. Months of fighting between the two sides had been sparked in March 2004 by Paul Bremmer's use of Order 14 to silence the cleric's low circulation newspaper, *al-Hawza*.

In sum, the IGI's approach to media regulation after the CPA's departure had something in common with that of US officials running the occupation in its early months. It was far removed from the one mapped out by international media freedom groups.

Conclusion

The country studies in this chapter are excessively brief. Yet they point towards the expanse of fertile analytical ground that may open up when actual policy targets are distinguished from declared needs. In the cases reviewed here, the terrain of policy-making was populated by domestic and foreign institutions defending an array of public and private interests. Sometimes, as the *New York Times* suggested about the Iraqi ban on al-Jazeera, private interests were pursued in the public's name. Sometimes public interests, such as those promoted by anticensorship organizations, were portrayed by others as the sectional interests of Western Imperialists and occupying powers. Analysing policy interventions in terms of their explicit and implicit rationales revealed interlocking relationships among players across the countries concerned. Thus US–Qatari military ties could be seen to influence policy towards al Jazeera, which in turn triggered responses in countries where al-Jazeera was watched. Contradictions between the US administration's professed objective of encouraging free expression in Arab countries and its practical resistance to unfavourable Arab media coverage of US military intervention affected the way the Saudi, Qatari and Iraqi authorities went about regulating the media under their control. In each case, despite signs of resistance from Qatari quarters, the duality was reproduced.

Indeed, a comparison of actual media policy targets over time, in this case before and after 9/11, showed more continuity than change, not least because the US administration's own need for Middle Eastern oil and military bases remained the same. In their essentially reactive stance to internal and external pressures, Saudi Arabia's ruling princes proved that acknowledging pressure is not the same as adopting new goals. On the contrary, as internal pressure for change increased, the government framed its version of the country's legitimate media needs more narrowly, reducing them to the age-old themes of national unity and tradition. In Qatar, al-Jazeera's Code of Ethics endorsed caution in reporting news for fear of making a mistake. In Iraq, media considered troublesome to the Interim Government were banned and intimidated, as they were under Saddam Hussein. 'Policy' may seem an overblown term for such *ad hoc* and sometimes inconsistent measures. But, if there is a mismatch between the term and the reality, it is a function of the vicious circle of vaguely worded media laws that keep autocrats in power in key Middle Eastern states. Media in the region remained trapped in this circle after 9/11 and the invasion of Iraq, as they were before.

Note

1   Sources used for detailed data in each of these country studies were so numerous that they are only cited individually here in the case of verbatim quotations. Principal sources for the section on Saudi Arabia were the country's English-language press, the Saudi Arabian Monetary Agency *Annual Report* for 2003, US State Department annual reports on human rights, and material from Arab media, including websites, reproduced by BBC Monitoring Services. Data relating to Qatar and al-Jazeera were largely culled from websites such as news.bbc.co.uk, mediaguardian.co.uk and english.aljazeera.net. The study on Iraq benefited from the *Iraq Media Developments Newsletter*, circulated by the Stanhope Centre for Communications Policy Research and accessible at www.stanhope.org/research/imdn.shtml

References

Abadi, J. (2004) 'Qatar's Foreign Policy: The Quest for National Security and Territorial Integrity', *Journal of South Asian and Middle Eastern Studies*, 27 (2) 14–37.

Abdullah bin Faisal bin Turki, (2003) Remarks to the Royal United Services Institute. London. 24 June. Author's transcript.

Abdullah, M. (2004) Personal communication to the author. Beirut, 11 June.

Al-Ali, M. J. (2002) Interview with the author. Amman, 1 March.

Al-Rashed, A.-R. (2002) 'Interview with Crown Prince Abdullah', Asharq al-Awsat, 11 May; Reproduced in *Middle East Economic Survey*, 45 (20), pp. 171-8.

Al-Rasheed, M. (1996) 'God, the King and the Nation: Political Rhetoric in Saudi Arabia in the 1990s', *Middle East Journal*, 50 (3), 359–71.

Ambah, F. S. (2004) 'Saudi Reformers Recoup After Blow', *Christian Science Monitor*, 22 March, p. 6.

Amnesty International UK (2000) *Saudi Arabia Business Briefing*. London: Amnesty International UK Business Group.

BBC (2004) 'Qatar Pledges Al-Jazeera "Review"', *news.bbc.co.uk*, 30 April.

Bevir, M. and Rhodes, R. A. W. (2002) 'Interpretive Theory', in D. Marsh and G. Stoker (eds), *Theory and Methods in Political Science*, 2nd edn. Basingstoke: Palgrave Macmillan.

Boyd, D. A. (1999) *Broadcasting in the Arab World: A Survey of Electronic Media in the Middle East*. Ames: Iowa State University Press.

Brown, C. (2001) *Understanding International Relations*, 2nd edn. Basingstoke: Palgrave.

Carey, J. (2003) 'Saudis Spending Millions to Improve Image in US', *Associated Press*, 28 October.

Collins, R. and Murroni, C. (1996) *New Media, New Policies*. Cambridge: Polity Press.

Curran, J. and Seaton, J. (1997) *Power Without Responsibility: The Press and Broadcasting in Britain*, 5th edn. London: Routledge.

Dabbous-Sensenig, D. (2002) 'Ending the War: The Lebanese Broadcasting Act of 1994', PhD thesis, Sheffield Hallam University.

Daragahi, B. (2003) 'Rebuilding Iraq's Media', *Columbia Journalism Review*, July/August, 45–8.

Davis, E. (1991) 'Theorizing Statecraft and Social Change in Arab Oil-Producing Countries', in E. Davis and N. Gavrielides (eds), *Statecraft in the Middle East: Oil, Historical Memory, and Popular Culture*. Miami: Florida International University Press.

Doumato, E. A. (2003) 'Manning the Barricades: Islam According to Saudi Arabia's School Texts', *Middle East Journal*, 57 (2), 230–47.

Dunleavy, P. (1991) *Democracy, Bureaucracy and Public Choice: Economic Explanations in Political Science*. Hemel Hempstead: Harvester Wheatsheaf.

Economist, The (2003) 'Arab Reform, or Arab Performance?', 19 July, 45–46.

FCO (2004) Personal Communication to the Author by Iraqi Operations Unit. London: Foreign and Commonwealth Office, 7 July.

Freedman, D. (2003) *Television Policies of the Labour Party 1951–2001*. London: Frank Cass.

Goodwin, P. (1998) *Television Under the Tories: Broadcasting Policy 1979–1997*. London: British Film Institute.

Gresh, A. (2003) 'Saudi Arabia: Radical Islam or Reform?', *Le Monde Diplomatique*, 4–5, June.

Gulf Times (2001) 'US Pressure on Al-Jazeera Slammed', 9 October.

Halliday, F. (2002) 'The Middle East and the Politics of Differential Integration', in T. Dodge and R. Higgott (eds), *Globalization and the Middle East: Islam, Economy, Society and Politics*. London: Royal Institute of International Affairs.

Hallin, D. C. and Mancini, P. (2004) *Comparing Media Systems: Three Models of Media and Politics*. Cambridge: Cambridge University Press.

Henry, C. M. and Springborg, R. (2001) *Globalization and the Politics of Development in the Middle East*. Cambridge: Cambridge University Press.

Herman, E. S. and McChesney, R. W. (1997) *The Global Media: The New Missionaries of Corporate Capitalism*. London: Cassell.

Hills, J. (1986) *Deregulating Telecoms: Competition and Control in the United States, Japan and Britain*. London: Frances Pinter.

———(2002) *The Struggle for Control of Global Communication: The Formative Century*. Urbana and Chicago: University of Illinois Press.

Hutchison, D. (1999) *Media Policy: An Introduction*. Oxford: Blackwell.

IMS (2003) *A New Voice in the Middle East: A Provisional Needs Assessment for the Iraqi Media*. Copenhagen: International Media Support.

Lukes, S. (1974) *Power: A Radical View*. Basingstoke: Macmillan Press.

O'Carroll, L. (2004) 'US Makes Al-Jazeera Complaint', *The Guardian*, 28 April.

Peters, B. (2003) 'The Media's Role: Covering or Covering up Corruption?', in R. Hodess, T. Inowlocki and T. Wolfe (eds), *Global Corruption Report 2003: Special Focus on Access to Information*. London: Transparency International/Profile Books, pp. 44–56.

Pincus, W. (2004) 'US Firm to Run Iraqi TV', *Washington Post*, 12 January.

Prokop, M. (2003) 'Saudi Arabia: The Politics of Education', *International Affairs*, 79 (1), 77–89.

Rabbani, M. and Hendriks, B. (2001) 'The Need for New Thinking in the *Intifada*: Interview with Edward Said', *Middle East International* 653, 29 June, 25–27.

Raboy, M. (2002) 'Introduction: Media Policy in the New Communications Environment', in M. Raboy (ed.), *Global Media Policy in the New Millennium*. Luton: University of Luton Press, pp. 3–16.

Razzouk, N. (2002) 'Tabloid Run by Saddam's Son Still Banned in Baghdad', *Middle East Times*, 21 November.

Rugh, W. A. (2004) *Arab Mass Media: Newspapers, Radio and Television in Arab Politics*. Westport CT: Praeger.

Said Zahlan, R. (1998) *The Making of the Modern Gulf States*. London: Ithaca Press.

Sakr, N. (2001) *Satellite Realms: Transnational Television, Globalization and the Middle East*. London: I. B. Tauris.

———(2004a) 'Al-Jazeera Satellite Channel: Global Newscasting in Arabic', in A. Sreberny and C. Paterson (eds), *International News in the Twenty First Century*. London: John Libbey Media, pp. 147–168.

———(2004b) 'Friend or Foe? Dependency Theory and Women's Media Activism in the Arab Middle East', *Critique: Critical Middle Eastern Studies*, 13 (2), 153–74.

———(2004c) 'Maverick or model? Al-Jazeera's Impact on Arab Satellite Television', in J. Chalaby (ed.), *Transnational Television Worldwide: Towards a New Media Order*. London: I. B. Tauris, pp. 66–95.

Sorbets, C. (1998) 'Debating National Policy', in D. McQuail and K. Siune (eds), *Media Policy: Convergence, Concentration and Commerce*. London: Sage, pp. 180–90.

TBS (2001) 'Interview with Sheikh Hamad bin Thamer Al Thani', *Transnational Broadcasting Studies*. (tbsjournal.com) 7.

Tunstall, J. (1983) *The Media in Britain*. London: Constable.

UNDP (2002) *Arab Human Development Report 2002: Creating Opportunities for Future Generations*. New York: United Nations Publications.

UNDP (2003) *Arab Human Development Report 2003: Building a Knowledge Society.* New York: United Nations Publications.

Whitaker, B. (2002) 'Selective Memri', *The Guardian*, 12 August.

────── (2003) 'Getting a Bad Press', *The Guardian*, 24 June.

White House (2004) *Partnership for Progress and a Common Future with the Region of the Broader Middle East and North Africa.* Washington: White House Office of the Press Secretary, 9 June.

Wilkin, P. (2001) *The Political Economy of Global Communication: An Introduction.* London: Pluto Press.

chapter thirteen

Media and Democracy Without Party Competition

ROBERT M. ENTMAN

Introduction

The media systems in most of the world's affluent democracies are converging toward the 'liberal', market-driven model most fully established in the USA. With the USA as case in point, this chapter argues that democracy will likely suffer as a result. The chapter suggests that the dominance of market forces in shaping media content has a specifically partisan effect: augmenting the ability of political parties most thoroughly embodying the interests of large corporations to dominate news agendas and government policy decisions. In the USA, and perhaps other affluent democracies, a '1.5-party system' may be developing. In this system, the imbalance between the dominant party and the leading opposition party is so great as potentially to transform the very character of established democratic institutions and processes, and of political communication itself.

Although important national variations remain, and unforeseen forces could certainly disrupt current tendencies, here roughly speaking are the transformative trends. The first three are well known and common across the globe:

- Increased exposure of media organizations to unfettered market competition (e.g. Hallin and Mancini, 2004: Chap. 8; Hamilton, 2004).

- Decreased investment in serious, 'hard' news by mainstream media and audiences alike (Gans, 2003; Patterson, 2002).

- Blurring distinctions between news and entertainment in the coverage and promotion of political leaders, issues, events and policies (e.g. Baum, 2003; Delli Carpini and Williams, 2001; cf. Meyer, 2002; Street, 2001; Gunther and Mughan, 2000).

The following, less-recognized but closely interrelated trends, consequences and causes of the first three, are most apparent in the USA, and they will draw the bulk of our attention:

- Ordinary citizens disengage from day-to-day politics, further diminishing market demand for serious news (e.g. Mindich, 2004).

- As attention to politics by major news organizations and the citizenry ebbs, elites from the party possessing superior infrastructure and resources for managing media images seizes firmer control of issue agendas and news frames.

- Since genuine public deliberation demands that party elites continuously and effectively contend over framing and interpreting reality (Entman, 2004), this partisan imbalance helps insulate the ruling party from accountability.

- As boundaries between mediated non-fiction and fiction formats dissolve, the ability of typically ill-informed and apolitical citizens to distinguish between the two diminishes, compounding their vulnerability to political manipulation.

In sum, and contrary to most observers who emphasize how media overtake the functions and influence of parties in general (such as Meyer, 2002), the argument here is that these developments *alter the field of party competition*, enabling one type of party to dominate, while diminishing the power of the other. Affluent democracies do *not* experience a decline of parties in general, but a rise of one and drop of another. The US electoral system essentially limits the competition to two parties. In multiparty systems, we might predict that similar forces will encourage parties to consolidate (just as market forces promote consolidation of media corporations). The bulk of effective power would be exercised by just two parties, one of them notably more successful.

For reasons discussed below, increased influence goes to those parties and elites desiring minimal state intervention in the 'natural' distributions of power, wealth and status as determined by the market (cf. Hallin and Mancini, 2004: 292–4).[1] These parties also promote media deregulation, which intensifies the media's exposure to untrammelled market forces. Not-so-incidentally, deregulation bolsters the other trends and redounds to those specific parties' political advantage. When a traditionally less market-oriented party does win power, the media are among the forces working to constrain its political options and forcing it to accept much of the market mantra.

Organized, consistent competition between the major political parties over the media's framing of issues and problems, or *party-competitive mediated democracy*, is the practical goal of most modern theories of democracy (see especially Dahl's, 1989, emphasis on the centrality of competitive information sources to real-world democracy, which he terms 'polyarchy'; cf. McChesney, 2000). Imperfect as the contributions of party competition and news media to genuine democracy have always been (see, for example, Bennett, 2004; Entman, 1989; Gans, 2003), the converging trends discussed here compound the shortcomings.

Regardless of whether it comes from a media product called 'entertainment' or 'news' (see Entman, 2005), citizens cannot reliably distinguish truth from fiction without a vigorous contest between contrasting frames of political reality. 'Frames' are narratives that select and highlight some aspects of reality and suppress others in order to promote a particular interpretation as truthful and relevant (cf. Entman, 2004). In the practice of political citizenship, pursuing truth does not require achieving scientific certitude. In simple terms, it requires that citizens be able to protect themselves from being fooled. More formally, effective citizens must have the ability to detect misleading frames – to reject narratives that might otherwise convince them to support the wrong leaders. Let us call news framing that helps citizens make the right choices and keeps them from supporting leaders who do *not* maximize the values and interests they want 'accountability news' (Entman, 1989; cf. Bartels, 2005; Curran, 2000: 148; Dahl, 1989).

Although most citizens will never pay close attention to politics, it is at minimum important that elites *believe* that many citizens have access to accountability news. Such perceptions can encourage leaders to behave as if they the public *might* hold them responsible. Leaders know accountability news potentially enables even the typically inattentive citizen to understand at least some impacts of government decisions on their lives and values. Its availability is self-reinforcing: as supply declines, citizens' grasp of the very need to watch TV news or read newspapers may weaken (cf. Mindich, 2004). As demand declines, the market signals media organizations to ramp up production of soft news, infotainment, and 'reality' TV – making it still less likely that citizens will stumble across accountability news and further emboldening leaders to govern without fear of close scrutiny.

There are of course countervailing forces, not least the internet and the newer cable, radio and satellite news outlets that may provide alternative perspectives. The internet clearly creates potential for political organization by geographically scattered publics that could influence the democratic process (Bimber, 2003; Dahlgren, 2001; Meyer, 2002: 118–24; Rojecki, 2002). However, there is little evidence as yet that these forces directly impact the day-to-day processes of governance in the way that the traditional mainstream media do (see, for example, Cook, 1998, on the USA, and Meyer, 2002, on Germany). Futhermore, the internet is as available to the dominant parties – and to conservative or reactionary religious organizations that in such countries as Italy and the USA have become indispensable electoral allies to those parties (see, for example, Domke, 2004: Frank, 2004). How much the internet will help to counteract the anti-democratic tendencies discussed here, and how much to promote them, remains an open question.

Media and US democracy in a 1.5-party system

With the foregoing as prelude, let us turn to a detailed case study of developments in the USA. The political theorist Sheldon Wolin has written:

> The Republicans have emerged as a unique phenomenon in American history of a fervently doctrinal party, zealous, ruthless, anti-democratic and boasting a near majority. . . . In ceasing to be a genuine opposition party the Democrats have smoothed the road to power of a party more than eager to use it to promote empire abroad and corporate power at home. . . . What is crucially important here is not only the expansion of governmental power but the inevitable discrediting of constitutional limitations and institutional processes that discourages the citizenry and leaves them politically apathetic (Wolin, 2003).

Is Wolin's harsh indictment justified? Consider two basic facts of American democracy and society. The first is rising income inequality and, more generally, class inequality and stratification. For example, between 1973 and 2000 the average real income of the bottom 90 per cent of Americans fell by 7 per cent while the income of the top 1 per cent rose by 148 per cent and the top 0.01 per cent by about 600 per cent – and this excludes capital gains from the stock market (Krugman, 2004). The second fact is the willingness of large majorities of Americans to support, accept or ignore this rising inequality. As conservative

New York Times columnist David Brooks (2003) has pointed out, 'The Democrats couldn't even persuade people to oppose the repeal of the estate tax, which is explicitly for the mega-upper class. Al Gore, who ran a populist campaign, couldn't even win the votes of white ~~males who didn't go to college, whose incomes have stagnated over the past decade.~~'

What allows this to happen above all is political disengagement by majorities of lower, working and middle class Americans, as opposed to the hyper-engagement in politics of the wealthiest individuals and interests (cf. Domhoff, 2002; Patterson, 2002). The deterioration of citizen participation in elections, the drop in the public's interest in politics and their political cynicism and general political malaise are deeply partisan matters. That is, mass disengagement is propelled by a decline in *highly publicized party competition over the framing of public issues* – what I termed earlier party-competitive mediated democracy. This deterioration threatens the basis of democratic deliberation and participation in the USA by making political detachment – ever a tempting course for ordinary citizens – an increasingly rational response. For when one party overwhelmingly dominates the agenda and framing of issues in the media, there is less reason to pay attention. And indeed the Democrats now function as approximately half a party, barely effective at sporadically contesting scattered elements of the Republican agenda.

The political circumstances of the American election year in 2004 provide evidence for this portrait. One poll (in 2003) found about three-quarters of respondents reporting that the Bush tax cut of 2001 did not add significantly to their after-tax income (American Enterprise Institute, 2004: 53). In point of fact, those cuts overwhelmingly benefited only the richest 1–2 per cent of taxpayers. Yet, polls suggested large majorities supporting Bush's tax cuts, especially the abolition of the estate tax, an act that shifted more of the tax burden to the 98 per cent of Americans not subject to such inheritance levies (Bartels, 2005). And as of early September 2004, polls found more Americans saying they trusted Bush than Kerry to handle tax policy (by 50 to 40 per cent in one poll, 52 to 38 in another).[2]

Then consider the multiplying problems in Iraq during 2004. There were continuing US casualties (and far more Iraqi casualties, civilian and military), almost daily terror attacks, and constant disruption of oil, electricity, water and other supplies. There were scandals over abuse at Abu Ghraib and other prisons; corruption and failures in reconstruction projects paid for by American taxpayers; and the revelation that Ahmad Chalabi, the main Iraqi adviser to the Bush administration, and its long-time choice to lead post-Saddam Iraq, was in all likelihood a spy for Iran. Yet Bush enjoyed a wide margin of approval for handling Iraq and the war on terror. By 57 to 35 per cent in one September 2004 survey (and 60 to 32 per cent in another), respondents voiced more trust in Bush than Kerry to handle the campaign against terrorism, and by 53 to 37 per cent (and 55 to 37), preferred Bush to lead the war in Iraq.[3]

Many US citizens supported the war on the grounds it made the USA safer from 9/11-style terrorism, based on dominant news framings that emphasized Saddam Hussein's possession of Weapons of Mass Destruction (WMDs) and active assistance to al-Qaida (see Kull, 2004). Such claims were supported by few terrorism or military experts outside the administrations of President George W. Bush and UK Prime Minister Tony Blair (indeed were opposed by many such experts *within* those administrations – e.g. Clarke, 2004; Wilson,

2004; cf. Mearsheimer and Walt, 2003). Nonetheless, war came, and arguably it did because few politicians from either party in the USA (or, for that matter, Britain) believed that they would be held to personal account for supporting or acquiescing to the fictions. And at least in the USA, the 2004 election campaign bore out that assumption.

The absence of an elite discourse of opposition, despite considerable privately held doubts about Iraq even within the Republican party (Entman, 2004; Woodward, 2004), the lack of a clear Democratic party counter-frame to the Bush White House's pro-war line, signals the decrepit state of partisan competition in America's mediated democracy. The failures of electoral politics and public discourse to reflect either the economic self-interests at stake in tax policy, or the national self-interests at stake in Iraq, mark a larger reality: the convergence of trends that may be propelling the USA (and perhaps other affluent democracies) toward a *de facto* 1.5 party system. In effect, one party comes to dominate the political culture and institutions, with only spasmodic and marginal contributions from the other.

The converging trends in the USA involve accelerating disengagement from politics by ordinary citizens, combined with a relentless campaign by one party to consolidate power over the backstage of institutional politics and the front-stage of media presentation. The most important new element of this move is the party's abandonment of the tacit, unwritten agreements that long governed the competition between Republicans and Democrats and allowed both real chances to win the White House and Congress, and also a share of power even when in the minority. The consequence is a serious disruption in the media's always-tenuous fulfilment of the core requirement of democratic citizenship: access to information that allows independent evaluation of the claims and frames of the ruling party (Dahl, 1989, 2000). Indeed, arguably, when one considers all the trends together, the USA has been experiencing the partial displacement of independent journalism by narratives rooted in fiction.

Citizen disengagement

Republicans identify the generic problem facing the USA as government itself, and the solution as private action in the market. A well-funded 30-year campaign to delegitimize the efficacy of public policy outside the realm of military action and crime control has convinced many people that government can only make things worse and waste taxpayer money in the process. These premises reduce political debate and policy discourse to an annoying distraction. The answer is always simple: cut the programmes, cut the taxes, rely on the market or, where necessary, on private charity and religion. As to foreign affairs, particularly in the wake of 11 September 2001, the message is equally clear: support the authorities (cf. Hochschild, 2003). Details of public policy become increasingly irrelevant if one accepts the frame.

As one small illustration, consider the changes in Table 13.1, showing even at the lower income levels and among Democrats and independents, support for government provision of jobs has dropped precipitously over the past quarter century. Table 13.2 shows the drastic fall in citizens who say they get no campaign information from newspapers, broken down demographically and politically. The working and lower classes are particularly remote by 2000, and Democrats and independents far more so than Republicans. The use of print media is a shorthand measure of political engagement but a useful one, and the decline of

	Year	
	1976	2000
Income		
Income 0–16th Percentile	19%	37%
Income 17th–33rd Percentile	30%	41%
Income 34th–67th Percentile	38%	53%
Income 68th–95th Percentile	51%	61%
Income 96th–100th Percentile	64%	50%
Partisanship		
Democrats (including leaners)	31%	40%
Independents & Apoliticals	38%	46%
Republicans (including leaners)	50%	66%

Table 13.1 Government Guaranteed Job/Standard of Living: percentage among demographic groups responding 'Each Person on Own'

* Entries are percentages of respondents placing themselves at 5, 6, or 7 on the 7-point scale. Wording of question: 'Some people feel that the government in Washington should see to it that every person has a job and a good standard of living. Suppose these people are at one end of a scale, at point 1. Others think the government should just let each person get ahead on his/their own. (1976 only: Suppose these people are at the other end, at point 7). And, of course, some other people have opinions somewhere in between, at points 2, 3, 4, 5 or 6). Where would you place yourself on this scale, or haven't you thought much about this?' See ftp://ftp.nes.isr.umich.edu/ftp/studies/nes48_02/data/cdf02var.txt.

print is compounded by changes even in television, the least demanding of media. Network news paid half as much attention to the 2000 election as they did to the 1988 (Patterson, 2002). Beyond this, the ABC, CBS and NBC news audience declined to the point that as the 2004 campaign heated up (late August–early September) just 16.3 per cent of television households (around 19 million households) tuned their televisions to one of the Big Three network news programmes on a given evening.[4] A couple of million other households caught the evening news on a cable news channel, but consider this: younger people were so detached that the median age of network news viewers was 60 (Mindich, 2004).

The result is a public that, despite increased formal education and use of the internet, remains poorly informed. The basic finding of Delli Carpini and Keeter's definitive book (1996) on the subject holds: the American public was no more knowledgeable politically in the late twentieth century than they were 50 years prior (confirmed by Somin, 2005; cf. Bartels, 2005; Mindich, 2004: Chap. 2). An uninvolved public reinforces the other trends.

	Year			
	1952	1984	1992	2000
Education				
Grade school/Some High School	35%	52%	52%	69%
High School Diploma	13%	26%	44%	55%
Some College, no Degree	6%	16%	30%	39%
College Degree/Post-graduate work	1%	8%	21%	31%
Partisanship				
Democratic (including leaners)	21%	22%	33%	45%
Independents & Apoliticals	41%	39%	47%	64%
Republican (including leaners)	15%	19%	33%	37%

Table 13.2 Growing percentages at all educational levels *not* reading newspaper coverage

Based on US National Election Studies responses to these survey questions. 1952: We're mainly interested in this interview in finding out whether people paid much attention to the election campaign this year. 1984: Did you read about the campaign in any newspapers? 1992 and 2000: (If R has read a daily newspaper in the past week). Did you read about the campaign in any newspaper? See ftp://ftp.nes.isr.umich.edu/ftp/studies/nes48_02/data/cdf02var.txt.

Violating the rules of the game to consolidate power

At the elite level, the party most closely tied to corporate interests and market ideology, the Republicans, have been firming up their power 'backstage', in institutional settings where real decisions get made (cf. Meyrowitz, 1986), and front-stage, in media presentations (Fritz *et al.*, 2004). This two-pronged, mutually reinforcing effort takes the form most significantly of disregarding the tacit rules of the political game not written into constitution or law. Until the 1970s, these norms made a degree of good faith bargaining between the two parties a reality (on the essential part played by these norms in making democracies work in practice, see the democratic theorists Dahl, 1989; Dahl and Lindblom, 1992; Truman, 1971). Now Republicans routinely treat the Democrats as political *enemies* rather than political opponents, with telling results for democracy (see Brock, 2003, 2004; Conason, 2003; Rampton and Strauber, 2004). For Republican leaders, Democrats' apparent desires to confiscate the resources of the wealthy and expand wasteful government programmes, while preferring secular society over religious, amount to an assault on the real America. These perceptions help convince Republicans that discarding the tacit traditions of political goodwill helps protect

American morality and civilization. Meanwhile Democrats see things in far less Manichean terms (cf. Lakoff, 2004). For instance, Bob Shrum, the senior adviser to Democrat John Kerry's 2004 presidential campaign, boasted of having helped his 'old friend', Republican Arnold Schwarzenegger, write his inaugural speech as governor of California (Anker, 2004) Schwarzenegger became governor after ousting a Democrat in a 2003 recall election. Schwarzenegger's recall campaign violated a long-standing unstated agreement that neither party would use a musty provision of the state constitution to overturn normal elections.

Whereas Democrats often try to cosy up to Republicans the reverse is rarely true. The 'Grand Old Party' (GOP) demands unswerving loyalty to its leaders, and disciplined support of its line. This difference in discipline is a deeply significant contrast between the parties that inflects all the other distinctions. Perhaps the most striking illustration of the overriding value Republicans place on discipline is the near-unanimous support of its politicians for George W. Bush's Iraq policy, despite the many harms it arguably did to the long-term maintenance of America's global hegemony, to efforts against terrorism, and to the stock market and other aspects of the domestic economy – all presumably top priorities for Republican political elites and their corporate and financial allies.[5]

Other examples of Republicans' determined violation of long-standing tacit agreements on political fair-play include their unprecedented battles to manipulate state and federal legislative district lines in such states as Texas (Kuttner, 2004; Toobin, 2003, 2004); their abandonment, particularly in the House of Representatives, of informal practices and formal rules that previously ensured a significant voice for the minority party (Kuttner, 2004); their partially successful effort to pack the formerly semi-independent judiciary with conservative ideologues while blocking appointments of even moderately liberal Democratic judges (Brock, 2003); their relentless pursuit of Bill Clinton's impeachment and removal from office over his (admitted) perjury in a civil suit of little relevance to Clinton's official duties or the mandate conferred on him by his re-election in 1996 (Toobin, 2002); their politicization or outright elimination of previously non-political processes of scientific data collection and policy analysis (e.g. Fritz *et al.*, 2004; Surowiecki, 2004); their efforts to minimize the electoral participation and power of African Americans (see Toobin, 2004); and their willingness to retaliate against critics in ways legal and on occasion perhaps illegal (Wilson, 2004; cf. Bennett, 2004; Entman, 2004).[6] In addition, although it would be wrong to idealize the honesty and civility of the past (Schudson, 1998), Republicans arguably set new precedents on this score during recent presidential campaigns (Fritz *et al.*, 2004; Jamieson, 1992; Jamieson and Waldman, 2002) (see below).

Minimizing the opposition party voice in the media

Republicans' backstage discipline bolsters the Democrats' weaknesses, their inability to significantly influence the course of legislation and other policy initiatives (such as the Iraq war) and this yields the third trend, the dissipation of oppositional presence in the media. The weaker the perceived impact of the opposition party on policy, the less relevant and newsworthy journalists will find them (Entman, 2004: Chap. 4). By weakening Democrats' impacts on policy, the GOP's disregard of the rules for backstage power-sharing diminishes the opposition party's ability to contend on equal footing for a media voice. The violation of tacit rules that once reflected and reinforced trust between party elites is thus compounded by Republicans' massively outmanoeuvring Democrats in the media arena. This trend is also self-reinforcing: tenuous control over media framing translates into less influence on government policy and vice versa.

Reflecting the structural and instrumental power of corporations in a capitalist economy, a power only magnified by globalization and its incessant pressure to elevate economic efficiency over other values in both the economic calculations of business executives (Johnson, 2003) and the political calculations of politicians who seek to maintain economic growth (especially Lindblom, 1977; also Coates, 1975; Domhoff, 2002; Miliband, 1969), the party most closely allied with the corporate world enjoys considerable advantages in the struggle to control media framing. Their edge is rooted in a deeper and broader financial base. Republicans' funding comes largely from corporate executives whose personal and organizational interests and ideologies coincide with the GOP's core beliefs (with some exceptions on social issues such as abortion). With superior funding comes a Republican willingness to exploit inherent weaknesses of journalism in monitoring and clarifying truth for an easily distractible citizenry (cf. Fritz *et al.*, 2004; Patterson, 2003). The Republican ideology and funding base allow them to remain disciplined around problematic claims, and thus to launch and withstand partisan attack, with far greater and more consistent effectiveness than is true of Democrats. Republicans closed ranks around Bush's Iraq war in 2003 based on specious assertions about Saddam Hussein's WMDs and connections with al-Qaida (Woodward, 2004). The debates over these policies featured little presence, let alone consistent, fundamental opposition, by the Democrats (Entman, 2004). Indeed, the top Democratic leader in both the House (Richard Gephardt) and Senate (Thomas Daschle) voted for Bush's Iraq war resolution in October 2002, as did the eventual 2004 nominees for president and vice president (Kerry and John Edwards).

Democrats too must obtain substantial funding from well-heeled organizations whose leaders and short-term interests fundamentally clash with the interventionist, redistributive beliefs and interests of the core Democratic coalition. Having to seek corporate money constrains Democratic opposition on many fronts.[7] In essence, it is easy for conservatives and Republicans, hard for Democrats and liberals, to raise money from the wealthiest corporate interests without compromising core party and ideological principles. By compromising, Democrats risk and often achieve the appearance of opportunism and weakness, and undermine the loyalty of certain natural constituents, such as union members and blue-collar workers (cf. Frank, 2004).

One example is the Democrats' failure to make an issue of the fact that American consumers pay two and three times more for prescription drugs than in any other industrialized country. Because the other countries all intervene to control drug prices, Americans subsidize by many billions of dollars drug research for the rest of the world.[8] The ramifications of this in the cost of health insurance and healthcare, especially to the middle and working classes, are enormous. But few Democratic politicians can make this a core appeal because so many need to solicit campaign funding from pharmaceutical companies and others for whom price controls are anathema.

Financial frailty limits Democrats' rhetorical options for appealing to independent voters and the disaffected half of the electorate that rarely turns out to vote at all. Those disengaged people often do not believe there is a significant difference between the parties, and Democrats frequently buttress that perception by their disorganized and weak rhetorical appeals. Reinforcing the electoral weakness, Democratic political consultants often work for corporations outside of election seasons. Whereas Republican consultants do not need to scrounge for commissions from unions or 'tree-hugging' environmentalists and similar liberal organizations, Democratic consultants must do their work while keeping in mind the need to remain acceptable to future corporate clients.

Democrats' financial vulnerability is compounded by a lack of an organized media machine that works exclusively for Democrats. On the other hand, aided by wealthy corporate and individual sponsorship, the Republicans have a vast apparatus of radio, print, cable television and think-tank outlets that pump out virtually pure pro-conservative and pro-Republican analysis and investigation. The importance of this partisan imbalance in the discourse-generating capacity of the two parties is inestimable. There are hardly any nationally circulated, consistently pro-Democratic and anti-Republican media outlets, commentators, television programmes, or widely quoted think-tanks. Yet dozens of such consistently Republican sources are available (Alterman, 2003; Brock 2003, 2004; Conason, 2003). Although the elite news organizations (ABC, CBS, CNN, and NBC television news, the *New York Times* and *Washington Post, Time*, and *Newsweek*) are neither pro- nor anti-Republican, a bevy of reliably Republican sources help the party move the parameters of debate to the right and, often, to set campaign agendas. To cite just a few of the more important: Fox News, radio host Rush Limbaugh, the *Wall Street Journal*, TV commentator and print columnist George Will, and the Heritage Foundation and many other think-tanks.

In part because of the media imbalance, Democratic elites must deal with a citizenry so misinformed on class-related issues that fully 19 per cent believe they are in the top 1 per cent of the income distribution, and 20 per cent more believe they will eventually be (Brooks, 2003; Bartels, 2005, also finds massive public ignorance about the distribution of wealth.). So two-fifths of Americans are immune to Democrats, including presidential nominees Al Gore (2000) and Kerry (2004), who opposed Republican tax cuts as benefiting mostly 'the top 1 per cent.' Large majorities of Americans of all income classes favoured abolishing the inheritance tax (Bartels, 2005) even though that meant in effect raising their own taxes. The widespread devotion among the middle class to the fiction that they are, or soon will be, rich has helped the Republicans to pass tax cuts shifting the tax burden from the affluent to the middle and working classes (Collins *et al.*, 2004; Johnston 2003).

Intermingling of Fiction and Fact in News and Entertainment

With the diminution of accountability news, the superior truth value of media content labelled as 'news' over that labelled as 'fiction' or 'entertainment' becomes suspect. Consider the purported $200 haircut President Clinton received in 1993 while aboard Air Force One at Los Angeles Airport (LAX) (cf. Entman, 2005). Widely portrayed as symbolic of Clinton's insensitivity and hypocrisy, the haircut neither cost $200 nor, despite news reports, did it delay masses of travellers on the tarmac (Byrd, 1993). In fact, the haircut cost under $150, perhaps well under (since Clinton was an established customer: Wallace, 1993), and air traffic was not delayed. The Pew Center nonetheless found that the story of Clinton's $200 haircut ranked as a major news story of mid-1993 in terms of public interest, with 18 per cent of people saying they followed the story 'very closely', compared with the 26 per cent who monitored Bosnia as closely, and 12 per cent the federal budget coverage. [9]

The *Washington Post*, which broke the haircut allegations on 20 May 1993 and covered 'the most famous haircut since Samson's' in *nine front-page stories* over six weeks, itself never prominently corrected its original allegations (Byrd, 1993). The haircut fiction never really died. Months later, as one example, comedian and talk show host Jay Leno uttered the following one-liner: 'Remember the good old days when Miss America had a $200 hairstyle and the President did his own?' As late as June 2004, *The Times* of London mentioned Clinton's $200 haircut as if it were a fact (Wapshott, 2004). Indeed the *Washington Post* story by ombudsman Joann Byrd, just cited, itself failed to correct the $200 figure, limiting its critique to the false claims of airport delays.

This example suggests that the differences in factual accuracy between non-fictional news and fictional entertainment are not always as great as journalists might like to believe. The less-than-clear line between fact and fiction holds even during election campaigns, when one might expect journalists to exert their greatest effort to clarify truth. Many recent campaigns in the USA were arguably decided – undecided voters were moved – by dubious claims or even demonstrable untruths. However we label them, these claims led undecided voters to cast votes that failed to maximize the values and interests they thought they were supporting. In other words, frames that fooled many voters were promoted by news media operating with their well-documented deficiencies. Although there may be no bright line separating truth from fiction, consider the following winning campaign themes and the larger frames for which they stood:

- 1984: 'It's morning again in America', 'President Ronald Reagan gave you a big tax cut.' (In fact, most Americans' real hourly pay stagnated or fell during Reagan's first term, and their taxes went up; cf.; Johnston, 2003; Krugman, 2003; Phillips, 2003.)

- 1988: 'Prison furloughs [Willie Horton] and the Pledge of Allegiance are key issues.'[10] (In fact, neither of these highly publicized campaign issues was ever considered by the victor, President George H.W. Bush, once in office.)

- 2000: 'Democrat Al Gore is a liar', 'Republican George W. Bush will give you a big tax cut.' (In fact, Gore's alleged lies were themselves fabrications (Jamieson and Waldman, 2002), and Bush's federal tax cuts not only yielded trivial amounts (or zero) for the majority of taxpayers but were cancelled out by state and local tax increases, and higher charges for health insurance, university tuition and the like; Collins *et al.*, 2004; Johnston, 2003; Krugman, 2003.)

The non-fiction media did not do much better when it came to clearly conveying truths about the candidates of 2004. The first big issue of the 2004 campaign arose in August, when the Bush team began framing Kerry as untrustworthy. Their attack, claiming Kerry did not deserve his combat medals from service in Vietnam, was contradicted by Kerry's own shipmates and official Navy records. In any case the assertions held little relevance to the choices before the voters, considering that Bush himself undeniably evaded Vietnam altogether (cf. Entman, forthcoming). Still, this negative framing of Kerry's personal character, based on fictional or at least highly questionable claims, attained massive publicity and appeared to inflict significant damage on Kerry's image (Clymer, 2004; Nagourney and Elder, 2004).

In 2004, as in the past, journalism often granted the best evidence of the historical record no more credence than the assertions of political spin doctors, thereby leaving the undecided, distracted, marginal voter with little consistent, repeated basis to decide between the two.[11] For instance, consider what Leonard Downie, Executive Editor of the *Washington Post* (one of the two most important newspapers in the USA) said about the controversy over Kerry, which was created by a group of conservative Republicans calling themselves 'Swift Boat Veterans':

> Downie said he believes the Swift Boat Veterans coverage had been fair and properly scrutinizing. 'We have printed the facts and some of those facts have undermined Kerry's opponents,' he said. 'We are not judging the credibility of Kerry or the (Swift Boat) Veterans, we just print the facts.'
>
> He defended a lengthy *Post* story that ran Sunday which appeared to give equal credibility to both Kerry's version of the events in Vietnam (which is supported by his crewmates and largely backed up by a paper trail) and the Swift Boat Veterans, despite the fact that previous stories in the *Post* and the *New York Times* had debunked many of the group's accounts.[12]

One reason the US news system fails to consistently convey truth (and often rather efficiently conveys something like fiction) is the oft-criticized 'objectivity' practices, the orientations implicitly endorsed above by the *Post*'s editor (see, for example, Bennett, 2004). These turn the journalist into something more akin to a stenographer than a clarifier of truth. But more important and far less understood is the dependence of news production on the competitive balance between the two major parties. The Republicans enjoy sufficient control over enough media that they can push material such as the Swift Boat innuendos onto the wider news agenda: their many outlets can report 'Those Swift Boat allegations really concern a lot of voters' and by repeating that enough, make it literally so – and thereby create an issue the rest of the media must cover (see, for example, Brock, 2004; Clymer, 2004).

Systematic and more or less equal competition between the parties is the *sine qua non* of balanced framing, of news that at least has the potential to decisively separate truth from fiction. *Without equivalently competing parties to cover, without equally skilled media management on both sides, the non-fiction media are incapable of clarifying truth for the distractible 'cognitive misers', the apolitical citizens lacking firm party identities who constitute the undecided electorate and decide every election's outcome.*

The American dilemma

In sum, political disengagement, the media's and public's diminishing attention to the realities of power and policy, perpetuate a downward spiral of faltering party competition and fading oppositional framing in the media. These help explain the majorities of Americans who acquiesce in domestic policies from which they lose income – and in a war that apparently did precious little to protect anyone from terrorism (Fallows, 2004). Acquiescence in dubious stories scripted by the Republican White House and Congress, with little effective resistance from Democrats, may explain why majorities of those Americans who voted (a mere half or less of eligible adults) kept Republicans in power in most state and federal elections from 1994 to 2004.[13]

Most Republican leaders sincerely think their innovations in policy and process serve the country's best interests. That may be a defensible argument, but unfortunately the USA is not having that argument. On the contrary, one product of these trends is an avoidance of serious public debate on the state of democracy.[14] And together the Democrats and the media find themselves abetting these trends, despite the obvious fact that they undermine the prestige and clout of both institutions.

The political and social sciences could also be complicit in the democratic breakdown. Conventional social scientists treat the two parties in the USA as similar entities, whereas the argument here is that in most ways that count, they are two quite different species of political animal. Just as the 'professionalization' in which journalists are trained (Hallin and Mancini, 2004) instructs them that objectivity requires treating the two main parties equally, so it is for social science. Yet as long as scholars neglect the fundamental ideological, organizational, behavioural and financial differences between the Democrats and Republicans that make only the latter a consistent, full-fledged partisan force in American national politics, mainstream scholarship will continue missing a defining feature of twenty-first-century American democracy. By treating the parties as analytical equivalents, scholars function as a mid-level force, themselves reinforcing the deterioration of party-competitive mediated democracy. This chapter is an effort to counter these tendencies, to sound a monitorial alarm (cf. Schudson, 1998; Zaller, 2003).

Beyond the American experience

These trends most definitely do not apply in a straightforward way to other media systems. As Hallin and Mancini (2004) suggest, tendencies toward Americanization will probably penetrate the affluent democracies of Western Europe and perhaps a few other countries, but to varying degrees and at varying speeds. The common denominator is the pressure of the market slowly undermining media systems where public service and other non-market values once prevailed.[15] But, returning to our starting point, it is above all the market that pushes systems in the US direction.

The key problem with relying so heavily upon the market can be stated simply enough: it is far from clear the ordinary citizen knows enough to demand accountability news (Entman, 1989; on the contradictions between market logic and that of democracy see also Baker,

Domke, D. (2004) *God Willing : Political Fundamentalism in the White House, the 'War on Terror' and the Echoing Press*. New York: Pluto Press.

Edelman, M. (1988) *Constructing the Political Spectacle*. Chicago: University of Chicago Press.

Entman, R. M. (1989) *Democracy Without Citizens*. New York: Oxford University Press.

——(2004) *Projections of Power: Framing News, Public Opinion and U.S. Foreign Policy*. Chicago: University of Chicago Press.

——(2005) 'The Nature and Sources of News', in K. Jamieson and G. Overholser (eds), *Annenberg Press Commission Report on Democracy and the Media*. New York: Oxford University Press.

——forthcoming: *Media Bias Scandals*. Seattle, WA: University of Washington Press.

Fallows, J. (2004) 'Bush's Lost Year', *The Atlantic*, October, 68–84.

Frank, T. W. (2004) *What's the Matter With Kansas: How Conservatives Won the Heart of America*. New York: Metropolitan Books.

Fritz, B., Keefer, B. and Nyan, B. (2004) *All the President's Spin*. New York: Simon & Schuster.

Gans, H. (2003) *Democracy and the News*. New York: Oxford University Press.

Graber, D. A. (2003) 'The Media and Democracy: Beyond Myths and Stereotypes', *Annual Review of Political Science*, 6, 139–60.

Gunther, R. and Mughan, A. (2000) 'The Media in Democratic and Non-Democratic Regimes: A Multi-level Perspective', in R. Gunther and A. Mughan (eds), *Democracy and the Media: A Comparative Perspective*. New York: Cambridge University Press.

Hallin, D. C. and Mancini, P. (2004) *Comparing Media Systems: Three Models of Media and Politics*. New York: Cambridge University Press.

Hamilton, J. T. (2004) *All the News That's Fit to Sell : How the Market Transforms Information into News*. Princeton: Princeton University Press.

Hochschild, A. (2003) 'Let Them Eat War', *Mother Jones*, (September/October).

Jacobs, L. R. and Shapiro, R. Y. (2000) *Politicians Don't Pander: Political Manipulation and the Loss of Democratic Responsiveness*. Chicago: University of Chicago Press.

Jamieson, K. (1992) *Dirty Politics: Deception, Distraction and Democracy*. New York: Oxford University Press.

Jamieson, K. and Waldman, P. (2002) *The Press Effect: Politicians, Journalists, and the Stories That Shape the Political World*. New York: Oxford University Press.

Johnson, C. (2003) *The Sorrows of Empire: Militarism, Secrecy, and the End of the Republic*. New York: Metropolitan Books.

Johnson, H. and Broder, D. S. (1996) *The System: The American Way of Politics at the Breaking Point*. New York: Little, Brown & Company.

Johnston, D. C. (2003) *Perfectly Legal: The Secret Campaign to Rig Our Tax System to Benefit the Super Rich – and Cheat Everybody Else*. New York: Portfolio Books.

Keane, J. (1991) *The Media and Democracy*. Cambridge: Polity.

Krugman, P. (2003) *The Great Unraveling: Losing Our Way in the New Century*. New York: Norton.

——(2004) 'The Death of Horatio Alger'. *The Nation*, 5 January

Kull, S. (2004) 'U.S. Public Beliefs and Attitudes About Iraq'. University of Maryland Program on International Policy Attitudes. www.pipa.org/OnlineReports/Iraq/Report08_20_04.pdf.

Kuttner, R. (2004) 'America as a One-Party State', *American Prospect*, 15 (2), 18–23.

Lakoff, G. (2004) *Moral Politics: How Liberals and Conservatives Think*, 2nd edn. Chicago: University of Chicago Press.

Lindblom, C. E. (1977) *Politics and Markets*. New York: Basic Books.

McChesney, R. (2000) *Rich Media, Poor Democracy*. New York. New Press.

Mearsheimer, J. J. and Walt, S. M. (2003) 'An Unnecessary War', *Foreign Policy*, 134, 51–61.

Meyer, T. (2002) *Media Democracy: How the Media Colonize Politics*. Cambridge: Polity.

Meyrowitz, J. (1986) *No Sense of Place: The Impact of Electronic Media on Social Behavior*. New York: Oxford University Press.

Miliband, R. (1969) *The State in Capitalist Society*. New York: Basic Books.

Mindich, D. (2004) *Tuned Out: Why Americans Under 40 Don't Follow the News*. New York: Oxford University Press.

Nagourney, A. and Elder, J. (2004) 'Bush Opens Lead Despite Unease Voiced in Survey', *New York Times*, 18 September, Sec. A, 1.

Patterson, T. E. (2002) *The Vanishing Voter*. New York: Knopf.

———(2003) 'The Search for a Standard: Markets and Media', *Political Communication*, 20 (2), 139–43.

Phillips, K. (2003) *Wealth and Democracy: A Political History of the American Rich*. New York: Broadway Books.

Pincus, W. and Millbank, D. (2004) 'Al-Qaeda-Hussein Link is Dismissed', *Washington Post*, 18 June, Sec. A, 1.

Rampton, S. and Strauber, J. (2004) *Banana Republicans: How the Right-Wing is Turning America into a One-Party State*. New York: Jeremy P. Tarcher.

Rojecki, A. (2002) 'Modernism, State Sovereignty and Dissent: Media and the New Post-Cold War Movements', *Critical Studies in Media Communication*, 19 (2), 152–71.

Schudson, M. (1998) *The Good Citizen: A History of American Civic Life*. Cambridge, MA: Harvard University Press.

Singer, P. (2004) *The President of Good and Evil*. New York: Dutton.

Somin, I. (2005) 'Political Ignorance and the Countermajoritarian Difficulty: A New Perspective on the "Central Obsession" of Constitutional Theory', *Iowa Law Review* 89, 1287

Street, J. (2001) *Mass Media, Politics and Democracy*. London: Palgrave.

Surowiecki, J. (2004) 'Hail to the Geek', *New Yorker*, 19/26 April, p. 70.

Thompson, J. (1995) *The Media and Modernity: A Social Theory of the Media*. Cambridge: Polity.

Toobin, J. (2002) *Too Close to Call*. New York: Random House.

———(2003) 'The Great Election Grab', *New Yorker*, 8 December, p. 63.

———(2004) 'Poll Position', *New Yorker*, 20 September, pp. 56–62.

Truman, D. B. (1971) *The Governmental Process: Political Interests and Public Opinion*, 2nd edn. New York: Knopf.

Wallace, A. (1993) 'Clinton's Hair Stylist Defends His Presidential Clip Job', *Houston Chronicle*, 20 June, Section A, p. 9.

Wapshott, N. (2004) 'Let Us Spray: How to Get Ahead in American Politics', *The Times of London*.

Wilson, J. (2004) *The Politics of Truth: Inside the Lies that Led to War and Betrayed My Wife's CIA Identity: A Diplomat's Memoir.* New York: Carroll & Graf.

Wolin, S. (2003) 'Inverted Totalitarianism', *The Nation*, 276, 19 May, 13–15.

Wᴀᴀᴀᴡᴀᴘɪ ʀ ᴜ/ᴜᴜ|ᴘᴜ Pᴜᴜ ᴜᴜ'ᴀᴜᴜ ᴀ. ᴜᴜ.ᴡ Nᴜᴀ. ᴊ|ᴜᴜᴜᴜ ᴄᴜ ᴏᴄᴜᴜᴜᴜ.

Zaller, J. (2003) 'A New Standard of News Quality: Burglar Alarms for the Monitorial Citizen', *Political Communication*, 20 (2), 109–30.

chapter fourteen

Selling Neo-Imperial Conflicts: Television and US Public Diplomacy

DAYA KISHAN THUSSU

Introduction

The primacy of television as a medium for the near global dissemination and consumption of both information and entertainment is now well established. Despite impressive growth in literacy rates across the world, billions of people still cannot read and write and largely depend on television as their window to the wider world. With the globalization of television and the proliferation of 24/7 news networks, powerful governments, such as the USA, have been forced to rethink their public diplomacy, particularly in the way warfare is covered on television, to market their version of events effectively to an increasingly heterogeneous and sceptical international viewing public.

This chapter examines television coverage of key post-Cold War military interventions, locating them within the context of a 'neo-imperial era' – one being shaped by the USA, the world's hyper-power, which has been acting with increasing regularity in an imperial fashion, culminating in the invasion and occupation of Iraq. Mapping a decade-and-a-half of US interventions in the post-Cold War period (1989–2004), the chapter explores the growing tendency among US-dominated global news networks generally to follow Washington's foreign policy agenda, couching imperial military actions in terms of 'humanitarian interventions' undertaken to promote freedom and democracy. Global television networks, operating in a ratings-driven and sharply competitive broadcasting ecology, are disposed to cover imperial military adventures in a simplified, not to say, sensational, way, presenting war and conflict as some kind of macabre entertainment. One result of this government–media dynamic is that there appears to be a growing crisis of credibility for Western media, especially among audiences in the non-Western world.

Media and neo-imperialism

The US-led invasion and occupation of Iraq – with the second largest known oil reserves on the planet – has rekindled debates about imperialism, a powerful discourse with its histories of rise, decline and fall, which has been reinvigorated in a new avatar at the beginning of the twenty-first century. Post 9/11, imperialism is back on the global agenda and seems to have permeated media discourses. British Prime Minister Tony Blair's former foreign policy advisor, Robert Cooper, has openly talked about a 'new imperialism' and the 'need for colonization' that would allow post-modern Western nations to impose order and stability around the globe (Cooper, 2003). The media-savvy historian Niall Ferguson has forcefully argued that the USA should not shy away from its imperial role and responsibilities in the era of globalization and that its presence in the world is a benign one and therefore should be celebrated (Ferguson, 2004). More liberal commentators such as Michael Ignatieff speak of a light-touch variety of Western imperialism. In this version of 'Empire Lite', humanitarian interventions by imperial powers – both current and of recent past – are to be encouraged to ensure peace and security in the world's conflict zones and for 'nation-building' (Ignatieff, 2003).

Others, such as Chalmers Johnson, see a more muscular dimension of the 'global pax-Americana', arguing that it has deep military logic, structured as it is around military bases – an 'empire of bases' – rather than colonies (according to the US Department of Defense, there are 725 official overseas US military bases dotted around the world) (Johnson, 2004; Posen, 2003). Among the 'sorrows' of the empire that Johnson notes are 'a state of perpetual war', supported by 'a system of propaganda, disinformation, and glorification of war, power, and the military legions' (Johnson, 2004).

It is also argued that imperialism underpins the US mission to create a seamless global market for free trade, one managed and controlled by Washington, the new Rome of twenty-first-century imperialism (Bacevich, 2002). To consolidate and expand this new empire, the USA should depend less on coercion than on persuasion, an indication of a growing realization that imperialism cannot sustain itself by military power alone. The mass media are crucial in making imperialism appear almost as a benign necessity to maintain global peace and order, to thwart 'rogue states' from acquiring weapons of mass destruction and to lead the 'war against global terrorism'. This imperial discourse has been promoted around the world, primarily through the medium of television, the most global of global media.

The globalization of the US model of commercial television and the multiplicity of dedicated news channels – partly as a result of deregulation and privatization of airwaves and partly the rapid innovations in information and communication technologies, particularly digitalization – has transformed broadcasting worldwide. In 2004, scores of dedicated news and current affairs channels operate round-the-clock, replicating the formula of 'real-time news' broadcasting established by CNN, which calls itself, with some justification, 'the world's news leader'. The leader has inspired an array of followers. Apart from BBC World, the commercially run 24-hour global news and information channel of the British Broadcasting Corporation, other news networks have a national or at best regional influence. Notable among these are: Sky News in Europe; Star News Asia, beamed from Hong Kong across Asia; Brazil's Globo News, part of TV Globo conglomerate; and the Qatar-based pan-Arabic network al-Jazeera. Among public broadcasters, Euronews, a collaboration among public service broadcasters in Western Europe; CCTV in China; and Doordarshan in India are other key examples of broadcasters with dedicated news networks.

The existence of global round-the-clock news networks has created a new genre of rolling news, one which is particularly sought after by media personnel and information bureaucracies around the world, especially at the time of an international crisis, such as a military conflict. The so called 'CNN effect' has spawned a debate, notably in the West about television's perceived powers to shape the foreign policy agenda (Robinson, 2002).

Television and public diplomacy

In his influential book, *The Paradox of American Power*, Joseph Nye argues that in order to achieve its geo-political and economic interests, the USA should flex its 'soft power' rather than its military muscle. Such an approach, he argues, is a key imperative for strengthening the US position in the world and for countering anti-Americanism (Nye, 2002). The mass media form a very significant part of this 'soft power' which the US government has skilfully used as part of its public diplomacy to legitimize imperial adventures. The US Department of State, *Dictionary of International Relations Terms*, defines Public Diplomacy to refer 'to government-sponsored programs intended to inform or influence public opinion in other countries; its chief instruments are publications, motion pictures, cultural exchanges, radio and television' (US Government, 1987: 85).

For the last half century, the US government has been successfully reaching an international audience as part of its public diplomacy, through its instruments of global communications including radio stations – both public, such as the Voice of America, and clandestine, such as Radio Free Europe and Radio Liberty (targeted at eastern Europe and Soviet Union) and Radio Martí (for Cuba) – which played a crucial role in the ideological battles of the Cold War. With the disintegration of the Soviet Union and the collapse of the communist bloc, such propaganda outfits were struggling for a role and the funding for public diplomacy was constantly declining; by 2001 it consisted of less than 4 per cent of the US government's overall international affairs budget. Despite the growing importance of television in implementing the foreign-policy agenda, the US Congress has reduced the budget for international broadcasting – from $844 million in 1993 to a proposed $560 million for 2004. In addition, in 1998 the US Information Agency (USIA), the umbrella body established in 1953 at the height of anti-communist propaganda to coordinate public diplomacy, was merged into the State Department (Hoffman, 2002).

However, the attacks of 11 September 2001 in New York and Washington revived the need for public diplomacy, the main aim of which then became to address the roots of anti-Americanism, especially among Arab and Muslim countries (Lennon, 2003). A former advertising executive, Charlotte Beers, was recruited as Undersecretary of State for Public Diplomacy and Public Affairs to lead US international public relations. In the wake of 9/11, one of her initiatives was to broadcast *Shared Values*, a series of video messages from Muslims eulogizing life in the USA and shown around the world. Other key initiatives included circulating more than a million copies of the brochure *The Network of Terrorism* which was translated into 36 languages, the most widely distributed public diplomacy document.

During the US invasion of Afghanistan in October 2001, Washington launched the round-the-clock Coalition Information Center, to manage news flow, later upgraded into a permanent Office of Global Communications, to coordinate public diplomacy. At the same time, a separate Pentagon Office of Strategic Influence was planned – though later scrapped – to wage secret 'information warfare', including distributing disinformation to foreign journalists.

In 2002, an Arabic-language popular music and news radio station, Radio Sawa ('Radio Together') aimed at a younger Arab audience, was launched as well as Radio Farda ('Radio Tomorrow' in Persian) which began transmitting into Iran. In January 2004, the Middle East Television Network al-Hurra (Arabic for 'The Free One') started broadcasting from Springfield, Virginia, as well as from a bureau in the Middle East, funded to the tune of $102 million by the Broadcasting Board of Governors (BBG), a US federal agency that supervises all non-military international broadcasting.

That broadcasting is central to promoting the US version of world events and to winning the battle for hearts and minds in the Muslim world is now an accepted truth: senior US officials publicly admit that 'the real tug of war in the Middle East is about broadcasting'. As Patricia Harrison, Assistant Secretary of State for Educational and Cultural Affairs told a House committee in August 2004:

> Television and video products continue to be powerful strategic tools for bringing America's foreign policy message to worldwide audiences.. . . We continue to produce 'good news' stories on reconstruction in Iraq and Afghanistan that American and foreign news editors have incorporated in their programs, and we are distributing Department-oriented videos to foreign media outlets worldwide (US Government, 2004).

With cuts in funding and a push to privatization, the US government appears interested in harnessing private media interests to enhance the effectiveness of public diplomacy. Peter G. Peterson, chairman of the Independent Task Force on Public Diplomacy, sponsored by the Council on Foreign Relations, in its 2002 report recommended creation of a 'Corporation for Public Diplomacy' as a possibility of public–private involvement in public diplomacy that could receive private-sector grants. Peterson has argued that 'the US leads the world in many industries crucial for winning hearts and minds abroad – television, digital technology, education and market research – and we must bring these to bear through reinvigorated public diplomacy' (Peterson, 2002).

On its part, the BBG too has accepted the market mantra. The BBG's 2002–2007 Strategic Plan, *Marrying the Mission to the Market*, uses the language of transnational media corporations. The plan talks of 'branding and positioning'; of 'target audiences' and 'marketing and promotion' (US Government, 2002: 23). There is also a clear realization of the potential for localization of media content to suit specific markets.

> Because every media market is different, a one-size-fits-all approach for US international broadcasting will not work. We must tailor everything we do for each of the more than 125 markets in which we operate. The news, information, and Americana we present; the language we speak; and the media we use must fully factor in local preferences and practices (US Government, 2002: 10).

Such a shift conforms to the changes in the media sector and in fact could strengthen the symbiotic relationship that exists between the US government and the American media as both champion corporate causes. The mass media, especially the elite media, need governments as much as the governments need them, symbolizing what may be termed a 'biennial dependency syndrome'. Since the global news networks – many part of huge media conglomerates – are not directly controlled by the government but rely on it for sources of information, they have greater credibility than would be the case for public media. Therefore governments are cautious not to antagonize news networks and they in turn tend to largely conform to the government line on contentious foreign policy issues, especially concerning foreign wars, as an overview of post-Cold War conflicts demonstrates.

Public diplomacy/private media: mutual dependency syndrome

Given the primacy of television as a means of global communication, the way the world's leading television networks cover conflicts acquires international significance. Despite a slow but significant contra-flow in tele-visual images from non-Western countries, the West, led by the USA, continues to dominate the world's news networks (broadcasters worldwide depend on news footage supplied mainly by two television news agencies – Reuters Television and Associated Press Television News), as well as other key sectors of international media (Boyd-Barrett, 1998; Thussu, 2000a; Tunstall and Machin, 1999). Coupled with the reach of such Anglo-American news networks as CNN and BBC World, this gives English-language news a headstart in international news, effectively a 'US/UK news duopoly' (Tunstall and Machin, 1999: 88).

As the new imperial order seems to be shaped by the USA (and vigorously supported by the UK), how US and UK television frames military interventions becomes crucially important. Though there are clear differences between the American and the British broadcasting norms (the latter being rooted in the ethos of public service broadcasting), when it comes to geo-political and economically important stories the difference can be more of degree than substance. British broadcasters (with notable exceptions such as *Channel 4 News* and BBC's *Newsnight*) tend by and large to follow the political agenda set by the USA, presenting more or less the same arguments, though in more measured tone and arguably a little more professionally.

If one examines the post-Cold War interventions, beginning with the regime change in Panama in 1989 up to the installation of a new regime in Iraq in 2004, interesting patterns emerge. The representation of these invasions, almost without exception, was framed in a discourse couched in the language of humanitarianism. Ostensibly, the aims were to promote peace, stability and democracy: the general tenor was moralistic and the responsible behaviour of the US troops was constantly underlined; the capacity of superior US weaponry, especially the 'smart bombs' with their precision and pinpoint accuracy, was routinely emphasized (Thussu, 2000b).

When the official residence of the President of Panama, Manuel Noriega, was seized in 1989 in Operation Just Cause – the first post-Cold War military intervention, heralding a 'new world order' – loud music was played as part of a major psychological warfare operation, giving the impression of a huge Hollywood set. Noriega, a close former US ally, was arrested and taken to the USA for a trial – the notion of state sovereignty was vindicated blatantly, and was the first indication that a new imperial order was being put in place to replace the bipolar world of the Cold War years.

With Operation Desert Storm, the 1991 invasion of Iraq, the notion of war as a spectacle was being globalized, as CNN's live reporting of the bombing of Baghdad brought, for the first time in history, military conflict into middle class living rooms across the globe. The almost surreal presentation, with Pentagon-supplied cockpit videos of 'precision bombings' of Iraqi targets, made the invasion appear as little more than a Nintendo exercise, prompting some to declare that 'the Gulf War did not take place' (Baudrillard, 1995). A year later, when US marines entered Somalia as part of Operation Restore Hope, they were greeted by batteries of television crews, beaming live the landing of imperial troops, timed with the evening news bulletins in the USA.

Operation Uphold Democracy followed this in 1994 undertaken ostensibly to restore to power Haiti's democratically elected President Jean-Bertrand Aristide (10 years later, in March 2004, in a striking example of imperial dictates for 'regime change', US troops deposed Aristide, forcing him to flee the country). A year later, US troops were in Bosnia as part of Operation Joint Endeavour – claiming to bring peace to the warring factions in former Yugoslavia. The 1999 Operation Allied Force, the 78-day bombing campaign against Yugoslavia, by the world's most powerful military alliance, the North Atlantic Treaty Organization (NATO), added a new dimension to the imperial discourse. NATO's first war created a significant precedent: that national sovereignty can be violated in defence of human rights, a principle that has profoundly affected imperial strategic thinking. Also, unprecedented in the history of warfare, the alliance 'won' the conflict without any loss of life on its own side, though the loss of life and property in Serbia was substantial.

By the time of the invasion of Afghanistan – Operation Enduring Freedom – just weeks after 9/11, in October 2001, the imperial powers had a new enemy: President Bush had declared an open-ended and global 'war on terrorism'. As Adam Curtis's series, broadcast on the BBC, argues, al-Qaida may be little more than an imaginary transnational terrorist network invented to suit geo-political interests of the US government, and 'the politics of fear' that characterizes the new imperial age may be a continuation of the Mutually Assured Destruction (MAD) of Cold War years (BBC, 2004). The 2003 Operation Iraqi Freedom, the invasion of Iraq, was claimed to be part of this wider often pre-emptive war which was justified as 'regime change' to suit imperial interests.

In almost all these military adventures, under the cloak of humanitarianism, the US government has advanced its geo-strategic interests, whether in Kosovo (by changing the nature of NATO from a relic of the Cold War to a peace-enforcer whose remit now extends way beyond its traditional North Atlantic territory), or in Afghanistan (which has given the US government entry into energy-rich Central Asian regions) or in Iraq (control of the world's second largest oil reserves and capacity to reshape the Middle East). Despite their specificities, common elements can be discerned in the coverage by global television news networks of the cases listed above. The US government's media agenda during these conflicts, essentially aimed at thwarting critical debate by reproducing the official line, can be discussed in six subsections.

Inundation with information – source-dependence

In virtually all cases the military interventions are presented in the context of how they fit into the US view of the world, with most reports being based on information provided, to a large measure, by official US sources. The coverage is dominated by the live broadcast of press conferences by Western military commanders, often shown in their entirety on networks such as CNN. In this way the imperial powers are able to project their version of the war to a global audience. As Jonathan Mermin has argued in his study of the media coverage of US military interventions in the 1990s, 'if the source of information on American foreign policy is the US Government, then what is being reported is not *the* story but *a* story, one told by a powerful interested party' (Mermin, 1999: 145, italics in original).

When in leading up to the 2003 Iraq invasion the Pentagon wildly exaggerated the power of the Iraqi Republican Guard, most reporters accepted it at face value. The Pentagon's impact can be so strong as to shape not only the coverage but also the language used by journalists. Such phrases as 'collateral damage' and 'surgical strikes' have already become part of war reporting in the 1990s. So when the Pentagon coined the phrase 'embedded', or proclaimed 'shock and awe', virtually all news networks repeated the phrases uncritically and routinely and thus internalized these terms.

The US government recognizes the effectiveness of this source dependence. The Department of Defense states unequivocally that

> Media coverage of any future operation will, to a large extent, shape public perception of the national security environment now and in the years ahead. This holds true for the US public; the public in allied countries whose opinion can affect the durability of our coalitions; and publics in countries where we conduct operations, whose perceptions of us can affect the cost and duration of our involvement (US Government, 2003).

Threat perception

To interest the public in distant wars, the US and UK governments have constructed a threat perception through the mass media. This is often done with the aim of projecting a particular leader who is claimed to have extraordinary powers to threaten imperial interests. Conflicts are invariably constructed within the frame of an 'us versus them' dichotomy – a reasonable, resolute and responsible West pitted against an irresponsible, illegitimate and unpredictable dictatorship. It scarcely matters who is being vilified: the villain of the piece can change as conflicts evolve – it could be a Noriega in Panama; a General Aideed in Somalia; a Slobodan Milosevic in Serbia; a one-eyed Mullah Omar in Afghanistan; a Saddam Hussein in Iraq; or a gun-wielding Osama bin Laden. Exaggerating threats emanating from a demonized opposition helps to personalize war to the extent that an entire country and its population can be reduced to one person. The Iraqi President Saddam Hussein, typically presented in the media as a megalomaniac, may not be as irrational as sometimes projected in Western media. John Simpson, the BBC's World Affairs Editor and one of the most experienced foreign affairs correspondents, noted after the fall of the Iraqi dictator that 'Saddam was never the crazed dictator of Western imaginings. He was rational, highly intelligent and thoroughly well-informed' (Simpson, 2003: 134).

The atrocity story

The atrocity story has a long history as part of war propaganda: during World War I, the Allies' propaganda machine invented the story of German soldiers bayoneting Belgian babies. In the first Gulf War propaganda played a crucial part in preparing public opinion for the inevitability of military involvement in Iraq. The most notable atrocity story in the media at the time concerned Iraqi soldiers killing scores of babies by removing incubators in a hospital in occupied Kuwait. A year later, it was revealed that the story was a complete hoax and part of a major propaganda offensive undertaken by the leading public relations firm Hill and Knowlton on behalf of the Kuwaiti government (MacArthur, 1992).

During 1999, the US government insisted that compelling humanitarian considerations had prompted them to take military action against Yugoslavia, accusing the authorities there of indulging in a genocidal campaign against the ethnic Albanian population of Kosovo. Leading up to the bombing, and during the NATO air campaign, Serbian atrocity stories formed an integral part of news bulletins. Media reports unquestionably reproduced the often exaggerated figure of number of people killed as a result of alleged Serbian atrocities – committed by Serbs against Kosovans but rarely by Kosovans against Serbs – provided by Western sources (Hammond and Herman, 2000). At one point, the claim was made that as many as 100,000 Kosovans had been massacred. However, the UN's International Criminal Tribunal for the former Yugoslavia could only find just over 2,000 bodies. Atrocities committed by the Taliban in Afghanistan were given prominent place on television networks, though the equally gruesome record of local supporters of imperial powers, namely the Northern Alliance, was largely ignored.

Disinformation/misinformation

In 1917, the US Senator Hiram Johnson famously stated that 'The first casualty when war comes, is truth.' As journalist Phillip Knightley has documented in his history of war reporting, disinformation is a regular part of wartime communication, but in the 1990s he also notes that governments have become much more adept at managing the media (Knightley, 2004). Given their dependence on military sources, the journalists tend to accept uncritically the information offered by the military. It is now known that only 10 per cent of 'precision bombs' during *Desert Storm* hit their targets. During the bombing of Serbia only 58 'confirmed' strikes took place against Serb tanks and personnel carriers and not 744, as stated by NATO, and the number of targets verifiably destroyed was a tiny fraction of those claimed by NATO's spin doctors. Yet the myths about 'surgical strikes', and a clean war continue to shape television's sanitized coverage which has tended to make wars appear as largely bloodless.

As a study published by the British science journal *The Lancet* showed, the invasion of Iraq and its aftermath may have claimed more than 100,000 Iraqi lives – a hundred times higher than casualties on the side of the so-called allies. Based on surveys comparing mortality before and a year after Operation Iraqi Freedom, the study attributes the deaths to what it calls 'invasion violence' (Roberts *et al.*, 2004). Yet, although the spiral of violence has continued and even intensified since the supposed liberation of Iraq there is little coverage of Iraqi deaths, reflecting the fact that they are not counted even as a statistic, while Western troops or civilians killed in Iraq receive prime-time prominence.

The invasion of Iraq has been the most extreme manifestation of a misinformation campaign at the service of imperial interests (Kamalipour and Snow, 2004; Miller, 2004). It is now evident that blatant lies were fed to the media to justify the invasion: that the Iraqi government was linked to the perpetrators of the attack on 11 September 2001; that it possessed 'weapons of mass destruction', which they could and would deploy, thus threatening not just the strategically vital Middle East region but the entire world. Although there was a great deal of scepticism about these claims, even among the multilateral bureaucracies – Hans Blix, the head of the UN Monitoring, Verification, and Inspection Commission (UNMOVIC), had expressed doubts about this position (Blix, 2004) – the media gave short shrift to any dissenters and kept representing these threats as real. As the subsequent revelations have shown virtually all the key arguments for the invasion of Iraq were based on misinformation, and, as has been pointed out, evidence of this was available even before the invasion if only the media had taken a more vigilant attitude (Kaufmann, 2004).

Jingoistic journalism

Though the journalists working for global news networks claim to be objective in their coverage of conflict situations, one can discern different levels of jingoistic journalism, from Panama in 1989 to Iraq in 2004, which seems to have reached a climax during the invasion of Iraq in 2003. The 'embedding' of reporters in military units – out of the more than 3,000 journalists covering the invasion, over 600 were embedded – was used to facilitate the dissemination of the Pentagon version of Operation Iraqi Freedom.

The uncritical, openly patriotic coverage of the 2003 Iraq invasion has received much criticism, but in fact patriotism has defined war coverage almost from the inception of modern media and in most countries. The idea of journalists 'going to war' with troops, eating, drinking and living with the military and experiencing life on the frontline has its origins in the Crimean war of 1853–1856. With Operation Iraqi Freedom we seem to have come full circle. Not surprisingly, the general tone of US television networks of 'cheerleading' and 'boosterism' with journalists donning on-screen flags and lapel pins and networks echoing Pentagon labels in their graphics and newsbars, as a new study has argued, gave a vivid but overall limited close-up view of the fighting (Seib, 2004). Monitoring the output from the main US television networks during the early weeks of the Iraq invasion, the Project on Excellence in Journalism found that the embedded coverage was 'largely anecdotal' and was 'both exciting and dull, combat focused, and mostly live and unedited'. Much of it, the report said, lacked 'context' but it was 'usually rich in detail' (Project for Excellence in Journalism, 2003a). Such detail – often concerning the progress of military campaigns – filled the airtime as networks vied with each other to prove their patriotism, with live interviews with soldiers and pilots returning from bombing raids.

War as entertainment

Given the fiercely competitive ratings battle that television networks have to contend with, journalists are under tremendous pressure to make war reporting entertaining. After the initial excitement of an imperial campaign the audience tends to lose interest in wars, forcing reporters to bring in a human-interest element in their coverage. It is not unusual to see imperial invasion presented as an entertainment show, drawing on Hollywood. The rescue of Private Jessica Lynch, who became an icon of the Iraq conflict and has since acquired the status of a minor celebrity, provided an example of mixing entertainment and information, with one news network actually calling her Jessica Ryan, no doubt influenced by the Hollywood film *Saving Private Ryan*. Lynch's capture by the Iraqis and 'rescue' by US special forces became a major media story of the invasion, but it was in fact a morale-boosting staged event for the cameras (Project for Excellence in Journalism, 2003b).

A BBC documentary later showed that the Iraqi doctors had actually looked after her well. One of the doctors who treated Jessica told the BBC: 'It was like a Hollywood film. They cried, "Go, go, go", with guns and blanks and the sound of explosions. They made a show – an action movie like Sylvester Stallone or Jackie Chan, with jumping and shouting, breaking down the doors' (BBC, 2003). The Iraqi lawyer who risked his own life to save Lynch was hardly mentioned in the media (Al-Rehaief and Coplon, 2003).

More enterprising television producers used the war to make the ultimate reality television programme. One key, though short-lived, example was the US entertainment show *Profiles from the Front Line*. Arguably the life and letters of embedded reporters during the Iraq invasion could also be defined as a type of reality TV show. The connection between US film factories and the military is not new and the boundary between information and entertainment – 'militainment' – is increasingly blurring (Burston, 2003; Der Darian, 2001; The History Channel, 2004).

In sum, the mainstream television news media, when covering imperial military actions, tend to accept uncritically the Pentagon's rationale for US military action against sovereign states, almost always in violation of international law and in most cases without authorization from the United Nations. The broadcasters give a disproportionate amount of air time to military commanders, government and political spokespeople and generally hawkish 'independent' experts at the expense of opponents of military action, thereby contributing to the legitimization of aggression, which is often couched in the language of humanitarianism and presented in a high moral tone. Actions are undertaken to stop atrocities and bring peace and stability to the 'rogue' states, most in the global South and populated by 'traditional' societies. The white knights of imperial powers are projected as responsible soldiers, equipped with superior weaponry, which with its pinpoint accuracy can miraculously avoid civilian casualties in a conflict. There is a tendency to personalize conflicts, with demonization of the opposition leader, portraying him as irrational and untrustworthy but wielding enormous power and therefore dangerous.

Discontents of neo-imperialism

Arguably, the US government has by and large succeeded in almost unilaterally redrawing the rules of international military intervention to further its own geo-strategic and economic interests. It has been able to do this and yet retain the moral high ground, thanks to a largely pliant media. Has US public diplomacy succeeded? There are indications that disjunctures and discontents are appearing within the imperial discourse and a growing resentment against imperial adventures around the world. A major international survey part of the Pew Global Attitudes Project conducted a year after the invasion of Iraq found that 'discontent with America and its policies has intensified' especially in the predominantly Muslim countries surveyed; anger towards the USA remains pervasive.

> An important factor in world opinion about America is the perception that the US acts internationally without taking account of the interests of other nations. Large majorities in every nation surveyed (except the US) believe that America pays little or no attention to their country's interests in making its foreign policy decisions. This opinion is most prevalent in France (84 per cent), Turkey (79 per cent) and Jordan (77 per cent), but even in Great Britain 61 per cent say the US pays little or no attention to British interests (Pew Center, 2004).

In the light of such antagonism, the need to revitalize American 'soft power' has acquired added urgency, argues Nye in a recent article, drawing parallels with the Cold War, which was won with a strategy of containment that used soft power along with hard power (Nye, 2004). This has been necessitated also by the availability of other media, as news technology advances and makes dissemination of information cheaper, to challenge the US version of reality. The emergence and growing importance of the pan-Arabic network al-Jazeera, whose coverage of both the Afghanistan and Iraq conflicts has made US public diplomacy less effective. The network has been able and willing to show the uglier side of war – with footage of death and destruction so assiduously avoided by US networks (Seib, 2004). In addition, the growing popularity of online journalism, reflected in the proliferation of news portals and 'blogs', has also affected international news journalism, changing the way people produce and consume news, making the traditional model of foreign correspondence obsolete (Hamilton and Jenner, 2003; Welch, 2003).

As the media outlets proliferate, the audience too is fragmenting. While most of the audience may generally be apathetic to distant wars, there is a minority that is active and feels a sense of betrayal by the mass media. The commercial and critical success of such documentaries as Michael Moore's *Fahrenheit 9/11*, to date the most profitable film documentary, and Robert Greenwald's *Uncovered: The War on Iraq*, commercially released in 2004, which refutes one by one the reasons given for invading Iraq, drawing on experts involved in the US foreign policy and defence establishments, points to the existence of this critical and increasingly global audience.

Despite the best efforts of US public diplomacy and private media, there appears to be a general discontent, within and outside the imperial centres – particularly pronounced in the Arab/Islamic world – with the media's role in covering conflicts, leading to a crisis of credibility within the media (Khalidi, 2004; Lynch, 2003). The public admission and apology by the *New York Times* to its readers about the newspaper's failure to cover the Iraq invasion adequately, points to this self-reflection within the journalistic community.

As the imperial power extends its sphere of influence it is likely that conflicts over the control of resources will intensify in parallel with the proliferation of new media outlets, forcing journalists to rethink their role in covering neo-imperial wars. Journalists have to come to terms with the reality that although state sovereignty may have been undermined under the neo-imperial order, the powerful notion of popular sovereignty has been gaining ground in an age of the globalization of market democracy. They have to realize that no people – traditional or modern, moderate or militant – will willingly accept imperial discourse, however attractively might it be presented. No amount of state-sponsored terrorism, violence and subterfuge is likely to suppress anti-imperial struggles – history teaches us that much at least.

References

Al-Rehaief, M. O. and Coplon, J. (2003) *Because Each Life is Precious*. London: HarperCollins.

Bacevich, A. (2002) *American Empire: The Realities and Consequences of U.S. Diplomacy*. Cambridge, MA: Harvard University Press.

Baudrillard, J. (1995) *The Gulf War Did Not Take Place*. Bloomington: Indiana University Press.

BBC (2003) 'War Spin', BBC 2, *Correspondent*, 18 May.

BBC (2004) 'The Power of Nightmares', BBC 2, 20, 27 October and 3 November.

Blix, H. (2004) *Disarming Iraq*. New York: Pantheon.

Boyd-Barrett, O. (1998) 'Media Imperialism Reformulated', in D. K. Thussu (ed.), *Electronic Empires – Global Media and Local Resistance*. London: Edward Arnold, pp. 157–76.

Burston, J. (2003) 'War and the Entertainment Industries: New Research Priorities in an Era of Cyber-Patriotism', in D. Thussu and D. Freedman (eds), *War and the Media: Reporting Conflict 24/7*. London: Sage.

Cooper, R. (2003) *The Breaking of Nations: Order and Chaos in the Twenty-First Century*. London: Atlantic Books.

Der Darian, J. (2001) *Virtuous War: Mapping the Military–Industrial–Media Entertainment Network*. Boulder, CO: Westview Press.

Ferguson, N. (2004) *Colossus: The Price of America's Empire*. London: Penguin.

Hamilton, J. M. and Jenner, E. (2003) 'The New Foreign Correspondence', *Foreign Affairs*, September/October.

Hammond, P. and Herman, E. (eds) (2000) *Degraded Capability – The Media and the Kosovo Crisis*. London: Verso.

Hoffman, D. (2002) 'Beyond Public Diplomacy', *Foreign Affairs*, 81 (2), March/April.

Ignatieff, M. (2003) *Empire Lite, Nation-building in Bosnia, Kosovo and Afghanistan*. New York: Vintage.

Johnson, C. (2004) *The Sorrows of Empire: Militarism, Secrecy, and the End of the Republic*. New York: Metropolitan Books.

Kamalipour, Y. and Snow, N. (eds) (2004) *War, Media, and Propaganda: A Global Perspective*. Evanston: Rowman & Littlefield.

Kaufmann, C. (2004) 'Threat Inflation and the Failure of the Marketplace of Ideas: The Selling of the Iraq War', *International Security*, 29 (1), 5–48.

Khalidi, R. (2004) *Resurrecting Empire: Western Footprints and America's Perilous Path in the Middle East*. New York: Beacon Press.

Knightley, P. (2004) *The First Casualty: The War Correspondent as Hero and Myth-Maker from the Crimea to Iraq*, 3rd edn. Baltimore: Johns Hopkins University Press.

Lennon, A. (ed.) (2003) *The Battle for Hearts and Minds: Using Soft Power to Undermine Terrorist Networks*. Cambridge, MA: MIT Press.

Lynch, M. (2003) 'Taking Arabs Seriously', *Foreign Affairs*, September/October.

MacArthur, J. (1992) *Second Front – Censorship and Propaganda in the Gulf War*. New York: Hill & Wang.

Mermin, J. (1999) *Debating War and Peace – Media Coverage of US Intervention in the Post-Vietnam Era*. Princeton: Princeton University Press.

Miller, D. (ed.) (2004) *Tell Me Lies: Propaganda and Media Distortion in the Attack on Iraq*. London: Pluto.

Nye, J. (2002) *The Paradox of American Power: Why the World's Only Superpower Can't Go It Alone*. New York: Oxford University Press.

———(2004) 'The Decline of America's Soft Power', *Foreign Affairs*, 83 (3), May–June.

Peterson, P. (2002) 'Public Diplomacy and the War on Terrorism', *Foreign Affairs*, September/October.

Pew Center (2004) 'A Year After Iraq War: Mistrust of America in Europe Ever Higher, Muslim Anger Persists', 16 March, Pew Research Center for the People and the Press. Washington. Available at: people-press.org/reports/display.php3?ReportID=206

Posen, B. R. (2003) 'Command of the Commons: The Military Foundation of U.S. Hegemony', *International Security*, 28 (1), 5–46.

Project for Excellence in Journalism (2003a) 'Embedded Reporters: What Are Americans Getting?' Available at: www.journalism.org/resources/research/reports/war/embed/default.asp

———(2003b) 'Jessica Lynch: Media Myth-Making in the Iraq War'. Available at: www.journalism.org/resources/research/reports/war/postwar/lynch.asp

Roberts, L., Lafta, R., Garfield, R., Khudhairi, J. and Burnham, G. (2004) 'Mortality Before and After the 2003 Invasion of Iraq: Cluster Sample Survey', *The Lancet*, 364 (9445), 30 October.

Robinson, P. (2002) *The CNN Effect – The Myth of News, Foreign Policy and Intervention*. London: Routledge.

Seib, P. (2004) *Beyond the Front Lines: How the News Media Cover a World Shaped by War*. Basingstoke: Palgrave.

Simpson, J. (2003) 'Saddam – A Dictator of Mass Destruction', in S. Beck and M. Downing (eds), *The Battle for Iraq*. London: BBC Books.

The History Channel (2004) 'Hollywood and the Pentagon', *The History Channel*, 19 June, 8 pm.

Thussu, D. K. (2000a) *International Communication – Continuity and Change*. London: Edward Arnold.

————(2000b) 'Legitimizing "Humanitarian Intervention"? CNN, NATO and the Kosovo Crisis', *European Journal of Communication*, 15 (3), 345–61.

Tunstall, J. and Machin, D. (1999) *The Anglo-American Media Connection*. Oxford: Oxford University Press.

US Government (1987) *US Department of State, Dictionary of International Relations Terms*. Available at. www.publicdiplomacy.org/1.htm

————(2002) *Marrying the Mission to the Market. Strategic Plan, 2002–2007*, Broadcasting Board of Governors. Available at: www.bbg.gov/bbg_plan.cfm

————(2003) 'Public Affairs Guidance on Embedding Media During Possible Future Operations'. Department of Defense. Available at: www.defenselink.mil/news/Feb2003/d20030228pag.pdf

————(2004) 'The 9/11 Commission Recommendations on Public Diplomacy: Defending Ideals and Defining the Message'. Patricia S. Harrison, Assistant Secretary of State for Educational and Cultural Affairs. Statement Before the House Committee on Government Reform: Subcommittee on National Security, Emerging Threats, and International Relations. Washington, DC August 23, 2004. Available at: exchanges.state.gov/news/2004/082304.htm

Welch, M. (2003) 'Blogworld: The New Amateur Journalists Weigh In', *Columbia Journalism Review*, 5, September/October.

Media Representations, Mediations and Influence

chapter fifteen ◀

The Information Society Debate Revisited

NICHOLAS GARNHAM

Introduction

In recent years the term 'information society' (IS) has come to dominate policy discourse around the world, not only in the field of communications and cultural policy, but across the whole field of economic and social policy. At the same time in academic discourse it has become a much favoured term with which to describe and explain what are seen as major contemporary economic, social and cultural trends.

The term has become ideological in two senses. First its use as a conceptual shorthand within academic discourse and policy analysis has the effect of giving a spurious unity to a range of observable trends with diverse possible explanations and consequences, and to a range of theoretical analyses with different intellectual roots and supporting empirical evidence, analyses which are in some cases mutually contradictory. Second this very conceptual promiscuity enables the term to act as a unifying rallying cry for a range of different, and often potentially antagonistic, economic and political interests.

Thus we cannot assume that those using the term 'information society' are all either making the same analysis of social structure and change or appealing to the same range of empirical data.

These differences are captured by a range of different terms under the broad IS umbrella; the knowledge economy/society which places a stress on human capital, science and technology: the digital economy/society which places a stress on the centrality of communication networks and information and communication technologies (ICT); the e-economy/society which focuses on the internet as the revolutionary change agent; the creative or entertainment economy/society which argues that it is the growth of media and the production and circulation of symbolic goods and services that are central.

Thus, in so far as there is a debate about the IS it is not, in my judgement, about whether it exists and what are its distinguishing features, whether good or bad. It is rather about what distinguishes the various versions of information society. How do they define the problems of social structure and development? What do they see as the main drivers of economic and social change? What policy prescriptions then result?

The major problem with the concept of the IS, whether as used in theoretical analysis or policy discourse, is that it does not refer to a single theoretical explanation of a set of economic, social and cultural changes nor to a specific delimited range of empirically testable phenomena. It encapsulates a range of different theoretical analyses which place their emphasis on different phenomena and thus are subject to a range of different empirical tests. At the policy level this can lead to important contradictions between both policy means and goals, all claiming to be in some way justified by the notion of an IS. To reject the notion of an IS is not to deny that there are observable and measurable processes of economic, social and cultural change affecting the world in which we live, processes to which those who use the term IS variously point as justification for their analyses or policy proposals. It is to deny that these processes of change have either the coherence to justify the notion of a new form of society or are of sufficient novelty and magnitude to justify the notion of a historical break or revolution equivalent to the shift from feudalism to capitalism or from agriculture to industrial manufacturing. It is however also the case that in many cases the claims made do not stand up well to empirical investigation and it is often the very vagueness with which the term is used that shelters its proponents from this necessary empirical test. It is for this very reason that it is important to unpack the IS concept into its various versions so that we can see what empirical data we might in fact use to test its credibility.

In brief we can distinguish the range of 'visions' of the IS according to the different interpretations of the term information (or knowledge); the role that knowledge or information plays within the economy; the emphasis on human capital, changes in labour market structure and the role of so-called information workers; the role of technology and especially ICTs; the changes in the structure and modes of operation of firms; the weight accorded to growth in the media and information sector. Above all we must distinguish between technologically determinist theories of IS where the development of a new technological paradigm around ICTs is the crucial driver and distinguishing feature and those that emphasize a general shift from fixed to human capital, from muscle power to brain power, with technology seen as a product and enhancer of this shift, in particular through the master concept of Innovation.

In particular it is important to note that the theory of the IS, as a theory of historical stages, derives, in a classic base/superstructure and forces/relations of production fashion from theories of an information economy (IE), itself variously labelled knowledge economy, digital economy, e-economy, creative or entertainment economy. Indeed in EU policy discourse the shift from information economy to information society was clearly politically motivated by a desire to sell a set of neo-liberal economic polices to the so-called social partners. IS fits better into a caring, supposedly socially responsible welfare capitalist model than IE. Hence the emphasis is on developing through public funding mechanisms socially beneficial uses of ICTs – now relabelled IS technologies.

For readers of this volume it is particularly important to stress that, in the present period, we need to tackle the political economy of media within the wider political economy of the IS. There are at least two indications that this is the case. During the period of 'irrational exuberance' that marked the so-called dotcom boom of the late 1990s the financial markets created a new sector, technology, media and telecommunications (TMT), under the assumption, erroneous as we shall see, that their economic dynamics and thus financial futures were as though one. Regulatory policy both in the USA, Europe and the

World Trade Organisation (WTO) is driven by a rhetoric that legitimates changes in intellectual property law, the deregulation of media and telecommunication markets and liberalization of world trade in cultural services as the removal of barriers to innovation and competition required for the development of the IS.

The political economy of the media is in particular linked to IS thinking in two specific ways. On the one hand it is argued that the media are a key growth sector, creating jobs and export earnings, and that therefore economic and regulatory policy in each country must be designed to ensure that supposed barriers to this growth and to national competitive success on global markets for media products and services are removed. It is this view that is captured in designating the creative or copyright industries as the focus of attention and in seeing the world wide web and multimedia as the revolutionary driving forces. On the other hand it is argued that the media sector's economic history, structure and dynamics are precursors for the whole economy as it becomes an IE, and as the centre of economic gravity shifts from producing material goods to producing, distributing and consuming symbolic goods and services. It is this view that is captured in the terms knowledge, weightless and digital economies.

Let me then turn to deconstructing IS discourse as a range of theories that try to explain what is happening to the capitalist economy and as a range of policy responses to problems thrown up by those developments. Sometimes these problems and responses will be found at a very general level among economists, corporate strategists and managers, and national and international policy-makers. For instance, how to explain, and then what to do about, stagnation, evidenced by falling rates of productivity growth and rates of profit in the leading industrial economies in the 1970s and 1980s. Or, and these are related, how to understand and respond to the implications of the shift from manufacturing to services. Sometimes they will stem from the interests of an industry and its lobbyists: for instance the marketing needs of ICT hardware and software industries or the investment needs, and intrasectoral competition of telecom operators.

Daniel Bell and the post-industrial society

It is now universally recognized that one of the key precursors to IS thinking was Daniel Bell's theory of the post-industrial society (PIS) (Bell, 1973, 2004). Indeed he himself substituted the term IS for PIS in the 1970s without making any substantive change to his theory. Thus it is important to stress that the core of Bell's argument is concerned with the shift from a goods to a service dominated economy. As he puts it, 'a post-industrial society is based on services'. This is important because it is the importance of services which in their turn determine both the way in which information, and its role in the economy and society, is thought about, and the associated changes in the nature of labour that are the PIS's defining characteristics. Information is central, according to Bell, because services are 'a game between persons. What counts is not raw muscle power, or energy, but information. The central person is the professional, for he is equipped, by his education and training, to provide the kinds of skill which are increasingly demanded in the post-industrial society' (Bell, 2004: 87). Bell is working here with a very general definition of information and a very wide definition of information workers. For Bell it is the general rise in the importance of human capital for economic performance, and thus of investment in the development of human capital through formal education and training rather than fixed capital investment in machines, that characterizes the IS. And the key category of information worker is the professional expert. In the PIS or IS, according to Bell, economic power passes from owners and controllers of financial capital to these new owners of specialist expertise. Thus Bell's version of the IS is primarily a story of professionalization and the formal certification that underpins the knowledge monopolies upon which professional power is based. It is also important to note that, contrary to the neo-liberal context within which the IS is now promoted, Bell argued that 'if an industrial society is defined by the quantity of goods as marking a standard of living, then post-industrial society is defined by the quality of life as measured by the services and amenities – health, education, recreation and the arts – which are now deemed desirable for everyone' (p. 87). And he went on to argue that because of the 'inadequacy of the market in meeting people's needs for a decent environment as well as better education and health' this would lead 'to the growth of government, particularly at state and local level, where such needs have to be met' (p. 88). The empirical evidenced drawn upon by Bell to support his effort at 'social forecasting' were employment data showing the growth of white-collar service sector jobs and of jobs requiring higher levels of education and training. His forecast of the economic, social and political problems thrown up by these developments were remarkably prescient and certainly fare better than many of his IS successors. In particular he pointed to the central productivity constraint, namely 'the simple and obvious fact that productivity and output grow much faster in goods than in services' (p. 96). This would lead in Bell's view to what others called the fiscal crisis of the state and the legitimation crisis, namely a rising social demand for public services the costs of which were inexorably rising, leading to increased taxes to a point where taxpayers were unwilling to pay the taxes necessary to fund the services they themselves demanded and increasingly expected. Secondly this would also lead to labour and other political struggles no longer being struggles with employers (or capital) over the distribution of surplus value, but with the state in various forms for a share of a restricted budget. Not only was this forecast prescient it also describes the very situation which, in my view, caused the growth of contemporary IS thinking within policy discourse. It is an attempt to escape, through for instance e-government, e-health or e-education, from these very dilemmas of low service sector productivity and the proportional growth of public expenditure.

The second major contradiction to which Bell accurately pointed was the increasing tension in service delivery between expert and lay person. On the one hand the increased professionalization of service delivery based upon educationally acquired expertise led to a desire for professional autonomy and to the relative value of human capital being dependent on embedded but scarce expertise. On the other hand increasingly educated consumers demanded greater access and accountability. It is of course around this contradiction and this field of social struggle that versions of the IS theory have been constructed. To take one key example, Lyotard's theory of the post-modern society (Lyotard, 1984) was based upon research on the impact of ICTs on universities in Canada and argued that the spread of ICTs would destroy the social and economic power of experts by making knowledge cheaply and easily available to everyone. We will return to this version of IS theory in a moment when we consider theories of the Third Wave and ICTs as 'technologies of freedom'.

When Bell made the terminological shift from PIS to IS it was associated with two ways of thinking about the role of information in society and the impact of ICTs. On the one hand he argued that the major driver of economic growth and contributor to value-added was now organized scientific and technical knowledge. Since the development of science-based industries in Germany in the late nineteenth century economic dynamism had come to depend upon what Castells has recently called informationalism defined as 'knowledge working upon knowledge' (Castells, 1996). The key figures were no longer inventors and entrepreneurs but teams of scientists and engineers working in university departments and the R&D labs of corporations. This specific vision of the economic role of information linked up, as we shall see, with Schumpeterian innovation theory to produce one current IS theory which stresses innovation, investment in R&D and the training of scientists and engineers at its centre. It also places a stress on the role of information and its management within the industrial sector rather than in services. ICTs, primarily computers, are then seen to play their role as enablers of scientific research and R&D. At the same time Bell argued, based upon his theory of the rise of the expert, that computing enabled, through its ability to model on the basis of large data sets, more efficient large-scale planning. It was thus diametrically opposed to current versions of IS theory which place a stress on uncertainty, bounded rationality and thus the very impossibility of planning. Finally Bell held out the hope that ICTs were a solution to the service productivity constraint because they enabled the mechanization of information work. This remains an important component, in my view perhaps the most important component, of the IS vision. And it is here that the vision is at its most vulnerable since promised rises in service sector productivity have, for good reasons, failed to materialize.

Post-Fordism

As with Bell's PIS thesis another influential contributor to IS thinking was a version of the service economy/PIS thesis. This is post-Fordism (Amin, 1994). The post-Fordists argued that the economic distinction between goods and services was no longer valid because increasingly the market for goods was in fact a market for immaterial values. This was the origin of those versions of IS that stress the 'weightlessness' of the economy, summed up in Negroponte's claim that we were moving from an economy of atoms to an economy of bits. Thus all economic sectors of production were now primarily information industries attempting to discover and satisfy consumer needs which were increasingly symbolic rather than material. This meant that demand was more volatile and unpredictable, as it had always been in the core symbolic goods or cultural industries, and that corporate success no longer depended on mass production and the search for least-cost efficiency through economies of scale, but on speed and flexibility of response to market demands. For many theorists at the time in the early 1980s the symbolic post-Fordist firm, the successor to General Motors as the quintessential Fordist firm, was Benetton. Such theories placed, as in Bell, a general stress on the growth of 'symbolic' work and workers, but the core activities were no longer science and technology, but marketing and design. Such theories led to the widespread focus on brands, rather than either products or firms, as the core of value added. They also linked to info economics and transaction cost analyses of the firm to feed into Castells concept of the network, the network firm and the project as the new cutting edge of the economy and the basis for Castells dubbing the IS the network society. Within this theory information is primarily data on consumers and competitors. The key characteristic of human capital is the soft, difficult to capture and measure, cultural know-how captured by the term creative. This theory was linked to theories of labour market changes and thus changes in social and cultural ethos through the supposed individuality and resistance to hierarchical and Taylorist forms of management of 'creative' workers. This theory has not stood up well to the test of history. In fact the majority of workers continue to work under hierarchical, Taylorist managers, even in the service sector. The major firms have continued to pursue economies of scale, if now on a global basis, and the associated process of concentration has proceeded apace.

One version of post-Fordism that stands up particularly badly to the empirical test is that which argued that the media or cultural industries, redubbed 'creative', were one of the key new economic growth sectors and generators of new forms of employment to substitute for the old blue-collar factory jobs lost in the process of deindustrialization that post-Fordism supposedly described. We will return to this issue, and the media-centric version of IS theory, shortly, but for the moment what is important to grasp is that the term of 'creative' economy associated with this analysis draws on two very different notions of the meaning of creativity, the meanings of information associated with it and their role in the economy.

The leisure society

It is worth mentioning briefly a now very *démodé* version of this shift in capitalist economies but one that had many connections to both the service and post-Fordist analyses, namely the leisure society. This held both that the rise in levels of productivity, and especially automation, were leading to ever shorter working hours and, as life spans lengthened, the working life as an ever smaller proportion of total life. Thus people were not only spending a greater proportion of their incomes on the satisfaction of symbolic life style needs but they also had much longer periods of leisure in which to enjoy their disposable income. Thus it was argued that forms of leisure enjoyment, including importantly the media and culture, were going to be growth markets. Unfortunately for this thesis the long-term trend to shorter working hours driven by the productivity growth of industrial capitalism appears to have reversed with the shift to service employment and the onset of the Information revolution. As a result conditions are not favourable to a growth in the Arts and Media sector and its current dynamics can better be explained as increasingly intense competition for stagnant or even declining consumption time. This is very important because a key use of the concept of IS within media studies is based upon this claim about expansion of the media and cultural sector and thus its status as a key growth sector of post-industrial, information economies. This is, I believe, a false or at least much exaggerated claim, but it has important policy consequences.

Schumpeterianism

A key feature of contemporary IS theory is the concept of innovation as central to economic growth, and the search for policies that, in a process of economic competition between nations and regions, will optimize the innovation process. It is here we find the stress on what Castells has dubbed 'informationalism' or 'knowledge working on knowledge' as the new spirit of capitalism and the associated focus on ICTs as both an exemplar and driver of an unprecedentedly rapid process of change. This focus derives from the school of political economic analysis known as Schumpeterianism (Schumpeter, 1934, 1939). I think it fair to say that if the *année glorieuse* of the post World War II boom, which ended with the oil shock of 1972, were dominated at both a theoretical and policy level by Keynesianism, the succeeding period of economic crisis and turmoil, to which the IS vision is a response, has been dominated by Schumpeterianism. Before examining this school I would like to stress that in assessing the IS vision it is useful to think of economic theories not as some general truth, either right or wrong, but as responses to real world problems. In order to understand their import and to assess their validity we need to understand the problem they are addressing and their adequacy in the face of that problem. Economic theories, and thus IS theories, are unlikely to be true for all time, both because the very complex interactive process that we call society will, in implementing the theory and the policies developed from it, throw up new and different problems and because, with hindsight, the problem may have been misdiagnosed. Thus Bell's analysis was a response to low service sector and especially public sector productivity, and the associated fiscal crisis of the state to which neo-liberal, market-based deregulatory theories and policies were one, temporarily hegemonic, response. Schumpeter's theories, as were Keynes', were a response to the Great Depression of the 1920s and 1930s. It is for precisely this reason that they were taken up again in response to the end of the long post-war boom.

The Schumpeterian response can be divided into two approaches: one that focuses on innovation and the entrepreneur, the other that focuses on long waves. Both have fed into IS thinking.

Schumpeter was arguing against the neo-classical school's static equilibrium analysis of the capitalist system, and of the business cycle which was a central feature of the system's dynamic. The neo-classicals argued that capitalism was driven by price competition and the search for efficiency. While Schumpeter acknowledged that such a process did indeed go on, he argued that such price competition and search for lower costs would inevitably result in stagnation as markets became oligopolistic and the return on investment was reduced to zero. As an alternative he argued that economic growth was fuelled by the competitive search for innovation in new products and processes. And contrary to Bell and others he argued that this search was not driven primarily by planned scientific and technological research but by entrepreneurial risk-taking. For Schumpeter the hero of capitalism was not the scientist or technologist but the entrepreneur. This is so because of the centrality of risk-taking. The concept of risk is central to IS thinking, and to the concept of information that results from it, as we shall see shortly when we look at the information economics school. In brief Schumpeter's argument was that no one could by definition know in advance whether an innovation was going to be successful. Innovation was by definition economically risky (we should note here that this is, of course, a central characteristic of media and information economics). But the rewards of successful innovation stemmed not from success in market price competition, but on the contrary from the fact that a successful innovation has for a time a monopoly. Thus the reward that makes the investment in the risk of innovation worthwhile is the super profits to be made from the monopoly rents accruing to successful innovation. This of course has profound implications for regulatory policy, particularly anti-trust, and for IP and patent legislation, since the time in which a monopoly can be sustained is crucial to the risk reward ratio and thus, this school argues, to the general dynamism of the economy. It is these Schumpeterian arguments that have been used to defend Microsoft against anti-trust action and were used to justify the inflated valuations of high tech and dotcom firms during the boom of the late 1990s. The battle of the corporate sector to strengthen and lengthen patent and IP protection in which they appeal to the idea of an IS is in essence a battle to lengthen the superprofits window and thus improve the risk reward ratio to innovation. The problem from an innovation perspective is that such a move also dampens rather than encourages future innovation by making both the sharing of information on which dynamic innovation is based more difficult and by raising market entry barriers to new innovations.

Long waves and the techno-social paradigm

This Schumpeterian, entrepreneur-driven innovation process is general and applies to all products and processes. It is not necessarily high-tech and the ICT 'revolution' would just be one among many such innovation processes. Indeed, one related school of thought, influential in regulatory policy, by linking Schumpeter to Hayek, argued for strict technological neutrality as between technologies. However Schumpeter was not just concerned with explaining capitalism's economic dynamism and the short-term business cycle. He was also concerned to explain, in the context of the long depression of the 1920s and 1930s, why there appeared to be long waves in economic development. Such long waves, of about 50 years duration, have since been named, after the Soviet economist who did most to establish their existence, Kondratieff waves. Here the explanation is firmly technological and technologically determinist. The best current statement of this position can be found in Freeman and Louca (2001).

This school argues that the historical development of capitalism has passed through successive cycles of long-term growth and stagnation associated with investment in the development and deployment throughout the economy of a series of general purpose technologies that transform both supply and demand across the whole economy. Freeman and Louca identify the following innovation clusters between 1780 and the present: water-powered mechanization of industry; steam-powered mechanization of industry and transport; the electrification of industry, transport and the home; the motorization of transport, civil economy and war; and computerization of the entire economy. Within such long-wave theory it is to this final wave of computerization that the name IS is given. It is an IS not just an IE because within this perspective long waves are characterized not just by a cluster of technological innovations but by the development of a techno-social paradigm – a set of institutions and social practices that make the successful deployment and exploitation of these technologies possible. And the creation of this paradigm is problematic, both because the necessary socio-cultural change may prove difficult if not impossible and because there may well be alternative viable paradigms. Thus previous waves have produced, or developed within, very different versions of capitalism. At one level it is a technologically determinist paradigm. The driving force of socio-economic change is investment in technological systems and the new utilities and/or radical changes in cost structure that result, but the general societal outcome is inherently open-ended and uncertain. For the purposes of the argument here it is important to stress that the key 'information' innovation is the microchip which works as a key innovation because it both produces new utilities – the ability to store, process and transmit information at unprecedented speeds and low costs – and thus produces a demand boom in its own right (the major beneficiaries of the high-tech boom of the late 1990s and early 2000s have been microchip manufacturing itself and the producers of equipment, not producers of 'information' or 'services' as these remain 'Fordist' material industries), but also powers process innovations that radically lower costs throughout the economy. It is here that, in my judgement, the case for an information long-wave boom is weak precisely because the impact of technological innovation on services has in general been, and is likely to remain, weak and thus the general model that was applicable to material, industrially dominated economies is probably not applicable to this current wave of innovation. This remains a question for research and debate.

Information economics

The fourth major input to IS thinking has been information economics and the analysis of the firm that has stemmed from it. The important point to stress is that this school derives from a different analysis of the role of information in the economy to that of Bell and others and as a result a different definition of the information worker and the role of ICTs. Starting with the work of Arrow (1979) and Machlup (1980–84) this school started by arguing against the neo-classical market model which assumed market actors were rational and that the knowledge upon which such rationality was necessarily based was costless. Arrow argued that market interactions were characterized by information asymmetry because information was not a free good but on the contrary information-searching cost both time and money. This had two important consequences. First that markets were games in which the cost of investment in information search had to be taken into account and second that market actors could skew the market in their favour through higher investments in or more efficient searching for information and its transformation into useful knowledge. Here innovation and the scientific and technological knowledge upon which it is based is merely a special case. It is also of course the case that such competitive information management may involve withholding information. A competitive process then led to both higher investments in information-related activities, including marketing and advertising, and thus to a rise in those employed in these activities. But note that these are essentially overhead costs. When applied to dynamic as opposed to static market interactions it also linked up with a general analysis of uncertainty in economic decision-making. Because economic decisions are necessarily taken within a time-dependant process economists, including importantly Keynes, argued that economic actions must necessarily be irrational in the sense that the outcomes could never be fully known and all economic decisions involve risk based upon calculations of probability of outcomes in interactions best understood as a game. We can immediately see that this is a very different vision to that of Bell and the computer as a tool of more efficient planning. But it links to post-Fordist theories of 'disorganized' capitalism, to management theories that stress flexibility and creativity as a response to uncertainty and to the more general appeals to chaos theory. It also, and this is important for the regulatory theory that has accompanied IS thinking, undercuts both all theories of efficient markets and rational choice, as well as the basic premise of most policy that we can match planned interventions to future outcomes.

Theories of the firm

This school of information economics then linked to theories of the firm. This is important because much of IS thinking focuses on changes in corporate structure and performance and is propagated by management consultants and gurus. We see this both in Castells' (1996) stress on the network firm and on a more general management discourse of corporate re-engineering, knowledge management, etc. Coase (1952) famously argued that the reason the firm existed was as a haven from market forces. It was because there were always costs, what became known as transaction costs – for instance the cost of lawyers to draw up contracts – and risks involved in market transactions that it was more efficient for firms to be set up as a series of bureaucratic relations between the the necessary inputs to a production process. This was particularly true when the exchange involved factors the quality of which was inherently difficult to assess and price, for instance white-collar labour time. Thus for Coase the firm in general and the large modern industrial corporation in particular was explained not primarily, as by Chandler (1977), in terms of efficiencies in the search for economies of scale, but in terms of savings in transaction costs. The result for Coase was that the firm as an economic institution was not explained by the superior efficiency of market outcomes but precisely its opposite. While investment in directly productive labour and plant, because there was a relationship between directly measurable inputs and outputs, was subject to the least cost disciplines of the market, the transaction costs school argued that not only the absolute proportion but also the relative cost of the corporate bureaucracy – broadly white-collar employment – rose and that this overhead cost was increasing the inefficiency of large corporations. This was a version of the low service productivity problem and a response, within the then contemporary environment of new managerialism thinking à la Galbraith (Galbraith, 1967), to the crisis of profitability in the US economy. The response to this analysis was a detailed analysis of these growing corporate bureaucracies – now retitled information workers – with a view to seeing which could be made subject to market disciplines by 'outsourcing' or replacement by ICTs.

Digitalization and the 'frictionless' economy

It is here we find the roots of that version of IS thinking that went by the name of the 'new economy' and that focuses on information and information work within the corporate sector and on the possible efficiency benefits to be gained from investment in ICTs. In particular the vision that placed the internet and e-business at its centre argued that the main impact of what, as shorthand, was referred to as digitalization came from what they called disintermediation and thus the stripping out of transactions and transaction costs both in the supply chain through e-business and in distribution through e-commerce. Here the empirical test of the IS vision is the extent to which disintermediation has in fact taken place, the returns both financial and in terms of enhanced productivity from ICT investment, corporate re-engineering, knowledge management, and all the other fads associated with this approach. I think it fair to say that current research would confirm that, while there are cases of success, in general the change has been much less dramatic and the impacts much spottier than the proponents of this vision claimed, and indeed continue to claim. So far as the media sector is concerned the issue is whether web-based distribution and transaction systems have or have not radically shifted the relationship between symbol production and consumption and thus the basic economics of the industry. In particular has it broken the power of the distribution-based conglomerates? The music industry is clearly at present the focus of this debate.

Technologies of freedom and the 'Third Wave'

A central component of the IS vision is that the economic, social and cultural developments that go to make up the transition to an IS are technologically determined by the rapid development and widespread adoption of ICTs. Within the Schumpeterian long-wave school the developments described as the IS are seen as the next long wave of capitalist growth based on a new techno-social paradigm founded on ICTs. Within this general argument ICT developments have little if anything to do with the cultural sector. They are rather the deployment of microprocessors and digital networks to produce a new generation of products and services and a new generation of process innovations in the production and delivery of other goods and services. The main beneficiaries of this new wave of growth have in fact been the ICT-producing sector itself, the financial services sector and the telecommunications industry. There is however a version of this technologically determinist argument that places the media and communication sector centre stage. This school argued that the mass culture that accompanied Fordism, and the rising relative real prices of cultural goods and services identified by Baumol and Bowen (1967), were due to the high costs of production and distribution both of which the ICT revolution radically reduced. According to this argument the domination of the cultural sectors by large oligopolistic organizations, whether in the private or public sector, was due to the high, capital-intensive costs of production and the scarcity, and therefore high cost, of distribution channels. It was then argued that new cheap recording and editing technologies in print, audio and audio-visual, and cheap and abundant, multifunctional digital network capacity via cables, satellites and later fibre optics and wireless, was radically altering what economists call the production function in the cultural sector, undermining the oligopolies and their high cost structures and thus at the same time the arguments for regulating them. ICTs were ushering in, it was argued, an era of cultural abundance and choice in which the original creator rather than the mediating middle men would be king. It is this version of post-industrialism, dubbed the Third Wave by Alvin Toffler (1981), that underpins the revolutionary hopes held out for the internet and the incantatory reference to the digital in much cultural discourse. This vision impacted on the cultural sector and cultural policy in two different and often contradictory ways. On the one hand it supported the idea of the culture and communications sector as the new leading growth sector of the economy driven, as historically such growth sectors have been, by radical improvements in function and reductions in costs. The problem however was that while distribution costs had in fact been radically reduced the costs of producing the cultural goods and services carried over these new high capacity networks had not. This then led to the argument, which is a central component of creative industry thinking both in the UK and the EU, that 'content is king', that the economic growth problem was not technological innovation but shortage of product to fill the networks and meet what was assumed to be an unsatisfied demand. In this vision it is cultural innovation that is the key and 'creative' workers narrowly defined (those in the arts and media) who are the key information workers. While it was network operators and equipment manufacturers who had made money in the first stage of this new growth wave it would increasingly be content producers who would reap the rewards. This became known as the hunt for the 'killer application'. In terms of competition between national economies on a global market it would be those who fostered their content-producing industries rather than those who controlled the technology who would capture market share and the resulting export earnings. This argument was then combined with a technologies of freedom argument for plurality and the decline of large intermediating corporations and with a post-Fordist argument for niche markets, to support deregulation and the bizarre proposal that the UK and Europe had comparative creative advantages *vis-à-vis* the USA because of their cultural heritage, a replay of Henry James in the age of the computer game.

At this point the policy argument led in two directions. On the one hand it favoured the creation of large, corporate national champions who could compete with US and Japanese companies on global markets for content. On the other it lead to a deregulatory argument and a policy in favour of small-scale creative entrepreneurs. Large corporations according to this argument were defined as uncreative, bureaucratic, etc. stifling the creative innovating energies of the 'creative workers'. This has led to particular contradictions in the field of intellectual property (IP) where the IP rights of large corporations have been extended on the grounds that only thus can the incentive to invest in new content be protected and as though it were protecting the rights of the original creators when in fact those rights and the returns from them are transferred under very unequal relations of contractual power from the original creator to the employing corporation. The current furore in the music industry over file-sharing is a good illustration of this contradiction.

The information/copyright/creative industries as the new growth sector

This version of IS theory has been particularly attractive, both to those who study the media and those who work in it, for obvious reasons. In my view this approach has (a) tended to take the propaganda (or wish fulfilment) of the media sector itself at face value, and (b) failed to distinguish the economics of content production from the economics of distribution. There has been a seamless move from the general post-industrial, Third Wave argument to seeing the media sector, now retitled the information industries, as the major economic beneficiaries of this development. The policy imperative is well captured in the title of a recent OECD report *Content as a Growth Industry* (OECD, 1998). In examining the reality of this argument we need first to be extremely wary of the slippery term 'creative' and thus the slide in the policy discourse from media or information industries to creative industries. No one of course can be against creativity. Its recent high valuation within IS discourse stems from (a) the high value placed upon innovation, (b) the stress in developed economies on the returns to human capital and its relation to a high skill/high value added strategy in the face of competition from cheap labour economies, and (c) the centrality in service-dominated economies of human to human relations rather than human to machine. It has little to do with creativity in the artistic or cultural sense, although the cultural industries and some sectors of education have adopted the creative industries' nomenclature in an attempt to capture the concept of creativity exclusively for themselves. In fact the claimed economic weight and growth prospects of the 'creative' industries rests largely on the inclusion of computer software and industrial design (Dept of Culture, Media and Sport, 1998). Within the media sector itself it is traditional print publishing that looms largest rather than the high-tech electronic sectors. So what is happening in the media sector? In order to understand the structure and dynamics of the media sector in relation to the larger economic context, whether of an IE or not, we need to make a crucial distinction that is too often ignored. The media industries serve two distinct markets: that for intermediate goods and services as well as that for final consumer demand or, as Marxists used to say, Dept 1 and Dept 2. This is important because central to classic political economy has always been the problem, in relation to the analysis of reproduction, the business cycle and crisis, of the coordination between Dept 1 and Dept 2. It is also important because information industry growth in recent years, as Charles Jonscher (1983) pointed out long ago, has been largely in business services *not* in final consumer demand. But it is the media as suppliers of goods and services to consumers in their leisure time that has dominated attention and analysis. The problem is further complicated in the media sector by advertising. Advertising is a business service. Its cyclical growth dynamic is determined by corporate profitability and the intensity of competition between firms. But it is an essential ingredient in the financing of consumer media. Thus the media sector marches to two tunes which, as the most recent cycle shows, are often out of sync. It is important to stress that there is a deep contradiction between the growth of business information services and of advertising on the one hand and the claims of the IS (read new economy) advocates that ICTs in general and the internet in particular make the economy more productive and efficient thus increasing consumer welfare by making markets more transparent and in Bill Gates' words 'frictionless'. In fact this claim does not stand up to any serious analysis, but if it were true the prospects for the media broadly understood would not be good.

So far as consumer media are concerned we can observe for the USA, supposedly the most advanced IS, over the last decade a modest growth above the growth rate of GDP (Veronis Suhler, 2001). A large component of this growth has been a cyclical boom in advertising (now followed by an equally severe slump) a large fraction of which was internal to the IS itself (dotcom advertising, etc.). But this growth has been largely a relative price effect since consumption itself has not risen proportionally. Indeed, it is better to understand recent media developments as intensified competition for stagnant demand than as driven by explosive demand growth. The result of this has been the rise in the price to consumers of each unit of media consumption time, in economic theory not a good recipe for dynamic sectoral growth. Of course the IS theorists were arguing that prices would fall because the cost of distribution was falling. This was central to the whole Third Wave, deregulation argument that saw the internet as the provider of nil cost information abundance. Unfortunately they overlooked both the rising relative costs of production (including, importantly, rising marketing costs) and the demand side. In fact rising disposable income has not been mainly channelled towards media demand growth. Rather it has gone to higher cost, but now affordable, ways of enhancing leisure, tourism, restaurants, interior decoration, fitness, and health and beauty. (It should not be forgotten that the largest service sector growth has been financial services, themselves a major driver of both ICT investment and IS boosterism.) The big media sector story of the last decade has not been growth in demand but a struggle for market share, which has taken the form of a struggle over distribution. If we look at US figures we see that the result has been declining margins, declining rates of return on capital and declining rates of profit, especially in the high growth sectors of cable and satellite. Beneath the froth we see a classic over-investment boom driven by a search for market share during a period of technological uncertainty in distribution. To this extent the media are part of TMT since it was this sector that fuelled the general over-investment boom that characterized the new economy period of irrational exuberance. In part this was a side-effect of developments in the telecom sector. Driven by regulatory induced competition and technological uncertainty network operators, both incumbents and new entrants, overbuilt networks and at the same time went in search of the increased traffic that would provide the economies of scale essential to make those network investments pay back. The economics of the sector are such that it was a 'last person standing takes all' game. As part of this strategy the telecom operators bought into the argument, at least temporarily, that it was media consumption that would eat up the bandwidth they were so profligately providing. Hence the content is king/content as a growth industry arguments and the search for so-called killer applications (Odlyzko, 2002). On the other side, the media industry bought into the convergence argument that digitalization enabled the exploitation of a range of content across delivery platforms and that to ensure economies of scale and scope it was necessary to be present on all platforms. Vivendi/Universal and AOL/Time Warner stand as decaying monuments to the fallacies of this strategy.

Conclusion

Those studying the media and media policy will increasingly be doing so within the context of the information society and theoretical and empirical claims made in its name. In assessing the theoretical and empirical validity of these claims they need first to recognize that the term does not refer to a single, coherent theoretical construct or empirical reality. When faced with the term, or its various analogues such as knowledge society, digital society, e-society or creative society, they need to ask in each case what theory of social change is being advanced and what are proposed as its main drivers. They then need to ask what empirical evidence, if any, is being used to support such claims and whether that evidence is either appropriate or adequate. When analysing its use in policy discourse, since as we have seen there are very different versions of the information society, they will then need to ask which version is being mobilized. How does it define the policy problem? On what dimension of the information society does it place its focus? And what policy prescriptions then result? Since the use of the term will often at this level be ideological, they then need to ask whose interests are being served by its usage in this way and in this policy context.

In distinguishing between the various possible versions of the information society they should focus on differences along the following main dimensions:

- How information and its role in the economy and society is conceptualized.

- How the category of information worker is defined and in relation to what changes in labour market structure.

- What role is attributed to information and communication technologies.

- Whether in thinking of the impact of ICTs the focus is on networks or content.

- And finally whether a major role is or is not attributed to the media.

For readers of this volume this last point is of particular importance because there has been a strong tendency within media studies to adopt a media-centric view of the information society and to assume that it is a theory that ascribes a central role to developments in the media and communication associated in particular with the development of ICTs, in particular the development of the internet, and that such a view is so obvious that it does not require empirical validation. I hope, if it has done nothing else, this chapter will have gone some way to dispel this illusion.

References

Amin, A. (1994) *PostFordism*. Oxford, Blackwell.

Arrow, K. (1979) 'The Economics of Information', in M. Dertouzos and J. Moser (eds), *The Computer Age: A Twenty Year View*. Cambridge, MA: MIT Press.

Bell, D. (1973) *The Coming of Post Industrial Society*. Harmondsworth: Penguin.

———(2004) 'Extract from Post Industrial Society', in F. Webster (ed.), *The Information Society Reader*. London: Routledge, pp. 86–102.

Castells, M. (1996) *The Rise of Network Society*. Oxford: Blackwell.

Castells, M. (2004) 'An Introduction to the Information Age', in F. Webster (ed.), *The Information Society Reader*. London: Routledge, pp. 138–49.

Chandler, A. (1977) *The Visible Hand: The Managerial Revolution in American Business*. Cambridge, MA: MIT Press.

Coase, R. (1952) 'The Nature of the Firm', *Economica*, 4, 386–405. Reprinted in G. Stigler and K. Boulder (eds), *Readings in Price Theory*, Irwin, pp. 331–51.

Dept of Culture, Media and Sport (1998) Creative Industries Mapping Document. London.

Freeman, C. and Louca, F. (2001) *As Time Goes By*. Oxford: Oxford University Press.

Galbraith, J. K. (1967) *The New Industrial State*. Boston: Houghton Mifflin.

Jonscher, C. (1983) 'Information Resources and Economic Productivity', *Information Economics and Policy*, 1 (1), 13–35.

Lyotard, J. F. (1984) *The PostModern Condition*. Minneapolis: University of Minnesota Press.

Machlup, F. (1980–84) *Knowledge: Its Creation, Distribution and Economic Significance* (3 vols). Princeton: Princeton University Press.

Odlyzko, A. (2002) 'Content is Not King', FirstMonday. Available at: www.firstmondaqy.dk/issues/issue6_2/odlyzko

OECD (1998) *Content as a Growth Industry* (DSTI/ICCP/IE(96)6/FINAL). Paris: OECD.

Pool, Ithiel de Sola (1990) *Technologies of Freedom*. Cambridge, MA: MIT Press.

Schumpeter, J. (1934) *The Theory of Economic Development*. Cambridge, MA: Harvard University Press.

———(1939) *Business Cycles: A Theoretical, Historical and Statistical Analysis of the Capitalist Process*. New York: McGraw-Hill.

Tofler, A. (1981) *The Third Wave*. New York: Bantam Books.

Veronis Suhler Stevenson (2001) *Communications Industry Report, 1996–2000*. New York: Veronis Suhler Stevenson.

chapter sixteen ◀

Comparative Ethnography of New Media

DANIEL MILLER AND DON SLATER

Introduction

The promise as well as the premise of ethnography has always been a trade-off, in that the more parochial method of participant observation is compensated for by a commitment to comparative analysis. In anthropology, the discipline most associated with ethnography, this is actually quite rare in practice. For the study of media, however, it is, if anything, even more pressing since so much of media studies stems from an immediacy of engagement with both commercial and policy-oriented practices, or from a particular sense of communication and connectedness that eschews such parochialism. In the case studies to be presented in this chapter the particular commitment to comparative work comes from a prior commitment to research the media as a tool of social development, since the work discussed was largely funded either by UNESCO or DFID (the UK Department for International Development). But the arguments to be made may hold for media studies much more generally, and particularly where ethnography can provide a more satisfactory sense of what people actually do with media as well as the best evidence for the consequences of media, matched by a desire to avoid any subsequent parochialism.

How then in practice can we move outwards from location-specific ethnographies of information and communication technologies (ICTs) in order to draw out their more general implications? This pressing question largely revolves around 'culture' and the status of 'culture' within contemporary social research: to what extent has a focus on the unique ('cultural') configuration of places come to limit our understanding of the more general impact of the media? In our case we have developed a series of ethnographic engagements with new media outside metropolitan regions.[1] This rolling programme has inevitably become increasingly comparative as more regions have been involved. Equally, it has become increasingly concerned with questions of development and poverty, as collaboration with both funding agencies and other researchers has pointed us in the direction of questions such as, 'How can ICTs help reduce poverty?' In this chapter we will use this engagement with policy concerns in order to question the identification of ethnography with the 'local' and the 'cultural'.

Situating comparative media research within the context of development and poverty reduction, as well culture and political economy, has made analysis considerably more complex than the questions from which we began in our first project, a study of the co-configuration of Trinidad and the internet (Miller and Slater, 2000). That study aimed to counter the extraordinary level of generalization about the internet that was emerging from metropolitan discourses in the late 1990s, particularly around notions such as virtuality, embodiment and cultural disembedding, all of which were taken to be properties intrinsic to the new technology. Locality (Trinidad and its diaspora) functioned as a test case for *difference*. To consider the project successful we needed only to substantiate the claim that the internet was configured differently in Trinidad than elsewhere, and that the concepts used to theorize the internet in northern discourses were inappropriate in Trinidad. In making this case, we grounded our arguments in alternative characterizations of the internet derived from Trinidadians' various understandings and uses of the new media. Above all, we concluded, the internet continued a longer Trinidadian history of material cultures that mediated the island's relationship to global modernity, acting both to extend and refine its identities in relation to its global position.

In this sense, we fit within a clear trajectory within consumption studies, media studies and technology studies: the assertion of local culture as a site of mediation, difference and agency. Rather than trace the 'impacts' of an already-given technology on an already-given place, we explored the co-configuration of the internet and Trinidad. The internet provided means and meanings through which on-going Trinidadian identities and practices were both continued and re-imagined, while the internet was assembled in a location-specific manner in Trinidad, and across Trinidadian social divisions. In this sense, the Trinidadian internet was approached by way of notions of 'culture' that are well established within anthropological traditions of ethnographic holism: the presumption of a totality of social relationships which it was our task to encompass. The entirely correct objection that this holism cannot assume pre-given and bounded communities (which is to unproblematically equate place with 'a culture') involved us in two intertwined strategies. Firstly, the various (and contradictory) notions of Trinidadian identity were not presumed but were ethnographically generated: 'being Trini' and 'representing Trinidad' were central to configuring the new media to an extent that actually took us by surprise. Secondly, in following the actors through their diverse identity projects, as mediated through new technologies, place became fragmented and dispersed in ways that are now entirely accepted within ethnography: families, businesses and politicians carved up both Trinidad and the internet in different ways, and – crucially – each mapped themselves differently onto the all-important relationship of Trinidad to global modernity and diasporic social relationships.

However, the problem turns out to be less about the equation of culture with place (the myth of bounded communities) and more about the equation of place with culture (the assumption – usually unspoken – that the local is 'cultural' and the global is 'political economy' or 'regulation'). This is because even after problematizing Trinidad as place and as culture, 'culture' would still have remained analytically as merely a signifier of local difference, had we left things at this point. The implications of ethnography would remain limited to asserting some (unspecified) degree of social agency and perhaps local resistance, on the one hand; and on the other hand, to adopting a vantage point from which to critique the metropolitan naturalization (and export) of a particular and technologically deterministic view of a new technology. To give an example (which we pursue further below) the Trinidad research could not be described as strictly culturalist at least in the sense that we invested much research energy, and several chapters, on the political economy of internet in Trinidad, including infrastructure provision, government policy, business practices and international regulation of telecommunications. Nonetheless, we took a somewhat populist position in relation to these issues, again generating our agenda and analysis largely in terms of what these processes meant for Trinidad/the internet within the evolving understandings and practices of different Trinidadians: our task was to identify local understandings and uses of media, and not to assess these as historical trajectories, or as possible development strategies. In point of fact we were not optimistic about some of the hopes and claims that Trinidadians expressed. However, we accepted that even the least realistic of these hopes nonetheless reflected local appropriations and therefore were valid to point up the main lines of differentiation between Trinidadian uses of the internet and those being generalized by the emerging northern literature.

In this chapter we will draw on some of our more recent research to problematize the association of place and locality with culture. This is also to problematize the association (and limitation) of ethnography to culture and locality: in our examples, the cure for ethnographic particularity is not so much multisiting as multiscaling. In the first case study we do this by presenting both 'political economy' and 'culture' explanations of local differences in media development, arguing that they are, indeed, two halves of an integral whole to which they should and could add up. This leads us to query, in the second example, the ways in which the global appears within the local, and 'political economy' appears within 'culture', and vice versa. In this example, both 'communities' and 'development agencies' are localities in which models of media and development evolve; analytically connecting these localities is more than a matter of marking difference but is rather a problem of opening up (hopefully democratic) dialogues over how to assess developmental possibilities.

Two stories: ethnography and political economy

Our 1999 research into the internet in Trinidad provided the evidence for rapid adoption and considerable interest in the new technologies, based on ethnographic research, rather than published statistics. We concluded that the proportion of the population who were accessing the internet was probably greater in Trinidad than in the UK in that year.

Five years later, again as part of a joint project which included Slater working in Ghana, Miller was engaged with a study in Jamaica (Horst and Miller, in press). Here the situation was very different. In several respects usage of the internet in 2004 was lower than Trinidad in 1999. Yet if we change media, the contrast works the other way. By 2004 Trinidad had achieved a respectable but not particularly impressive penetration of mobile phones at around 300,000. By contrast, by the end of the same year Jamaica had over 2 million subscribers out of a population of only 2.6 million. These figures provide all the grist one needs to the mill of comparative research. How can we account for these striking differences? Our aim in this chapter is not just to provide two answers to this question but to consider the different ways in which such answers might be provided.

So let us start with story one. Let us say we are not ethnographers but students of media production, business and its wider political economy. How could this approach resolve our differences? As it happens there is a common starting point to the two situations, in as much as most of the Caribbean share an extremely powerful media institution in the form of Cable and Wireless (from now on CW), which dominated the region during the colonial period. In almost every case CW has been regarded as a highly conservative incumbent trying to protect its own interests and delay the development of new technologies that might harm its profitability, as well as more generally oppose the liberalization of the telecom industry (e.g. Miller and Slater, 2000: 117–43; Stirton and Lodge, 2002). In this respect it is not dissimilar from dominant incumbent companies elsewhere, for example BT in the UK. From that common starting point, there were marked differences in the actions of both the state and key companies that could provide a plausible explanation for why Trinidad went for the internet and Jamaica for the mobile phone.

The first major distinction comes in the response of the two governments. In 1999 the Trinidadian government had created excellent conditions for the widespread use of the internet. Of particular importance was the decision to abolish all duties on the importation of computers and related equipment, along with a decision to provide interest-free loans to public sector workers to help them afford computers. Ministers in the government had family who were in the forefront of companies developing high-end web construction services on an international basis. In general also there was a liberal sentiment that spread through the country in relation to giving access to the internet as part of a nationalist ideal that the whole country needed to be geared towards this technology of the future and not left as a peripheral region. So what we encountered was a very liberal attitude reflected in school children being allowed to remain on site overnight to use the school internet access with no censorship as to what they did online, and companies allowing their internet to be used by workers for their private communications after working hours. All of this created a climate for a high level of knowledge and enthusiasm that was reflected in our ethnography. This coincided with the high point of the commercial hype around internet use where every business was being told that if it was not online it had no real future as a business. Trinidad was flooded with management consultants who resembled the Pentecostal missionaries in their zeal to spread the word that there was no future without the internet. So the state, working together with commerce, provided the basis for rapid internet expansion.

The same year, 1999, was critical for the fate of the mobile phone. Since 1995 the World Trade Organisation (WTO) had been pushing for liberalization in the telecoms sector and Trinidad was expected to be the first major Caribbean state to grant licences to companies that might challenge the dominance of CW. As it happened, however, internal wrangling and arguments delayed this event in Trinidad by some five years, so that mobile phone liberalization was in effect stalled. By contrast, the Jamaican government under the influence of a minister of commerce with a strong interest in telecommunications and liberalization, decided to go ahead and auction off licences for the development of mobile phone networks. Hovering in the wings was a new company called Digicel, founded by Denis O'Brien one of the Celtic Tigers who had made a fortune in the liberalization of the Irish media and had turned to the Caribbean for his next venture (Boyett and Currie, 2004). He had expected to launch in Trinidad, but seeing the way the wind was blowing turned instead to Jamaica. Having bid US$47.5 million, they set up a network of mobile phone poles that for the first time covered the remote rural areas of Jamaica, and came up with a different pricing policy. Soon after the launch it was clear that Digicel would exceed even its own wildest ambitions. By 2004 it had sold a million phones in a country with a population of 2.6 million, while CW, which already had a 300,000 scale mobile phone operation in the country, during the same period had not even reached half a million. Between them and a smaller third company they had reached virtually every household in the country. In our rural study in very remote hillsides in central Jamaica, only households with no one under 65 years old seemed to be entirely without a mobile phone.

How had Digicel achieve this? Especially considering a huge incumbent advantage which meant that phone calls from Digicel to landlines or to what was then the main mobile service were several times the price of CW mobiles and more than ten times the price of using a landline. Firstly, it was favoured because of considerable resentment by many in the population against CW which was seen as having been very slow even in providing fixed phones. Many parts of our rural site had no landlines at all. CW was also seen as heavy handed, for example in failing to deal with complaints. And there was widespread suspicion that the monthly bills were constantly higher than could be accounted for from the calls made. They were seen as the legacy of a colonial and hierarchical company that had treated the country badly, abusing its monopolistic position and its influence over the government.

Digicel, by contrast, brought in a totally new kind of management, flat not hierarchical, with a culture of treating workers very differently, its senior executives seen to muck in, its 'fun days' were more popular, and generally it was seen as trying to get its workers involved in the excitement of the launch. Indeed, Boyett interviewed most of the main players at this earlier period, and they all tell it like some great adventure story. They relish their tales of apparently insurmountable difficulties in getting the towers up on time with their imported materials, getting everything else in place, being prepared for the launch. These Irish executives felt like pioneers in the wild west, part of what they saw as a new adventure, rather than venture capitalism (Boyett, personal comment).

Digicel simply got a whole lot of things right. They hired an experienced marketing figure, namely the Jamaican who had masterminded the rise of the beer *Red Stripe*. Digicel advertising and marketing is replete with Jamaican rasta colours, or national colours. They did brilliantly in their choice of sponsorship from dancehall to a key televised schools competition. Recently they sponsored a local version of *Pop Idol* based on the public voting for their favourite musician using their Digicel phones. They also launched many new initiatives such as texting and internet access through the phone with considerable lead-in periods where the service was free, emulating many internet features by phone under labels such as digichat or digidate.

The competition had a major effect on pricing. It is easy today to get a decent handset for under £20, and it is often cheaper to phone a mobile in the UK from Jamaica than from within the UK. Having said that not everything the company thinks was essential to its success survives ethnographic scrutiny. For example, they presumed that being an Irish, i.e. not an English, company, with its colonial connections, helped get them established in Jamaica, but we have not yet found a single customer that knows that Digicel is Irish.

Still, the story sounds complete – understand the role of liberalization, of the state, of regulation, of the particular commercial companies involved, of their business and marketing acumen, and it seems to have entirely explained the discrepancy between the two countries. A sense of the wider political economy, a knowledge of the industry and research based on reading the local press and business news seems to be sufficient for this purpose. There then is story one.

But there is another story (Horst and Miller, 2005). Our research on business and the state was only one element in our research. Most of our work was concerned with the ethnography of usage. So let us start story two. Miller and Slater (2000) argued also for a particular 'fit' between the internet and Trinidadian culture. Most of that book consists of detailed evidence for a particular propensity for Trinidadians to go online and identify with the internet – how it related to their highly successful education system, their fluid and articulate modes of expression, their confidence of a local presence in the global ecumene, and so forth. But why is it then that Jamaicans do not use the internet, especially since they have actually put so much money into mobile phones that for some it has become their most expensive household utility?

Jamaica's use of the internet is paltry, even where it is available. In urban Portmore, an extension of the capital Kingston and one of our two ethnographic sites, there are only four internet cafés for 200,000 people, of which one is free access provided by a non-governmental organization (NGO). Yet in much more impoverished countries these can be found at every street corner. There are internet kiosks at post offices and libraries that are basically completely unused. So irrespective of availability there is a clear difference in demand and desire present here.

As in all successful ethnography the main lessons come from the failures. We went into Jamaica with the idea of paying careful attention to the precise genres of phone conversations and with a determination to actually listen to the details. We found almost nothing worth studying. Then we became excited because in 2004 Digicel introduced a system by which people who had no credit left on their phone could text up to 30 others to try to persuade them to call back. We thought this would be a excellent route to contextualizing Jamaican use within anthropological work on systems of reciprocity as they worked for low-income households. But once again the material we encountered showed no evidence of working in the ways we had anticipated and, once again, our ethnography failed.

In the end it was a combination of such failures that we feel really unlocked for us the door to the prevalent relationship Jamaicans have with the mobile phone. Together with reference to some classic anthropological work on kinship (Smith, 1988), which demonstrated that Jamaicans know and name a much wider network of kin than in many other societies, but without the common concern for the precise structure of these relationships. We also noticed that many Jamaicans know, without looking, just how many names they have in their mobile phone address book, and quite often this was a hundred or more. So we began asking people if we could go through every single name and find out how often they phoned them and what the nature of their connection was. In the event this technique, combined with the wider ethnography, allowed us to construct a picture of the way low-income Jamaicans employ the phone within what locally is termed *link-up*. That is, they use the phone to keep in touch with very large numbers of people through short calls, based around that familiar Jamaican phrase '*wa gwaan*' (what's going on?)

We also started to uncover how these link-up phone calls corresponded to much wider practices concerned with the nature of relationships. To give three examples. This use of the phone related closely to the way people involve large networks in their economic lives, for example the way children are often helped by money coming in from a wide range of sources, not just biological parents. This is symptomatic of the way money plays a major role in intra-household and family relations, the complex forms of debt and loans, as well as a kind of low-level intensive cajoling system that again tended to share resources widely.

Secondly, there is the incredibly complex network of sexual or potential sexual liaisons that are facilitated by the phones and reflected in phone address books, with categories such as babymothers, partners, second principle current girlfriend, etc. Also very elaborate hierarchies where, for example, better looking individuals always tend to be the recipients of phone calls without having to phone back, and much flirting and innuendo and collecting of possible contacts that are constantly kept up through these short '*wa gwaan*' phone calls.

Thirdly, there are many other networks working on similar principles, such as how the extensive system of small Pentecostal churches keep themselves going, or how rural transport systems have been re-configured by phone systems to integrate with new systems of communication. Phone costs are also justified through their employment in contacting relatives abroad and requesting remittances, which is a vital part of the current economy and without which some of the rural areas we worked in would probably be depopulated by now.

We now have a book-length study of the specific Jamaican relationship with the mobile phone (Horst and Miller, in press) that can parallel the prior study of the relationship between Trinidadians and the internet. This provides a detailed point by point account of the specific propensities that lead to them favouring one media over the other. For example, the antipathy to landlines, which has recently led to so many of these phones being abandoned, is not just a reflection of the costs, which can actually work out considerably cheaper, but is more to do with a resistance to certain regimes of intra-household sharing required by landlines combined with a premium on privacy required by the way people conduct relationships, and more generally a radical individualism and mobility that seems to fit closely with this preference for mobile phones in particular.

If we put the two studies together we can see many good grounds for accounting for the difference in usage. Trinidadians like to talk, at length, at great length, and they are also more comfortable with writing and typing, which reflects their greater wealth and advanced education system. Their focus was on fewer relationships, but relationships that become very intense, so that the internet soon became a major route leading towards marriage. The internet fitted a highly collective sense of sharing and using each machine to bring many others on board, and to express an intense nationalism. These were just some of the ways in which the internet could become characteristically Trinidadian, just as there are now many reasons why one can see the mobile as characteristically Jamaican.

So once again we have a story that quite comfortably, in and of itself, can on the basis of comparative ethnography more than account for the differences between the two sites and their relationship to the two media. But there are two stories. What implications does their juxtaposition bring to the process of analysis? Well, it seems to us clear that an individual researcher could very easily have worked on just one of these stories and simply assumed that their story was entirely sufficient.

As such these stories would be testimony to the disciplinary and methodological divides between ethnography and political economy, between the study of consumption and production, between the study of use and the study of infrastructure. As such there is a lesson from their juxtaposition: that we need somehow to bring them back into a conversation with each other, even if the exact terms of this relationship are not always clear.

Furthermore, were we to start to intertwine the two stories we would find that there is a deeper problem which is not so much disciplinary or methodological as 'topographical': what really distinguishes the two stories is that the local story appears as a story about culture whereas the global one appears as a story of political economy. From the more global perspective, locality is merely the culturally homogeneous object of different policies and technologies; from the ethnographic perspective, locality may appear simply as different cultures. Neither is correct, yet together they give the false sense that our task is to synthesize culture and political economy. Is not the problem rather the way in which they have been separated off into two different analytical scales – the local and the global?

This additional point is best made by systematically reversing the two stories. Could we analyse the commercial and governmental developments as though this was an ethnography of local cultural forms, and could we analyse what we have termed local cultural propensities as an aspect of the wider political economy? Both of these are entirely possible. The advantage of such a reversal would be not just to enhance academic understanding, but also to understand how local policies have developed in the past and perhaps should develop in the future.

Firstly, let us take what we described as local cultural proclivities. The obvious next stage is to ask why these are indeed distinctive, and how they came into being. To answer these questions we have to turn precisely to the wider political economy and study the history of governments and colonialism and political structures. For example, Trinidad is an oil country which has been able to use money obtained from the sale of oil since the 1920s to invest in an extremely successful education system. It is hardly surprising that this has led to an impressive ease and ability of even quite low-income Trinidadians when it comes to the use of computers. Trinidad has become in essence a largely middle-class society, whose diaspora consists mainly of professionals such as doctors and lawyers. Jamaica simply never had that kind of money. The economy has been in the doldrums for a considerable time, not helped by the entrenched nature of political divisions and decades of destructive political patronage and clientelism. Even the government's own assessments during 2004 and reported in the local press suggested considerable failures in the education system. As a result even basic confidence with the computer keyboard is often lacking and there is much less self-confidence with respect to appropriating the internet. There is also a much greater sense among low-income households of an oppressive 'system' that holds people back and that makes the struggle to master such opportunities hardly worthwhile. By contrast the struggle to merely get by has been that much tougher and has meant that complex social networks have developed, which are maintained as flexible and extensive – precisely the networking that helps account for the specific use made of mobile phones. Indeed, Smith, who originally described this kind of loose and pragmatic networking with respect to kinship showed how they were linked to still deeper and older issues to do with the nature of British colonialism and slavery (Smith, 1988).

So what could have been dismissed as merely fortuitous localisms labelled 'culture' can also be understood as the deep imprint of the history of political and economic trajectories. But the same process can work in reverse. The story of business and government in Trinidad and Jamaica is not simply a story of global capitalism. For example, there has been one major study of the internal culture of Digicel itself (Boyett and Currie, 2004) which reported on the marked changes in the way Digicel itself had to adapt to working in Jamaica. In some ways it had to abandon its 'new' capitalism ideals and pick up various more hierarchical and class-based systems simply to fit within Jamaican ways of doing commerce. This was part of a wider process of becoming generally more Jamaicanized, which meant considerable shifts from the original business plan as conceived by the Irish management. In a similar way our earlier study showed how the way the internet spread in Trinidad often had little to do with commercial companies *per se*, since much of it was achieved by small-scale ISP activity that broadened out to small-scale entrepreneurial ventures such as a proliferation of training schools and small internet cafés that followed very Trinidadian ways of doing things. All of this reinforced the arguments made in one of our starting points, a book called *Capitalism: An Ethnographic Approach*, in which Miller (1997) argued more generally that it was just as important to understand the localized nature of capitalism and business itself as it was to undertake the ethnography of consumption. He concluded that we needed to radically critique the concept of capitalism and appreciate that actually what we studied were plural capitalisms, which themselves were highly localized in nature.

So the starting point of this chapter, which implied that the study of political economy is always top-down and the study of consumption is always bottom-up, is found to be quite misleading. Understanding why governments and commercial bodies took the decisions they did was just as much an ethnographic challenge as appreciating the economic and political conditions for cultural preferences. Indeed, one can constantly observe this constant flow between two regimes that might otherwise be appropriated by different academic disciplinary regimes. Take for example the issue of pricing. On the one hand, it is clear that given the complexity of determining the costs within something as fluid and dynamic as the telecoms industry what is represented to the consumer as price when justified as cost is merely a strategy of representation. Digicel employees often point to the pricing policy as a key to their success; for example, at launch they introduced pricing per second rather than per minute. This makes far more sense when you realize that Jamaicans use the phone for a multitude of short calls, with an average length of only 19 seconds, to a mass of different people. It also found that billing services were more or less entirely rejected in favour of pre-paid cards mainly to the value of one pound.

Pre-paid cards were seen as essential to the ability to have individual control over the phone and to understand the relationship of cost to usage. But more than this, it developed a localized trade in phone cards, often bought and resold at the street level, or gifted. For example, an individual can simply phone the scratched number to their boyfriend to pass over the benefit, which allows pricing to become part of kinship and social network studies rather than conventional approaches to pricing. At the same time a study of the regulatory frameworks in the telecom sector (e.g. Stirton and Lodge, 2002) makes one equally question whether the legitimation that companies provide for their pricing of services has any stronger link to some ultimate cost. So is price part of the study of political economy or part of the study of kinship?

So to conclude, the problem is the tendency in much of academia to see capitalism as best understood in terms of its own internal logic, assumed to be largely an instrumental logic, while consumers are studied in terms of something remnant, often termed 'culture'. As a result capitalism is often assumed to be homogenizing, often an instrument of globalization, while culture is thought to be the basis of global heterogeneity and diversity. Yet capitalism when subject to ethnography appears to be just as much an instrument of heterogeneity, i.e. part of the study of culture not opposed to it. Similarly thinking that an ethnographic description of localized difference is of itself an understanding of difference is a surrender to an unwarranted parochialism.

ICTs and development

We can now apply to the idea of 'development' the same questions we raised above in relation to capitalism and locality. The two research programmes on which we draw for the following discussion (UNESCO's ICT for Poverty Reduction or ictPR and DFID Information Society) themselves arise from contradictions and shifts within what might be called a global culture of ICT and development. Particularly over the 1990s, development agencies such as UNESCO and DFID operated within the context of global excitement over the internet, the information society, the new economy and other ICT-driven models of economic and social development that was reinforced at all levels of their operations (such as liaison with national governments and local NGOs). Indeed, ICTs often appeared as a general solution to all development problems, the task of agencies being simply to work out implementation strategies in order to widen access to skills and technology as quickly as possible, and in order to find appropriate implementations in specific areas such as health, education, agriculture and so on.

As ICT excitement subsided, the assumption that these new technologies are simply the inevitable and benign future of development gave way to an often crude and polarized opposition: either a continued assertion that ICTs generate development (and that lack of ICT access will deepen the social exclusion of the south), or a frustration that money thrown at ICTs is wasted in not directly addressing 'real needs' (digging wells, providing medicines, etc.). Put this way, the central question becomes: How can we identify and measure the 'impacts' of ICTs, and specifically the effectiveness of the ICT interventions funded by agencies? To a considerable extent, this grafted the entire issue of ICTs onto the 'monitoring and evaluation' industry within the development (and corporate) sector, whose aim is largely to conduct 'baseline studies' and 'needs assessments' at the start of projects, followed by implementation and self-evaluation methods aimed at connecting project development to meeting targeted needs (and hopefully encouraging community participation in both project and self-monitoring), and ending with final evaluation studies to assess the impacts of the ICT intervention. There are a huge number of such models on offer, each more or less attempting to marry two linked but not entirely compatible considerations: on the one hand, the need for measurements and indicators that can assess the effectiveness of particular funded interventions, compare ICT interventions across the agencies' different regional involvements, and keep specific projects focused on agreed objectives and models; on the other hand, the need for interventions to be targeted on objectives that are locally generated, locally relevant and are connected to local participation.

Hence, the immediate context out of which these two projects emerged focused strongly on methodology. In our involvement with both UNESCO and DFID, ethnography seemed to address two problems inherent in previous approaches. Firstly, understanding the relationships between ICTs and poverty reduction cannot be reduced to a question of 'direct impacts' (as more progressive monitoring and evaluation approaches themselves recognize). Ethnography promised instead to investigate the full range of social relationships around local communication and information, and situate this within local understandings and experiences of poverty. Secondly, and in keeping with this approach, ethnography would reverse the direction of most monitoring and evaluation: rather than trying to develop comparative understandings of what does and does not 'work' by applying global indicators in specific localities, it would attempt the reverse: to generate understandings of both poverty and communication locally, and then bring these understandings within common frameworks for analysis.

In other words, the supposedly macro-context of development agencies and development discourses that permitted these research projects needs to be studied as a changing political and organizational culture that framed ICTs, targets, methodologies and practices – the very 'question' of ICTs. Ethnography itself enters the scene in terms of contestations over the nature of knowledge and control within the development community itself; in particular, sections of both UNESCO and DFID felt the need for exploratory or basic research that attempted to make complex connections between ICTs and possible poverty reduction, on the basis of more detailed and localized understandings of poverty processes and communication/information processes. As a way out of the global questions (and measurements) as to whether or not ICTs 'work' in a generic sense, the strategy was to explore the processes in which they participate, or potentially participate. As one of the ictPR founding documents put it very well, 'if ICTs are the answer, what was the question?'.

Conversely, if we now turn to the actual ethnographies – first to the ictPR projects in South Asia, and then to Ghana – we find local people acting as development theorists, often asking very similar questions about the relationships between ICTs and poverty reduction, and often generating similar debates. That is to say, the ethnographies were inevitably concerned not simply with local cultural framings of ICTs but also – and intrinsic to these framings – with how localities think through development strategies in relation to ICTs as a global phenomenon.

Across all the ictPR sites in South Asia (rural and urban), local people framed ICTs in terms of global discourses that are not dissimilar to those of the development agencies, not least because they are partly mediated through those agencies and collaborating NGOs. Computers, the internet and mobile phones are widely understood as an inevitable future, as signifiers of a modernity from which local people will either profit or be excluded. The sources of this common sense are already extremely diffuse: in the absence of direct personal encounters with ICTs, this framing is conveyed through media representations (above all film and TV); through the buzz of word of mouth and narratives of familial ICT-related successes and failures, through national, state and local policies and politics; and – not least – through the discourses and practices of locally involved donors and NGOs. For example, in most of the project communities, it was clear that the ICTs that were suddenly made to appear in the locale were at least as significant as material cultural objects as tools to use: computers objectified a relationship with global modernity and the future which most locals believed to exclude them. People frequently said that ICTs are not 'meant for' poor people, or lower castes or women; access to ICTs through centres identified them with the most prestige global technologies. Moreover, the presence of ICTs in a UNESCO sponsored centre (rather than a local private computer school) embodied what were clearly understood as new patterns of social and economic capital in the information age: it is through the most modern objects that one connects the local to the global in terms of a flow of funding but also of foreign visitors (researchers, journalists, UNESCO team members) to the locality and a flow of local people to meetings and conferences.

There were some people – particularly among the poorest – who took a line close to the negative view of ICTs within development discourse. They are simply the latest development hype, which can have no direct impact on urgent needs:

> Prem: What will poor people do by learning computers? If we go to learn computers who will feed our stomach. Poor peoples spend their life as a labourer. None of us here has time for computer. We will starve if we don't work for a day. Anyway what is the use of learning computers. Hey, Nima, let's go for work, why do we need to waste our time here? We are not going to benefit anything out of it. It's the same old thing, they simply document, nothing will happen practically . . . (Fieldnotes from Darjeeling researcher: group discussion in outlying village).

However, this was very much a minority view (even amongst those as poor and illiterate as Prem). Most people embraced the association of ICTs with an inevitable future, and therefore as the necessary context for their own concepts and strategies of poverty reduction and social improvement for themselves and their families. In this respect, new technologies are an additional burden on families – they are experienced and communicated to them as a new and urgent requirement of modern life. The clearest manifestation of this was extraordinary investment in computer training for their children on the part of even extremely poor families. The 'need' for ICT skills does not arise from a clear sense of how they might impact on income or opportunities, directly or in practice, and is indeed often based on little or no direct experience of any of these technologies. Rather, it arises from an analysis of development in which the key to advancement is believed to be educational qualifications because certificates are the key to the central aspiration: advancement into secure and preferably white-collar employment in a civil service job or in the administration of a large and stable company. This pattern of aspiration is largely inherited from the colonial and post-colonial days. Buying computer tuition for one's children is the latest in a long line of massive educational investments, a list that has included proportionally huge expenditures on fees for English medium schools, private tuition, English classes or secretarial training and typing, each of them has a period the price of trying to keep up with the constant march of modernity, and preparing one's children to survive and hopefully advance in 'the modern world'. Today, educational advancement includes – and requires – computer and internet skills.

For example, Meenakshi, living in a rural Tamil Nadu village, is illiterate, separated from her husband and living on coolie wages of about Rs500 a month. Nonetheless she is spending Rs30 a month on private tuition for her daughter, plus the cost of transport and school meals, and she is involving herself and her daughter extensively in an ICT initiative sponsored by UNESCO. Meenakshi simply knows that the ICT involvement in particular, as well as the overall connection to modernity that the project constructs, is the best thing she can do for her daughter. However, her understanding of these connections between ICTs, education and future employment is based on little direct experience of any of them. She had not seen the inside of an office until recently, when as part of her project activities, she had been inside a bank. Hence Meenakshi conceptualized a leap from field work to information society by way of the category that she understood most clearly: white collar office work that is secure (rather than daily and unreliable) and that is indoor rather than outdoor:

> Researcher: What do you want your daughter to do?
> M: I would like her to become an office worker. But I don't know. She is studying well. I don't want her to work in the hot sun. She should work in a cool place. Working in the hot sun and getting low pay is horrible.
> R: How are you going to educate your daughter?
> M: I can educate my daughter up to SSLC in Varakalpattu. After that I have to send her to Cuddalore or Nellikuppam. Government is giving free bus pass. I have to spend little more. I will educate her. It is the only aim of my life
> (From researcher's notes, Tamil Nadu).

As in the development agencies themselves, and often in mediated connection to them, a parent like Meenakshi was attempting to conceptualize a direct translation of ICTs into personal and collective development without a clear sense of the social mechanisms through which that translation might actually be produced. In her case – and this was by far the most common throughout the field sites – ICTs were made to fit within an older view of social advancement through educational credentials into secure employment, preferably white collar. That continues to be the gold standard of aspiration, despite a widespread awareness that this pattern of advancement (to whatever extent it was realistic in the past) is now being rendered obsolete as privatization and deregulation render government jobs and secure private ones increasingly scarce.

However, we can contrast this development analysis with another that was prevalent among active participants in the ICT projects. Development agencies, parents of participants and some of the very poor might focus on the direct impacts of ICTs, either pointing to education as their mechanism or denying any impact. For most participants, at least most of the time, the emphasis was on the indirect benefits of their involvement, and this led to often new ways of conceptualizing poverty reduction strategies within new understandings of modernization that evolved from their encounters with new technologies.

This is best explored through an example. Seelampur is an historically Muslim district of New Delhi. An ICT project for young women was set up in the *Madrasa* – a religious education institute – under the protection of a very powerful *Maulana*, the leader of local religious education, who used this alliance with prestige new technologies and their extension to women to mark himself out as modern and proactive. This patronage constituted the Seelampur centre as virtually the only public space that most of these girls were allowed to enter. The project had originally been set up to provide ICT training linked to marketing and vocational training. The community has strong traditions of sewing, embroidery and dress design. The idea was to develop these craft skills and business expertise, supported by computing (for example, creating CD-ROMs for skills training, designing patterns on computer). However, within days of opening, the project was completely rethought in relation to the women's demands. While non-ICT based tailoring classes went on in the hallway outside the centre, the girls at the computers explored multimedia: they drew pictures, recorded stories and songs, made computer animations, held discussions and debates which they fed into their visual work on computers. The visual languages they employed included everything from Hindu mythology and Muslim history, through Bollywood, Disney cartoons and women's magazines.

On the one hand, the ICT centre was embraced as a space of freedom with little or no reference to vocation or earning. It was about the experience of new ways of doing things and being with others, of expressing oneself and enjoying an expanded field of possibilities. This sense of freedom, of course, cannot be attributed simply to working with ICTs, and the creative use of ICTs itself partly arose from the way the space was constituted to enable this framing of technologies: however clichéd the term has become, Seelampur was experienced as 'empowering', a space that generated new ways of relating to the world, building up a sense of new capabilities and possibilities. This certainly led to tensions: most symbolically, parents of participants were upset that Seelampur did not (at the beginning) give out certificates to show that the young women had completed a structured course, while the participants themselves focused on the value of the experience rather than the formal result.

On the other hand, where centre activities did connect with thinking about jobs and employment the women articulated their futures in unpredictable ways. It was striking that in interviews and conversations the young women's ideas of ICT-related work was much closer to graphic design, fashion design and interior design as we might understand them in the north than to traditional craft or artisanship – they had basically reinvented the culture industries, and were sometimes scathing about the ghetto of traditional crafts. They articulated a version of modernity in relation to ICTs rather than seeing ICTs as a tool to further traditional poverty reduction strategies.

Local appropriations and uses of ICTs asked the same questions about development and poverty reduction that were asked in the funding agencies themselves. Indeed, both field sites and funding agencies were characterized by similar tensions between global discourses, which framed ICTs as 'the inevitable future', and struggles to conceptualize specific social mechanisms that might connect up – directly or indirectly – ICTs and poverty reduction. This replication arises both from the extent to which field sites and agencies are in direct communication and from the extent to which they inhabit the same world of technically defined visions of the future, and the need to define development – personal or social – in relation to prestige technologies and technical skills. We could not make ethnographic sense of these local appropriations of ICTs unless we regarded local people as development theorists; and conversely, we need to consider the development agencies as development *cultures*.

We can underline this perspective by briefly comparing the ictPR experience with research in Ghana. Firstly, Ghana certainly shares with the South Asian sites the global discourses that frame ICTs as 'the future'. Ghana's recent governmental ICT strategy promises a leap from an agricultural economy to an information society by 2025, envisaging ICT interventions in every aspect of the social fabric. However, Ghanaian public discourse is generally permeated with a sense of missed opportunity. As the first independent African state, under the charismatic leadership of Nkrumah, and with considerable human and natural resources, there is a sense that it should have had a leadership role within Africa and a significant international presence, as well as considerably more developmental progress. ICTs often appear as Ghana's historic last chance to achieve this position.

At the same time, at least in urban Ghana, frustration over lack of development is targeted both on the state and on donor-dependency. Although neo-liberal structural adjustment and deregulation à la the Washington consensus is not necessarily popular, it has considerable sympathy: ICTs in particular represent a sector of dynamic and excited entrepreneurialism, a new level playing field of enterprise in which those who are talented and opportunistic can finally make it, and make it in relation to a prestige articulation of global modernity. The popular demands are for deregulation of telecommunications as the only route both to modernization of ICTs and to the modernization of Ghana through the release of local energies and talents.

This situation is very different from the South Asian one just described. At the local level, the institutions that people imagine or construct around ICTs involve large numbers of small businesses – little mobile phone operations, innumerable internet cafés, phone decoding businesses, and so on. Development has come to mean the emergence of entrepreneurial spaces which are understood as both private capitalism and as social enterprise, as community development.

At the same time, personal internet use replicates and perpetuates some older and traditional strategies of development and social advancement, just as in South Asia, but of a very different sort. In our urban field site, as in much of Ghana, social advancement means leaving Ghana. Every conversation ends up revolving around exit strategies and comparisons of the bright future abroad and the lack of reward at home. Hence huge amounts of investment go into planning to get away and into accumulating foreign social capital – contacts, networks, invitations, visas, etc. Equal energy is devoted to enforcing the social obligations of those abroad: a major use of all forms of communications – but now especially mobile phones and the internet – is to keep up the flow of remittances and other symbolic and material benefits from friends, relatives and contacts abroad.

Hence an example of Ghanaian internet use that might correspond to the South Asian stress on ICT credentials would be something called 'comsor': the word comes from the pre-internet days when hundreds of letters would be sent to foreign schools and universities and to scholarship funds in the hope of securing education abroad. Today, the main use of websites that we have found is a continuation of comsor – endlessly surfing for educational opportunities outside Ghana. This is second only to chatting online in an attempt to accumulate foreign social capital in the form of chat partners in Europe and North America.

Overall, the South Asian projects and the Ghanaian field sites exhibited two different appropriations of ICTs in relation to development. They had in common an overarching sense of ICTs as keys to the future (both personal and regional) and this sense is replicated in complex ways from the local through the global. At the same time, popular appropriations of this sense of the future took different forms: in South Asia, a tension between traditional educational routes to social advancement, on the one hand, and a more open ended exploration of social and technical innovation on the other; in Ghana, the use of ICTs to intensify equally traditional but very different routes to advancement – maximizing foreign social capital. In both cases, however, the local ICT uses and framings are always already saturated with development discourses, models and strategies, and these must extend considerably our sense of what it means to talk of local cultural difference.

Conclusion

We have used two short comparative examples, drawn from much wider projects, to place ethnography, culture and locality in relation to two very global themes: capitalism and development. This chapter reflects our own disciplinary experiences. In the case of sociology, and cultural and media studies, there is a strong tendency to treat locality (and localized ethnography) as a cultural mediation of global processes, and therefore as a marker of cultural differences that signify social agency or resistance. At the extreme, ethnography and its findings fill a largely theoretical function within metropolitan academic debates. By contrast, although anthropology claims to be a comparative discipline, in practice it is based on the detailed and descriptive ethnography of individual case studies, written up according to a relativist framework, which stresses the unique elements of each situation. Hence, the commitment to an internal holism tends to negate the initial ideal of comparison, since it renders each case incommensurable with any other case, although, as we have shown, it can and should be applied to the local variants of what are viewed as global institutions, such as capitalism.

There is no reason, however, why specific genres such as the study of media need to fall into the same dualisms. On the one hand, if we push sociology's concern with social agency to its logical conclusions we are inevitably concerned with local actors not simply as markers of cultural difference but as reflexively engaged in the same range of practices and understandings we expect to encounter at the more 'macro' levels. On the other hand, it is possible to use ethnography comparatively, and with respect to global phenomena while recognising that the use of comparison promotes generality at the expense of the degree of specificity (and sometimes regional parochialism) that anthropological ethnography increasingly espoused.

Acknowledgements

The research in Jamaica was carried out together with Dr Heather Horst. The Ghana research was conducted in collaboration with Janet Kwami. Both the Jamaica and Ghana research are funded by DFID and are part of a larger four-country comparative ethnography being conducted by Miller and Slater in collaboration with Jo Tacchi (CIRAC, Queensland University of Technology) and Andrew Skuse (Adelaide University). The South Asia research was conducted with Dr Jo Tacchi, funded by UNESCO and in collaboration with a large research and support team based both in UNESCO and in the individual ICT projects.

Notes

1 The two authors have pursued a rolling programme of ethnographies of ICTs in non-northern places over the past six years:

- A study of the internet in Trinidad, conducted by Miller and Slater in 1998–1999 (Miller and Slater, 2000)

- Ethnographic monitoring and evaluation of a community multimedia project in rural Sri Lanka, funded by DFID, conducted in collaboration with UNESCO by Don Slater, Jo Tacchi (CIRAC, Queensland University of Technology) and Peter Lewis (LSE). See Slater *et al.* (2002).

- ictPR – ICTs for Poverty Reduction programme funded by UNESCO. This project comprised the setting up of nine innovative ICT centres in South Asia (India, Sri Lanka, Bangladesh, Nepal, Bhutan), each with full-time local ethnographers supported by Don Slater and Jo Tacchi. See Slater and Tacchi (2004).

- Information Society, funded by DFID. Four-country comparative ethnography of relationship between ICTs and poverty reduction: Jamaica (Daniel Miller); Ghana (Don Slater); South Africa (Andrew Skuse) and India (Jo Tacchi). To be completed June 2005.

References

Boyett, I. and Currie, G. (2004) 'Middle Managers Moulding International Strategy: An Irish Start-Up in Jamaican Telecoms', *Long Range Planning*, 37, 51–66.

Horst, H. and Miller, D. (2005) 'From Kinship to Link-up: Cell Phones and Social Networking in Jamaica', *Current Anthropology* 46(5).

———(in press) *The Cell Phone: An Anthropology of Communication*. Oxford: Berg.

Miller, D. (1997) *Capitalism: An Ethnographic Approach*. Oxford: Berg.

Miller, D. and Slater, D. (2000) *The Internet: An Ethnographic Approach*. London: Berg.

Slater, D. and Tacchi, J. (2004) *Research: ICT Innovations for Poverty Reduction*. New Delhi: UNESCO.

Slater, D., Tacchi, J. and Lewis, P. (September 2002) *Ethnographic Monitoring and Evaluation of Community Multimedia Centres: A Study of Kothmale Community Radio Internet Project, Sri Lanka*. London: DFID/UNESCO.

Smith, R. T. (1988) *Kinship and Class in the West Indies*. Cambridge: Cambridge University Press.

Stirton, L. and Lodge, M. (2002) 'Regulatory Reform in Small Developing States: Globalisation, Regulatory Autonomy and Jamaican Telecommunications', *New Political Economy*, 7, 437–55.

▶ chapter seventeen

National Prisms of a Global 'Media Event'

CHIN-CHUAN LEE, JOSEPH MAN CHAN, ZHONGDANG PAN AND
CLEMENT Y. K. SO

Introduction

It is often claimed that media discourse represents 'a site of symbolic struggle', but what are the processes, significance and limits of that struggle? As a global 'media event' (Dayan and Katz, 1992), the transfer of Hong Kong from British to Chinese sovereignty on 1 July, 1997 provided such a site and moment for opposing *national* media communities to express, and thus reinforce, their enduring values and dominant ideologies. More than 8,000 journalists and 776 media organizations from around the world congregated in this bustling city to witness an event of presumed global significance. Journalists were interested not in Hong Kong *per se*, but in China as an emerging and hostile power. They participated in the embedded ideological struggle among various modern 'isms': East versus West, capitalism versus socialism, democracy versus authoritarianism. What marked for China a national triumph over colonialism was, in the eyes of most Western journalists, 'a menacing, authoritarian Chinese government, its hands still stained by the blood of Tiananmen Square, riding roughshod over freewheeling, Westernized Hong Kong' (Chinoy, 1999: 394).

Foregrounding a barrage of news events as a rupture requires interpreting its meaning against a background of continuities. Van Ginneken (1998:126) puts it so well: 'What the fireworks of international news illuminate or leave in the dark is the historic panorama beyond them.' This chapter examines, from a comparative perspective, how international journalists took part in a post-Cold War ideological discourse through making sense of a 'media spectacle' (see Lee *et al.*, 2002, for a full study). This event underwent a transformation – thus robbed of conflict, suspense and theatrical appeal – but it did not prevent the world media, cum various national cultural arms, from plunging into discursive struggles to promote the legitimacy of their national regimes.

Despite much talk about the growing globalization processes, we argue that international news-making is inherently domestic and paradoxically *national*: the same event may be given distinct media representations by various nations through the prisms of their dominant ideologies as defined by power structures, cultural repertoires, and politico-economic interests. The process of 'domestication' (Cohen *et al.*, 1996; Gans, 1979) brings various happenings in distant places and renders them familiar and intelligible to home audiences. The conversion of a global agenda into a home agenda involves treating foreign news as an extension of domestic news, selectively framing issues or topics through the lens of professional norms, national interest, cultural repertoire and market dynamics. In most foreign policy issues, this frame tends to revolve around a state-defined 'national' perspective that may suppress 'local', ethnic, sub-national and other alternative voices. Even though the set of people to be interviewed in an event, mostly from the ranks of the elite plus some token 'ordinary folks', is likely to be small and highly overlapping, journalists use different national narratives to insert the present into a highly ideological perspective on the past and the future. In foreign news, therefore, media differences *between* nations tend to override the media's ideological divide *within* a nation.

International news-making and discursive struggles

The handover of Hong Kong stood for a concentric circle of relevance and vested interests to various national discursive communities and was thus open to divergent media construction. International news-making follows the same logic of domestic news-making, but under different political conditions. It is widely accepted that the media produce and reproduce the hegemonic definitions of social order. There are four general claims to this overall thesis. First, 'news net' of the media corresponds to the hierarchical order of political power and the prevailing belief system that defines this order (Tuchman, 1978). Occurrences outside the centralized organizations or standard genres would not be recognized as news. Second, even in a democratic society, news production must inevitably epitomize the capitalist mode of production and serve the financial–ideological structure and interests of the dominant class (Murdock, 2000), race (Gandy, 2000) and gender (Press, 2000). Third, the ideology of journalistic professionalism, as enshrined by the creed of objectivity, is predicated on an unarticulated commitment to the established order (Gitlin, 1980; Said, 1978; Schlesinger, 1979; Tuchman, 1978). News media 'index' the spectrum of the elite viewpoints as an essential tool for domestic political operation (Bennett, 1990; Cook, 1998). In a similar vein, Donohue *et al.* (1995) maintain that the media perform as a sentry not for the community as a whole, but for groups having sufficient power and influence to create and control their own security systems. Fourth, when elite consensus collapses or is highly divided, or when there is strong mobilizing pressure from social movements, the media may have to reflect such opinion plurality (Chan and Lee, 1991; Hallin, 1986; Page, 1996). Such plurality does not, however, question the fundamental assumptions of power in society.

The international order being more anarchic, the *state* – rather than specific individuals, classes or sectors within a country – acts as the repository of 'national interest' (Garnett, 1994), as the principal maker of foreign policy, and as a contestant in international news discourse (Snyder and Ballentine, 1997: 65). Operating as 'little accomplices' of the state (Zaller and Chiu, 1996), the media rely on political authorities to report foreign policy-cum-national interest. Moreover, the media, the domestic authorities, and the public tend to perceive the international news reality through shared lenses of ideologies, myths and cultural repertoire. The media resolve around the head of state, foreign ministry and embassies to make news because these institutions are assumed to have superior if not monopolistic access to knowledge about what national interest is abroad. Foreign news agendas are even more closely attuned to elite conceptions of the world than domestic news agendas. The US media therefore tend to 'rally around the flag' in close alliance with official Washington (Brody, 1991; Cook, 1998), especially when the country is in conflict with foreign powers. By this process of 'domesticating' foreign news as a variation on a national theme (Cohen *et al*, 1996), the media serve to sharpen and legitimize national perspectives embedded in the existing order of power and privilege. Gans (1979) maintains that in the US media, foreign news stories are mostly relevant to Americans or American interests, with the same themes and topics as domestic news; when the topics are distinctive, they are given interpretations that apply to American values. Media domestication is an integral part of the international political economy.

News media participate in a broader discursive process in constructing the domestic elite's images of 'the other' and legitimizing the state's effort in safeguarding geo-political interests abroad (Said, 1981, 1993). They produce a local narrative of the same global event through the employment of unique discursive means of rhetoric, frames, metaphors and logic. In 'tangling' with distant contestants in the game of international news-making, they impute different causes and effects to reality to advance national interest and promote national legitimacy. During the Persian Gulf War, CNN became a stage for the US and Iraqi governments to verbally attack each other, paving the way for and extending the eventual armed conflict (Kellner, 1992). Unlike the institutional struggle in which central authority allocates tangible material resources (Jabri, 1996: 72), the discursive struggle wins or loses symbolically in terms of expression of preferred values and orders. The latter may be mobilized into an institutional struggle while the former may derive its legitimacy from a discursive struggle (Edelman, 1971; Gamson, 1988; McAdam *et al.*, 1996). During the Cold War, the superpowers contested over intangible public opinion, images and rhetorical discourse in order, ironically, to prevent the hot wars of guns and missiles (Medhurst, 1990).

The making of a media event

The script for the handover of Hong Kong had already been written in the Sino-British Joint Declaration in 1984. The predictability of its prescheduled nature facilitated 'calendar journalism' (Tuchman, 1978). Such events may neither require much enterprising journalistic effort (Sigal, 1973) nor satisfy the 'entertainment logic' of the television age (Altheide and Snow, 1979). Worse yet, since bad news is good news, the world media had concocted various hypothetical worst-case scenarios of Communist takeover but the handover turned out to be smooth and peaceful. The large presence of international journalists in a crowded island became a story – a media spectacle – more important than the event itself. A Canadian journalist compared this 'thin massive event' to 'a small pellet of fish food being attacked by 8,000 piranhas'. *Newsweek*'s bureau chief, when asked, agreed that thousands of competitive egos probably ended up talking to the same set of 20–50 people in town, but the *Daily Telegraph* reporter defended this practice as an inherent logic of journalism and no different from covering South Africa or Bosnia.

According to Dayan and Katz (1992), a media event may fall into one of three categories: a contest, a conquest or a coronation. In spite of consuming efforts made by the dismayed international journalists, the handover story did not seem to rise to various qualifications of a spectacular media event. As it began, the event seemed to contain all the exciting elements of a conquest or those of a contest. As the event went through a process of transformation during its life cycle, elements of a contest and conquest receded and the media began to focus on it more as a coronation.

First, a contest 'pits evenly matched individuals or teams against each other and bid them to compete according to strict rules' (Dayan and Katz, 1992: 33). Media events of this type should generate much excitement over the process of competition and reduce the uncertainty about its outcome. The Sino-British rows over sovereignty negotiations and Governor Patten's democratic reforms began to fade in significance as Hong Kong inched toward the handover.

Second, a conquest refers to great men and women with charisma who 'submit themselves to an ordeal, whose success multiplies their charisma and creates a new following' (Dayan and Katz, 1992: 37). Indeed, all of China's official and media proclamations hailed Deng Xiaoping, the paramount leader, as the ingenious author of the 'one country, two systems' idea, through which the previously impossible task of reclaiming Hong Kong became a reality. Thus, Chinese heroes roundly beat British imperialist villains. As a favourite icon that provided an occasion for journalists and their sources to 'refigure cultural scripts' (Bennett and Lawrence, 1995), China's official television constantly showed a picture of Margaret Thatcher falling on her steps in front of the Great Hall of the People. The Prime Minister had just emerged from her first excruciating encounter with Deng, during which he lectured her that China would not take humiliation from foreign powers any more. That showdown forced both sides to embark on painful negotiations leading finally to the handover. This icon was coined in 1982. By 1997, Thatcher had retired from public life and Deng was already dead, but the image lived on as a soothing symbol of China's conquest over its injured national psyche. China's media were also fond of flexing military icons to relish the story of national strength in front of the doubting world.

A coronation, a third kind of media event, deals in 'the mysteries of rites of passage' which 'proceed according to strict rules, dictated by tradition rather than by negotiated agreement' (Dayan and Katz, 1992: 36). Media coverage of a coronation serves to pledge allegiance to the political centre and to renew contract with it. Persons of authority are signified and dignified by costumes, symbols, titles and rituals. Media presentation, which tends to be reverent and priestly, enacts the tradition and authority that are usually hidden from everyday life. A prime icon of Hong Kong's handover coronation was a picture of the brief moment at midnight of 30 June, seemingly frozen in history. The Union Jack was being lowered, and the Chinese flag being raised. All principal actors – including Prince Charles, President Jiang, Governor Patten and Chief Executive Tung – were solemnly arrayed on the stage to commemorate a change in the authority structure and to usher in formal absorption of Hong Kong into the motherland. In spite of its historical significance this still moment produced no lively journalism.

The media event thus transformed, journalists must do something to save the integrity of their paradigmatic structure: repairing part of the assumptions, culling more supporting data, dismissing contrary evidence, or trying to fit their stories into generic narrative structures of media events (Bennett *et al.*, 1985; Chan and Lee, 1991). Above all, they must 'hype' up the event in the hope that their domestic audiences may find reasons to participate in the media rites and rituals. Aronson (1983: 23) defines 'hype' as 'the merchandizing of a product — be it an object, a person, or an idea – in an artificially engendered atmosphere of hysteria, in order to create a demand for it, or inflate such demand as already exists'. Through the display of repetitive, familiar and exaggerated images often out of the context, hyping creates a mythical ritual that is confirming of the dominant ideological framework (Nimmo and Combs, 1990).

National media prisms

To understand these national narratives, we take a 'constructionist' approach to 'framing analysis' (Gamson, 1988; Gamson and Modigliani, 1987, 1989; Pan and Kosicki, 1993) and examine the newspaper and telecast accounts from two weeks before to one week after the handover. These frames serve as an organizing scheme with which journalists provide coherence to their stories and through which some critical issues can be discussed and understood. Gitlin (1980: 7) writes, 'media frames, largely unspoken and unacknowledged, organize the world both for journalists who report it and, in some important degree, for us who rely on their reports'. We first deconstructed each national media account into what Gamson and Lasch (1983) call a 'signature matrix', a device that lists the key frames and links them to salient signifying devices. We then reconstructed their major theses into genotypical categories – or what Gamson calls 'ideological packages' – replete with metaphors, exemplars, catch phrases, depictions, visual images, roots, consequences and appeals to principle.

In a nutshell, national jingoism of China's mouthpiece contrasted sharply with the fear and doubt of all other national media systems. Western media accounts revealed a common commitment to democratic values and widespread ideological aversion to the People's Republic of China (PRC). But they also differed in matters of national interest. The US media banged the democracy drums while the British media exhibited considerable imperial nostalgia. The Australian and Canadian media emphasized the unique significance of Hong Kong to their countries. The Japanese media were intensely concerned with economic interest but not democratic issues. The ideological gaps that stratify the media's taste cultures on domestic issues became blurred on a remote foreign reality like Hong Kong. All in all, several lines of ideological contestation were engaged.

The United States: new guardian of democracy

The USA views itself as 'a righter of wrongs around the world, in pursuit of tyranny, in defense of freedom no matter the place or cost' (Said, 1993: 5). The collapse of the Soviet Union has left the USA as the only superpower and made the PRC a major hurdle to reconstructing the US-dominated international order (Burchill, 1996). In a controversial thesis, Fukuyama (1992) asserts that the end of the Cold War marks the total exclusion of viable systemic alternatives to Western liberalism that is the 'only coherent political aspiration'. As the *Chicago Tribune* lamented in a typical editorial (1 July, 1997), 'There is sadness in seeing this jewel of

Asia transfer to the hands of a dictatorial regime, only 10 years after the fall of the Berlin Wall.' This postulated East–West contest was given credence by vivid memories of the Tiananmen crackdown, which stood out as the most potent point of media reference. Because of, or notwithstanding, its human rights abuse, China has stepped in to fill the psychological void of the USA for a new enemy.

The media proclaimed that the USA had taken over Britain's 'guardian responsibility' to protect the treasured capitalist enclave from Communist atrocity. While pledging to link the preservation of Hong Kong's freedoms to Washington's policy toward China, President Bill Clinton declared a 'positive engagement' policy aimed to 'draw China in' rather than to 'shut China out'. This policy was widely criticized (for example, *The Washington Post*, 24 June) for sniffing up a version of the old 'quiet diplomacy' excuse for doing nothing about China's human rights violation, or even emboldening China to trample on Hong Kong's freedoms. With the British gone, the conservative Republican chairman of the Senate Foreign Relations Committee, Jessie Helms, wrote in the *Wall Street Journal* (25 June) urging the USA to 'employ tactics well beyond legal challenges' until China lived up to its commitments.

This 'new guardian' role was obviously based not on sovereignty or territorial claims, but was justified on ideological grounds. As the *New York Times* columnist Thomas Friedman put it vividly, the return of Hong Kong to China was 'not just a slice of the West given back to the East', but also 'a slice of the future being given back to the past' (15 December, 1996). CBS News cast Hong Kong's handover, however, as part of a big story about China striving to be a world superpower. Not only did its serious-looking anchor, Dan Rather, travel to Hong Kong by way of revisiting, reminiscing about, and reporting from Tiananmen Square, thus linking the handover to the crystallized symbol of Communist repression, but Bob Simon, as a key member of the network's coverage team, was a 'war correspondent' renowned for his coverage in the Middle Eastern and Bosnian theatres but with little knowledge of China. Wearing a safari outfit, Simon told Rather: 'A Communist regime gets control of a piece of real estate without firing a shot.' The network frequently pegged the handover story to library footage of the Tiananmen Square bloodshed, as if to create an emotional *déjà vu* against Communist dictatorship and to foretell the horror of life in post-colonial Hong Kong. The *South China Morning Post* gave the four globe-trotting US celebrity anchors a simple test on name recognition and found them 'decidedly hazy on some general knowledge of Hong Kong' (Buerk, 1997). Ignorance made them even more reliant on a stock of stereotypes.

The Washington Post doubted editorially (1 July) that 'authoritarian China' could succeed in using Hong Kong as a model to bring 'democratic Taiwan' back into the fold, and urged that the people of Taiwan be allowed to decide their future. Citing China's violation of agreements with Tibet, a writer implored that 'policy-makers in the free world' keep a 'vigilant watch on Hong Kong' (2 July). *The Washington Post* compared the Hong Kong handover to communist North Vietnam's takeover of the capitalist South, even though the British did it with a style or – in the words of CBS correspondent Simon – 'without a tail between legs'. Next to the Tiananmen crackdown, Singapore and its authoritarian patriarch, Lee Kuan Yew, emerged as a favourite media metaphor. Singapore's *Straits Times* chided 'the British nation's surrogate mourner [in Hong Kong] – the western media, human rights lobbyists and crusading politicians in Washington and parts of the European Union'. The *New York Times* along with others noted, disapprovingly, the new Chief Executive Tung's fondness of Singapore's authoritarian system. The outgoing governor Patten got a lot of media mileage out of lashing at Lee Kuan Yew as an 'eloquent advocate of authoritarian government' not particularly Asian or Confucian (The *Washington Post*, 25 June). Thus, international politicians and media fought an ideological battle at the site of Hong Kong on the occasion of its sovereignty transfer.

The new Cold War was translated into a local fight over the erosion of Hong Kong's fragile democracy (especially the dismantling of the elected legislature) and existing freedoms. A *New York Times* editorial (1 July) declared, 'By habit and ideology, Beijing is quite capable of quashing freedom in Hong Kong.' It predicted (25 June) that China's critics would have 'a major confrontation in the next few years with Communist hardliners who never met a publication that they did not like to censor'. The media repeated Patten's railings against Hong Kong's business elite, most of them having obtained foreign passports, for switching allegiance to Beijing. Major democratic leaders such as Martin Lee, who spoke English eloquently, were favoured media icons. *Wall Street Journal* editorials (26 June and 1 July) criticized harshly Beijing's behaviour in seeking to gain 'absolute control' in Hong Kong and condemned German, French and British leaders for kowtowing to Beijing (2 July).

While it was common to make out Hong Kong as the target of abuse and negative influence from China, the US media also invoked a complementary frame – deriving from the famous Greek 'Trojan Horse' mythology – to suggest that Hong Kong would be a harbinger of economic, even political, change for China. The *New York Times* (1 July) stated that the Red Star over Hong Kong might be the end of Maoism. On the same day, foreign affairs columnist Friedman argued that Hong Kong would be the future of China 'when it grows up'. He also warned (3 July) that if China did not live up to its obligation, it 'will be punished by that most brutal, efficient and immediate of diplomatic tools: the ATM machine'. Depicting Hong Kong as 'the tail that wags the dragon', he was referring to the threat of withdrawing more than US$100 billion in foreign investment in the city, most of it in highly liquid funds. In a similar vein, former Prime Minister Thatcher wrote in the *Wall Street Journal* (27 June) that Hong Kong would mark 'a new impulse toward freedom and democracy in China and the rest of Asia'. She also referred to Hong Kong in a CNN interview as a 'small crystal ball for a big solution' and 'an example and a flagship of what Chinese can accomplish'.

Britain: imperial nostalgia

The Tiananmen crackdown provided an impetus for Britain to harden its policy towards China. When Chris Patten arrived in 1992 as the last Governor, he vowed to abandon a decade of British appeasement and acquiescence policy and, instead, to implement last-minute democratic reforms as a British legacy in the colony. China was so infuriated that it denounced him as a 'sinner of millennium' (Dimbleby, 1998; Patten, 1998). Verbal warfare was a daily media fare. Patten's rhetorical eloquence did much to inspire local and international media conjecture about the horrible scenarios of life under Chinese rule.

The British media seldom broached, much less apologized for, the morality of the colonial origin, but focused on the current 'bright' conditions of Hong Kong. Prime Minister Tony Blair apologized to Ireland in 1997 for the nineteenth-century potato famine, but his Foreign Secretary, Robin Cook, said that Britain would not apologize for what it did in the Opium War. 'Imperial nostalgia' reigned high. The media echoed British officials in claiming that their small island nation – or, alternatively, the Empire – had 'brought civilizations to the world', and, specifically, left marvellous legacies in Hong Kong: liberty, prosperity, the rule of law, and a clean and efficient civil service. The *Times* (1 July) stated that many Hong Kong Chinese looked back 'with gratitude', and Britons could reflect 'with pride' on what they and their ancestors had contributed to Hong Kong and to 'dominions and colonies over which the Union flag once flew'. Former Prime Minister Thatcher, calling herself 'an unashamed defender of the record of the British Empire', argued in the *Wall Street Journal* (27 June) that Hong Kong's lifestyle would be 'an impulse toward freedom and democracy in China'.

Extolling Hong Kong as 'a Chinese success story with British characteristics', Patten (1997) emphasized in his monthly radio programmes and public speeches that Hong Kong would become the only decolonized place with less democracy. 'Because men who set off from our islands conquered the world', the *Daily Telegraph* asserted editorially (30 June), English is now the world language of commerce, law, science and universal model for good government. 'Hong Kong is Britain's creation', it continued. To the *Financial Times* (30 June), Hong Kong people under British rule enjoyed better government and greater opportunities than Beijing had yet provided for its own people. 'If this is a (national) disgrace', it asked, 'whose is it?' These media depictions, while substantially true, presented a truncated and skewed history that lost sight of Britain's own anti-democratic record in the colony. They also shockingly exemplified what Said (1993) portrayed as the imperial construction of Orientalism in relation to 'primitive' or 'barbaric' peoples: 'You are what you are because of us; when we left, you reverted to your deplorable state' (p. 35).

The BBC called Hong Kong 'the best-run' and the 'most successful' of the countries of the British Empire. All major media accentuated Britain's presumed role in safeguarding Hong Kong's freedom, by echoing official rhetoric or by personifying Patten. On the day of the handover, the media prominently quoted Prince Charles as telling Hong Kong people, 'We shall not forget you, and we shall watch you with the closest interest as you embark on this new era of your remarkable history.' Patten was portrayed as the symbol of ability, character and political courage to 'stand by the principle of liberty against the angry power of China' (The *Times*, 1 July). Both the BBC and ITV underscored his characteristically strong rhetoric: 'Hong Kong people are to rule Hong Kong. That's the promise. That's the unshakable destiny.' (Patten also exchanged fire in the British media with his detractors, those 'China Hands' in the Foreign Office who accused him of undermining British interests by being belligerent to Beijing.) The *Times* claimed that Britain had secured a firm commitment from world leaders to watch over China (23 June). It depicted Prime Minister Blair as someone who 'talks tough with Beijing leaders' and Foreign Secretary Cook as 'freedom's watchdog in former colony' (1 July). The *Guardian* observed more soberly in an editorial (30 June), 'After all the superlatives have been spoken, we must not let our attention (on this matter) drift away'.

Patten had wanted to convince British and international public opinion of Britain's ability to withdraw from Hong Kong 'with at least a modicum of dignity and honour' (Dimbleby, 1998). He appeared to have well achieved this mission in view of the overwhelmingly celebratory, if also sad and sentimental, media characterization. The media used plenty of pictures and titbits related to British cultural icons or colonial symbols. A Black Watch soldier was shown rehearsing a Highland dance for a Hong Kong farewell concert. The pageantry was filled with coloured uniforms, military bands, regiments in formation and the Union flag. Above all, the BBC praised the departing Royal Yacht with the tone of a romantic lover: 'thousands of various kinds of ships move through [the glass canyon of Hong Kong] everyday, but none is as pretty as Britannia! After 80 state visits in her 47 years of service, she has not seen a quite as emotional departure as this one'. Of the British departure, a *Times* (1 July) subheader read: 'tears mingle with the rain as retreat is beaten'. The *Daily Telegraph* spread a headline across pages two and three: 'Britannia sails into the night as the flag of freedom is lowered for ever'. Lowering of the Union flag for the last time in Hong Kong, said The *Times* editorially (1 July), 'recalled an almost forgotten sense of duty and responsibility, good government and dedication to the peoples over which the British once held sway'.

China: nationalism and its discontent

The Chinese authorities harnessed the media to a gala of 'national ceremony' full of patriotic emotions but, mindful of historical precedents, were determined to contain mass euphoria. Media extravaganzas were tightly orchestrated. Of the 16 media units chosen to cover the handover, the 'big three' – China Central Television (CCTV), the *People's Daily* and the Xinhua News Agency – accounted for the lion's share of the 610-member entourage. All of them strictly followed official policy and news guidelines. The party-state accorded special advantage on the big three and facilitated their access to pro-China sources in Hong Kong.

The media interpreted reclaiming Hong Kong as the culmination of national triumph over Western colonialism – a Chinese dream that could not have been realized without strong Communist leadership. The event marked an end to 150 years of national humiliation and a beginning of the reunifying process with Macao and Taiwan into the big 'Chinese family-nation' (*guojia*). This framework placed a micro local report about the handover in the macro context of Chinese history. The media adopted a linear historical script that started with British takeover of Hong Kong in 1842, flowed continuously to unjust domination of a weak and corrupt China by Western imperialists, and ended up with the 'China is strong again' theme. The media gave little credit to what the British had accomplished in Hong Kong. Nor was the handover put in the context of the general decolonization trend in the world: in fact, after 1949, it was Mao himself who decided not to change British jurisdiction over Hong Kong because China needed the port to circumvent the Western blockade, and this later became a topic of Moscow's ridicule in the 1970s. The Chinese media never acknowledged these historical interruptions.

The media recreated a highly politicized myth of the Chinese as a family-nation. National festivities being a family affair, patriotic expressions were mingled with the rituals of ancestral worship. CCTV featured a family memorial of Lin Zexu, an official whose burning of confiscated British opium triggered the Opium War, with 300 descendants gathered in his hometown to read a eulogy and recite a pledge of patriotism to their distinguished ancestor. CCTV and the *People's Daily* emphasized that the handover was a day of national jubilation for all 'children of the Yellow Emperor' around the world who should be united as closely as 'flesh and bones' in the 'big motherland family'. For days, the *People's Daily* carried special sections featuring various overseas Chinese communities, one by one honouring the return of Hong Kong, taking special care to reflect geographical balance in a global appearance. CCTV sent 22 crews to cover strategically selected cities within China and from global Chinese communities, whose activities were synchronized to construct a mythical concept of 'Chinese' that transcended spatial divide, ethnic differences and political rifts.

The 'children of the Yellow Emperor' were to be embraced by Mother China from Beijing. Visually revealing was the 'countdown clock' at the centre of Tiananmen Square, where CCTV depicted the frantic scenes of national flags, fireworks, folk and ethnic dances, accompanied by the sound of the national anthem and thunderous acclamations from the crowd. CCTV's anchors declared that the countdown clock had forever 'erected a monument in people's heart' and this was a spectacular 'festival of the century' for the Chinese nation. The official media kept emphasizing that Hong Kong would be even more prosperous under the care of the motherland's 'one country, two systems' policy, and that Macao and Taiwan would follow suit.

In contrast, since the people in Hong Kong had no say over the fate that the PRC and Britain negotiated on their behalf, the media showed enormous ambivalence about this forced union. While praising British achievements in the colony, they also paid lip service to national dignity but evinced little enthusiasm for becoming a member of the Chinese family-nation. The main concern was whether China would indeed honour its promise to prevent 'one country' from interfering with 'two systems'. Hong Kong people identified with Chinese culture but rejected the Communist system, as an *Apple Daily* editorial (1 July) asserted. A columnist asked rhetorically (24 June), 'Why do so many people feel unsettled and alienated as Hong Kong bids farewell to colonial rule?' Public opinion polls were often reported to show widespread fear about losing liberty, democracy and human rights under Chinese rule, a fear that *Ming Pao* (1 July) attributed to the Tiananmen crackdown as its worst source. The *South China Morning Post* (1 July) editorially urged China to leave the 'Hong Kong virus' alone.

The defensive and subdued Taiwan media largely echoed their government in rejecting the PRC's 'one country, two systems' policy as a solution to national division. Instead, Vice President Lian Zhan, in a CNN interview, proposed to adopt what he called 'one country, one system – a better system', meaning Taiwan's flourishing democracy. He told NBC's Tom Brokow that Taiwan is 'part of China, but not part of the PRC' (*China Times*, 22 June). Appealing to international media for sympathy and rebuffing Beijing's nationalist lure, the leaders insisted that Taiwan would not be absorbed as a province of the PRC and that Taipei and Beijing be treated as two equal sovereign states under one nation. While expressing satisfaction at Hong Kong's returning to 'the Chinese nation' (*minzu*), the head of Taiwan's Mainland Affairs Committee reiterated that Taiwan, unlike Hong Kong, was a sovereign state, not a local government of the PRC. If the PRC tried to link the 'nation' and the 'state' as a big happy family headed by Beijing, Taiwan's media would seek to delink them. The pro-independence *Liberty Times* treated China and Taiwan as two separate political entities; to them, the distinction between a nation and a state was irrelevant. It prominently reported a 'Say No to China' rally (24 June) with a headline that read 'Opposing Chinese Annexation'.

Canada and Australia: the diaspora

The media in Australia and Canada – Hong Kong's new diaspora – shared Western pessimism but also developed their own news agendas. Neither country is a global power. Canada has absorbed more than half a million immigrants from Hong Kong, mostly affluent middle-class professionals who uprooted themselves to escape the prospect of Communist rule. Australia too has absorbed Hong Kong immigrants to a lesser extent, and many Australians remember Hong Kong fondly as their take of the East. The Australian media called for a foreign policy more independent from the USA and Britain, while the Canadian media played up their special ties with Hong Kong.

The Australian media focused on what China could do to harm Hong Kong as well as what Hong Kong could do to change China. The best-case scenario would be for China to become more like Hong Kong, and the worst-case scenario would be for Hong Kong to sink into a mainland mire of corruption, disrespect for the rule of law, and restraint on press and other freedoms. An Australian Television (ABC) programme contrasted 'modern' Hong Kong people's despising view of China and 'backward' mainland Chinese's patronizing view of Hong Kong. Two of its feature stories (17 June and 30 June), one with footage of the Tiananmen massacre, mocked Hong Kong business for working with 'their new Communist bosses rather than running for cover with their second passports'. The third special feature story (1 July) was introduced by asking if the Red Flag over Hong Kong 'signals a new game plan for organized crime and its export to Australia'. One in four of ABC's stories made reference to Taiwan's position.

Australia has been striving for a more independent foreign policy. Earlier in 1997 it refused to support the USA and Britain in condemning China's human rights at a United Nations forum in Geneva. In attending the swearing-in ceremony of Hong Kong's Provisional Legislature, Foreign Minister Alexander Downer put it bluntly: 'Gone are the days when Australia does just what Washington and London want us to do' (*Weekend Australian*, 14–15 June). Former Prime Minister Malcolm Fraser wrote in the *Australian* (17 June) charging that 'British and US attempts to establish a Western-style enclave in Hong Kong and to impose Western conditions on China will contribute nothing to stability in East Asia and the Western Pacific'. He called for an open appraisal of Western policy in this region. In response, a historian commented that Australia's position was not on a higher moral ground, but simply based on 'a different set of national interests to pursue in the international arena' (20 June).

As neighbours and allies, Canada has much in common with the USA but has always been struggling to come out of Big Brother's shadow and establish its own identity. The Canadian media were characteristically suspicious of China's respect for liberty and democracy. In a CBC Pacific Rim Report (20 June), after China's minister for Hong Kong affairs Lu Ping gave a speech, a local businessman reacted that he would trust Lu in terms of business but not human rights. The programme host remarked that 'the right to make money will be protected, but [I'm] not sure about human rights'. The media favoured Hong Kong's democratic camp. But privately many Canadian journalists had faulted their American colleagues for carrying the Holy Grail as 'the only interpreters' of democracy.

The media stressed the special ties between Canada and Hong Kong. Not only do Toronto and Vancouver have a distinct Chinese flavour, Cantonese is now the third most widely spoken language spoken in Canada. So, what happens in Hong Kong has a very direct bearing on what happens in Canada. Jonathan Manthorpe of Southam News said: 'Hong Kong is a domestic story for us. I sometimes feel I am in the Richmond West bureau of the *Vancouver Sun*.' There are so many Canadians living in Hong Kong (estimates say 200,000) that it is impossible for journalists not to bump into their fellow citizens. CBC was keen to mention the Canadian identity of its interviewees in Hong Kong ranging from a radio broadcaster, a newspaper columnist, a lawyer, to a billionaire. The *Globe and Mail* (3 July) quoted Chief Executive Tung as telling the visiting Foreign Affairs Minister Lloyd Axworthy his wish to strengthen the special bilateral relationships, as they both attend the Canada Day that happens to be the first day of Tung's administration in operation. One editorial theme of Fairchild Television Canada was the 'Canada–Hong Kong sentiment' while another illustrated how Canadian commodities, interests, and technology had taken root in Hong Kong.

Japan: money, not democracy

As befitted their international image, the Japanese media were intent on preserving much of Japan's economic benefits in the region, while demonstrating little concern for local democratic aspirations. It has been observed that elite integration between the Japanese government, commercial–industrial conglomerates, and the media is so powerful – much more so than in the USA – that the media tend to echo the government–corporate views (Pharr and Krauss, 1996). Historically, Japan's 'least offensive' policy in foreign diplomacy has placed economic benefits above ideological interests (Ozaki and Arnold, 1985). Inasmuch as human rights are not a guiding spirit of Japan's foreign policy, its leaders have questioned the idea of applying Western standards of democracy to countries such as China (Kesavan, 1990). During the Tiananmen crackdown, the US media zealously sided with the protesters as if to score ideological victories, but the Japanese media were reluctant to challenge the Chinese authorities in order to protect Japan's economic gains (Lee and Yang, 1995).

Most Western media that had been based in Hong Kong to report about China moved their offices to Beijing after the PRC normalized its relations with the USA in 1979. But the Japanese have continued to maintain a large contingent of reporters in Hong Kong – efficiently, if quietly, gathering economic intelligence about South China. They do not get excited about China's democracy or human rights unless politics means money and trade. During the Hong Kong handover, a *Yomiuri Shinbum* reporter confided that his editor would have scolded him for wasting the space if he dwelled on the themes of democracy. For this reason, when he requested an interview with Democracy Party leaders, he was given a cold shoulder. Several of his Japanese colleagues have corroborated his accounts. However, the democratic concerns in Hong Kong were too intense for the Japanese journalists to ignore, so they said that the Western media had focused their attention on Hong Kong's democracy.

Conclusion

International news making is a form of ideological contestation. Media domesticate foreign news in the light of their own national interest and cultural assumptions. Three outstanding theses – and discursive battles – can be revisited. First, what is the nation-state? The international media were uneasy about the PRC's strengthened role in the geo-political order. But within Chinese societies, it provoked heated debates about the political and cultural meanings of China and being Chinese. In laying claims to official legitimacy, the PRC media constructed China as a unified nation-state that was centred in Beijing yet supposedly inclusive of global Chinese communities as common descendants of mythical ancestry. The helpless Hong Kong media displayed ambivalence about being part of the Beijing-defined nation-state. The Taiwan media sought to delink 'the nation' with 'the state', claiming that there were two equal sovereign states within one Chinese nation.

The second theme regarded the interpretation of colonialism and nationalism. Media tied their narratives selectively to larger historical frameworks to achieve interpretative coherence. Holding the Opium War as *the* point of historical reference, the echo chamber of the PRC media tried to *essentialize* British colonialism as evil while upholding nationalism as supreme; the handover of Hong Kong was touted as national triumph over Western imperialism. History was thus made invariant, decontextualized, temporally frozen, and incapable of change and rupture. On the contrary, the British media sought to *de-essentialize* colonialism by emphasizing that the British had created in Hong Kong a stable and prosperous enclave against relentless national turmoil in the PRC (Patten, 1997, 1998). This media framing directed attention to reassessing the virtues of nationalism and colonialism in the context of concrete and changing historical experiences rather than fixed ideological assumptions. On the receiving end, the Hong Kong media were reminiscent about positive British legacies; while accepting Chinese nationalism as a cultural goal they distrusted its political practice. As the next target of China's pressure, the media in Taiwan endorsed bringing British colonialism to an end but rejected the PRC brand of nationalism as expansionist and hegemonic. Interestingly, US, Canadian and Australian media all referred tangentially to their own British colonial past but defended British accomplishments in Hong Kong as part of Western civilizations.

Third, the handover energized media struggles between systems and ideologies. The PRC found itself being renewed as a villain in the post-Tiananmen era and in the post Cold-War order, while both US and British media underscored their new and old guardian roles toward Hong Kong. The PRC media contended that the 'one country, two systems' would protect Hong Kong's capitalism within China's socialism as if 'two systems' were totally compatible with 'one country'. On the contrary, prevailing scepticism led the international media to make three sorts of prognosis: (a) Hong Kong's democracy and human rights would be seriously eroded under authoritarian Chinese rule; (b) Hong Kong would become another Singapore – economically prosperous but politically controlled; and (c) Hong Kong's capitalist prosperity would not be viable without democracy.

What has happened since the handover? The global media were inaccurate in predicting that Hong Kong would be politically unstable but economically vibrant. In fact, China has kept its hands off Hong Kong until a massive anti-government protest broke out on 1 July, 2003, but an Asian financial crisis sent Hong Kong's economy into a tailspin barely a year after the handover. The USA shifted its policy of containing China to 'engaging' positively with China by adroit application of carrots and sticks, culminating in the strategy of integrating China into a global order, or – as some media commentators put it – 'dissolving China into the civilized world' (Lee, 2002). President Bush re-targeted China as a major enemy, but the war on terrorism has muted the policy controversy. China eagerly embraces the dream of global capitalism: acceding to the World Trade Organization and hosting the 2008 Olympics are being viewed as signalling China's coming of age on the world stage, while more and more capitalists have become the Communist Party's newly ordained members (Lee, 2003). Britain eyes a greener pasture: Prime Minister Blair did not 'talk tough' to Beijing; he refused to meet with democratic activists but received business tycoons in the former colony. Having tried to keep 'two systems' from the harm's way of the 'one country', Hong Kong finds its media saddled with self-censorship, indecency and vulgarization (Lee, 2000).

Taiwan is more than ever disillusioned with China's unification pressure. A more independent foreign policy for Australia is easier said than done. Canada retains strong ties with Hong Kong, but the significance has receded to the background. Japan keeps up its economic, but not democratic, interest in Hong Kong. Except on rare (mostly bad) occasions Hong Kong has been pushed off the radar screen of the global media. In sum, all Janus-faced small truths or half-truths do not seem to add up to the whole truth. Even in the unlikely event of unequivocal evidence, the media struggle will continue to refract different ideological light.

References

Altheide, D. L. and Snow, R. P. (1979) *Media Logic*. Beverly Hills, CA: Sage.

Aronson, S. M. L. (1983) *Hype*. New York: William Morrow.

Bennett, W. L. (1990) 'Toward a Theory of Press–State Relations in the United States', *Journal of Communication*, 40, 103–25.

Bennett, W. L. and Lawrence, R. G. (1995) 'News Icons and the Mainstreaming of Social Change', *Journal of Communication*, 45, 20–39.

Bennett, W. L., Gressett, L. and Haltom, W. (1985) 'Repairing the News: A Case Study of the News Paradigm', *Journal of Communication*, 35, 50–68.

Brody, R. A. (1991) *Assessing the President: The Media, Elite Opinion, and Public Support*. Stanford, CA: Stanford University Press.

Buerk, S. (1997) 'Anchors Aweigh in the Great Ratings War', *South China Morning Post*, 30 June, p. 23.

Burchill, S. (1996) 'Liberal Internationalism', in S. Burchill and A. Linklater (eds), *Theories of International Relations*. New York: St Martin's Press, pp. 28–66.

Chan, J. M. and Lee, C-C. (1991) *Mass Media and Political Transition: The Hong Kong Press in China's Orbit*. New York: Guilford Press.

Chinoy, M. (1999) *China Live*. Lanham, MD: Rowman & Littlefield.

Cohen, A. A., Levy, M. R., Roeh, I. and Gurevitch, M. (eds) (1996) *Global Newsrooms, Local Audiences: A Study of the Eurovision News Exchange.* London: Libbey.

Cook, T. E. (1998) *Governing with the News: The News Media as a Political Institution.* Chicago: University of Chicago Press.

Cox, R. W. (1984) Social Forces, States, and World Orders: Beyond International Relations Theory', in R. B. S. Walker (ed.), *Culture, Ideology, and World Order.* Boulder, CO: Westview Press, pp. 258–99.

Dayan, D. and Katz, E. (1992) *Media Events: The Live Broadcasting of History.* Cambridge, MA: Harvard University Press.

Dimbleby, J. (1998) *The Last Governor.* London: Warner Books.

Donohue, G.,Tichenor, P. J. and Olien, C. (1995) 'A Guard Dog Perspective on the Role of Media', *Journal of Communication*, 45 (2), 115–32.

Edelman, M. (1971) *The Politics of Symbolic Action.* New York: Academic Press.

———(1988) *Constructing the Political Spectacle.* Chicago: University of Chicago Press.

Fukuyama, F. (1992) *The End of History and the Last Man.* New York: Free Press.

Gamson, W. A. (1988) 'A Constructionist Approach to Mass Media and Public Opinion', *Symbolic Interactionism*, 11, 161–74.

Gamson, W. A. and Lasch, K. E. (1983) 'The Political Culture of Social Welfare Policy', in S. E. Spiro and E. Yuchtman-Yaar (eds), *Evaluating the Welfare State: Social and Political Perspectives.* New York: Academic Press, pp. 397–415.

Gamson, W. A. and Modigliani, A. (1987) 'The Changing Culture of Affirmative Action', in R. G. Braungart and M. M. Braungart (eds), *Research in Political Sociology.* Greenwich, CN: JAI Press, vol. 3 pp. 137–77.

———(1989) 'Media Discourse and Public Opinion on Nuclear Power: A Constructionist Approach', *American Journal of Sociology*, 95, 1–37.

Gandy, O. H. Jr. (2000) 'Race, Ethnicity and the Segmentation of Media Markets', in J. Curran and M. Gurevitch (eds), *Mass Media and Society.* London: Arnold, pp. 44–69.

Gans, H. J. (1979) *Deciding What's News: A Study of CBS Evening News, NBC Nightly News, News Week and Time.* New York: Pantheon.

Garnett, J. C. (1994) 'The National Interest Revisited', in K. W. Thompson (ed.), *Community, Diversity, and a New World Order.* Lanham, MD: University Press of America, pp. 87–110.

Gitlin, T. (1980) *The Whole World is Watching.* Berkeley: University of California Press.

Hallin, D. (1986) *The 'Uncensored' War.* New York: Oxford University Press.

Jabri, V. (1996) 'A Structurationist Theory of Conflict', *Discourses on Violence: Conflict Analysis Reconsidered.* Manchester, UK: Manchester University Press, pp. 54–89.

Kellner, D. (1992) *The Persian Gulf TV War.* Boulder, CO: Westview Press.

Kesavan, K. V. (1990) 'Japan and the Tiananmen Square Incident', *Asian Survey*, 30, 669–81.

Lee, C-C. (2000) 'The Paradox of Political Economy: Media Structure, Press Freedom, and Regime Change in Hong Kong', in C-C. Lee (ed.), *Power, Money, and Media: Communication Patterns and Bureaucratic Control in Cultural China.* Evanston, IL: Northwestern University Press, pp. 288–336.

———(2002) 'Established Pluralism: U.S. Elite Media Discourse on China Policy', *Journalism Studies*, 3, 383–97.

———(2003) 'The Global and the National of the Chinese Media: Discourses, Market, Technology, and Ideology', in C-C. Lee (ed.), *Chinese Media, Global Contexts.* London: RoutledgeCurzon, pp. 1–31.

Lee, C-C. and Yang, J. (1995) 'National Interest and Foreign News: Comparing US and Japanese Coverage of a Chinese Student Movement', *Gazette*, 56, 1–18.

Lee, C-C., Chan, J. M., Pan, Z. and Clement Y. K. So (2002) *Global Media Spectacle: News War over Hong Kong*. Albany. State University of New York Press.

McAdam, D., McCarthy, J. D. and Zald, M. N. (eds) (1996) *Comparative Perspectives on Social Movements: Political Opportunities, Mobilizing Structures, and Cultural Framing*. New York: Cambridge University Press.

Medhurst, M. J. (1990) 'Rhetoric and Cold War: A Strategic Approach', in M. J. Medhurst, R. L. Ivie, P. Wander and R. L. Scott (eds), *Cold War Rhetoric: Strategy, Metaphor, and Ideology*. New York: Greenwood Press, pp. 19–27.

Murdock, G. (2000) 'Reconstructing the Ruined Power: Contemporary Communications and Questions of Class', in J. Curran and M. Gurevitch (eds), *Mass Media and Society*. London: Arnold, pp. 7–26.

Nimmo, D. and Combs, J. E. (1990) *Mediated Political Realities*. New York: Longman.

Ozaki, S. and Arnold, W. (1985) *Japan's Foreign Relations: A Global Search for Economic Security*. Boulder, CO: Westview Press.

Page, B. (1996) *Who Deliberates? Mass Media in Modern Democracy*. Chicago: University of Chicago Press.

Pan, Z. and Kosicki, G. M. (1993) 'Framing Analysis: An Approach to News Discourse', *Political Communication*, 10, 55–75.

Patten, C. (1997) *Letters to Hong Kong*. Hong Kong: Government Printer.

———(1998) *East and West*. London: Macmillan.

Pharr, S. and Krauss, E. S. (eds) (1996) *Media and Politics in Japan*. Honolulu: University Press of Hawaii.

Press, A. L (2000) 'Recent Developments in Feminist Communication Theory: Difference, Public Sphere, Body and Technology', in J. Curran and M. Gurevitch (eds), *Mass Media and Society*. London: Arnold, pp. 27–43.

Said, E. W. (1978) *Orientalism*. New York: Pantheon.

———(1981) *Covering Islam*. New York: Pantheon.

———(1993) *Culture and Imperialism*. New York: Knopf.

Schlesinger, P. (1979) *Putting 'Reality' Together: BBC News*. Beverly Hills, CA: Sage.

Sigal, L. V. (1973) *Reporters and Officials: The Organization and Politics of Newsmaking*. Lexington, MA: D.C. Heath.

Snyder, J. and Ballentine, K. (1997) 'Nationalism and the Marketplace of Ideas', in M. Brown, O. Cote, Jr., S. M. Lynn-Jones and S. E. Miller (eds), *Nationalism and Ethnic Conflict*. Cambridge, MA: MIT Press, pp. 61–91.

Tuchman, G. (1978) *Making News: A Study in the Construction of Reality*. New York: Free Press.

van Ginneken, J. (1998) *Understanding Global News*. Thousand Oaks, CA: Sage.

Zaller, J. and Chiu, D. (1996) 'Government's Little Helper: US Press Coverage of Foreign Policy Crisis, 1945–1991', *Political Communication*, 13, 385–405.

chapter eighteen

Women and Race in Feminist Media Research: Intersections, Ideology and Invisibility

LINDA ALDOORY AND SHAWN J. PARRY-GILES

Introduction

Throughout the 1960s, 1970s and into the 1980s, many liberal feminists emphasized the political, legal, and social inequalities that existed between women and men (Arneil, 1999; Whelehan, 1995). Feminists from this second wave of US feminism often treated gender and race/ethnicity as distinct categories, homogenizing 'woman', perpetuating dualist reasoning (black/white, masculine/feminine) of modernist thought, and further marginalizing women of colour (Fraser, 1989; Glenn, 1999). As a result, 'men of color stood as the universal racial subject', and '[w]hite women were positioned as the universal female subject' (Glenn, 1999: 3). Valdivia (1995) argues similarly that feminist work has centred largely on white women, and ethnic and race studies, while growing in number, have focused primarily on African-American men. In US popular culture and media, such homogenization and dualism depicted black women, for example, as 'all woman and tinted black', or 'mostly black and scarcely woman' (Gaines, 1988: 19).

We believe this homogenist and binary thinking reduces women and persons of colour to unproductive stereotypes, furthering the presence of sexism and racism in media studies. Instead, we encourage an emphasis on the differences among women in scholarship and in political practice. Other feminist scholars have also promoted a more 'multicultural feminism' (Shohat, 1998: 2), where 'the term "women" applies to differently situated individuals . . . who occupy a spectrum of identities as well as positions of power' (Valdivia, 1995: 9). Zinn and Dill (1996: 321–2) use the concept 'multiracial feminism' to impart 'race as a primary force situating genders differently'. They contend that the concept of 'difference' has replaced 'equality' as the central force in US feminist theory, demonstrating a significant shift in feminist scholarship and activism over the past two decades (p. 322).

Such commitments, which stem from third-wave feminism, moved many scholars toward developing what has become known as theories of '*intersectionality*' (Valdivia, 1995; Zinn and Dill, 1996). Such intersectional commitments presuppose that studies of women should always be connected with considerations of race and class, characteristics that work together to define a person's particular subject position. West and Fenstermaker (1995: 11) suggest no one can 'experience gender without simultaneously experiencing race and class.' The main assumption is that race and gender are mutually constitutive' and 'relational' (Glenn, 1999: 9; McLaughlin, 1998: 85; Pellegrini, 1998).

We argue in this chapter that this move toward intersectionality makes media studies research more complex, more realistic, and more sensitive to cultural contexts, all of which are significant factors in improving media scholarship.[1] The goal of this chapter, then, is to review feminist media literature that works to disrupt (and in such cases perpetuate) such binary reasoning and interrogate the media as a complex system of gender, race and economics, which allows 'violence and inequities to continue' (Farrell, 1995: 643).

Similarly, we are attuned to issues of 'transnational affiliations' and 'diasporic nationalisms' related to 'gendering practices, class formations, sexual identities, [and] racialized subjects' (Grewal and Kaplan, 2001: 52). Such a 'multiplicity of relations' (Mouffee, 1992: 372) complicates matters of oppression and resistance as an individual can 'occupy both dominant and subordinate positions and experience advantage and disadvantage' because of race, class, gender and/or sexuality, as well as matters related to globalism, nationalism and localism (Weber, 2001: 105). We argue, however, that while feminist media scholars are making considerable progress in offering a more multicultural and global feminism in relation to progressing nations such as India, such research still often reflects the binaries of modernism and the hegemony of Western feminism that, well intentioned or not, can dominate feminist politics and scholarship. In the process, such scholarship often reinforces the power of elite white/anglo males and, in certain instances, elite white/anglo females while rendering certain women of colour in particular developing nations more invisible, particularly in relation to the African continent. As Flores and McPhail (1997: 115) warn, 'discourses [can] continue to maintain a binary opposition between the dominant and the marginalized, an opposition which may limit or obscure our understanding and comprehension of the complexity of difference, and preclude the possibility of moving away from the rhetoric of "us against them"'.

Specifically, we centre our attention on research that takes a cultural studies approach to feminism and the media, particularly to matters of media production, representation and audience reception (Henderson, 2001; Shohat and Stam, 1996). We note the ways that media production, representation and reception disrupt and/or perpetuate structures of domination. For example, some cultural studies scholars analyse media texts to study the ways that the media serve as sites of resistance for persons often oppressed within their local and/or global communities. Other studies examine whether specific audiences accept 'preferred' meanings offered by media producers, whether they resist or oppose the preferred meanings altogether, or whether they negotiate the preferred meanings that media producers generate. While media producers construct certain, preferred meanings in the media texts they produce, it is not necessarily the meanings received by audience members. Cultural studies scholars explore this meaning-making process from production through representation to reception and track the meanings that are created, negotiated and received, examining how such meanings change over time.

We define feminist research as scholarly work that critically examines gender and power relations and uses feminist theories as analytical frameworks. This chapter focuses on gender and race studies that have examined women and their interactions with, and representations in, the media. This limitation thus is necessary to constitute a limited, relevant review of literature, but there are also weaknesses inherent in our delimiters. First, not all feminist media literature is represented here, and not all topics are represented. There is an emphasis on popular media, political communication, news and journalism in a US context most noticeably yet not exclusively. We are also aware that certain, critical areas of scholarship have been de-emphasized, particularly health communication, pornography, advertising, and new technology or internet studies from an appropriate multiplicity of international contexts. In this chapter we first detail themes that emerge in the research on intersectionality in media production, media representation and audience reception. We end with a discussion of the scholarly implications for feminist media research.

Media production

In general, research on women, race and ethnicity in the context of media production has been limited, compared with the amount of research conducted on media representation. Media production is most often studied by feminists through ethnography that highlights women as producers of alternative media and through observational studies, surveys or interviews that examine women in media professions who struggle against racism and sexism to influence media production. Other studies accentuate the ideological influences that production has on media content.

Women producing media

Feminists have for decades challenged mass media portrayals of women by forming independent media sources and channels (Opoku-Mensah, 2001; Riano, 1994), or what Smith (1993: 61) calls 'women's movement media'. Riano (1994) argues that the process of creating alternative media forms make women the primary subjects of struggle and change in communication systems, by developing oppositional and proactive alternatives that influence language, representations and communication technologies. Using ethnography, researchers explore these media in order to illustrate how they offer alternatives to dominant meanings produced through media and how they construct sites of resistance (Baehr and Gray, 1996). Examples of this research include Byerly's (1995) historical description of the women's feature service in world news, Bhandarker's (1995) case study of female foreign news correspondents from developing countries, and Ruiz's (1994) examination of video and radio productions by Native Aymara women in Bolivia. These and other studies (Kawaja, 1994; Lloyd, 1994; Mensah-Kutin, 1994; Rodriguez, 1994) indicate that women working as cultural producers of media play crucial roles as conduits of social change. The authors integrate race, ethnicity, globalization and colonization into understandings of gendered media production. For example, Shafer and Hornig conducted a study of women journalists in the Philippines who were 'primary actors in using the press to hasten the downfall of President Ferdinand Marcos between 1982 and his exile in 1986' (Shafer and Hornig, 1995: p. 177). Rodriguez (1994) conducted ethnographic and participative research on women producing videos in Colombia. One video involved women from Ciudad Bolivar, a 'barrio' in Bogota, and their work with community day-care centres. A second video was produced by women working to transform a maternity clinic into a worker-owned institution because they were exploited as employees. Rodriguez found several significant changes in the women she worked with. First, the women began focusing on the nuances of their everyday lives. Second, the women who were originally enamoured with the media and popular culture became familiarized with production processes. Third, the women found themselves reconstructing roles of power among themselves, giving voice to some women who were invisible in the communities. Finally, the stories told on the videos were sources of collective strength and empowerment to the women.

In her edited book on women in grassroots communication, Riano (1994) offers a typology of media production efforts by women; she constructs four major frameworks: development communications, participatory communications, alternative communications and feminist communications. Development communications originate from outside the control of the community and are delivered through government, international development institutions, or non-governmental organizations (NGOs). In participatory communications, women are seen as participants in the process that enables them to take control of their lives and influence public policies through media production. Alternative communications is the development of means other than commercial media or vertical, one-way communication systems. Finally, feminist communications take on gender as a central, analytical dimension, where the main concerns are the ways in which gender influences the nature of participation and communication production and the mediation of gender in women's and men's experiences of subordination. Riano explains that these frameworks overlap and address issues of gender, race and globalization in different ways. Riano maps out this typology to counter prevailing myths of participation, communication and democratization while challenging how differences are ignored in current proposals of participatory communication.

Within the body of work on women-produced media are examples of participative action research, where scholars assist participants in producing and analysing alternative media forms (Mensah-Kutin, 1994; Rodriguez, 1994; Stuart and Bery, 1996). Stuart and Bery (1996), for example, helped women in Bangladesh produce a video to increase awareness about domestic violence. The authors explain: 'In exploring less brokered forms of communication, we produced programs with real people speaking from their own experience on issues of general concern' (p. 304). They argue that participative video enhanced the 'bottom-up' strategies used by global women's organizations.

Women inside mainstream media

Feminist media scholars have also examined the ways that female professionals work to change policies and media content from inside popular media outlets. Much of the research has concluded, however, that in terms of overall numbers and distribution across and within specific occupations, women media workers are disadvantaged in the male-dominated field

(Baehr and Gray, 1996; Creedon, 1993). Empirical research offers minimal evidence of a direct correlation between the number of women working in mainstream media and the increase in productive representations of women. Baehr and Gray (1996) demonstrate that institutional and professional constraints inhibit progress for women in the male-dominated media industry. They maintain that a specific women's perspective or aesthetic could radically transform discriminatory structures and practices in media institutions.

Production studies that intersect race and gender centre on the ideological constraints and oppressive work practices for women. In her examination of the television series *Any Day Now*, aired on the US cable network Lifetime, Lotz specifically focuses on how executive producer Nancy Miller bisected race and gender for the two female characters on the show. Lotz finds through her observations and interviews of the show's producers and writers that Miller's struggles with the network indicate 'how American society tries to separate aspects of identity into discrete categories, barricading the intersections that offer more complex understandings of identity in contemporary US culture' (Lotz, 2004: 295). Lotz explains that originally the show was sold to the US broadcast network, CBS, who then cancelled production, citing fears that US audiences were not ready to see two female characters confront interracial friendship and racism. Miller adjusted the vision of her show at a time when drastic changes were taking place in the economics and competition between US broadcast and cable television stations. Seven years after CBS cancelled production, the cable network Lifetime – a channel targeting women – aired the drama with Miller as the producer. Miller still encountered challenges because Lifetime's executives did not wish to focus on character conflicts arising from racial differences between women. Lotz concludes that television networks are still maintaining a separation of identities in order to appease audiences. Even with niche networks such as Black Entertainment Television (BET) in the USA, relatively broad audiences are sought. According to Lotz, 'Voices such as Miller's may have difficulty receiving distribution because they recognize intersections more specific than those currently served by networks' (p. 299).

Ideological influence of media

Other media production studies focus on ideological influences in relation to matters of race, ethnicity and gender. Acosta-Alzuru's work on Venezuelan telenovelas is one of the most intricate and comprehensive examinations of the impact of media production on media content and audience reception. Telenovelas are Spanish language television shows featuring dramatic content and a continuous story line. In her study, Acosta-Alzuru interviews head writers, actors, and the producer of a popular Venezuelan telenovela, *El Pais de las Mujeres* (The Country of Women). Taking a cultural studies approach, Acosta-Alzuru also examines the content of the telenovela for its representations and interviews both male and female audience members in Venezuela. The author finds that the writer and producer of the show intentionally portray strong female characters who are often victims of patriarchal oppression. The producer wanted to show 'women's redemption and, in some way, use a flashlight to light the way for those who still don't know how to redeem themselves' (Acosta-Alzura, 2003: 274). Even though the producer and writers set out to honour Venezuelan women by presenting them as protagonists of their own stories, the head writer said he did not want a feminist telenovela. Acosta-Alzuru concludes that feminism is seen as a threat to the established social order in Venezuela. Thus, even though the producers develop story lines for female characters who are strong and who reflect real problems, the meanings presented still maintain the hegemonic ideals of womanhood. Such ideological commitments exhibited by the producers clearly impact the representations that circulate in media discourse.

Media representation

Examining the intersectionality of gender, race and ethnicity has occupied the attention of scholars interested in the study of media representations, which communicate images of power and control (Fair, 1996), connect 'meaning and language to culture' (Hall, 1997: 15), and function as sources of 'desire, memory, myth, search, discovery' (Hall, 2000: 32). Grossman and Cuthbert (1996: 431) contend that the 'politics of representation is also always a politics of the material' and Rony (1996: 8–9) maintains that the media serve as a site where gender and race are represented as 'natural categories' in relation to the global, national and the local. While such representations can 'reinforce mental structures and images to constrain, dehumanize, and disempower particular individuals in both First- and Third-World cultures' (Heung, 1995: 83), they also 'can play a more coherent and transformative role in the social construction and reconstruction of difference, diversity, and dialogue' (Flores and McPhail, 1997: 107).

Representations as mediated stereotypes

One way that the media organize power is through stereotypical representations, which reinscribe social rules and roles that are often simultaneously sexist and racist (Fair, 1996) – troubling images that some believe are harder to detect in visual representations than in the written or spoken word (Wallace, 1990). Multicultural feminists commonly accentuate the sexualization of women in film, music videos, advertisements, news and other television genres. In the USA, scholars often attend to the ways in which black women are hyper-sexualized in the media (hooks, 1996). Wallace (1990) suggests that black women are more likely to be featured as performers in music videos or as fashion models than they are to be given roles with speaking parts. In hip-hop, for example, Perry charges that 'the visual image of black women . . . rapidly deteriorated into one of widespread sexual objectification and degradation', especially in music video images that are often controlled by record company executives (Perry, 2003: 137). Hooks explains that black women participate in such practices because 'the black female body gains attention only when it is synonymous with accessibility, availability, when it is sexually deviant' (hooks, 1992: 66). When black women are featured as lead characters in film, such sexualizations still persist. Bobo, for example, talks of Shug as the 'licentious cabaret singer' in the 1985 Steven Spielberg film, *The Color Purple* (Bobo, 1995: 73). Writing about Martin Lawrence's Fox television show, *Martin*, Zook (1999: 64) suggests that the relationship between Lawrence's character and his on-screen girlfriend, Gina, was really about 'power and patriarchal desire'.

The conflation of black women's sexuality and class with electoral politics is the subject of other media scholarship about the news media. Linking sexualization with drug use and welfare dependency, for example, Reeves constructs the image of the 'crack mother as an out-of-control black sexuality' that emerged during the presidential years of Ronald Reagan (1981–1989) (Reeves, 1998: 110). Visions of the black teen welfare mother were pervasive in US television news throughout the 1980s and 1990s – images that combined with black men as absentee fathers to further the '[r]acial coding parading as commonsense populism [which] associated blacks with negative [sexual] equivalencies . . . affirming the repressed, unspeakable, racist unconscious of dominant white culture' (Giroux, 1998: 46). Even the news media coverage of professionally successful black women can reflect overt sexualizations. Vavrus studied the news coverage surrounding Anita Hill's 1991 testimony before the US Senate Judiciary Committee concerning Clarence Thomas's Supreme Court nomination. She asserts that the press coverage of Hill's testimony 'pathologized her sexuality', as journalists and pundits debated, for example, one psychiatrist's view that Hill was 'diagnosed as erotomaniacal, a disorder characterized by the presence of sexual desire so strong that it overwhelms sufferers' (Vavrus, 2002: 63). Such constructions reflect the nineteenth-century ideology that women who entered the US public sphere and politics in particular were sexually provocative and promiscuous.

Sexuality and race also collide with colonialism, nationalism and class in other scholarship on media representations (Durham, 2001; Luthra, 1995; Parameswaran, 2001). Writing about US popular representations of Native Americans, Bird juxtaposes those found in the classic Western films of the 'squaw' that is 'sexually convenient', with the 'American Indian princess' as portrayed by Disney's *Pocahontas* – the non-threatening symbol of the 'virgin land' possessed by the white/anglo males (Bird, 1999: 72–4). Luthra intersects matters of colonialism, race, gender and sexuality when examining the US media coverage of Third World women over matters of population control during the Reagan administration. Within such coverage, Luthra contends, 'Third World woman' were depicted as 'mysterious, inaccessible, [and] oppressed', which helped justify 'foreign intervention in the international population arena'. Such images work to normalize First World power over women of colour and their sexuality to restrict the growing number of poor that might destabilize Western sovereignty (Luthra, 1995: 197, 211). Further emphasizing US international power, Parry-Giles and Parry-Giles (in press) focus on popular representations found in the US television drama, *The West Wing*, a fictional narrative about the US presidency. The authors emphasize how Russia is personified by a female leader whose sexual advances are decidedly rebuked by the white male political officials of the west wing, communicating a disgust and distrust of contemporary Russia attempting to rebuild its international prestige in the post-Cold War era.

In addition to accentuating women's sexuality, other critics note that Third World women or poorer women of colour in the USA and Britain are often portrayed as victims in need of Western benevolent aid. Fair shows that men are portrayed as 'producers' while women are depicted as helpless and dependent on international aid in US press coverage of famine in Ethiopia and other parts of Africa (Fair, 1996: 11–12). Parameswaran situates *National Geographic*'s 1999 millennium issue in a globalized context as she examines the Western gaze toward women of colour and black women in the USA. She concludes: 'the *Geographic's* facile accounts of women as symbols, consumers, peddlers, and mute victims of global culture become the dominant narratives of femininity' (Parameswaran, 2002a; 300). Furthering such images of black women's disempowerment globally, Omenugha examines British newspaper coverage of 'African women', noting the common visual images of 'destitution, victimization, poverty, sickness, and wretchedness' (Omenugha, 2003: 15). Such transnational images deny women of colour a sense of agency, justifying international intervention and control in the increasingly global environment.

Images of Third World victimization are sometimes associated with 'primitive' visualizations – depictions that work in opposition to images of progress that often accompany characterizations of white/anglo women. When examining The Body Shop's advertising campaign entitled *Mamatoto*, for example, Grossman and Cuthbert note how non-Western women of colour are usually featured in outdoor settings, including a forest or desert surrounded by animals, as they bathe infants. Conversely, the images of white women in the same advertising campaign are mediated through computer-generated graphics that are highly stylized. Such differences, the authors suggest, 'informs and reinforces the ideological juxtapositions of progress and primitivism, science and folklore, knowledge and ignorance that discursively marks the boundaries between "us" and "them" throughout *Mamatoto*' (Grossman and Cuthbert, 1996: 438).

In some cases, feminist scholars juxtapose portrayals of Third World and First World women (Grossman and Cuthbert, 1996), while other scholars destabilize images of white/anglo female dominance, demonstrating how they are empowered in one context and disempowered in another (Durham, 2001). Durham, for instance, interrogates the ways that South Asian symbols of femininity (e.g. nose rings, mehndi, and bindis) are appropriated by white/anglo women and promulgated throughout US popular culture. As a result, Durham (2001: 213) suggests, 'The US mass media's presentation of Indian femininity as a substructure for White female sexuality serves to legitimate the hegemonic construction of Western superiority over Asian culture'. Willis reveals other ways that US white/anglo women are symbolized in dominant ways by studying how film and television drama commemorate their political contributions to the African-American civil rights movement (1950s and 1960s). Referring to white women as 'protofeminists', Willis suggests that they are portrayed as 'a medium for the transformation of racial consciousness of the men around her'. While such images can be read as productive on the one hand by writing white women into the activism of the civil rights movement, Willis accentuates the ideological ambiguity of the texts, concluding that 'the central focus on the progressive women downplays white resistance to integration in general' (Willis, 2001: 100, 113–14). Vavrus (2002) uses former US first lady Hillary Rodham Clinton as a case study, and contends that Clinton, 'a privileged white woman with fairly conservative politics . . . comes to be the poster child for feminism', communicating more restricted images of contemporary feminism. Thus, while white/anglo women are often imbued with power in a global context, such power is restricted in a US political context, demonstrating the contestation and complexities surrounding matters of domination and subordination as researchers seek to integrate intersectional perspectives in their media scholarship.

For many scholars, the stereotypes of women's sexuality, victimization, primitiveness and empowerment are often transported globally and locally through representations of women's bodies. Heung details how 'colonization operates by taking over land and bodies'. In assessing films by Asian and Canadian film makers, Heung says that for Asian women especially, ideologies of gender, race, ethnicity, and sexuality place their bodies under the burden of erasure while also marking them as receptacles of projected cultural meanings' (Heung, 1995: 90). Likewise focusing on the mediation of Third World women, Fair contends that 'women in Africa often . . . are depicted only in terms of their bodies . . . embodying inferior qualities of womanliness compared to their white Western counterparts' (Fair, 1996: 7). Juxtaposing the portrayal of women in India by centring attention on issues of age and globalism, Parameswaran demonstrates how the 'older Indian woman's body and posture announce her alignment with tradition'. Younger women's bodies, conversely, reflect 'an androgynous firm body' reflective of 'cosmopolitan modernity', communicating a 'bold assertiveness, feminine youthfulness' against images of 'gentle passivity and the slack middle-aged body' (Parameswaran, 2002a: 291–2). Durham concludes that when white women's bodies replace those of Indian women in the mediation of South Asian culture, 'the cultural appropriation of Eastern cultures as trends, styles, or exotic sexual displays can be understood in terms of issues of imperialism and dominance' (Durham, 2001: 205).

Representations as sites of political resistance

Even scholars who expend considerable energy isolating and destabilizing destructive images of oppression and submission also accentuate productive images of empowerment. As Durham suggests, historically oppressed communities and nations are making their presence felt in 'subversive ways'; Durham turns to India as a case study where its image is moving from one of 'swamis, gurus, or poverty-stricken laborers' to 'highly employable scientists, engineers, doctors' (Durham, 2001: 212). Bobo (1995) similarly insists that social movements, with clear connections to political activism, can do their work through media texts. Parry-Giles and Parry-Giles (in press) illustrate such political work by discussing how US civil rights organizations worked toward the diversification of television cast members in the late 1990s. Responding, at least in part, to such diversity calls, *The West Wing* places white women and people of colour in positions of political power. As a result, white women serve as presidential political and legal advisers, influential members of Congress, feminist activists, and as the president's press secretary. Women of colour, although less visible than men of colour in this presidential narrative, are still depicted as the National Security Adviser and the Secretary of Housing and Urban Development. While limited, such representations work to change the face of US television, demonstrating the potential impact of political activism. *The West Wing* also features significant debates over global feminist matters, including the trafficking of teen prostitutes worldwide, population control and abortion rights, and the complicit role of the US government in the violence against women in the Middle East. *The West Wing*, thus reflects the contention offered by Carter, Branston and Allan about television news, where 'privileged news celebrities' can 'allow a range of feminist debates to be articulated' with considerable emotion that might have previously been 'disallowed' (Carter *et al.*, 1998: 7–8).

Several scholars also indicate ways that representations of black women destabilize disempowered images previously discussed. In particular, several reveal how black women in music are taking greater control over their own image-making. Gaunt highlights DOJJ, an African-American rap artist, who exudes images of independence and financial success that work against the typical sexualized or welfare mother stereotypes. In the process, she, along with other women in 'gangsta rap', co-opt 'the male voice and the male dress and use male privilege and space to deconstruct codes of gender identity as a sign of access' (Gaunt, 1995: 302). Further focusing on self-empowerment representations, Zook links another African-American rap artist and actor, (Queen) Latifah, to 'nontraditional representations of femininity, sexuality, and power' (Zook, 1999: 69), likewise prompting discussion about feminism and lesbianism. Latifah works with the activist group, Intelligent Black Women's Coalition; her voice and activism are reflected in the media representations of her, which resist the typical sexual victimization images that often pervade music videos in particular. Perry notes that feminism began to infiltrate hip-hop during the 1980s. The images that newer artists such as Alicia Keys and India Arie project in their songs and their videos evidence 'intelligence and integrity rather than expensive clothes, liquor, and firearms', defying visual sexual images that 'may be implicated in the subjugation of black women' (Perry, 2003: 140).

The disruption of historical images of colonization is also part of global political activism; media scholarship reflects such political commitments. Shohat and Stam urge that '[j]ust as the media can eroticize and "otherize" cultures, they can also promote multicultural coalitions'. In a contemporary context, they contend, the media is more 'multicentered, with the power not only to offer countervailing representations but also to open up parallel spaces for alternative transnational practices' (Shohat and Stam, 1996: 145). More specifically, Parameswaran (2001) demonstrates through the images of the 1996 Miss World pageant how local communities can impart influence in a global context, destabilizing the hegemonic control of the West and demonstrating that the media can serve as a site for counter-hegemonic causes. As Parameswaran and other multicultural feminists reveal, by integrating questions of race, gender, class, sexuality, globalism, nationalism, and localism, we see a much more contested terrain than previous scholarship generated during the second wave.

This contestation means, though, that certain women hold greater representational power than others in the mediated discourse of the global village. Parameswaran (2002a) showcases the polysemic images at work through her interrogation of *National Geographic*, which reflects the legacy of imperialism and juxtaposes women against women through representations of progress and disempowerment. Parameswaran illustrates how white/anglo women 'luxuriate in the freedom of pursuing ethnic culture and attractive Asian women express independence of style' as Asia is aligned with 'the vitality of modern progress'. Conversely, black women become 'the canvas on which the magazine etches poverty and disenfranchisement' in a US context while Africa, through its absence in the millennium issue, 'remains anchored to the amorphous state of extinction' (Parameswaran, 2002a: 313). While some scholarship on hip-hop accentuates the limited gains that US black women have made in the politics of representation, other multicultural feminists reveal the near invisibility of African black women in a global media context, illustrating the political work yet to be done.

Media reception

Cultural studies scholars who focus on audience reception are interested in understanding how people make sense of media and how media experiences affect daily life. While cultural studies scholars believe that the media can have potentially powerful effects, they also argue that audiences actively construct meaning when they interpret media. In fact, studies show that people use media to construct identities, gain knowledge and resist authority (Tracy, 2004).

According to Baehr and Gray (1996), questions of audience are never far away from any feminist work on the media. The number of studies on women's experiences with popular and mass media has increased over the past 20 years (Frazer, 1987; Gray, 1996; Gregg, 1992; Hobson, 1989, 1990, 1996; Press, 1990, 1991; Radway, 1984; Rakow, 1988; Seiter *et al.*, 1989), but there has been limited focus on interconnected experiences of women as gendered and raced subjects. The studies that connect race and gender often examine audiences for their differences in media consumption and reception. Cultural studies scholars also work to ascertain whether female audiences negotiate meanings from media texts or resist the preferred meanings offered by media producers.

Readings of media as 'different'

Many intersectional audience reception studies highlight difference in the ways that women of colour make meaning of media (Bobo, 1995; Harris and Hill, 1998; Munoz, 1994; Osborne, 2004). Bobo and others (Collins, 2000; King, 1988) suggest, for example, that black women face 'multiple jeopardy' because of their status as black and female, and, for the most part, because of a specific class hierarchy. Bobo contends that this multiple jeopardy is not additive, but rather an incremental process where racism is multiplied by sexism and then multiplied by classism (Bobo, 1995: 205). Reid (1989) argues that most studies of African Americans are based on the assumption that there is a relatively homogeneous black perspective and that most African Americans have similar views on political and social issues. Reid instead isolates the factors that lead to differences in attitudes toward television among young black women in London. She conducted a series of interviews with these women and found that gender, class and race influenced the viewing choices and attitudes towards television programmes. Darling-Wolf (2003: 153) similarly claims that there exists a theoretical recognition of the complexity of national and individual identity formation, but relatively few studies have attempted to determine how members of marginalized groups might experience processes of globalization.

In Darling-Wolf's study of Japanese women's meaning-making of popular Japanese media, a preference for Westerners' physical attributes was a significant element in the study's findings. Darling-Wolf spent eight months living in Japan and completed 40 interviews with 29 women ranging in age from 16 to 81. She found unanimous agreement among participants that white Western women presented in Japanese magazines and film were more physically attractive than Japanese women. She quoted one of the participants: 'That's the kind of beauty we pursue' (p. 166). However, Darling-Wolf also notes that this preference for white/anglo women's beauty did not mean that participants approved of white women's presence in the Japanese media environment. She argues that this racial hierarchy increases the alienation, remoteness and longing that the Japanese women feel toward representations of attractiveness in their favourite media (p. 107).

Negotiated and oppositional readings of media

Many studies explore how certain audiences negotiate between meanings produced in media texts and meanings construed within the audiences' subjectivities. Tracy (2004), for example, found in her study of fourth-grade girls that racial and gendered identities, as well as friendship histories, affect and are affected by the girls' use of popular music. Tracy spent ten months and an average of three to four days a week with the girls in their school. She conducted group and individual interviews, observations, surveys and participated in school events. She concluded, 'While the girls negotiated their own identities when engaging with music in the lunch room and/or in their dance groups, dominant racial and gendered belief systems continued to affect their ways of seeing and being with others in other contexts' (p. 46). In Tracy's study, some participants claimed certain girls were 'acting black'; there was also gender allegiance against boys who wanted to interfere with the girls' dancing at recess. In arguing for the necessity of intersectional work, Tracy writes about one participant who identified herself as 'African American black and half white girl': 'If we were to judge Vanecia based on her skin color or gender alone we would most likely make assumptions that don't fully represent her day-to-day experiences' (p. 47). Durham (1999, 2004) also examines how gender, race and ethnicity interact with middle-school girls' readings of popular media in the USA. After conducting interviews and participant observations at one predominantly white school and one predominantly Latina school, Durham found that girls at both schools preferred mainstream media to Spanish-language media. While the potential for resistance was a subcurrent in her findings, Durham suggests that the girls accept the meanings preferred by their peer groups, in particular those reflecting heterosexual norms and behaviours. Durham (1999: 211) argues: 'The research indicates that while race and class were differentiators of girls' socialization and concomitant media use, the differences highlighted the ways in which their different cultures functioned to uphold different aspects of dominant ideologies of femininity'.

One of the most cited audience reception studies that integrates race and gender is Bobo's (1995) research on the representations of black women and the reception by black women of the US films, *Daughters of the Dust*, and *The Color Purple*. She describes her study as concerning not only the ways black women make sense of media texts but also with their battles against systematic inequities in all areas of their lives. Bobo conducted interviews with groups of black women and showed some of the groups the film, *The Color Purple*, and some of the groups the independent film, *Daughters of the Dust*. Bobo was particularly concerned about interpreting religious attitudes and beliefs, given the centrality of religion in many black women's lives. She also considered the differences between what she found and what other scholars maintain for marginalized groups. According to Bobo, 'If more contact was made with those who participate in a range of everyday activities and who watch and view a variety of cultural forms, then there would be a greater understanding of the ways in which audiences negotiate their existence in a society not of their making but with some attempts at control' (p. 100). Bobo's participants noted the disparaging images of blacks in *The Color Purple*, yet still appreciated and enjoyed the film. By identifying with the women characters in the film, this audience felt that 'finally somebody says something about us' (p. 101). Similarly, participants appreciated the film *Daughters of the Dust*, a story of four generations of black women, but also commented on the lack of reality in the film. Bobo concludes that 'black women cultural consumers' are part of an interpretive community, and, as such, are cogent and knowledgeable observers of the social, political and cultural forces that influence their lives (p. 204).

Other studies have featured telenovelas and their impact on gender, ethnic and feminine identity construction (Acosta-Alzuru, 2003; Munoz, 1994; Rivero, 2003). Rivero (2003) uses focus groups of Colombians, Mexicans, Puerto Ricans, Colombian Americans and Mexican Americans living in Texas to explore meaning-making of an extremely popular telenovela titled, *Betty*. Rivero argues that *Betty* creates a space for gender/cultural identification and provides a source of contestation regarding ideologies of female beauty. Similarly, Acosta-Alzuru (2003) finds that Venezuelan women described a Venezuelan telenovela as emphasizing qualities, rights and struggles of Venezuelan women; at the same time, these women denounced the idea that feminism was a useful tool. As the author put it, in the consumption of the telenovela, feminism is divorced from messages that seek to empower women and improve their living conditions because of the negative opinions that are socially constructed in Venezuela about feminism and its place in society. In Munoz's exploration of how women living in a Columbian barrio perceive and use telenovelas, she found that the women illustrate a sensibility that is expressed 'from a time and a logic that is not contemporary with those in the center of modernity' (Munoz, 1994: 97).

Colonialism and cultural imperialism in audience reception

Other research examines the connections among colonialism, language and media reception. Parameswaran (1999, 2002b) explores the social constructions of Western romance novels by Indian girls. She conducted group and individual interviews and participant observation over a period of four months with 42 young Indian women living in South India. She found some major themes that defined how these girls made meaning of their sexual and ethnic identities. First, the English-language medium of Western romance fiction reminded participants of the imported books and comics they read as children. Second, the romance novels was viewed as resources to improve English language skills. Third, reading Western romance novels was viewed as an expression of class privilege. Parameswaran concluded that the legacies of colonialism continue to prevail but that Western cultural forms in the Third World do not necessarily cause global cultural homogeneity. Such heterogeneity is dependent on factors such as language, the form of media, and the differences of class, gender and cultural capital.

Durham's (2004) work also articulates the relationship between media and girls of immigrant diaspora groups. She focuses on immigrant South Asian teenage girls and their media preferences and interpretations. She found through focus groups that the girls preferred Indian movies and music over US popular culture. Her conclusions bring together the impact of ethnicity, race and gender on sexual identity and media use: 'The cultural constraints on their lives – both the real restrictions imposed by their parents and the subtler cultural cues that tie female chastity to family honor and the preservation of Indian traditions and heritage – worked to facilitate a critical reading that must be distinguished from the sort of unthinking refusal to recognize the ideological content of media texts . . .' (p. 155). Such studies evidence the power of the local over the global.

Conclusion

In this chapter we have shown how theories of intersectionality have developed and can produce scholarship that highlights the complexity of political and personal identity. Such intersectional commitments produce research that is more sensitive and more realistic to women's everyday lives. Problems, though, still persist in studies of media production, representation and audience reception, particularly in the ways that certain characteristics defuse the political force of sexuality and race and perpetuate the monolithic stereotypes that disrupt political progress. Some scholarship also continues to reify the Third and First World binaries that third-wave feminism seeks to disrupt. For example, much of the current research has not yet developed a thorough and sensitive way to intersect race with sexuality. Pellegrini contends that through US films such as *Bar Girls* (1995), *Boys on the Side* (1995) and *Watermelon Woman* (1996), lesbian difference is articulated through racial difference, accentuating distinctions of race that blunts the level of intimacy expressed between women, ultimately promoting a sense of 'sisterly solidarity' instead. Pellegrini (1998: 254, 256) observes that moving 'from sexual difference to racial difference does not disrupt binaries but [simply] displaces them'.

Political (in)visibility is an on-going issue for women. Studies of middle- to upper-income white/anglo women situated in a US context are more common. McLaughlin offers an example in her analysis of the O.J. Simpson murder trial in the USA. She argues that the news coverage of this early 1990s trial and its outcome 'pitted race against gender, racial solidarity against domestic violence' as people either galvanized around the black male defendant as a victim of a racist prosecution or expressed solidarity with the white/anglo female murder victim of domestic violence. In the end the news media's concern over domestic violence was fleeting, showing the definitional force of race, masculinity and celebrity and the continuing challenge for feminists in 'overcoming the exclusion of women from representational space' (McLaughlin, 1998: 85, 89).

Obstacles also persist for women who labour in a persistently patriarchal institution of media production. Even as a more diverse community of women gain greater visibility in media production worldwide, the scholarship reviewed in this chapter reveals that the media perpetuate common stereotypes that further diminish women's power. Women's inclusion in media production therefore does not guarantee progress. Media stereotypes about gender and race and monolithic representations continue even as more women of colour work within media, produce alternative media, and gain more visibility in representations. As Casey *et al.* (2002: 48) predicted, media centre more on 'maintaining social and ideological systems' rather 'than changing them'.

An on-going problem is the hegemonic gaze of white, Western feminists, such as ourselves, toward women and issues from other racial, ethnic and colonized backgrounds.

Grewal and Kaplan (2001: 54) explain the problem in these terms: 'in a transnational framework, US multiculturalists cannot address issues of inequities and differences if they presume the goal of progressive politics is to construct subjects, feminist or womanist, that are just like themselves'. Another concern is that a large percentage of the feminist scholarship is published in the West, which promulgates Western academic and feminist ideologies and offers privileged access to 'global village' media and scholarly outlets. At the same time, critiques are being raised about 'upper-middle class "Third World" women . . . unilaterally represent[ing] "other" working class sisters, or diasporic feminists operating within First World representational practices' (Shohat, 1998: 8). Writing from a Western location perpetuates the First/Third World juxtaposition, making transnational coalitions more difficult to sustain and normalizing First World dominance by reiterating its empowerments.

On a positive note, the research we reviewed demonstrates that theories of intersectionality are elevating the complexity of feminist media research and furthering commitments to understanding 'difference'. Such research is decidedly more global as multicultural feminists committed to counter-hegemonic gains are becoming more visible in scholarly projects. As Tucker insists, 'An elaborate web of discursive structures now enmeshes' race and feminism, 'along with many other related concepts and categories, in an inextricable field of multiple meanings, representations, and narratives that have put an end to an identity politics consisting of competitive individual, immutable, and categorically succinct entities' (Tucker, 1998: xi). We end with a call for additional feminist media research that further interrogates existing forces and constraints of dominant ideologies and attends to the intersectional complexities of gender, race, class, sexuality, nationalism and (post)colonialism.

Note

1 Our understanding of 'race' is guided by Winant's conception that 'The meaning of race is utterly variable among different societies and over historical time,' yet 'race is a significant dimension of *hegemony* that is deeply infused with power, order, and indeed the meaning systems of every society in which it operates'. Winant (1994:2–3) concludes that 'Not only is the social racialized, but the racial is socialized, such that identity itself is, so to speak, color coded.'

References

Acosta-Alzuru, C. (2003) ' "I'm Not a Feminist . . . Only Defend Women as Human Beings": The Production, Representation, and Consumption of Feminism in a Telenovela', *Critical Studies in Media Communication*, 20 (3), 269–95.

Antler, J. (ed.) (1998) 'Introduction', *Talking Back: Images of Jewish Women in American Popular Culture*. Hanover, MA: Brandeis University Press.

Arneil, B. (1999) *Politics & Feminism*. Oxford: Blackwell.

Baehr, H. and Gray, A. (1996) *Turning It On: A Reader in Women & Media*. London: Arnold.

Bhandarker, V. (1995) 'Female Foreign News Correspondents from Developing Countries Reporting from Washington, D.C.', in D. A. Newsom and B. J. Carrell (eds), *Silent Voices*. Lanham, MD: University Press of America, pp. 199–214.

Bird, S. E. (1999) 'Gendered Construction of the American Indian in Popular Culture', *Journal of Communication*, 49 (3), 61–83.

Bobo, J. (1995) *Black Women as Cultural Readers*. New York: Columbia University Press.

Byars, J. and Dell, C. (1992) 'Big Differences on the Small Screen: Race, Class, Gender, Feminine Beauty, and the Characters at *Frank's Place*', in L. F. Rakow (ed.), *Women Making Meaning: New Feminist Directions in Communication*. New York: Routledge, pp. 191–209.

Byerly, C. M. (1995) 'News, Consciousness, and Social Participation: The Role of Women's Feature Service in World News', in A. N. Valdivia (ed.), *Feminism, Multiculturalism, and the Media: Global Diversities*. Thousand Oaks, CA: Sage, pp. 105–22.

Carter, C., Branston, G. and Allen, S. (1998) *News, Gender and Power*. London: Routledge.

Casey, B., Casey, N., Calvert, B., French, L. and Lewis, J. (2002) *Television Studies: The Key Concepts*. London: Routledge.

Collins, P. H. (1999) 'Moving Beyond Gender: Intersectionality and Scientific Knowledge', in M. M. Ferree, J. Lorber and B. B. Hess (eds), *Revisioning Gender*. Thousand Oaks, CA: Sage, pp. 261–84.

———(2000) *Black Feminist Thought: Knowledge, Consciousness, and the Politics of Empowerment*. New York: Routledge.

Creedon, P. J. (1993) *Women in Mass Communication*, 2nd edn. Newbury Park, CA: Sage.

Darling-Wolf, F. (2003) 'Media, Class, and Western Influence in Japanese Women's Conceptions of Attractiveness', *Feminist Media Studies*, 3 (2), 153–72.

Durham, M. G. (1999) 'Girls, Media, and the Negotiation of Sexuality: A Study on Race, Class, and Gender in Adolescent Females', *Journalism and Mass Communication Quarterly*, 76 (2), 193–217.

———(2001) 'Displaced Persons: Symbols of South Asian Femininity and the Returned Gazed in US Media Culture', *Communication Theory*, 11 (2), 201–17.

———(2004) 'Constructing the "New Ethnicities": Media, Sexuality, and Diaspora Identity in the Lives of South Asian Immigrant Girls', *Critical Studies in Media Communication*, 21 (2), 140–62.

Fair, J. E. (1996) 'The Body Politic, the Bodies of Women, and the Politics of Famine in the US Television Coverage of Famine in the Horn of Africa', *Journalism & Mass Communication Monographs*, 158 (August), 1–42.

Farrell, A. E. (1995) 'Feminism and the Media: Introduction', *Signs*, 20 (3), 642–5.

Ferree, M. M., Lorber, J. and Hess B. B. (eds) (1999) *Revisioning Gender*. Thousand Oaks, CA: Sage.

Flores, L. S. and McPhail, M. L. (1997) 'From Black and White to *Living Color*: A Dialogic Exposition into the Social (Re)Construction of Race, Gender, and Crime', *Critical Studies in Mass Communication*, 14 (1), 106–22.

Fraser, N. (1989) *Unruly Practices: Power, Discourse, and Gender in Contemporary Social Theory*. Minneapolis: University of Minnesota Press.

Frazer, E. (1987) 'Teenage Girls Reading *Jackie*', *Media, Culture and Society*, 9 (4), 407–25.

Gaines, J. (1988) 'White Privilege and Looking Relations: Race and Gender in Feminist Film Theory', *Screen*, 29 (4), 12–27.

Gaunt, K. D. (1995) 'African American Women Between Hopscotch and Hip-Hop', in A. N. Valdivia (ed.), *Feminism, Multiculturalism, and the Media: Global Diversities*. Thousand Oaks, CA: Sage, pp. 277–308.

Giroux, H. A. (1998) 'White Noise: Toward a Pedagogy of Whiteness', in K. Myrsiades and L. Myrsiades (eds), *Race-ing Representation: Voice, History, and Sexuality*. Lanham, MD: Rowman & Littlefield, pp. 42–76.

Glenn, E. N. (1999) 'The Social Construction and Institutionalization of Gender and Race: An Integrative Framework', in M. M. Ferree, J. Lorber and B. B. Hess (eds), *Revisioning Gender.* Thousand Oaks, CA: Sage, pp. 3–43.

Gray, A. (1996) 'Behind Closed Doors: Video Recorders in the Home', in H. Baehr and A. Gray (eds), *Turning It On: A Reader in Women and Media.* London: Arnold, pp. 118–29.

Gregg, N. (1992) 'Telling Stories About Reality: Women's Responses to a Workplace Organizing Campaign', in L. Rakow (ed.), *Women Making Meaning.* New York: Routledge, pp. 263–88.

Grewal, I. and Kaplan, C. (2001) '*Warrior Marks*: Global Womanism's Neo-colonial Discourse in a Multicultural Context', in M. Tinkcom and A. Vallarejo (eds), *Keyframes: Popular Cinema and Cultural Studies.* London: Routledge, pp. 52–71.

Grossman, M. and Cuthbert, D. (1996) 'Body Shopping: Maternity and Alterity in *Mamatoto*', *Cultural Studies*, 10 (3), 430–48.

Hall, S. (ed.) (1997) 'The Work of Representation', in *Representation: Cultural Representations and Signifying Practices.* London: Sage, pp. 13–64.

——(2000) 'Cultural Identity and Diaspora', in N. Mirzoeff, *Diaspora and Visual Culture: Representing Africans and Jews.* London: Routledge, pp. 21–33.

Harris, T. M. and Hill, P. S. (1998) '*Waiting to Exhale* or Breath(ing) Again: A Search for Identity, Empowerment, and Love in the 1990's', *Women & Language News*, 21 (2), 9–14.

Henderson, L. (2001) 'Sexuality, Feminism, Media Studies', *Feminist Media Studies*, 1 (1), 17–24.

Heung, M. (1995) 'Representing Ourselves: Films and Videos by Asian American/Canadian Women', in A. N. Valdivia (ed.), *Feminism, Multiculturalism, and the Media: Global Diversities.* Thousand Oaks, CA: Sage, pp. 82–104.

Hobson, D. (1989) 'Soap Operas at Work', in E. Seiter, H. Borchers, G. Kreutzner and E. M. Warth (eds), *Remote Control: Television, Audiences, and Cultural Power.* New York: Routledge, pp. 150–67.

——(1990) 'Women Audiences and the Workplace', in M. E. Brown (ed.), *Television and Women's Culture: The Politics of the Popular.* Newbury Park, CA: Sage, pp. 61–71.

——(1996) 'Housewives and the Mass Media', in H. Baehr and A. Gray (eds), *Turning It On: A Reader in Women and Media.* London: Arnold, pp. 111–17.

Hooks, B. (1992) *Black Looks: Race and Representation.* Boston: South End Press.

——(1996) *Reel to Real: Race, Sex, and Class at the Movies.* New York: Routledge.

Kawaja, J. (1994) 'Process Video: Self-reference and Social Change', in P. Riano (ed.), *Women in Grassroots Communication: Furthering Social Change.* Thousand Oaks, CA: Sage, pp. 131–48.

King, D. K. (1988) 'Multiple Jeopardy, Multiple Consciousness: The Context of a Black Feminist Ideology', *Signs: A Journal of Women in Culture and Society*, 14 (1), 42–72.

Lloyd, L. (1994) '*Speak* Magazine: Breaking Barriers and Silences', in P. Riano (ed.), *Women in Grassroots Communication: Furthering Social Change.* Thousand Oaks, CA: Sage, pp. 251–9.

Lotz, A. D. (2004) 'Barricaded Intersections: *Any Day Now* and the Struggle to Examine Ethnicity and Gender', in R. A. Lind (ed.), *Race/Gender/Media: Considering Diversity Across Audiences, Content, and Producers.* Boston, MA: Pearson, pp. 294–300.

Luthra, R. (1995) 'The "Abortion Clause" in U.S. Foreign Population Policy: The Debate Viewed Through a Postcolonial Feminist Lens', in A. N. Valdivia (ed.), *Feminism, Multiculturalism, and the Media: Global Diversities.* Thousand Oaks, CA: Sage, pp. 197–216.

McLaughlin, L. (1998) 'Gender, Privacy and Publicity in "Media Event Space"', in C. Carter, G. Branston and S. Allan (eds), *News, Gender, and Power.* London: Routledge, pp. 71–90.

Mensah-Kutin, R. (1994) 'The WEDNET Initiative: A Sharing Experience Between Researchers and Rural Women', in P. Riano (ed.), *Women in Grassroots Communication: Furthering Social Change*. Thousand Oaks, CA: Sage, pp. 441–44.

Mouffe, C. (1992) 'Feminism, Citizenship, and Radical Democratic Politics', in J. Butler and J. W. Scott (eds), *Feminists Theorize the Political*. London: Routledge, pp. 369–85.

Munoz, S. (1994) 'Notes for Reflection: Popular Women and Uses of Mass Media', in P. Riano (ed.), *Women in Grassroots Communication: Furthering Social Change*. Thousand Oaks, CA: Sage, pp. 84–101.

Omenugha, K. A. (2003) 'Photographs of African Women in British Newspapers: Graffiti?', *Media Report to Women*, 31 (2), 15–20.

Opoku-Mensah, A. (2001) 'Marching on: African Feminist Media Studies', *Feminist Media Studies*, 1 (1), 25–34.

Osborne, G. E. (2004) ' "Women Who Look Like Me": Cultural Identity and Reader Responses to African American Romance Novels', in R. A. Lind (ed.), *Race/Gender/Media: Considering Diversity across Audiences, Content, and Producers*. Boston, MA: Pearson, pp. 61–8.

Parameswaran, R. (1999) 'Western Romance Fiction as English-Language Media in Postcolonial India', *Journal of Communication*, 49 (3), 84–105.

———(2001) 'Global Media Events in India: Contests Over Beauty, Gender and Nation', *Journalism & Communication Monographs*, 3 (2), 53–105.

———(2002a) 'Local Culture in Global Media: Excavating Colonial and Material Discourses in *National Geographic*', *Communication Theory*, 12 (3), 287–315.

———(2002b) 'Reading Fictions of Romance: Gender, Sexuality, and Nationalism in Postcolonial India', *Journal of Communication*, 52 (4), 832–51.

Parry-Giles, T. and Parry-Giles, S. (in press) *The Prime-Time Presidency: The West Wing and U.S. Nationalism*. Urbana: University of Illinois Press.

Pellegrini, A. (1998) 'Women on Top, Boys on the Side, But Some of Us are Brave: Blackness, Lesbianism, and the Visible', in K. Myrsiades and L. Myrsiades (eds), *Race-ing Representation: Voice, History, and Sexuality*. Lantham, MD: Rowman & Littlefield, pp. 247–63.

Perry, I. (2003) 'Who(se) Am I? The Identity and Image of Women in Hip-hop', in G. Dines and J. M. Humez (eds), *Gender, Race, and Class in Media: A Text-Reader*. Thousand Oaks, CA: Sage, pp. 136–48.

Press, A L. (1990) 'Class, Gender and the Female Viewer: Women's Responses to *Dynasty*', in M. E. Brown (ed.), *Television and Women's Culture: The Politics of the Popular*. Newbury Park, CA: Sage, pp. 158–80.

———(1991) *Women Watching Television: Gender, Class, and Generation in the American Television Experience*. Philadelphia, PA: University of Pennsylvania Press.

Radway, J. A. (1984) *Reading the Romance: Women, Patriarchy, and Popular Literature*. Chapel Hill: University of North Carolina Press.

Rakow, L. F. (1988) *Gender on the Line: Women, the Telephone, and Community Life*. Urbana: University of Illinois Press.

Reeves, J. L. (1998) 'Re-covering Racism: Crack Mothers, Reaganism, and the Network News', in S. Torres (ed.), *Living Colour: Race and Television in the United States*. Durham, NC: Duke University Press, pp. 97–117.

Reid, E. C. (1989) 'Viewdata: The Television Viewing Habits of Young Black Women in London', *Screen*, 30 (1–2), 114–21.

Riano, P. (1994) 'Women's Participation in Communication: Elements for a Framework', in P. Riano (ed.), *Women in Grassroots Communication: Furthering Social Change*. Thousand Oaks, CA: Sage, pp. 1–29.

Rivero, Y. M. (2003) 'The Performance and Reception of Televisual "Ugliness" in *Yo soy Betty la fea*', *Feminist Media Studies*, 3 (1), 65–81.

Rodriguez, C. (1994) 'A Process of Identity Deconstruction: Latin American Women Producing Video Stories in P. Riano (ed.), *Women in Grassroots Communication: Furthering Social Change*. Thousand Oaks, CA: Sage, pp. 149–60.

Rony, F. T. (1996) *The Third Eye: Race, Cinema, and Ethnographic Spectacle*. Durham, NC: Duke University Press.

Ruiz, C. (1994) 'Losing Fear: Video and Radio Productions of Native Aymara Women in Bolivia', in P. Riano (ed.), *Women in Grassroots Communication: Furthering Social Change*. Thousand Oaks, CA: Sage, pp. 161–78.

Seiter, E., Borchers, H., Kreutzner, G. and Warth, E. M. (eds) (1989) 'Don't Treat Us Like We're So Stupid and Naïve: Towards an Ethnography of Soap Opera Viewers', in *Remote Control: Television, Audiences, and Cultural Power*. New York: Routledge, pp. 223–47.

Shafer, R. and Hornig, S. (1995) 'The Role of Women Journalists in Philippine Political Change', in D. A. Newsom and B. J. Carrell (eds), *Silent Voices*. Lanham, MD: University Press of America, pp. 177–98.

Shohat, E. (ed.) (1998) 'Introduction', *Talking Visions: Multicultural Feminism in a Transnational Age*. New York: MIT Press, pp. 1–63.

Shohat, E. and Stam, R. (1996) 'From the Imperial Family to the Transnational Imaginary: Media Spectatorship in the Age of Globalization', in R. Wilson and W. Dissanayake (eds), *Global/Local: Cultural Production and the Transnational Imaginary*. Durham, NC: Duke University Press, pp. 145–70.

Sloop, J. M. (2004) *Disciplining Gender: Rhetorics of Sex Identity in Contemporary U.S. Culture*. Amherst: University of Massachusetts Press.

Smith, M. C. (1993) 'Feminist Media and Cultural Politics', in P. J. Creedon (ed.), *Women in Mass Communication*, 2nd edn. Newbury Park, CA: Sage.

Stuart, S. and Bery, R. (1996) 'Powerful Grassroots Women Communicators: Participatory Video in Bangladesh', in D. Allen, R. R. Rush and S. J. Kaufman (eds), *Women Transforming Communications: Global Intersections*. Thousand Oaks, CA: Sage, pp. 303–12.

Tracy, P. J. (2004) ' "Why Don't You Act Your Color?": Preteen Girls, Identity, and Popular Music', in R. A. Lind (ed.), *Race/Gender/Media: Considering Diversity Across Audiences, Content, and Producers*. Boston, MA: Pearson, pp. 45–52.

Tucker, M. (1998) 'Foreword', in E. Shohat (ed.), *Talking Visions: Multicultural Feminism in a Transnational Age*. New York: MIT Press, pp. xi–xiii.

Valdivia, A. N. (ed.) (1995) 'Feminist Media Studies in a Global Setting: Beyond Binary Contradictions and into Multicultural Spectrums', *Feminism, Multiculturalism, and the Media: Global Diversities*. Thousand Oaks, CA: Sage, pp. 7–29.

van Zoonen, L. (1999) *Feminist Media Studies*. London: Sage.

Vavrus, M. D. (2002) *Postfeminist News: Political Women in Media Culture*. New York: State University of New York Press.

Wallace, M. (1990) *Invisibility Blues: From Pop to Theory*. London: Verso.

Weber, L. (2001) *Understanding Race, Class, Gender and Sexuality: A Conceptual Framework*. Boston: McGraw-Hill.

West, C. and Fenstermaker, S. (1995) 'Doing Difference', *Gender & Society*, 9 (1), 8–37.

Whelehan, I. (1995) *Modern Feminist Thought: From the Second Wave to 'Post-Feminism*, New York: New York University Press.

Willis, S. (2001) 'Race as Spectacle, Feminism as Alibi: Representing the Civil Rights Era in the 1990s', in M. Tinkcom and A. Vlllarejo (eds), *Keyframes: Popular Cinema and Cultural Studies*. London: Routledge, pp. 98–110.

Winant, H. (1994) *Racial Conditions: Politics, Theory, Comparisons*. Minneapolis: University of Minnesota Press.

Zinn, M. B. and Dill, B. T. (1996) 'Theorizing Difference from Multicultural Feminism', *Feminist Studies*, 22 (2), 321–31.

Zook, K. B. (1999) *Color by Fox: The Fox Network and the Revolution in Black Television*. New York: Oxford University Press.

▶ chapter nineteen

Viewing and Reviewing the Audience: Fashions in Communication Research

TAMAR LIEBES

Introduction

Any evaluation of audiences should start with a disturbing doubt about the continuing validity of the term. On the threshold of an era in which pressing a button summons any song, stock number or *Star Trek* episode on display anywhere in the house (Livingstone, 2004), and 'grazing' and 'on demand' viewing replace the viewing of broadcast television for 'time famine' victims (Ellis, 2000), the notion of audience (or the activity of 'audiencing') as some form of a solidarity group, or as a form of involvement in a text which one has not summoned or invented oneself – a text that can surprise – becomes problematic.

The danger to audiences posed by their possible disembodiment into individual dreams bubbles, or their disappearance into time-shift recorders who never find time to view, is not as close as the technologies that allow for it. As Livingstone reminds us, the conditions underlying identity, sociality and community are slower to change than technologies. We know that the Olympic games, or, *mutatis mutandis*, any large-scale disaster close to home, finds us attending as faithful audience members, be it within the community, the nation or even the globe. These examples however also suggest that the term 'audiences' is too general. 'Fans' may be more fitting in the case of football, and 'public' in the case of an al-Qaida attack (Dayan, 2001).

But, whether television viewing as we know it is seriously threatened, the acutely destabilizing transformations of communication technologies suggest that the concept of 'audience' should be studied in tandem with its counterpart: the dominant media and genre it faces. Those changing technologies also suggest that the way in which audiences are situated – is everyone looking simultaneously at the same content, are they viewing alone or together, are they talking or silent, is the transmission live or recorded – is inseparable from the characteristics of the media they interact with, marked by their technological and institutional characteristics, and the ways in which they perceive their consumers.

The larger picture suggests that the contemporary media environment holds two types of threats to audiences. One is the abundance of what is offered, chasing viewers to an endless choice of niche channels and time-shift options, all of which may operate as a boomerang, pushing us to turn on good old broadcast television, and find out what is playing (Ellis, 2000). The second threat is the internet, confusingly entitled the new media environment. It is important to show why the term 'audiences' is not applicable to the internet before the changing audiences of broadcast media can be discussed.

Why internet users are not 'audiences'

The internet should not be seen as the latest electronic mass medium, continuing the chain of cinema, radio and television with their varying social contexts of viewing. It is rather an umbrella, multipurpose technology, loaded with a broad range of disparate communication functions, such as shortcutting mediators in the management of daily life. What does 'audience' have to do with buying food, or medicines, or booking tickets (activities for which the internet acts as a virtual supermarket, pharmacy and box office), or with operating as an archive, or a weather forecaster or private library? The internet's facilitation of downloading songs or pornographic movies – its capacity to provide any fantasy within the distance of one mouse click – may be the closest to audiencing since it has a pleasurable text in its midst. But this is only one of a multitude of uses provided by the internet, and more closely related to shopping in a video store (often used for a furtive private act, unacknowledged, let alone discussed). Being part of an audience, it seems to me, requires some form of real or potential sharing of an acknowledged (vocal or visual) text, with the variations of 'togetherness' in time and place depending on the medium, the genre and the situation of contact, accompanied by the knowledge that others are (or have, or will be) viewing.

The tendency to think of the internet as a medium that transforms the concept of audiences stems from the activity that characterizes its users. But this activity should not be confused with the capacity for the 'oppositional' or subversive 'activity' of audiences. Interacting with the internet is part of the full control exercised by users, which also restricts users' involvement. The breakthrough contribution of cyberspace to social communication lies not in offering space for audiencing but in offering new spaces for interpersonal interaction, in which one's own texts are created. Thus, the internet is a technological alternative to the cellular phone for 'one-to-one' talk, or as a virtual space for 'many-to-many', or 'one-to-many' chats, all of an anonymous kind – somewhat equivalent to encounters with strangers in a train, sports club or political meeting. Modelled on 'real' conversations, these internet communications constitute novel ways for getting to know people, making friends, or discussing social issues, including texts of popular culture. As any peep into chat sites of popular soaps should reveal, the internet, at its most social, provides additional spaces in which audiencing can be discussed, or rather 'worked through' (Ellis, 2000), ironically serving as another proof for the fact that soaps are still viewed in real time, in their regular slot. Thus, among its multiplicity of tasks, cyberspace supplies additional locales for debating shared experiences of audiencing.

So the internet does touch on audiencehood at the one pole of facilitating the option of radical individualistic consumption of popular cultural products, and at the opposite pole by facilitating talk about television viewing (that is, about audiencing). It does not, however, fulfil the need of viewing texts over which audiences have no control, and/or texts that enable the suspending of disbelief.

Television audiences: a three-phase history

Assuming that in spite of the dramatic transformations in the media environment, audiences are still (and should be) alive, as do the technologies that nurture them, what follows is a review of the changes undergone by mass media audiences and the ways in which these changes were defined and studied. This look at audiences starts with showing that the emphasis on audiences rather then on communication as a system (consisting of message, receiver and effect) is misplaced. It is important to maintain that audiences, and researchers in their wake, operate within the options and constraints of what is being offered – that is, in interaction with the medium and its social organization, with the attributes of the audiences determining those of the dominant media, and vice versa. The change in the image of audiences over the history of communication research suggests that this image is correlated with particular phases of the development of mass media, characterized by the degree of choice and versatility of use offered by those media at various stages.

A very useful scheme to define audiences can be drawn from the categories offered by John Ellis as a way of looking at the history of television and its implicit audience from the supply side. Although Ellis's categories relate only to stages undergone by television, they also are relevant to the development of radio, television's predecessor as the dominant electronic mass medium. Coming from a technological psychoanalytic perspective, Ellis defines the implicit audiences of television's first and second historical phases as 'citizen' and 'consumer'. For the present, unlabelled phase, I propose 'juggler' and sometime 'witness'. Ellis's scheme also can be used to examine the way in which mass communication research has defined the audience it studies during these three periods.

Scholars disagree about the right approach to audiences. Although everybody agrees that 'the audience' is a construction, the arguments focus on how audiences act (and react), and on the ideological implications. Central actors in the debate are Ang (1996), Morley (1991), Livingstone (1998, 2004), and Curran (1990). Rather than considering what they have in common, these scholars tend to argue with each other.

This chapter will follow Ellis's scheme in dividing the history of communication research into three periods, and how broadcasters situate audiences. This provides a framework for three layers of analysis: (1) how communication research defined and studied audiences in these phases; (2) the current critique of this work by scholars from different perspectives, and (3) my own view of these critiques and of what should be done.

Ellis's three phases

The history of television, according to Ellis, is marked by a progression through three eras, moving from 'scarcity' to 'availability' to 'plenty' (Table 19.1). Each phase carries an image of the audience. Scarce television addresses audiences as a unified mass of 'citizens' while available television addresses them as individual 'consumers'. Today's television of plenty

Ellis's Broadcasting Phases	Audiences Seen As	Dominant Research Paradigms
Scarcity	Citizens	Powerful effects
Availability	Consumers	Active audiences
Plenty	Jugglers	Ethnography

Table 19.1

seems to be addressing lonely 'jugglers' somewhat paralysed by endless choice, offering viewers to either commute between isolated niches or view broadcast television as 'impotent witnesses'.

The early scarcity phase, characterized by a dominant public broadcast tradition in Europe and three nationwide channels in the USA, was one of standardized mass-market consumerism. The development of public service and nationwide networks broadcasting, with an oligarchic focus, articulated a sense of the imagined (national) community, and promoted stability and continuity. Moulding itself to 'the patterns of everyday life', defining and standardizing clock-times, working schedules and national press, at the expense of regions and minorities, television infiltrated into everyday conversations, providing a shared national culture, with the BBC 'bringing special prominence to the artistic, sporting and ceremonial events' (Scannell and Cardiff, 1991). At the same time, television could address people intimately, as individuals, and could thereby represent the audiences *vis-à-vis* powerful politicians.

Thus, the implied audiences in the era in which the whole nation was watching mostly the same programmes were undifferentiated mass audiences, consisting of citizens that nationwide television unified as an imagined community, or imagined polity.

The era of availability, into which television moved during the 1980s and the end of the Cold War, coincided with a more diverse consumer market, and the destabilization of the structure of media institutions. This era is marked by the switch from a limited number of channels to a multitude of channels, delivered mainly by cable, and the accentuation and commodification of 'every available differences in the name of choice' (Ellis, 2000). In terms of its view of the audience, this change meant that television moved from 'definitive programming broadcasting to a mass audience' in the first era to the introduction of diversity of choice and to niche markets. The question, 'What did you think of that programme last night?' was replaced by 'Did you see that programme last night?' In this context, says Ellis, television does not cease to matter; it provided an important social forum in which complexities and anxieties were explored. Television plays a part in trying to reconcile differences, but also to 'develop the process of differentiation' by 'promoting the consumerism of choice through its display of opinions and styles'.

In the phase of availability, the experiences of witness, giving modern citizens 'a sense of complicity with all kinds of events in their contemporary world' takes a new form. Television, says Ellis, is particularly effective in involving viewers with distant events because, unlike other media, it 'introduces both the experience of witness and the mechanism of fiction'. But unlike the first centralized phase, the programming of any one channel 'no longer aims to be definitive'. Instead, audiences participate 'in a vast inchoate process of working through'. Thus, whereas this aspect of television's performance still assumes audiences of broadcast television are politically concerned human beings and not only individuals in search of a particular brand of pleasure, television's 'working through' poses a problem for the witnessing it offers. At the end of the day, the intense process of digesting events leads to liberation from further concern – another alternative to the one offered by Lazarsfeld and Merton (1948) by their concept of television's dissuasion from social action by overloading audiences with information.

The current phase of plenty introduces a qualitative change in the nature of broadcast television. It is an era in which viewers are free to ignore the programming of nationwide channels, and seek the programmes they crave from a menu of several hundred channels.

The audiences constructed by these changes are poor-rich consumers who, confronted with this abundance of infinite choice and experiencing 'time famine', face 'choice fatigue'. Thus, according to Ellis, worn-out audiences, feeling nostalgia for pattern and habit, return to broadcast television. Paradoxically, in this era of extreme choice, broadcast television, which had carved out a domestic niche in the era of scarcity, and later developed the role of a forum for working through social pressures, is now distinct in its sense of co-presence with its audience, addressing us at the moment of relaxation, away from choice fatigue, in the moment when 'you turn on the TV to see what's going on'.

Defining audiences: the dominant paradigm

As stated above, adopting the tripartite division suggested by Ellis for the evolution of the supply side of media is a useful scheme for looking at the changing conceptions of the audience in communication research at each phase, including the degree of their correspondence with Ellis's implied audiences. In the phase of scarcity, radio and then television address 'citizens' who in the period of availability turn into 'consumers' and in the phase of plenty become 'jugglers' (my label). The dominant research paradigms, roughly corresponding in time to the three phases, are the traditions of powerful effects, active audiences and postmodern ethnography.

Ellis's implicit audiences in these three phases can be matched with the images produced by audience research, and at the ways in which they remained in the collective memory of communication scholars. One research paradigm does not replace an older one at each phase. Instead, the various paradigms co-exist all along but do not become dominant at the same time.

Citizen: the lonely crowd

The image of the audience underlying the work of the powerful effects tradition, looking apprehensively at the potential influence of radio, the first mass medium to reign in the USA, does not fit with Ellis's image of audiences as citizens. In opposition to Ellis's image of audiences joining the nationwide imagined community from the safety of their suburban homes, research at the phase of scarcity (first on radio and later on television) was based on the image of audiences as isolated individuals, in a mass society, vulnerable to direct effects. However, the questions that motivated a lot of this research – Is the process of decision-making by voters amenable to persuasion by the mass media? Can media be used to counteract prejudice? Can media develop an appreciation for music? – show the researchers' concern with the relationship between the new, powerful medium and citizenship.

At the root of the belief of powerful medium and passive audiences is the political and social climate in Western societies between the world wars. The dominant perception was that of a mass society, characterized by the loss of faith in human rationality, with radio listeners as isolated individuals, alienated from the communities to which they belonged and prone to radical demagogy. This perception of the passivity of audiences was exacerbated by the recognition of the new medium's accessibility. Radio was seen as 'distinguished from all other kinds of communication by its capacity to reach all groups of the population uniformly' (Freidson, 1954). And even then, it should also be noted that this initial idea of powerful effects went in two directions. On the one hand there was the threat of political populism (motivated by the fear of propaganda by fascist groups) and the threat of popular culture (motivated by the fear of mass media's signalling the end of elitist canonic culture). On the other was a great pedagogic potential for closing educational gaps and making classical music accessible by radio (Lazarsfeld and Merton, 1948).

However, the findings of these researchers led them quite early on to lower both their fears and their expectations in regard to the new mass media. For better and for worse, research showed that audiences were not as isolated and as amenable to influence as the researchers had imagined. Much like the image of the citizen viewer in Ellis's phase of scarcity, audiences were found to be listening to radio together within the family (recall Woody Allen's *Radio Days* (1987)), going to the movies with another person, and discussing the programmes socially.

Thus, at the outset, communication researchers within the phase of scarcity were mostly concerned with effect. Assuming a helpless, passive audience, they went to work to examine the degree of exposure to cinema, radio and television. Audiences were seen as waiting to be influenced – to vote (when exposed to media campaigns), to buy something (via advertising), to fight prejudice (via anti-racist cartoons) and to escape the Martians (in Orson Welles' 'reality show' of an invasion from Mars). The discovery that effect was not uniform soon led to the downgrading of the idea from 'powerful' to 'limited' effects. A good example is Cantril's (1954) study of Welles' radio drama posing as a 'live' broadcast of Martian creatures invading the USA, in which the notion of powerful effects was disproved by the discovery that the show did not scare all of its listeners. Differences between 'believers' and 'non-believers' were related to listeners' degree of critical ability and to differences in education. In another study, Jastorf and Cantril (1954, cited by Curran, 1990) convincingly demonstrated that audiences are heavily defended against messages that contradict their existing perceptions. The study looked at two groups of students viewing a film of their universities playing each other at football. The two groups were found to have seen two different games.

Each side counted the fouls differently, in favour of their team, indicating that perceptions were influenced by socially shared predispositions.

Thus, the logic of the route undertaken by the 'strong effects' tradition led in the direction of tilting the balance between media and audiences in the direction of the power of the audience. Starting from counting heads, to identifying audience profiles, to looking at audience reasons for listening and viewing and at their understandings of what they are seeing, the findings led researchers to map out the various influences on people's decisions on what to buy and for whom to vote. Thus, the early campaign studies carried out by Lazarsfeld *et al.* (1948) led to the discovery of selectivity in exposure to media and messages, and to the centrality of interpersonal communication in the process of decision-making, providing major clues to contradict the belief in powerful effects.

Selectivity plays a role first in answering the question of *who* is in the audience, and later becomes more central in the uses and gratifications tradition, which follows (at least logically) the early exposure tradition, but moves from seeing audiences as passive to acknowledging activity. Then the *why* question was introduced. Researchers set out to discover why people listen to classical music or quiz programmes. Their research was a major shift away from anonymity and demographics because it shows awareness of the relevance of people's roles and interests. Researchers also discovered that the most effective way of influencing selection was not by promotion on media but by talking to family, friends and colleagues. This was the basis for the discovery of the effect of interpersonal communication on decision-making and, with it, the realization that members within these networks act as 'opinion leaders' (Katz and Lazarsfeld, 1955).

The assumptions of the ubiquity, simultaneity and anonymity of audiences thus were dispelled with the discovery of selectivity and the salience of sub-groups such as family, friends or religious communities, all of which created barriers to protect audiences from strong effects. So much for mass society and isolated lonely audiences. It should be noted, however, that the rhetoric of protection from the effects of radio and television does not imply that a barrier is always a good thing. As proven by studies of the reception of anti-racist messages – such as the exposure to prejudiced characters in cartoons (Kendal and Wolf, 1949) and in television series (Vidmar and Rokeach, 1974) – barriers can also prevent people from accepting a more enlightened perception of social reality than the biased view they have contracted in their own social environment.

Methodologically, the empiricist positivistic approaches were motivated by the ambition to adopt the approaches that had proved successful in the natural sciences in measuring and predicting phenomena, and fitted with the researchers' aims in the study of campaigns, searching for direct links between exposure to a specific message and subsequent behaviour. Nevertheless, qualitative methods such as in-depth interviews and the writing of autobiographies were deployed from the outset. As early as 1933, sociologist Herbert Blumer asked people to write compositions on how films had influenced their lives. His work invoked a variety of insights into the subjects' perceptions of how viewing films had affected their moods and emotions, the meaning of love in their eyes, and much more. Although this study did not result in pointing to particular effects, it provided subtle insights, not dissimilar to the ones gleaned from observation in later periods in which the idea of popular culture as a 'tool kit,' that is, as a resource to draw on (Swidler, 1986), was introduced. Another example is Herta Herzog's (1941) seminal study of radio listeners of soap operas (probably designed as an exploratory study for generating hypotheses for a formal quantitative study), which consisted of in-depth interviews with housewives. 'On Borrowed Experience' led to rich insights concerning the housewives' motivations for listening ('supplying legitimacy for crying' was one), identification with the characters and the ideological implications of the narratives. Despite Herzog's image as the founding mother of gratifications research, she deserves to be considered the founder of the ethnography of reception.

Consumer: the active audience

The tradition of the active audience or the study of audience reception coincides with Ellis's second television phase of availability. He defined this phase as a 'diverse consumer's market, which accentuates and commodifies every available difference between citizens in the name of choice'. The 1980s introduced more television channels, less public broadcasting and more television sets in each house. Also influential is the *Zeitgeist* characterized by the flourishing of cultural studies, with its erasing of the hierarchical distinction between elite/quality culture and popular consumerist culture.

The study of audience activity, or involvement, or critical ability – all ways of describing the focus of communication research from the beginning of the 1980s – looked at the ways in which audiences 'read' or 'negotiate the meaning' of media texts. If the discovery of audiences' selectivity and sociability led to finding how audiences make use of texts according to the different roles they assume and the varying interests they have, now audience power was perceived by the capacity of decoders or 'readers' to interpret media texts from their own, potentially subversive, perspective.

Thus, the dominant paradigm has shifted from audiences as users of texts to the process of reception, based on the idea that viewers are capable of creating a plurality of meanings, and allowing for the possibility of oppositional, or subversive decodings. In this context, media texts are seen as triggers for conversation, as catalysts in the negotiation of identity and, ultimately, as the site of struggle over social and cultural issues. This struggle takes a new form for European audiences faced by ever-growing imports of popular American TV series, giving rise to a new kind of concern with effects, this time from the threat of 'cultural imperialism', and shifting the focus of studying audiences from questions of withstanding hegemony within the culture to questions of withstanding the smooth, plastic, readymade entertainment from the USA. Alarmed European scholars at the beginning of the 1980s organized emergency meetings under the slogan 'Europe fights back' (Liebes and Katz, 1992; Silj, 1988).

Ellis's implied audience of this period can be deduced from television's effort to supply 'specialized tastes or needs by a diversified marketing'. The widely varying interests of these consumers are now considered significant to individual 'multiple and shifting' identities, and self-fulfilment, establishing their styles from a vast range of possibilities. On its face, the emphasis on the opening up of choice, giving new legitimacy and status for individual lifestyles and shifting preferences, seems to be more connected with the implied choice of uses and gratifications rather than with multiple readings. But considering that negotiating the meanings of texts, within viewers' subcultures, is closely connected with the negotiation, sometimes the discovery of various aspects of identity – as a woman or a feminist or a member of a cultural diaspora – leads to the understanding that trying on identities via shared media texts is no less connected with Ellis's new style audiences. Multiple interpretations, made in different social contexts, are compatible with Ellis's (former?) citizens, who, by now, identify themselves 'with fragments of society', as male or female, young or old, gay or straight, belonging to a city, a region, an ethnic group or a religious or political organization, 'rather than with the increasing mythical mass'. They can find their own favourite text (and stay within a community of 'fans'), and/or negotiate with 'mainstream' texts from their own perspective (Gross, 1998). The latter has the additional advantage of remaining in dialogue with other groups.

Indeed, the diffuse array of studies of reception, rooted in different theoretical approaches at the beginning of the 1980s, focused on particular communities or sub-cultures. Janice Radway's romance readers belong to a 'fan' community of the popular feminine genre of the romance. Dave Morley's viewers of *Nationwide* news are part of a community of factory workers and Israeli fans of the American soap opera *Dallas* belong to various cultural groups (Jewish immigrants from Morocco and Russia, and Israeli Arabs). A closer look at three such studies shows they share basic assumptions and are interested in similar questions. All three were concerned with observing the process of reception in the social context in which it occurred, and assumed that meanings were made within relevant social networks. In Ellis's terms, these studies demonstrate that various genres address and activate particular aspects of audience identity, and that the legitimacy, at this phase, of addressing viewers as consumers with varying tastes, including genres heretofore considered unworthy, is shared by broadcasters and researchers.

Beyond Ellis, all three studies are concerned with the power to resist or oppose hegemonic meanings. The potential of subversive readings, and their political potential, becomes a major issue. For Radway's romance reader the daily hour with book in hand became (physically and symbolically) a 'room of her own' within patriarchy, marking a niche, or time slot, signalling the reader's time off as wife and mother. Radway says readers see textual meaning as reflecting their frustration with their lives and, more important, allowing for hope for change in the future, which is where the subversive potential comes in. Reading the romance is thus seen as a (pre-) feminist rebellion against the imposition of the roles of wife and mother in favour of lover, and the fulfilment of the need for nurturance (Chodorow, 1978). Liebes and Katz's *Dallas* viewers were found to commute between playing 'sophisticated' and 'naïve' readers (Eco, 1979), that is, between 'suspending disbelief' and acting as 'outsiders', or oppositional critics of the genre and the producers' ideology, capable of exposing textual manipulation ('they would like us to think that the rich are unhappy').

Does the shared interest in meaning from the readers' perspective suggest a convergence between the 'dominant' and 'critical' traditions? Some critical scholars say yes; the radicals say no. Morley (1997) sees a *rapprochement* of the critical to 'mainstream' scholars in the former 'offering counter evidence to a simple minded "dominant ideology" thesis' by observing or drawing out the ways in which audiences can resist the 'preferred' meanings of texts (Hall, 1985). For Radway, convergence between literary and media scholars occurred in the shift from the literary studies of eliciting implied ideal readers from texts to the acknowledgement of 'real' readers, and to the social uses of the act of reading. From the 'dominant' end, scholars of uses and gratifications reinstated the meaning of texts and decoding, which they had gradually abandoned in their elaborate mapping of the plurality of uses, and, methodologically, instead of asking closed questions (after the fact), which impose given categories of analysis, audience decodings were observed within the social context of reception.

Thus, in the eyes of scholars of reception, audiences have potential or realized critical abilities, and a plurality of ways of getting involved in texts, and of incorporating them into real life. The latest twist, in the present phase of plenty, has shifted from the ethnography of audiences to an ethnography of life in the home, in which interaction with various mass and individual media is looked at in the context of a host of social activities. This shift in focus means that contemporary media research looks at audiences as individual users of new media technologies, not as a community of decoders of shared texts (Livingstone, 2004).

Juggler: itinerant witness

The age of plenty provides endless options for activity, but raises the issue of how activity should be defined. According to Ellis, traditional broadcast television, now more than ever, connects viewers to the real world as 'actively passive' witnesses. With its capacity for liveness and intimacy, accompanied by direct address, and carrying a sense that others are watching at the same time, television, he argues, allows us 'to experience events at a distance', creating a situation of powerless complicity, in which 'we cannot say that we do not know'. However, we remain safe but helpless, 'able to over-look but under-act'.

Beyond the case of broadcast television, it may be argued that 'activity' is also problematic in the context of the new options of radically individual viewing, and in forms of interactions on the web. Being witness to a distant reality on television, choosing one's own fantasy, and interacting with others on the internet may all be seen as 'active passive'. In the case of powerless watching of the world outside, as in diving into an isolated bubble, not connected to any social context, and in virtual chatting on the internet (often identified as a possible indicator for the lack of ability for social interaction in reality), audiences lack any form of commitment (Pinchevski, 2003). If anything, choice only weakens commitment. Ang (1996) sees activity at the era of plenty as imposed on audiences by endless choice, 'sentencing' audiences to some form of action. However, there is nothing subversive about it.

Whereas the emphasis of research shifts from meaning and reception of specific texts to the juggling between competing channels and old and new communication media, it seems scholars are unsure how to proceed conceptually and methodologically. It is yet to be decided whether all or any of various uses of the internet can be entitled audiencing. There also is uncertainty about how to proceed methodologically. Livingstone (1998) professes having grave doubts about continuing to do ever 'thicker' descriptive ethnographies, tentatively suggesting comparative studies (which, of course, can be done only by more rigorous methods).

The image of the audience: critical recall

Critical historiography sees audience research as a story of progress, a kind of morality play, in which researchers (as well as 'their' audiences) advance from the ignorance and arrogance of the early traditions at the dark age of 'powerful effects', notorious for their image of passive audiences and omnipotent medium, to the phase of availability, marked by scholars' acknowledgement of viewers' activity and by the shift from effects and uses to oppositional readings and subversive involvement. Arrival at the present phase of plenty marks a new insecurity for scholars, who, guided by rightful humility and respect for audiences, are faced with the theoretical need to distinguish between television audiences and internet users, and the urgent methodological need to redefine the ethnographic turn, in an awkward situation in which discourse about the problems of ethnography continues side-by-side with the continuing carrying out of new ethnographic studies (Livingstone, 1998).

Looking backward, one way of considering (or, rather, discarding) the era of powerful effects turns out to be ignoring it altogether, and starting from reception studies as the beginning of 'audience research' (Alasuutari, 1999; Livingstone, 1998). Another is to provide what James Curran (1990) sees as 'a caricature' description of early research. Thus, critical accounts of the first 'lonely crowd' era of scholarship see it as dominated by the belief in a 'hypodermic needle' theory, an image that has become the symbol of the early scholars underestimating viewers.

Particularly scathing about what they see as the simplistic and paternalistic approach of early media researchers, coupled with their bias in favour of the broadcasting institutions in the service of which they worked, are Dave Morley and Ien Ang, authors of what are seen as the canonic texts of the second-phase media research (Livingstone, 1998). Their image of the first generation highlights the slogans of stimulus-response and hypodermic needle to illustrate the 'simplistic notion of direct effects' of radio and later television on helpless and passive viewers (Morley, 1991). Thus, in summarizing early research Morley argues: 'The whole tradition of effects studies, mobilizes a hypodermic model of media influence, in which the media are seen as having power to "inject" their audiences with particular messages which will cause them to behave in a particular way.'

The difference between perspectives from the right and the left, according to Morley, vary only by reasons: the former ascribe the audiences' passivity to the loss of 'traditional values' in mass society, and the latter to the inculcation of false consciousness, to ensure that viewers would 'remain politically quiescent'. Paradoxically, within this paradigm, says Morley, audiences are seen both as 'zombies' or 'glass eyed dupes' addicted to the media's junk food, and as prone to commit violence. More generally, early researchers are commonly accused of serving the establishment in managing audiences. Television, says Ang, is 'one of the most powerful media of modernity', and the dominant paradigm's 'neverending concern with "effects" and "uses" ' betrays implicit ideological connivance with the modernist framework, and the tendency 'to serve either the media industry, its clients, or the official guardians of society and public morality'. Specifically, Ang denounces early research for 'offering scientific knowledge about the audience' for the powers that be in order to figure out 'what could be done in order to "administer" the audience' for preserving social order. Ang's damning conclusion of the maltreatment of audiences by the dominant paradigm research is that it had caused the reification of viewers:

> as the invisible, silent, majorities of the suburban wasteland, subjected to the objectifying gaze of social sciences and authoritarian arbitrators of taste, morality and social order . . . The relative autonomy of the 'receiving end' outside and beyond the mass communication order was unthinkable; the audience was merely a function of the systemic design, and privatized reception completely subjected to the requirements of centralized transmission. This of course was the source of the image of the 'passive audience' (Ang, 1996: 47).

Ang dumps together effects and functions as part and parcel of the same approach, seeing 'uses' as ascribed by media messages. Other accounts regard the uses and gratifications tradition, which emerged with the discovery of selectivity in exposure, retention and memory, as a slightly more enlightened approach, indicating a shift of focus from the effect of media *on* audiences to their use *by* audiences (Morley, 1991). Ang, however, does not grant any points to the early scholarly concern with the various uses of media by audiences, answering a variety of needs for different groups. The introduction of 'use' as diametrically opposed to 'effects', as is often done, is mercilessly discarded, 'because they share the same functionalist framework'.

This tradition also is reproved by these accounts for 'its emphasis on individual psychological meanings rather than social and ideological ones' (Seiter *et al.*, 1991). And both traditions, the one known for 'hypodermic' effects and the other for individualistic gratifications, are severely criticized for assuming the possibility of conducting 'neutral' and 'objective' research, and for their use of quantitative methods accompanying this unsophisticated perspective. This 'positivist' and 'functionalist' scientific approach, Ang argues, makes it impossible to think 'what it means, in qualitative cultural terms, to be a television audience'. In a similar spirit, Seiter reprimands scholars who continue to do 'an enormous number of quantitative studies . . . insistent on proving the researcher's neutrality and objectivity' that 'have proven quite inadequate for the task of understanding television viewing'.

Thus, the first phase of communication research, including the discovery of selectivity and social networks, is not relevant for the critical recall of audience research. For the radical critics, history starts with reception studies, or audience ethnography, which is thought to have adjusted the balance between television and viewer (Livingstone, in press). Scholars who have been part of this new turn regard it in retrospect as 'the period in which empirical audience research has become prominent in media studies', audiences were saved 'from their mute status as "cultural dopes"' (Brundson, 1991), and they gained recognition 'as active meaning makers' (Ang, 1996).

Does critical historiography consider the shared interest in audience reception at the beginning of the 1980s as providing common ground for researchers from various theoretical and methodological perspectives? Do they see this phase as some form of convergence between mainstream and critical scholars? Here, the critical narrative is more tentative than in the case of the total rejection of the effects tradition, perhaps because, unlike the earlier phase, the historians of the 1980s were in it themselves. Some, implicitly or explicitly, lean towards seeing reception as convergence, shared by similar concerns and insights; for the radicals, convergence is not an option.

On the conciliatory side, a corpus of studies, published at the beginning of the 1980s, such as Morley's (1980) news viewers, Radway's (1984) romance readers, Ang's and my own work, with Elihu Katz (Liebes and Katz, 1992), of *Dallas* viewers (the first three marked by Livingstone as the canon of reception studies), are seen as sharing the premises that characterize the period at the outset, and influence later studies. All share the assumptions that the audience is always active and that the content is always open to various interpretations. The soft belly of convergence, unsurprisingly, is the methodological issue that draws the fire of anti-convergence critics (Liebes, 1989). As the research questions moved away from effects to decodings, and, possibly, empowerment, new methodologies had to be enlisted to catch a glimpse of the process, *in situ*, by the least obtrusive means. This caused a methodological shift away from macro studies of political economy (for the neo-Marxists), and away from textual analysis (for the literary scholars), and from formal positivistic methods (for mainstream scholars) towards adopting ethnographic and quasi-ethnographic approaches. Those new approaches brought with them a host of new questions. Is activity an artefact of the method? How unique and/or generalizable is any particular setting? How can the interference of the researcher's presence with the 'normal' context of audiencehood be minimized? Moreover, the theoretical issue of the relationship between these micro-narratives and the macro-political or cultural frame remained unsolved.

The most determined voice of the objectors to convergence is that of Ien Ang (1996) who remains suspicious of liberal audience research, charging it with having a 'hidden agenda' of 'political, commercial usefulness', and with 'objectifying' audiences. Words such as 'scientific enterprise', 'findings', 'generalizations', 'empirical' and 'systematic', Ang warns us, signal danger. Her main arguments for continuing the war over the living room are: (1) mainstream researchers are not aware of the power relations underlying the interaction between scholars and audiences; (2) liberal pluralists see individuals as free and uninhibited by external power whereas critical scholars see the 'negotiation' as over-determined by the concrete conditions of audiences, forcing them to conceive of the 'conjectural determination of audiencehood', and (3) from the perspective of critical scholars, the aim of liberal researchers to achieve a generalizable map of all the dimensions of audience activity is both undoable and misses the point of standing by audiences.

Critical historiography, revisited

Critical historiography may be questioned on a number of accounts. First, labelling the early research as 'effects tradition' and the reception phase as 'audience research' ignores the fact that the communication process includes both. Effect needs a message and subjects, and effectiveness can be established only by testing it on the audiences (of groups or individuals) targeted. Whether effect ends up on top and audience underneath or the other way around, all research traditions engaged in studying mass media are concerned with studying the effect of messages/texts on audiences. (There are, of course, researchers such as Modleski, 1984, or Ang, 1985, or even Radway, 1984, who basically derive effects by studying 'implied viewers', as will be discussed later.) Second, the title of 'effects tradition' invokes the image of 'audiences' as disembodied numbers measured by exposure to be studied by abstracted empiricism. But as it turns out, these disembodied audiences managed to make their mark at the outset, turning the tradition of powerful effects into a tradition of limited effects.

Third, as Geertz (among others) reminds us, any human actions and perceptions should be studied and understood within their social and historical contexts. Reading through some of the original research suggests the theory of powerful effects and the concern about propaganda and mass persuasion was derived from the mass society model, dominant in the political climate between the two world wars, according to which uprooted and alienated individuals in modern society, unable to cope with their freedom, were seen as easy prey for rabble-rousers or fascist leaders. Radio, used by Hitler and Stalin to mobilize the support of the masses, had demonstrated it was all-powerful. Never before in history could one voice talk to everybody at the same time. At the receiving end there was a newly emancipated society, at the end of the period of mass immigration, in which people, confronted with choice that they did not know how to handle, were seen as particularly vulnerable.

Fourth, the way by which critical theories draw a one-dimensional picture of the early research as a simplistic belief in powerful effects, or ignore its contribution to the understanding of audiences altogether, underestimates the process by which the theory of powerful effects led to audience studies intended to see if audiences could be controlled remotely. In his effort to reinstate the importance of the first generation 'tradition of effects studies', James Curran (1990) reminds us that 'far from having been "dominated" by the hypodermic model . . . its main thrust ever since the 1940s was to assert the independence and autonomy of media audiences, and dispel the widespread notion that people are easily influenced by the media'. Moreover, the effects research was the first to develop the same insights that reception studies claim to have invented, arguing, 'the predispositions that people bring to texts crucially influence their understanding of these texts'. Any casual look at the effects studies shows that by no stretch of the imagination could they be filed under 'hypodermic needle' studies.

In the accounts of critical theory, the discovery of audience 'activity' belongs exclusively to the 'receptionists' generation. It can be argued that this title belongs to the earlier school of uses and gratifications, that it had discovered the mechanism of selectivity (in exposure, recall and interpretation), which serves as defence against effects. This ancestry is belittled, however, and the activity it allocated to audiences is sometimes seen as 'pseudo activity', thus ensuring the exclusivity of reception theorists as pioneers of audience empowerment.

Ang's rhetorically brilliant discourse in which she divides the world between scholars who are 'for' and 'against' audiences raises some serious questions. Her attack on liberal methodology is more convincing than her guidance as to how research *should* be done. The warning against seeing audiences as 'uninhibited by external power', the pronouncement of audience talk as 'over-determined' by external conditions, and the instruction to critical scholars to use 'conjecture' in their interpretations, is too close to suggesting that audience talk should not be taken seriously, thereby handing over power to the researchers. There is something disquieting in condemning researchers who treat audiences' words seriously as 'objectifying' them, and in instructing scholars seen as 'on the side of audiences' to make their own inferences, in the name of viewers. Paradoxically, respect for audiences means that researchers should not take seriously what they say.

Although Ang is a staunch advocate of ethnography as a methodology, and she instructs scholars to thoroughly immerse themselves in ever 'thicker' specific contexts, her own convincing insights into the melodramatic identification in describing viewers' involvement in soaps (Ang, 1985, 1996) emerge out of the text alone. A number of 'thin' quotations from viewers' letters (which on their own do not reverberate with the meanings that Ang assigns to them) serve to illustrate her in-depth analysis. If there is conjecture here, it is building a house on sand. Textual analysis, or rather, one based on one's own experience as viewer, provides the more solid basis. This also is not surprising when considering that important insights into human emotions are inspired by purely theoretical, literary or dramatic texts. In other words, it is legitimate to argue that implied viewers are sufficient for extracting convincing interpretations about involvement. Ironically, then, when it comes to it, real audiences are superfluous. The 'thickest' ethnography does not guarantee any such brilliant insights. Can we tell if these insights are true? We can only judge if they have the power to convince us as readers.

Next, there is the meaning of 'activity'. Studies by Ang (1996) and Radway (1984) focus on deriving oppositional readings from involvement. Other studies (such as those by Morley, Livingstone, and Liebes and Katz) are more directly concerned also with critical ability. Radway, like Herta Herzog (1941) before her, psychoanalyses her romance readers by reading their interpretations as clues to their unhappiness. Accordingly, she concludes that once romance readers come to understand that is it their domestic unhappiness and the false hope promised by the romance that motivates their pleasure, they would be set free. In other words, the potential for activity lies in eventually seeing the light – that is, acquiring feminist consciousness. Both Ang's and Radway's audiences experienced vicarious, temporary liberation from a harsh reality by identifying with the heroines of fiction, which was not that different from Herzog's soap opera audiences (Liebes, 2002). Although Herzog belongs to the 'strong effects' generation and is labelled as a pioneer in the gratifications tradition, while Ang and Radway are critical scholars, the three have a lot in common. They endow feminine genres with status, listen to the talk of audience members, and psychoanalyse women's subconscious. Moreover, careful reading indicates that Radway and Ang, declared champions of ethnography, rely more heavily on the text for analysing audiences than does Herzog.

Is there a future for audiences?

The present phase of the 'wandering juggler' is one in which the term 'audience' itself has collapsed into 'a provisional shorthand for the infinite, contradictory, dispersed and dynamic practices' (Livingstone, 2004), and the forecast for its future is unclear. Two questions that have yet to be answered relate to theory (Can we continue talking about audiences?) and to methodology (What is the right way to do audiences research?).

Methodologically, as Livingstone (1998) details, we seem to have reached a dead end. The politically correct way at this point, inspired by postmodernism and cultural studies, is to do ethnography. By now it is no more the ethnography of audiences but that of the lifeworld as reflected in the household, with the implication that the legitimacy of studying the interaction between media and audiences (that is, identifying oneself as a media scholar) is put into question. Researchers are summoned to become anthropologists, or, in broader terms, sociologists. Thus, the real danger may be the disappearance of communication researchers rather than the audience.

But whether or not the field survives, audience research is at this methodological dead end, Livingstone argues. First, there is the technical and perhaps insurmountable problem posed by current anthropology's demand that observations be unobtrusive and context-bound, leading to thick descriptions, with purist critical researchers warning against falling into the trap of generalization. Is it heresy to suggest that this model is technically unrealistic? Can research be conducted unobtrusively while peeping over the shoulder of a teenager who insists he or she is not performing for the researcher? And how does the distortion of the picture by the researchers' presence in the subjects' homes compare with the distortion of anonymous answers to questionnaires into which certain parameters of context are introduced? Even if a researcher manages to be a fly on the wall, Livingstone questions the significance of what is seen. Is it idiosyncratic or generalizable into something that holds for most contemporary audiences? Ang confesses that radical contextualism is not interested in building a theory of the audience but in telling stories to illustrate 'positioned truths', or stories that reinforce the researcher's ideological commitment. The weakness of this kind of research lies in the danger that it reifies the researcher's perception and blocks new discoveries – for example, in the way that the effects tradition was surprised by selectivity.

This does not mean that media ethnographers should be converted into positivist researchers. Yet raising anti-canonic questions is essential to remembering that the latest fashion in audience research has entrenched itself within ever-stricter limitations. Geerz, whose 'thick description' was once a cornerstone in the new approach, had no fear of analysing case studies in order to extract insights into the way in which the culture works as a whole.

While the methodology of audience research may be in deep trouble, there is enough evidence to believe in the future of audiencehood. Looking back, it seems that the concept of choice was central to the debate over activity all along. In the first phase of citizen and lonely crowd, choice was facilitated by selectivity, which, in the age of scarcity meant choosing *whether* to be exposed to certain messages, *how* to look at what one is seeing (recall the contradictory views of football fans cited earlier), *what* to remember, and *how* to interpret. Thus, choice, in the form of selectivity, could be exercised even when the offering was limited. In the phase of consumer, television began offering a multiplicity of choice defined in terms of texts and genres for fans and for cultural groups. Addressing women, young people, or cultural diasporas, these texts infiltrated into group culture through conversation, contributing to the debate over identities (Liebes and Katz, 1992). And by listening to audiences, researchers could understand how texts infiltrate into the lives of viewers.

The monstrous dimensions of choice in the present phase are leading in two opposite directions. As indicated by Ellis, jugglers can choose between retreating to any obscure, esoteric, isolating niche, or joining the lonely crowd as citizen and/or consumer by turning to broadcast television. In the era of the lonely juggler, says Ang (1996), activity, dictated by time shortage and the enormity of choice, produces fickle, recalcitrant and unpredictable audiencehood, and although activity cannot be fully controlled, it has lost the subversive potential of the consumer phase. The juggler's isolation, with the virtual contacts introduced by bedroom TV sets, the internet (and cellular phones) separating parents and children, and wives and husbands, erased the earlier effect of television bringing families closer together in the home (Meyrowitz, 1985). In addition, the choice in the ever-expanding multiplication of technologies, feeding on one another, acting as unstoppable golem, results in endowing users with maximal control, but at the same time undermining the pleasure of viewing. Facing a multitude of choice, and fully aware that viewing anything means missing everything else, users are pushed to a nervous form of sound-bite-style sampling rather than getting involved in one continuing text – television's socialization for immediate gratifications gone crazy. In this choice-governed environment, good old broadcast television still provides some solace in its capacity to rally the family to view old or new favourites, or live (ceremonial or disastrous) events, and by connecting individuals with the reality outside and with sometimes interactive entertainment.

In addition to isolating users, the internet's 'one to one' ability to immediately supply choice-obsessed customers with a chosen content also undermines a major aspect of the pleasure of TV viewing, namely the element of suspense. Whereas texts such as quiz or game shows, in which the script allocates viewers with a role, is interactive by the genre's definition, hijacking the text by using the remote control (to zap among programmes, or watch two or more narratives intermittently), or by downloading a favourite text or genre, skipping forward and backward, or zooming to the episode's end to discover the villain's identity, undermines our experience as bona fide 'naïve' viewers. Taking charge does not allow for the pleasure of being led through, of being surprised, of getting lost in the story – all of which depend on letting go of the wheel. In other words, while the text produced by downloading or time-shift recording is the result of each viewer's actions, watching television consists of what is happening outside of the viewer's control. Television may provide a surprise, a text or a genre previously unknown to the viewer, and therefore something he or she could not seek. Control over the medium only weakens the involvement with the text. In comparing how viewers engage with film versus television, Beverley Houston (1985) argued that the technology of the remote control, seen then as empowering viewers, only contributes to their frustration. Putting the viewer in the cockpit, with the freedom to skip among various alternatives so as not to miss anything, turns viewers into 'tourists', not 'citizens' (Booth, 1982). Constantly haunted by the sense of missed opportunities, zappers skip from one territory to another, never remaining long enough to settle or to suspend disbelief. A text that loses its capacity to surprise loses its grip over the spectator. Thus, interacting with the medium may interfere with our interaction with the text. At the end of the day (every day), broadcast television still offers some solace from the traps of lonely, relentless choice by connecting families or individuals with real or imagined, beautiful or terrible, dramas, or real dramas such as 9/11 (Blondheim and Liebes, 2002). When the hype around the non-stop invention of new choice technologies calms down, relief in escaping from the freedom of lonely juggling may ensure the continuation of broadcast television and of unchanged, sometimes inactive, audiences, the way they were.

References

Alasuutari, P. (1999) *Rethinking the Media Audience*. London: Sage.

Ang, I. (1985) *Watching Dallas*. London and New York: Methuen.

————(1996) *Living Room Wars: Rethinking Media Audiences for a Postmodern World*. London and New York: Routledge.

Blondheim, M. and Liebes, T. (2002) 'Live Television's Disaster Marathon of September 11 and Its Subversive Potential', *Prometheus*, 20 (3).

Booth, W. (1982) 'The Company We Keep', *Daedelus*, 111 (4), 33–59.

Brundson, C. (1981) 'Pedagogies of the Feminine: Feminist Teaching and Women's Genres', *Screen*, 32 (4), 364–81.

Cantril, H. (1954) 'The Invasion from Mars', in W. Schramm (ed.), *The Processes and Effects of Mass Communication*. Urbana: University of Illinois Press.

Chodorow, N. (1978) *The Reproduction of Mothering: Psychoanalysis and the Sociology of Gender*. Berkeley: University of California Press.

Curran, J. (1990) 'The New Revisionism in Mass Communication Research: A Reappraisal', *European Journal of Communication*, 5, 2–3.

Dayan, D. (2001) 'The Peculiar Public of Television', *Media, Culture and Society*, 23, 743–65.

Eco, U. (1979) *The Role of the Reader: Explorations in the Semiotics of Texts*. Bloomington: Indiana University Press.

Ellis, J. (2000) *Seeing Things: Television in the Age of Uncertainty*. London and New York: I.B.Tauris.

Freidson, E. (1954) 'Communication Research and the Concept of the Mass', in W. Schramm (ed.), *The Processes and Effects of Mass Communication*. Urbana: University of Illinois Press.

Gross, L. (1988) 'Minorities, Majorities and the Media', in T. Liebes and J. Curran (eds), *Media, Ritual and Identity*. London and New York: Routledge.

Hall, S. (1985) 'Encoding and Decoding', in S. Hall *et al.* (eds), *Culture, Media, Language*. London: Hutchinson, pp. 128–38.

Herzog, H. (1941) 'On Borrowed Experience: An Analysis of Listening to Daytime Sketches', *Studies in Philosophy and Social Science*, 9 (1), 65–95.

Houston, B. (1985) 'Viewing Television: The Metapsychology of Endless Consumption', *Quarterly Review of Film Studies*, 9, 183–95.

Katz, E. and Lazarsfeld, P. (1955) *Personal Influence*. New York: Free Press.

Kendal, P. and Wolf, K. (1949) 'The Analysis of Deviant Case Studies in Communication Research', in P. Lazarsfeld and F. Stanton (eds), *Communication Research 1948–1949*. New York: Harper.

Lazarsfeld, P. and Merton, R. K. (1948) 'Mass Communication, Popular Taste and Organized Social Action', in L. Bryson (ed.), *The Communication of Ideas*. New York: Harper, pp. 93–125.

Lazarsfeld, P., Berelson, B. and Gaudet, H. (1944) *The People's Choice*. New York: Columbia University.

Liebes, T. (1989) 'On the Convergence of Theories of Mass Communication and Literature Regarding the Role of the "Reader"', in B. Dervin and J. M. Voigt (eds), *Progress in Communication Sciences*. New Jersey: Ablex.

————(2002) 'Herzog's "On Borrowed Experience": Its Place in the Debate Over "Active"/"Regressive" Consumers', in E. Katz *et al.* (eds), *Are There Any? Should There Be? How About These? Canonic Texts in Media Research*. Cambridge: Polity.

Liebes, T. and Katz, E. (1992) *The Export of Meaning: Cross Cultural Readings of Dallas*. Cambridge: Polity.

Livingstone, S. (1998) 'Relations Between Media and Audiences: Prospects for the Future', in T. Liebes and J. Curran (eds), *Media, Culture, Identity*. London: Routledge.

Livingstone, S. (2004) 'The Challenge of Changing Audiences: Or, What is the Audience Researcher to do in the Age of the Internet?', *The European Journal of Communication*. March.

———(in press) 'The Changing Nature of Audiences: From the Mass Audience to the Interactive Media ﬂﬂﬂ, ﬂﬂ ﬂ ﬂﬂﬂﬂﬂ ﬂﬂ ﬂ, ﬂﬂﬂﬂﬂﬂﬂ ﬂﬂﬂﬂﬂﬂﬂ ﬂﬂ ﬂﬂﬂﬂﬂ ﬂﬂﬂﬂﬂ ﬂ ﬂﬂﬂﬂ ﬂﬂﬂﬂﬂﬂﬂ

Meyrowitz, J. (1985) *No Sense of Place*. New York: Oxford University Press.

Modleski, T. (1984) *Loving with a Vengeance: Mass Produced Fantasies for Women*. London and New York: Methuen.

Morley, D. (1980) *The Nationwide Audience*. London: British Film Institute.

———(1991) 'Changing Paradigms in Audiences Studies', in E. Seiter *et al.* (eds), *Remote Control*. London: Routledge.

———(1997) 'Theoretical Orthodoxies: Textualism, Constructivism and the "New Ethnography" in Cultural Studies', in M. Ferguson and P. Golding (eds), *Cultural Studies in Question*. London: Sage.

Pinchevski, A. (2003) 'Ethics on the Line', *The Southern Communication Journal*, 68 (2), 152–66.

Radway, J. (1984) *Reading the Romance*. Chapel Hill, NC: University of North Carolina Press.

Scannell, P. and Cardiff, D. (1991) *A Social History of British Broadcasting 1922–1939*. Oxford: Blackwell.

Seiter, E., Borchers, H., Kreutzner, G. and Warth, E-M. (1991) Introduction in Ellen Seiter *et al.* (eds), *Remote Control*. London: Routledge.

Silj, A. (1988) *A Est di Dallas: Telefilm Usa ed Europei a Confronto*. Rome: Rai, Vpt.

Swidler, A. (1986) 'Culture in Action', *American Sociological Review*, 51, 273–86.

Vidmar, N. and Rokeach, M. (1974) 'Archie Bunker's Bigotry: A Study of Selective Perception and Exposure', *Journal of Communication*, 24 (2), 240–50.

chapter twenty

Political Communication in a Changing World

PETER DAHLGREN AND MICHAEL GUREVITCH

1. Introduction

We start by stating the obvious: political communication as a system and as processes never takes place in a vacuum: it is always shaped by a variety of contextual, historical factors. Political communication as an academic sub-field emerged several decades ago, and it was shaped in part by what the system and processes of politically relevant communication looked like at the time. It was also formed by the prevailing theoretical traditions and research trajectories. Much has changed since then – both within the system and processes of communication, as well as what can be deemed relevant academic horizons. In this chapter our aim is sketch an overview of some of the key changes that have taken place within political communication as it is manifested in Western democratic societies. We will also probe some contemporary theoretical horizons that we feel can be mobilized to enhance the study of political communication.

In Section 2 we offer an overview of some of the key transformations in the realm of power and politics in Western democracies; these changes alter the premises for democracy, as well as the conditions for political communication. Among the themes we address here are the changes in the formal structures of political systems; the democratic engagement of citizens, as well as cultural changes. Many of these developments point to a destabilization of political communication.

In Section 3 we take up more specific changes as reflected in the institutions and actors that shape political communication in the West. Here we look in particular at how journalism is evolving and the impact of new kinds of actors in the field of political communication.

Section 4 focuses on a major technological development that is dramatically reconfiguring political communication, namely the emergence of the internet. There has been a good deal of debate around this theme, which we summarize. Moreover, it is not least via the internet that the need to rethink traditional political communication becomes apparent. The changes taking place to some extent render the established horizons of political communication analysis inadequate. Contemporary developments force us to reflect on such basic themes as the nature of politics, the relationship between formal and informal politics, the interface between the political, the personal and the cultural, as well as alternative modes of citizenship, democratic organization and the strategies of communication.

The final section strives to stake out some new analytic terrain within the study of political communication. Basically, if political communication has largely taken a systems perspective as its analytic point of departure, we propose to complement this with a perspective that underscores agency, that puts the citizen as a social actor in the centre. To this end, we cull a number of useful concepts from contemporary cultural theory; these help us develop a view of citizenship as agency, as well as an analytic framework that illuminates the preconditions for such action. We call this framework civic culture. This framework is not intended to replace traditional political communication and its system perspective, but rather to merge with it to offer a better understanding of political communication from the standpoint of citizens' everyday lives.

2. Politics and power

Models of democracy

If we begin with the perspective of political systems, we need to keep in mind that the overarching concept of 'Western democracy' can refer to societies that actually have rather different political traditions and cultures. Hallin and Mancini (2004), for example, distinguish between what they see as three loose models or ideal types among actually existing democracies, where not least the character of the political communication systems vary. In what they call the Mediterranean or polarized pluralist model (exemplified by Italy, Spain, Portugal and Greece), capitalism, industrialization and political democracy developed later, with the absolutist state, the Church, and the landed aristocracy playing important roles into the twentieth century. In the north/central European or democratic corporatist model (the Benelux countries, Germany, Austria, Switzerland and Scandinavia) these power centres of the *ancien régime* had become weaker, and we find a tradition of power-sharing and a culture of compromise, along with the emergence of a welfare state during the twentieth century (with Germany and Austria picking up on this development in the post-war years). In the North Atlantic or liberal model (the USA, the UK, Ireland and Canada) we find democracies and media systems that to varying degrees manifest the traditions of classical liberalism – and not least are often cited as normative examples.

These ideal types are of course approximate; other countries could be added to exemplify each model, and some nations sit uneasily within the scheme: France can only be slotted into the Mediterranean model to a certain degree, and the phrase 'Anglo-American' deflects some very important differences between the UK and the USA. The reason for briefly mentioning these distinctions is to underscore the point that there is not one unified model of democracy – we find several versions – and that variations in systems of political communication must be understood to a large degree in relation to the historical patterns of social and political evolution. The trends we mention below are – to various degrees – common to all versions of democratic systems.

Politics, power and participation in late modern democracies

We note first, at an overarching level, that the past two decades or so have witnessed an *increase in the power of market forces* – on a global scale – in shaping societal development (see Hertz, 2001, for one of many accessible introductions to this theme). While the relationships between capitalism and democracy have always been complex and variable, we suggest that this contemporary trend arguably diminishes the terrain and efficacy of formal political systems. Globally, we see a paradox: on the one hand, there is a rising demand for formal democracy in societies where this tradition has been weak or absent. On the other hand, the logic of market mechanisms tends to subordinate most other considerations and value schemes. One of the consequences of this development is that market forces increasingly compete with, and possibly also sap the vitality of formal political systems of Western nations, by rendering them more reactive than proactive. The margins of governmental manoeuvrability – the policy options available – become narrower. At the same time, *ideological differences between parties have become less pronounced*. Political parties have become more *voter-oriented* rather than *member-oriented*. Citizens' identification with specific parties has become looser, and market forces have been given greater free reign in shaping societal development. In somewhat simplified terms, for many people the political system appears increasingly stagnant, reactive rather than proactive. The driving power behind these developments appears to lie more with the economy and technology than with ideology.

Among citizens, the arena of official politics does not command the degree of support and participation it had in the past. Voter turnouts are decreasing; party loyalty is in decline, especially among the young. One sees signs of a growing contempt for the political class. Ideological visions seem to be on the decline, and a corrosive climate of cynicism is emerging in some places. Of course, there *are* notable exceptions to these trends, as illustrated, for example, in the presidential campaign of 2004 in the USA. Election campaigns typically tend to raise the political temperature and to invigorate otherwise semi-dormant political sentiments among citizens. But even so, the climate of increased fears about security in the USA – both national and individual – as well as pervasive economic uncertainties resulted in heightened political passions and consequent political polarization of the citizenry.

We should keep in mind, however, that we are talking about *trends and not detailed realities*, and that these trends vary in strength between countries. Yet there is nothing to suggest that these trends will be reversed, and they may even intensify. In regard to political disengagement, we can look at this from several interrelated standpoints: attitudes towards politics; the political system itself; and larger changes in the cultural frameworks of society. At the attitudinal level, we can distinguish three dimensions. *Distrust* signals a critical distancing, an active dimension of disengagement that rests on a clear negative evaluation of the political system or at least the alternatives that it offers. *Ambivalence* suggests some degree of involvement, but the motivation for participation and voting is simply not strong enough to overcome the inertia of non-involvement. Alternatively, when a strong motivation exists, it is mitigated by a sense that the efforts required for engagement are simply too great. Here we may also conceptually include an uncertainty about which party to vote for, with non-voting the easiest resolution to the dilemma. *Indifference* is of another order. It implies a disinterest in the formal political system altogether, an 'alienation' that can psychologically place 'politics' as an activity on par with, say, 'sports', 'music' or other forms of free time activity, and in the comparison, politics is perceived as the least interesting.

Evidence suggests that among the politically disengaged, distrust, while certainly present, is not the dominant sentiment. Likewise ambivalence, while operative, does not appear to be the major factor. Rather, indifference seems to be the psychological condition that best describes most of those who are disengaged and manifest a deep sense of the irrelevance of democratic procedures. We will return to this perspective on civic agency later in this discussion.

The ostensible political apathy and disaffiliation from the established political system visible within many democracies may not necessarily signal a disinterest in politics *per se*. Instead, many observers suggest that this may in fact represent *a refocusing of political engagement outside the parliamentary system*, or even embody new definitions as to just what constitutes the political. In this emerging mode of 'new politics', the boundaries between politics, cultural values, identity processes and individual self-reliance measures become more fluid (Bennett, 2003a, 2003b, develops this theme further). 'New politics' is characterized by personalized rather than collective engagement, and a stronger emphasis on single issues than on overarching platforms or ideologies. We also see frames of reference and engagement beyond the borders of the nation-state, as evidenced by, for example, transnational social movements, such as the alter-globalization movement, and diasporic communities. These developments, while still evolving, suggest the need for new ways to think about the contemporary political landscape.

Cultural changes

Cultural changes have also played an important role in fostering political disengagement. It is not easy to identify these changes as directly linked to political disengagement. Rather, these trends appear to coexist with tendencies towards political disengagement. (A modern classic on the theme of disengagement from civil and political life is found in Putnam, 2000.) Three intertwined trends may be identified here.

First, increasing *fragmentation* of a shared common culture is evident. Societies are becoming more pluralistic and differentiated along several lines: class, ethnicity, patterns of media consumption, cultural interests, life styles, etc. Shared political horizons are not easily integrated into people's everyday lives when such socio-cultural heterogeneity increases.

Second, *consumerism* has become all-pervasive. This is not limited to the consumption of goods and services, nor even to the many symbolic dimensions attached to it (e.g. social status). Consumerism is also a way of life that suggests that life strategies, large and small, are for the most part individual rather than collective. Moreover, consumerism is characterized by enormous differences in purchasing power, which stands in contrast to the universalistic ideals of democratic citizenship. The bases for collective political activity thus become weaker. The position created for the citizen within the logic of political discourse becomes all the more that of a consumer. Political ideas are to be 'bought', and politics itself increasingly manifests attributes of market logic (Kantola, 2003).

Third, *individualism* can be seen in part as an outcome of the above. Individual autonomy, lack of enthusiasm for authority figures, a disinclination to become a part of large organizations or entities where one sees little chance of influencing their direction, are all growing tendencies that make the task of traditional political parties more difficult. Political participation in the form of voting can be understood as a perceived normative duty as well as an expressive act. Both the norm and the need to express oneself in the context of large institutions such as political voting seem to be on the decline in the context of the developments we have referred to. Instead, social horizons tend to emphasize personal life and the graspable local milieu. Consequently the involvement with abstract 'isms' declines.

In a related mode, we observe processes of the *erosion of traditional institutions* that have taken place over a period of several decades. Observers have noted a general loosening of the impact that traditional institutions have on individuals: the family, school, church, neighbourhood and even political parties can no longer take for granted the authority and role in socialization that they have held in the past. While we should be careful not to exaggerate this argument, it appears that this major trend in late modernity is of considerable significance for democracy and political communication. The modern citizen is not only characterized by a stronger degree of individualism, but he/she is socialized by institutions whose impact has become more muted in recent decades. As the older horizons decline in significance, this creates new challenges in how to politically address or appeal to the citizenry.

Destabilized political communication

Blumler and Gurevitch (2000) also underscore another important development, namely that *the geography of political communication is in flux*, as the significance of traditional national borders becomes weakened. This should by no means be taken as a premature obituary for the nation-state, even if that entity is playing a relatively less commanding role in the wake of contemporary processes of globalization. The authors instead argue that politics in the globalized world, and the communication processes that transmit them, are less likely today to be confined by national borders. Political issues increasingly take on a transnational character (e.g. the recent war in Iraq), and global media in turn can impact on the political agenda of specific nation-states. Moreover, looking at the extra-parliamentarian arena, many of the actors – social movements, non-governmental organizations (NGOs), activist groups, etc. – work explicitly in transnational contexts.

The consequences of all these transformations in power and politics run deep, raising concerns about the integrity of the political communication system. Destabilization encompasses several, at times oppositional tendencies. On the negative side we might expect inefficiency, unpredictability and a decline in the truthfulness and explanatory mission of political communication. Also, the centripetal forces of private capital are coalescing under the prevailing neo-liberal order, drawing power away from the formal political arena and thereby constricting and weakening democracy. On the positive side, we would place such trends as the increase in the range and diversity of political voices as well as new modes of political engagement and definitions of what constitutes politics. Furthermore, cultural heterogeneity may suggest dispersions and openings that can be developed for democratic gains. Destabilization can thus extend the reach of political communication through civic communication, as well as through horizontal communication between citizens. Yet, again, it must be acknowledged that from a systems perspective, too much dispersion and multi-vocality undercut political effectiveness and hamper governance.

The flux that we can observe in the overarching domain of power and politics impacts on – and is also an expression of – the changes taking place with political communication. The next section continues the discussion by looking at the major contemporary trends that are manifested specifically within political communication.

3. Evolving patterns of political communication

Journalism remains the primary form of political communication, but it is undergoing transformation as the conditions of the media evolve. Thus, for example, journalism is increasingly losing its privileged status as an institution whose purpose is to serve – and help define – the common good (see, for example, Allan, 2004, and Campbell, 2004). In the context of commercial logic the media are merely one commodity among others. Media organizations generally are not prioritizing news departments with their investments, and news organizations often face difficult financial times. However, there are also some particular developments at work within journalism that we should note. We must keep in mind that the various tendencies do not all point in the same direction: they are in some cases quite contradictory, and the overall drift in political communication needs to be understood in terms of sets of deep tensions (see, for example, Bennett and Entman, 2001).

First, *proliferation*: the sheer amount and density of journalism and other information outlets available to citizens is increasing. The flow and availability of information is so ubiquitous, so crowded, that the competition for attention is becoming an ever-important feature of public culture. At the same time, the vast majority of media output is not journalistic in nature, and the competition for attention must also be understood as one between journalism and non-journalism. Among the oceans of information flowing through the traditional media, only a small portion can be deemed journalism and the attention it gets may be even disproportionately smaller.

Second, *journalism is becoming more heterogeneous* – with varying standards and sets of news values – and is aiming at ever-smaller target audiences. There is a wide range in quality: today audiences can find both outstanding manifestations of quality journalism as well as rock-bottom currents. The heterogeneity is manifested not least in the proliferation of various forms of journalism on the internet (see below).

Another important feature, which in a sense is somewhat paradoxical in relation to the above points, is that *the audiences for traditional news media outlets and traditional journalistic formats are declining*. This is most noticeable in the newspaper industry: the national press in many democracies have seen their markets contract in the past decades. In broadcasting, economic pressures have resulted in less serious traditional news as well as a *decline in diversity* of points of view expressed (Campbell, 2004), deriving from both programming patterns and genres, as well as ownership patterns within broadcasting industries.

At the same time, *the distinctions between journalism and non-journalism (popular culture) are becoming blurred*; the hybrid genre of 'infotainment' (e.g. talk shows and docu-dramas) is pervasive, along with a trend towards the popularization of journalism. The shift away from an 'elite' press toward audio-visual formats in much public culture can also be understood as an expression of popularization.

Popularization can be and often is a positive development when it makes the public sphere available to larger numbers of people via more accessible formats and styles of presentation. Alternatively it takes up topics and experiences from the realm of private experience and introduces them as important and contestable topics within the public sphere.

All too often, however, popularization reflects commodification, and in practice means sensationalism, scandal, personification and excessive dramatization, *derailing civic-oriented news values*. Such trends are at the heart of much of the controversy within journalism today, and they have evoked vehement critique not least from journalists committed to journalistic ideals and values. The increasing influence of powerful market forces results in increasing marginalization of normative considerations, i.e. journalistic values that do not enhance short-term profits (cf. Baker, 2002).

Online journalism ranges from major news organizations that have gone online, such as newspapers and CNN, to net-based news organizations (usually without much or any own original reporting, such as Yahoo! News), to alternative news organizations such as Indymedia and Mediachannel, as well as one-person weblog sites (known as 'bloggers'). The growth of journalism on the net manifests also the many forms that contemporary journalism can take. For example, in the case of bloggers, raising questions about the definitions and the boundaries (if any) between journalism from non-journalism, this genre contributes individual perspectives and eyewitness testimony, and also sidesteps editorial filtering. Yet, with the 'blogosphere' becoming so extensive, certainly much of what we find there is of questionable quality in terms of political communication. Moreover, seen from the perspective of what we might call communicative logistics, the vitality to democracy of such online contributions must be weighed against the resultant cacophony of voices.

Other actors and forces are making themselves felt in political communication. Today, a lot of journalism originates with non-journalists. An emerging stratum of professional communication mediators is altering the way journalism gets done and the way political communication takes place. An expanding occupational group of professional communicators, 'spin doctors', public relations experts, media advisers and political consultants using the techniques of advertising, market research, public relations and opinion analysis have entered the fray to help economic and political elites shape media messages to their advantage. Such developments further blur the distinctions between journalism and non-journalism. While in principle this might be viewed as opening the doors for progressive movements to get their messages onto the media agenda, in the long run the question of resources and influence determine whose messages get across.

Political communication is increasingly being geared to *smaller and smaller specific target groups*. Thus, political communication is increasingly addressing smaller, well-defined niche groups, based on specific and often quite narrow socio-cultural parameters. This can certainly enhance the capacity to formulate messages in a more specific manner, yet it may also result in the diminution of a shared public culture. These trends dovetail with the more general patterns we find at the socio-cultural level, where media audiences are increasingly characterized by fragmentation (horizontal differentiation) and *stratification* (vertical differentiation). The latter involves a growing distinction between what we might call informed elites and entertained majorities.

Evidence suggests that the executive branches of some Western democracies are making increased use of *news management and direct communication to the general public*. After 9/11 the Bush administration in the USA has intervened in dramatic ways in shaping the political atmosphere of the country, with its 'war on terrorism' mantra and an array of laws (under the umbrella of the Patriot Act) that curtail the civil liberties of citizens (Kellner, 2003). In Britain, the Blair administration's 'New Labour' government has been engaged in a 'permanent campaign' in the media to manage and steer opinion (Franklin, 2004). In Italy, the economic dominance of prime minister Silvio Berlusconi in the media landscape has given him unprecedented power to influence the political climate (Ginsbourg, 2004).

Perhaps most significantly, there is *a growth of other forms of political communication among a wide variety of civic groups*, movements and NGOs. In particular, this engagement is greatly facilitated by the internet and other ICT's (Information and Communication Technologies, e.g. mobile telephony), as we discuss further below. Thus, for example, in the 2004 US election campaign political groups not formally associated with the political parties, such as Moveon.org or the notorious 'Swift Boats Veterans for Truth', raised large amounts of money used, in large part, for producing and broadcasting political advertisements in support of one candidate or the other.

In taking account of important transitions with political communication, we must also mention the events of 9/11 and their aftermath. While we still lack the distance of historical perspective, it is clear that these events had important consequences for the systems and practices of political communication. We can note first that the trauma itself – the suffering and the pain it caused – quickly moved from being simply 'news' to being incorporated into a mode of political communication generated by the Bush administration. This mode underscored the 'war on terror', which in turn involved polarizing opinion not just in the USA but also around the world. The use of 'patriotism' to silence critics, the climate of fear that was generated, the attacks on civil liberties, and the emerging journalistic frame of militant Islam versus the West has had enormous impact. There has been – especially in the USA and the UK – a massive effort on the part of the governments towards news management and spin, including outright lies. The control that the military, and then editors and journalists exercised over reporting is also a part of this picture. Events have modified the momentum of these developments; several major media have publicly recanted their failure to exercise a more critical journalistic approach in their coverage. Alternative news and bloggers on the net became activated as never before. While the long-term effects of all this are still not certain, we must retain these events in our analytic perceptions.

As can be seen, there are many force-fields of tension here and there is considerable evidence to justify deep concern about the future of political communication and democracy. At the same time, as suggested above, we find significant counter-trends, a robust contribution that potentially enhances the democratic character of political communication.

A significant part of the terrain where these tensions, as well as the democracy-enhancing developments, are taking place is on the internet, to which we turn in the next section.

4. The internet and political communication

While the discussions about the poor health of democracy intensified during the 1990s, the internet was rapidly leading a media revolution. It did not take long for many observers to connect the two phenomena in an optimistic spirit. That new ICTs are impacting on all spheres of life in late modern society is of course no news, but there remains in fact some ambiguity as to the extent to which they are enhancing democracy (cf. Anderson and Cornfield, 2003; Castells, 1998; Jenkins and Thorburn, 2003). One's understanding – and perhaps even appreciation – of this ambiguity grows as one's insight into the complexity of democracy's difficulties deepens.

One of the first things to note is that the use of the net for political purposes is clearly minor compared with other purposes to which it is put; politics on the net is completely overshadowed by consumerism, entertainment, non-political networking, chat, etc. Furthermore, in terms of civic discussion and deployment of the net as a new arena for public spheres, the communicative character of the political discussion does not always promote the civic ideal; much of it is isolated and disjointed; its contributions to democratic opinion formation cannot always be assumed.

At the same time, we note that the present architecture of the net offers available space for many forms of civic initiative. The internet is becoming integrated with the established system of political communication, yet it is also being used to challenge established power structures. Even the efforts of some more overtly authoritarian regimes around the world to curtail the democratic uses of the net have not been fully successful, though inventories of the mechanisms of control are sobering. The progressive and subversive role of the net should not be overestimated; 'closed systems' can short-circuit the potential gains to be had by online political conversation (Fung, 2002). Yet, for those with access and political motivation, and who are living within open, democratic societies, the internet still offers very viable possibilities for civic interaction. Seen from a systemic view, however, its potential must be qualified, and it cannot offer any quick fix for democracy, a position that Blumler and Gurevitch (2001) affirm elsewhere.

Yet, given the variations in democratic systems and cultures around the world (cf. Hallin and Mancini, 2004), and the pace of social, political and technological change we should not expect to arrive soon at some simple, definitive answer to the questions. The sprawling character of online political communication can be seen as contributing to the destabilization of the systems of political communication, creating certain practical difficulties for the functioning of democracies. At the same time, as noted, this proliferation has a positive side if it offers openings for new developments, particularly in the realm of extra-parliamentarian politics. Indeed, thus far the evidence seems equivocal; moreover, the conclusions one might derive are inexorably tied to the assumptions one holds about the character of democracy. Rather than yielding any fast answers, we should acknowledge that the issue of the internet and political communication now has a central place on the research agendas and in the intellectual inquiry of political communication scholars.

There is a strong argument that the internet has not made much of a difference in the ideological political landscape; it has not helped mobilize more citizens to participate, nor has it altered the ways that politics gets done. Even the consequences of modest experiments to formally incorporate the internet into the political system with e-democracy have not been overwhelming. E-government efforts to incorporate citizens into discussions and policy formulations usually have a decisive top-down character (cf. Malina, 2003, for a discussion of the UK circumstances), with discursive constraints that derive from the elite control of their contents and the contexts.

Internet and new politics

This evidence cannot be dismissed lightly, but what should be emphasized is that this perspective is usually anchored in sets of assumptions that largely do not see beyond the formal political system and the traditional role of the media in that system. Indeed, much of the evidence is based on electoral politics, especially in the USA. While the problems of democracy are acknowledged, the view is that the solutions lie in revitalizing the traditional models of political participation and patterns of political communication, rather than relying on the internet to bring about such revitalization.

Other scholars alternatively take as their point of departure the understanding that we are moving into a new, transitional era in which the certitudes of the past in regard to how democracy works have become problematic. Democracy is seen to be, precariously, at a new historical juncture. Few observers would dismiss the central importance of electoral politics: a more robust democracy will not emerge by blithely side-stepping traditional, formal structures and procedures. However, one phenomenon that challenges the certitudes of the traditionalist view is the massive growth in what we can call advocacy or issue politics, often in the form of on-going campaigns. Some of the advocates are large and powerful interest groups; others take the form of social movements or have a more grass roots character. Many represent versions of 'new politics'; such politics can materialize all over the social terrain, and manifest itself in many contexts, including popular culture.

It is probably here where the internet most obviously makes a potential contribution to political communication. There are literally thousands of websites having to do with the political realm at the local, national and global levels; some are commercial, many are not; some are partisan, most are not. We can find discussion groups, chat rooms, alternative journalism, civic organizations, NGOs, grass roots issue-advocacy sites as well as voter education sites. One can see an expansion in terms of available communicative spaces for politics, as well as an ideological breadth compared with what exists in the mass media. Structurally, this pluralisation not only extends but also disperses the relatively clustered and constrained spectrum of political communication in the mass media.

If the internet facilitates an impressive communicative heterogeneity, we should not ignore the negative side of this development, namely fragmentation, with various groups veering towards disparate islands of political communication. There is a risk that they will remain in their respective cyber-ghettoes. This threatens to undercut a shared public culture and the integrative societal function of political communication, and may even foster intolerance where 'voluntary communities' have little contact with – or understanding of – one another.

In the arena of new politics the internal became not only relevant, but central: it is especially the capacity for the 'horizontal communication' of civic interaction that is paramount. Both technologically and economically, access to the net (and other new technologies, such as mobile phones) has helped facilitate the growth of large digital networks of activists (see, for example, Van de Donk *et al.*, 2004). At present, it is in the crevices deriving from the changes in the media industries, in socio-cultural patterns, and in modes of political communication that we can begin to glimpse new trends where the internet clearly makes a difference. In their recent survey of the available research Graber *et al.* (2002: 3–4) note

> . . . the literature on interest networks and global activism seems particularly rich in examples of how various uses of the Internet and the Web have transformed activism, political pressure, and public communication strategies . . . Research on civic organizations and political mobilization is characterized by findings showing potentially large effects of new media and for the breadth of directly applicable theory.

Set in relation to the population as a whole, the numbers involved here may not seem overwhelming, but the embryonic patterns taking shape in political communication now may, with historical hindsight, prove to have been quite significant.

The net's impact: summing up

The internet promises and delivers a lot. It can empower, it can widen our worlds, it can offer us seemingly endless amounts of information, and it can help us get in touch with people who share our interests. It can entertain, it can tantalize, it can tempt. It can also absorb and engulf us, drenching us in more information than we can ever use. It can promote our identities as consumers, but also, with some effort on our part, allow us to cultivate our identities as citizens. Will the net help deliver a better democracy? The net does have a capacity to enhance the public sphere, though thus far it seems not to have dramatically transformed political life. It allows for new communicative spaces to develop – alternative public spheres – even if the paths to the centres of political decision-making are often uneasy to discern.

Its structural features make any thought of universalism highly unrealistic, yet at the same time only a small part of all net activity at present has to do with politics and the public sphere. The internet clearly offers opportunities for the motivated. The questions today are not so much how the internet will change political life, but rather what might motivate more people to see themselves as citizens of a democracy, to engage in the political and – for those with access – to make use of the possibilities that the net still offers? Some of the answers may be found on the net itself, but most reside in our real social and cultural circumstances.

If one of the key problems facing democracy today is the decline in civic participation, it is worth considering how circumstances impact on engagement, i.e. to look at what kinds of conditions might foster or hinder such participation. Seen from the standpoint of political communication, this leads us to consider citizenship as a mode of agency, thereby complementing the dominant systems perspective. What are the factors that are relevant in this regard? What kinds of resources – not least in media terms – might be important for people to act as citizens? We explore these questions in the final section, under the theme of civic culture.

5. Merging perspectives: systems and culture in political communication

Traditional political communication

Political communication as a field of study has traditionally focused on the interaction between the formal actors within the political communication system – political institutions/actors, the media and citizens. Election campaigns, political journalism, public information and the perception of politicians among voters are a few of the research themes that frequently appear within such research. Over time, it has become apparent that there are some difficulties and limitations built into this approach.

First is its traditional view of politics. Most studies within political communication tend to work from the assumption that the 'political' is being played out in the interaction between these three sets of actors in the political communication process. On the one hand this appears to be quite an encompassing view, but on the other hand it could be regarded as rather narrow. By focusing on the interaction between the formal actors in politics it tends to deflect attention from other actors and activities that could potentially play an important and interesting role in the political process, such as extra-parliamentarian actors. Moreover, this tradition tends to ignore other forms of mediated communication in which politics can be relevant and important – e.g. films, talk shows – assuming a firm boundary between the political and the non-political. Generally, from the perspective of this research tradition, political communication – and politics itself – tends to be decontextualized from other domains of lived, everyday life.

Another feature of this research tradition is its tendency to focus on the citizens' opinions and knowledge of politics. While these remain important, they put too much emphasis on the informational aspect of citizenship, while ignoring other, subjective aspects of citizenship. With inspiration from contemporary cultural theory, such aspects of citizenship that relate to our identities could turn out to be of great interest. Even though ideas stemming from cultural theory and notions of late modernity inspire us here, they in turn are also problematic in some ways. One such problem is precisely their reluctance to focus on citizens and politics in the traditional sense. We refer also to the discussions above, where we have indicated the importance of macro-cultural changes for the contemporary practices of political communication, as well as for politics. Not least, the newer forms of political engagement underscore the importance of a personal sense of the political self.

Thus, what follows is an attempt to synthesize elements from both the political communication tradition and some currents from cultural theory, to provide a more nuanced framework for the analysis of communication processes in modern democracies. Our emphasis is on the theme of citizens' political engagement.

Integrating cultural theory and political communication: civic cultures

We begin with an overview of what we call the civic cultures perspective (Dahlgren, 2000, 2003, 2005) as a way to conceptualize the factors that can promote or impede political participation. We use the plural form to underscore that there are many ways of enacting, or 'doing', citizenship in late modern society. Here we can only sketch the contours of the perspective, but we hope it may offer some suggestive new ways to think about political communication.

Our starting point is the notion of political agency, viewing citizenship as a mode of individual and collective action, and probing the cultural conditions of such agency. Citizenship as a concept traditionally builds upon a set of rights and obligations, historically evolved in society, and underscores universalism and equality. In the modern world it has usually been linked to the nation-state. More recently, citizenship has become an object of contemporary social theory (cf. Isin and Turner, 2003). For our purposes, a major strand of such studies highlights the subjective side of citizenship, as a dimension of our identities (cf. Clarke, 1996; Isin and Wood, 1999).

This perspective argues that civic agency requires that one can see oneself as a citizen, that this social category be a part of one's sense of self – even if the actual word 'citizen' may not be a part of the vocabulary. This identity has to do with a sense of belonging to social/political entities and with the perceived possibilities for meaningful participation in societal development. In other words, a civic identity relates to belonging and to doing. While citizenship still generally evokes the notion of a subjectivity that is positioned publicly, with the increased blurring of the boundaries between public and private, citizenship as an identity can become increasingly interlaced with other dimensions of the composite, multidimensional self. In other words, we have many 'selves', operative in different situations; for democracy to function, there must also be some version of the 'civic self'.

To highlight citizenship in terms of identity leads us to ask: What are the cultural factors that can impact on this identity, and promote (or hinder) people's perceptions of their civic selves? What cultural factors might counteract civic indifference? Cultures consist of patterns of communication, practices and meaning; they provide taken-for-granted orientations – factual and normative – as well as other resources for collective life. These patterns are internalized, they exist 'in our heads', as it were, guiding and informing action, speech and understanding. We can thus think in terms of civic cultures – cultural patterns in which identities as citizens are an integrated part. Civic cultures, to the extent that they are compelling, operate at the level of taken-for-granted, everyday realities. We should note that the idea of civic culture tends to link up with notions of 'strong' or 'radical' democracy; it emphasizes participation and 'deliberation', as well as a view of citizenship that is associated with neo-republicanism (cf. Barber, 1984; van Gunsteren, 1998; Mouffe, 1992).

We can think of civic cultures as resources, as storehouses of assets which individuals and groups draw upon and make use of in their activities as citizens. Civic cultures are potentially both strong and vulnerable. They can shape citizens; they can serve to empower or disempower. They sit precariously in the face of political and economic power. They are shaped by an array of factors: the nature of the legal system, factors of social structure, economics, education, organizational possibilities, infrastructure, spatiality, can all have their impact. Even dramatic changes in the political climate can impact on civic culture, as witnessed in the USA after 9/11. For our purposes here, however, we emphasize the media factors that can shape civic culture.

A dynamic circuit

The concept of civic cultures does not presuppose homogeneity among its citizens, but it does suggest the need for minimal shared commitments to the vision and procedures of democracy, which in turn entails a capacity to see beyond the immediate interests of one's own group. Needless to say, this is a challenging balance to maintain, in the context of plural late modern societies. However, different social and cultural groups can express civic culture in different ways, theoretically enhancing democracy's possibilities. Groups and their political positions are always to some extent in flux, and thus civic cultures are never static.

Conceptually, civic culture can be modelled as an integrated circuit of six dimensions that interplay with each other. The first three are familiar from the established tradition of political communication; the latter three are more associated with contemporary cultural theory. They are: (1) knowledge and competencies, (2) values, (3) trust and affinity, (4) practices and traditions, (5) spaces and (6) identities. Identities as citizens is the key dimension for us here, but it is clearly interdependent upon the other five. Thus the civic culture found among wealthy suburbanites near a large metropolitan area will probably have a different character than one prevalent in an impoverished rural area. In both cases it is fully possible that the civic respective cultures can be strong or weak. We would assume, however, that the media and the modes of political communication prevalent in each context would be significant. Each dimension can be the start for empirical inquiry: the mass media as well as interactive media can be studied to see in what ways they contribute to or hinder each of these dimensions.

Knowledge and competence

Knowledge, in the form of reliable, referential cognizance of the social world is indispensable for the vitality of democracy. A subset of knowledge is competencies, and in particular, the skills to deal communicatively in the socio-political world are pivotal. Some degree of literacy is essential; people must be able to make sense of that which circulates in the public sphere, and to understand the world they live in. Education, in its many forms, will thus always retain its relevance for democracy, even if its contents and goals will vary and often need to be critically examined.

While it seems rather obvious that people must have access to reliable reports, portrayals, analyses, discussions, debates and so forth about current affairs, it is also becoming more challenging to specify access to knowledge, as socio-cultural heterogeneity increases and as the media landscape evolves. What do citizens need to know today? That question does not have a final, universal answer. Modes of knowledge are evolving, especially among the young, in keeping with cultural changes. New media technologies can promote new modalities of thought and expression, new ways of knowing and forms of communicative competencies. Thus, precisely what kinds of knowledge and competencies are required and by whom for the vitality of a civic culture can never be established once and for all. Furthermore, access also includes issues of linguistic capacity and cultural proximity. This of course reiterates the need for diversity within public communication, to accommodate and incorporate different groups.

Values

Clearly values must be anchored in everyday life; a political system will never achieve a democratic character if the world of the everyday reflects anti-democratic dispositions. We can distinguish between substantive values, such as equality, liberty, justice and solidarity, and procedural ones, such as openness, reciprocity, responsibility, accountability and tolerance. In short, democracy requires civic cultures that underscore commitment to democracy's ideals and rules.

The mass media largely tend to reinforce the commitment to democratic values (even by invoking them in sensationalist scandals), and it can be argued that support for the democratic rights of individuals is something that is spreading globally via media representations. In regard to the new interactive media, it can be argued that the virtues of democratic communication are espoused, though market logic and increasing state intervention may well be hampering the fulfilment of these values.

Trust and affinity

We have in mind here a minimal sense of commonality among citizens in heterogeneous late modern societies, a sense that they belong to the same social and political entities, despite all other differences and conflicts. They have to deal with each other to make their common entities work, whether at the level of neighbourhood, nation-state or the global arena. If there exists a nominal degree of affinity, for example, conflicts can then become enacted between 'adversaries' rather than 'enemies', as Mouffe (1999) puts it, since an awareness of a shared civic commonality is operative. Affinity is, in a sense, a modest criterion, certainly not as ambitious (or unrealistic) as 'community'.

Civic affinity blurs into civic trust. Here too we aim for a modest level. Certainly a degree of trust in government and other major institutions is important, but in the civic context we must also add trust between citizens. Putnam (2000: 136) distinguishes between 'thick' trust based on established personal relationships, and 'thin' trust, the generalized honesty and expectations of reciprocity that we accord people we do not know personally but whom we feel we can have satisfactory exchange with. Without such affinity and trust there can be no civic networking, for example.

The media's contributions to affinity and trust must be seen as mixed. If journalists reveal misdeeds among elected officials, such officials obviously no longer deserve trust. Increasingly, however, the media seem to encourage cynicism towards both the institutions and the values of democracy – and even towards themselves. Civic affinity seemingly gets only limited help from the mass media, but on the internet, for example, we find many networks, movements and other collectivities which are predicated on trust and affinity.

Practices and traditions

Democracy must be embodied in concrete, recurring practices – individual, group, and collective – relevant for diverse situations. Such practices help generate personal and social meaning to the ideals of democracy. Elections can be seen as a routine form of practice in this regard, but civic culture requires many other practices, for example organizing campaigns, holding meetings and mobilizing actions.

One of the key practices of civic culture is discussion. Discussion among citizens can be seen as the continuation of political communication beyond the mass media, or alternatively phrased, as a cornerstone of the public sphere. We can empirically investigate civic talk by examining, for instance, its various discursive modes, its spatial and contextual sites and settings, its social circumstances. We might look at what tacit rules are operative in these contexts, and how mechanisms of social etiquette about talk can either promote or hinder the practices of public discussion. Eliasoph (1998) reveals the troubling socio-cultural patterns that inhibit discursive civic practices in American civic culture, contributing to what she calls the 'evaporation' of the public sphere. Stromer-Galley (2002), however, finds that the internet can be used in part to overcome such socio-cultural obstacles.

Talk has been associated with democracy and opinion formation from the start; civic engagement starts with discussion. By talking to each other, citizens shape their opinions and can thus generate a collective will. Though citizens' interaction may at times be wanting in terms of deep knowledge and well-thought-out opinions, it is still important to underscore the central role of talk for maintaining the life of democracy. Even the looseness, open-endedness of everyday talk, its creativity, its potential for empathy and affective elements, are indispensable for the vitality of democratic politics. There is an innate democratic strength in the messiness and unpredictability of everyday talk. 'The political', and thus the individual's role as citizen, is never an a priori given, but can emerge in various ways within informal everyday speech, establishing the links between the personal and the political.

Across time, practices become traditions, and experience becomes collective memory. Today's democracy needs to be able to refer to a past, without being locked into it. New practices and traditions can and must evolve to ensure that democracy does not stagnate. The mass media obviously contribute here by their selective representations (and exclusions) of on-going political life, including its rituals and symbols. They can stimulate civic talk in various ways. Yet the newer media increasingly take on relevance as more people make use of the newer possibilities and incorporate these as part of their political practices (e.g. activist mobilization via the internet). A good deal of civic discussion today takes place on the internet, not only in explicit public forums, but also within varieties of online journalism and within the networking of activist organizations and mobilization.

Spaces

In the context of everyday life there are innumerable spaces, sites and settings in which people may meet and interact as citizens. It could be argued that these civic spaces are declining, as the shopping mall becomes the dominant new spaces, and large screen TV drowns out conversation in some traditional spaces for civic encounters, such as bars. At the same time, new spaces can be – and sometimes are – opened up. Certainly there are tensions between private and public spaces. In the late modern world, we often find the democratic challenge of making public certain spaces that have been privatized in the economic sense. For example, in the early 1990s, municipalities in Sweden became legally treated as 'corporatized', and thus city councils could close its doors to citizens while making decisions. Newer interactive media of course offer communicative spaces for civic interaction, and these have become crucial for most political groups, organizations and movements working outside the parliamentarian parties. Even here we see how commercial portals may serve to drive out politics, or domesticate political discourse in keeping with their own interests.

Identities

This brings us back to identities. It should be clear by now that this sense of self is predicated on the interplay with the other dimensions of civic cultures. Thus, values may reinforce affinity and trust, which in turn can encourage certain practices, and these practices may have positive impact on knowledge.

Generally, it can be said that the mass media have become increasingly weaker in fostering identities of citizenship among its audiences, as the prime identity promoted by the media is that of consumers. It is in the domain of consumption where we are being empowered, where we make choices, where we create ourselves. To be sure, being a citizen and a consumer are not always antithetical. Citizens need to consume, and consumption at times can be politically framed, e.g. the anti-sweatshop movement. Yet there is a fundamental distinction between consumption, which is predicated on the fluctuations of the market, and the universality embedded in the notion of the citizen. Democracy cannot be reduced to markets.

The changing world

What we have presented in this chapter are basically snapshots from a reality that is in constant transition. The basic contours of society, politics, power, culture, the media landscape, journalism: all of these are in many ways fluid and evolving as historical circumstances change. Thus, political communication is never static. Moreover, as we suggested in the previous section, these changes prompt us to explore newer analytic paths to better grasp contemporary political communication.

At the same time, we must not lose sight of all the continuities. Here we would mention the role of technology. It has long played an important role in shaping political communication, and continues to do so. But its role remains that of offering possibilities, of setting conditions. Despite the intensity of various communication revolutions over recent decades, communication technology continues to play a role that is formative yet never deterministic. The internet, for example, is a tool, but in itself does not automatically drive history onto a predetermined path. We see how its use and the role that it plays vary across cultures, how its architecture is contested and how efforts to regulate it vary considerably. Yet nobody could ignore its central importance.

The role of the nation-state remains a key fixture of continuity, in the sense that it still organizes much of political and economic life. Certainly there are changes: the European welfare state has been reduced in its scope of activities in the neo-liberal era. More generally, there have arisen realms of political activity and political communication that seemingly bypass the nation-state. At the micro level, there are forms of local political engagement that sneak under the nose of the nation-state. On the global level, there are actors and activities that bypass the nation-state: NGOs and especially transnational corporations in some important instances eclipse the nation-state on the international arena, as does the EU to some extent. But to announce the nation-state's demise is clearly a silly exaggeration.

As in the case of all intellectual endeavours involving analysis of the modern world, we enhance our study of political communication today to the extent that we can develop a mindset that can see, appreciate and make use of the tensions between change and continuity. This tension is of course always open to different interpretations, but keeping this basic dynamic in our sights can only add to the payoff in our analyses.

References

Allan, S. (2004) *News Culture*, 2nd edn. Maidenhead, UK: Open University Press.

Anderson, D. M. and Cornfield, M. (eds) (2003) *The Civic Web: Online Politics and Democratic Values.* Lanham, MD: Rowman & Littlefield.

Baker, C. E. (2002) *Media, Markets and Democracy.* New York: Cambridge University Press.

Barber, B. (1984) *Strong Democracy: Participatory Politics for a New Age.* Berkeley: University of California Press.

Bennett, W. L. (2003a) 'New Media Power: The Internet and Global Activism', in N. Couldry and J. Curran (eds), *Contesting Media Power.* Lanham, MD: Rowman & Littlefield pp. 17–37.

———(2003b) 'Lifestyle Politics and Citizen-Consumers: Identity, Communication and Political Action in Late Modern Society', in J. Corner and D. Pels (eds), *Media and Political Style: Essays on Representation and Civic Culture.* London: Sage, pp. 137–50.

Bennett, W. L. and Entman, R. (eds) (2001) *Mediated Politics in the Future of Democracy.* Cambridge: Cambridge University Press.

Blumler, J. and Gurevitch, M. (2000) 'Rethinking the Study of Political Communication', in J. Curran and M. Gurevitch (eds), *Mass Media and Society*, 3rd edn. London: Edward Arnold, pp. 155–72.

———(2001) 'The New Media and Our Political Communication Discontents: Democratizing Cyberspace', *Information, Communication and Society*, 4 (1), 1–14.

Campbell, V. (2004) *Information Age Journalism.* London: Edward Arnold.

Castells, M. (1998) *The Power of Identitiy.* London: Blackwell.

Clarke, P. B. (1996) *Deep Citizenship.* London: Pluto.

Dahlgren, P. (2000) 'Media, Citizens and Civic Culture', in M. Gurevitch and J. Curran (eds), *Mass Media and Society*, 3rd edn. London: Edward Arnold.

———(2002) 'In Search of the Talkative Public: Media, Deliberative Democracy and Civic Culture', *Javnost/The Public*, 9 (3), 5–26.

———(2003) 'Reconfiguring Civic Culture in the New Media Milieu', in J. Corner and D. Pels (eds), *Media and Political Style: Essays on Representation and Civic Culture.* London: Sage.

Eliasoph, N. (1998) *Avoiding Politics: How Americans Produce Apathy in Everyday Life*. Cambridge: Cambridge University Presss,

Franklin, D. (2004) *Packaging Politics. Political Communication in Britain's Media Democracy*, 2nd edn. London. Edward Arnold,

Fung, A. (2002) 'One City, Two Systems: Democracy in an Electronic Chat Room in Hong Kong', *Javnost/The Public*, 9 (2), 77–94.

Ginsborg, P. (2004) *Silvio Berlusconi: Television, Power and Patrimony*. London: Verso.

Graber, D., Bimber, B., Bennett, W. L., Davis, R. and Norris, P. (2003) 'The Internet and Politics: Emerging Perspectives', in H. Nissenbaum *et al.* (eds), *The Academy and Internet*. New York: Peter Lang.

Hallin, D. C. and Mancini, P. (2004) *Comparing Media Systems: Three Models of Media and Politics*. New York: Cambridge University Press.

Hertz, N. (2001) *The Silent Takeover: Global Capitalism and the Death of Democracy*. London: Arrow Books.

Isin, E. F. and Turner, B. S. (eds) (2003) *Handbook of Citizenship Studies*. London: Sage.

Isen, E. F. and Wood, P. K. (1999) *Citizenship and Identity*. London: Sage.

Jenkins, H. and Thorburn, D. (eds) (2003) *Democracy and New Media*. Cambridge, MA: MIT Press.

Kantola, A. (2003) 'Loyalties in Flux: The Changing Politics of Citizenship', *European Journal of Cultural Studies*, 6 (2), 203–17.

Kellner, D. (2003) *From 9/11 to Terror War*. Lanham, MD: Rowman & Littlefield.

Malina, A. (2003) 'e-Transforming Democracy in the UK. Considerations of Developments and Suggestions for Empirical Research', *Communications: The European Journal of Communication Research*, 28 (2), 135–55.

Mouffe, C. (ed.) (1992) *Dimensions of Radical Democracy*. London: Verso.

———(1999) 'Deliberative Democracy or Agonistic Pluralism?', *Social Research*, 66, 745–58.

Putnam, R. (2000) *Bowling Alone: The Collapse and Revival of American Community*. New York: Simon & Schuster.

Stromer-Galley, J. (2002) 'New Voices in the Public Sphere: A Comparative Analysis of Interpersonal and Online Political Talk', *Javnost/The Public*, 9 (2), 23–42.

van de Donk, W., Loader, B. D., Nixon, P. and Rucht, D. (eds) (2004) *Cyberprotest: New Media, Citizens and Social Movements*. London: Routledge.

van Gunsteren, H. R. (1998) *A Theory of Citizenship*. Boulder, CO: Westview Press.

Index

The letter n represents a textual note and t a table.